DOMINIQUE PERRAULT

DOMINIQUE PERRAULT

Gallimard

for Gaëlle

TABLE OF CONTENTS

"I don't reason so much in terms of shadows"

By Nina Leger

The day I was asked to write a text about the architect, the roof of the warehouse below my apartment opened up. It formed a mouth, perhaps an eye, around which the roof buckled, threatening to collapse at any moment.

It's very open, said the woman on the phone, no doubt to persuade me to accept the commission, and from my balcony I could see that, yes, it was very open indeed.

"Here, I would like to talk about ruins in the present. And even in the future."[1]

Perhaps it was the imminent collapse of the roof that convinced me to accept the commission—something was undoubtedly going on—but I think that, more than this present on the brink, it was the past that pushed me, and the memory of a time when I was still living in Paris and spent four years sitting in a building designed by the architect. I had found a place for myself there and hadn't really moved on, so to speak.

"For when we return to a place after considerable absence, we not merely recognize the place itself, but remember things that we did there, and recall the persons whom we met and even the unuttered thoughts which passed within our minds when we were there before."[2]

The building in question closed every evening, so I had to leave and go home for the night, but every morning, as soon as it opened, I'd arrive, sit myself down, and spend the rest of the day contemplating.

My neighbors did the same thing, because that's what people do in a library: seated at their tables, they spread out their minds in front of them, contemplate their thoughts, put them in order, they request books so as to find new thoughts, they take notes from their heads to their computers, they correct, erase, archive, and, sometimes, they make their heads into books. I myself was doing a thesis on perspective, in other words on emptiness and infinity, which is to say, in a sense that escaped me at the time, on the Bibliothèque Nationale de France.

"The universe (which others call the Library) is composed of an indefinite and perhaps infinite number of hexagonal galleries, with vast air shafts between."[3]

Many have said that the four corner towers of the Bibliothèque Nationale de France built by the architect imitate open books. I don't think so. First, because it is unusual for books to stand open at a right angle—try it yourself at home—and second because the architect is not a literalist: his buildings do not imitate the objects they house. No, the corners are there to create emptiness, a void that didn't exist before the Bibliothèque Nationale de France invented it by enveloping it.

The building spent its time reflecting itself around this void. That's what the void is for, that's what symmetry is for, as well as all the glass surfaces in which other glass surfaces were multiplied, like so many images of the building inserted into the building itself. Now, what is a library if not a physical architecture doubled by another virtual and infinite structure, made up of the limitless collection of books, the foundations of which are summed up in the marvel that is the library catalogue?

Some buildings house bodies, others house infinity. This is true of libraries, theatres, archives, museums, universities, psychoanalysts' offices, and, of course, all the rooms in which we sleep.

"The first thought is placed, as it were, in the forecourt; the second, let us say, in the living room; the remainder are placed in due order all round the impluvium and entrusted not merely to bedrooms and parlours, but even to the care of statues and the like."[4]

"Ewha," said the woman on the phone.

The second time we spoke, I once again stationed myself on my balcony. Beneath my feet, the eye had grown. The missing tiles gave a glimpse of the grey framework and the milled wood.

Ewha, a university for women in Korea, a university… I interrupted her: underground. Not exactly, she corrected, but I wasn't listening any more. Okay, I said.

It was already okay because of the library, and it became even more so with the university. A friend told me about it one evening, after one of my Bibliothèque days. We'd go to the cinema together often. He'd meet me at closing time and I'd slip from the library into the cinema without realizing it, so that in my memory, the two blend together. The library was able to hold all the scenes from all the films, just as it could house all the pages of all the books.

We were sitting in the red armchairs facing the white screen when my friend told me that the architect had also built a university. It was one of Korea's biggest in terms of both prestige and attendance, and he had decided to build it under the landscape, rather than on top of it.

You walk up, said my friend, you're looking for a tower, a grand staircase, a colonnade, but there's nothing, nothing but a hill. I remember his hands imitating the gentle movement of the ground as it rose. Then the houselights went out and my friend's hands disappeared.

> "When it was proclaimed that the Library contained all books, the first impression was one of extravagant happiness."[5]

It's not quite that, the architect explained when I first met him.

We were in a hole—an old quarry whose walls were now covered with grass that formed a fixed green swirl around us. Along with the sky, it was the only thing we could see.

Some time had passed since my conversation with the woman on the balcony. A few mornings earlier, I'd been woken by the sound of things being broken. Opening the window, I saw two workmen sitting astride the roof, busy demolishing it. They were tipping one tile after another into the hole, which thanks to them was growing bigger. It was a melodious and easy act of destruction, requiring only a series of flicks of the wrist. The less roof there was, the better I could see the tiles smashing. At the end of the day, the tile-strewn ground looked up at the sky.

It's not quite that, the architect explained,
we didn't build the university in the hill,
we built the hill, or rather,
we restored it
because it had been there
before,
it had been razed and we returned it to its rightful place, it's not
a university buried under a hill but
a building from which a hill was born,
rather than an architectural conception, it's a conception
of the landscape.
We created a hillock, we
opened it in two with a trench and that is how you enter:
downward.
This trench has been renamed valley by the students
and nowadays they speak
of the valley of Ewha.

I listened as the architect's sentences created spaces. Each suggestion was a line, each silence an interval.

Four years ago, maybe five, he continued,
the students occupied the valley,
they settled in and
they didn't budge.

Like me, I thought. Like me in the Bibliothèque Nationale de France. The students had found their place in one of the architect's buildings and had set about making a life for themselves there but, unlike me, they had found a way of staying there even at night because, if the University closed its doors, it was impossible to close the valley and the students couldn't be put outside because they were there already. So they had slept there and I was curious about the dreams they might have had in this structure that was an exterior, this room under the stars. Maybe, if I was a bit crafty, I could sneak into the warehouse and sleep on the tiles and under the sky; and maybe I'd have the same dreams as the women students of Ewha.

Of course they slept, replied the architect, but above all they fought, they demanded
the impeachment of the President
of the University.
Their movement spread
from the valley to the whole country and
to all the young people who demanded
the impeachment of the President
of Korea.
The Ewha students won,
The youth of Korea won
and it all
began in the valley.

The architect showed me an image of the valley on his phone. I thought of a sculpture by Michael Heizer called *Double Negative*, a double trench cut into the rock on either side of a collapse, and then of another one, *Levitated Mass*, a sort of open-air corridor dug into the ground into which you descend and then climb back up again. The slope is gentle, as are the walls and the ground. But above the point where the descent becomes an ascent is perched an enormous rock.

To get into Ewha University, continued the architect, climbing back up the slope,
you have to go down
as much as twenty metres below ground, down until the landscape
disappears and I believe
that this disappearance made possible an appearance.

Perhaps the students wouldn't have had the idea of a revolution if the University had been at ground level.

> "I removed what little there might be which might be a mountain range twenty miles away. I got rid of that too and was left with nothing except light, just the sky."[6]

In order to go and write my thesis at the Bibliothèque, every morning I had to go down the outside staircase that leads to the main entrance, then take an escalator, then another—both going down. I then reached the area reserved for research, but no matter how far down I went, I'd end up at the level of a garden, or rather a forest, planted between the four towers. My subterranean expedition brought me back to horizon level, and for a long time this paradox seemed to me to be one of the possible expressions of the library. A horizon beneath the horizon.

We emerged from the well of lawn. In front of us stretched a building so beautiful that the division of the world between heaven and earth seemed to take place at the exact point of this short white strip. I had never seen architecture so compact and yet so immaterial. The play of light and shadow that it produced was so precise and so clear that I was sure that if the building had dissolved before our eyes, the light and shadow would have remained in the landscape and outlasted, for a moment at least, the disappearance of their material support.

We reached this villa, which the architect hadn't built, which was designed by someone else, and which he bought as it was falling into disrepair.

Have you ever heard of Jean Dubuisson? asked the architect, stroking a huge black dog that had come to greet him.

I had never heard of Jean Dubuisson.

A second black dog entered the room, a lookalike of the first, and also stood at the architect's feet. They looked like two large, rough rocks resting on the white marble, and something about their presence reminded me again for a moment of Heizer's *Levitated Mass*.

Inside the villa, nothing could be opened or closed, there were no pegs, no rotation was possible, all you could do was slide the planes. The space transformed, the same way light ebbs and flows. All the movie scenes that I remembered taking place in the Bibliothèque Nationale de France could have been set in this house, built by someone other than the architect, and yet so reminiscent of him.

He planned to deposit his archives there. Naively, I'd imagined that he would entrust them to the Bibliothèque Nationale de France, but perhaps a place that you built yourself has been part of your future for too long to ever be able to contain your past.

> "The only architectural form we would have liked to propose was […] a fog bank wandering over the plain."[7]

When I got home, there was no roof at all, in other words no tiles and no framework either. The ground had been cleared, the warehouse had never been so close to non-existence and, at the same time, it was saturated with possible futures. What was to become of it?

Before it was decommissioned, the warehouse had housed a moving company—which I suppose means trucks and all kinds of containers that might help people move their lives from one place to another. A friend who lived in the building next door to mine had told me that he secretly dreamed of getting his hands on the warehouse and turning it into a theatre. The dimensions were perfect, he said. There seemed to be a secret link between theatre and moving house, one that surely had something to do with the ability to keep changing the scenery infinitely.

A backhoe and two lorries were sleeping between the walls. Concentrating, I tried to guess what mission they had been assigned, but when I left, nothing had moved. I had an appointment in Paris with the architect

> "That zero panorama seemed to contain *ruins in reverse*, that is—all the new construction that would eventually be built […] because the buildings don't *fall* into ruin *after* they are built but rather *rise* into ruin *before* they are built."[8]

We met at the agency's offices on a Saturday. Like the warehouse, it was deserted, but all the work surfaces were covered with projects in progress and gestating shapes. Upside-down ruins were strewn on the tables and the silence made the space bigger.

I marvelled at the models—their precise beauty, but also the simple fact of their existence: so, people still built models? Projects are made by cutting and pasting and not just on-screen in computer-generated images?

Models are extremely important, the architect explained,
in fact,
of all the visions,
of all performances,
of all the projections,
it's the model that matters most, and that is a fine thing, because
the model
is a paradox:
the larger the project, the more you have to miniaturize it, so the larger you build, the smaller the model seems to be.

We stood bending over a white cardboard model and I marvelled that you could make trees with scissors.

Nanako did this one, she's been working at the agency
for over twenty years and every time we have to present a model,
she packs it, she makes it
a Japanese package,
and it's very beautiful, but sometimes very difficult to undo,
so we turn up in front of the clients with our sublime package
and we struggle,
but elegantly, right,
to get the model out of its paper,
it's rather funny, it's like a staging,
a not entirely voluntary one,
of the birth of the world.

Behind the bay window, a bluetit alighted in a pine tree, which was an enormous event for us, having adapted our perception to the scale of the model.

We went down to the basement of the offices, where large illuminated panels showed views of projects. We stopped in front of the Gangnam intermodal hub in Seoul. Work was ongoing, the architect had just got back. It was huge and, for the moment, empty.

We dug a gigantic trench and covered it up
with metal plates.
Cars drive over it, you can't
interrupt traffic during construction, there are at least
four times four lanes
passing by,
can you imagine
the infernal racket,
and so I was down there,
in this excavation that we decided on,
in the din of the cars and I said to myself,
But what have we done?
It happens sometimes, when construction has begun
and it is impossible
to turn back the clock.

Standing in the empty office, in front of the calmly luminous image, I listened to the architect describe the world turned upside down, I listened to him tell me all the things that must be destroyed when you have to build, I listened to him admit what violence is needed when, like him, you want to open up the earth to bring light in—because that was what was going to happen in Gangnam, the space where the noise of the cars had rushed in was going to become a space for light, a place as serene and luminous as the panel that foreshadowed it and in front of which we were standing.

But for now, concluded the architect,
it's a mess.

Next to Gangnam, another panel showed the new Villejuif station, which had just been completed. Once again, the architect had dug a building, a light well several dozen meters deep, and I thought to myself how astonishing he was, this architect who insisted on digging when he was asked to build, how surprising it was, this *idée fixe* of bringing daylight underground.

I thought for a moment of my bare warehouse, about the daylight spreading over this floor that had probably never seen it before, and I wondered how the rock felt when exposed to the sun for the first time. How do the particles of the subterranean world experience this first contact? Inevitably, the atoms react, the energy of the light acts on that of the rock and the rock surely transforms the light in return, but perhaps we're not just talking about a reaction here, perhaps the hitherto subterranean rock is also gripped by an emotion when this thing that didn't exist suddenly pounces on it.

"Unforgettable.
Fragment of sunlight fills the prison.
An opening in the horizon.
Life bursts."[9]

The architect offered to show me how deep light can venture underground if you know how to make a path for it.

He led me to a white screen and, turning on the projector, said we were going to watch fictions. The profile of Villejuif appeared with, beneath it, where the underground station was now, a cross-section of the Pantheon in Rome.

It's a collage, he said,
it's a fiction and its function
is revelation.

Before I saw the Pantheon installed below ground level, I had forgotten—had I ever known?— that it was nothing more than a cavity built to let in light. On an empty square, they built another void with a hole at the top. Light enters. The beam of its rays project a circle of light onto the walls and floor of the building, which has become a darkroom. This is what the millions of visitors to the Pantheon come to see: a disc of light moving through the darkness.

We put the Pantheon underground, continued the architect,
to show that light enters
and goes a long way.
Fiction
helps see things more clearly.
He paused and added, I'll be right back.

While I was waiting for him I took out my phone. My neighbor had written, "End of suspense, start of work" with a photo of a van parked in front of the warehouse with the words "Couvreurs Azur"[10] on it. The possibilities were closing in: there would be no new building in place of the warehouse, just one roof replacing another. In a while, the ground would stop seeing the sky and I was both relieved and disappointed.

The architect came back carrying some large printed sheets. He had something to show me. It was another collage. It featured Le Corbusier's Cité Radieuse embedded in the ground like the churches hewn from the rock on the Lalibela plateau in Ethiopia.

Well, since you live in Marseille... he said, smiling at me, and I smiled back because I live in Marseille almost by chance, a coincidence in which the Cité Radieuse played a role—that of an apparition catching, cutting through the light of a July afternoon, when I went past it on the bus and it popped up like an immense sign, such that ever since, despite all the reasons that seem more solid than an apparition, I've been convinced that it was the reason for my coming. What would have happened if, instead of rising above me, it had lain beneath my feet?

A few weeks before I received the commission, I returned to the Cité Radieuse for the first time since my arrival in Marseille. Now I had a way of making regular visits: I'd found a shrink there. I'd arrive well ahead of schedule and wander through the spaces, watching the light slide across the reddish-brown wooden panels, wandering through the corridors lit by dim lamps reflected in the black floor, and casting my mind back to the Bibliothèque Nationale de France. I told myself that the most interesting part of the therapy took place before I entered the consulting room, in my secret conversation with the building. During the session, I turned my head to the side as I spoke to get a better look at the mountains and the tall white buildings flowing into the evening. Seeing the collage the architect had handed me, I asked myself: would my unconscious be darker, or would it be brighter by contrast, if, from the armchair where I was sitting, instead of a landscape, I could see a wall, perhaps crossed by a ray of light falling from the heights?

I don't reason so much in terms of shadows, said the architect,
I think in terms of light.

"What with all that digging and digging, you eventually improve."[11]

When I got back to Marseille, I ran out onto the balcony. Three triangles of framework like three successive pediments were installed inside the building. It was yellow and soft in the sun. I took a photograph and sent it off. The base of the triangle is the bottom chord, its other two sides are the rafters, the architect replied.

I should have been writing, relating our talks, talking about all the things he had built, but I spent my days on the balcony watching the roofers as they gradually completed the framework. I told myself that it was the only chance I'd have to see that in-between space, between the ground and the roof, that soon it would be covered by tiles.

Besides, I couldn't concentrate on what the architect had done: I was too busy with what he had dreamed. I saw the sheets in his hand again and wondered why these collages, these radiant cities and buried pantheons, why Ewha embedded under the Avenue Foch, why the gardens of Versailles at the foot of the towers of Créteil, why the Washington Monument under the Invalides, why put into images these double worlds that could never be built because they juxtaposed buildings that had already been built in different places.

The architect's fictions didn't invent anything completely—no building, no site—they started from existing elements and imagined their coming together. In this collision of the distinct, something new appeared. I had to see the Panthéon buried under Villejuif to understand this.

There is no white page,
no,
what already exists counts,
even in fiction, especially in fiction, the architect told me in words that could have been spoken by a writer,
there are no more blank pages and invention
is only of interest

if it composes and
recomposes.
For me, fiction has
a critical function,
a speculative function,
and a revelatory function, but that
is something I've already said.

He had already said it about fictions, and I remembered that he had also said it about Ewha, when he talked about having to descend in order to enter, that from the valley you could no longer see the surrounding landscape and that from this place a revolution was born, as if hiding the world could give you the idea of changing it.

I thought this was one way of understanding his work. By obliterating part of an overall situation, or by creating a new whole with two parts taken from separate situations, he was putting things back into play, re-launching thought, escaping imposed orders and fixed structures.

In his letters, Michelangelo distinguishes between the kind of sculpture that he considers authentic and another that he despises. The sculpture he despises begins in emptiness and adds, it proceeds, as he writes, "*per via di pore*." The sculpture that he esteems and practices is that which begins with fullness—that of a block of marble, for example—and which removes and thus creates "*per via di levare*." Therein lies true sculpture, he says, in the gesture that embraces what is and makes its way through it, creating by removing, not adding, but metamorphosing what is.

I had always thought of architecture as a way of installing fullness in emptiness. I now understood that it was also a way of making emptiness speak in a different way, of giving it a different form, a different depth and a different light.

"It's a real architectural problem.
But also a grammatical problem."[12]

One day, the roof closed and the warehouse ceased to exist in my eyes.
It took me a while to notice that a circular
opening,
quite unusual,
had been formed
in the roof,
an opening for which the only possible reason was
to let light in.

1 Emmanuel Hocquard, *Ruines à rebours* (Bordeaux: Éditions de l'Attente, 2010).
2 Quintilian, *Institutio Oratoria*, trans. H. E. Butler (New York: G. P. Putnam's Sons, 1922), Book 11, Chapter 2, Paragraph 17, 221.
3 Jorge Luis Borges, "The Library of Babel" [1941], *Labyrinths*, trans. James. E. Irby (New York: New Directions, 2007), 51.
4 Quintilian, *Institutio Oratoria*, Book 11, Chapter 2, Paragraph 20, 223.
5 Borges, "The Library of Babel," 54–55.
6 Michael Heizer, "Interview with Julia Brown," *Sculpture in Reverse* (Los Angeles: Museum of Contemporary Art, 1984), 38.
7 Archizoom, "Competition project for the University of Florence," *Domus*, no. 509 (April 1972).
8 Robert Smithson, "The Monuments of Passaic," *Artforum* VI, no. 4 (December 1967).
9 Hélène Bessette, *La Grande Balade* (Paris: Gallimard, 1961).
10 This translates as "Azure Roofing Company," which evokes the idea of a cloudless sky as a roof.
11 Kiyoko Murata, *Le Coureur et les Rêves* (Arles: Actes Sud, 2024).
12 Hocquard, *Ruines à rebours*.

1

2

3

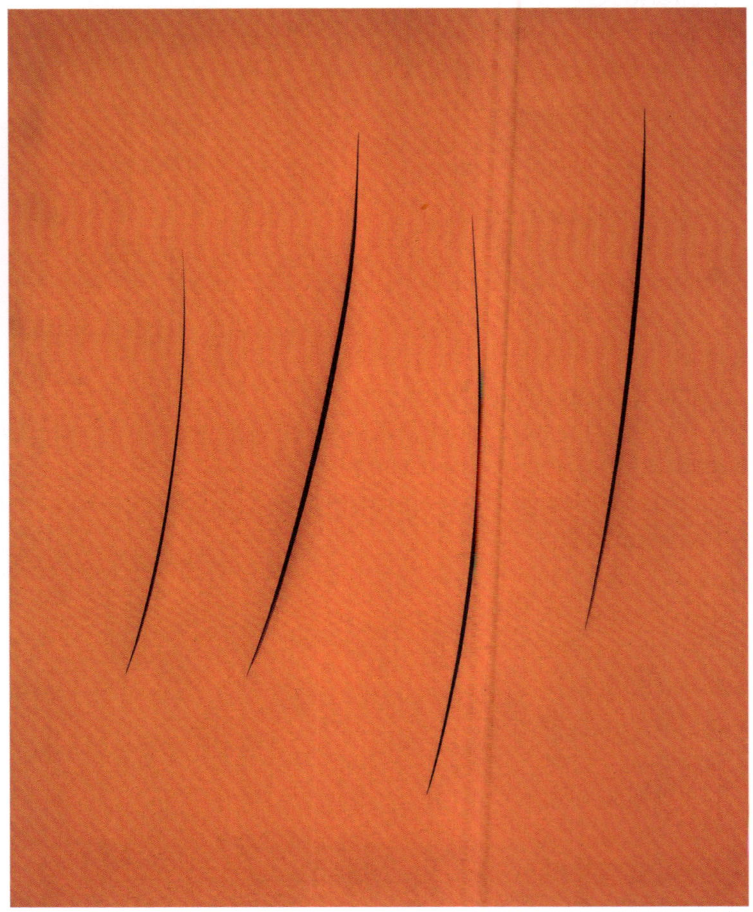

4

1 Le Corbusier, *Grande nature morte Indépendants*, 1922. Lacquer on canvas, 114 x 146 cm. Moderna Museet, Stockholm.
2 Larry Bell, *Untitled*, 1966. Tin-plated glass, chromed metal, and Plexiglas, 132 x 51.3 x 51.3 cm. Centre Pompidou-Musée National d'Art Moderne.
3 Michael Heizer, *Double Negative*, 1969, two trenches displacing 240,000 tons of earth, rhyolite, and sandstone, 427.2 × 15.24 × 9.14 m. Mormon Mesa, Moapa Valley, Nevada, US.
4 Lucio Fontana, *Concetto spaziale attese 1+1-111XY*, 1962. Emulsion on slashed canvas, 92 x 73 cm. Collection Les Abattoirs-Frac Occitanie Toulouse.

"There is no architect who is not an artist"

Interview with Éric de Chassey

Éric de Chassey
The architecture school where you studied was located within the École des Beaux-Arts. But even though they shared the same premises, the two were completely separate. A paradoxical situation. Does this mean that there is a difference between architecture and the creation of an art object and that, for you, this difference is important? Or are the boundaries porous? I am thinking here of Le Corbusier because he's a major historic example, but he's far from the only one (fig. 1). If you think back to the Renaissance, to the seventeenth or eighteenth centuries, you find a considerable number of people who were simultaneously architects, designers, painters, and sculptors. With Le Corbusier and a few others, there is still the idea that fine arts and architecture are distinct, but that in spite of that there are constant crossovers between them. Do you see a real separation? And if so, where would you locate it?

Dominique Perrault
An architect is not an artist in the sense that an architect doesn't produce a pure work of art. With an architect, the separation doesn't exist at the start of the design process but occurs during the implementation process. In the creative process, their attitude is that of an artist, then afterwards, it's applied art. Architecture is applied art, meaning that it embodies an ensemble that is not conceptually autonomous, and its grandeur, like its servitude, lies in being useful. This does not give it access to the dimension of art, for which utility is not required.

É.d.C.: However, there are many works of art (paintings, sculptures, etc.) that are useful by virtue of the very idea that guides them. If you make a stained-glass window for a church, it's generally for a specific place, with a clearly defined function. It's not the same approach as architecture, but the processes have much in common. You could say that it's also applied art.

D.P.: Decorative art, rather.

É.d.C.: Does the visual dimension of architecture take precedence in the actual work process? The very beginnings of a project, with sketches, start with a visual form; they propose a visual solution for a place. To what extent does this dimension come first?

D.P.: Some things come to me immediately when I'm creating, with more or less value in terms of expression and perception. I can use lines as well as models, as in the work for the Fondation Pinault on the Île Seguin, where we covered this pile of boxes with a whole range of materials. At the start, there's always some kind of élan, which may later be criticized because it's not necessarily suitable. The result is not necessarily sufficiently resilient to survive the time-frame of an architectural project, which can take five years when things are moving quickly, but is generally closer to ten. These first moments are very important because they carve out routes, entire processes. My relationship to contemporary art is not a question, it's a way of approaching subjects, understanding and conceptualizing them. When we fitted out Denise René's gallery on the Right Bank, in 1991, she let us use her space for the first exhibition. Gaëlle Lauriot-Prévost and I produced around twenty pieces, some of which are still worthy of being looked at today, which were the fruit of a completely conceptual process, halfway between the pictorial and the sculptural—they were reliefs placed under a veil of black gauze. When you arrived, all you could see was a dark surface, and as you got closer, shapes gradually appeared. Behind them, there were also aerial photos and an installation of highly conceptual objects, for example a glass plate placed on a plan and covered with a filtering black sheet. This approach is a constant.

É.d C.: Speaking of abstraction, I have the feeling that, compared to many contemporary architects, you're not really interested in the question of architecture that talks, or in the fact that the building embodies a form of discourse, figurative or otherwise.

D.P.: If I take the example of the Bibliothèque Nationale, the media really latched on to the literal image of the four open books.

É.d.C.: I just can't see that image; I don't see those open books.

D.P.: The reality is the disappearance of a parallelepiped, which was the volume that had to be built. It was really a punishment to construct a building with such a volume: three times the size of the Centre Pompidou! This had not insignificant consequences for the development of the neighborhood. Now, I buried this cube, I embedded it in the ground. The four towers are the four corners of the

parallelepiped. The volume between these four angles is embedded in the ground, so it's totally abstract. One source of inspiration for this is Robert Morris and his four glass cubes [*Untitled Mirrored Cubes*, 1965], a real abstract dimension between presence and absence. This underpins all the projects.

É.d.C.: Is this something you need or is it just a facilitator?

D.P.: No, I need it.

É.d.C.: Is an artist's work on one of your buildings fundamentally different from what you do when you intervene in a pre-existing situation, in a place that's never pristine, with a context in which you have to find how to fit in, while meeting a set of specifications?

D.P.: It's wonderful when the encounter with artists turns out well in these architectures, such as railway and metro stations, which are works of civil engineering. Michelangelo Pistoletto, for example, created huge frescoes in Naples on the theme of travel. It's a sublime work, consummately intelligent and poetic. His two frescoes give the project its full meaning: forty meters deep, on either side of the set of escalators, we are faced with two frescoes, thirty meters long and three or four meters high, which almost invite us to continue your descent. Another fantastic example is Piotr Kowalski's sculpture of a thirty-meter spire parallel to the Earth's axis in front of the École de l'Innovation Technologique building in Marne-la-Vallée. We could also mention the work on Innsbruck's town hall, in which a dozen artists were involved, including Isa Genzken, who drew an ear on the level of the municipal council chamber, on the gable wall opposite. These things are not innocent...

É.d.C.: Are the other arts present, consciously or unconsciously, as sources, memories, or whatever, at different moments of the creative process? Or does the focus remain on the question of architecture as a specific issue?

D.P.: The entire emotional dimension is constantly present. Architects have a bit of a split personality. In any case, that's how I experience my profession. The architect thinks, transcribes this web of emotions, then builds. And when all this becomes operational, the criteria, the very language, and the methodology are completely different. It's applied art. And that is a very fine definition.

É.d.C.: Let's consider a slab of glass like the one you used for the collage for the Arc de Triomphe. Can the work of artists who have used glass, like Larry Bell for example (fig. 2), be thought of as specific inspiration for a specific project?

D.P.: Let's look to Claude Rutault on the question of absence, which is a real subject for me. In all the work on the relationship with the soil, there are of course questions of sustainability and resilience. But there is also the question of invisibility, and Rutault embodies this work on a certain form of disappearance. When, in a real stroke of genius, he covered the raw canvas stretchers in the Hôtel Berlier with a sheet of glass, so that the city could be reflected, he produced a major work, in the conceptual sense. When I develop these strategies of the glass floor, I feel an immediate closeness to him, in terms of reading, understanding, and emotion. For me it's quite immediate.

É.d.C.: In short, then, architectural creation is supported, nourished, even almost founded, on works that do not belong to architecture. Let's stay with what you were saying about Rutault. Can we say that his work gives you ideas as an architect, or that, knowing his work, you see affinities with your own?

D.P.: Both. There's no precedence. It's part of my sensory world. When I see Michael Heizer's work in relation to the land and Ewha University, they are twin gestures.

É.d.C.: But is there anything more than a similarity? In general terms, can Heizer's work—I'm thinking of *Double Negative* (fig. 3) here, of course—provide an architect with solutions when he's thinking about a given situation?

D.P.: The answer is yes. Heizer absolutely does provide answers, through the formal, physical dimension, but also through the gesture of revealing places and what stems from that. If he doesn't dig into his hill, it doesn't exist and, therefore, the act of digging into this earth sets the scene for an entire landscape. With a limited gesture—even if it takes a few bulldozers and a Caterpillar—he sets in motion a whole piece of desert. It's exactly the same thing for an architect: with our buildings, we reveal places, we set in motion processes that transform them. Not only is there the aesthetic question of how to intervene on the physical, but there is also everything this entails in this kind of intervention. To me, there are no limits to the use of these references, this culture, this nourishment. I appropriate this substance, I manipulate it, I put it back, I redeploy it, in a very free way. What I'm trying to say is that these are foods, but they are not images.

É.d.C.: There we have it, you've said it: it is the processes that interest you more than the images.

D.P.: The processes and their physicality. You can't not feel something when you walk down these vertical labyrinths to get to the water in India. They transport you. In everything we are talking about, there is a notion of transfiguration. Heizer's creations in the desert are a way of transfiguring dead earth.

É.d.C.: This point of view is interesting because it suggests that we could link Heizer or Lucio Fontana to the cut, to revelation, which is of course extremely apt for the latter (fig. 4). What's important is the opening up of space in front and behind, the revelation of space. In your architectural work, when you dig, it looks like a cut, only it's also done in order to connect a certain number of things. Works of art interest you when they are clearly linked to your concerns, such as connecting rather than separating.

D.P.: One of my convictions is that in architecture, abstraction liberates. It's a source of free interpretation. It allows you to re-read what exists, the notion of reversibility, of reinterpretation. You can reinterpret an abstract form, but you can't reinterpret a figurative building,

be it postmodern or deconstructed. And this is typically linked to questions of Conceptual Art, of installation.

É.d.C.: It's true that a great deal of historical abstraction was linked to a very prescriptive project. This was the case, in a way, when Kazimir Malevich thought that the black square, or rather the black quadrangle, constituted the beginning of a complete reorganization of the world.

D.P.: Architecture is prescriptive, whether it likes it or not. Indeed, that is its main point. If you want shelter, you need a roof and walls; if you want to enter a place, you need a door; if you want some light, you need a window. There is no choice. But if you develop a notion of abstraction—impossible by definition, because architecture is totally physical—if you do some conceptual work on this physicality, which you can't and don't want to escape, because you absolutely need it, you're going to take it out of itself and take it beyond what it is in the functional or constructed sense of the term.

É.d.C.: Does this mean that at the very moment of conception, there is the idea that what has been built could, one day, have a completely different function from its original one?

D.P.: Yes, the future of a building is the transformation of that building into another building.

É.d.C.: In a text that goes back a bit now, you say that the question for the architect is no longer history, but territory and geography. What is the first thing you do when you start a project: analyze the place or the space?

D.P.: The place.

É.d.C.: If you're post-minimal, it's the place and not the space.

D.P.: Yes.

É.d.C.: I'm referring to Barnett Newman's phrase: "My drawing declares the space."

D.P.: As soon as I started school, people talked to me about space. At first, I'd look up, looking for the rocket. But for me, place has meaning. It's a bundle of information. When I work on a subject in a place, knowing what it's going to be—a library, for example, in a European capital—is enough for me to get to work. I don't go see the site, for fear of damaging it if it's great, or coming back in despair if it's ugly. My protocol is to follow my ideas and only afterwards do I go and see the site, but by then I already have an imaginary vision, one that can be contradicted or, on the contrary, elevated and amplified. I then begin to have a real exchange with the site and I enter data into the program elements. The richer the data, the richer the project. But at first I need a kind of blank slate, a distance, which leads quite naturally to the historical, geographical, artistic, and scientific references we mentioned. I can't work on a project that has been touched by the agency before I begin, not because what is proposed isn't interesting but because I'm already lost.

É.d.C.: This is why we could say that the term "installation" or "installing" is apt, given that, since the 1950s and 1960s, an art installation is something that is autonomous from a specific place and is conceived in terms of its general modalities. Then, once you arrive in the gallery and see it for real, you realize that you're going to have to adapt.

D.P.: What would you say about work that's floor-bound, like Urs Fischer's? For me it's installation. I have always found this kind of intervention on a gallery floor deeply affecting. It gives the place, which was rather inert, an intensity, a life of its own, and it creates a different kind of nature. My work effectively consists in changing nature into another kind of nature. I construct the landscape as an integral part of the project and the inscription, because all these buildings, even if their form is elementary, have echoes in their position, their settings. It's quite precise, in fact it's extremely precise.

É.d.C.: You can have things that are barely visible but that completely change the place, but we've been talking for a while now around this very complex relationship, around this question: where does this change, which isn't necessarily a demiurgic gesture, or which certainly isn't—

D.P.: ... or that at least tries to keep itself from being—

É.d.C.: this change occurs, while still allowing freedom? I recall that in your book *Groundscapes*, there is an illustration of a plate on the floor, a work by Carl Andre, with the idea that you can transform an entire space simply by applying a very, very thin layer of a material. But have I understood correctly?

D.P.: Perfectly. These are extremely limited gestures. On a horizontal surface, you place another horizontal surface and the reading of the original one becomes more dense, lives differently. Architecture has this capacity for the most radical transformation.

É.d.C.: These same questions apply to a certain form of abstraction, Rutault's in particular. The commonality is that successful architecture requires that the subjectivity of the architect does not prevent the subjectivity of those who are going to live in the architecture from having free rein. Have you ever done a museum?

D.P.: We have entered a lot of competitions for museums. We won some of them, but they never came to fruition. We did a project for the Centre Pompidou in Metz using this prism. We covered it with panels of metal fabric and you could enter the intermediary space of the museum through the gaps in the corners. I reworked this approach comprehensively in the project for the Fondation Pinault on the Île Seguin, which marked the moment when metal textile really became an element of architectural design, taking its place both as a building material and as an artistic device. We then went on to work with Daniel Buren (fig. 5) along the edges of the island, using fountains and curtains in metal fabric over which the water slid to recreate the wall of the Renault factory.

É.d.C.: Daniel Buren is older than you. Were you interested in his work from the 1960s and 1970s, such as the strips of fabric with just one stripe painted over?

D.P.: Yes, absolutely, thanks to an architecture teacher I had at the École des Beaux-Arts called Philippe Sers, an art historian.

É.d.C.: Sers was one of the pioneers of the history of revolutionary architecture, particularly that of Bolshevik Russia, but he is also a great historian of abstraction—in particular, he has written several books on Wassily Kandinsky and Alexander Rodchenko. Finally, what is it that interests you in the work of Loris Gréaud (fig. 6)?

D.P.: It's Loris himself. Because he has an extremely strong relationship with architecture. We're currently working on the idea of a buried house for him. The studio where he works today is a posthumous work by Claude Parent. And Loris has always been interested in architecture, even when he had his big exhibition at the Palais de Tokyo in 2008. He had to be an architect, or at least to not be afraid of architecture.

É.d.C.: That's interesting: I ask you why you're interested in an artist's work and you say, because he's interested in architecture and, in fact, he's an architect...

D.P.: In a word, there is no artist who is not an architect and no architect who is not an artist.

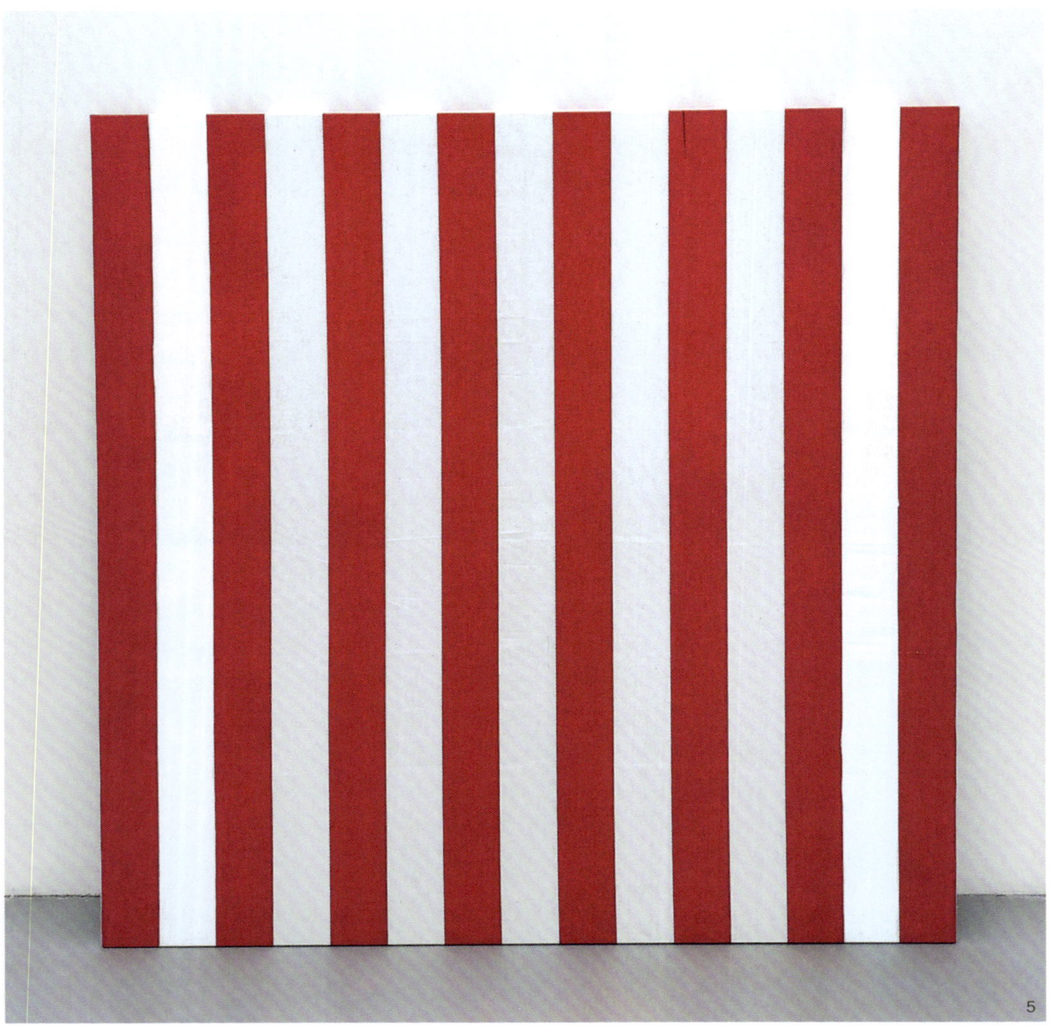

5

5 Daniel Buren, *Untitled*, December 1971. White acrylic paint on white and red striped fabric stretched on frame, 231 × 202 cm. FNAC 2013-0008 (11), donation Yvon Lambert, on deposit with the Centre national des arts plastiques.

6 Loris Gréaud, */dʌv/*, 2021–23. Installation, basalt funerary slab, grey paresol glass, raw concrete, taxidermized dove, soundtrack. Variable dimensions. Donation Domaine de Frapotel.

6

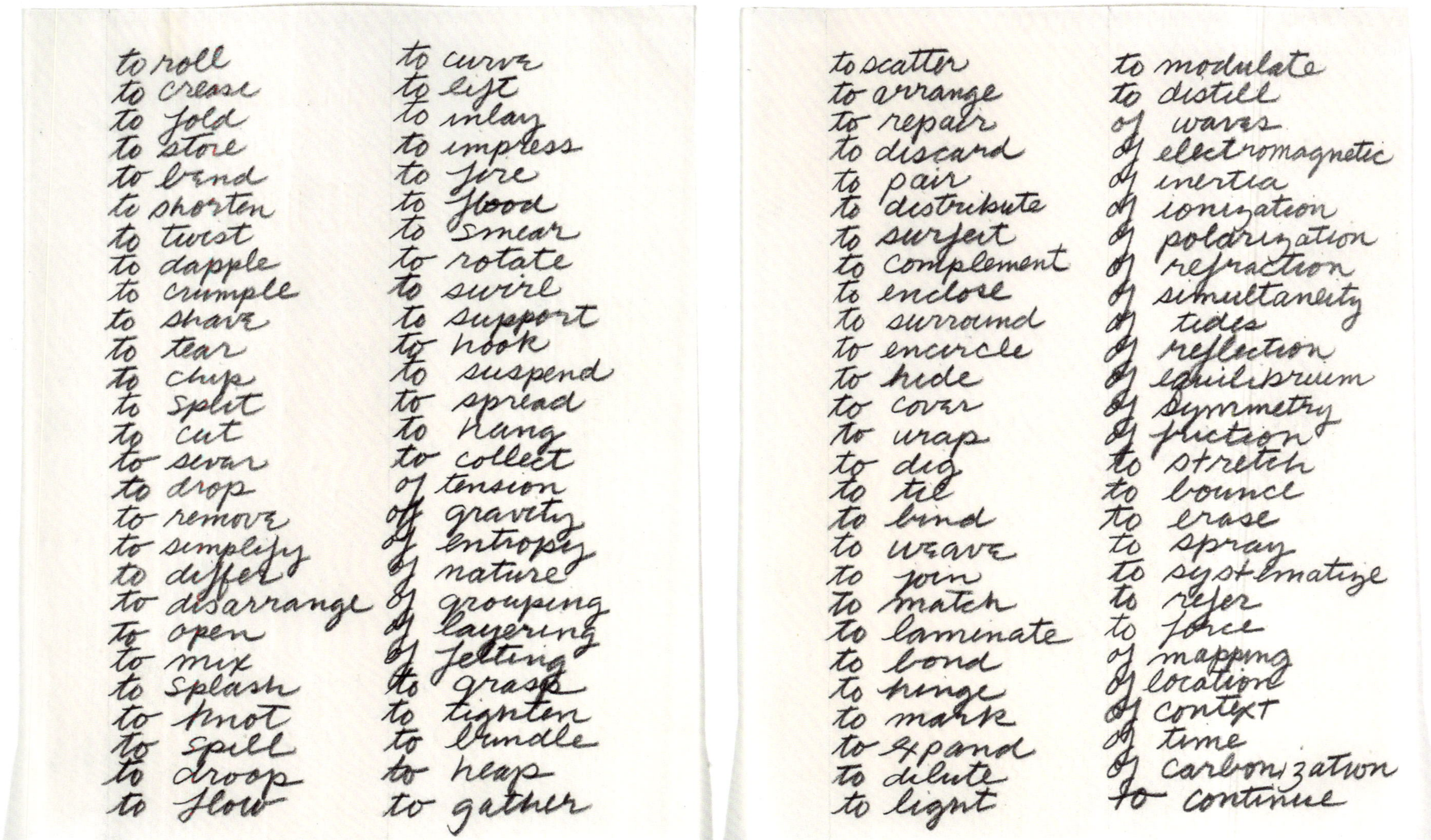

to roll
to crease
to fold
to store
to bend
to shorten
to twist
to dapple
to crumple
to shave
to tear
to chip
to split
to cut
to sever
to drop
to remove
to simplify
to differ
to disarrange
to open
to mix
to splash
to knot
to spill
to droop
to flow

to curve
to lift
to inlay
to impress
to fire
to flood
to smear
to rotate
to swirl
to support
to hook
to suspend
to spread
to hang
to collect
of tension
of gravity
of entropy
of nature
of grouping
of layering
of felting
to grasp
to tighten
to bundle
to heap
to gather

to scatter
to arrange
to repair
to discard
to pair
to distribute
to surfeit
to complement
to enclose
to surround
to encircle
to hide
to cover
to wrap
to dig
to tie
to bind
to weave
to join
to match
to laminate
to bond
to hinge
to mark
to expand
to dilute
to light

to modulate
to distill
of waves
of electromagnetic
of inertia
of ionization
of polarization
of refraction
of simultaneity
of tides
of reflection
of equilibrium
of symmetry
of friction
to stretch
to bounce
to erase
to spray
to systematize
to refer
to force
of mapping
of location
of context
of time
of carbonization
to continue

1

1 Richard Serra, *Verb List*, 1967
Pencil on two sheets of paper, 25.4 x 21.6 cm each
The Museum of Modern Art, New York, 843.2011.a-b.
Gift of the artist in honor of Wynn Kramarsky

Cutting into the void

Interview with Barry Bergdoll

Barry Bergdoll
I'd like to start our conversation by considering the verbs chosen for the four sections of the book—situating, mapping, writing, rewriting—because you hesitated over other words before choosing these terms to structure this retrospective, to look back over your entire architectural journey, as if echoing American sculptor Richard Serra's famous *Verb List* (fig. 1). Here, words are actions.

Dominique Perrault
We decided early on to use verbs because from the outset in an architect's process there are actions and movements. There was the same almost unpremeditated movement, for example, when I started work on the Bibliothèque Nationale project. One of my teachers and mentors at the École des Beaux-Arts, the German architect Martin Schulz van Treek, taught me how to make projects out of modelling clay. As a member of the German school, he didn't calculate in square meters, but translated his architectural program into cubic meters. Using a big kitchen knife, he cut the clay into a basic shape, a parallelepiped.

B.B.: It's the exact opposite of the doctrine associated with the École des Beaux-Arts, which for much of its history considered the plan as essential. Every project begins with the plan, and volumes follow from the plan.

D.P.: Exactly! And that had some immediate physical consequences for the resulting volumes. If there was some modelling clay left over, it meant the program wasn't finished, and if there wasn't enough, that meant the volume was already too big. When I was working on the Bibliothèque Nationale competition, I designed my model around a hypothetical neighborhood since it hadn't yet been built. I worked up my volume from modelling clay, which was the size of a shoebox. When I saw how this volume towered over everything, I thought: "That's not possible," and I pushed it down, physically, I crushed it. Hence the idea of embedding the project in the ground, making it disappear. The volume of a structure has to be acceptable, "sustainable."

B.B.: So you didn't start by "digging," you started by assembling the volumes... So then what was the relationship between the program rendered in three dimensions and the extravagant gesture of the four towers?

D.P.: At the time—and perhaps this isn't quite so true today—I found it very inspiring to define an elementary geometric form and have a conception that was sufficiently agile for the whole program to fit into it. Inside, this created quite unexpected, even unprecedented, devices and forms of organization. It wasn't a matter of adding together the elements in the program but of finding ways for them to work together physically in order to stay within this predetermined volume, which in turn wasn't an isolated volume, because it worked with urban issues, landscapes, dimensions, and silhouettes. The program is just one given—one material, I would even say—among others. In finding its proper place, it in turn creates places specific to it.

B.B.: You describe an exercise in assembling volumes in relation to a program almost as if the composite form emerged from this sculptural act. But in many projects—particularly the library—the image is so strong that it's hard to imagine it didn't play an essential role. Does the image direct or does it emerge along the way?

D.P.: Image is important, for sure. It allows us to read what the architect has written, and this is true of all projects. The Bibliothèque, which is thirty years old in 2025, is part of the history of architecture. Sometimes I think it's actually the last building of the modern movement. Today, the question of image is perhaps less in the forefront, because my projects are more concerned with complementarity, and even absence in some cases. The Bibliothèque was really a declarative project. I tried to fit everything in around the garden and have just one public square, but we were in the middle of abandoned industrial land and a large space, with the void of the garden at center and the library around it, would not have been able to visually inspire the development of the neighborhood we see today. The swimming pool and velodrome project in Berlin (fig. 3) that came right after the library is absolutely radical: the buildings really do disappear, because the whole thing is embedded in the ground. Then, of course, there's the Ewha project in Seoul (fig. 2), where the building constructs a landscape and then disappears beneath it.

B.B.: It's an absolutely fascinating sequence that generated other projects.

D.P.: But it took me a while to understand that—first, we had to build the library, which, after all, was quite a big deal! Then I had to free myself from that, in a way, which took time. Today, I see the library in terms of an initiation, because it contains just about every concept I've worked on since, including the question of materials, because that is where metal weave, which didn't exist in architecture, first made its appearance. In my lectures, I always joke that I'm still thirty-six, which is the average age of young architects, because I designed a project with a sustainability that is celebrated today: with a garden, a place of biodiversity and an island of coolness, using the resilience of the underside, wood for the public space and solid materials for the interior, without paint or primer, creating a pedestrian esplanade on which people dance: the program of a young architect of today, you might say.

B.B.: Let's look again at these three sites, all very different, which can be grouped together under the term "situating." In a way, the Library is a hill, so it's a mixture of dug-out and built-up, whereas Berlin is submerged, and in Seoul you had to dig into the hill as if you were building a valley.

D.P.: From a conceptual viewpoint, it's about conceiving geographies. This is a fairly unprecedented approach for architects, because to construct buildings like these you actually have to design the civil engineering. These are infrastructures that shape the ground and build networks.

B.B.: Like the great heroic public works of yesteryear?

D.P.: Absolutely. There is no separation between infrastructure and architecture. The Villejuif station encapsulates this idea of infrastructure that becomes architecture, linked to its specific calculations, of the civil engineering, technical installations, soil resistance, and so on. I chose the cylinder, which is a pure form. The staging of the infrastructure comes about through the architectural elements that intersect within the cylinder. This approach doesn't really exist in the world of architects. When the building is above ground, it is called architecture; when it's below ground, we don't call it anything. It's untitled.

B.B.: That reminds me of the architect Étienne-Louis Boullée, who is seen as the great visionary of the late eighteenth century, with his astonishing panoramic projects that were as much landscape design as architecture. He was proud to claim that he had invented two types of architecture: an "architecture of shadows" and a "buried architecture." Could we say that, engineers aside, we had to wait for Dominique Perrault for his dream to come true?

D.P.: I don't know about having to wait for Perrault, but it's true that my work is marked by a certain mistrust of architecture as an object in itself. I'm wary of architecture seen in terms of global solutions. Today, I have developed a kind of response that always seeks to go beyond architecture itself. To come back to Boullée's words, it's about getting the world above to live with the world below, as a whole, in the same way that you can't separate the roots from the tree. That's why the question of soil is so important. Perhaps it has something to do with my origins in the land. I come from the center of France. As a teenager, I did geological research amidst the volcanoes of Auvergne, collecting stones in the mines, and to do that, I had to draw a map.

B.B.: Thinking about the former Museum of Public Works built by Auguste Perret, which unfortunately no longer presents maquettes of civil engineering projects, I wonder what a museum of Dominique Perrault's models and projects would be like? How do you make a model of something that is half underground? How do you convey this relationship to the site?

D.P.: Building in the ground is nothing new. It's a theme that's been explored since the dawn of time. An exhibition showing the devices used by architects and engineers to reveal what I have defined as the *groundscape* would be fantastic. I'm thinking of the impressive model of the Opéra station that was displayed at the Cité de l'Architecture et du Patrimoine in the exhibition "Métro! Le Grand Paris en mouvement." That would be a great theme for an architecture biennale.

B.B.: If we take the Bibliothèque-Berlin-Seoul sequence, what is the relation to the site? Do you begin work on each project with certain forms in mind, or does the encounter with the site generate the device? These are two different questions. How do you represent one of these projects, when a large part of the site is underground and can't be represented by traditional models, and at the same time the projects have forms that are so present, so simple in a way, that they are very easy to remember. I can close my eyes and picture the projects in my mind's eye.

D.P.: The ground level is changed by the intervention. This is a very important issue when it comes to writing the project. In the process, we define the level of the ground, which is not the ground floor, which is not the ground of the city, but a displaced ground. This introduces the notion of thickening the ground. This is a very illuminating element between the nineteenth-century city and this work on the thickening of the ground that coincided with the emergence of the metropolis. The nineteenth-century city established a clear separation between what was below and what was above, with all its ways of dwelling and working, its streets, squares, and so on. We can see this very clearly in drawings from the Haussmann era and how they evolved, and you can also see the evolution of the underground, with all the technical and energy networks, the metro, etc. For the projects we're talking about, we made cuts that went as far as fifty meters deep, in Villejuif, Naples, and Seoul, in order to connect all the layers of infrastructure. These are projects where the ground line becomes plural, it multiplies. At Ewha, the topography of the valley created a gentle slope, which made it possible to engage with a ground line at almost every level. It's a building dug into the ground that you walk through horizontally. I believe in this architecture, in its sensitivity to the site.

B.B.: The idea of the nineteenth-century French city is an interesting one: underground you put the services and everything you shouldn't see but that makes everyday life above ground function. In so doing you bring everyday life into the ground. You occupy in a civic way the space where the machinery used to run, where the servants often worked...

D.P.: The ground is a common good. It has been seen as a place of denial, of anxiety, an opaque world in which anything can be hidden. But actually, it's all about "bringing to light" what's below ground in order to appropriate it, and turn it into a project! This term "mise à jour"—literally "bringing to light," but also "updating"—says a lot. There is a programmatic update, but also in the physical sense, bringing to light by opening a space to natural light, and environmentally, too, updating our cities' resilience.

B.B.: In other words, what we weren't supposed to see. The extraordinary thing about the university in Seoul is that a very, very strong gesture, a site that is very complicated but at the same time very strong and civic, was made by digging. When you think of all the public squares like that, every time you dug pedestrian zones, underground, you created hell, such as the Forum des Halles in Paris in the 1970s. Very few of them worked.

D.P.: My projects are intimately linked to geography, to a site, to a context—ultimately, to an "already there" that is not contained within the existing architecture. In all the work of incision, whether circular, linear, or otherwise, the creation of a geography is what allows the redeployment of the existing geography, which will be of a different nature. Then come questions of landscape, questions about the presence or absence of the architectural object in these landscapes. Villejuif is an "iceberg" project, because it's a station that is a bit like a market in a city. The visible part of the station resembles a small, open hall, accessible from all sides. It's practically a public space, and then you discover this depth and vitality. You're not standing over an abyss. You're really surveying a world of movement and light.

B.B.: On the surface, we're talking about the scale of a small neighborhood center, but in depth we're in the infrastructure of a metropolis. In terms of the activities that take place there and the scale, we have two completely different dimensions: on the one hand, the creation of a large square, a podium framing a garden below; on the other, an urban intervention connected to complex systems of transport, networks, and, of course, the landscape of the Seine.

D.P.: These two dimensions do seem very far apart, but if they can't cohabitate, the metropolis won't work: you can't read this notion of a very large territory. Anyone who lives in a metropolis doesn't know it as a whole—it's so huge. Who knows the Île-de-France, this metropolis of twelve million inhabitants called Paris? Nobody, but we do have a mental map of it. I'm always fascinated by this, the measure and excessiveness inherent in the areas in which we live. In the "Mapping" section of this book, a more theoretical approach was developed as part of the international workshop on Greater Paris called "Hôtel Métropole": how could we develop a map that connected to a person living in Greater Paris, rather than an administrative map—a personal map on the theme of "migration," of movement? At the time, this approach was misunderstood because of the ambiguity surrounding the term "migration." When you live in a metropolis, there are times (of separation, illness, etc.) when you can't *inscribe yourself* at once in order to redefine your life, so you need places that can create a kind of antechamber before that re-inscription in the city. So we drew a map resembling the sky, with constellations identifying the major facilities that are needed. On this map, the constellations revolved around a point called "Hôtel Métropole." The idea was to situate a building where people could live, work... Today, this is what we call *co-living* and *coworking*. We defined a network with these metropolis hotels that would enable us to have the services we need at certain times in our lives close at hand. Thinking in networks is mapping.

B.B.: You mention the hotel. Today, a hotel is a place where tourists are stored, whereas the great hotels of the nineteenth century were public squares, with lobbies that served as hubs for both the resident population and people passing through. The ground floor was a sample of the city. Your Bibliothèque is the only one that follows the very precise program of a library, but conceived with a focus on being much more open to the public: it creates a large public square that people walk through, it organizes a neighborhood even for the people who will never come inside. It's something of a prefiguration of this idea of a metropolis hotel.

D.P.: This brings us back to my doubts about architecture. Is it capable of producing an open system? Architecture is an art that creates the forbidden by building walls that, while they protect, also separate. The architecture I design is a permanent critique of the presence of walls. We could imagine walls made of metal fabric: a filtering wall but not a wall that excludes, one that allows different worlds to live together. Imaginary cities built of fabric. When you talk about this public square, you're talking about a proposition that isn't immediately linked to a library. A library's vocation isn't to offer a public space, especially not a public space that allows you to walk through the library. The attitude here is really paradoxical. I would like to talk about the work done on the *mairies*, annexes of the Paris Hôtel de Ville, when the city expanded. The town halls in these new arrondissements were home to a very hospitable system of facilities: the market that gravitated around it, the square, the boys' school, the girls' school, the fire station... It was extremely sophisticated and it was organized and disorganized according to the geography of the place where the town hall instituted republican power. This was not a closed bastion. You could get inside—that's what you were saying about a hotel—it's a refuge. The courtyard of the town hall is active, an extension of public space. At the end of my studies, I worked on another typology, this time introverted, when I studied the convents on the Faubourg Saint-Germain in the eighteenth century, another territorialization of power but, this time, in enclosed spaces. A network of one, two, three, four or five convents was created, which then controlled the development of the neighborhood. The library is a hybrid of these two strategies of territorialization. It is introverted, what with its cloister, like the convents of the eighteenth century, and extroverted, with its public space, like the buildings of the Republic in the nineteenth century. It is a paradoxical monument, without walls, railings, or perimeter colonnades.

B.B.: Can you expand on what you mean by "I have a horror of walls"?

D.P.: Building means building walls, whether they're made of wood, straw, concrete, metal, or any other material. It's one of the primary acts of architecture. It's not the only one, because architecture is also about creating roofs, another symbol. Building a wall is an act of separation, an authoritarian act that is violence but not aggression, because walls provide shelter. The primary act of architecture, its duty, is to protect, but the wall excludes. On the one hand, it is absolutely expected; and, on the other, it generates exclusion, because either I'm *in* or I'm *out*, it's physical, there's no negotiating. Whereas when we do the work of architecture as a work of geography, the question of the wall disappears.

B.B.: If we were to design the models for a future Perrault exhibition in a museum of public works, since we are somewhat in the spirit of civil engineering as architecture, where would the walls be? They're buried underground and we don't have a mental image of their position. It could be the beginning of a whole underground city that goes on for kilometers. We don't know where the limits are, even though they will define the invisible site and withstand all the pressure, be it the bed of the Seine or the movement of the land. The three projects we've mentioned are extremely strong gestures of inscription. You can project images of the form and experience when you're there, but you can't draw the contours of the project that are deeply embedded in the site. If you agree with this idea that in every project there is a tension between its strong visual representation, which gives us a clear mental image, and the reality of a network of underground connections that extends beyond it, how would you situate the station at Villejuif from this perspective?

D.P.: In Villejuif, the cylindrical wall is an infrastructure that constructs and asserts the boundary. The idea is to build an interior that we will call "architecture," which will accommodate all public and technical uses in a single volume, without walls. The public space extends into the first two floors of the station. You can exit from below to head for the park, for the hospital. There are multiple available floor levels. The project has a lot to do with mobility, it's a symphony of movement: I go up, I go down, I move around. The Villejuif station is a metaphor for perpetual movement, a kinetic Piranesi. There are hundreds of elements in motion: the people, but also the escalator steps, the elevators, the movements of the light, that of the metro. It's incessant. The wall has completely disappeared. You can feel the cylindrical shape surrounding you, but you can't see it. It frees up an empty space in which everything circulates without galleries, tunnels, or partitions: a three-dimensional open space bathed in the same natural light.

B.B.: In many of your projects, the question arises: where are the limits of the project? They're a bit hazy, indefinable.

D.P.: This connects with the question of scale. As the limits are not established, neither is the perception of scale. Scale is the result of inscription, but it doesn't inform us about anything. It is the dimension of the voids, that is to say, the spaces between things, that inscribes us, that enables us to read what is written, drawn, or built.

B.B.: Did the training that you mentioned at the start of our conversation have anything to do with landscape? It's very common these days to form a team with an architect and a landscape architect so that these two disciplines can complement each other in one way or another. But it seems to me that the landscape-design aspect of your work grew out of your architecture and your gestures.

D.P.: Which always leads to some robust discussions with landscape architects! I think that we need to build pieces of nature, which architecture invites us to do with its own particular means of construction. The cloister of the Bibliothèque is one example of this. We built the landscape using crane tracks, lifting equipment, and trucks that delivered trees twenty-five meters tall and thirty years old. It was a genuine construction operation, just like what you would do for a building. Planting the pine trees posed some real engineering questions, because the root ball of a pine tree weighs three tons, but its trunk weighs nothing and its needles even less. So we invented a machine, a bit like Leonardo da Vinci, creating a support along the trunk of the tree so that it could be lifted without breaking because of the difference in weight. And then we planted them vertically with cranes on the esplanade, twenty meters below.

B.B.: Did you have any idea, when you thought up this project, of how complicated it was going to be?

D.P.: No. We were lucky to have the remarkable expertise of an agricultural engineer who was also an adventurer and explorer. He was won over by the audacity of the idea of transplanting a piece of Normandy forest to the very heart of the Bibliothèque Nationale de France. Nature is no longer natural. Today, everyone agrees that the planet is totally known; there is no virgin land left. To preserve nature, we need to protect it, but we also need to build it.

B.B.: An English book published more than seventy years ago, *The Making of the English Landscape*,[1] shows the extent to which, apart from a few mountains, there is not a single kilometer of England that was not shaped by man, even though the English say they love the countryside because it is natural.

D.P.: Building nature is not an ecological offence, it's even a duty. Today, the area occupied by nature is shrinking because of urbanization, pollution, and climate change. So, in my projects, I build a nature by trying to use the device of a building that, when it disappears, will leave more room for the landscape and the void.

B.B.: That also brings to mind this idea of context, which you alluded to and which you don't like very much, the idea of inscribing something in a very delicate way. When you've described Ewha, you've stated that it entails "removing an incredible amount of earth in order to put it back." Once this absolutely heroic work of civil engineering is finished, once the plans are handed over, it's very contextual, but the transformation has been radical.

D.P.: In our typo-morphological education of a city, context refers to an analysis often linked to a historical approach to an urban fabric, determined by definition. Today, the notion of urbanity is disappearing.

That's why I replace the notion of context with that of place, which is more indeterminate and more complex.

B.B.: You work as an architect in Paris, where the urban context is extremely strong and in many places still framed by the system created by Haussmann. How does a Parisian architect work in the context of a city like New York or Seoul? How do you work in urban situations as diverse as those of Europe, America, and Asia?

D.P.: The question of geography, in the sense of the map, is not the same. The map of Paris, as it is constructed, is obviously very different from that of New York, and Seoul is something else again. In New York, there's a kind of conquest. It's a city of pioneers, so the grid is significant in terms of its inscription. Mapping New York means drawing a grid. And then building in New York is deforming that grid. This brings to mind the cities of Sicily, as studied by Bernard Huet. Their urban grids are fascinating to observe and are altered for reasons linked to the production of the city, but also because of topography. Topography and cartography seem inextricably linked. That's why the question of geography recurs so insistently. To me, Ewha is a geography project: the construction of a landscape allows what is "already there" to become permanent. A few years ago, 25,000 female students staged a protest against the university president. They stayed for three weeks, day and night, in the valley, at the heart of our project, and secured her dismissal. This was a historic event. This telescoping of a geographical fact and a historical fact is, in my opinion, the exact definition of public space.

B.B.: How has way you work evolved since the Bibliothèque Nationale? Are there attitudes in your current projects that were already written into your approach at the time? Is everything a natural outcome of this evolution, with moments when you take the approach deeper and challenges arising from other commissions?

D.P.: Commissions these days are quite varied. In Europe, it's more a case of rewriting and intervening in existing places, in cities that are already very well established. In the Middle East and Asia, commissions arise for completely new buildings and new city districts. On the other hand, as regards the Bibliothèque, there has been a path, a furrow that has been dug and is developing as a creative resource: what I call the Groundscape. This path obviously intersects with other themes. Versailles is certainly the most emblematic example. In terms of size, the intervention was relatively modest, but still we enlarged the château! The accommodation of thousands of visitors was rethought and reorganized by the creation of a "dessous." This "underneath" made it possible to extend the architecture of the château without affecting its existing, protected national heritage. Then there's the "rewriting" part, which we discuss in this book and which has been a major part of our work during the past ten years, based on existing buildings that we transform, for reasons either of use or adaptation. For example, the three Pont-de-Sèvres tower blocks, which were scattered around one another, were brought together by a large communal lobby that can accommodate the 5,000 people who work there. The existing structure was "flipped" by means of a rather sophisticated geometrical design. A set of hexagons captures and reflects the light on their facets, so that there is no longer a north facing façade. The communal space introduces a social dimension, an effect of comfort at the heart of these buildings. All this is achieved through additions, because in order to work on what's already there, we need to produce a new element that complements it, so that it can be given a new lease on life. Acting on something that's already there doesn't mean "leaving it there." You have to develop a project that provides a different interpretation.

B.B.: The same can be said for the whole of the Ile de la Cité. There is a continuous movement in this part of Paris, which in the eighteenth century was the city's most densely populated. Most of its inhabitants were driven out by Haussmann's operations and it became home to major institutions that have nothing to do with one another, each of which forms an internalized world in which people are cared for, punished, judged, or blessed. Paris is the world's most important tourist destination, an astonishing number of people pass through it, and all the work consists in imagining public space, which is now a bit haphazard and scattered. Does restoring mean reworking what's already there or transforming it completely?

D.P.: "Rewrite" is the word I'd use to return to its collective dimension, to provide, from a political point of view, a new reading of the Ile de la Cité, considering the whole island as a monument and not as a juxtaposition of monuments or institutions. From an institutional point of view, the only power that can bring all these institutions to the table is the presidential power. A reorganization of the State could also find an answer based on the Ile de la Cité...

B.B.: You also thought of "restoring" as one of the four actions, which is maybe not quite what people would expect of you. In his dictionary, Viollet-le-Duc inserted, not to say "inscribed," the word "restoration." This was the first dictionary of architecture to contain an article on "restoration." And it begins as follows: "Restoration: feminine noun. Both the word and the thing are modern." What would be your definition of the word "restoration," which I don't think you understand the same way as Viollet-le-Duc did?

D.P.: In the end, rather than the verb "to restore," I preferred "rewrite." Rewriting as both a duty to protect and a duty to create. In "rewriting" there is "I protect," and therefore the heritage dimension, and at the same time, "I create." There is obviously understanding and respect, sometimes admiration, for "what is there," for heritage, whether it's Versailles or the Montparnasse Tower. But to ensure that "what is there" remains, so that it can be put to other uses, so that the economic balance needed to keep it alive can be achieved, we need to work creatively to give it contemporary value and relevance. The Montparnasse Tower is a manifesto and an experimental project in the "Rewriting" chapter. What's really interesting about this tower is that it can't be restored on a like-for-like basis, because it's a completely monofunctional, standardized object, with a repetitive, standardized plan. We need to be able to demolish the interior so the building can breathe, all the while protecting the façade. That's why the project consists in connecting another tower alongside the Montparnasse Tower, on the same site, merging with the existing tower. This assembly makes it possible

to break up 15,000 square meters inside the tower, and thus offers new possibilities for living and working there.

B.B.: So, we're talking about digging upwards, right?

D.P.: Exactly! And this also gets rid of the obsession with the height of the Eiffel Tower. This restoration project, working with what already exists, requires more sensitive planning, which needs to be written and rewritten in order to account for its topography and to map it. Everything fits together.

B.B.: Is it frustrating to have to classify a project under one theme in this book, when it fits under several rubrics and overlaps with others?

D.P.: This approach may seem imperfect, but it opens up new ways of reading and linking different projects, and shows their complexity. It allows us to go beyond the chronology of a traditional monograph.

B.B.: It means questioning the evolution of your thinking on one or more themes, through this very interesting juxtaposition of projects that may be thirty years apart, because there are also things that change...

D.P.: A work has to be positioned and repositioned on the loom each day. It's a permanent weaving of the same warp, the same thread, but different each time. You don't forget anything, you write and rewrite.

B.B.: As a historian of nineteenth-century French architecture and urban planning, I'm intrigued by your take on the contradictory legacies of Haussmann and the modernist city. Do you think it is possible to draw on both in a critical analysis, perhaps to transcend the opposition between them created by the postmodernist quest for the "European city," promoted by a whole school of thought in the 1980s and beyond, particularly in the movement associated with Maurice Culot?

D.P.: We're engaged in a dialectical process, but also a structural one that is constantly constructing and reconstructing the architectural object. This critical reading partakes of the principle of revealing what is and anticipating what will be. At the Poste du Louvre, built by the architect and theorist Julien Guadet, a conceptual approach installs a solid periphery with a self-stabilizing stone façade and delivers an interior made entirely of flexible metal "Meccano" that lends itself to all kinds of purposes. It's not modern. It's not postmodern. It's not typo-morphological, it's not historicist. With this rewriting, Guadet becomes wildly contemporary.

B.B.: It seems to me that there is a difference between the concept of "enhancement," an act of careful restoration to restore the grandeur of a somewhat forgotten monument, and the process of intervention that reveals entirely new aspects and potential in a building.

D.P.: Restitution is not revelation. Architecture is admirable when it reveals. Architecture without this virtue is useful, but it doesn't transport us.

B.B.: Do you encounter similar situations in Asian cities in the sense that, culturally, Asians have a different relationship with buildings and heritage, as a civilization in which things are replaced every thirty years? When you have to conceive a very large-scale project in an Asian city, do you feel totally free, without all the constraints of European heritage and urban planning?

D.P.: The notions of urban fabric and urban continuity do not exist in Asian cities the way they do in our European cities. And yet these cities, most of which are becoming metropolises or even megalopolises, are building a history that also has geographic roots. This is perhaps what explains a certain abstraction of the map, which we Europeans see as offering an unprecedented conceptual freedom. The independence of architectural structures transforms them into objects that are tossed about by political and economic forces, sometimes with no clear plan, vision, or meta-urbanity. This complex urbanity could be symbolized by a theatre in which the stage is the cartography/topography and the buildings are the actors, in a written and rewritten narrative that defines their presences or absences.

B.B.: How do you perceive Berlin in relation to this analysis? A building of Olympic dimensions, designed for movement, with swimming and cycling, which almost disappears in the center of a garden?

D.P.: The concept behind the Berlin project stems from a political choice. It was conceived as part of Berlin's bid to host the 2000 Olympic Games. I absolutely wanted to make a gesture that was the antithesis of the 1936 stadium. A place that was not a celebration of political power. We planted an apple orchard. The two sports halls were built into the heart of it. They disappear. They create clearings with their roofs that are flush with the ground, like pools with a metallic sheen. The architecture disappears. It was for this ethical and aesthetic reason that the project was chosen.

B.B.: It's a great gesture, an anti-heroic heroic gesture.

D.P.: It's a definition of architecture.

1 William George Hoskins, *The Making of the English Landscape* (London: Hodder & Stoughton, 1954); reprinted several times by Penguin Books since 1970.

2

3

5

4

2 Ewha Women's University, Seoul South Korea, 2004–08, study model, scale 1:500.

3 Olympic velodrome and swimming pool, Berlin, 1992.

4 Aérogare des Invalides, Fondation Giacometti, 2017–30.

5 Piazza Garibaldi, Naples, 2004–15, 2017–19.

SITUATING

Critique of the fundamentals

Architecture always benefits from examining its own roots. Serious architectural action is critical action. What could be more essential than the floor, the wall, the roof, and the façade? Trace them, raise them, and architecture appears. Demarcative, supportive, and protective, they undoubtedly form its foundation; at the same time, they divide it by imposing their separative language, their limiting structural logic. Each imposes its authority on the other, and together they form a coalition of as many self-blocking prerogatives. They are thought to be irrevocable and immutable, yet they are merely architectural modalities and by no means finalities. Constrained by its own limits, this system must enter into crisis and deconstruct itself.

If the floor ceases to be conceived as a dividing plane, its surface gives way. It then opens up its underside like a new architectural domain, blurring the relationship between the intra and the extra, the infra and the supra. In these spaces thus freed, new topographies emerge.

If the wall—this powerful archetype of the founding gesture—ceases to be a secant plane in space, a tool of subdivision, in the underground domain, as a support structure, countervailing the pressure of the earth and rocks, it no longer separates space: it opens it up in front of it, clearing a constructive void. In a reversed logic, it no longer constrains the interior volume, but guarantees and protects it.

Finally, the infiltration of architecture into the subcutaneous depths of the city redefines or abolishes the very function of the façade and redefines the notion of the roof.

The subsoil is swallowed up by reductive, strictly logistical assignments and issues. It is a largely under-qualified space, devoted primarily to accommodating everything that would clutter the city above ground and needs to be concealed: network infrastructure (energy, water, transport of goods and persons, sewers, ventilation) and storage space, including parking. The ground is thus defined in crude terms: a volume that can be dug out at will, a windfall of space that can be spent without counting the cost, in a context in which urban land is in increasingly short supply.

Moving the city below ground level is an impoverished approach to architecture and urban planning. The point is not to live underground! We don't perceive the fictions and alternatives concealed in these still-hermetic spaces. Adding something more to architecture and to the city. Each must rethink its program and create a new dialectic between superstructures and infrastructures. Architecture infiltrated underground creates new urbanities, radically changing the fabric of the city, the way it is perceived, and the very practice of the architect-urban planner.

For architecture to take issue with itself, to embolden itself in critical deconstruction, is for it to free itself from that which encases it and ultimately contributes to the architectural object's over-assertion and unmooring from topography and territory. Yet, that it needs to steer clear of soliloquizing and formal rhetoric goes without saying. The most crucial issue is inscription.

The autonomous, single object fails to anchor itself and fails the territory when it descends haughtily from its leaden sky to fix itself solitarily. Instead, we need to work at the heart of complexities. Architecture as a discipline must no longer think in terms of objects, but of places.

Groundscape, the landscape of the ground

Groundscape designates a new register of spaces, to be discovered in the topography of a place. A new scale of landscape that launches architecture into other dimensional arcana and opens it up to bold experimentation. Groundscape is a generative concept, an operator of architectural conversions. It is radical because it works on syntaxes at the root level, on visual lexicons, predicates, aspects, and perceptions. Architecture as a discipline is broadened, as is the spirit of the constructive gesture and the design itself. Groundscape opens onto new architectural intelligences. As a laboratory of potential architecture, it generates other phenomena, other fictions, other poetics of spatial play. However strongly characterized an architect's grammar may be, its language deepens through neologism.

Bringing the ground and the subsoil back to the heart of architectural design is part of the arsenal of means at our disposal. Groundscape broadens the horizon of action beneath our feet like a vivid image of the powers of architecture: it is, one might say, a deep deposit in its mental soil. A field of action capable of changing the morphology of the city and renewing it through its root system.

Thought is catalyzed by constraint. In this case, for architecture, the constraints of the ground: its resistance, its ultra-dense matter, its opaque compactness against light, and even the prejudices that weigh on underground space. We need to activate new engineering resources, a holistic approach to geology, and a different culture of sub-surface places.

Groundscape does not presuppose a minimum depth. It is generic and, above all, a transfiguration of the city's subcutaneous depth, a revision of the interfaces between below and above, within and without, inverted topographies, constructive emptiness, circulations, volumetrics, and scenographies of light. It constitutes an architectural and mental landscape that extends and amplifies our visible world.

Abstract architecture

Architecture strengthens itself when it challenges itself, its postulates and its lexemes (floor, wall, façade, roof). It needs to further radicalize this self-contestation by extending it to its phenomenality. To put its authority—an oh-so-ambiguous term—on the line is to take a path of boldness and discernment.

Architecture must slip free of itself like an abstraction. Clarity is the visible form of the idea. No one enters here who is not a geometer. The beauty of spacing and disappearance. By eclipsing the entire mass of its volume in the ground, the Bibliothèque Nationale de France François-Mitterrand silences its absence in the Parisian riverside landscape. Its presence is dematerialized in the monumental void between its four corner towers. This void is itself hollowed out by a second cloister-forest. With the void comes full power! The architecture is excavated like a landscape added to the city. The whole site, this relief turned towards the depths, becomes extra-dimensional. Hidden from view, by subtraction, the library is nonetheless firmly rooted in its territory. It frees it from the over-assertions and sovereignties of the architectural object. The subterranean deployments of the library carry with them a major and paradoxical challenge: the enhancement of the architectural inscription and at the same time the denial of the foundation, its de-inscription.

At its highest degree of abstraction, architecture ceases to be a nagging presence. It must be conceived more as a landscape than as an object. By seeping into the ground, architecture brings forth new relationships to space. The beauty of the gesture is to introduce transparency and fluidity underground, to let the light in.

Architecture from below

The urban plot is remodeled by its new underground extensions, its stratifications and spacious volumes. By freeing itself up from below, it reduces the density of its surface. The space for use is reprogrammed by being excavated.

Groundscape situates the building in an overly mineral and overly dense urban environment, and rebuilds links by means of spacing and rooting. The ground line no longer demarcates anything. The entire reading of the architectural device is modified when it is elaborated in strata that can be penetrated by light. Images of depths have no assigned dimensions. They can move effortlessly from the small to the large. From microcosm to cosmos. A place infiltrating the ground that becomes architectural plenitude touches on something timeless. Here we are dealing with the anthropological structures of human culture. In buried architecture, the mental archetype of the cave is charged with prohibitions and superstitions. The bowels of the earth have always been a place of initiation and anxiety. Their imaginary world conjures great images of the tellurian power of plate tectonics.

Combating Dante's vision of hell by opening it up to heaven and flooding it with light.

Confrontation

The terrain shapes the architectural project. It serves as a lever for thought. It situates it and connects it to its ground. It is through the choice of a site that architecture becomes exact. Nothing is dictated; everything is configured in a sensory equation.

Topography always involves perceptual issues. The encounter involves the experience of the place, a phenomenology of its reality. The aim is to grasp the totality of what we see. Not a fragmentary perception of forms, objects, or facts, but a vision of the general meaning. At first, the land and the territory speak to us silently—at times loudly. On each occasion, the question is posed in new terms.

Site logic versus architectural logic. Confrontation is a necessary step. An edge-to-edge dialectic. A relation of tensions, from which something apt, precise, and memorable must emerge. If it only accompanies the rhythms and lines of a topography and landscape with homological agreements, architecture exposes itself to the anemia of tautology. In order to transform one place into another, it must operate dialectical contrasts, even refigurations. To become simultaneously something else, architecture, its site, and its landscape must compare forces, without yielding to or absorbing each other. Symbiosis is neither indistinct nor homogeneous, but a complex unity of interdependencies and mutualities, through which two alterities find it advantageous to associate and metabolize each other.

Topography does not hamper architecture. It transcends itself when it becomes an architectural idea. That is when emotion is generated. An unformulated experience of the work.

Geometry, a partial landscape

During the Renaissance, the theory of the arts accorded pre-eminence to mimesis. If poetry and painting excel at conveying what is dispersed in the world as contingencies, it is by refraining from imitating it, from copying its appearance.

We must abstract what we see and perceive. Reject the simulacrum. Then we reach the principle, and fiction becomes exact, be it a portrait, a landscape, or a sonnet.

Such is architecture's relation to topography. Architecture substitutes its own organicity for geological matter.

Architectural concepts and ideas should be as clear-cut as possible. Radicality is capable of transfiguring a place and taking its nature to another level of reality. The most beautiful harmony comes from what differs; all things come to be through discord.

When a process takes place between geometry, nature, and material, architecture acquires a radiance. That the abstraction of form is so far removed from the aspects of nature is precisely what allows architecture to connect with nature as if it had actually emerged from its order—without it being possible to tell which of the two has needed this new identity more.

When a place undergoes this metamorphosis, the architecture truly acquires meaning in its parts and as a whole. It embodies the spirit of the place through belonging. *To belong to. To go along with.*

P. 30 Sketch, Villejuif-Gustave Roussy station, 2016.

MUSEUM CENTER
LAUSANNE, SWITZERLAND
2015

The site, which brings together the Museum of Photography and the Museum of Contemporary Design and Applied Arts, draws its strength from the way it is viewed from below, evoking a root network inspired by the topography of archaeological digs. Sculpted like a marble quarry, the floor reveals a complex layering of platforms and rooms designed to accommodate all kinds of exhibitions. On the surface, the only visible structure is a minimalist, transparent hall, suggesting that the heart of the project is articulated below. This architectural device is a discreet way of accompanying the Musée des Beaux-Arts as part of the overall museum complex. Seen from the upper street looking down onto the site, the glass roof gradually disappears towards Lake Geneva, merging architecture and landscape.

1 Fiction by DPA. Collage: Hiroshi Sugimoto, *Indian Ocean, Bali* (1991); Mies Van Der Rohe, Neue Nationalgalerie (1968); and Sivrihisar quarry, Turkey.

2 The surface of the museum's frosted roof visually extends the surface of Lake Geneva.

3 The interior spaces, inspired by marble quarries, are made up of cubes that punctuate the space by playing on effects of volume, stratification, and cutaways.

1

3

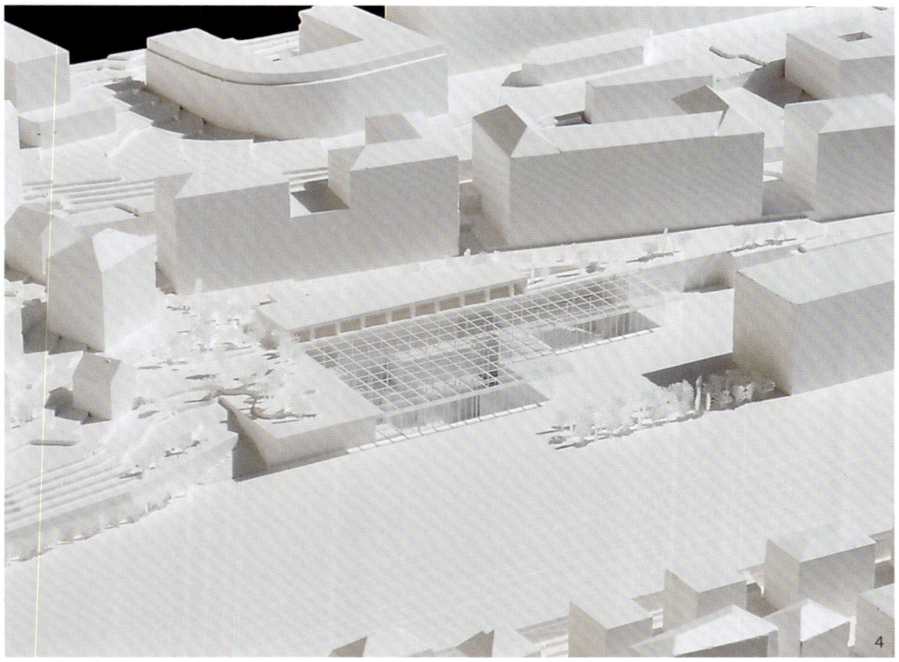

4

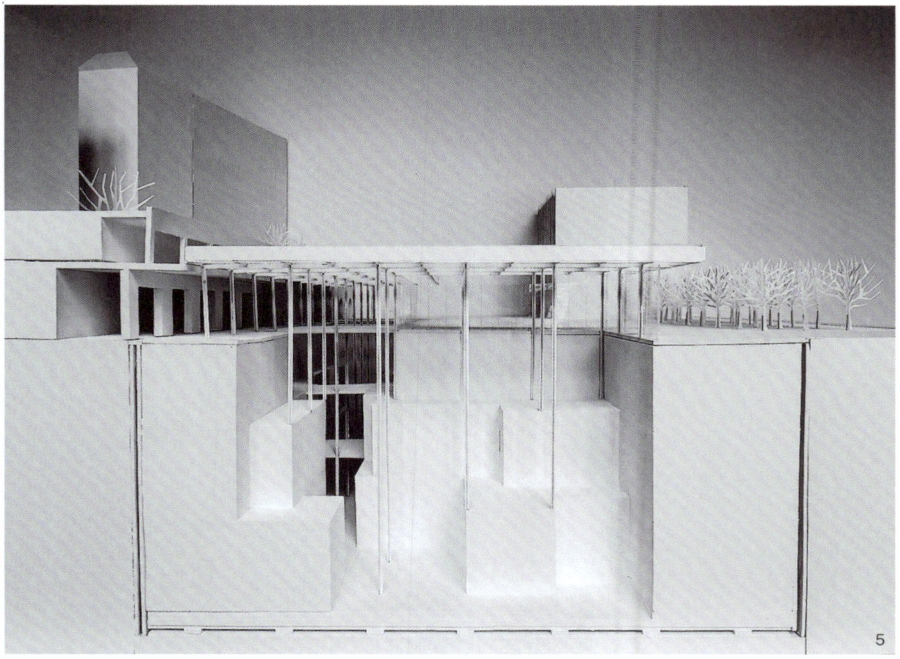

5

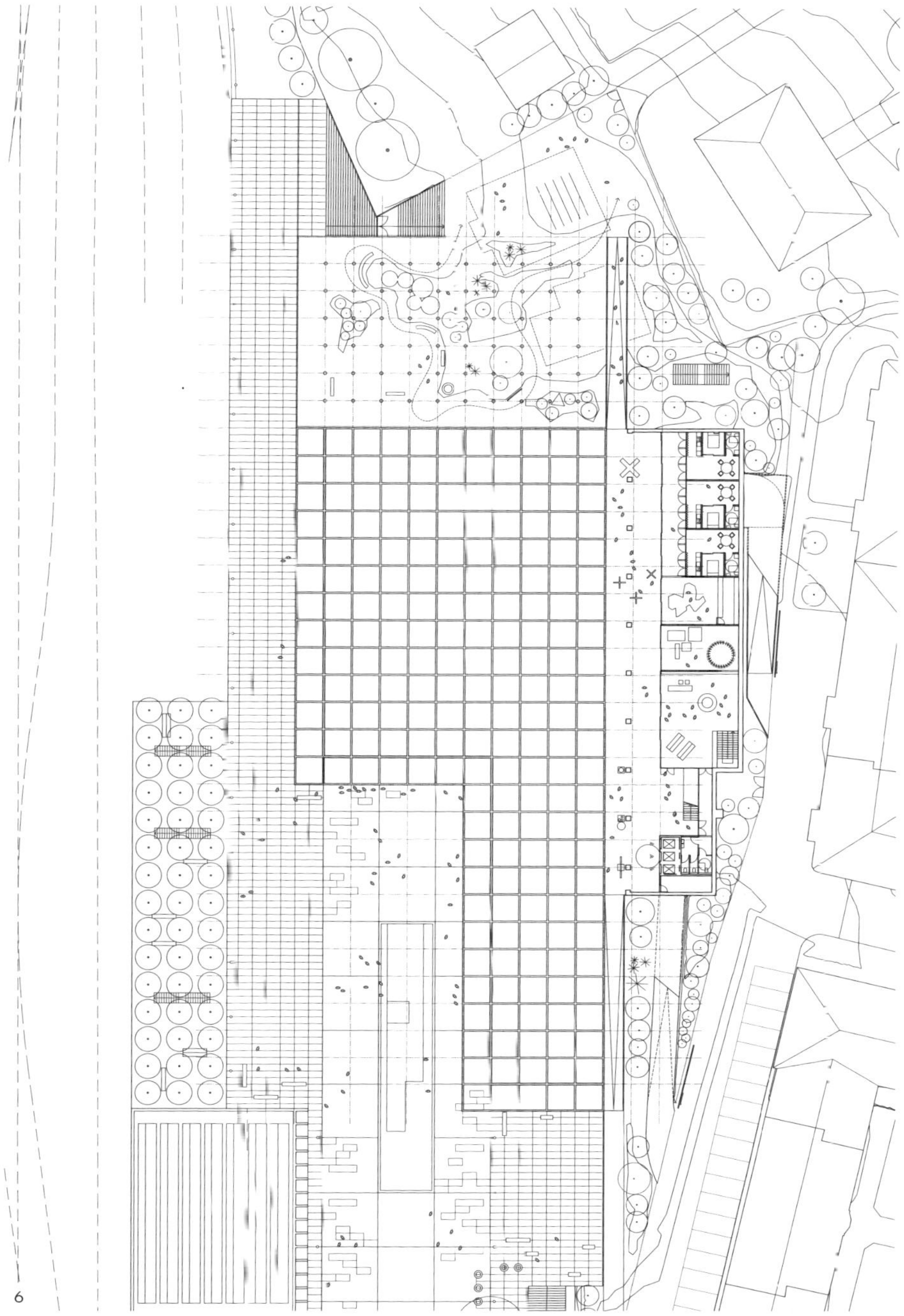

6

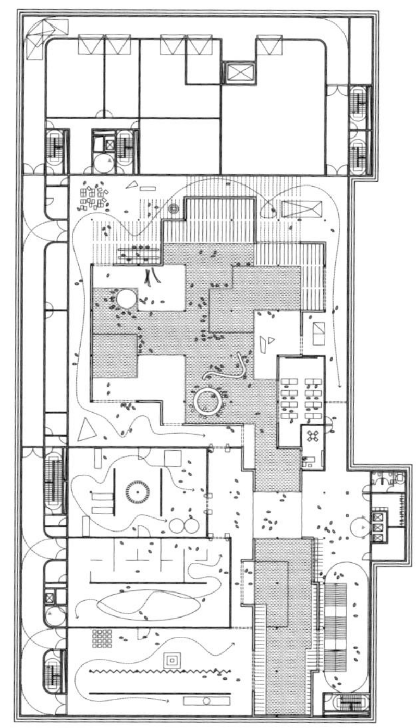

7

1, 2 Aerial views before intervention.
3 Aerial view after intervention.
4, 5 Models of top and underside, scale 1:500 and 1:100, 2015.
6 Plan of glass roof.
7 Plan of sculpted spaces below
8 Section through the depths of the museum.

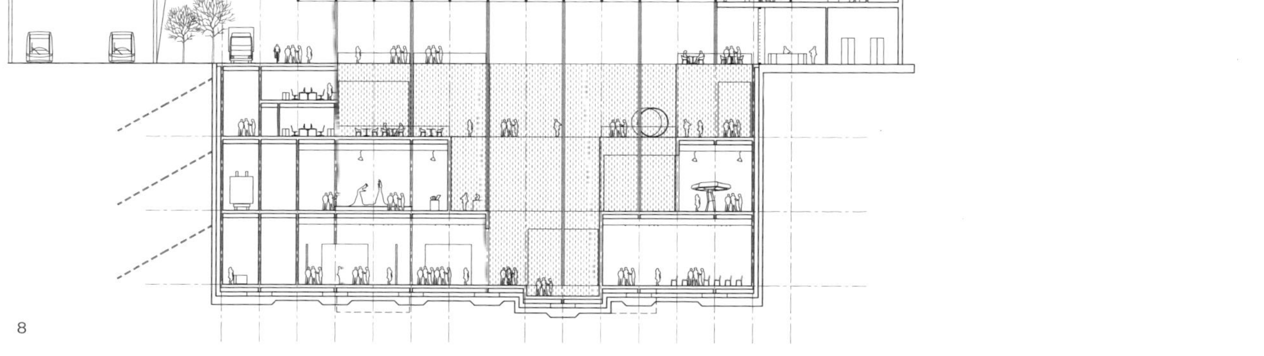

8

USINOR-SACILOR CONFERENCE CENTER

SAINT-GERMAIN-EN-LAYE, FRANCE

1988–91

The essence of this conference center project is to build on what was already there by enhancing the landscape and preserving the Château Saint-Léger. The new facilities and extensions are subtly integrated beneath and around the building, under a glass disc that reflects its image while recreating the hollowed-out natural level. In perfect harmony and forming a coherent "whole," the refurbished château becomes a functional space and houses meeting rooms, which can be reached via a light footbridge spanning its moat.

1

2

MUSEUM OF ETHNOGRAPHY

BUDAPEST, HUNGARY

2016

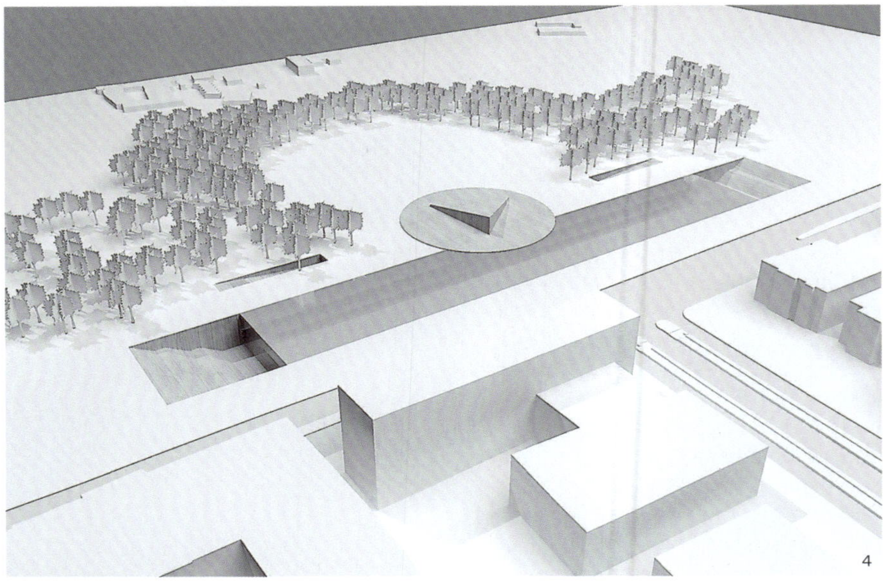

4

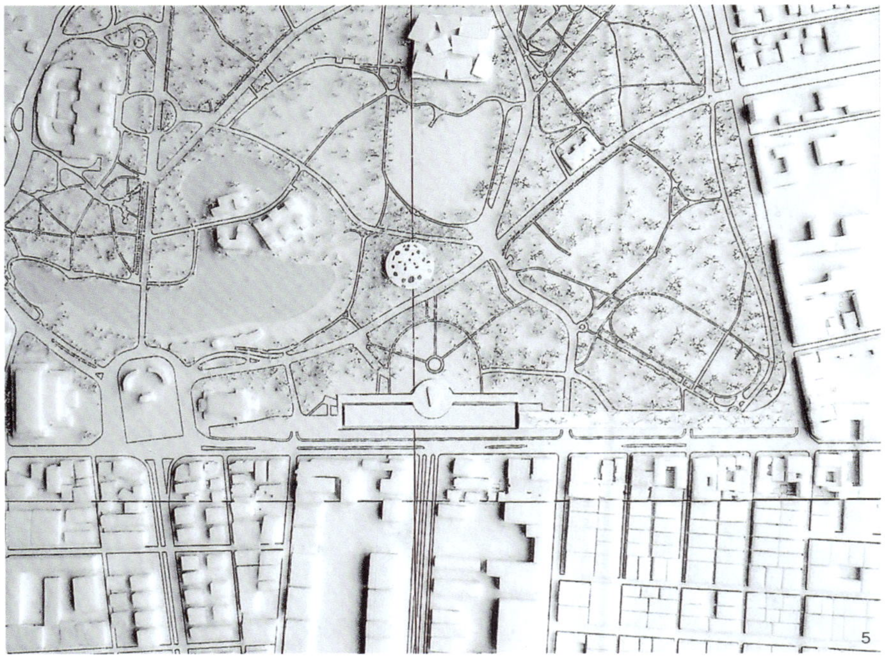

5

6

7

To preserve the view over the natural landscape of Budapest's Városliget Park, the Museum of Ethnography is integrated into the site by a thick glass floor, flush with the ground of the park and creating the illusion of a shimmering body of water. This play of reflections on the surface enhances the impact of the memorial to the uprising of 1956. As you approach, what appears to be an expanse of liquid turns into a glass prism. This instrument for the diffraction of images and light, linked to the public space, invites us to enter a world where light is architecture. Once inside, visitors move between heaven and earth, floating weightlessly above the museum's topography.

8

1 Cutaway of the entire project, preservation of the château and extension from below, 2016
2 The château on its glass disc.
3 Aerial view before intervention.
4 Embedding of the museum in the park.
5 General model of the neighborhood around the museum, scale 1:2,000, 2016
6 The museum's main entrance.
7 Topographical section.
8 Under the glass ceiling.

PASSAGE DE L'ÉTOILE – ARC DE TRIOMPHE

PARIS, FRANCE
2017

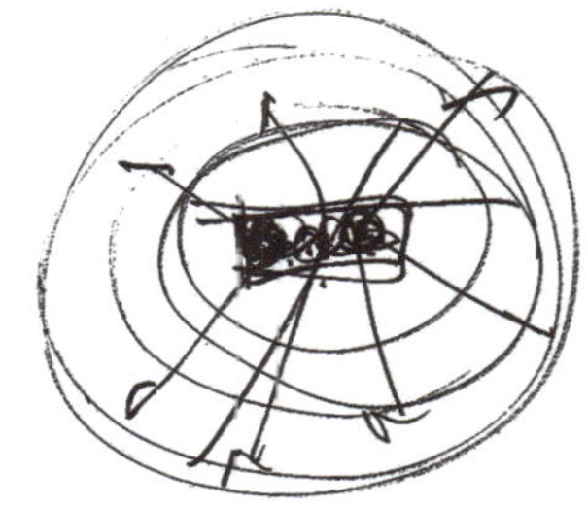

1

2

3

4

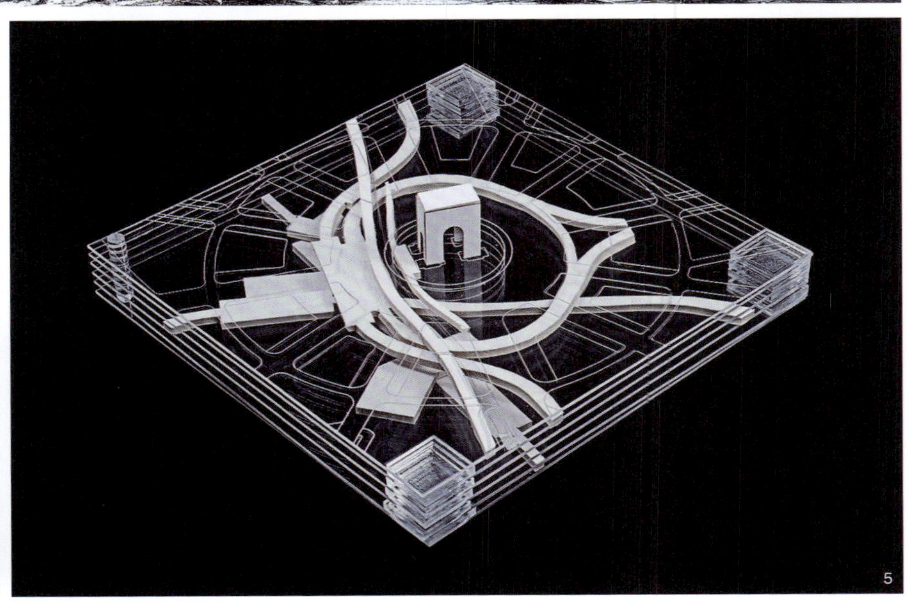

5

The fiction that stages the Arc de Triomphe introduces an operational strategy that replaces the paved surface with a concentric glass floor. This device establishes a connection between the underground networks and the aerial space of the city, anchoring the monument in the Parisian soil while generating new spaces dedicated to commemorative ceremonies. This optical lens amplifies the monument's visual impact, multiplying its reflections and redefining its topographical tie to the city. At the foot of the Arc de Triomphe, the opening dug into the circumference, reveals an unprecedented low-angle view. This architectural gesture reinforces the symbolic power of the monument, which is freed from its traditional function, and reinvents its commemorative role. A new dynamic emerges, sublimating the memorial experience and conferring on the site an emotional depth it previously lacked.

6

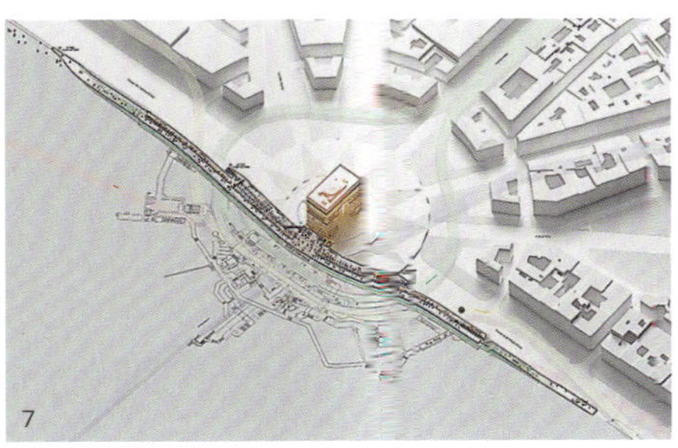

7

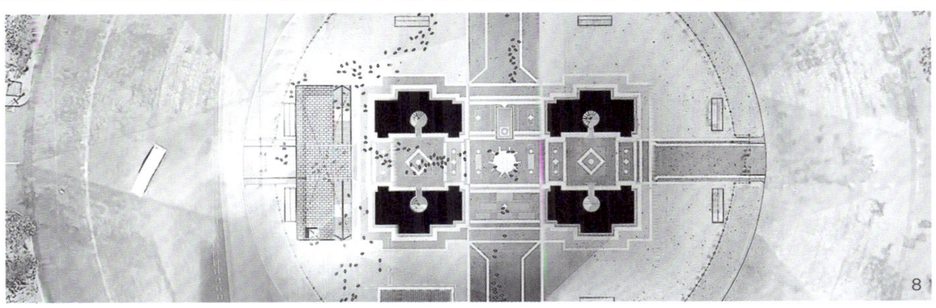

8

1 Sketch, 2018.
2 Fiction by DPA. Collage: Arc de Triomphe (1806–36) and *The Tomb of the Via Appia*, Giovanni Battista Piranesi (1756).
3 Panoramic view of the Arc de Triomphe, 1920.
4, 5 Transparent views revealing the networks. Model, scale 1:5,000, 2017.
6 The new plaza at the foot of the Arc de Triomphe.
7, 8 Plan and cross-section of the area under the Arc de Triomphe.
9 Below ground, the open and bright plaza does not detract from the image of the monument.

9

YEULMARU CITY OF CULTURE AND ARTS

YEOSU, SOUTH KOREA
2009–12

The Yeosu City of Culture and Arts is a line extending between two points of reference: following the pronounced undulations of the land, it links the observatory at the summit of Mount Mangma to the peak of Jangdo Island, at the southernmost tip of Korea. This long promenade, carved into the landscape like a furrow, is both an open-air art gallery and a belvedere providing views of the sea. The galleries and cafés along the way are more than just functional spaces; they are part of the landscape, accessible even when there are no scheduled events. At the heart of this composition, the Philharmonic is rooted in the hill, crowned by a grand staircase. This fusion of art, architecture, and landscape transforms every step into a sensory and cultural experience.

1

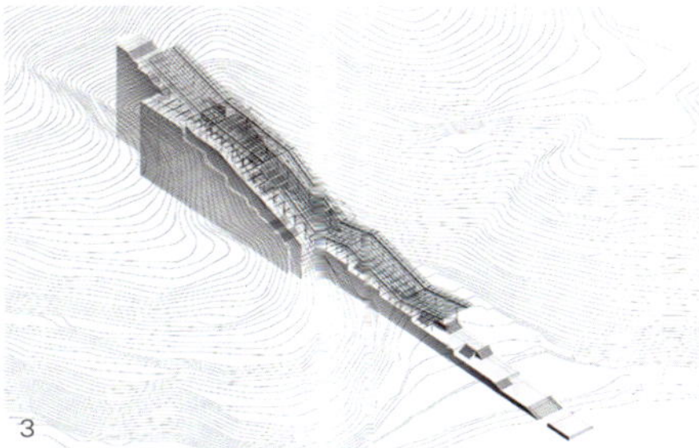

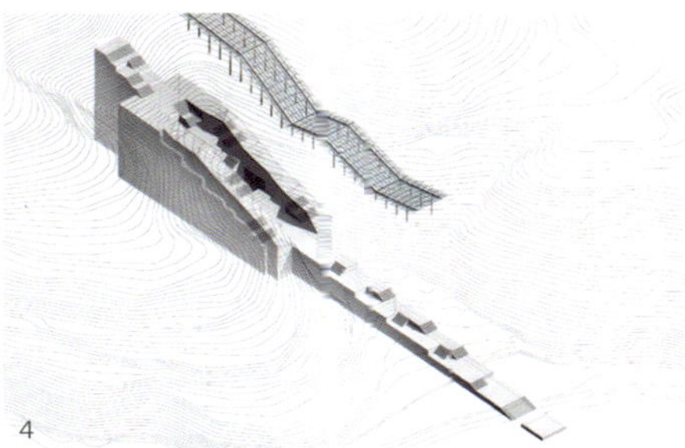

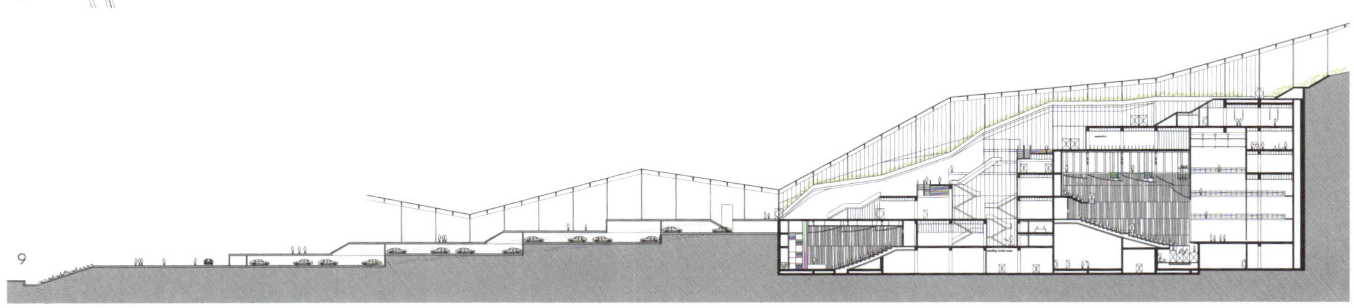

1, 2 The City of Culture and Arts traces a route linking the two peaks on the site: Mangma Observatory and Jangdo Island.
3 Overall axonometric view.
4 Exploded axonometric view of the cultural spaces embedded in the ground, under the canopy.
5 The canopy accompanies and protects the promenade.
6 The site under construction 2011.
7 On Jangdo Island, the promenade is transformed into open galleries housing exhibition spaces.
8 Topographical map.
9 Cutaway view of the music rooms embedded in the ground.

EWHA WOMEN'S UNIVERSITY

SEOUL, SOUTH KOREA
2004–08

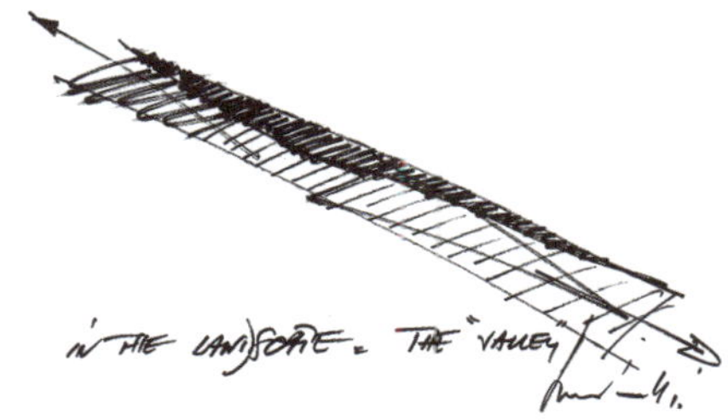

1

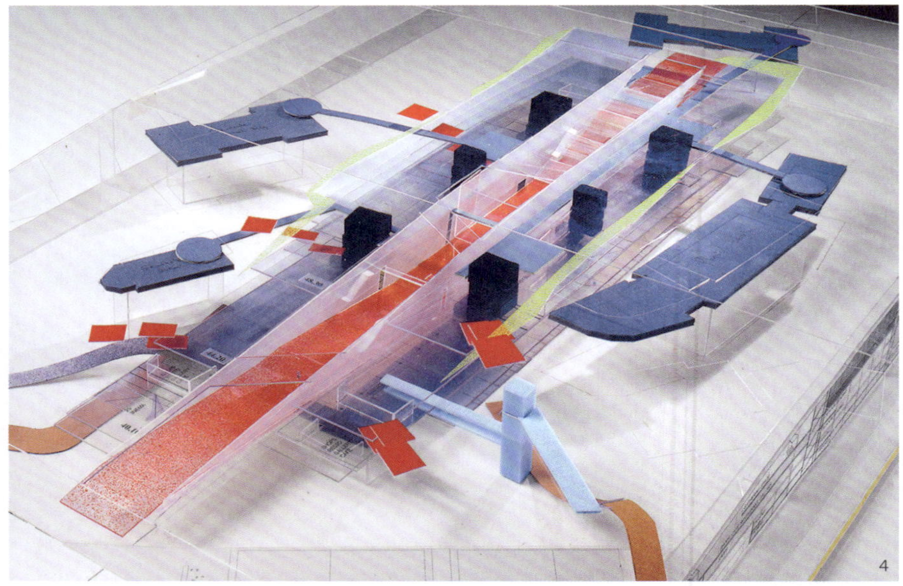

4

The project reconstitutes the original topography that disappeared when the campus was first built and creates a natural link between the university valleys and the Korean capital: by integrating a vast esplanade grafted onto the city, it conceals its structure within a hill crowned by a park. A deep fault line runs through this new topography, acting as a dynamic public space. The mixed program is organized around this structuring open space, in which informal uses encourage interaction and appropriation by its users. At night, the illuminated furrows diffuse a soft glow, transforming the façades into moving, almost liquid surfaces. A theatre of light and shadow comes to life, sublimating the site's unique territorial dimension. During the day, the volumes take on a solid appearance, evoking a marmoreal texture.

5

1 Sketch, 2004.
2 Historic view of the site, 1930s.
3 View of the site before intervention, 2004.
4 Relative position of existing and new networks. Model, scale 1:500, 2005.
5 Model, scale 1:500, 2005.
6 The valley running through the heart of the campus.

1, 2 Excavation and construction of the infrastructure at the heart of the campus, 2007.
3 Earth-retention buttresses.
4 Architectural reconstruction of the original hill.
5 The new campus landscape.
6 Topographical section of the valley.

5

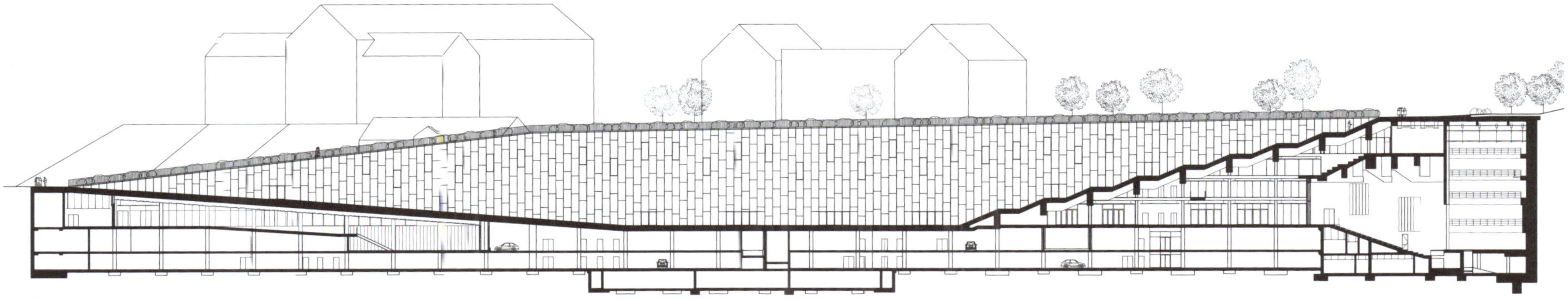

6

1 The valley is a public space that extends the district's urban plan into the heart of the university campus.
2, 3 Cross-sections. Distribution of functions on either side of the valley.
4 The grand staircase/amphitheater.
5 The valley opens onto the city.

"Architectural excavation is a political act: it challenges the logic of the monumental object."

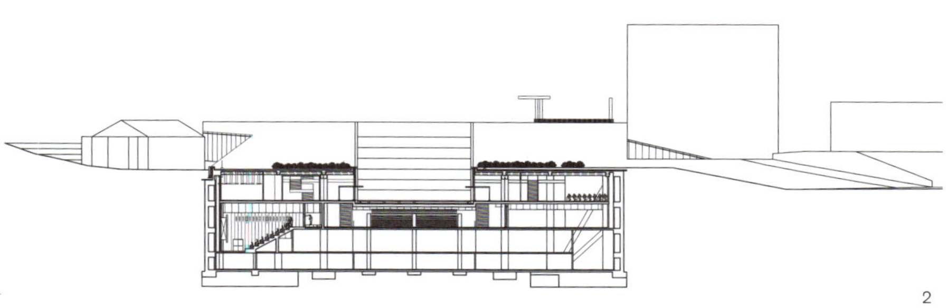

2

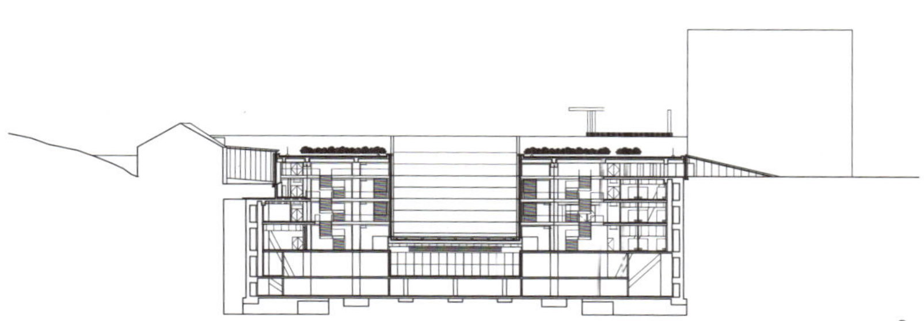

3

4

5

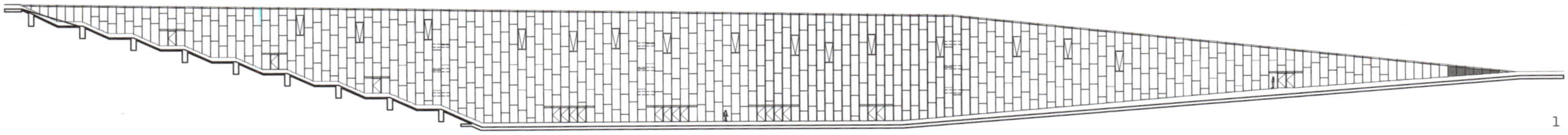

1

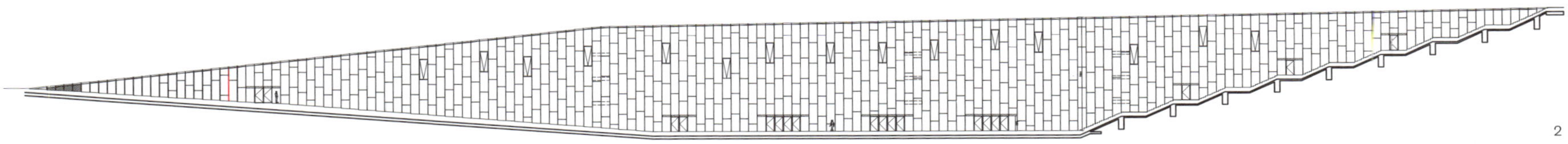

2

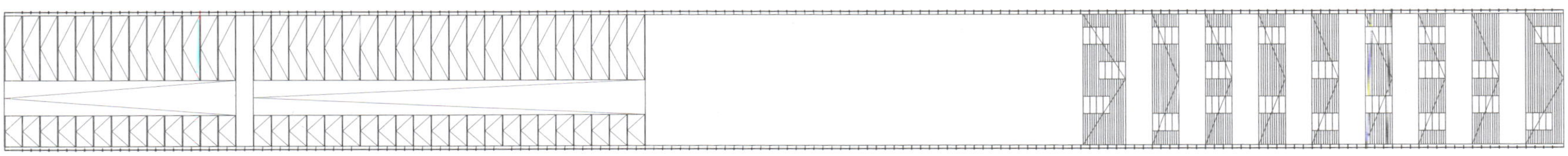

3

1, 2 Glass façades along the valley.
3 Topographical plan of the valley.
4–7 Detail of mirror-polished stainless-steel façade structures.
8 The transparency of the curtain wall, seen from inside.
9 Axonometric detail of curtain wall.
10, 11 Walkways alongside the glass façade.

4

5

6

7

8

10

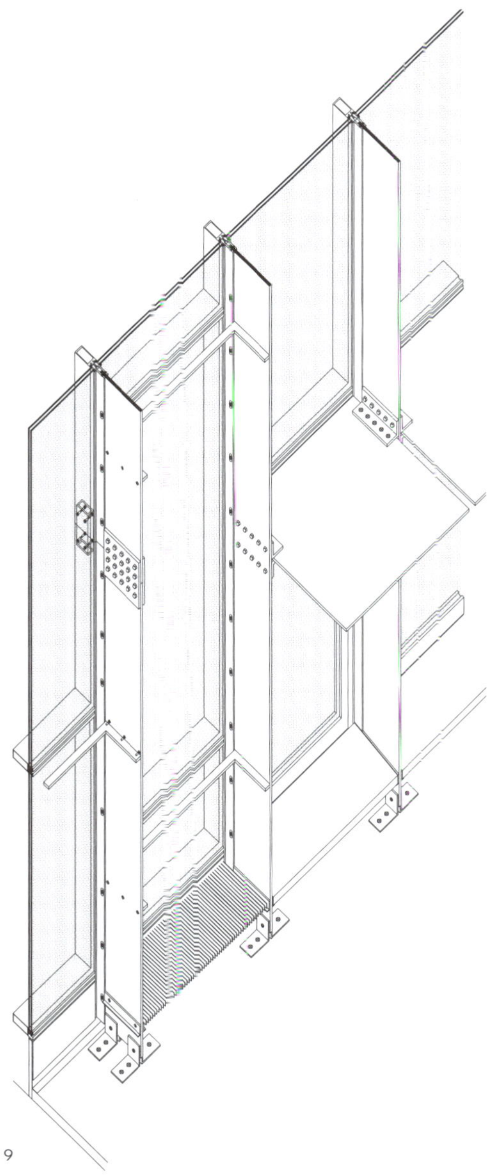

9

11

9
7
5
3

10
8
6
4

LONDON 2012 OLYMPIC VELOPARK

LONDON, UNITED KINGDOM
2007

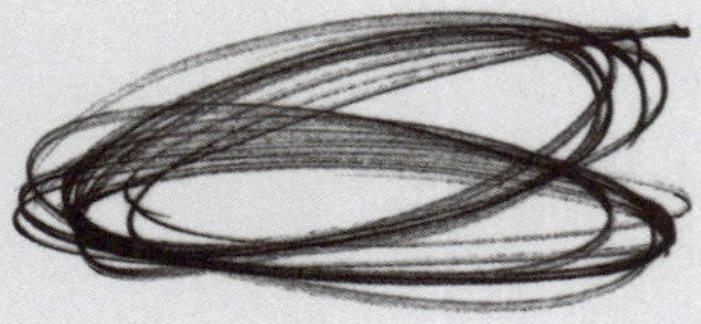
1

Inspired by Land Art, the project fuses architecture and landscape. The circular roof of the velodrome, walkable and covered with trees and shrubs, slants upward, rising above the ground to offer panoramic views of the Olympic complex and the city of London. Beneath this natural extension of the topography, a sculpted crater houses the cycle path and bleachers. The site, conceived as a fluid experience, can be experienced both above and below ground, abolishing any separation between interior and exterior.

2

3

4

OLYMPIC SKATING RINK

BEIJING, CHINA
2016

The intention of the project was to create an open landscape by avoiding the addition of a new object in Beijing's Olympic Forest Park. By raising the ground, two sloping roofs, shaped like half-discs, emerge naturally from the ground. A fine incision under the skin allows the sports equipment to slide under each of the plates, integrating it into the site. Far from being limited to one-off use, this evolving architecture stimulates the social life of the town: the accessible roofs become living public spaces, which also house a field of solar collectors, providing sustainable energy to power the ice rink.
By breaking with the conventional typology of stadiums, this exploratory process aspires to create a project marked as one of the most resilient in the history of the Olympic Games.

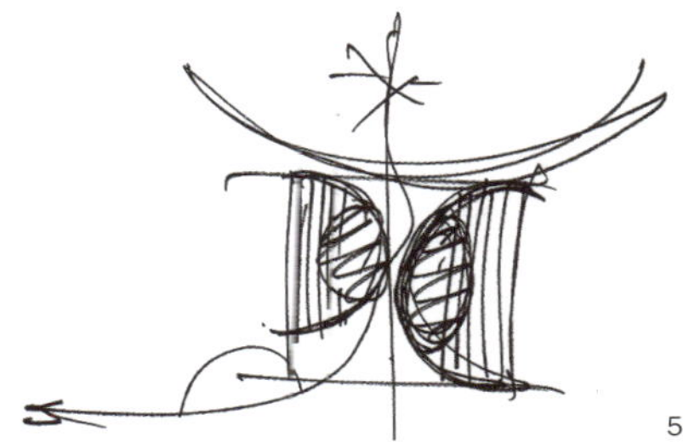
5

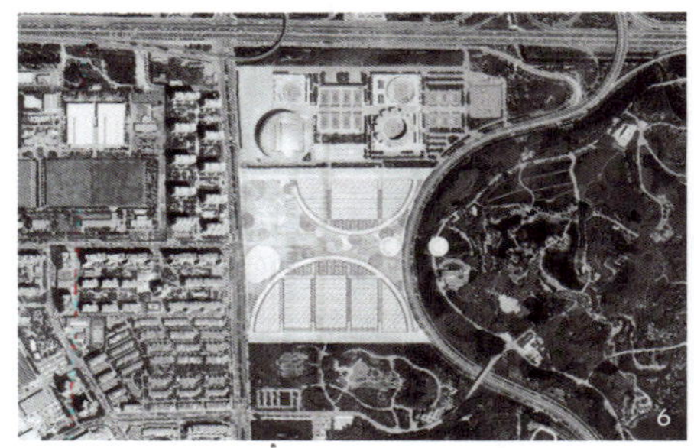
6

7

1 Sketch, 2007.
2 Beneath the raised structure.
3 The ground becomes architecture.
4 Architecture turns into a hill.
5 Sketch, 2016.
6 Location of the project on the Olympic site.
7 The two raised structures facing each other. Model, scale 1:500, 2016.
8 Vast, multi-level public space connecting the two buildings.
9 General plan of the sports areas.
10 Speed-skating ring.

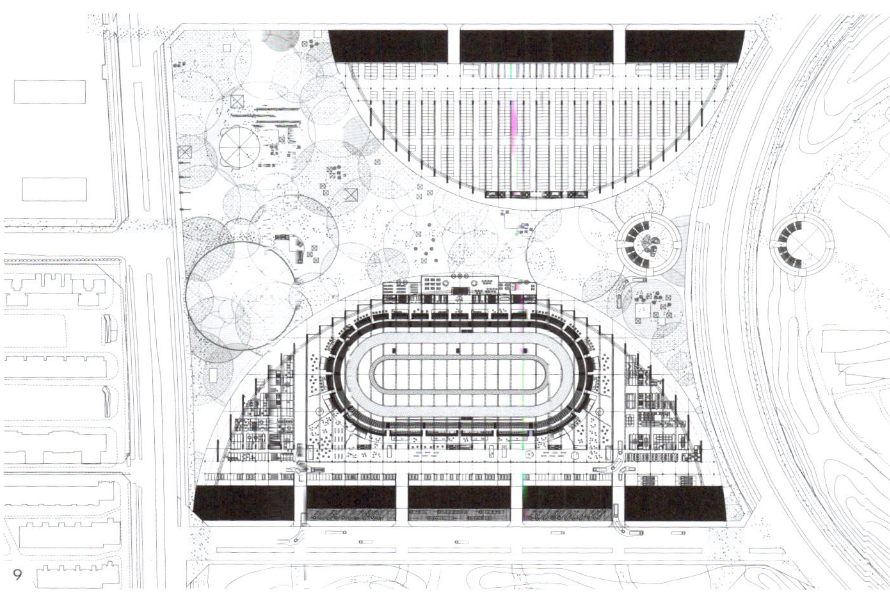

CENTRO DE CREACIÓN CONTEMPORÁNEA DE ANDALUCÍA

CORDOBA, SPAIN

2005

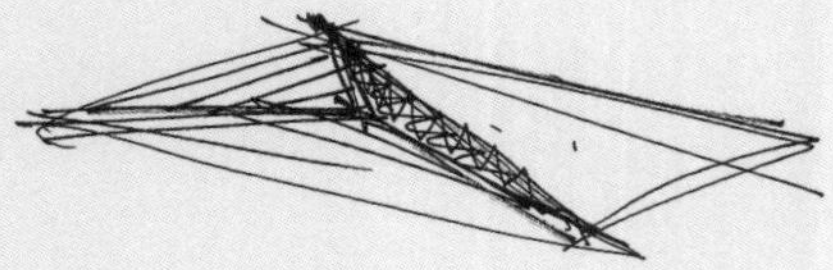

1

The project is anchored by a radical gesture that strongly evokes the role of the slit in the work of the artist Lucio Fontana. Its rectangular footprint is split into two triangular surfaces: one slopes slightly, while the other rises, forming a fold whose roof is an urban amphitheater. This structural fold houses the museum, which is easily accessed from the gently sloping public square.

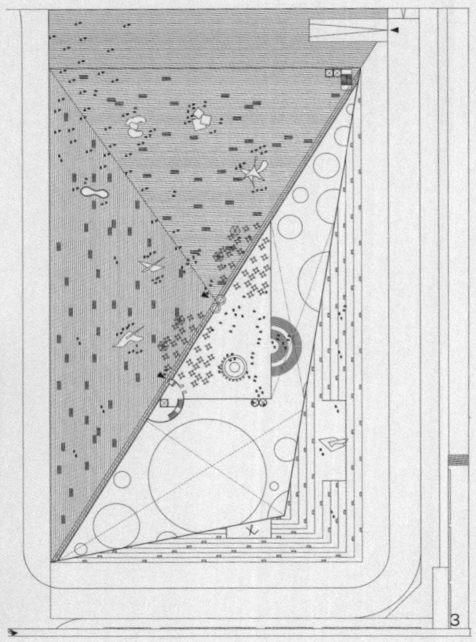

3

4

MERCEDES-BENZ CAMPUS

STUTTGART, GERMANY

2012

5

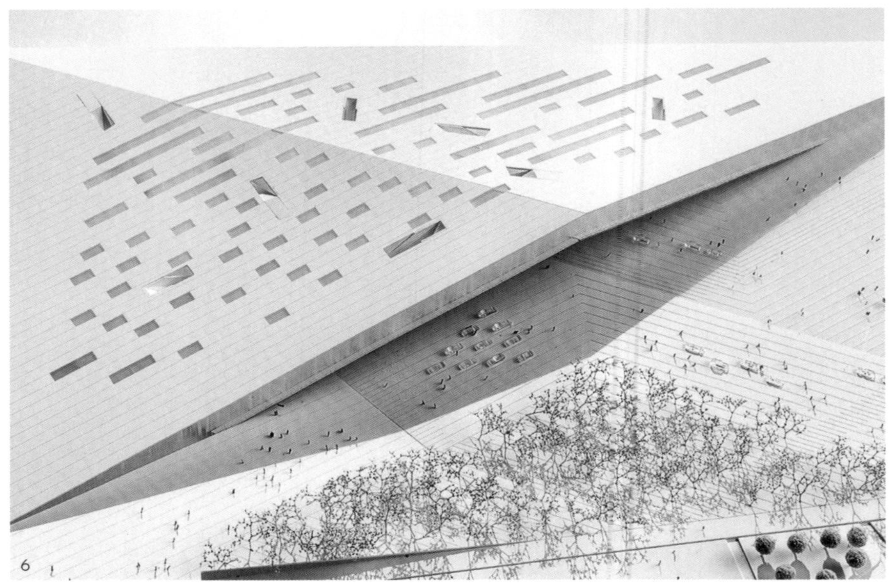

6

1 Sketch, 2005.
2 The Centro de Creación Contemporánea de Andalucía-C3ᵅ in Miraflores Park.
3 Plan of the roof level. The fold allows the architecture to be either a roof or bleachers.
4 Two triangular surfaces oppose and complement each other. Concept model, scale 1:500, 2005.
5, 6 The building/landscape rises up to extend the public square below, creating a natural access to the campus. Competition model, scale 1:100, 2012.
7 Plan of the ground floor.
8 Section illustrating the relationship between the slab and the natural ground.
9, 10 View of the kinematics of the interior spaces.
11 The building/landscape offers a host of scenic spaces. Concept model, scale 1:200, 2012.

The museum is set in the landscape as a structure shaped by the relief of the land, which is transformed into a dynamic topography. Designed around a wide public esplanade, it is notable for a deformation of the ground that raises a triangular slab with planted slopes. This uplift, exploited to its full extent, forms the main space of the museum. The forecourt, conceived as an extension of the surrounding area, inserts itself beneath the structure. The museum is reached via a series of ramps, escalators, and elevators suspended in this vast covered hall. In this way, the landscape-cum-building functions like a large theatre, offering both indoor and outdoor stages.

7

9

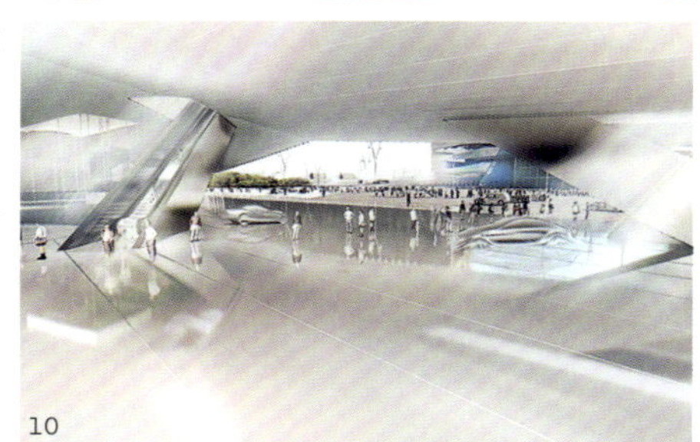

10

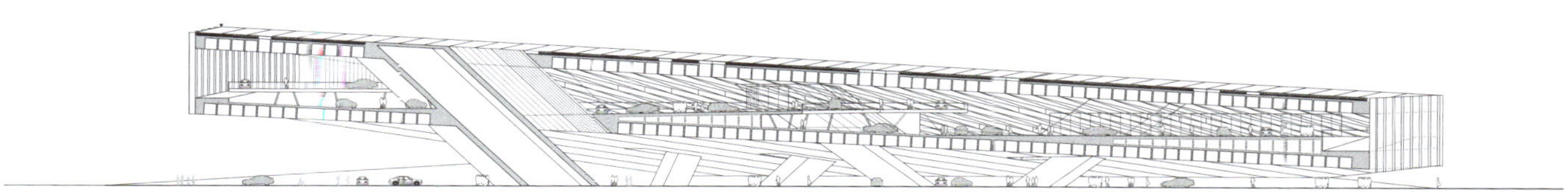

8

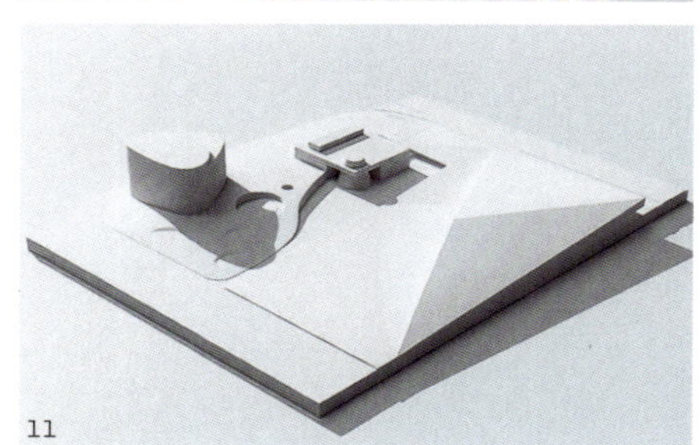

11

VILLA ONE

SAINT-CAST-LE-GUILDO, FRANCE

1993–97

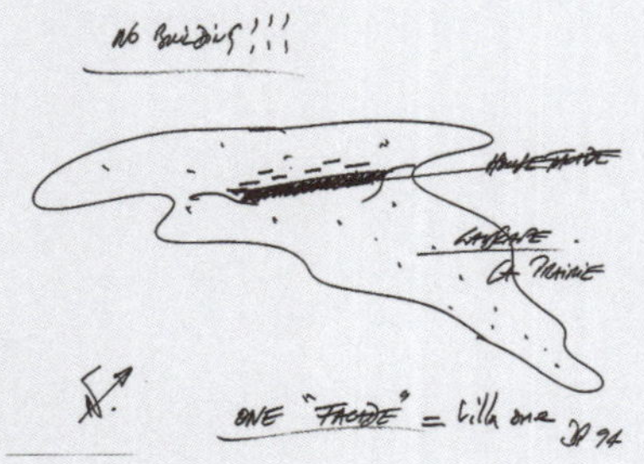
1

Villa One fits discreetly into the landscape, blending into the depths of the ground and revealing its existence only through its long, south-facing glass façade. This architecture, oscillating between presence and absence, questions the role of the landscape as a unifying element between architecture and nature. It is an invitation to constantly renewed experimentation, inspiring us to feel, understand, and imagine new ways of living in symbiosis with our environment.

2

3

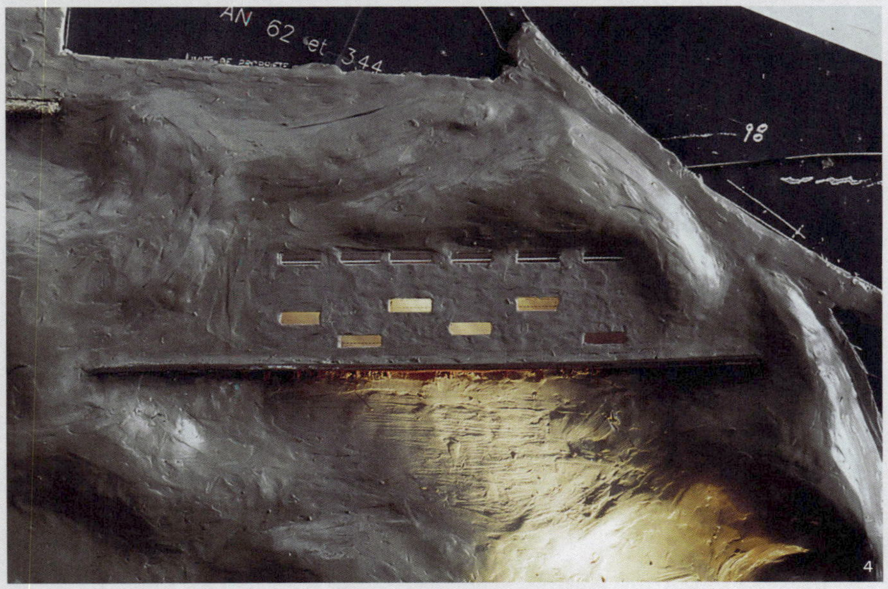

4

DOUBLE DECK – DOME-ESPLANADE OF THE ÉCOLE POLYTECHNIQUE FÉDÉRALE DE LAUSANNE

LAUSANNE, SWITZERLAND

2023–27

Called "Double Deck," this project reinvents the esplanade at the heart of the campus by deepening the ground to allow the introduction of new modular lecture halls that can accommodate up to 500 people, which is vital for the university's development. This infiltration into the ground and its planted extension transform the site into a vast plaza that is also a garden and a belvedere, a new public space offering views of the Alps and the surrounding landscape. The two levels thus created, converting the infrastructure of the former underground car parks, include additional cycle paths and pedestrian walkways. This strategy redefines the topography of the site, blurring the boundary between what is above and what is below, creating a peaceful, lively campus center.

6

7

8

9

10

1 Sketch, 1993.
2 Villa One is inserted by incision into an enclave by the sea.
3 The glass wall forms the villa's city façade.
4 Topographic model, scale 1:200, 1993.
5, 6 The campus of the École Polytechnique Fédérale de Lausanne, a densely populated part of the city.
7 Embedding the project at the heart of the campus.
8-10 The new esplanade overlooking the Alps.

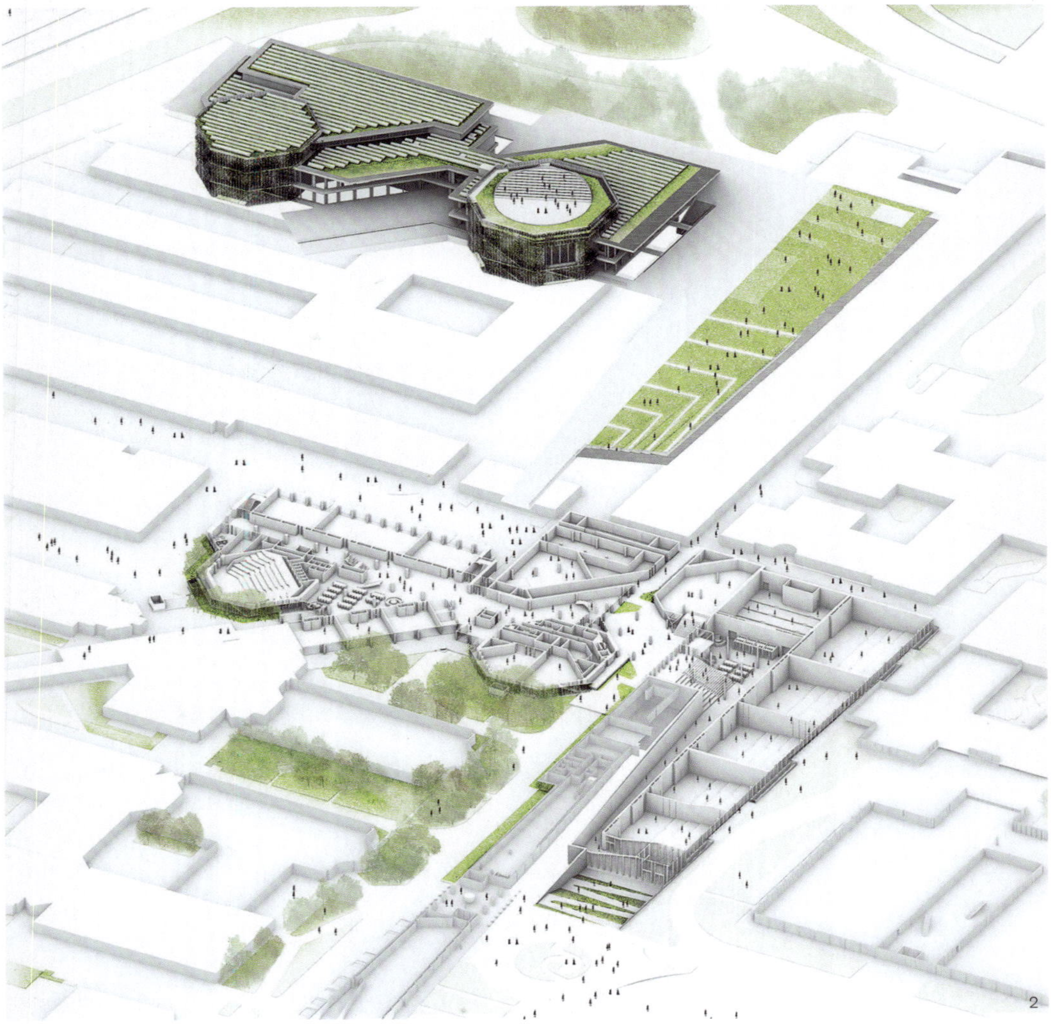

1 The cupola building and esplanade.
2 Exploded axonometric view showing the superposition of functions in a double deck.
3, 4 Interior views of study areas.
5 Topography and volumes of the new campus.
6 Access to the lecture halls.

5

6

MUSEUM OF VEGA BAJA

TOLEDO, SPAIN
2010

Toledo's archaeological museum is set in the natural topography of the undeveloped Vega Baja area. Placed in direct dialogue with an archaeological field, its architecture reflects its forms, like an architectural tautology.
The museum structures are set beneath an artificial hill, their presence suggested by their roofs, which are flush with the earth. This offers visitors a twofold experience: a walk on the surface reveals a 360-degree panorama of Vega Baja, linking the archaeological sites, the surrounding town, and the history they tell. This open-air space, a veritable outdoor museum, showcases the visible past, while the buried museum preserves its memory. The decision to bury the building also serves to naturally moderate the bursts of high temperatures that are characteristic of Toledo's climate.

2

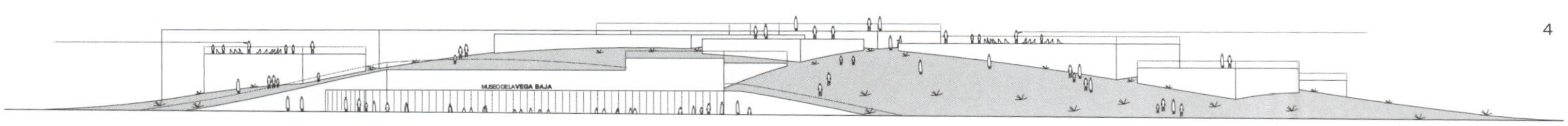

4

"Architecture strives,
as we do, to resist time."

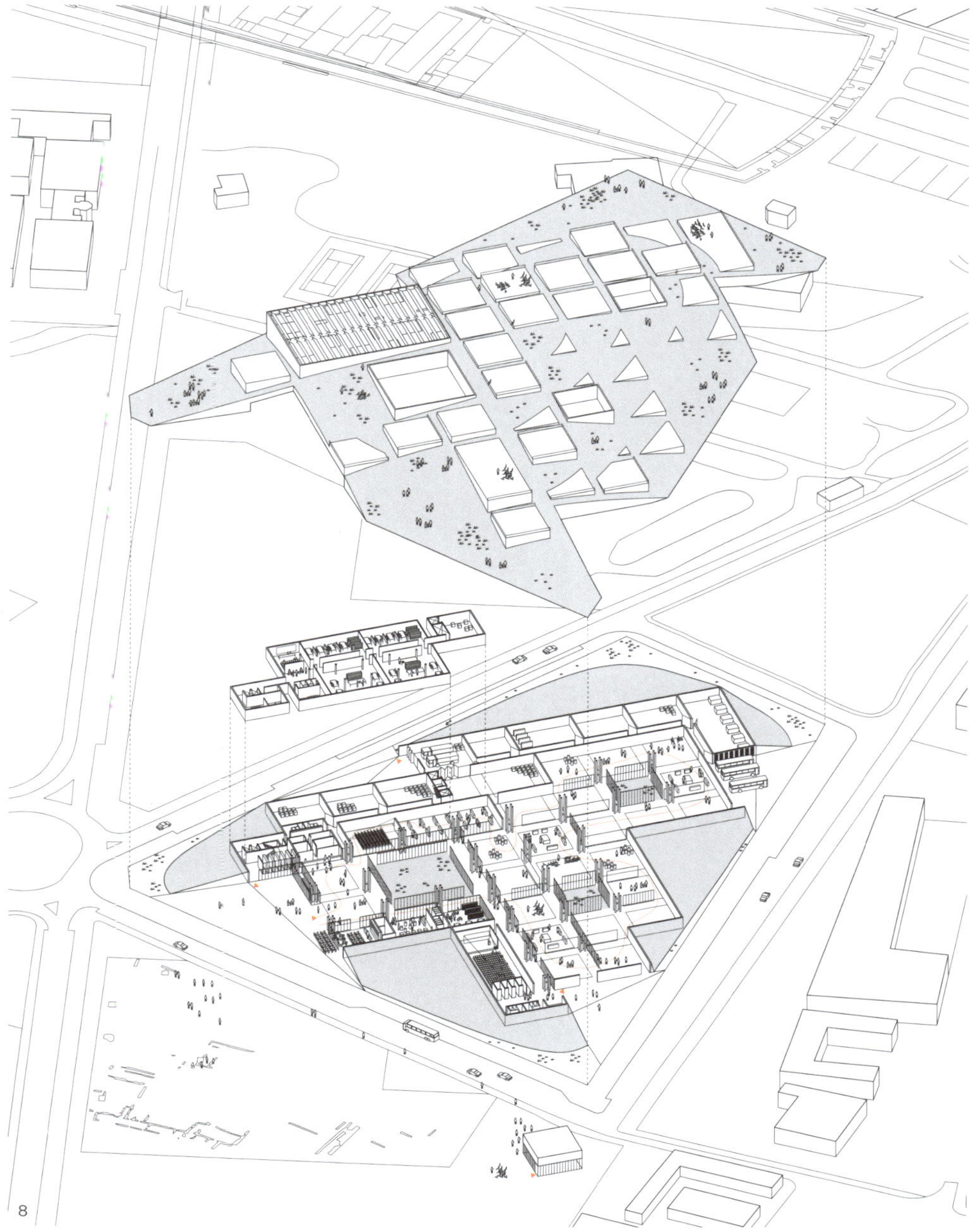

8

6

7

1 General view of the museum's main entrance.
2 The archaeological site.
3 Position of the project shown on an aerial photograph of the site.
4, 5 Façade and cross-section showing the different functional layers of the museum.
6 Relief model revealing the museum's architecture. Concept model, scale 1:500, 2010.
7 Mysterious, subdued light envelops the interior spaces.
8 Axonometric cutaway view of the interior and exterior layers.

5

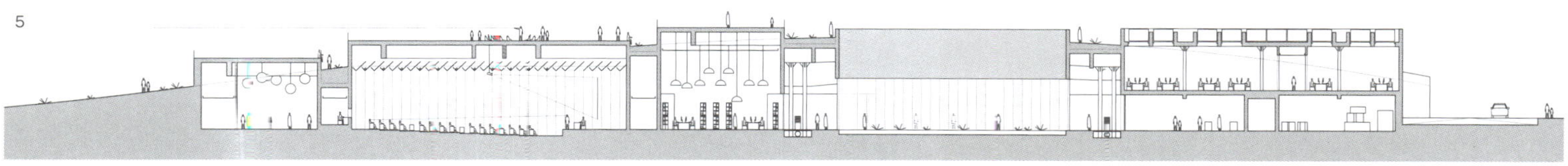

OCTOPUS – UPGRADING THE SALERNO QUARRIES

SALERNO, ITALY

2009

The Salerno project reconstructs the ground of a large open-cast quarry using a process of accumulation and subtraction inspired by the very mechanisms at work in the site's formation: like a stack of strata, the structure clings to the excavated walls, leaving gaps at certain points between the building and the rock. A natural flora develops here, reintegrating the soil into the natural life cycle and repairing a landscape damaged by industrial activity. The architecture is like a natural concretion with multiple flexible tentacles, stretched in multiple directions and with an organic plasticity in symbiosis with its environment. An extension of the topography, the multicultural and multimodal facility houses vast public spaces, embodying the idea of connection and transforming the quarry into a living space, anchored in its territory.

1 The abandoned quarry.
2, 3 The hollow space left by industrial exploitation is reinvested by a sprawling, octopus-like architectural device.
4 Geological-style cross-section of the building.
5, 6 Positioning of new ground strata. Model, scale 1:1,000, 2009.
7 A project between earth and sky.

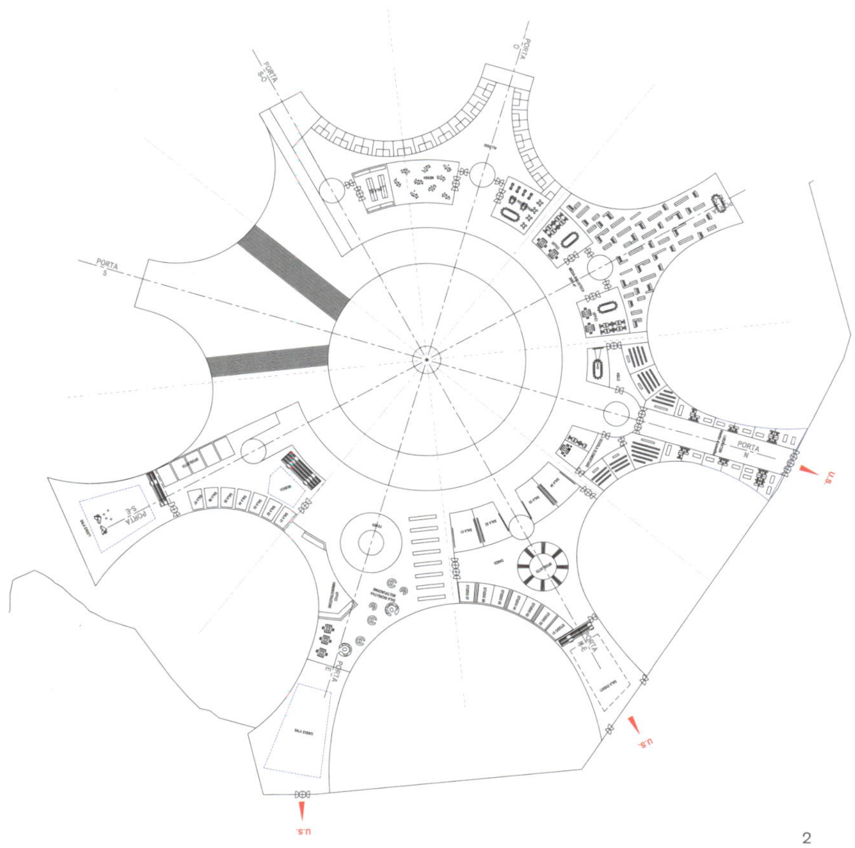

2

1

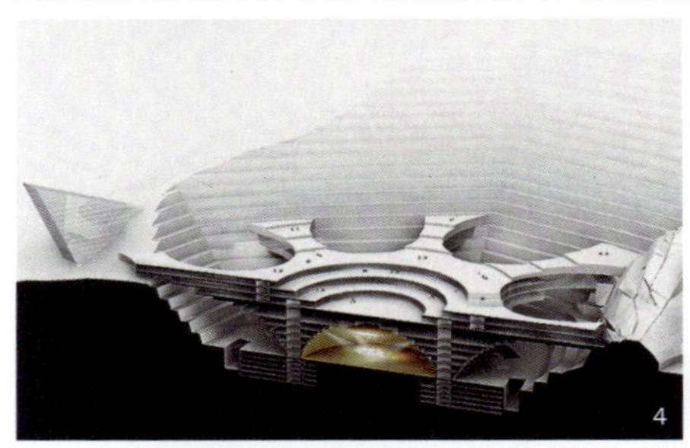

4

5

3

6

7

SANCTUARY OF NOTRE-DAME-DU-LAUS

SAINT-ÉTIENNE-LE-LAUS, FRANCE
2012

The sanctuary is a "landscape in the landscape": a deep notch in the mountain floor creates an open-air hollow. At its heart, the cross-shaped church unfolds like a bas-relief, with its pews and aisles sculpted into the rock. On the periphery of this place of prayer, open to the sky and symbolically linked to the sun and stars, is a peristyle offering privacy for pilgrims and protection from the elements.

This new topography creates a natural link between the house of Saint Benoîte Rencurel and the existing basilica of Notre-Dame-du-Laus. The intensity of this delicately integrated project, in which the architecture fades into the background to preserve the original relief, appears most vividly when seen from the summits of the Hautes-Alpes mountains.

1

2

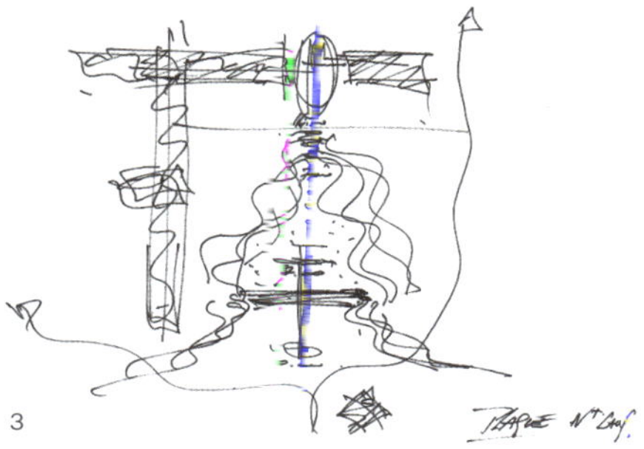

3

1 Route through the sanctuary, from village to church.
2 Open/covered. The shrine welcomes pilgrims.
3 Sketch, 2012.
4 The historic site, 1980.
5 Plan of the new Notre-Dame-du-Laus.
6 The pilgrimage and the new church.
7 Relief model, scale 1:500, 2012.

4

5

7

MONTAGNE DU PARC

BRUSSELS, BELGIUM
2013

1

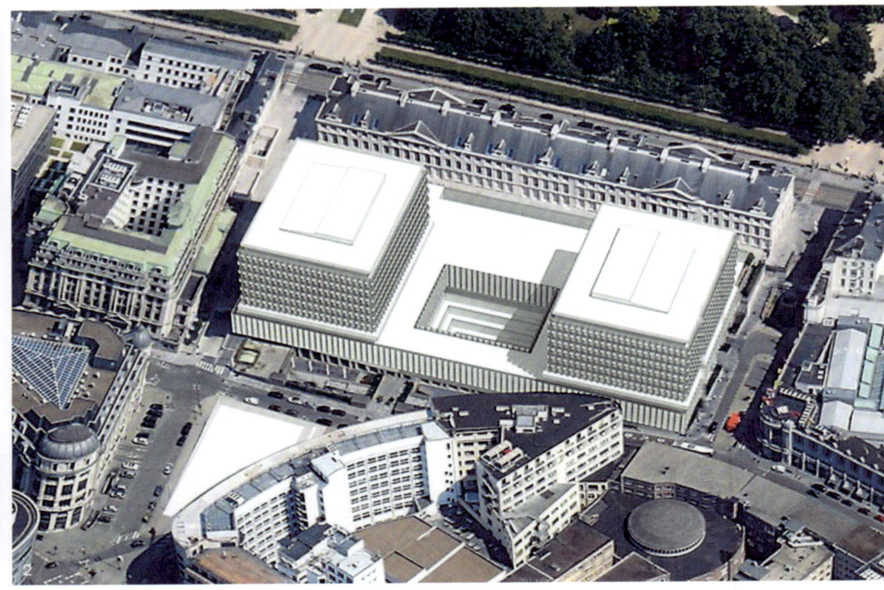

2

1 Aerial view before intervention.
2 Aerial view after intervention.
3 Rather than rising into the sky or creating a block of buildings, the project seems to erase itself by digging into the ground.
4 The entrance to the Montagne du Parc.
5 Between above and below, a levitating building.

3

4

The new building has opted for a controlled form of discretion: it sits like a negative image between the twin metal cubes built on the site in the 1970s. This creates a physical and functional link between the volumes without compromising the original architectural quality. The hollowed-out base opens up the public space in this new unitary whole. At its heart, a sunken garden serves as a light well, naturally irrigating all the levels. This architectural rootedness reinforces the presence of the new establishment in the prestigious royal district of Brussels, establishing a respectful dialogue with the surrounding heritage.

5

LIGHTWALK – GANGNAM INTERMODAL TRANSIT CENTER

SEOUL, SOUTH KOREA
2017–30

The Lightwalk is a radical, minimalist line that is deeply integrated into the territory and the ground of the city, in the manner of a powerful Land Art intervention. This architectural gesture marks the epicenter of a gigantic urban hub, connecting multiple modes of transport: bus, metro, train, car, taxi, and bicycle. This great gallery plays a key role in the regeneration of the heart of Seoul, choked by its density, by linking existing buildings and new constructions. Rooted in the ground, the Lightwalk uses a revolutionary optical instrument that, like a Fresnel lens, diffuses beams of natural light through the different strata of the subsoil. Above ground, a planted promenade and a vast central park link the neighborhoods while signposting access to the various transport stations.

1

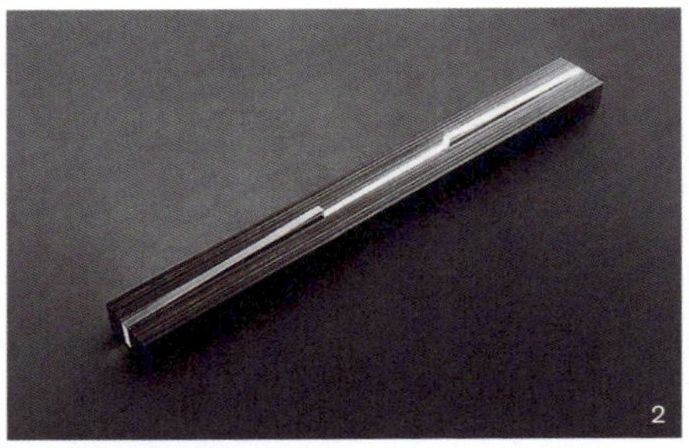

2

1 Sketch, 2017.
2 Concept model, scale 1:1,000, 2017.
3 Jeong-Ho Kim, *Suseonjeondo*, 1897. Map of Suseon (old Seoul).
4 Perfectly rectilinear, the project aligns with a major axis of the capital.
5 Fiction by DPA. Collage, embedding Joseph Paxton's *The Great Victorian Way* (1855) below ground.
6 Tokujin Yoshioka, *Rainbow Church*, 2013, Tokyo.
7 Do Ho Suh, *The Perfect Home*, 2002. Suspended fabric sculpture.
8 Site under construction, 2023.
9 Yeongdong-daero, a major artery in the Gangnam district.

3

5

6

7

8

9

"Architecture that sinks into the ground does not flee from the light; it redefines its relationship with it."

1 Overall view of the project.
2 Plan of planted areas and inter-neighborhood landscape.
3 Plan of the gallery connecting the two metro stations.

pages 74-75
4 "Greenland" public space and entrances to Gangnam Intermodal Transit Center.
5 Gangnam's new public square in winter.

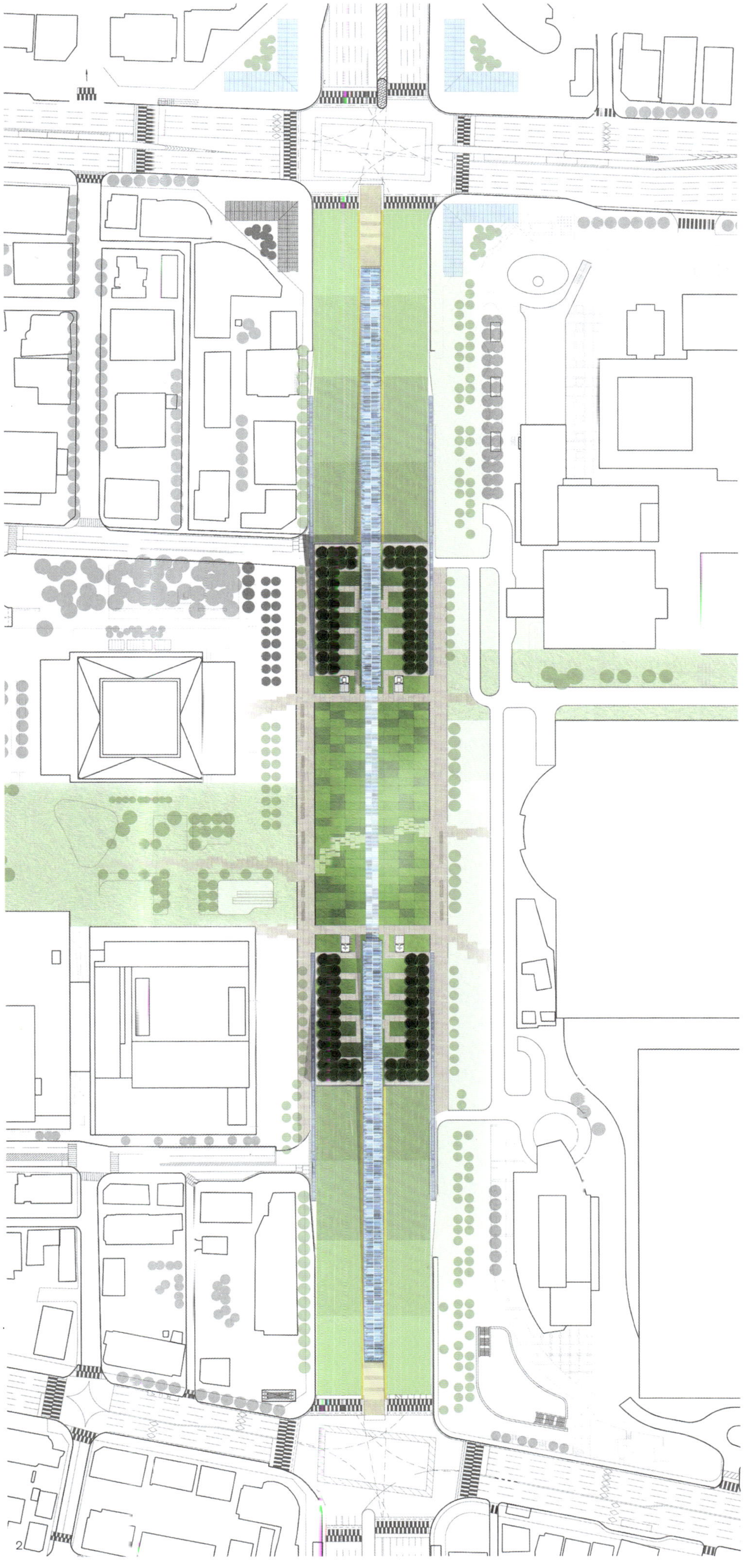

2

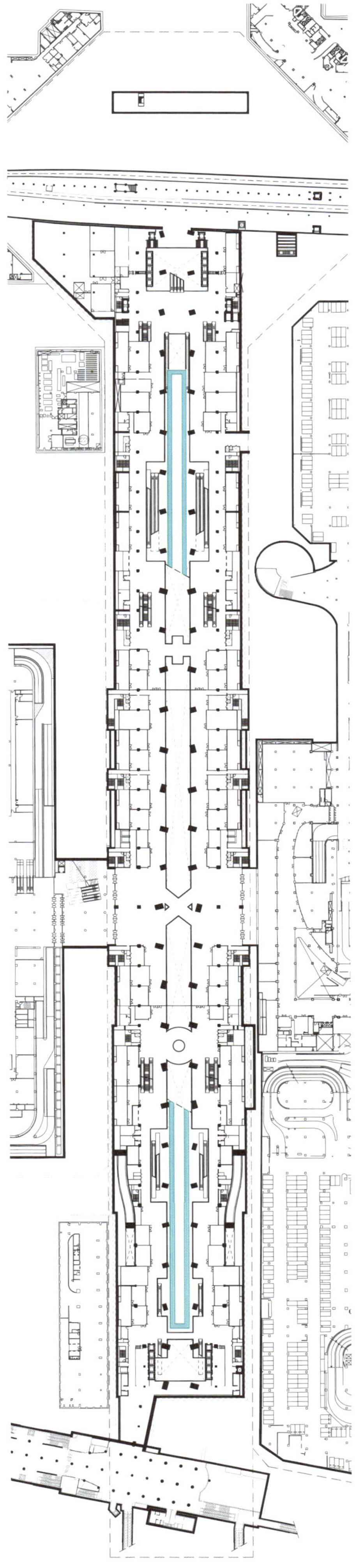

3

4

5

1

2

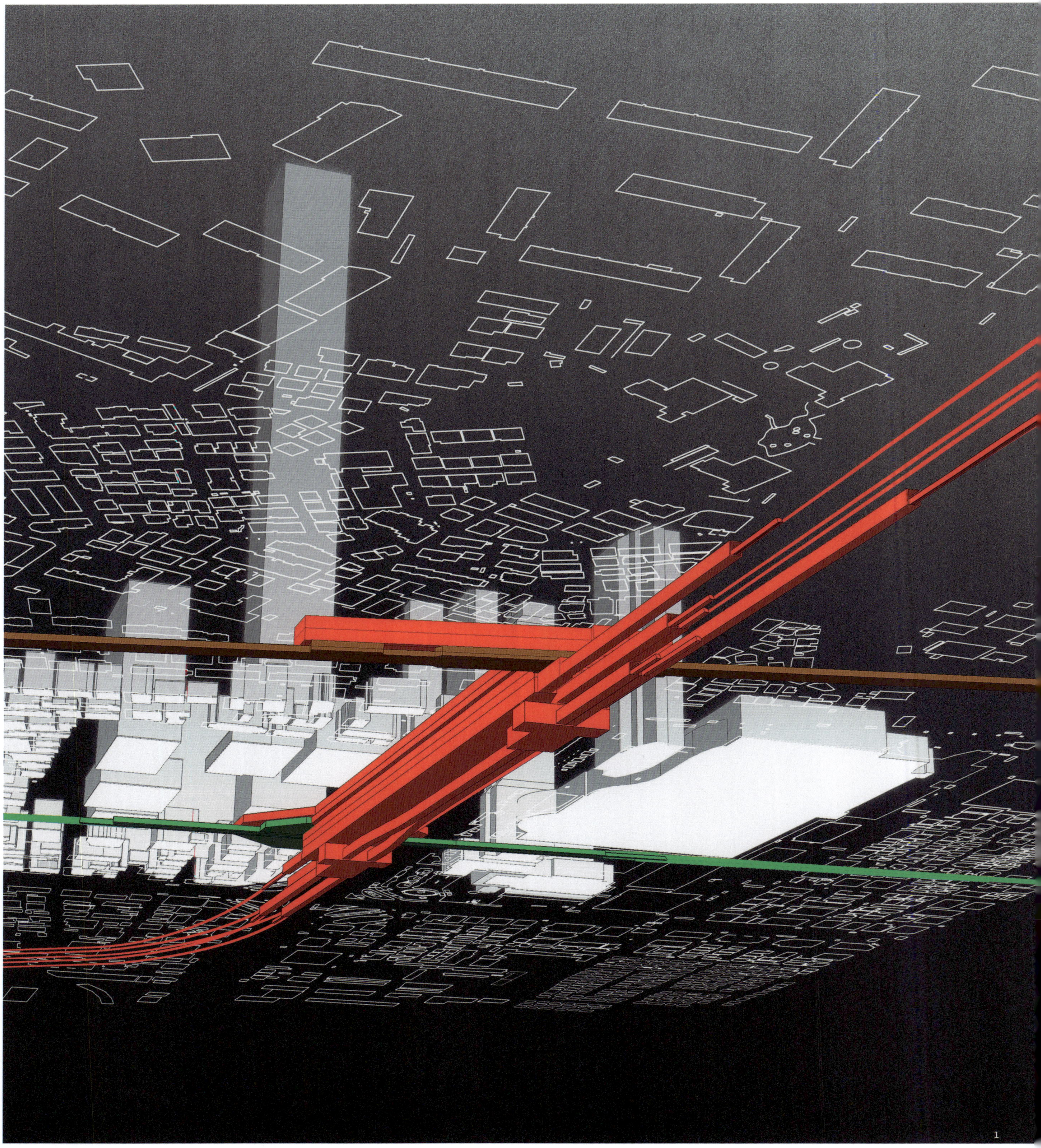

1

1 The city above and the city below: urban fabric and infrastructure.
2 Cross-section illustrating the transformation of a wide avenue into a mobility hub.

pages 76-77
1 Longitudinal section of the central gallery with light from the glass beam.
2 Longitudinal section through the central gallery.

FORUM

SAMSEONG
SPIRAL
← FORUM
DROP-OFF
택시 승강장
WAY OUT
출구

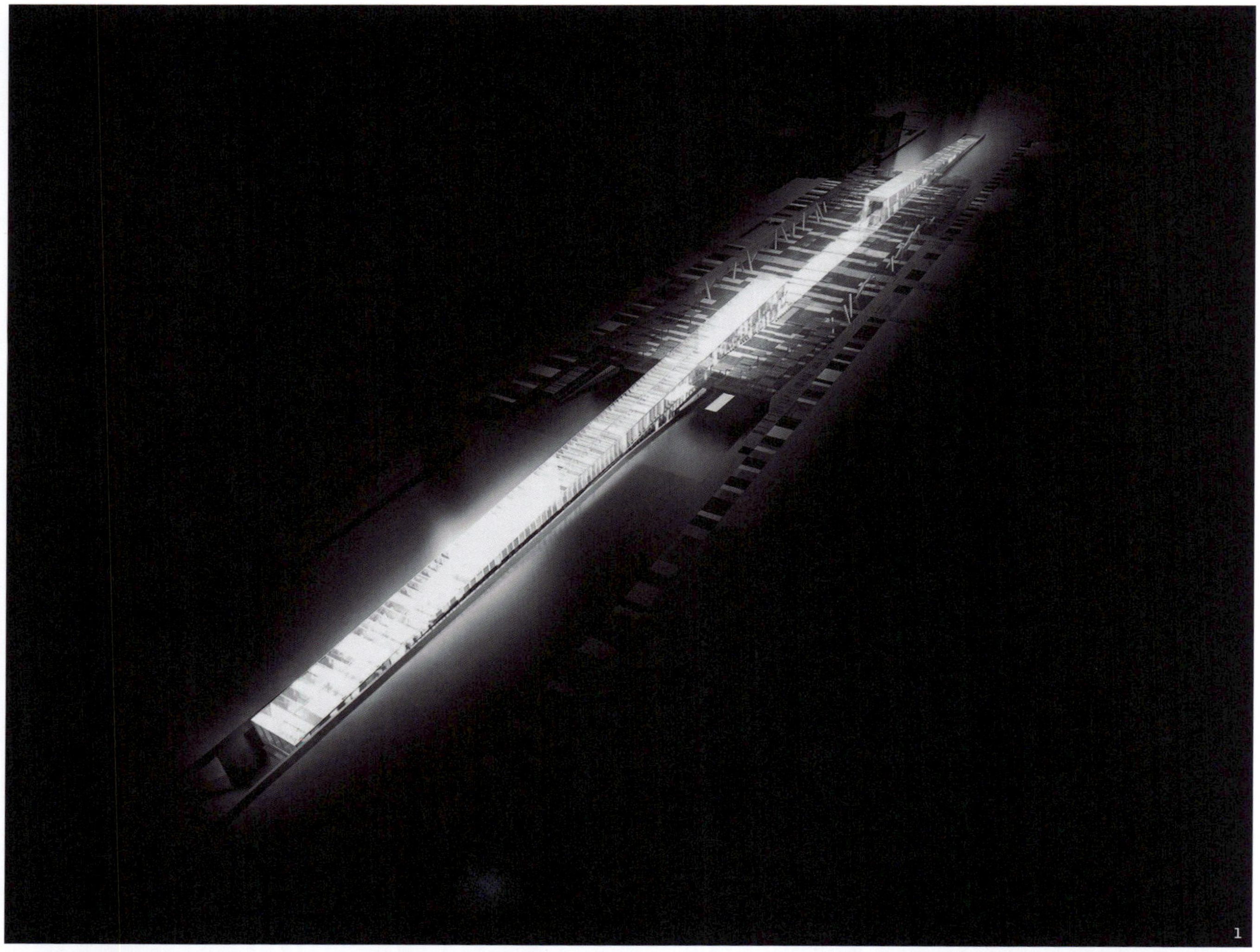

1

2

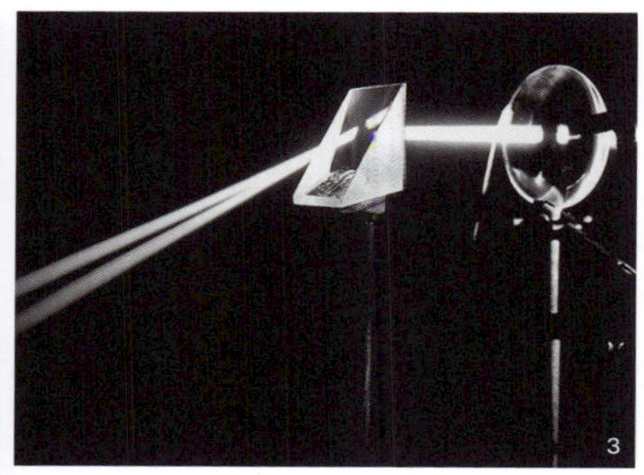

3

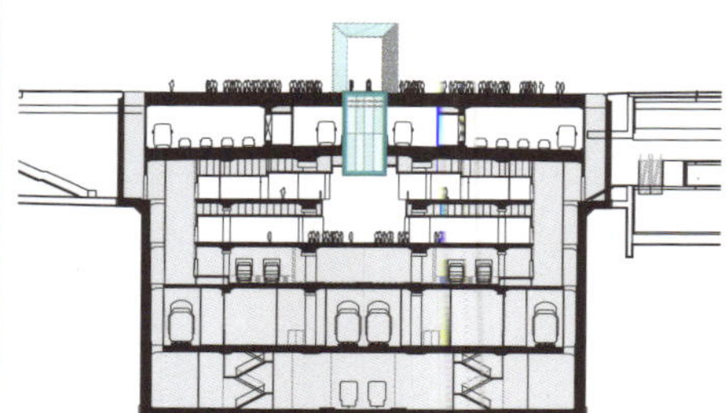

4

7

6

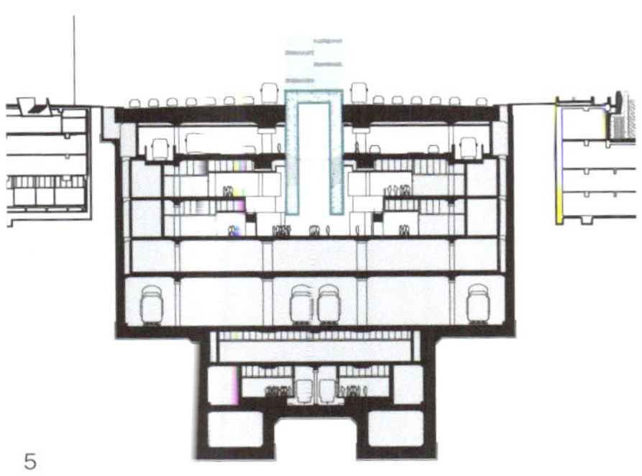

5

8

1 Night vision: a streak of light.
2 Light filtered and diffracted by the prism of the glass beam.
3 Fritz Goro, *Crystal Prism Producing Two Diverging Beams*, 1945, London.
4,5 Cross-sections and glass beam.
6 Glass beam study model, scale 1:50, 2018.
7 Play of reflections and mirrors at the entrances to the Gangnam Intermodal Transit Center.
8 Breaking down the beam's glass prism.

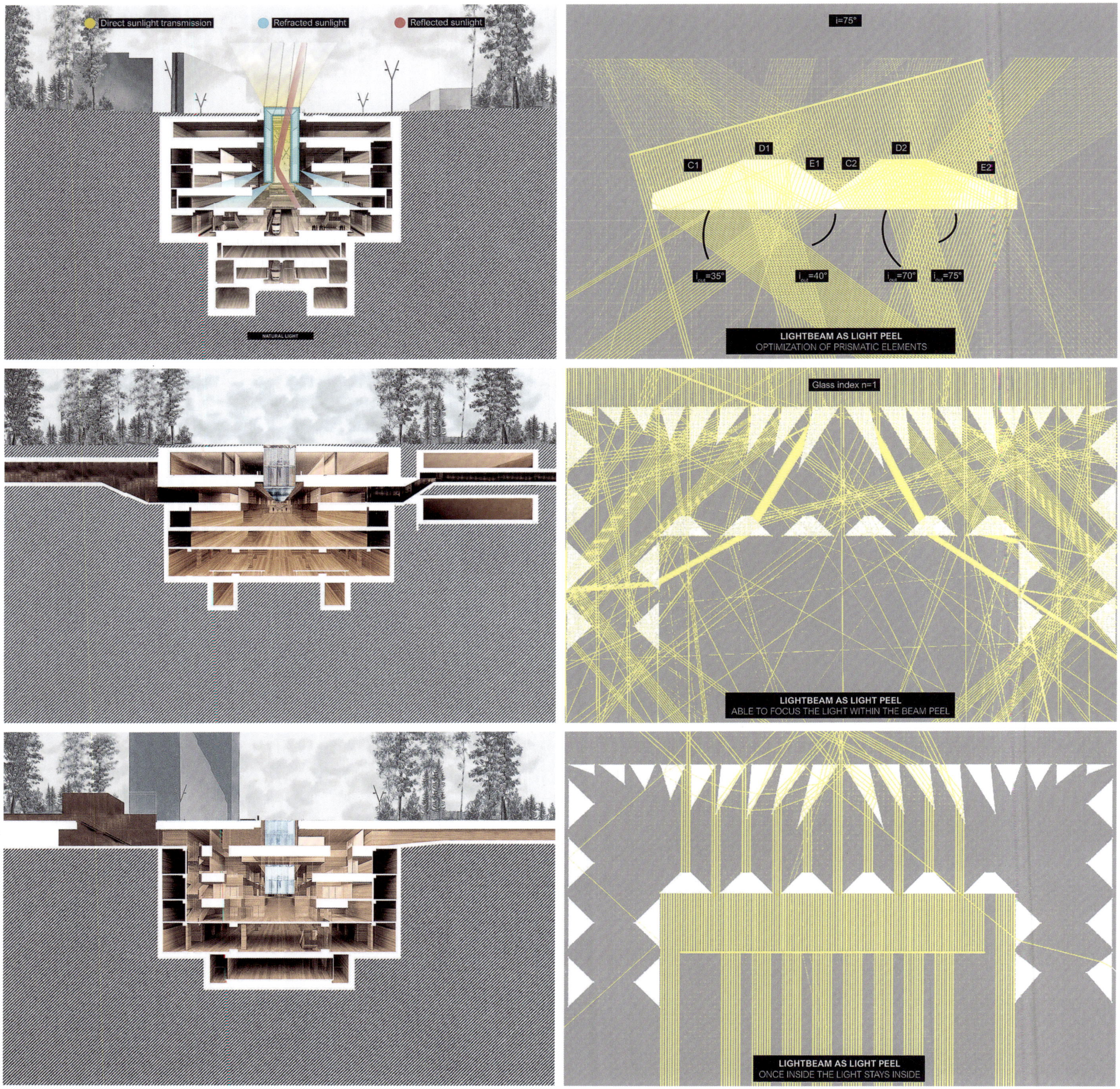

Set of physical studies of light and heat transmission.

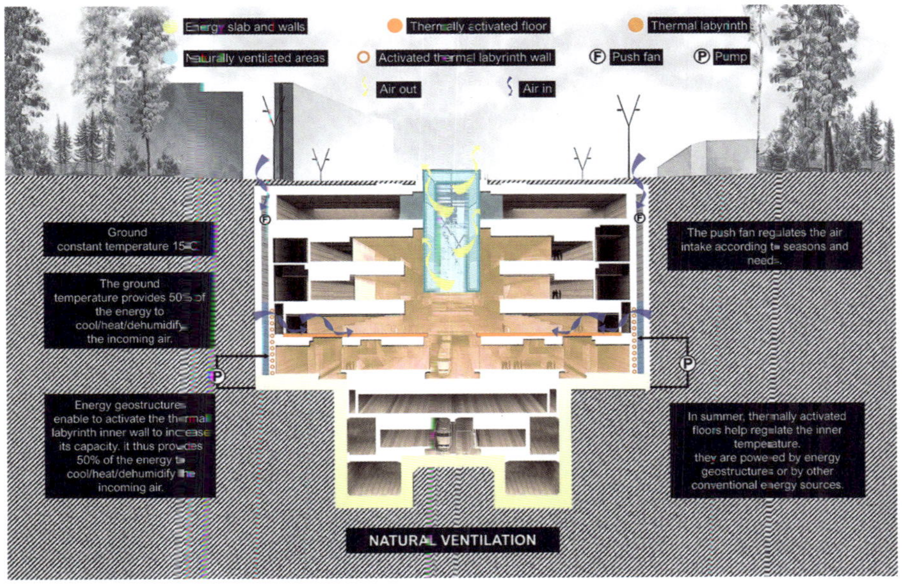
Energy slab and walls
Naturally ventilated areas
Thermally activated floor
Activated thermal labyrinth wall
Thermal labyrinth
Push fan
Pump
Air out
Air in
Ground constant temperature 15°C
The ground temperature provides 50% of the energy to cool/heat/dehumidify the incoming air.
Energy geostructures enable to activate the thermal labyrinth inner wall to increase its capacity. it thus provides 50% of the energy to cool/heat/dehumidify the incoming air.
The push fan regulates the air intake according to seasons and needs.
In summer, thermally activated floors help regulate the inner temperature.
they are powered by energy geostructures or by other conventional energy sources.
NATURAL VENTILATION

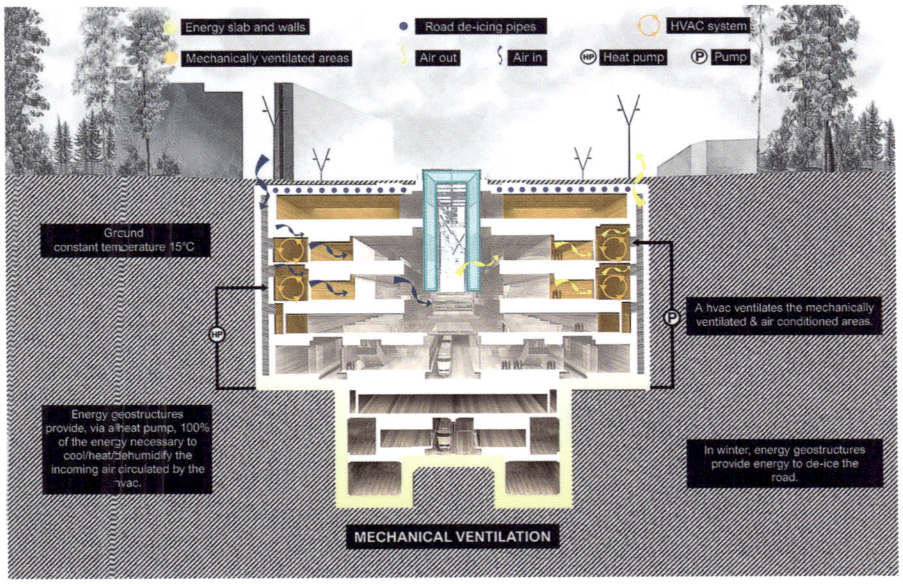
Energy slab and walls
Mechanically ventilated areas
Road de-icing pipes
Air out
Air in
Heat pump
HVAC system
Pump
Ground constant temperature 15°C
Energy geostructures provide, via a heat pump, 100% of the energy necessary to cool/heat/dehumidify the incoming air circulated by the hvac.
A hvac ventilates the mechanically ventilated & air conditioned areas.
In winter, energy geostructures provide energy to de-ice the road.
MECHANICAL VENTILATION

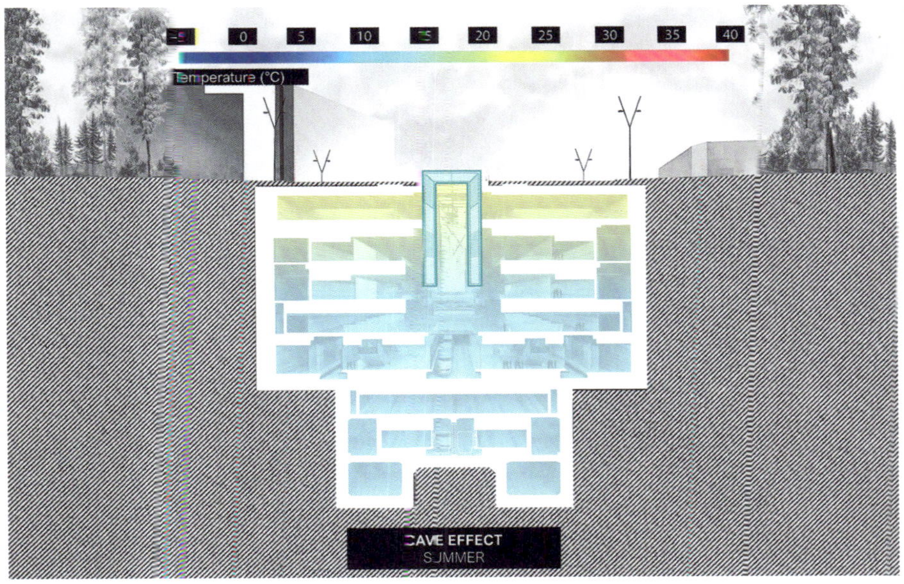
-5
0
5
10
15
20
25
30
35
40
Temperature (°C)
CAVE EFFECT
SUMMER

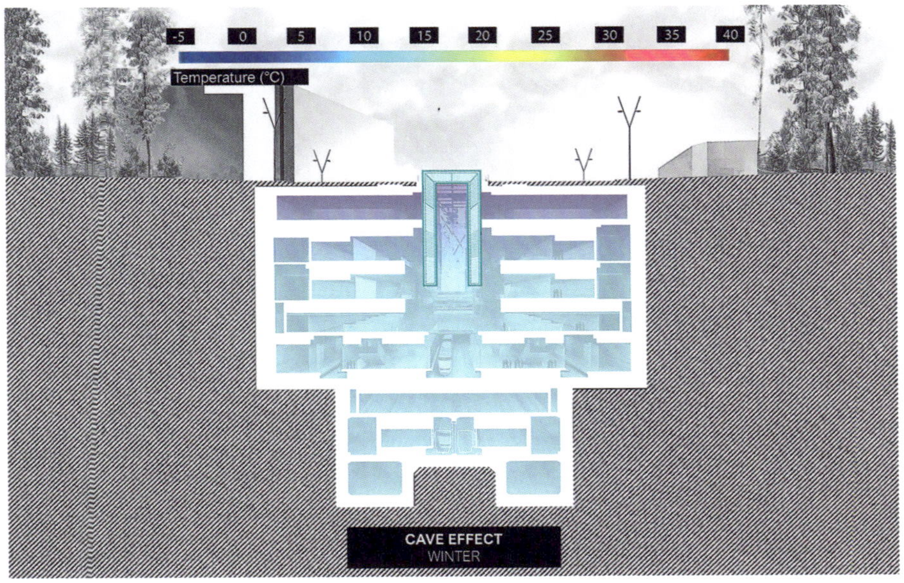
-5
0
5
10
15
20
25
30
35
40
Temperature (°C)
CAVE EFFECT
WINTER

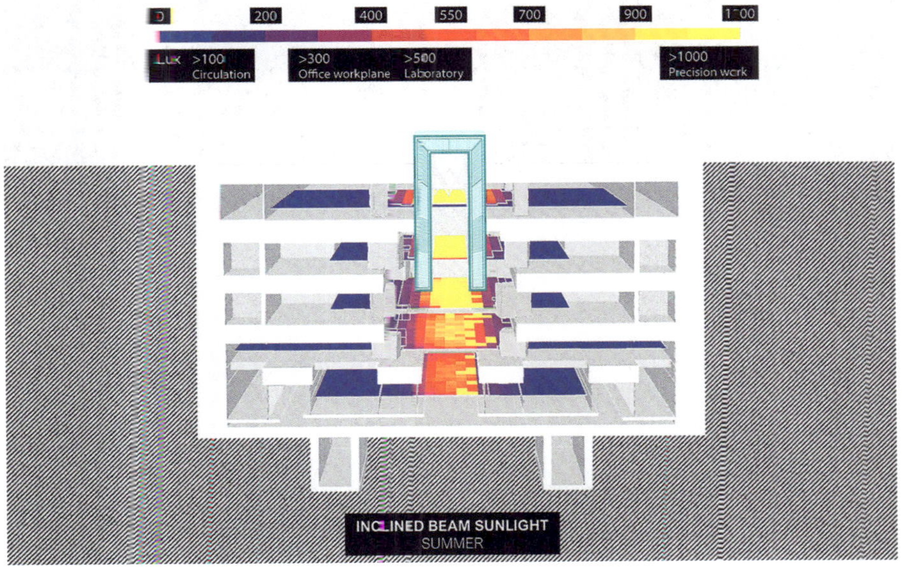
0
200
400
550
700
900
1100
Lux >100 Circulation
>300 Office workplane
>500 Laboratory
>1000 Precision work
INCLINED BEAM SUNLIGHT
SUMMER

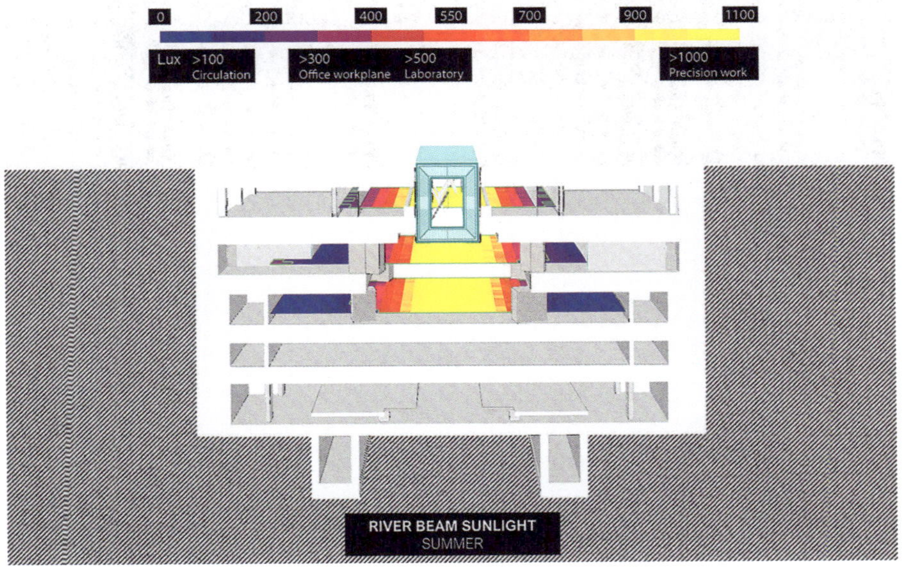
0
200
400
550
700
900
1100
Lux >100 Circulation
>300 Office workplane
>500 Laboratory
>1000 Precision work
RIVER BEAM SUNLIGHT
SUMMER

PIAZZA GARIBALDI

NAPLES, ITALY

2004–15 / 2017–19

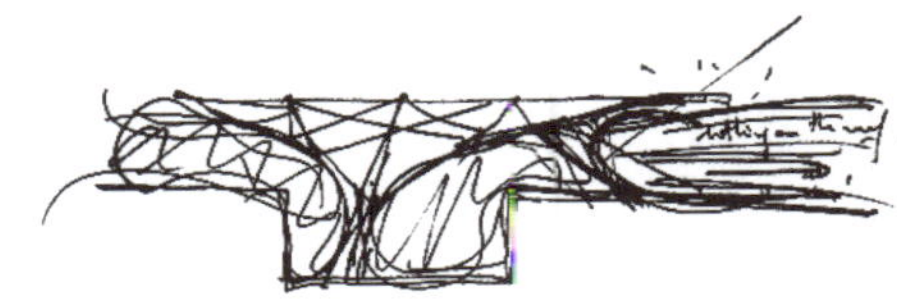

1

As part of the transformation of Piazza Garibaldi, which includes the addition of a new underground metro station to the scheme, a large open-air living gallery is embedded eight meters below the surface of the square. This monumental furrow cuts right through the emptiness, infiltrating and sliding underground to connect to the complex network of galleries linking the many stations in this intermodal hub. Highlighting the historic axis that stretches from the railway station to the statue of Garibaldi, tall metal trees spread their branches to provide shade for both the underground gallery and its above-ground surroundings. In the central shaft of the metro station, the walkways bend, turn, and interact with the light of the Neapolitan sky, which seeps through the city floor to the platforms.

2

3

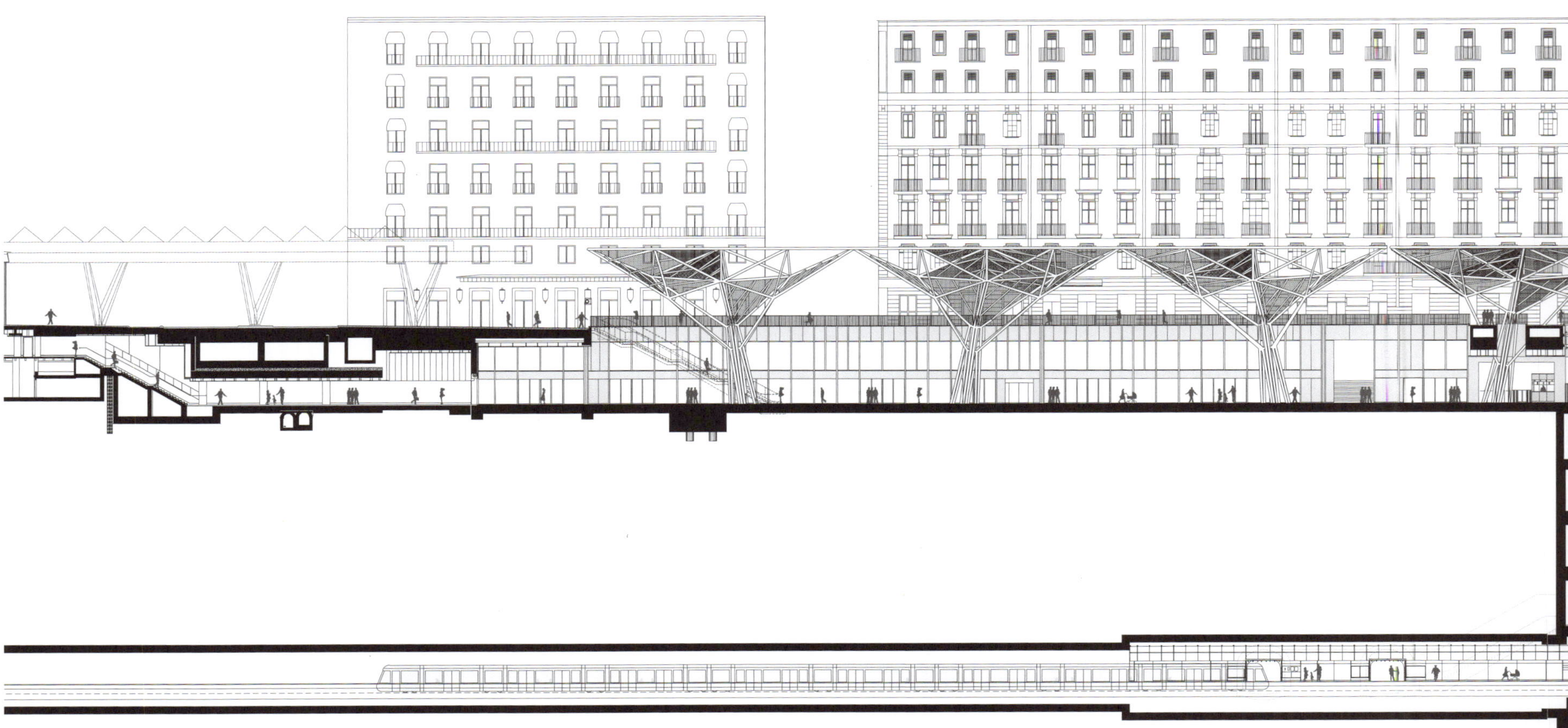

5

4

1 Sketch, 2004.
2 Historic photograph, 2000.
3 Concept: cover/open.
4 Natural/artificial. Metal trees and living trees.
5 An underground gallery to reduce the depth of the metro station and connect it to other forms of public transportation.

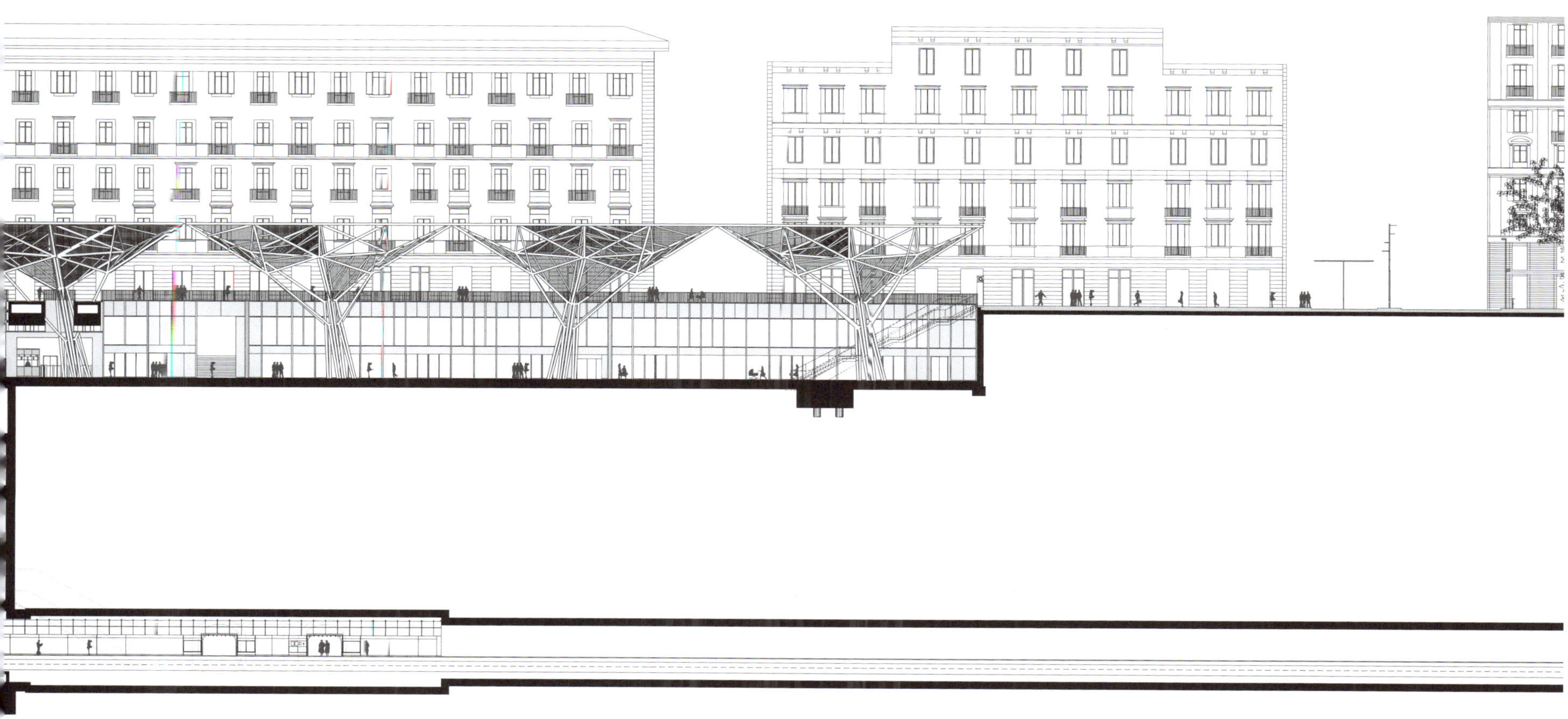

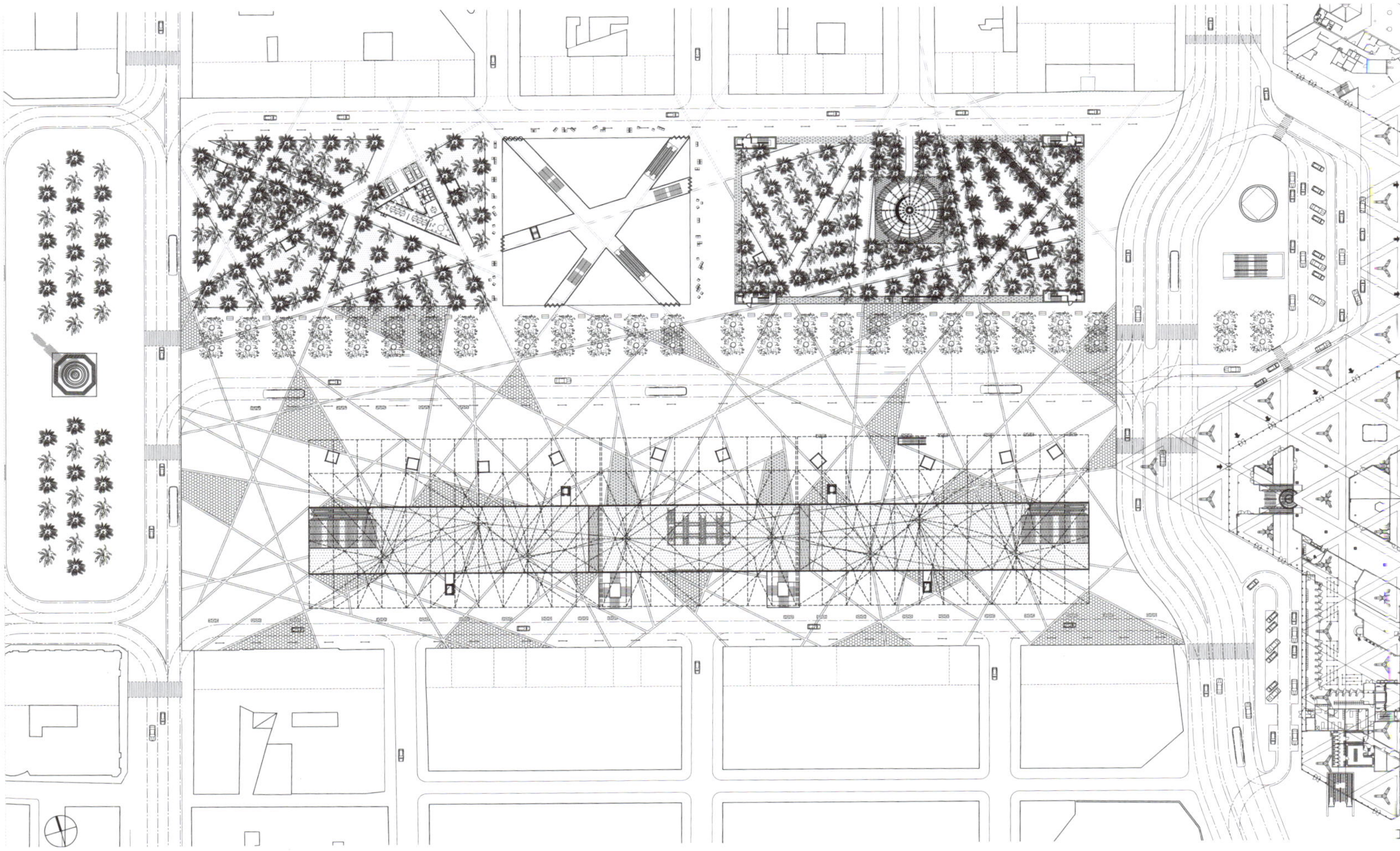

1

2

1 Plan of Piazza Garibaldi.
2 Study model, between nature and architecture, scale 1:250. 2007.
3 Sketch, 2004.
4 Study model of the metal tree, scale 1:50, 2006.
5 Plan of the shadow device with shade cloths.
6, 7 Metal structure and canvas shades.

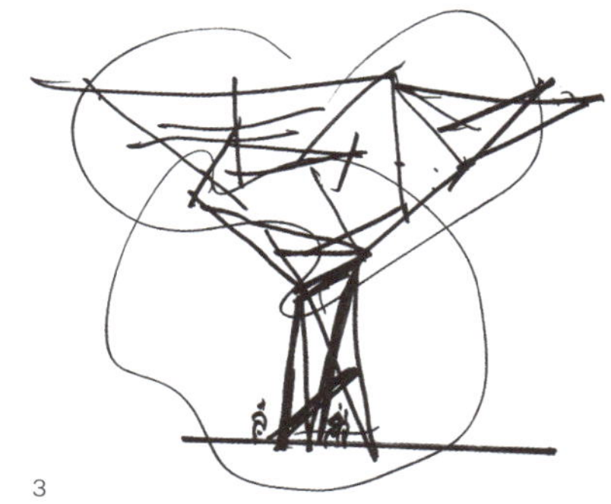

3

4

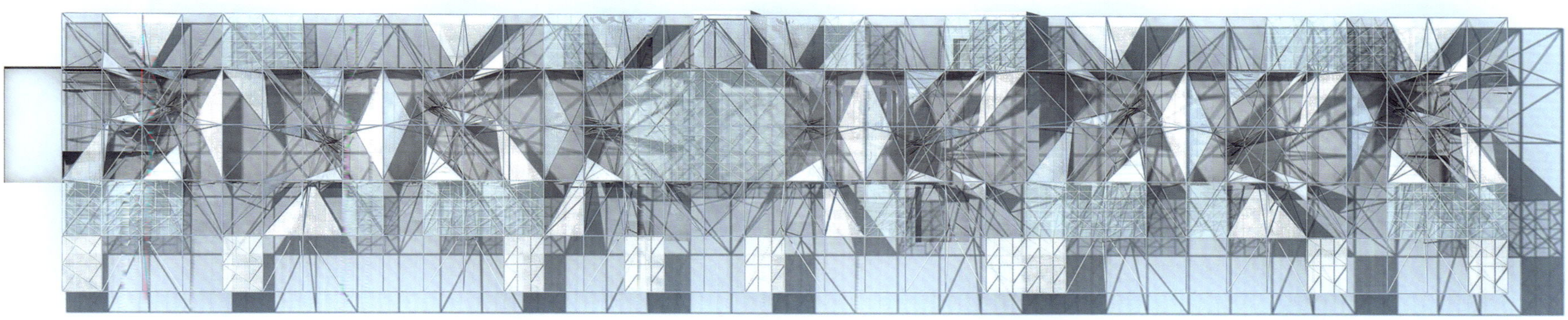

5

6

7

HOTEL IDEAL
BAR
PIZZERIA
Free Wi-Fi

VILLEJUIF GUSTAVE-ROUSSY STATION

VILLEJUIF, FRANCE

2013–25

Envisaged as a connector between the world above and the world below, the architecture of the station elevates the infrastructure and the moment of travel: erasing the boundaries between open and closed space, opening its floor to the public space of the street, it raises no built frontage to confront the city but instead allows air and natural light to circulate down to the platforms fifty meters below. An invitation to “travel within the journey,” the route is designed to be tranquil, but not bland: the flights of escalators and staircases form an extraordinary Piranesian space that seeps into the flesh of the territory and extends the vertical dynamics of access to the transport networks with the movements of the city.

1 The station and Gustave Roussy hospital.
2 Fiction by DPA. The Pantheon of Rome beneath the hospital.
3 Block plan of the station and its public spaces.
4 Natural light penetrating to a depth of 50 meters. Model, scale 1:500, 2015.

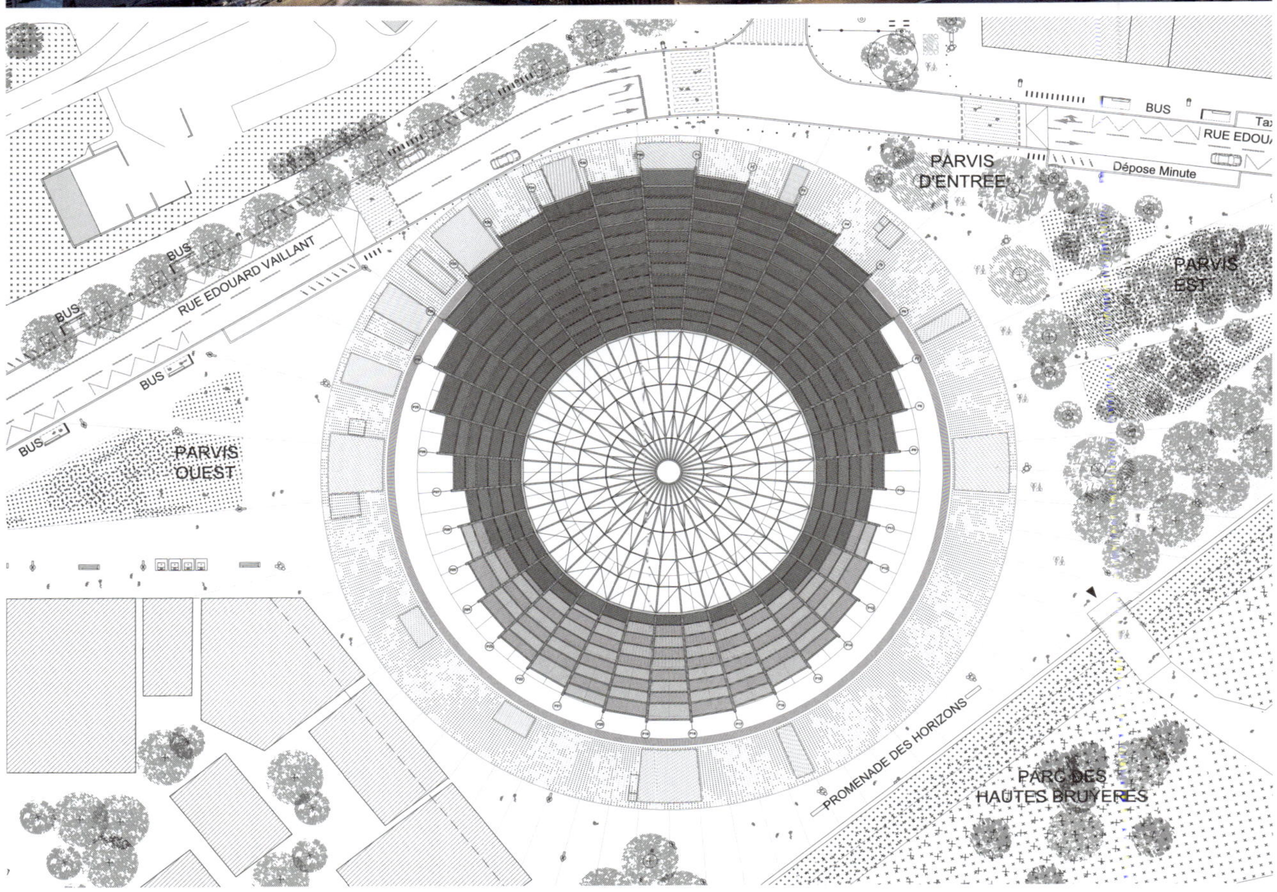

1

2

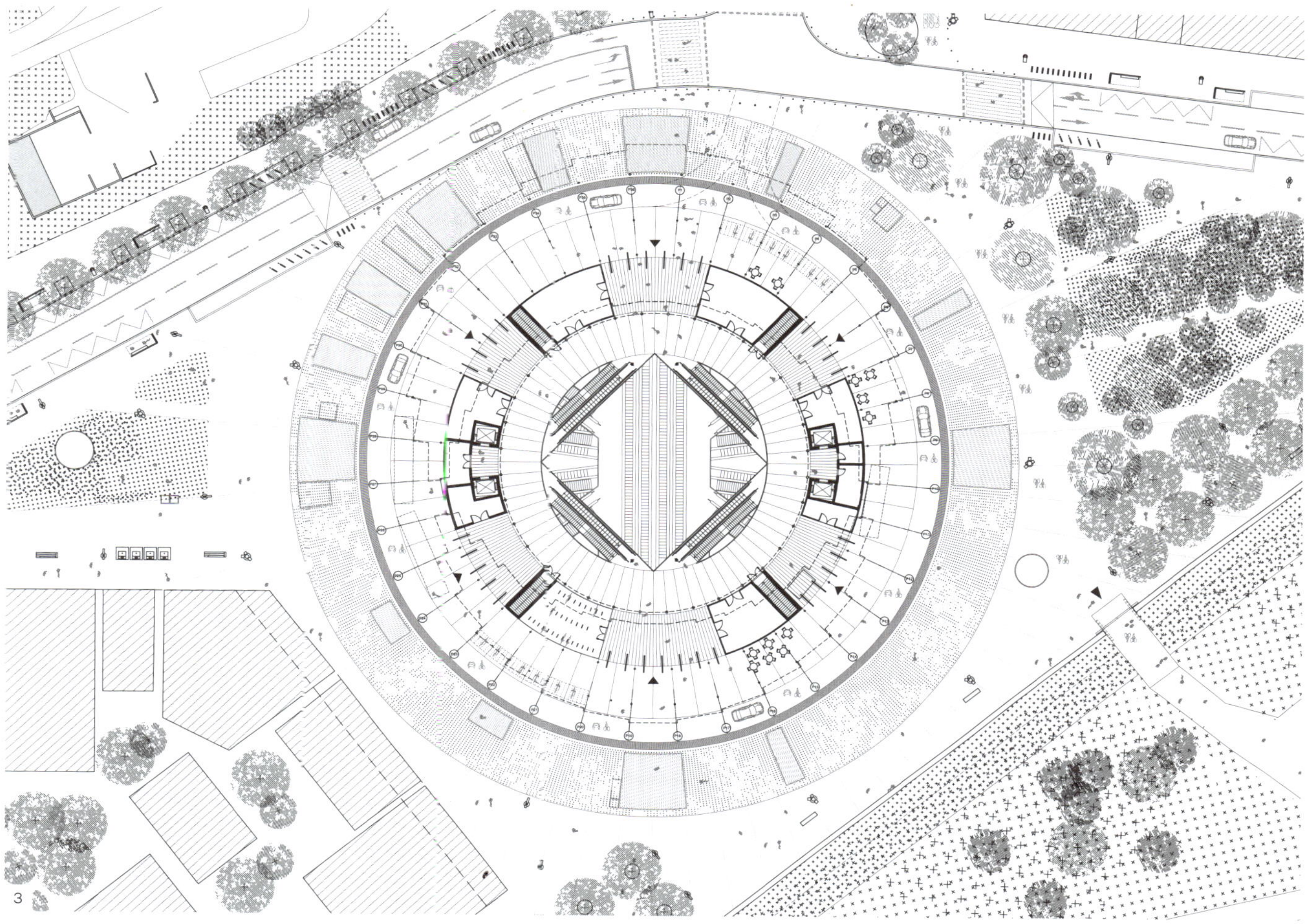

1 No tunnels or galleries, no shadows: everything is visible, accessible, and luminous. Model, scale 1:500, 2015.
2 Vertical succession of ring-shaped plans.
3 Street-level plan.
4 View of the escalators connecting the station's nine levels.

BOMECON.NL

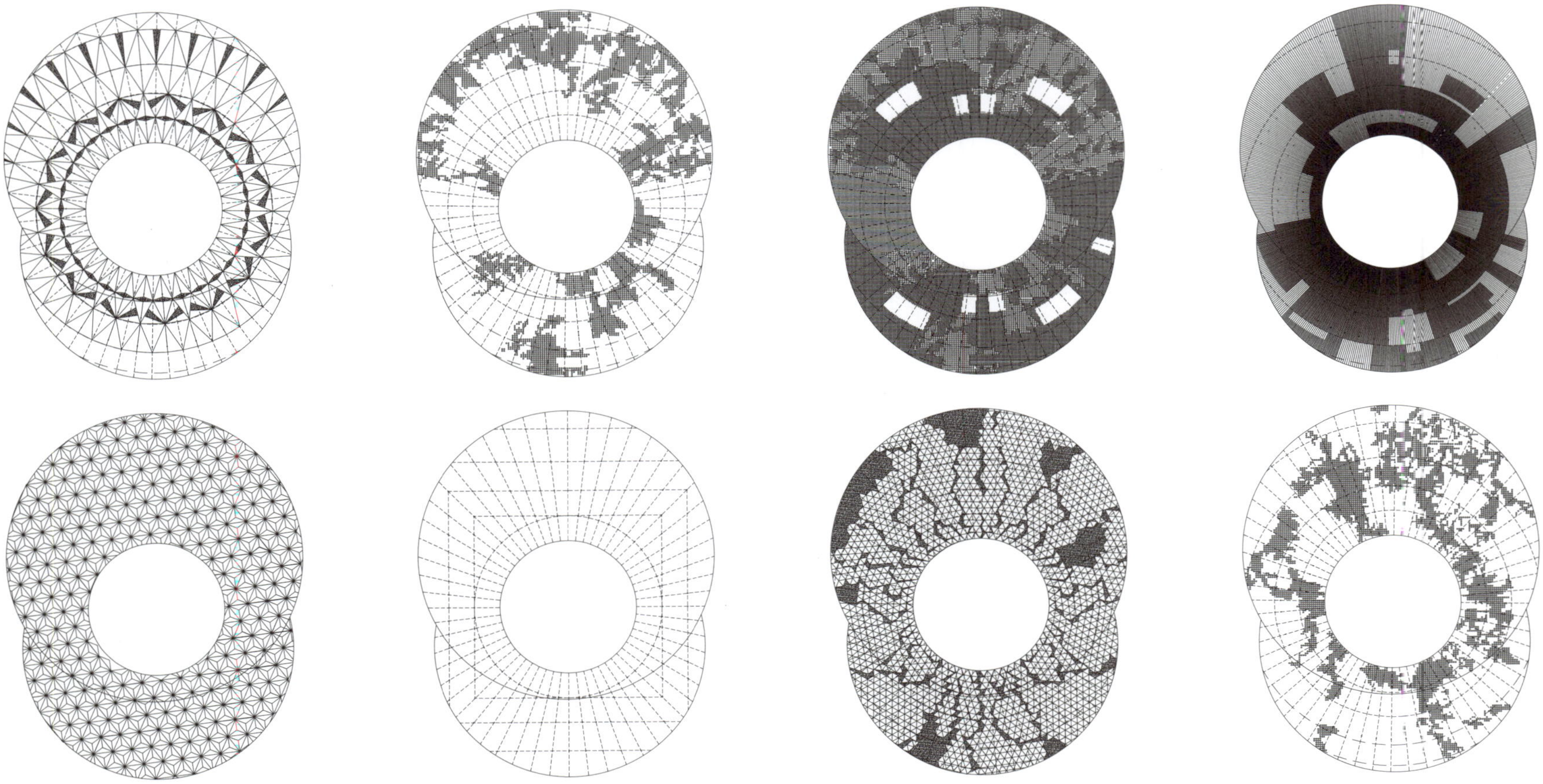

1

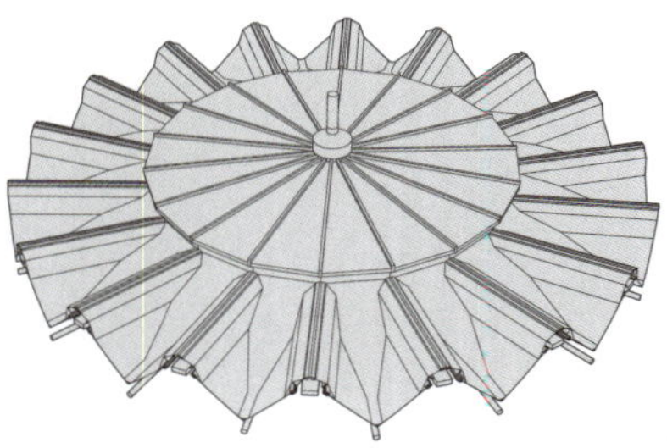

2

3

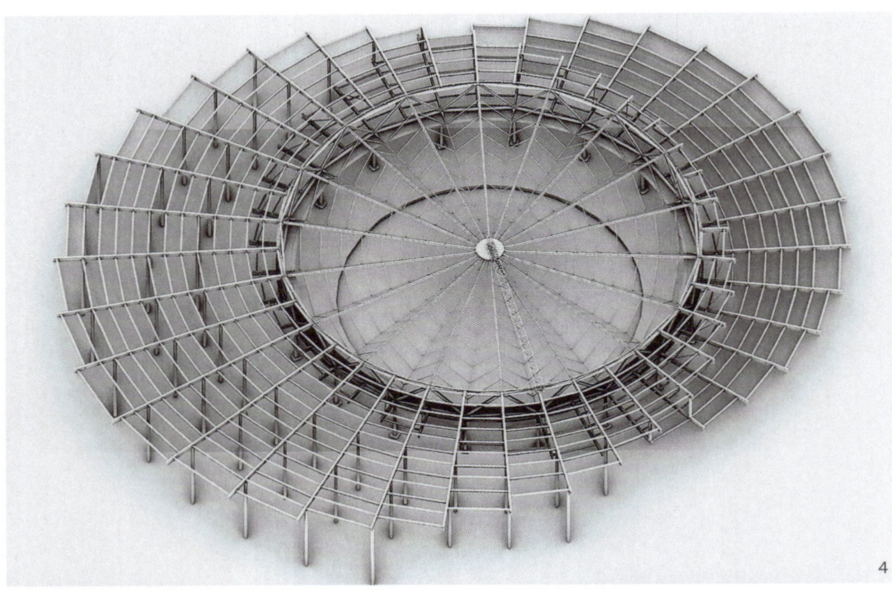

4

5

6

7

1 Studies for halo-shaped roofs.
2-4 Studies for the overhanging structures of the roof's eye.
5-7 Pleated roof in metal fabric.
8 View of the transparent roof membrane from the hospital.

Plan du quart
Station map
Plan de la
station

1 The interplay o lights and mirrors dematerializes the architecture.

2-4 Views of the various platforms for transfers between metro lines.

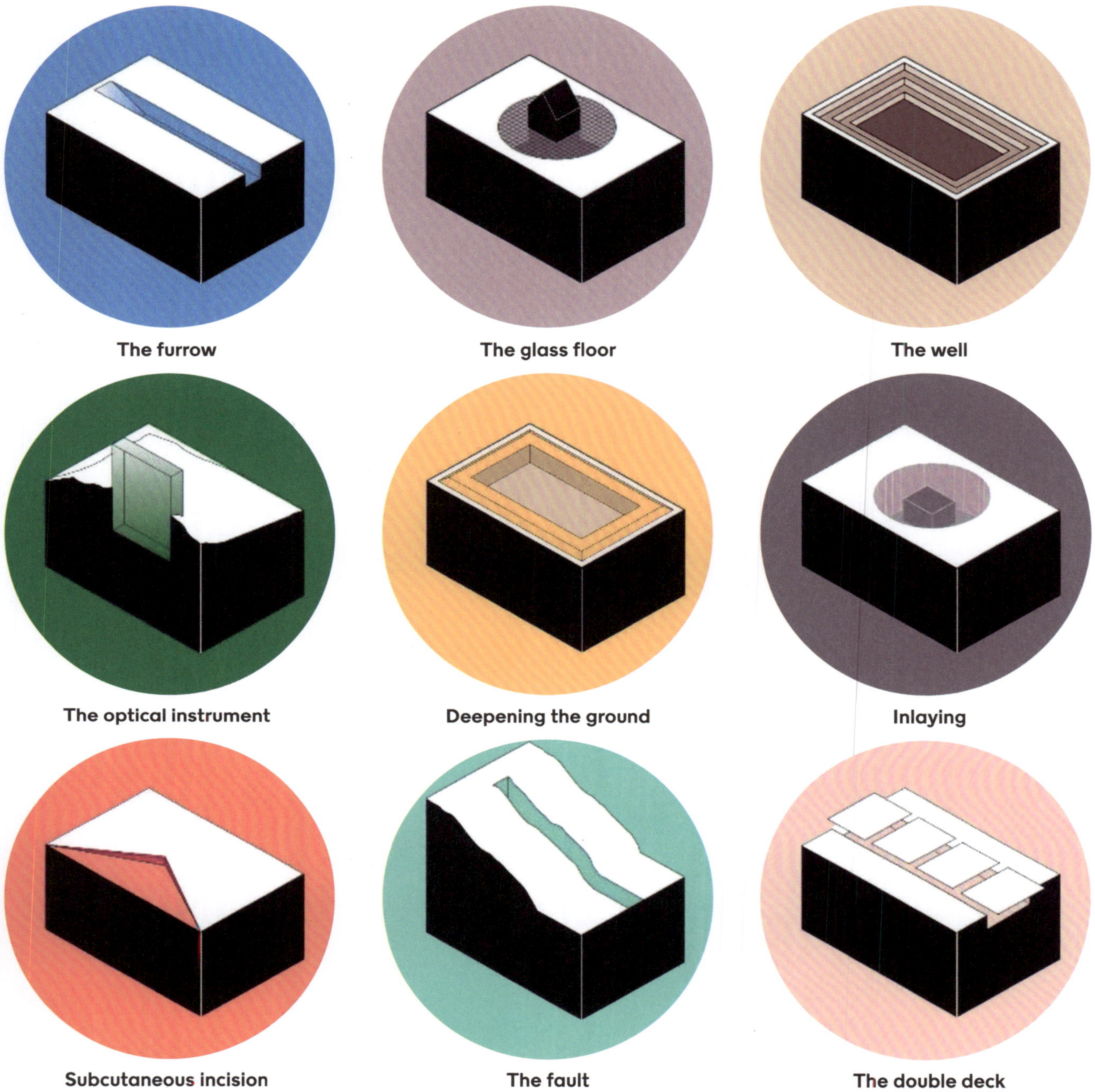

1

Groundscape typologies: a grammar for inhabiting the ground
Beneath the surface of the land lies a world of possibilities, of new places, already existing or to be created. The groundscape is the last space to be conquered by our cities, offering a powerful catalyst for urban networks, naturally ideal thermal inertia, respect for the landscape, enhancement of heritage, and a unique palette of light. By playing with reliefs, hollows, openings, and overlays, the groundscape offers a range of different typologies, each expressing a particular relation to the ground, to light, to movement, and to perception. These groundscape figures are more than just formal games: they ask a fundamental question about how we inhabit the density of the world. Reconciling space and matter, the groundscape typologies invite us to rethink our relationship with the ground, not simply as a support but as a living, sculptable, habitable material. The different typologies offer a spatial grammar for working on the relationship between man and the earth, between architecture and landscape.

1 Research on Groundscapes began in the late 1980s and led to the definition of nine categories for land occupation and use; nine operating strategies. This typology constitutes a kind of toolbox that can be applied and adapted to very different contexts.
2 "Turning the table."

"Groundscape arch tecture breathes through its roots."

2

3

4

6

7

8

9

1

2

1

The furrow

Unlike a straightforward excavation or cavern, the furrow cuts delicately into the ground, forming a long, continuous notch that inscribes a line in the continuity of the ground. Tracing a path, this furrow is like a linear writing of the ground, its strength lying in the relation it establishes between the horizontality of the landscape and the depth of the architectural space.

1, 2 Ewha University campus under construction, April 2007.
3 Christo and Jeanne-Claude, *Running Fence, Sonoma and Marin Counties, California*, 1972–76. Centre Pompidou, Paris.
4 Christo and Jeanne-Claude, *Running Fence, Sonoma and Marin Counties, California*, 1972–76. Smithsonian American Art Museum, Washington, DC.
5 Carey Young, *Body Techniques (after A Line in Ireland, Richard Long, 1974)*, 2007.
6 Michael Heizer, *Double Negative*, 1969–70, Nevada Desert.
7 Painted Canyon in Riverside County, California.
8 Richard Long, *Walking a Line in Peru*, 1972.
9 Francis Alÿs, *Untitled (When Faith Moves Mountains)*, 2002. The Museum of Modern Art, New York.

5

1

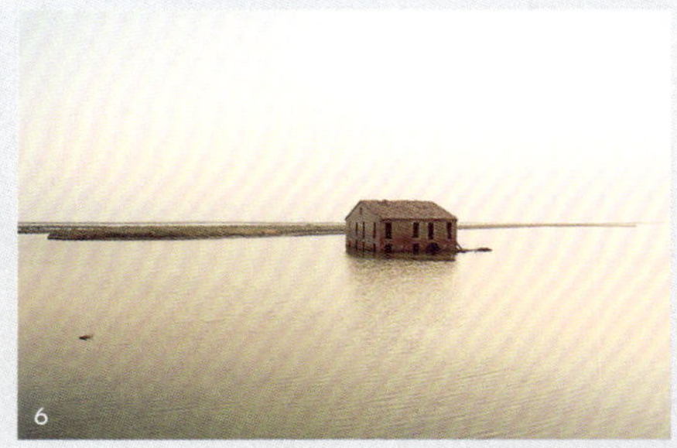

6

7

8

2

The glass floor

The glass floor introduces a diaphanous horizontality that shifts the gaze and the light towards what lies beneath our feet. Transforming the floor into a viewing surface, it acts as a threshold between two worlds: above and below, bringing the subterranean space within the realm of perception

2

9

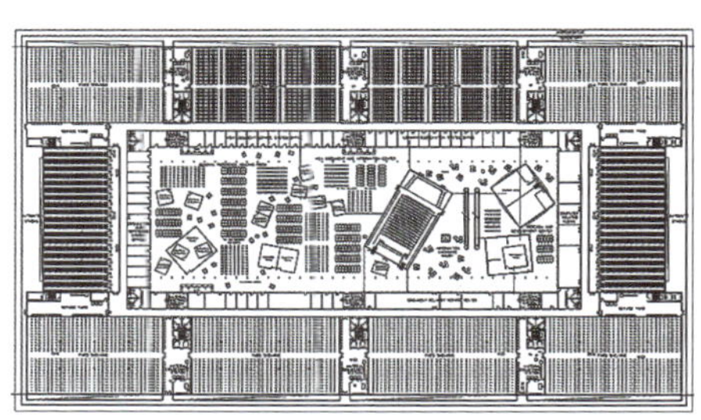

3

10

1-3 Kansai-Kan National Library, Kyoto, 1996.
4 Regina Silveira, *Abyssal*, 2010, Atlas Sztuki, Lodz, Poland.
5 Philippe Ramette, *Rational Exploration of The Undersea: The Contact*, 2006.
6 Luigi Ghirri, *Argine Agosta: Comacchio*, 1989.
7 Leandro Erlich, *The Swimming Pool*, 2010. 21st Century Museum of Contemporary Art, Kanazawa, Japan.
8 Mathias Haker, *Mirror, Mirror on the Floor*, 2014.
9 Olafur Eliasson, *Your glacial expectations*, 2012. Kvadrat, Ebeltoft, Denmark (photography: Annabel Elston).
10 Gerry Barry, *Skycircle*, 1978.

3

4

5

6

7

8

9

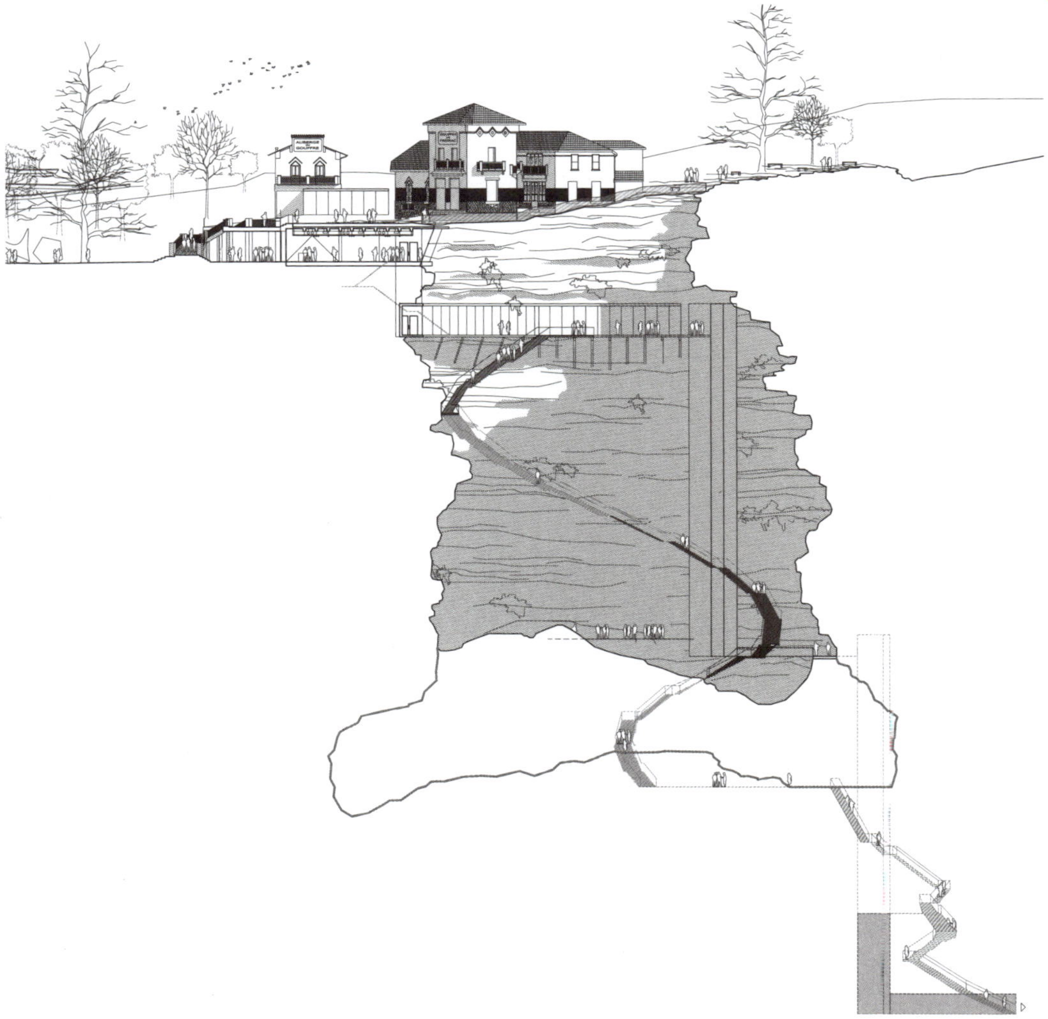

1

2

3
The well

The well is a pure vertical excavation, a deep, vertical opening that draws light and air down into the substance of the ground. It is a concentrated gesture that connects the depths to the infinity of the sky, offering a powerful sensory link between earth and sky in a direct relationship.

1, 2 Modernization of the Gouffre de Padirac chasm infrastructures, Padirac, 2016.
3 Detail of the planning and construction concept for the Messe Wien exhibition and congress center, Erlach & Mossburger, Austria.
4 Step well, first quarter of the 8th century, Abhaneri (Rajasthan), India.
5 Adalaj Stepwell built for Mahmud Begada, 1499, Gujarat, India.
6 Diavik Diamond Mine, Canada. Photo: Jason Pineau, 2007.
7 Mikhael Subotzky and Patrick Waterhouse, *Looking Up the Core, Ponte City*, 2008, Johannesburg.
8 Manfred Hermer, *Ponte City*, 1975, Johannesburg.
9 Peter Neve, *Parkhaus Rödingsmarkt*, 1965, Hamburg.

4

5

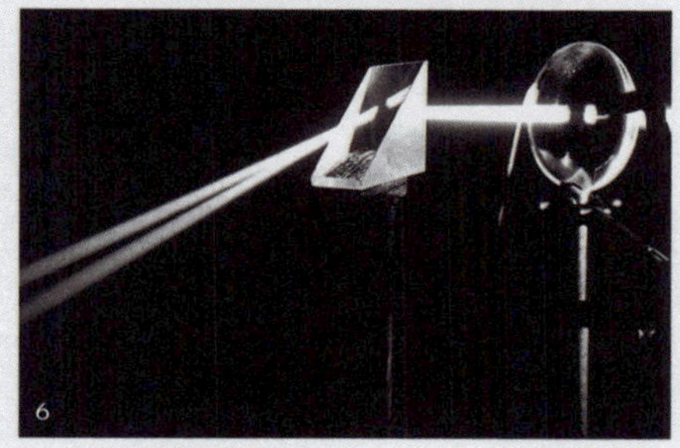

6

7

8

9

10

1

4
The optical instrument

The optical instrument is not a crude crack but a sophisticated window, a perception device integrated into the ground. Staging a piece of sky, landscape, or architecture, it transforms an underground space into an observation chamber. The ground becomes a screen, a membrane sensitive to what is happening above and below.

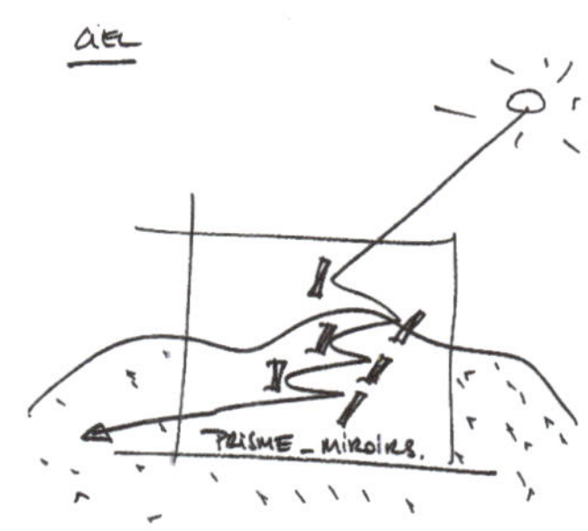

2

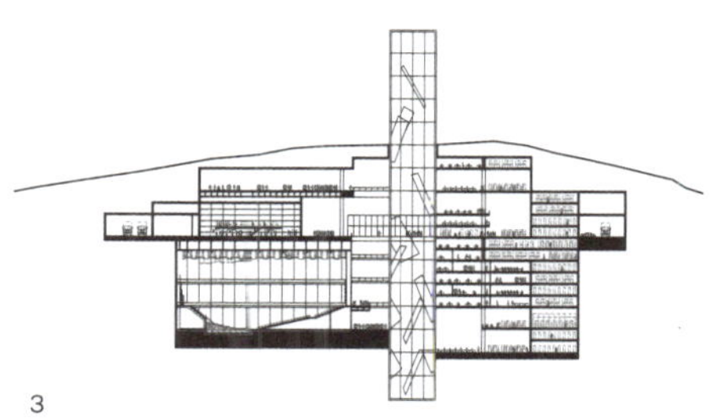

3

1-3 City of Culture of Galicia, Santiago de Compostela, 1999.
4 Harald Haraldsson and Super Nature Design, *Prisma 1666*, 2011, Shanghai.
5 J.A. Houston, *Newton Investigating Light*, c. 1879.
6 Fritz Goro, *Crystal Prism Producing Two Diverging Beams*, 1945, London.
7 Dmitri Kessel, *Light Refracting through Piece of Clear Material*, 1941.
8 Ivan Navarro, *Tuning*, installation, Templon Gallery, Paris, 2015.
9 James Turrell, *Acro Red*, Projection Piece, 1968.
10 Augustin Mouchot, Parabolic Solar Energy Concentrator, 1878, Exposition Universelle, Paris.

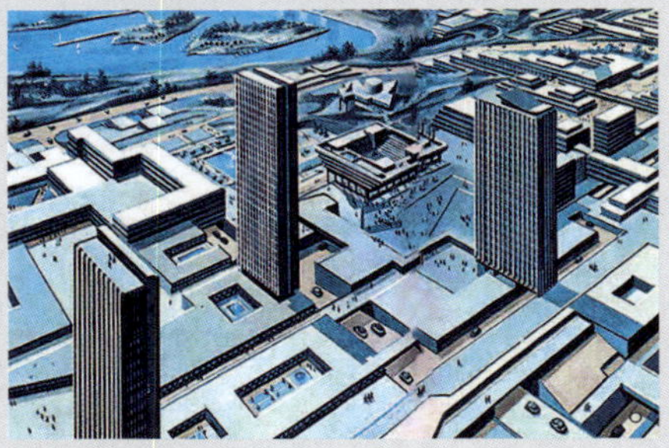

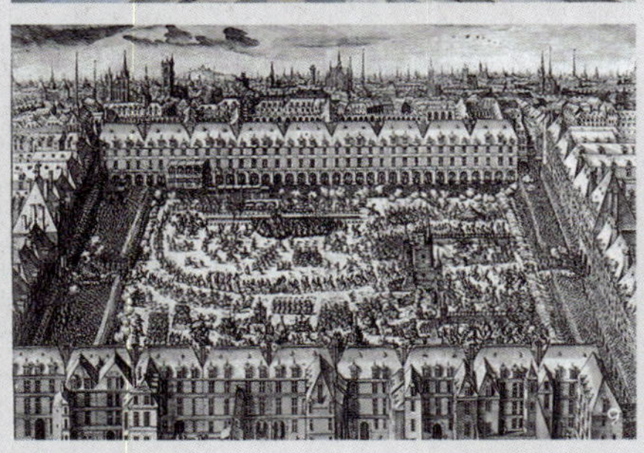

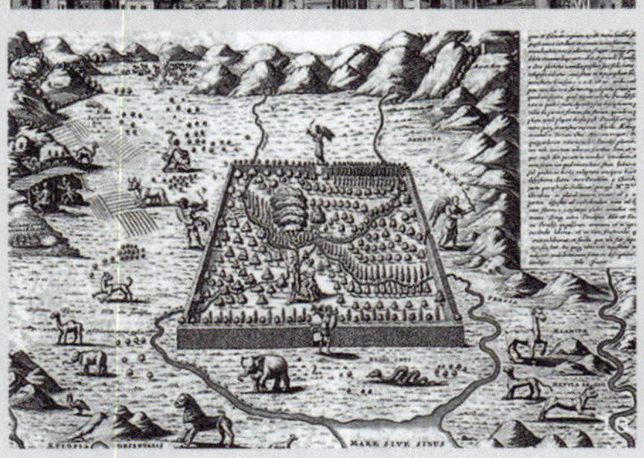

5
Deepening the ground

Deepening the ground consists in considering the ground not as a simple surface but as a material to be developed, dug out, and layered. The ground becomes a world in itself, a complex volume generating layers of habitat and redefining the relationship between inside and outside, between the buried and the open. The architecture melts into this thickness, creating places between surface, depth, and landscape.

1-3 Bibliothèque Nationale de France, Paris, 1993.
4 Kader Attia, *Pascale, Fernand Pouillon, Algiers*, 2012, lightbox.
5 Raine Karp and Riina Altmae, Linahall, Tallinn, Estonia, 1980.
6, 7 Photographs from the article "Paris in 20 Years" published in *Paris-Match*, no. 951 (July 1, 1967), pp. 44–45 and 52–53.
8 Magdalena Jetelová, *Domestication of a Pyramid*, Warsaw, Poland, 1991.
9 Claude Chastillon, *Carrousel on the Place Royale in Paris for the Wedding of Louis XIII and Anne of Austria*, 1612.
10 Atanasius Kircher, *Topographia paradisi terrestris juxta mentem et conjecturas authoris*, c. 1675.

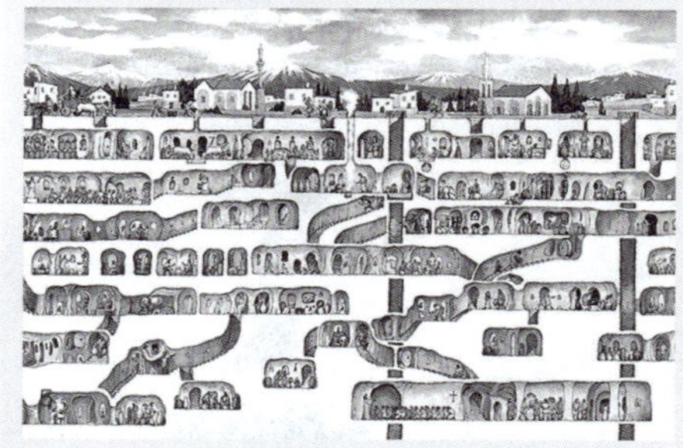

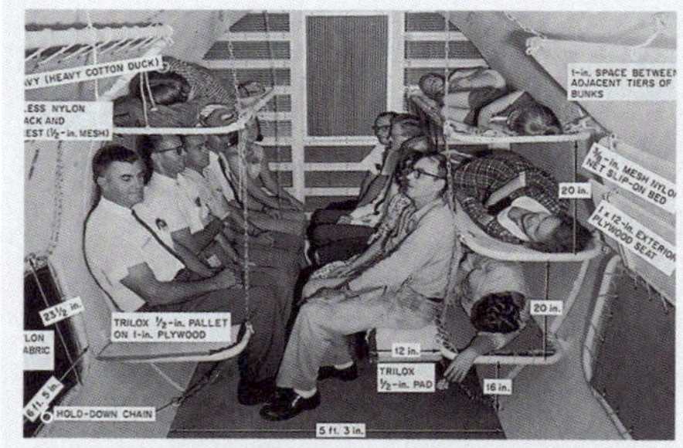

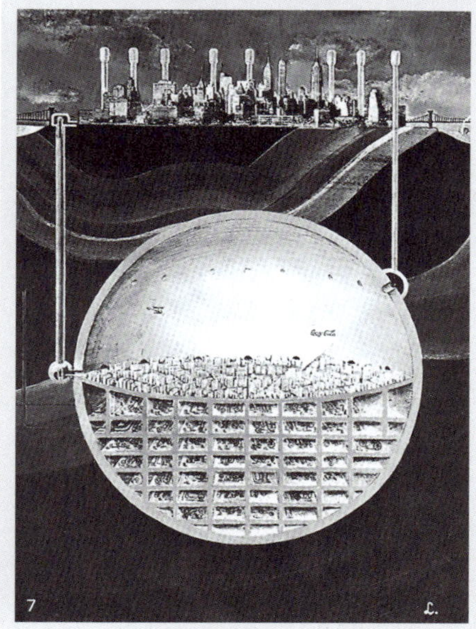

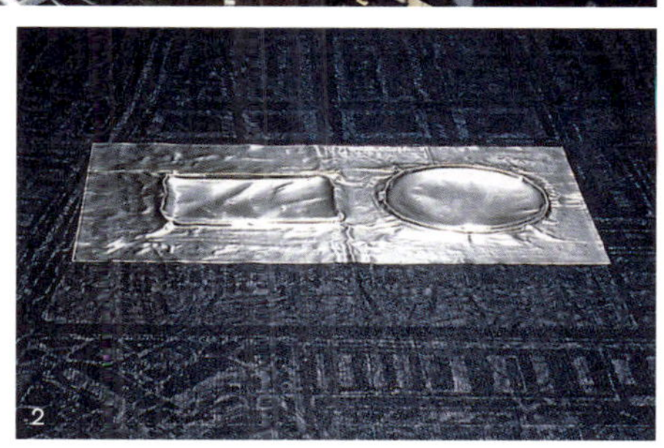

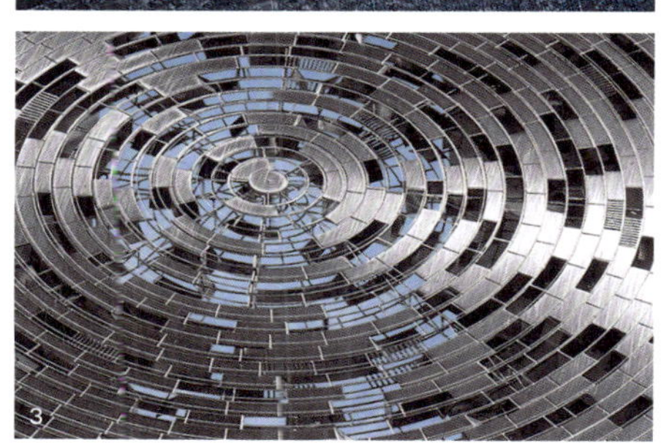

6
Inlaying

Inlaying, in close contact with the ground, is a gesture that creates a strong anchoring effect: the architecture seems to be inserted into the matter of the ground. Unlike the incision or the fault, the inlay is architecture embedded in the ground, rather than placed upon it, and sinks in and embraces the earth like a jewel in its setting.

1-3 Olympic velodrome and swimming pool, Berlin, 1992–99.
4 John Portman, *Hyatt Regency Hotel*, Atlanta, 1967.
5 Underground city of Derinkuyu, Nevşehir Province, Turkey.
6 Occupancy test in a model for the Oak Ridge National Laboratory bomb shelter.
7 Oscar Newman, *Underground City*, 1969.
8 Paul Maymont, *Paris sous Seine*, 1960–63.
9 Interior of the volcano where the base of *Spectre* is located, designed by Ken Adams for the James Bond movie *You Only Live Twice*, Larry Ellis, Pinewood Studios, Buckinghamshire, October 28 1966.

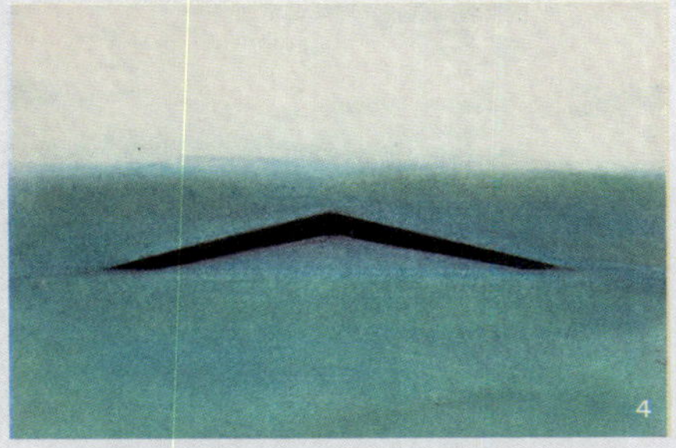

4

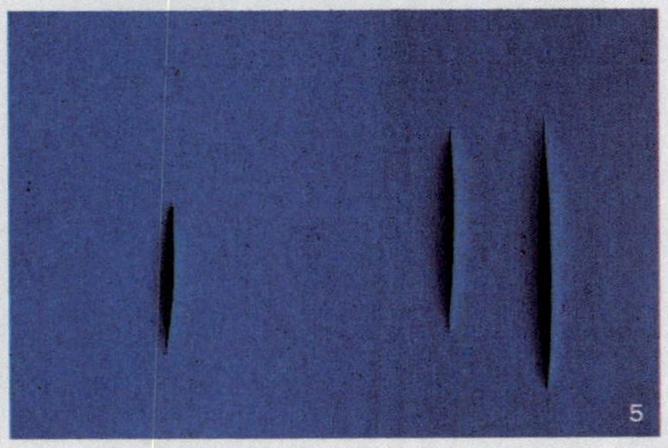

5

6

7

8

9

10

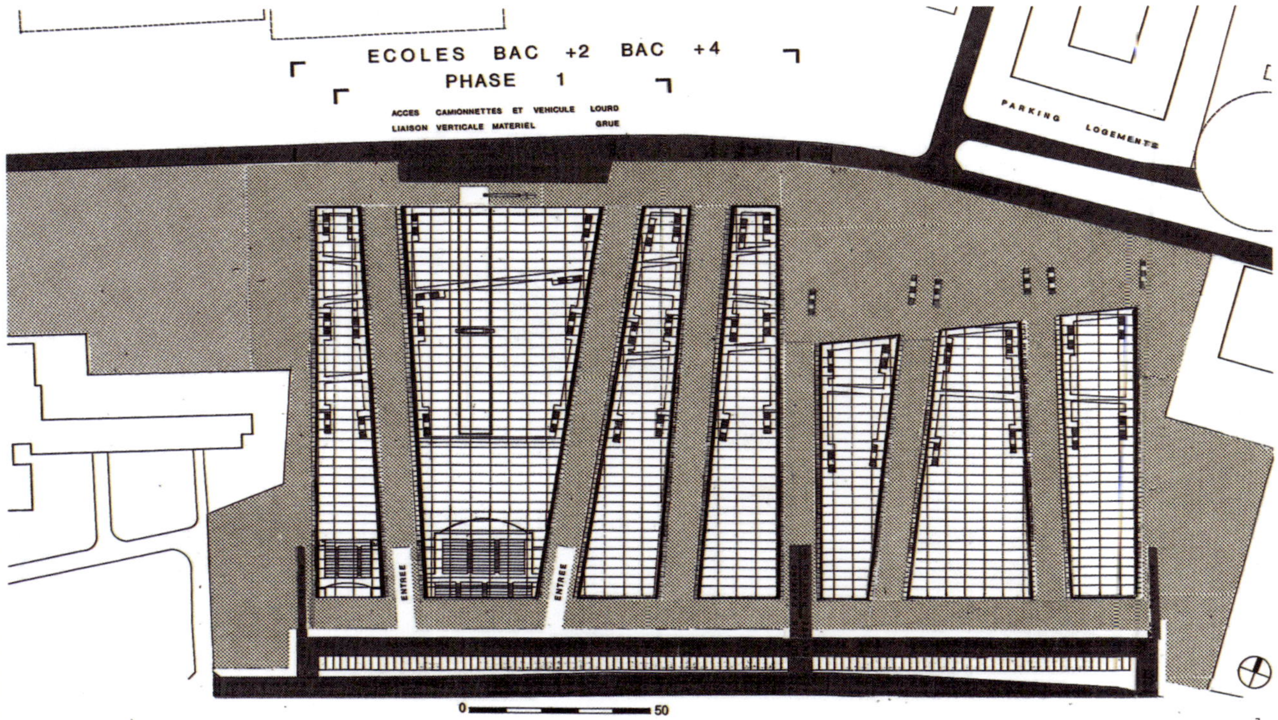

1

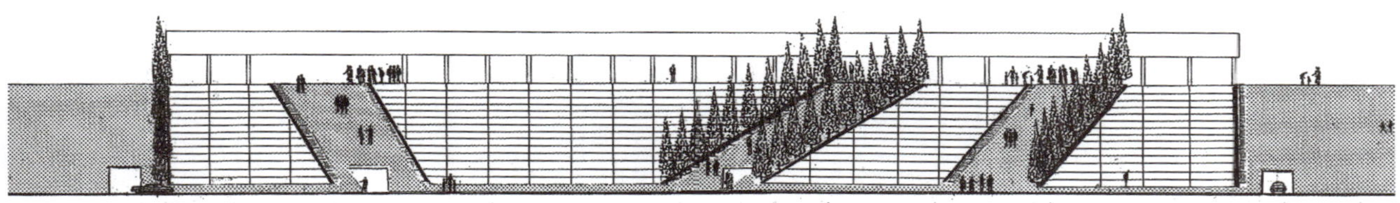

2

3

7

Subcutaneous incision

The subcutaneous incision is a discreet gesture, a slit flush with the ground, which does not cut deeply but skims the surface. It creates semi-buried, protected spaces that are hidden beneath the skin of the ground, yet remain connected to light and air, and appear progressively as one approaches. This figure creates a tension between presence and absence, and questions the way in which architecture can "inhabit" the landscape without imposing itself.

1-3 French Institute of Advanced Mechanics, Clermont-Ferrand, 1989.
4 Maya Lin, proposal for the design for the Vietnam Veterans Memorial, National Mall, Washington, DC, 1981
5 Lucio Fontana, *Concetto spaziale, Attesa, Blue*, 1959.
6 Lucio Fontana, *Concetto spaziale, Attesa*, 1960.
7 Tilla-Durieux Park, Berlin, Germany.
8 Maya Lin, Vietnam Veterans Memorial, National Mall, Washington, DC, 1982.
9 Tadao Ando, Water Temple for Awaji Island, Japan, 2013. Photographed for *Openhouse Magazine* by Ken Conley, 2013.
10 Robert Smithson, *Partially Buried Woodshed*, 1970.

4

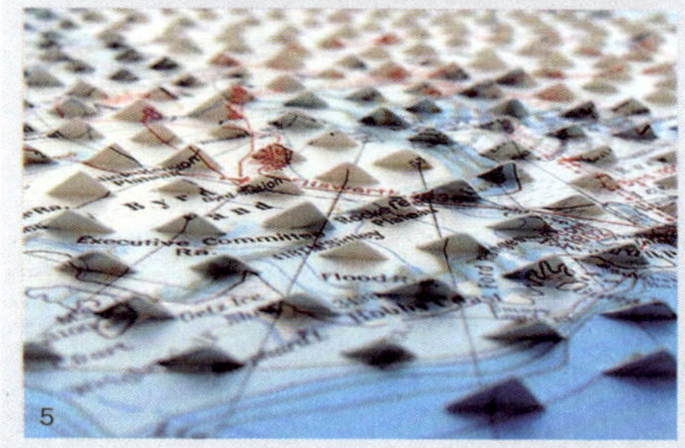

5

6

7

1

8

8
The fault

The fault is a deep vertical tear, revealing the raw material of the ground. It creates spectacular spaces where the sky and the light seep into the depths. This figure dramatizes the relation to the terrain, creating partitions, natural walls, and cast shadows. It can be a space of passage or an inhabited canyon opening onto the outside world.

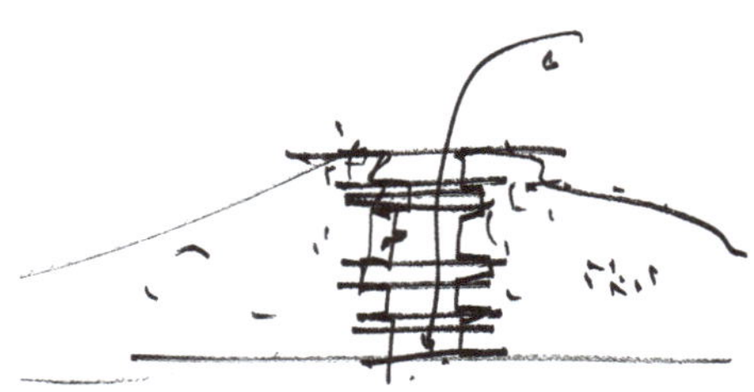

2

9

3

10

1-3 Antuoshan Museum Park, Shenzhen, China, 2013.
4, 6 Maya Lin, *Storm King Wavefield*, 2009, Storm King Art Center, New Windsor, New York.
5 Shannon Rankin, Untitled, 2009.
7 Michael Heizer, *Levitated Mass*, 2012, Los Angeles County Museum of Art. Photographed by Doug Pray, 2013.
8 Karanlik Kilise Monastery, Göreme Valley and rock sites in Cappadocia, Turkey.
9 Michael Heizer, *Double Negative*, 1969–70, Nevada Desert.
10 Richard Long, *Throwing Snow into a Circle. Seven Day Walk in the Glärnisch Massif*, 1991, Switzerland.

4

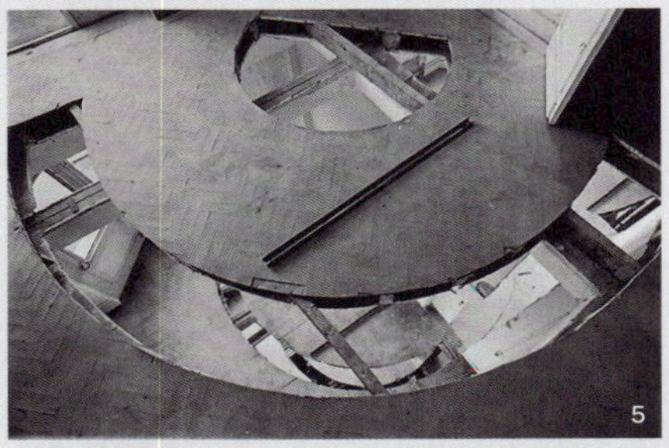

5

6

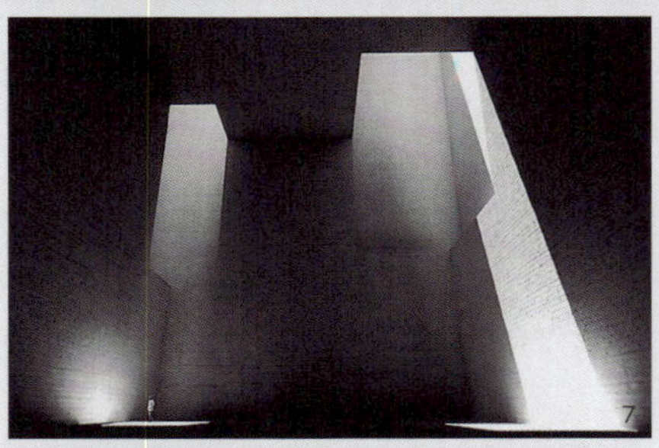

7

8

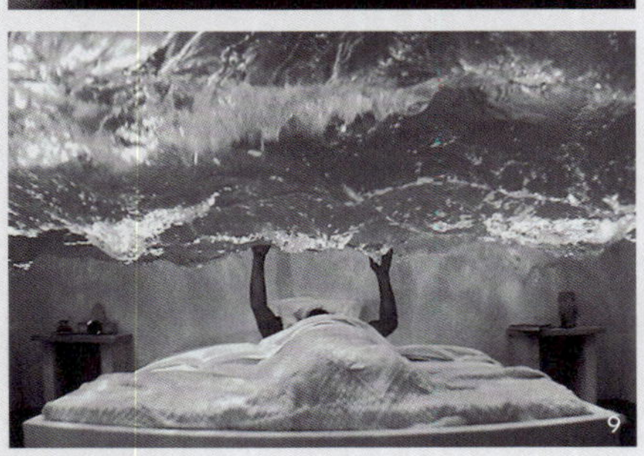

9

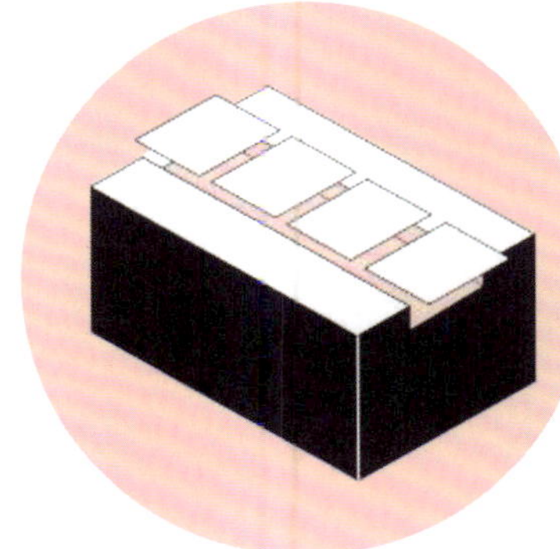

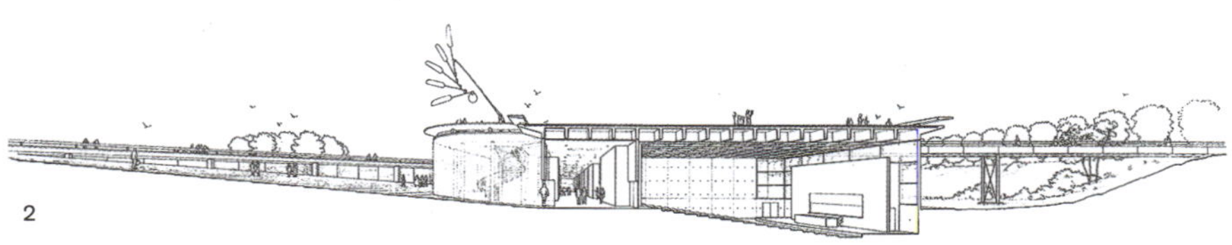

2

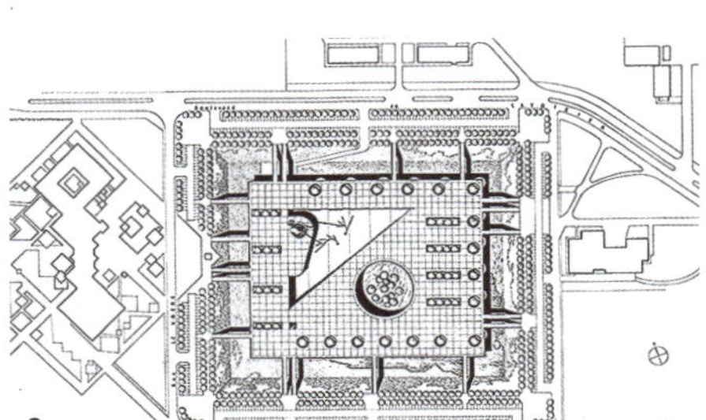

3

9

The double deck

The double deck is a figure in which the floor is split, stratified over several levels. Beneath the visible surface, an inhabited floor develops above and below. The double deck is a way of making the ground denser without suffocating it, using depth to multiply uses. It is a thick floor that increases the capacity of a site without saturating the surface.

1-3 University of Angers, Law and Arts Faculty, Angers, 1985.
4 Gordon Matta-Clark, *Conical Intersect 2* (documentation of the action *Conical Intersect*, Paris, 1975), 1977.
5 Gordon Matta-Clark, *Office Baroque* (documentation of the action *Office Baroque*, in Antwerp, 1977), 1977.
6 Uwe Kils, *Iceberg*, 2005.
7 Eduardo Chillida, *Montaña Tindaya*, 1996, Fuerteventura, Canary Islands.
8 Giuseppe Perugini, Nello Aprile, and Mario Fiorentini, Memorial to the Martyrs of the Ardeatine Caves, 1944–49, Rome.
9 Luc Besson, *The Big Blue* 1988.

10 Le Corbusier, Model of the Plan Voisin, 1925.
11 Fiction by DPA. Le Plan Voisin by Le Corbusier, 1925, versus *Groundscape*, 2014.

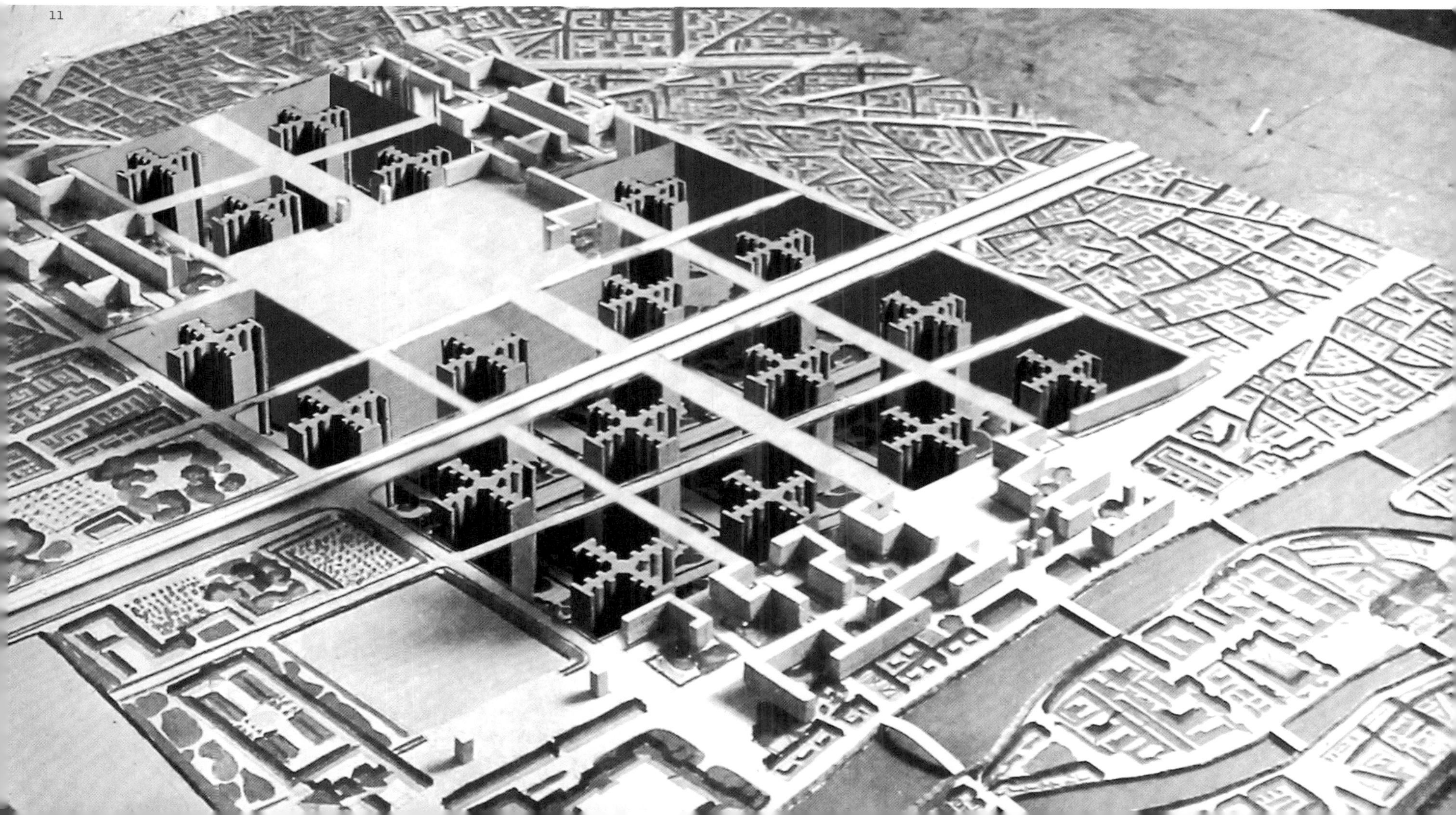

MAPPING

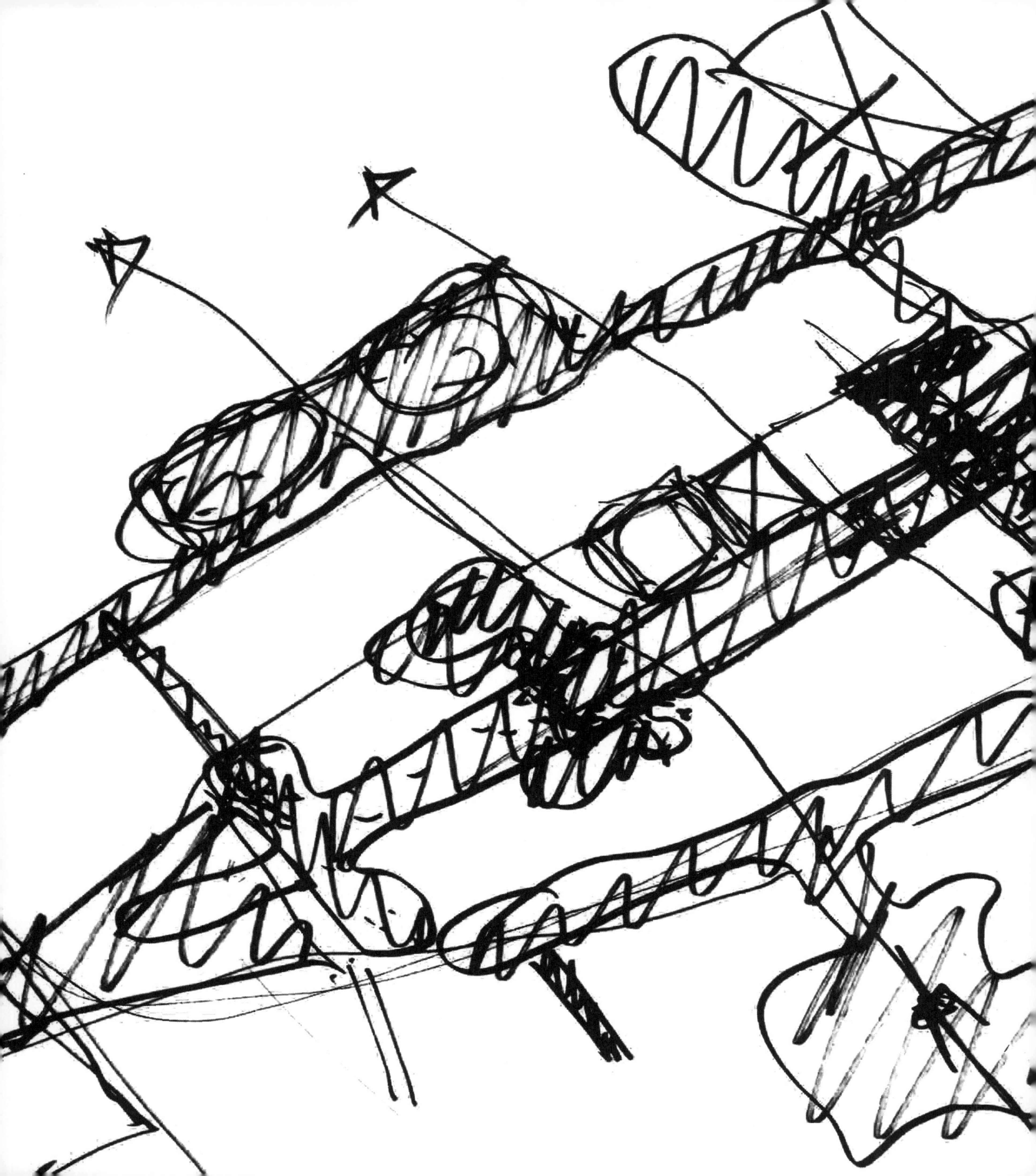

Collective intelligence

The metropolis is not the city. All planners must be aware of this. The metropolitan phenomenon exceeds its limits. We are entering into a new physiology. This leap in scale calls for a leap in sagacity and imagination.

For many years the city imposed a radioconcentric, hierarchical, and centripetal model on its territory, subordinating it without fully understanding its synergies, its capacities for union and solidarity, its polycentric disposition, and its plural identities. We therefore need to invent a new map for this geography. The very notion of the peri-urban is an ill-fitting one, because it continues to index the metropolis to the behavior of the city. The very idea of periphery needs to be challenged. Urbanity needs to change paradigms and gears.

The architect-urbanist and developer work in areas marked by discontinuity, desynchronization, and inequalities. There are places where electricity doesn't flow. No energy switching. Without a global vision, certain master plans, with their reduced and unarticulated area, short-circuits the metropolis.

The Olympic and Paralympic Village raises questions about the public developer's vison of the metropolis: does the planning, which France once excelled at, now expect its construction sites to generate a territory of their own? From the Olympic precinct to the metropolitan district that the Village is expected to become—such is its source code—a leap of scale is not a leap into the void.

The ambition of the Village is to durably inscribe its neighborhood within its zone of influence, to transfer within it the energy released by the metropolis. Conceived as an innovative, mixed-use pilot district, it is nonetheless beset by the shortcomings and contradictions of public commissioning. Not the least of its legacy is the revelation within it of enclaves and self-blocking mechanisms. This impediment needs to be remedied with a crowbar, equipped with both patience and a blade. By rescaling collaborative intelligence and freeing the making of the metropolis, responding with a salvo of future.

At both neighborhood and regional scales, any development strategy requires a proactive approach, unified management, and appropriate tools. And, above all, a vision, a way of thinking. Governments understand the demands of the metropolis. But to think in terms of the commons, we must think organically. Unfold the map and move away from the perimeter of the plan. The failures of long-term support, tunnel vision, or silo thinking, as the case may be, leads to slipshod connections, to a juxtaposition of projects with no trajectory strategy. The metropolis is a political project in the most demanding sense.

Metropolitan geographies are multiple. Within the global system, a host of sub-systems are constantly in motion, attracting, distancing, interweaving, or remaining mutually silent. Superimposed scales, overlapping plates, multidimensional tensions that must be assimilated if we are to take action.

New intensities are constantly being promised to the city and the metropolis. The Grand Paris Express is the emblem of this in the Paris region: the biggest civil engineering project in Europe. Here, public planning seems to be in full swing. In an age of high uncertainty, its project for an inclusive network-region has the merit of being intelligible. But beyond its two hundred kilometers of automatic lines and its sixty-eight new stations, beyond its extraordinary public transport engineering, it can only be understood in the context of the metropolitan project. The connectivity of a brand new metro calls for collective aspirations for a new urban experience, and for territorial and social justice. The metropolis is building a new mental geography, a vector of belonging. An imaginary and a non-administrative narrative. This is where Greater Paris comes into play.

That collaborative intelligence should surpass itself in collective intelligence.

Resuming the flow

Sometimes, as cities grow and change, they turn away from their geography and see it as an obstacle to their plans. Cut off from their map, they lose their territorial coordinates. A number of cartographic studies are examining the synergy between a river and metropolitan redevelopment. These are just some of the planning methods that can be used to get abandoned urban areas back on their feet.

In 1992–95, just a few months after the creation of the Nantes urban district—the future Nantes Métropole—an exploratory study into the regeneration of Ile Sainte-Anne proposed making it the new beating heart of the city, instead of the abandoned port and disjointed neighborhood currently found there. And so the Ile de Nantes was born. Over the course of the twentieth century, the urbanization of Nantes had turned its back on the river. The aim now was to regenerate a lost relationship, on a different scale.

The "Bordeaux les deux rives" pilot project (1992–99) concerned a site with similar challenges. Commissioned by the City of Bordeaux, it too proposed an urban reappropriation of the two riverside districts that had hitherto been pitted against each other: a bourgeois, Left Bank of stone buildings and an industrious, working-class, plant-filled Right Bank. Adding another Pont de Pierre was a fictional way of staging the bonding of the two banks.

The master plan for the future Hangang district in Handan links together three programs: development of the banks of the Qin River, redevelopment of an industrial site, and urban ecology. These operational axes are very similar to those of the Olympic Village, where the urban project consisted in "returning the site to the Seine." Repairing a broken link, as in Nantes and Bordeaux. The great industrial cathedrals that structured the area in the twentieth century had abruptly turned their backs on the riverbanks.

New confluences and urbanity

As defined in the mission statement issued by François Hollande, the "Paris Île de la Cité 2040" initiative is rare enough to merit a mention. In this instance, the State did not commission a report from its senior civil servants, but entrusted an architect and town planner and the President of the Centre des Monuments Nationaux with a forward-looking and imaginative project. The production of a possible fiction. Thirty-five proposals were submitted, with the aim of regenerating the nerve center of the capital. Reconciling the island with its geography and urban hospitality. Once again, this was a project of reconquest and reconnection.

The fact that the Île de la Cité in the heart of Paris is an unidentified urban object is no small paradox. The fault lies in the brutality of its development, the overbearing presence of institutional and administrative buildings, and the artificial nature of its relation to the riverbanks. Locked up in its hull of a stone vessel, the island had broken with its surroundings, going against the current of the city.

In fact, the link with the river began to break down in the Middle Ages, when it developed organically with no or precious little planning. Then Haussmann cut up the city, deprogramming the very notion of urbanity. The island district was levelled in places, starved in others, while institutional enclaves swallowed up public space.

Once again, it is a matter of questioning urban morphology and the map beyond the plan. Engaging in a global architectural, cultural, and social reflection. So that the disjointed and saturated "Island of Monuments" may become a living and unified "Monument Island."

Urbanity is a civility to which the architect-urbanist and the developer are obliged. Let's move beyond the perimeter of the island: creating a neighborhood means creating a society. If living together includes the hospitality of the city, it is first and foremost a requirement for shared citizenship. A metropolitan area is insufficiently integrated if it does not itself integrate. Interconnecting areas means combining individual wills into a general will supported by residents and public authorities. The notion of the commons is transversal and exists on interweaving scales. From access to public services to equality of membership, without discrimination. From freedom of mobility to territorial justice. From diversity (housing, activities) to democratic plurality. There is indeed a right to a metropolis, with national stakes.

The notion of urbanity crystallizes and unites. Every metropolis invests it with its meaning and its fullness. It draws its map.

No cursed sites

Our urban realities are rich in new opportunities that can multiply the range of programs on offer. Each site addresses its own territory, the extant, its markers of identity, its stories.

Reallocating a site means recharging it with new uses and new affects. More than just adding value to property or rehabilitating a building, it consists in reinscribing it through a new syntax. *Resetting* from a blank page is brutal and a dilapidation of legacy. No place is fated to undergo loss and neglect. The rewriting of an industrial site creates a palimpsest favorable to the city.

Abandoned, unwelcoming, resistant places raise crucial questions about the development of cities, about the fate reserved for the plethora of buildings constructed in the twentieth century (numerically superior to anything built in the history of humanity), about the metabolization of past experiences, about building the city on the city and against sprawl.

Diversity

Mixed-use neighborhoods are more robust than those with restricted programs, which, until the 1960s, sacrificed themselves to the model of the functional city and its spaces assigned by specialty (work/living/circulation/recreation). Deprived of fertile connections, the sectors thus created suffered from hypo-urbanity: a locked-in future. This zoning skewed the city, conceived as a high-performance machine. Organicity turned on its head. The commons paid the price for the full powers given to the plan at the expense of the map and of geography.

The programmatic layer of the future Hangang district deploys the principle of mixed use through precise planning tools and development systems adapted to the city's evolving nature. Like a Mendeleev's table organizing chemical elements by electronic configurations and properties, the urban grid and its checkerboard system of blocks adjust to the city's behavior. As with Mendeleev, it not only divides up the fundamental substances that are known, but also deduces atomically those that have yet to be discovered. Its logic is exploratory and predictive. Flexible and open to the experiments of urban matter, it allows the future to happen. So many Petri dishes in which urbanity is cultivated. The grid also sets a scale for urban planning: from the cellular level to the whole organism. Urban physiology gains in symbiosis.

Period coordinates

The city and the metropolis are a given: we can no longer do without them, and there will be no turning back. By 2050, they will be home to the vast majority of humanity. There are many factors that make them attractive: the scale and diversity of the services and facilities on offer, economic vitality, the concentration of institutional and private centers of power, cultural wealth, protection, and asylum. These evolving entities crystallize crucial questions about the future of societies, transformations in lifestyles, and the anthropization of the environment.

The architect-urbanist has always been asked to read the future of the city. Today, however, they have to contend with the brutalization of history, a series of interconnected cumulative crises, whose speed of acceleration society and the State struggle to anticipate. The metropolis of the future belongs to this time of unprecedented—and unpredictable—rupture. New relationships to housing, energy, transport, culture, services and work, to nature, natural disasters, not to mention war, will generate powerful societal changes that will impact all levels of governance.

To speak of resilience is to confront the many issues linked to our vulnerability, which will lead to formidable ethical, economic, political, and cultural trade-offs. Today it behooves us to grasp at once the questions of ecosystems and human interactions, the protocols of reciprocity and multi-scale solidarity. To be receptive to the possibility of accident. More than in the past, the imperative of anticipation and adaptation requires that we incorporate the notion of fluidity into architectural and urban design.

The active map

To generate the right kind of territorial transformation, we need to be able to approach the experience of the city and the metropolis. In a word, its phenomenology.

The nature of geography has changed. The flow of data is bringing to light realities that have gone under the radar of the plan. The urban landscape has been transformed into a global datascape—a landscape of information, an extension of the universe of data, enhanced by the Geoweb and now artificial intelligence. If we want to tackle the fine substance of metropolises and profile their futures, we need to invent new kinetic and forward-looking cartographies that are attentive to the organic. Capture streams and tensions. Identify force fields and polarities, distortions and connections. Diagnose atonia. Scan mobilities and networks of activities. So many data streams through which to perceive the regular pulsations and arrhythmias of the metropolis. A territory is by nature heterogeneous and contradictory. A development strategy requires knowledge and modelling tools capable of informing the decision of a public planner grappling with reality.

Geography goes beyond the world of maps. A metropolis is above all a complex of *situations*. The term seems clear-cut and effective to me. Let's imagine an atlas of one hundred urban ecosystems likely to gain autonomy within the metropolitan fabric. One hundred maps of interventions with a view to a cohesive and mutually supportive Greater Paris. Each configuration would conceive of the territory as a nervous system. Creating a territory means working on energy points and nodes, connective fibers and innervations, while assimilating the living principle of discontinuities, interfaces, and unconstructed spaces. The contemporary metropolis is not the continuity of the expanded city.

Metropolitan catalysis

Each new project fits into a network like a chip in a printed circuit board. In this sense, it has the value of a generic device, at the crossroads of architecture and regional planning. It is a tensor of urbanity, an operator of conversions. Its efficiency lies in its ability to process the field of information in its geographical area to offer a response to its shortcomings. To do this, it relies on the mapping of volatile, time-limited flows and uses.

Devices capable of acting as territorial tensors must be invented. Diversity would be the source code and the occupant, the free interpreter. A reformulation of modern hospitality. Microcosms connected to their territory. Places of encounter, incubation, and emulation, reconciling intimacy and community, clean and shared, in a new model of living. Intelligent technologies now make it possible to optimize the management of spaces and services—which can be modulated according to need—as well as interactions between users and the personalization of their experience.

In the spirit of tactical urbanism, such projects are intended to act on their fabric through points of stimulation and acupressure, in order to trigger beneficial chain reactions. Through these projects, the architect-urbanist tests the urban potential of areas that are still mute in terms of their metropolitan destiny, by reprogramming existing facilities that have hitherto been mutually silent. Geographical proximity is transformed into urban situations. This is an example of the experimental construction of urbanity and the fertile crystallization of the *datascape*.

In today's context of multiple transitions—societal, economic, environmental, technological—the agile and ingenious city is essential. Its ecosystem is synergistic.

There is one prerequisite for any urban project: an intelligent map. It is the only real framework for development. The plan is just an extract.

P. 120 Sketch from the "Île de la Cité 2040" mission study, 2016.

THE ATHLETES' VILLAGE – PARIS 2024 OLYMPIC AND PARALYMPIC GAMES

SAINT-DENIS AND SAINT-OUEN, FRANCE

2017–26

The Olympic Village reveals a long-forgotten area on the banks of the Seine, transforming a former industrial site into a vibrant new part of Greater Paris. Connected to the Grand Paris Express transit system, the project restores meaning to the historic routes and paths perpendicular to the Seine that concrete platforms had obliterated. The Halle Maxwell and the Cité du Cinéma, both of which also face the Seine, have been reinvented to bring everyday life into the district. A welcome consequence of this transformation: the site has been returned to its natural state. Following the original topography, the Village slopes gently from the Pleyel station to the banks of the river. Designed from the outset to be reversible after the Games, this multi-program project is above all part of a long-term urban strategy: to create a sustainable neighborhood, open to all, rooted in its territory.

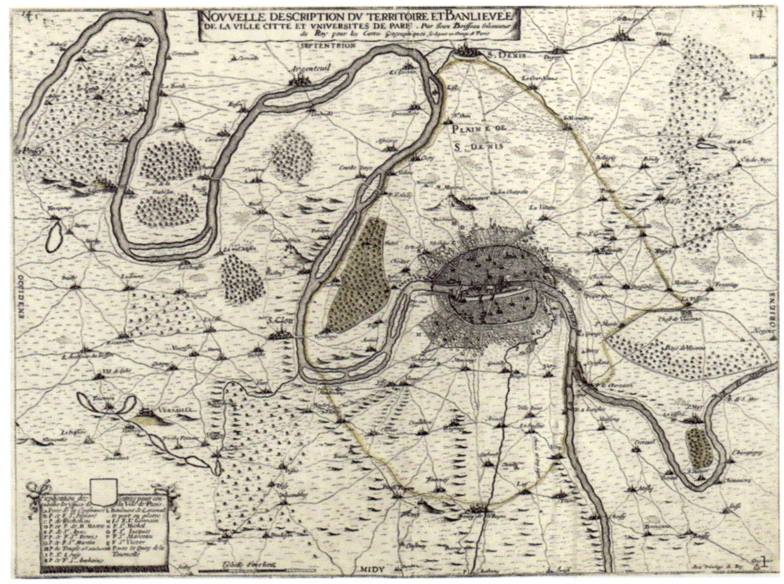

1 Map of the territory of Île-de-France and geography of the Seine valley by Jean Boisseau (the king's illuminator), 1640.
2 Aerial view of Saint-Denis and electric power plants, industrial heritage of the site, 1940.
3 Aerial view of the site before construction, 2010.
4 Relief model of the Athletes' Village on Île-Saint-Denis, Saint-Denis, and Saint-Ouen, scale 1:1,000, 2017.
5 Fiction by DPA. Collage of boat-islands.

"The periphery is not what surrounds but what has been deliberately exiled from sight and thought."

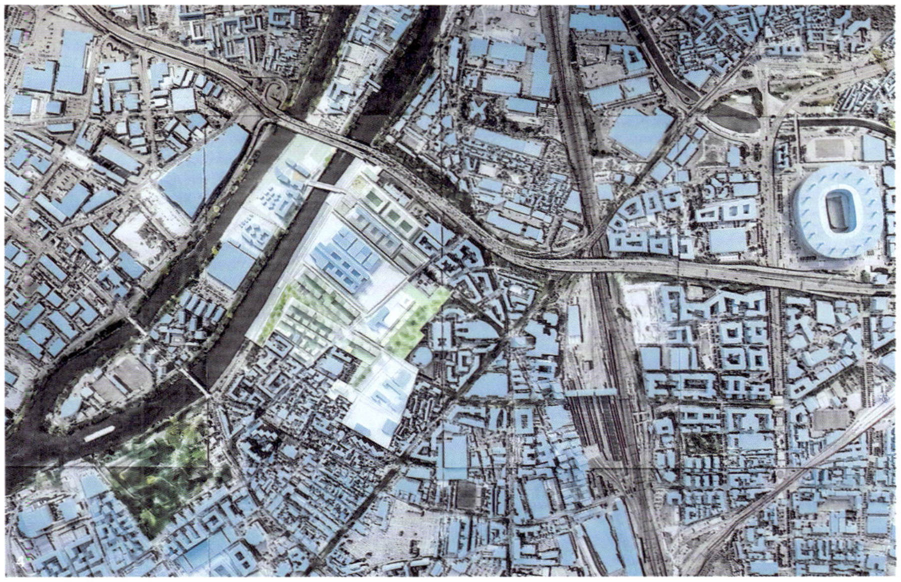

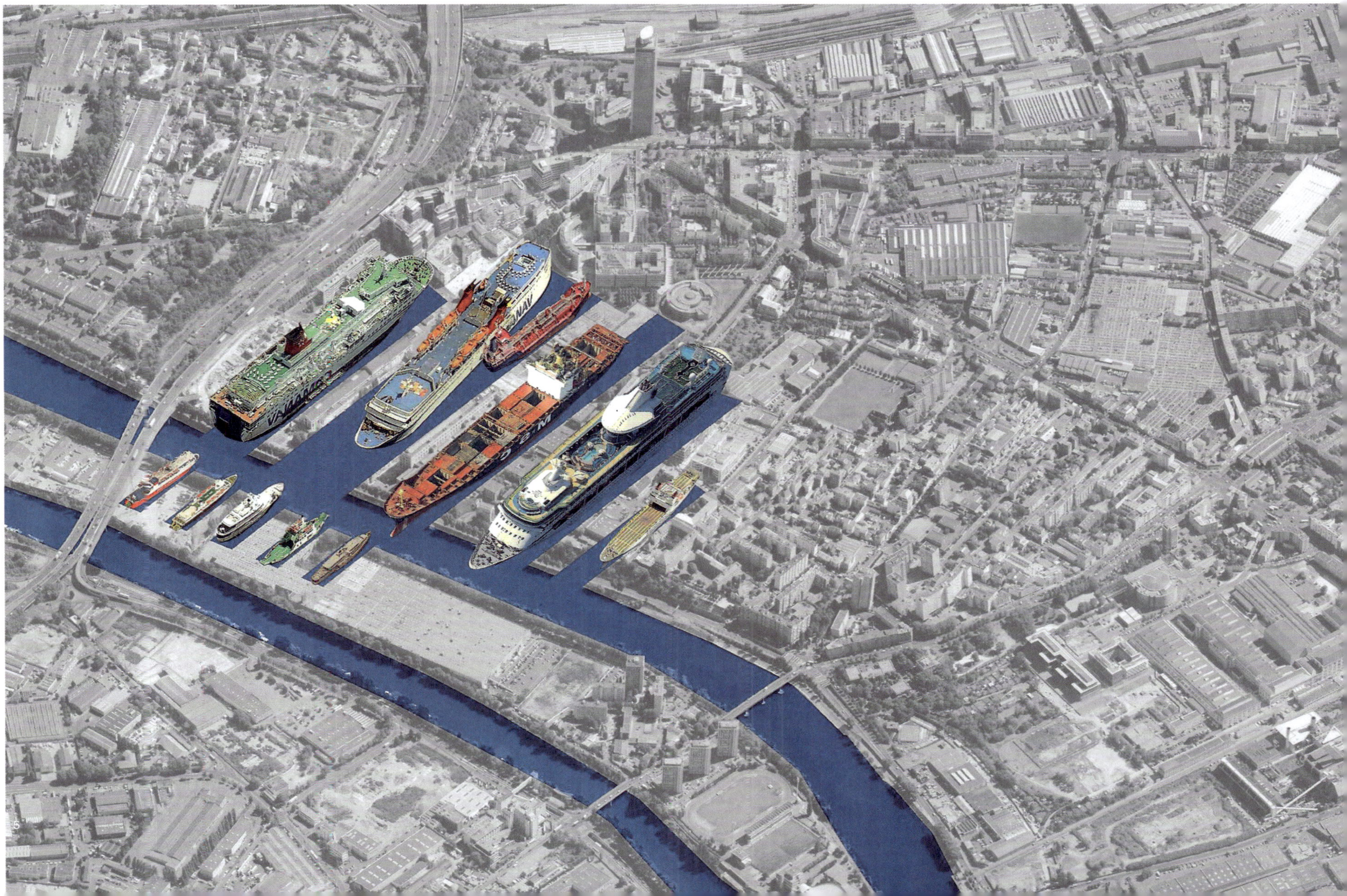

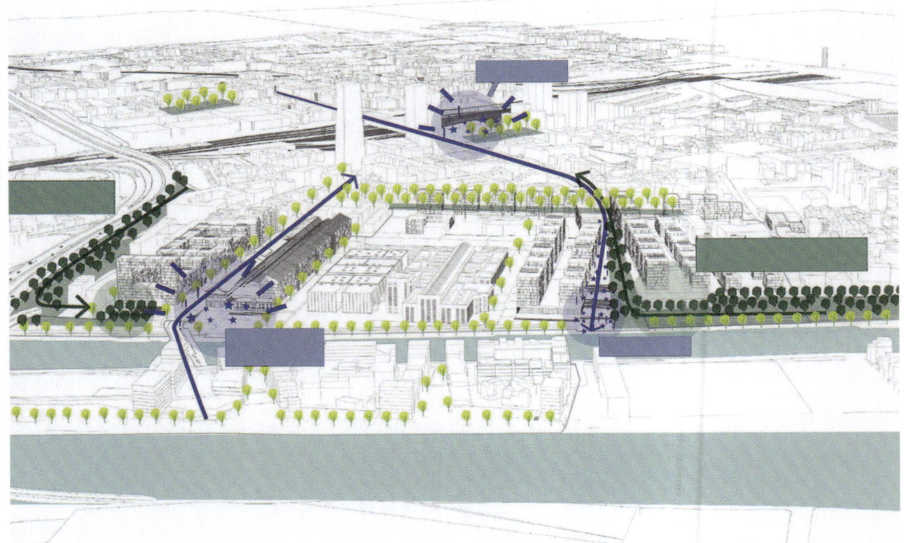

2

3

4

5

6

1 Fiction by DPA. Collage of Hokusai, *The Great Wave of Kanagawa*, 1831, and the Athletes' Village.
2 Joining the Seine.
3 Master plan of the Athletes' Village, the green network leading to the water's edge.
4 The Olympic Seine/reversible city.
5 Fiction by DPA. Collage of architectural signs of the Olympic villages.
6 Master plan of boat-islands perpendicular to the river.
7 Detailed cross-section of the Mail Finot.
8, 9 Detail of the play of floor materials of the Mail Finot.
10 Topographical study of the soil layers in the Olympic district.
11 Implementation of mobility and universal accessibility.

7

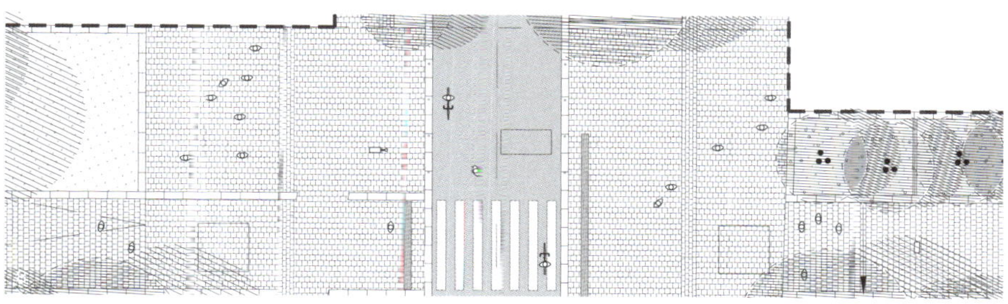

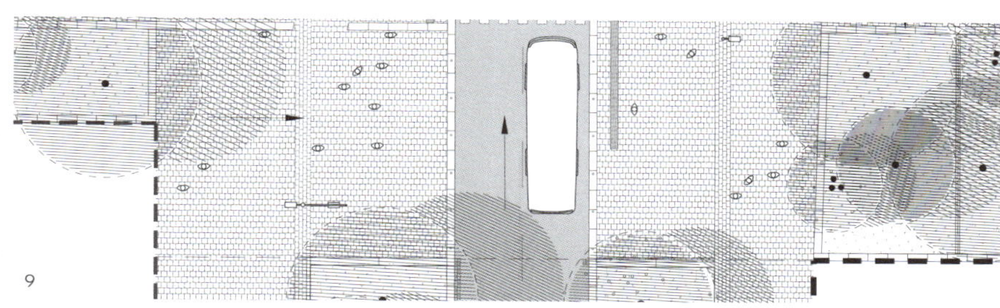

9

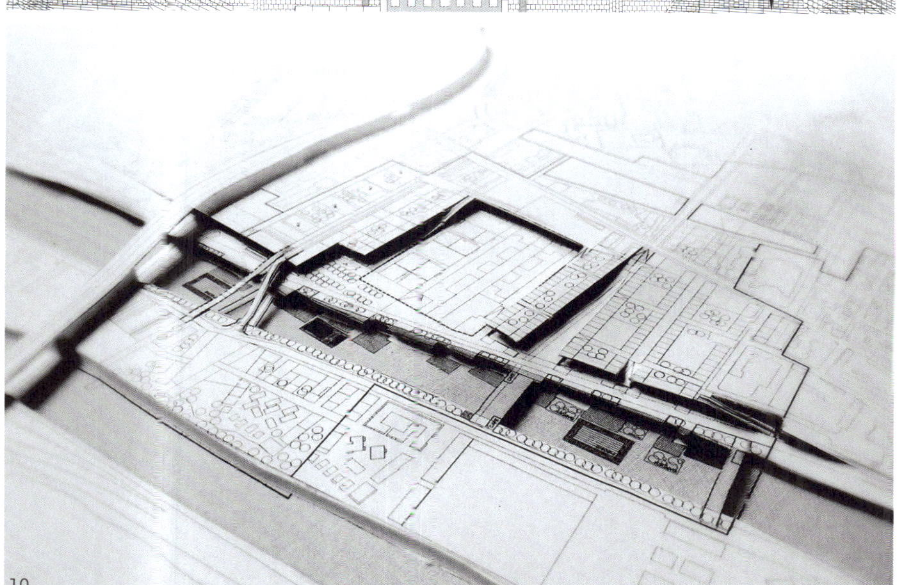

10

11

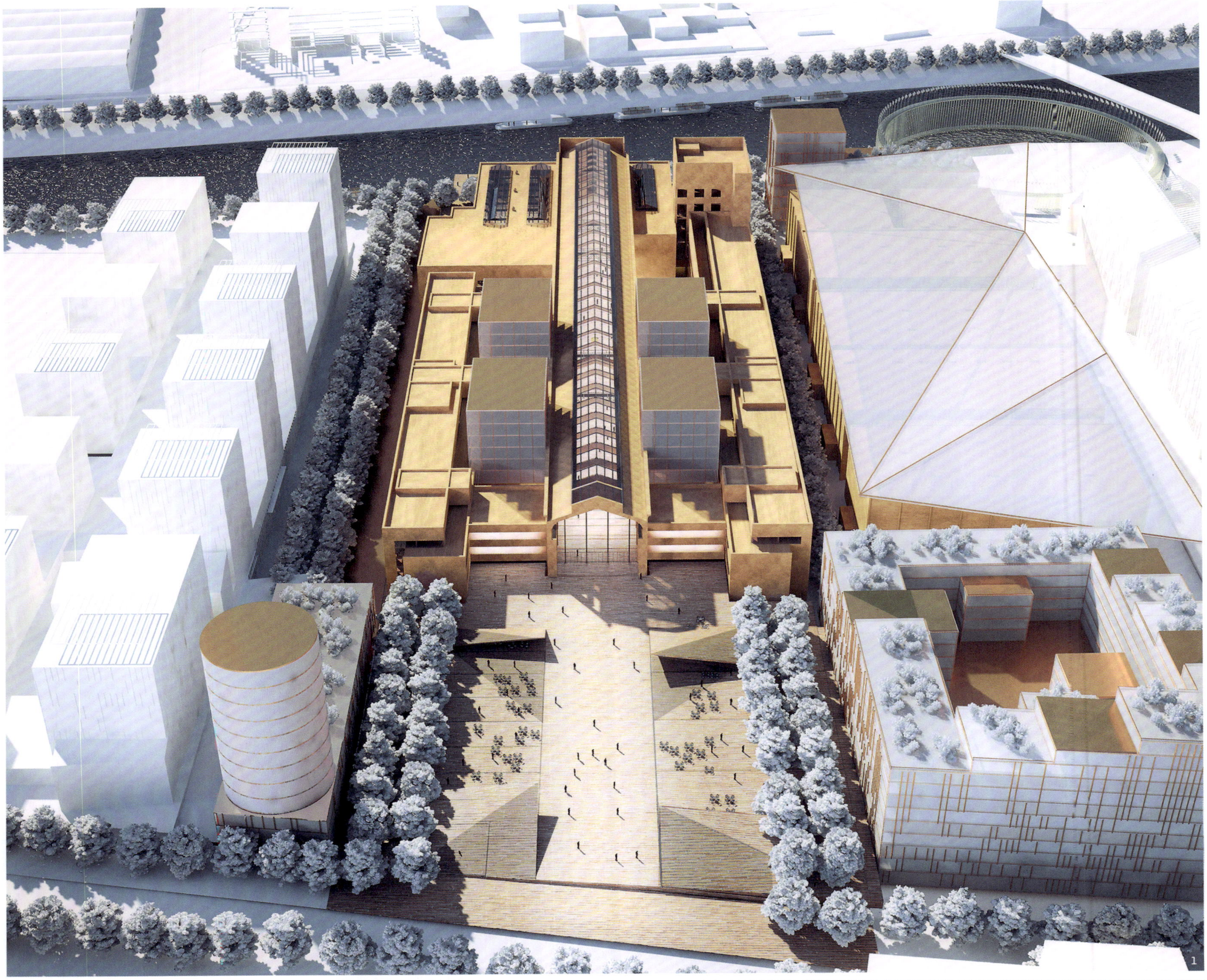

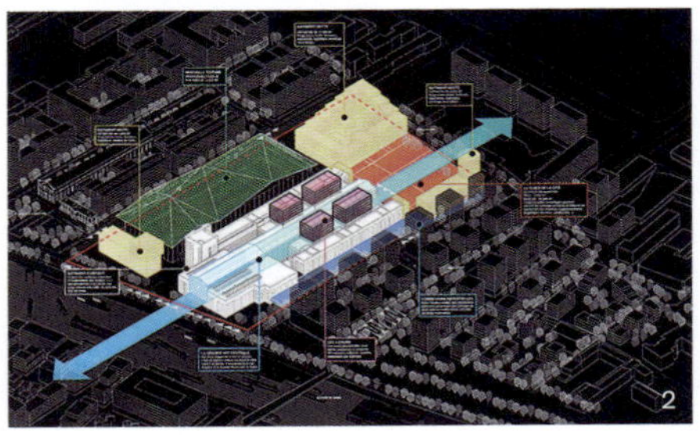

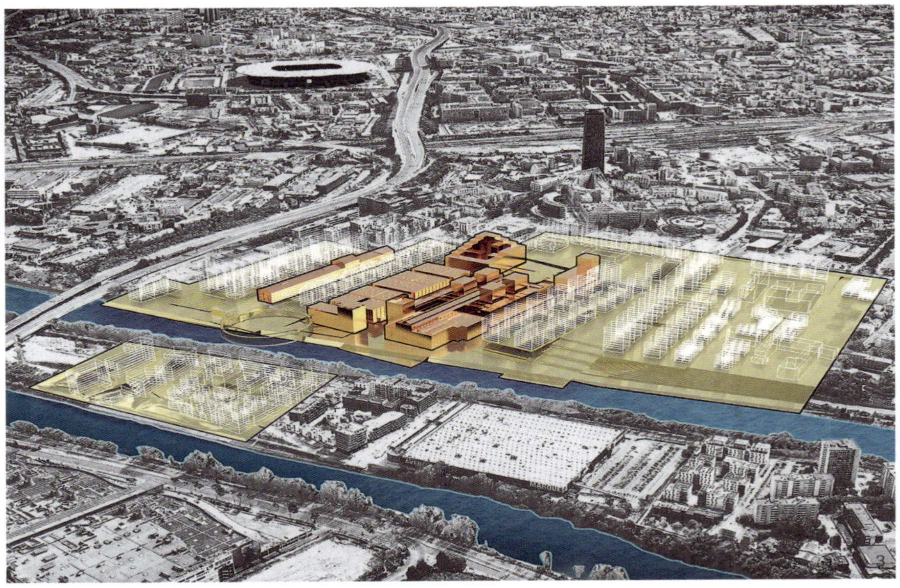

1 At the heart of the district, the current Cité du Cinéma is intended to become an integral part of the legacy of the Paris Games.
2 Strategic location of the Cité du Cinéma nave.
3 The Cité du Cinéma: the heart of the Olympic district.
4 Fiction by DPA. The large nave, longer than Tate Modern's, hosts a variety of cultural, sporting, and educational programs.

p. 132-33
1 Fiction by DPA. Jean-Luc Godard's *À bout de souffle* (1960), projected in the nave of the Cité du Cinéma.
2 A thousand hands build the city.

PARIS
Les Saveurs du Monde
World Flavors
Boissons
Beverages
Bebidas

1

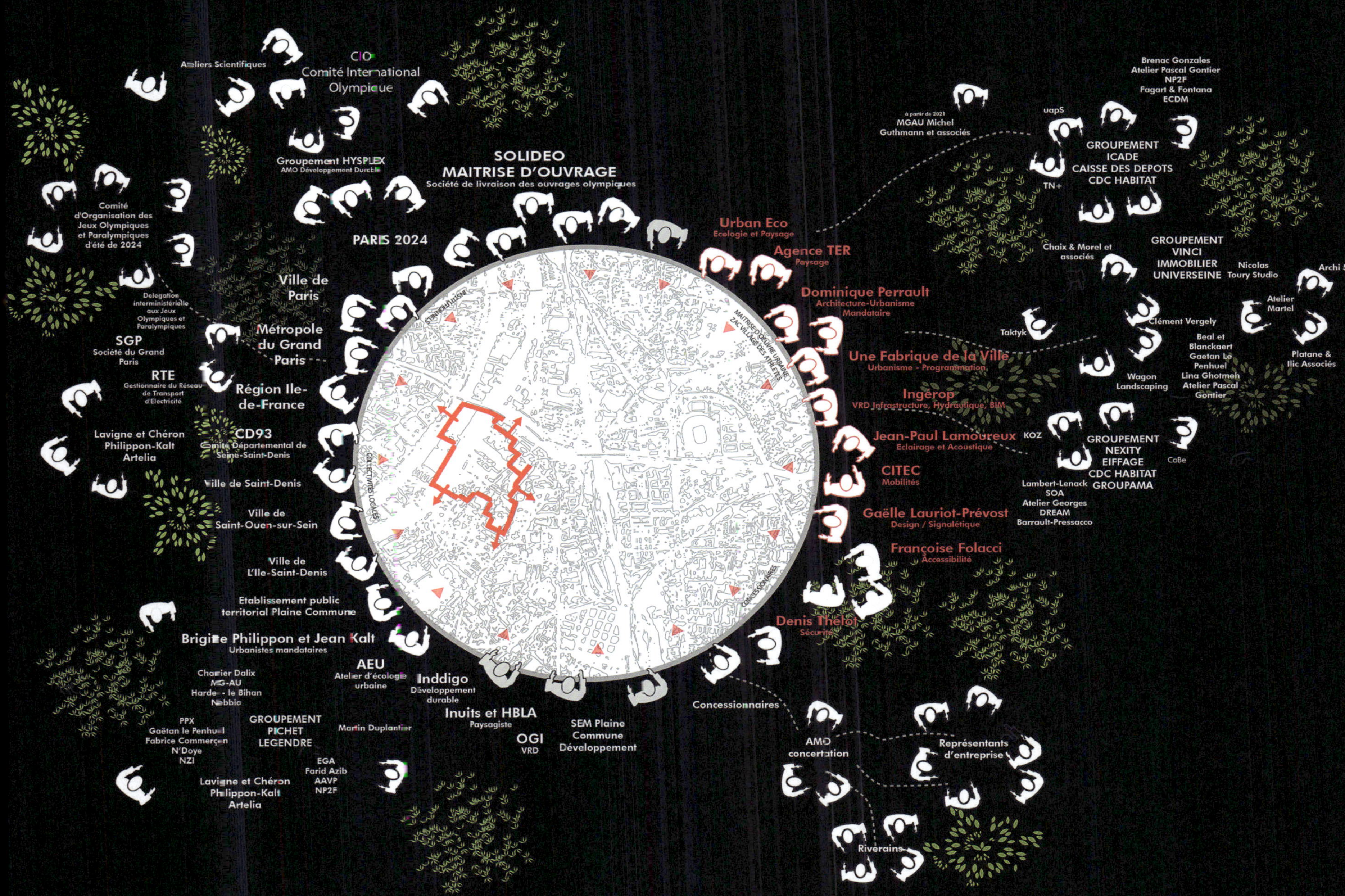
CIO
Comité International Olympique
Ateliers Scientifiques
Groupement HYSPLEX
AMO Développement Durable
SOLIDEO
MAITRISE D'OUVRAGE
Société de livraison des ouvrages olympiques
PARIS 2024
Comité d'Organisation des Jeux Olympiques et Paralympiques d'été de 2024
Delegation interministérielle aux Jeux Olympiques et Paralympiques
SGP
Société du Grand Paris
RTE
Gestionnaire du Réseau de Transport d'Electricité
Lavigne et Chéron
Philippon-Kalt
Artelia
Ville de Paris
Métropole du Grand Paris
Région Ile-de-France
CD93
Comité Départemental de Seine-Saint-Denis
Ville de Saint-Denis
Ville de Saint-Ouen-sur-Sein
Ville de L'Ile-Saint-Denis
Etablissement public territorial Plaine Commune
INSTITUTIONNELS
COLLECTIVITÉS LOCALES
MAITRISE D'OEUVRE URBAINE ZAC VILLAGE DES ATHLETES
CONCESSIONAIRES
Brigitte Philippon et Jean Kalt
Urbanistes mandataires
Chartier Dalix
MG-AU
Hardel - le Bihan
Nebbia
PPX
Gaëtan le Penhuel
Fabrice Commerçon
N'Doye
NZI
GROUPEMENT PICHET LEGENDRE
Martin Duplantier
EGA
Farid Azib
AAVP
NP2F
Lavigne et Chéron
Philippon-Kalt
Artelia
AEU
Atelier d'écologie urbaine
Inddigo
Développement durable
Inuits et HBLA
Paysagiste
OGI
VRD
SEM Plaine Commune Développement
Urban Eco
Ecologie et Paysage
Agence TER
Paysage
Dominique Perrault
Architecture-Urbanisme
Mandataire
Une Fabrique de la Ville
Urbanisme - Programmation
Ingérop
VRD Infrastructure, Hydraulique, BIM
Jean-Paul Lamoureux
Eclairage et Acoustique
CITEC
Mobilités
Gaëlle Lauriot-Prévost
Design / Signalétique
Françoise Folacci
Accessibilité
Denis Thélot
Sécurité
Concessionnaires
AMO concertation
Représentants d'entreprise
Riverains
à partir de 2021
MGAU Michel Guthmann et associés
uapS
TN+
Brenac Gonzales
Atelier Pascal Gontier
NP2F
Fagart & Fontana
ECDM
GROUPEMENT
ICADE
CAISSE DES DEPOTS
CDC HABITAT
Chaix & Morel et associés
GROUPEMENT
VINCI
IMMOBILIER
UNIVERSEINE
Nicolas Toury Studio
Archi 5
Atelier Martel
Taktyk
Clément Vergely
Wagon Landscaping
Beal et Blanckaert
Gaetan Le Penhuel
Lina Ghotmeh
Atelier Pascal Gontier
Platane & Ilic Associés
KOZ
GROUPEMENT
NEXITY
EIFFAGE
CDC HABITAT
GROUPAMA
CoBe
Lambert-Lenack
SOA
Atelier Georges
DREAM
Barrault-Pressacco

BUSAN EXPO 2030 MASTER PLAN

BUSAN, SOUTH KOREA

2023

South Korea's second-largest city and the world's ninth-largest port, Busan is an extraordinary metropolis, set between mountains and sea, industry and nature. The master plan for the 2030 World Expo makes use of the artificial harbor land, previously reserved for container storage, to invent a new part of the city. The pavilions, with their free and organic forms, are set in a rigorous composition, with nature featuring prominently: parks, squares, and gardens occupy a large part of the site. Open to the bay and the city, these platforms are uniquely extroverted. Ultimately, this area reclaimed by the World Expo is destined to become a vibrant district of Busan, continuing the momentum of transformation initiated by the event.

1

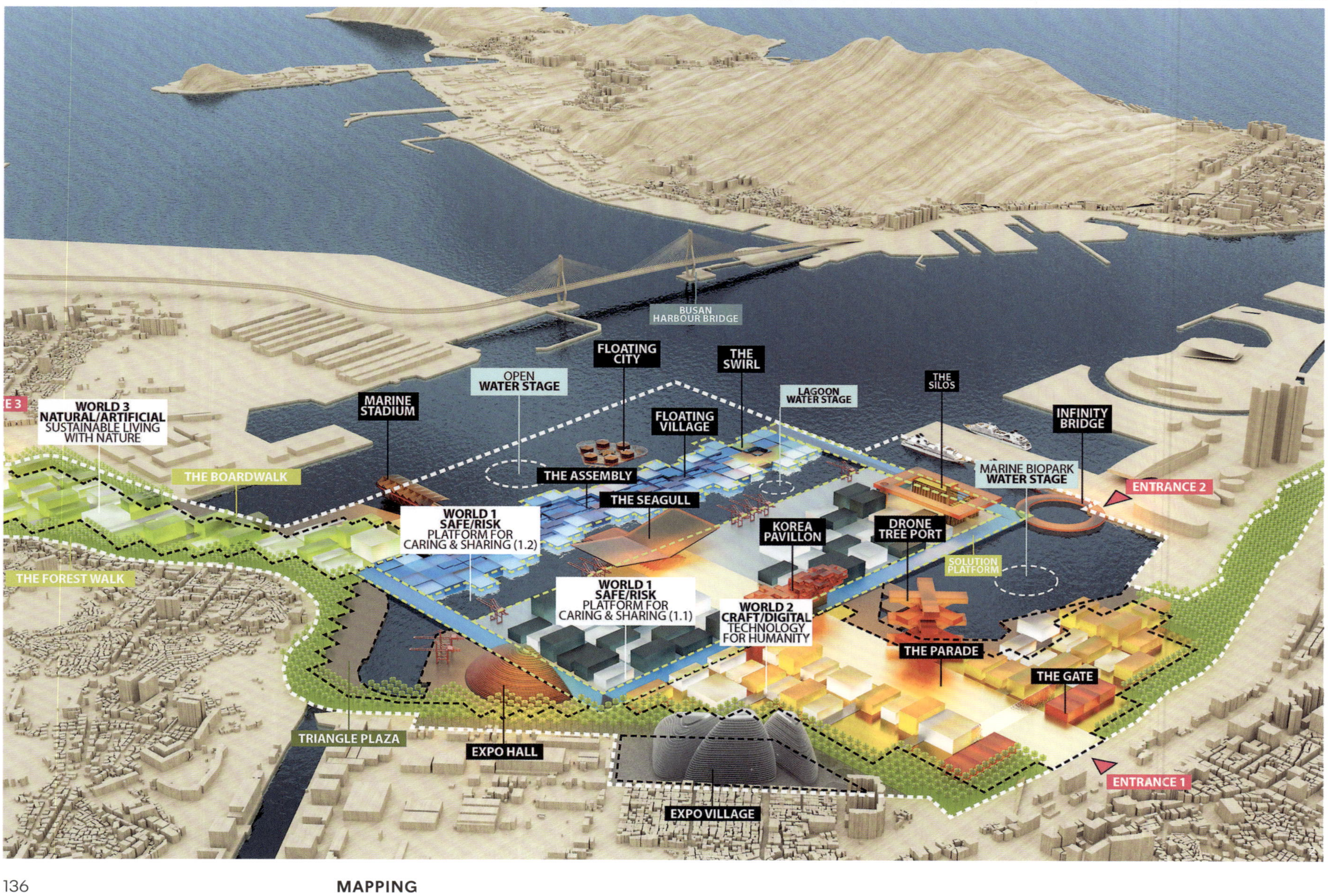

1 Fiction by DPA. Concept for an international platform between land and water.

2-3 Model and strategic plan for the development of Expo 2030 in Busan, featuring its different worlds and pavilions.

1

3

1-3 Initial state, 2023. The future exhibition site extends around the port.

4 Two worlds are identified: the first, in green and yellow, includes the main entrance and the emblematic exhibition building; the second, in blue, is built around the water and the site's port heritage. Master plan study model, research into initial ideas for intervention, scale 1:5,000, 2009.

5-7 Schemas of the various master plan concepts: the grid, the parade, and the world.

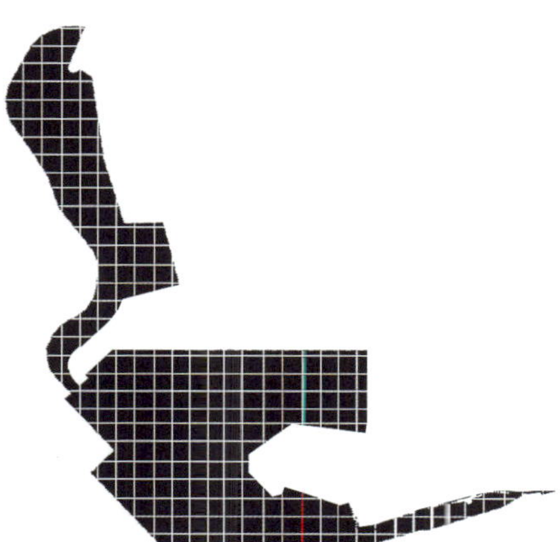

5

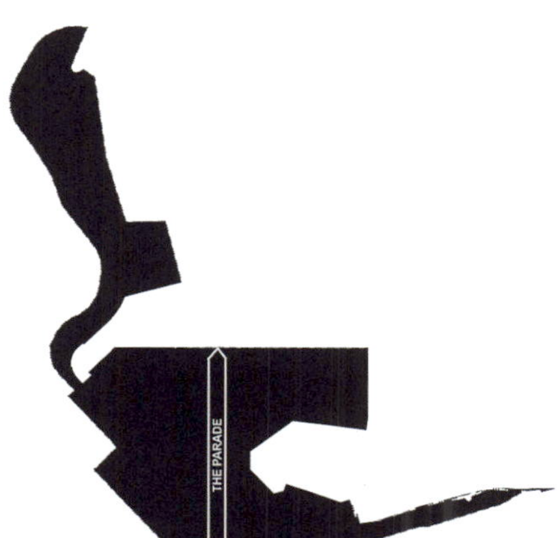

6

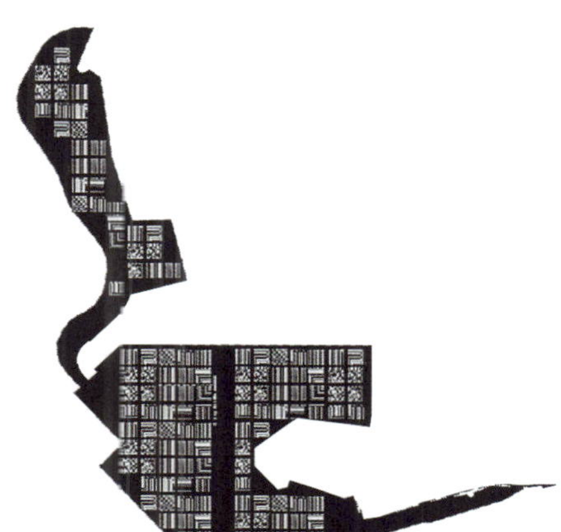

7

KX72

“Read data currents as others read ocean currents.”

SHENZHEN INSTITUTE OF DESIGN AND INNOVATION

SHENZHEN, CHINA

2021–23

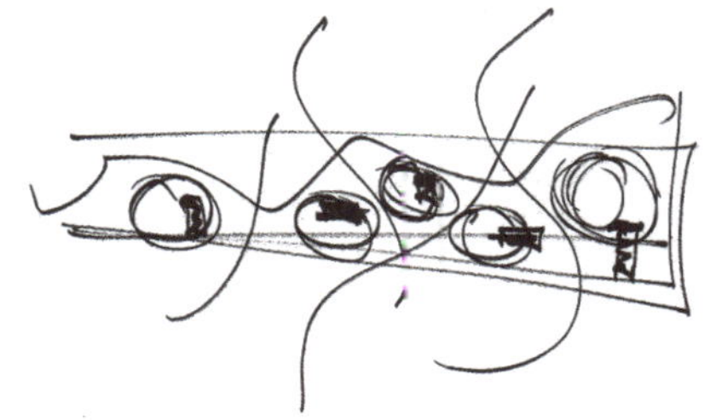

1

2

Clinging to the mountainside of Shenzhen, the Institute of Innovation and Design is conceived as a city landscape. Taking the form of a vast French-style park, the building unfolds across the site through a jumble of terraces and patios, linked together by a network of intersecting pathways. On the border between a wild forest and the urban fabric, this large university "village" blurs the boundaries between inside and outside, study space and living space. You can move around as if in a park, rest as if in a refuge, learn as if in an agora. The whole forms an inhabited cartography, a place in osmosis with the landscape, to the point of dissolving into the surrounding nature, in a radical way of conceiving a campus: inhabiting nature and letting nature inhabit the city.

3

1 Sketch, 2020.
2 Relief model, halfway between map and plan.
3 An existing site on a mountainside.
4 Constructing the landscape as an enlargement of the map.

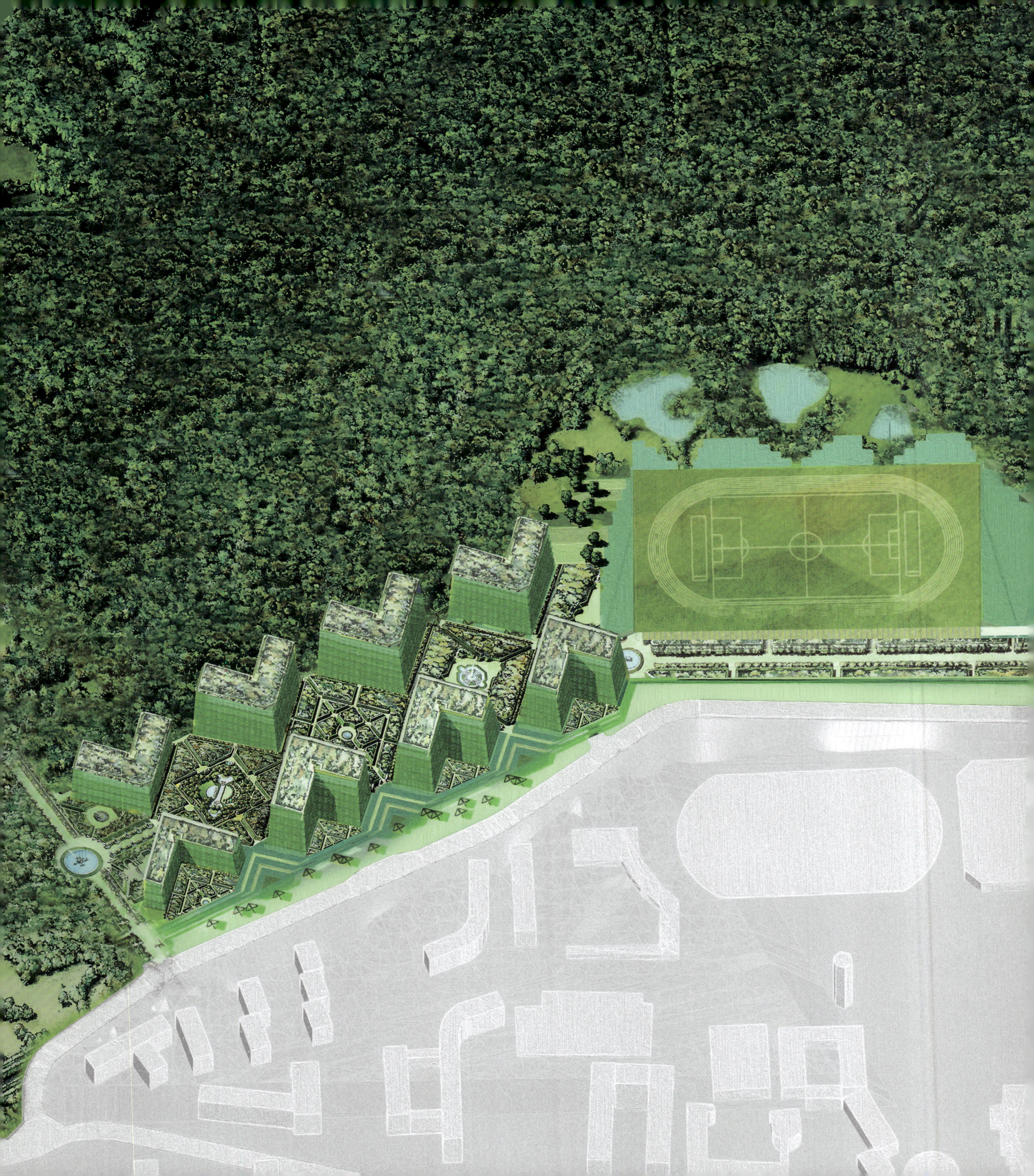

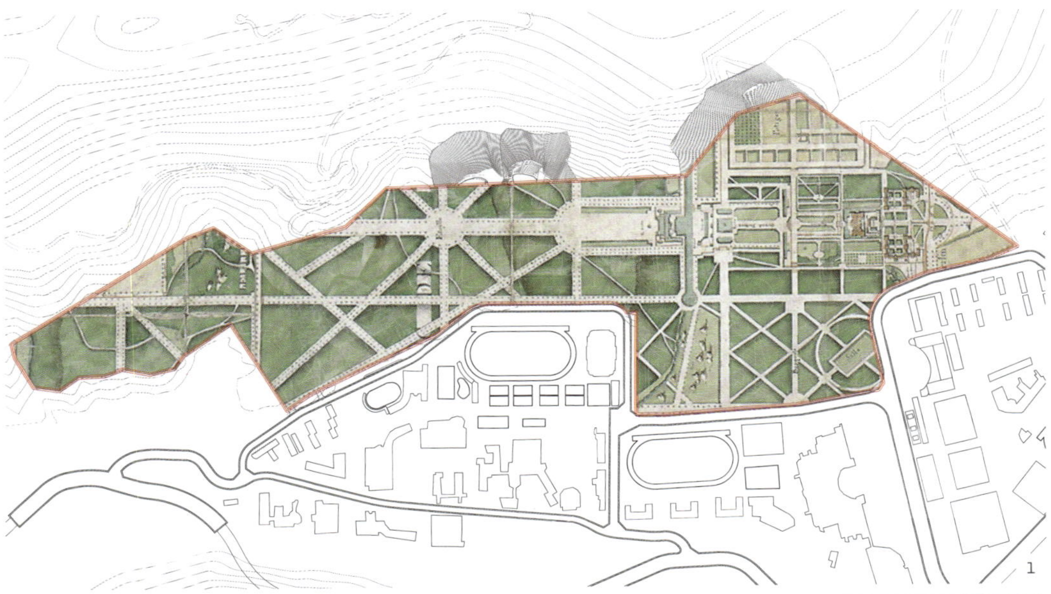

1

"The beauty of a city is measured by its ability to embrace what it never intended to be."

3

1 Fiction by DPA. Plan of the gardens of the Château de Versailles inserted into the site plan.
2 Insertion of the project in an aerial view of the existing site. The linear layout and dimensions of the project echoes major French planning projects, such as the development of the gardens at Versailles.
3 Axonometric illustrations of the pavilions.

4 Research diagrams inspired by the natural character of the site.
4.1 Eye of light.
4.2 Canopies.
4.3 Shelter with a view.
4.4 Covered walkway.
4.5 Protective flooring and elevation.
4.6 Climbing ladder.
4.7 Stepped topography.

4.1

4.2

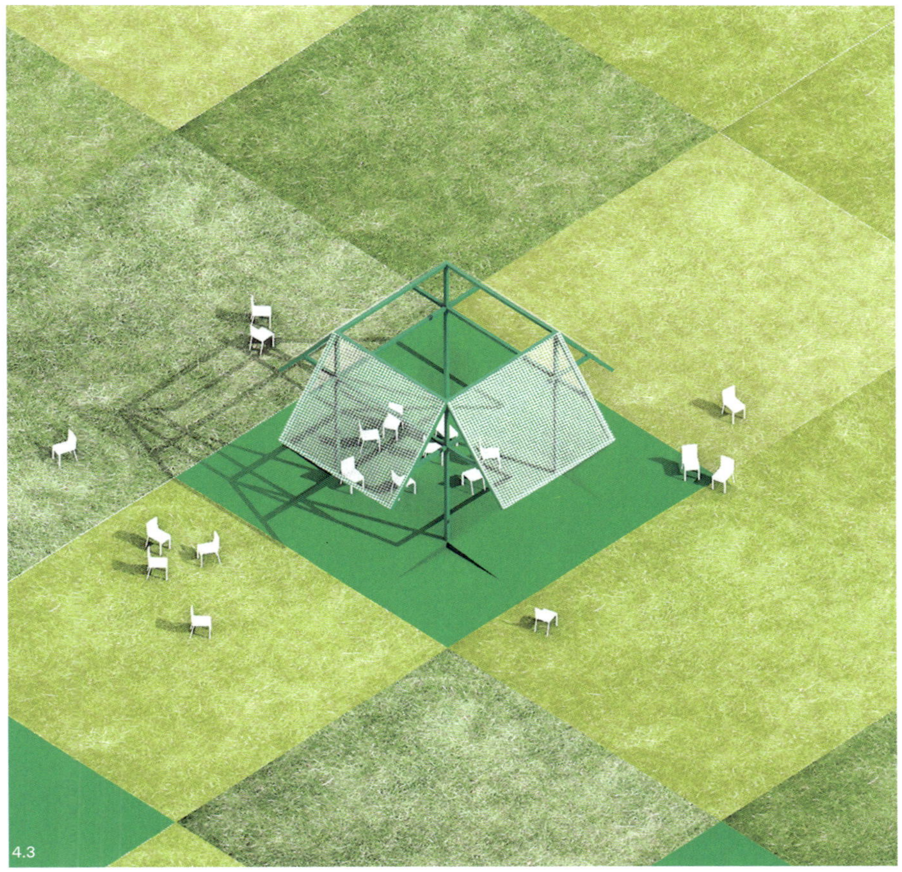

4.3

4.4

4.5

4.6

4.7

1

2

3

4

5

6

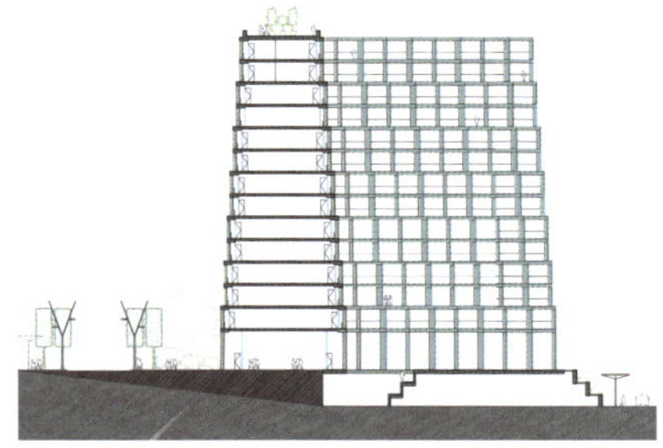
7

8

9

10

11

1 The library's roof garden and central skylight.
2 The library's central foyer and staircase
3 The library's central light well.
4 The library's entrance.
5 Long panorama showing the assembly of architectural elements that make up the landscape.
6 Overall view of the residential towers, with public facilities on the first floor.
7-9 The architecture of the student residences.
10 Fiction by DPA. Collage: the stadium and sports facilities in the natural landscape.
11 View of the administration tower, its structure and materials.

MULTIFUNCTIONAL DISTRICT

SOFIA, BULGARIA

2009–10

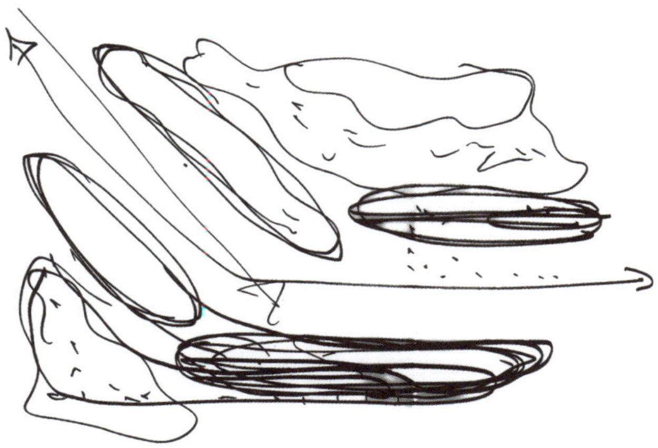

1

The creation of a new part of the city, offering a second heart for Sofia, is based on a twofold reading of the territory: the hidden cartography of ancient routes and the mountainous topography that surrounds the Bulgarian capital. The project draws a horizon line below which the ground rises up, organizing blocks and buildings according to programs, resources, and opportunities.

The traces of the neighborhood, erased by industrialization, re-emerge as the invisible foundations of this new urban fabric, connecting fragments of the past to future uses. A park-garden preserving the existing trees runs through the heart of this area, forming the backbone of the urban landscape by establishing a vast and continuous public space.

2

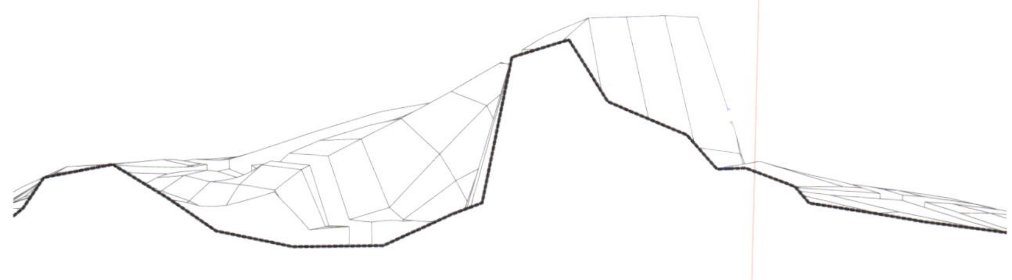

4

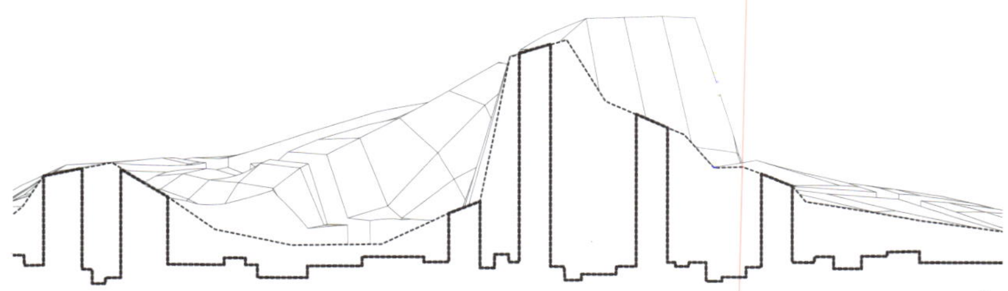

5

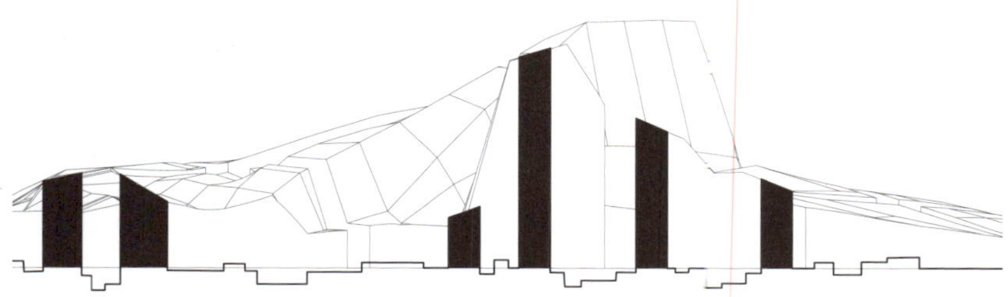

6

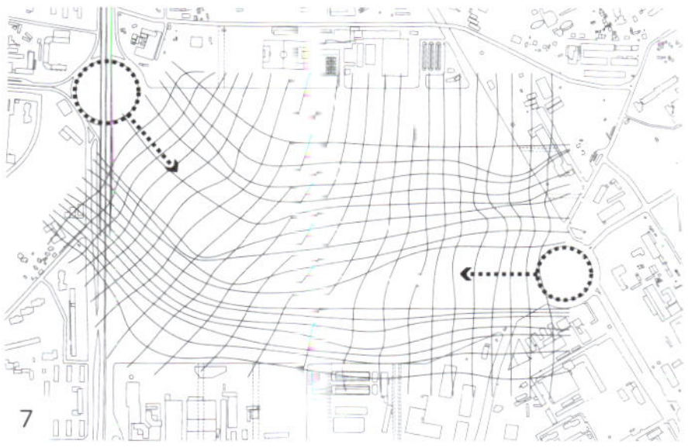

1 Sketch, 2009.
2 Plans of green spaces in Sofia.
3 Satellite view of the site.
4-6 Architecture is a device for creating a specific landscape and relief.
7 Contours, new topography.
8 Urban fabric.

9 The park at the heart of the project. A river runs through the park, its width varying with its position: in the center of the site, a huge pond is created.
10-11 Sports and play areas integrated into the project to revitalize the site.
12 The urban fabric was designed with its environmental context in mind: wind, sun, views, and existing landscape features.

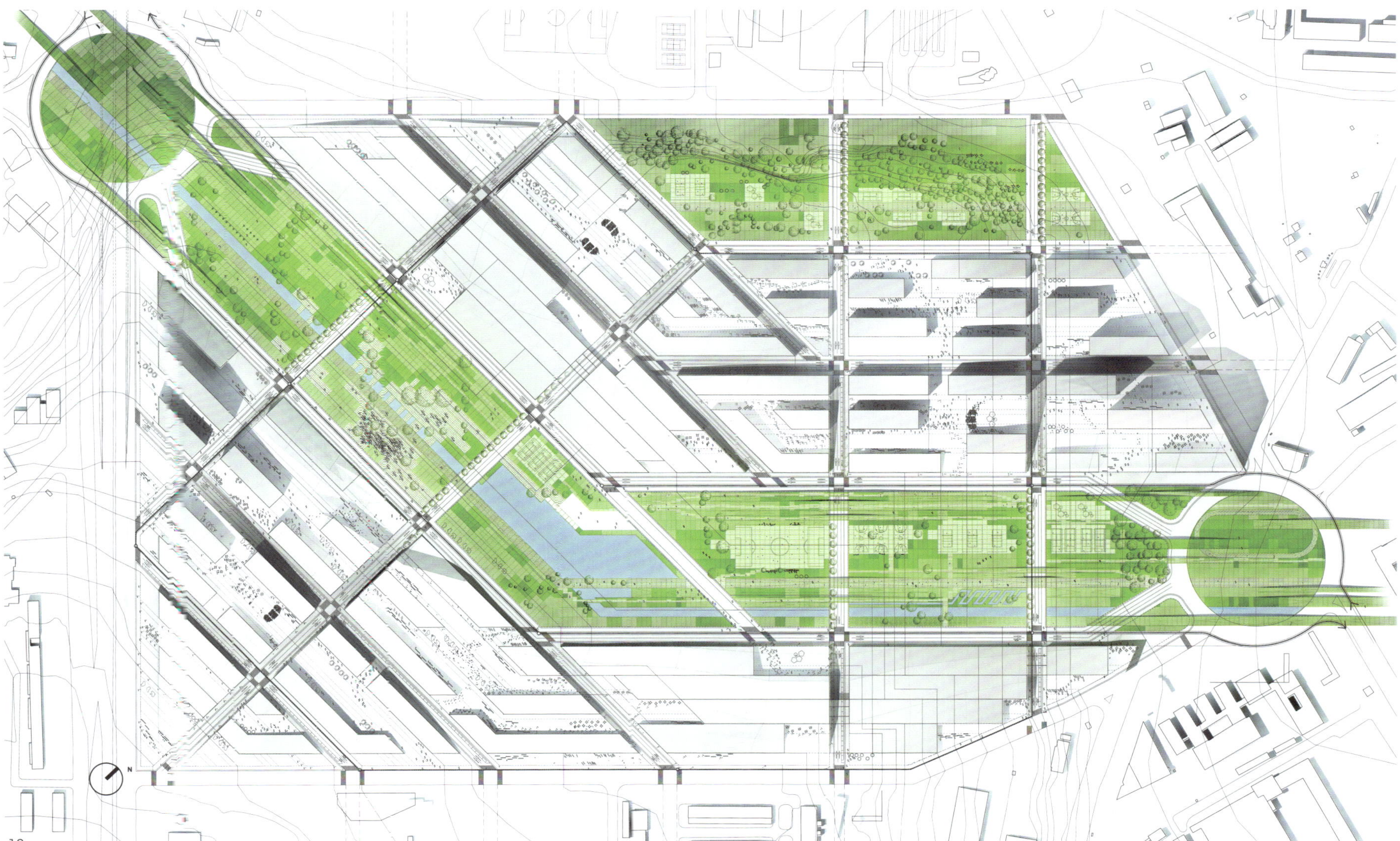

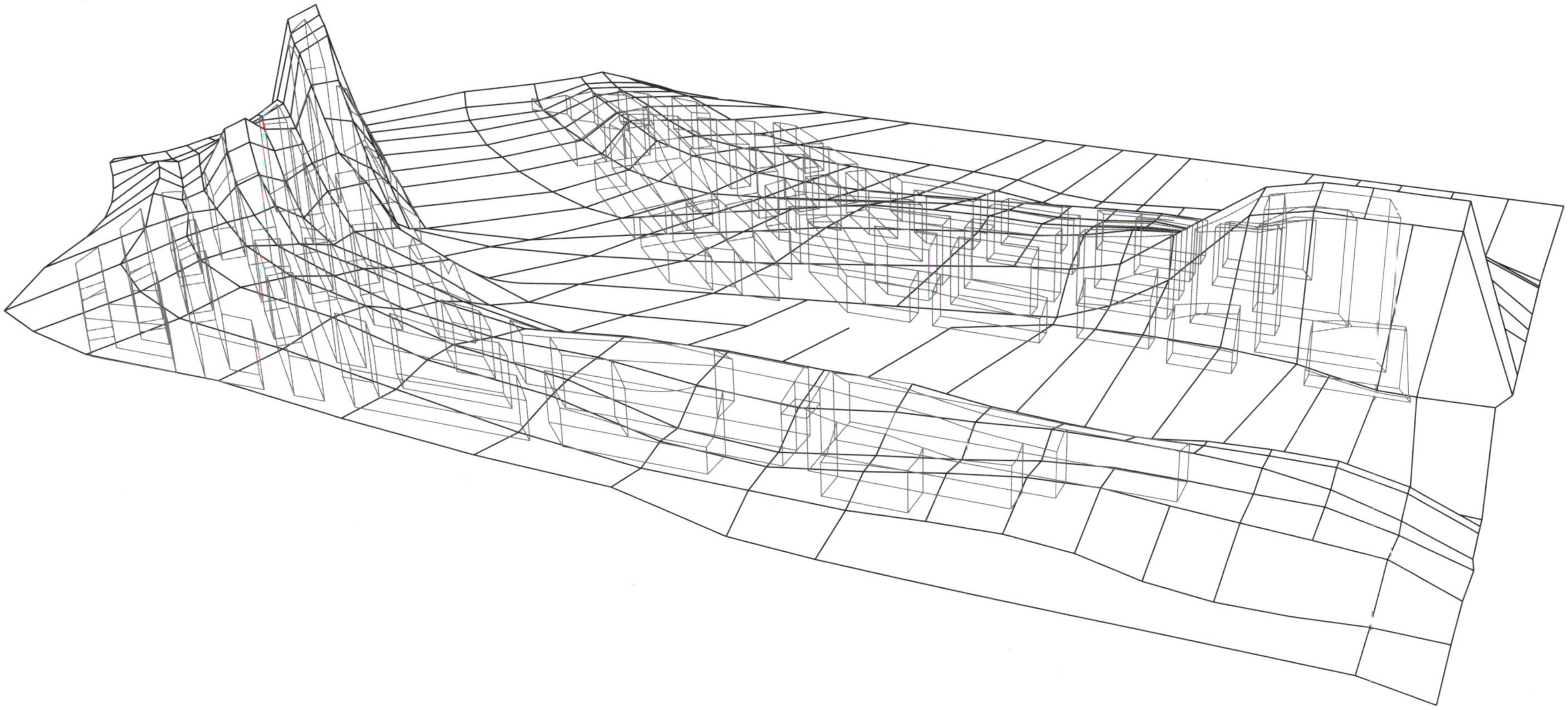

1

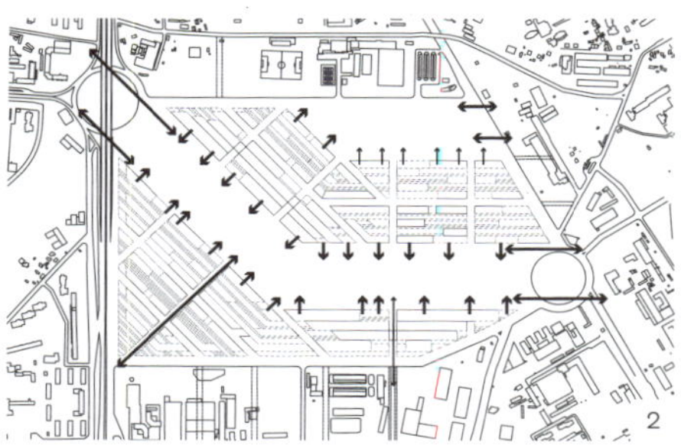

2

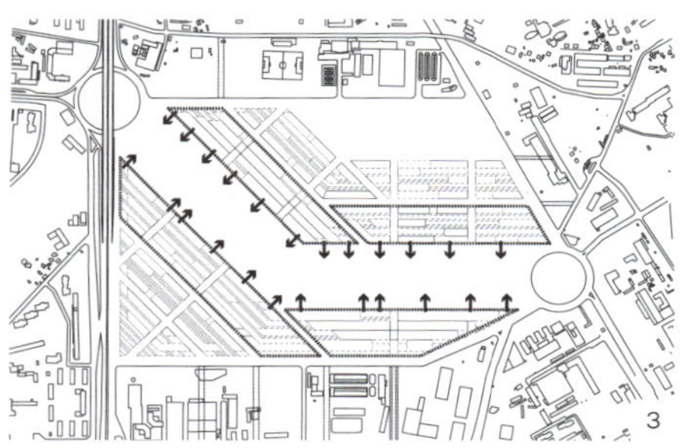

3

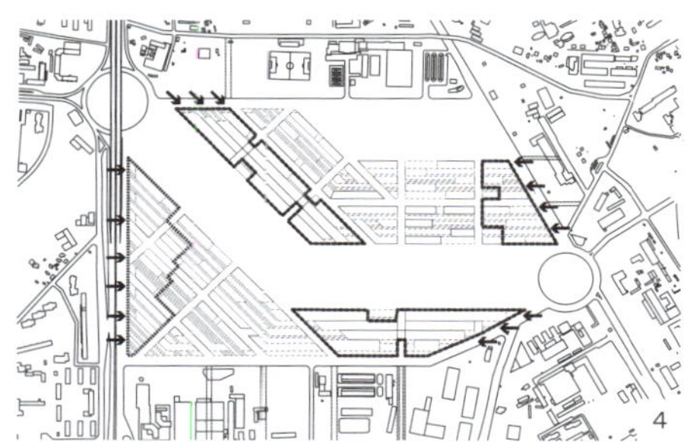

4

1 Experimental model for the silhouette of the new district.
2-4 Schemas exploring interactions between different programs.
5 Architectural ensemble evoking the rolling relief of a small mountain.
6-7 A biomorphic approach to the relief model Scale model 1:1,000, 2009.
8 Lateral view of the new district.
9 Transversal view of the new district.
10 View at the heart of the new district.

6

7

8

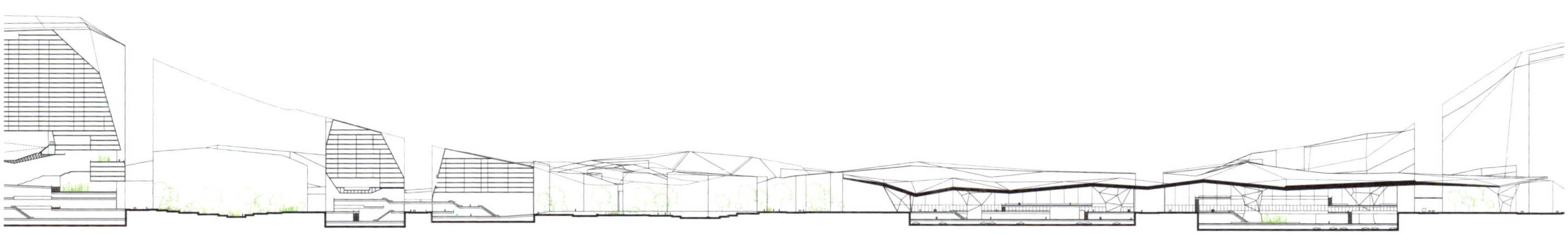

9

10

METROPOLIS? – VENICE ARCHITECTURE BIENNALE

VENICE, ITALY

2010

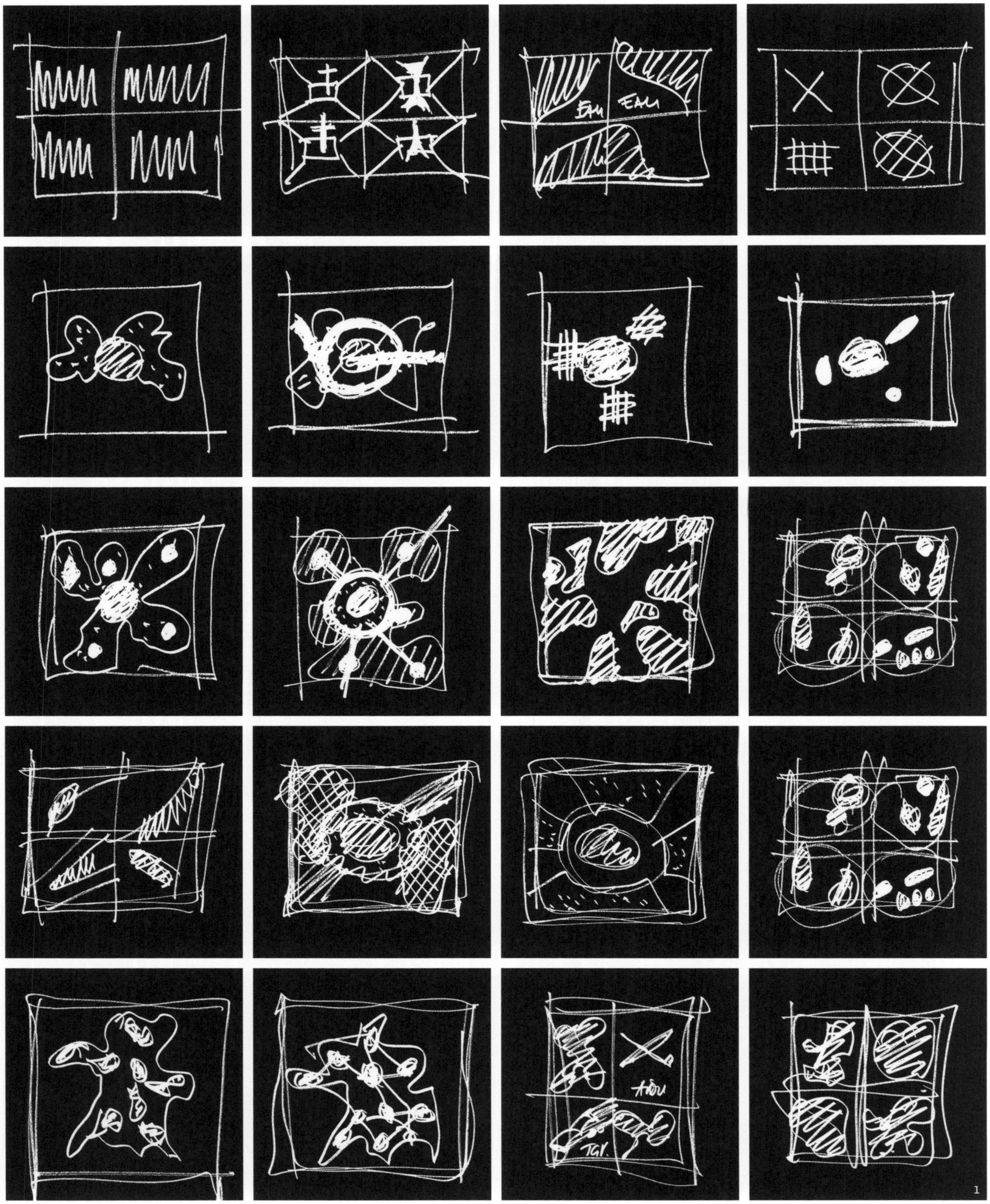

1

1 Typology of voids, sketch, 2020.
The metropolis is not a city, but a territory essentially made up of free, open, or available spaces. The revelation, transformation, and protection of these voids are all strategies, projects, or actions offered by metropolises to those who govern, imagine, and inhabit them.

2 Sketch, 2020.

3 Poster for the "Metropolis?" pavilion exhibition.

4-6 French pavilion at the "Métropolis?" exhibition.

2

"Metropolis?" is a reflection developed for the 2010 Venice Biennale, presented in the French Pavilion. The project explores the metropolis not as a built mass but as a territory structured by the void, which is no longer seen as a lack but as an active, foundational material. In the face of the saturated historic city, the metropolis opens up free, fertile spaces capable of accommodating new uses, new forms of mobility, and new ways of living. Fullness and emptiness cease to be opposites and become interdependent, revealing not what separates but what connects. In this way, a metropolitan cartography is being redrawn, free of administrative borders and rooted in the actual practices of the territory. In this vision, the void becomes the liveliest, most inhabited space, open to invention and sharing, a space for collective projection as much as for individual freedom.

3

4

5

6

1

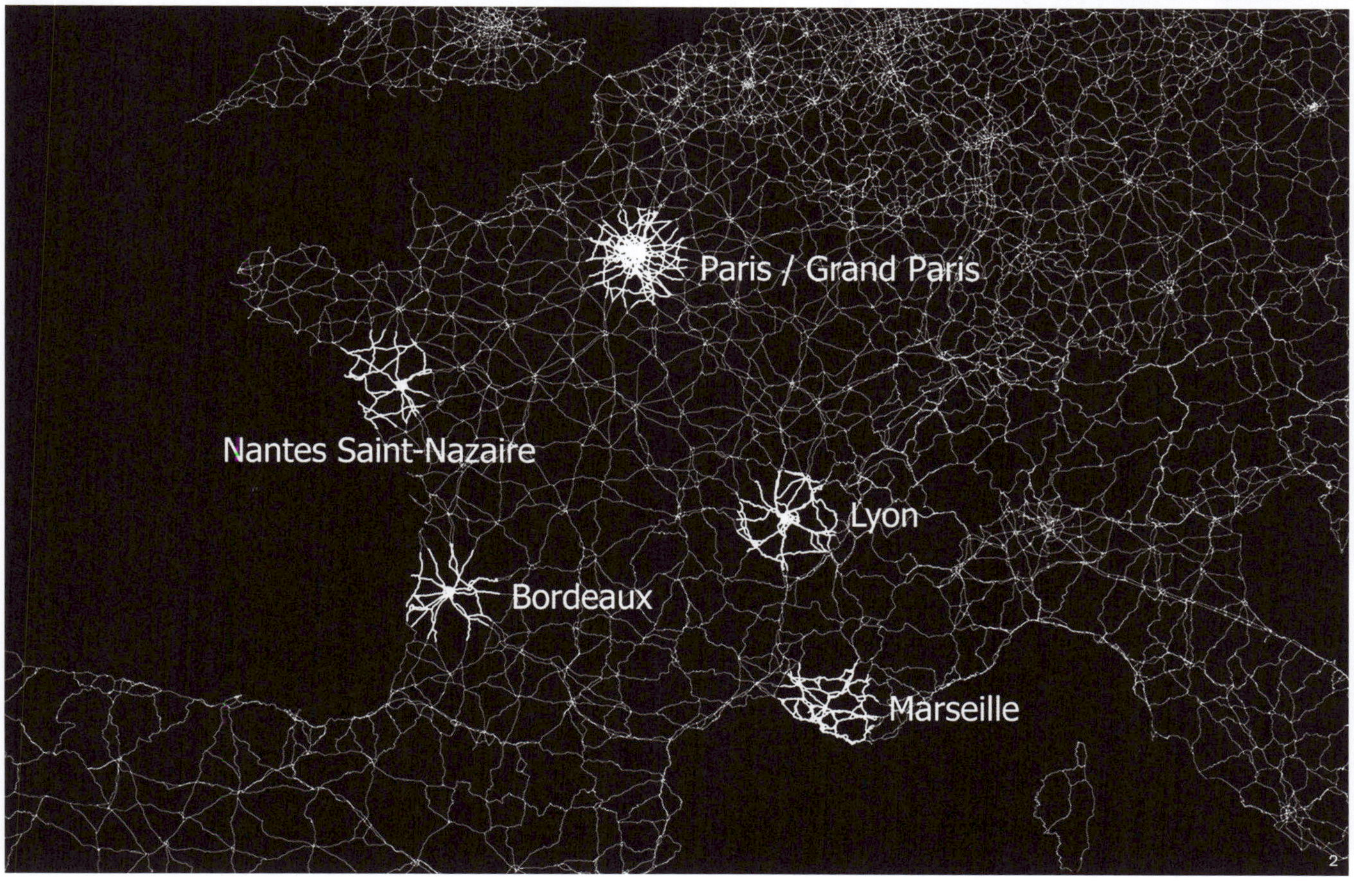

Paris / Grand Paris
Nantes Saint-Nazaire
Lyon
Bordeaux
Marseille

2

3

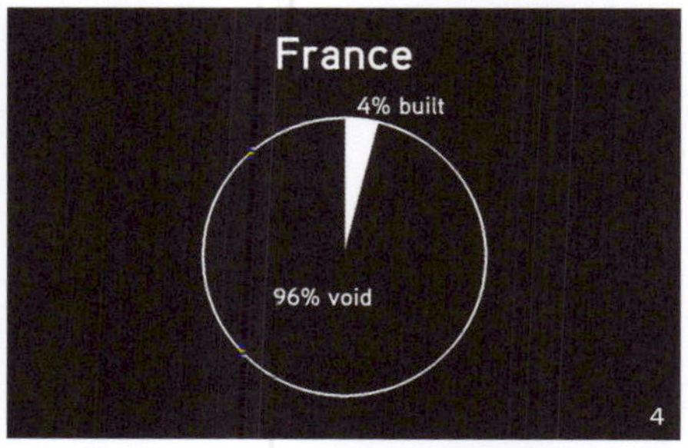

France
4% built
96% void

4

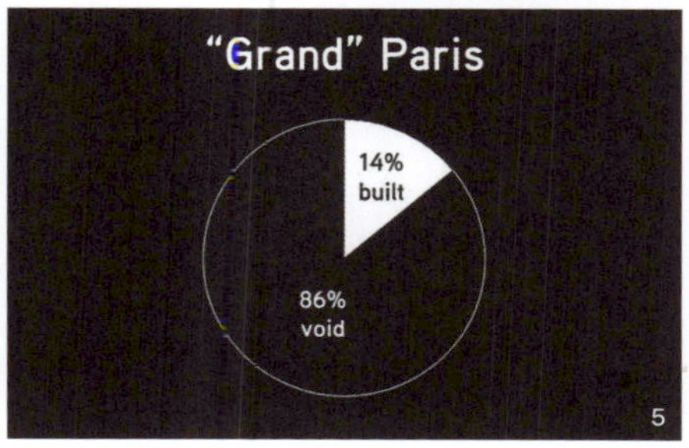

"Grand" Paris
14% built
86% void

5

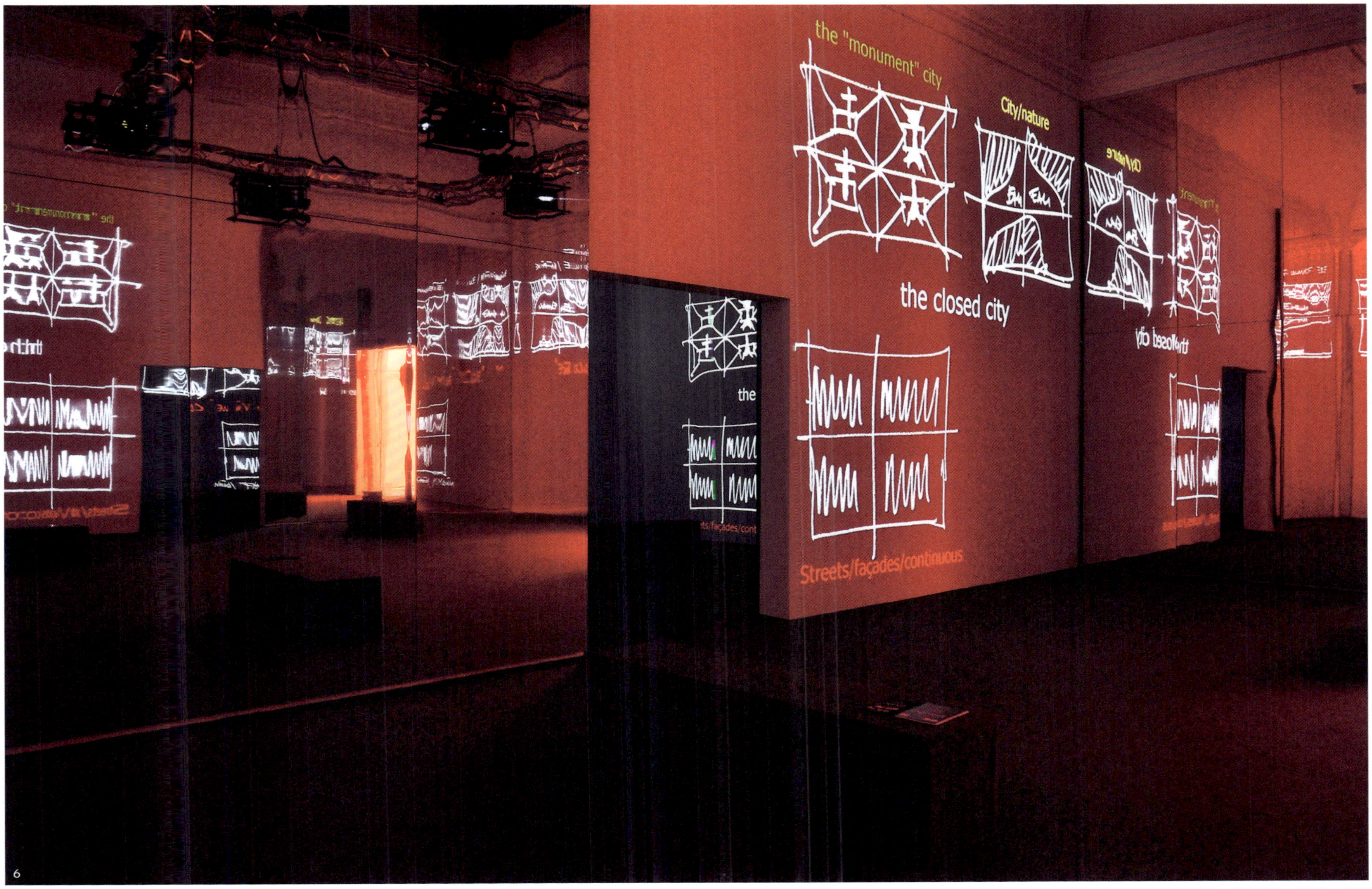

6

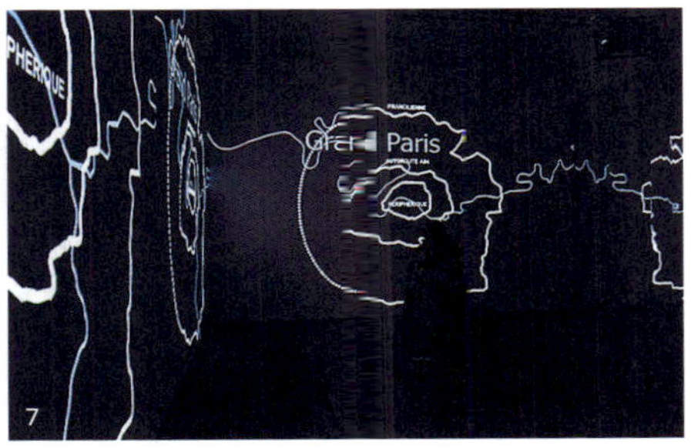

7

8

9

10

1–9 Exhibition layout. At the center of the Pavilion: the film *Métropolis*, made by Richard Copans especially for the Biennale. The viewer is plunged into the heart of the substance of metropolises, which end up merging, evidence that these new territories belong to another cartography, another mental map.

10 Mock-up of the exhibition (foamboard, mirror-effect aluminum foil, paper), 2010. The pavilion, deliberately left empty, hosts a "multiplex"-style staging articulated in three exhibition sequences: Métropolis, Grand Paris, and a bonus sequence questioning the metropolis-world.

CROSSROADS, BUILDING THE RESILIENT CITY – SEOUL BIENNALE OF ARCHITECTURE AND URBAN PLANNING

SEOUL, SOUTH KOREA

2019–21

The Seoul Biennale is an experimental, responsive laboratory in which architecture confronts the complexity of the world, and architecture, urban planning, science, art, engineering, and philosophy meet and collide. Its manifesto, "Crossroads: Building the Resilient City," traces five themes, confronting the contradictions that structure our times: above and below, heritage and modernity, natural and artificial, safety and risk, traditional and digital. Five fault lines that refuse compromise in order to generate hybrid, radical projects capable of opening up new paths towards a sustainable, resilient planet. The scenography itself becomes a terrain of friction: a huge grid, like a chessboard, accommodates in each of its squares a position in which the diversity of forms, materials, stories, and experiences composes a cartography of futures waiting to be invented. This is an invitation for architecture to become once again a political art form.

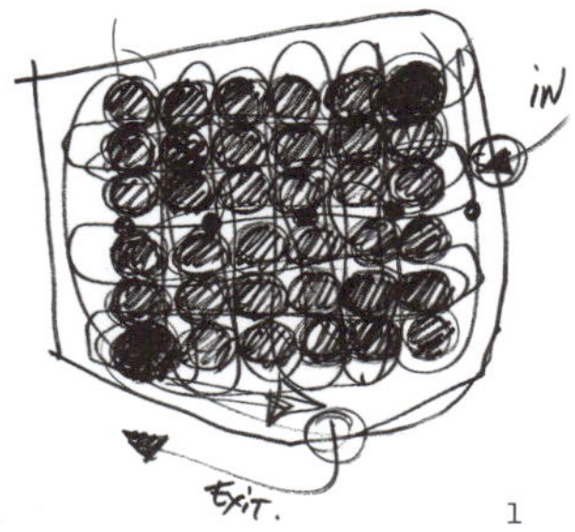

1

1 Design sketch, 2020.
2 The "six crossroads" that illustrate the Biennale theme.
3 Poster for the 2021 Biennale of Architecture and Urbanism.
4 Fiction by DPA. The Above X Below crossroad goes deep into the stratifications of the city, questioning its space and limits.
5 Study for the exhibition design.
6 Exhibition design for the first floor.

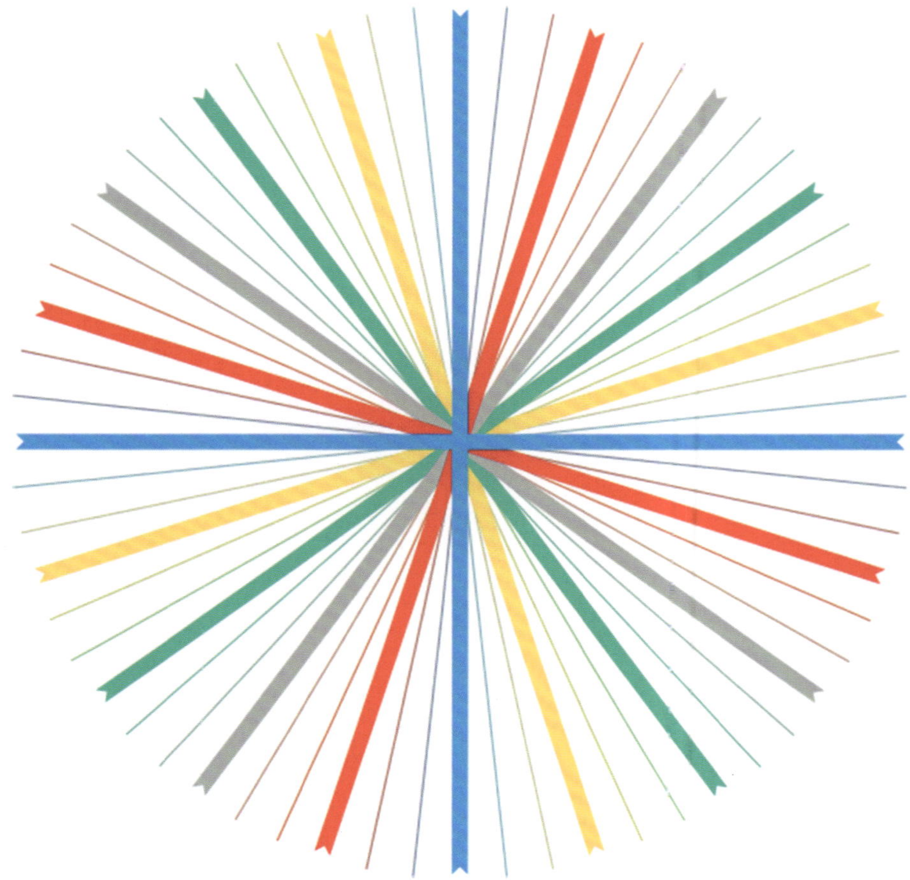

BUILDING THE RESILIENT CITY

2

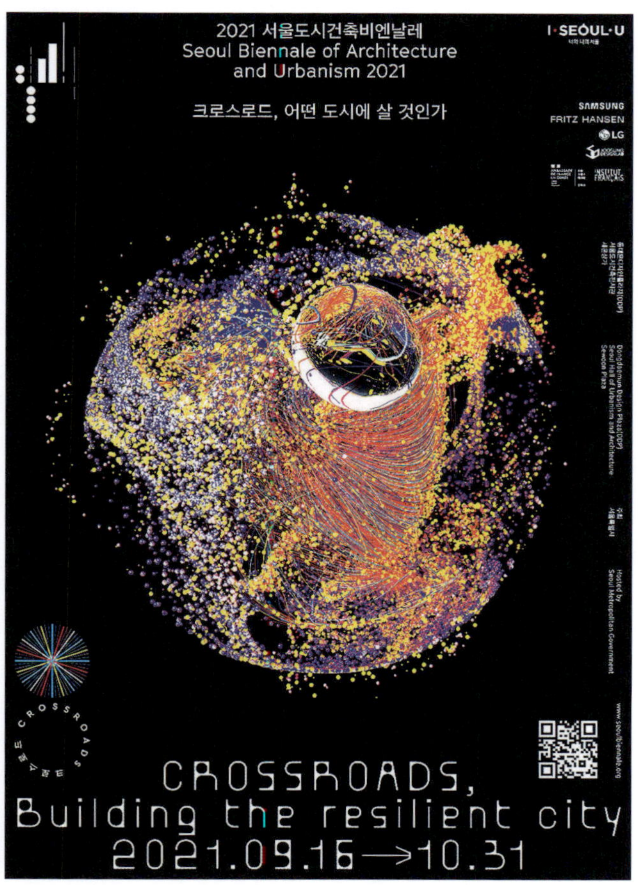

3

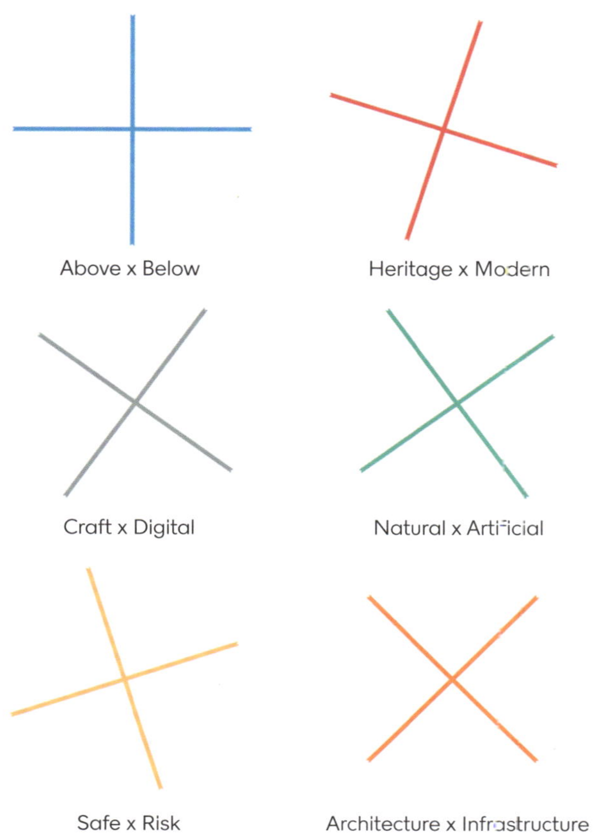

4

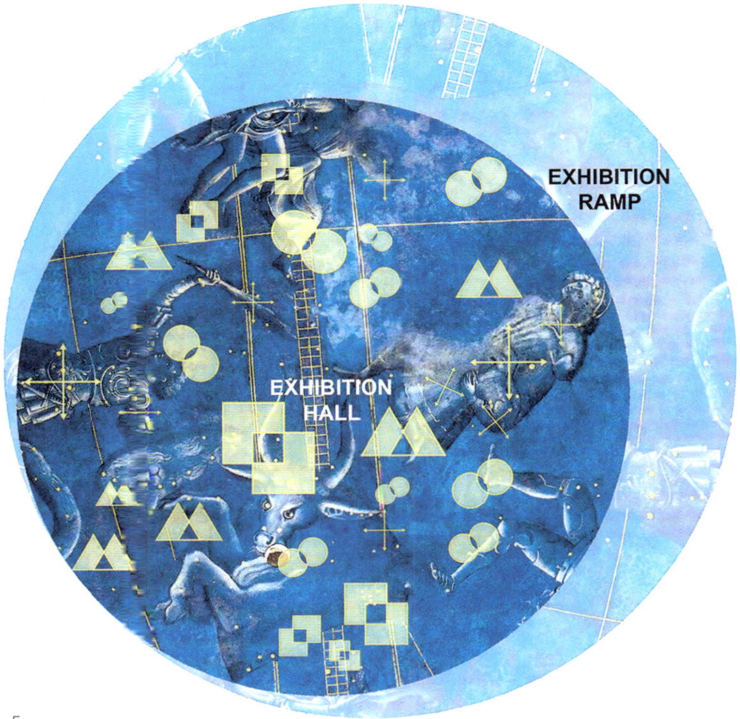

5

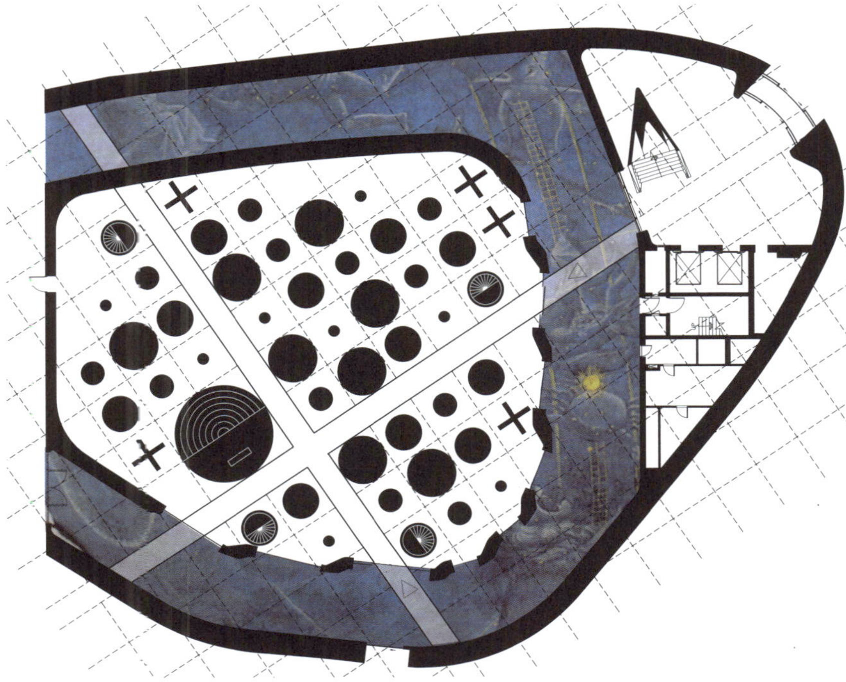

6

1

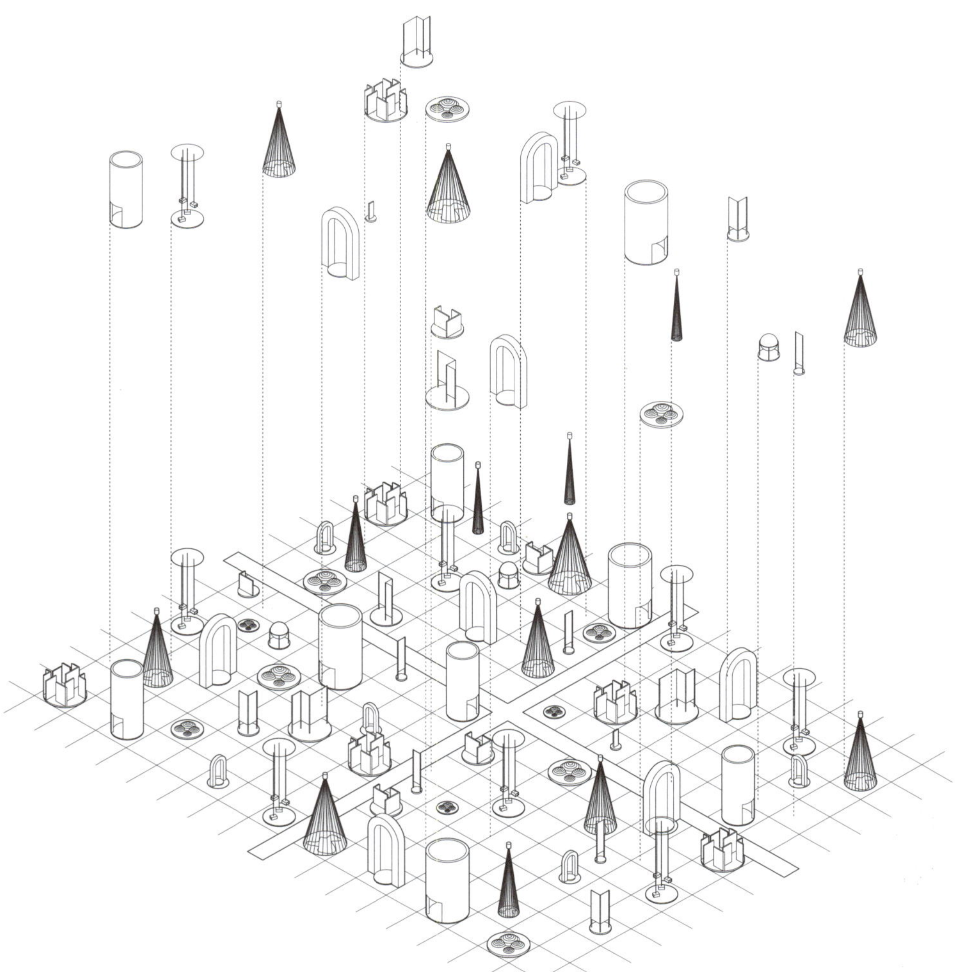

2

"Our cities suffer less from a lack of technical solutions than from a deficit of shared wonder."

1 The checkerboard map can be transformed into a line, and its horizontal surface into a spiral. All these mutations produce new maps, without leaving behind the elements of which they are composed.
2 Schema of the thematic exhibition as a chessboard. Circles 4 meters in diameter on the floor present the various works in the manner of chessboard pieces.
3 Installation models.

3

THE INFORMAL CITY 비공식적 도시
PORT-AU-PRINCE BAI
FONTAMARA

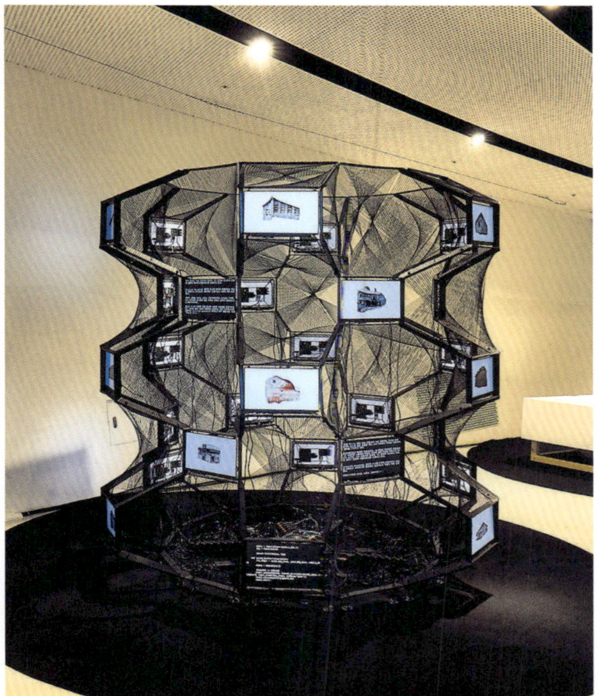

도시전 계속
Cities Exhibition continues
안전 × 위험
SAFE × RISK
글로벌 스튜디오 피난처
Global Studios Refuges
출구
서점

HANGANG DISTRICT MASTER PLAN
HANDAN, CHINA
2020

The master plan involves the radical transformation of a neighborhood of the historic town of Handan, a composite area combining heterogeneous architecture and the remains of a once-powerful iron and steel industry. To tame this complexity, the project is based on a rigorous grid, inspired by Mendeleev's periodic tables: a grid measuring 100 meters by 100 meters marks out the site, like a founding gesture reactivating the ancestral act of establishing a town and giving it a new scale. This grid becomes the matrix of a balanced territory: it organizes heights and densities, articulates built-up areas and large parks, accommodates major infrastructures, and frees up breathing spaces in the landscape. Each square of the grid becomes a project unit, capable of accommodating new programs while preserving the industrial and urban heritage. In this way, the old factories are transformed into cultural sites and traces of the past irrigate the future district. Conceived as an open and reversible tool, this method combines rigor and flexibility: a framework capable of absorbing change and accompanying Handan in its transformation. Without denying its history, the city thus invents a new form of modernity.

1

2

1, 2 Photographs of the existing site. The area concerned, which represents about a quarter of the surface area of the historic town of Handan, is made up of highly heterogeneous built elements and a significant industrial heritage.

3 Guidelines for opening up the industrial site in the heart of the town.

4 Collage, map of New York superimposed on the Handan metropolis.

5 Collage, map of Paris superimposed on the Handan metropolis.

6 Guiding principles to promote the porosity of the urban fabric within the Handan metropolis.

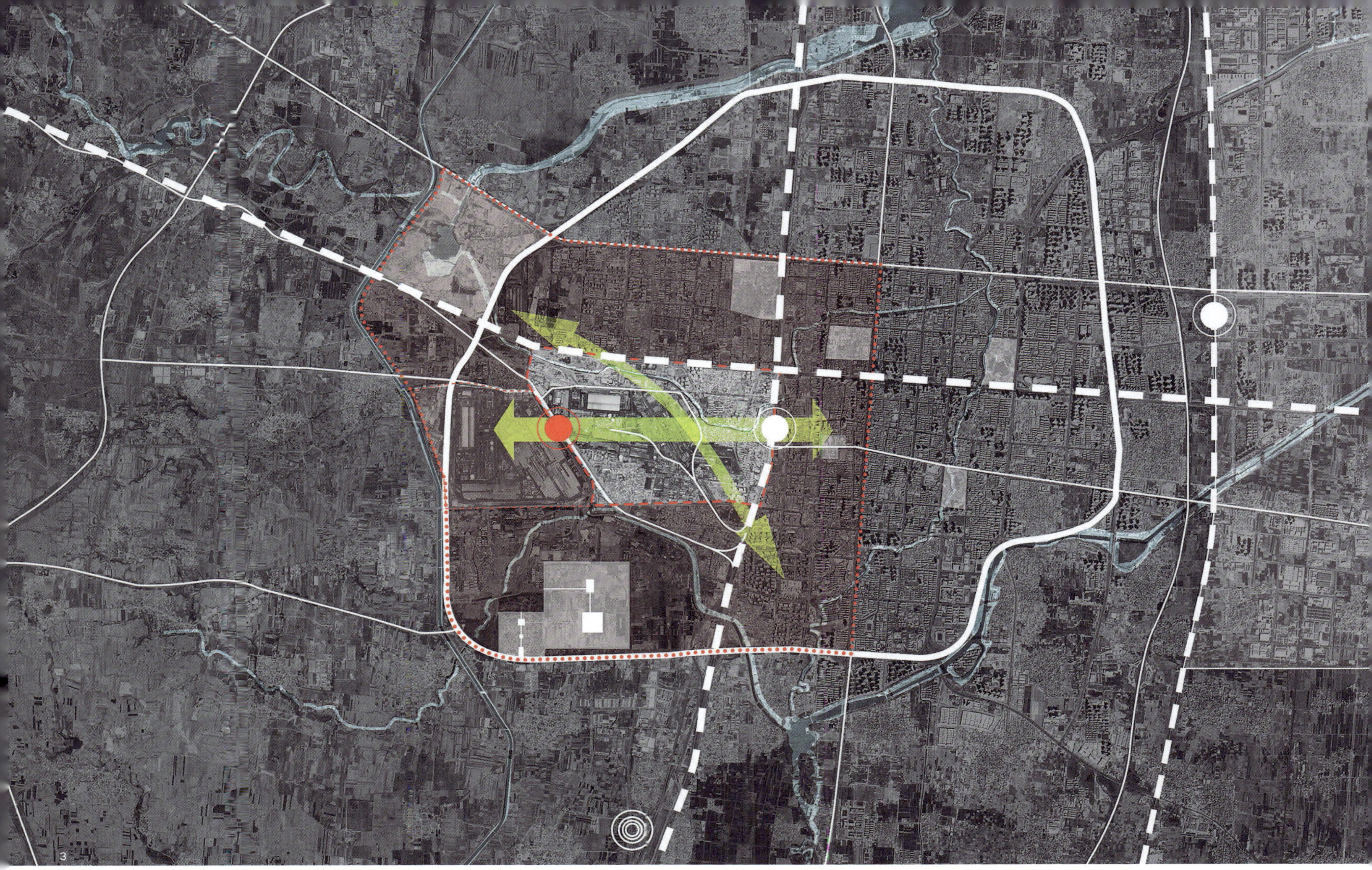

3

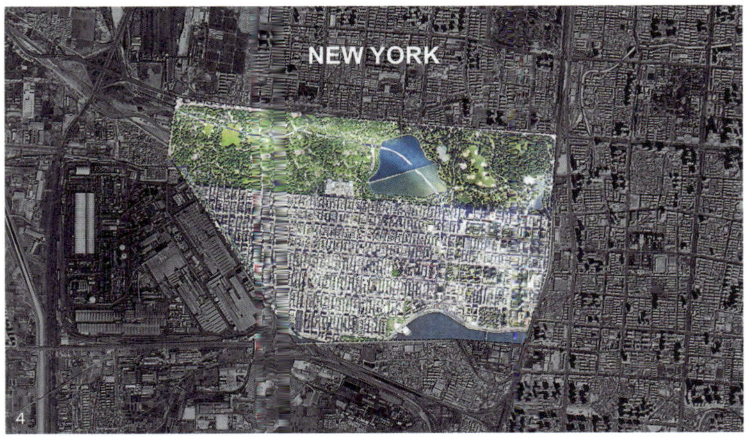

4

5

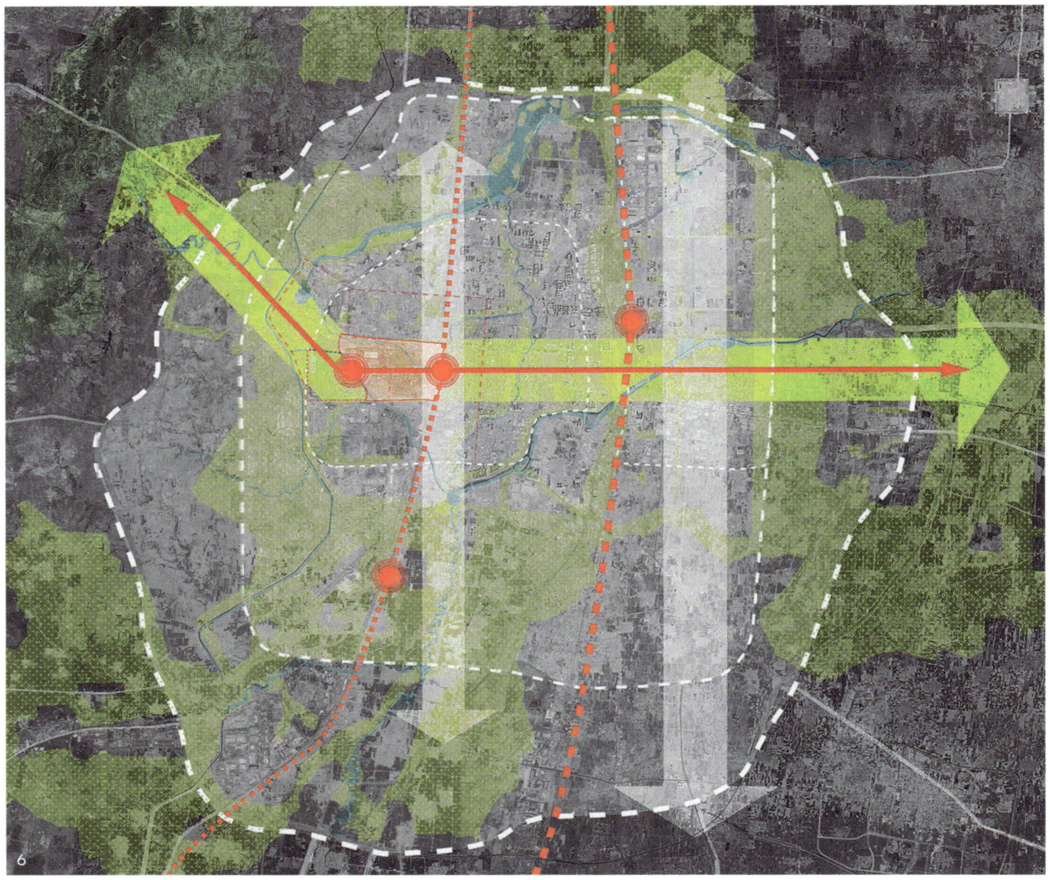

6

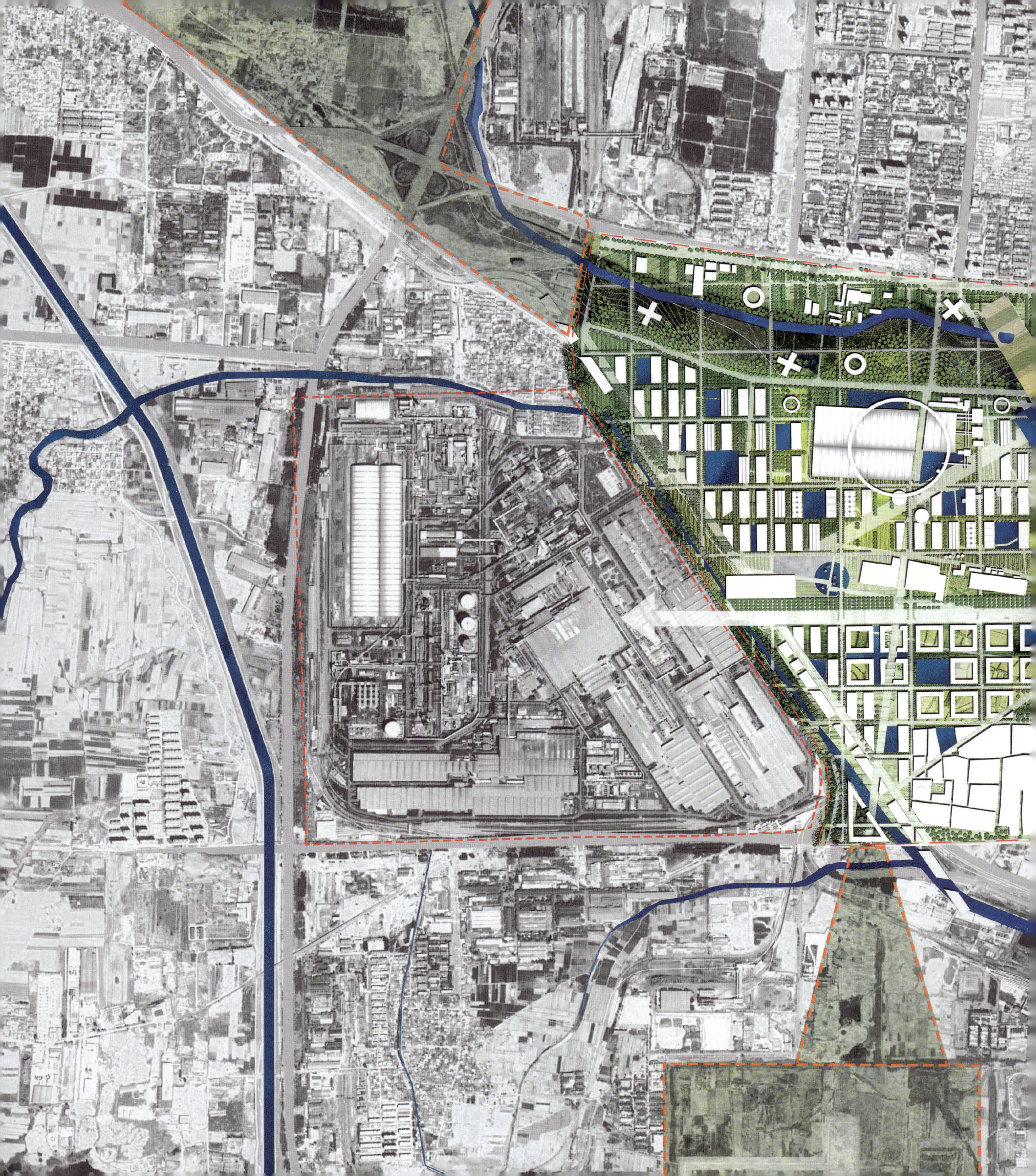

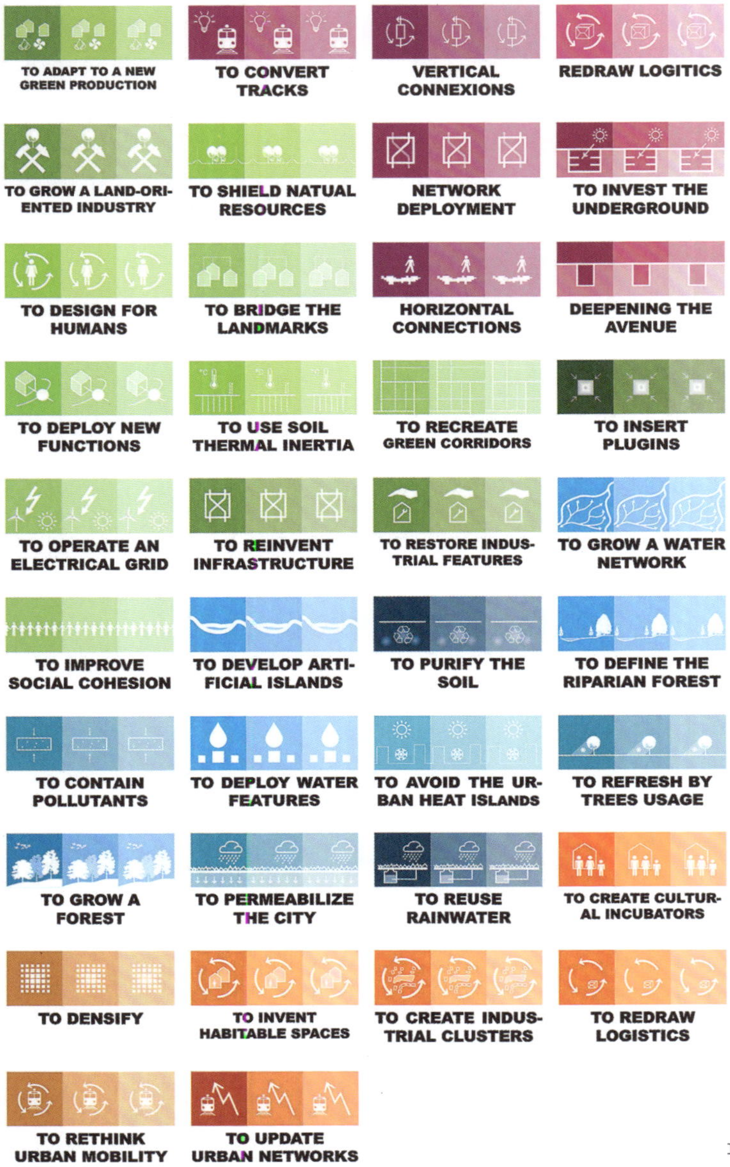
TO ADAPT TO A NEW GREEN PRODUCTION
TO CONVERT TRACKS
VERTICAL CONNEXIONS
REDRAW LOGITICS
TO GROW A LAND-ORIENTED INDUSTRY
TO SHIELD NATUAL RESOURCES
NETWORK DEPLOYMENT
TO INVEST THE UNDERGROUND
TO DESIGN FOR HUMANS
TO BRIDGE THE LANDMARKS
HORIZONTAL CONNECTIONS
DEEPENING THE AVENUE
TO DEPLOY NEW FUNCTIONS
TO USE SOIL THERMAL INERTIA
TO RECREATE GREEN CORRIDORS
TO INSERT PLUGINS
TO OPERATE AN ELECTRICAL GRID
TO REINVENT INFRASTRUCTURE
TO RESTORE INDUSTRIAL FEATURES
TO GROW A WATER NETWORK
TO IMPROVE SOCIAL COHESION
TO DEVELOP ARTIFICIAL ISLANDS
TO PURIFY THE SOIL
TO DEFINE THE RIPARIAN FOREST
TO CONTAIN POLLUTANTS
TO DEPLOY WATER FEATURES
TO AVOID THE URBAN HEAT ISLANDS
TO REFRESH BY TREES USAGE
TO GROW A FOREST
TO PERMEABILIZE THE CITY
TO REUSE RAINWATER
TO CREATE CULTURAL INCUBATORS
TO DENSIFY
TO INVENT HABITABLE SPACES
TO CREATE INDUSTRIAL CLUSTERS
TO REDRAW LOGISTICS
TO RETHINK URBAN MOBILITY
TO UPDATE URBAN NETWORKS

1

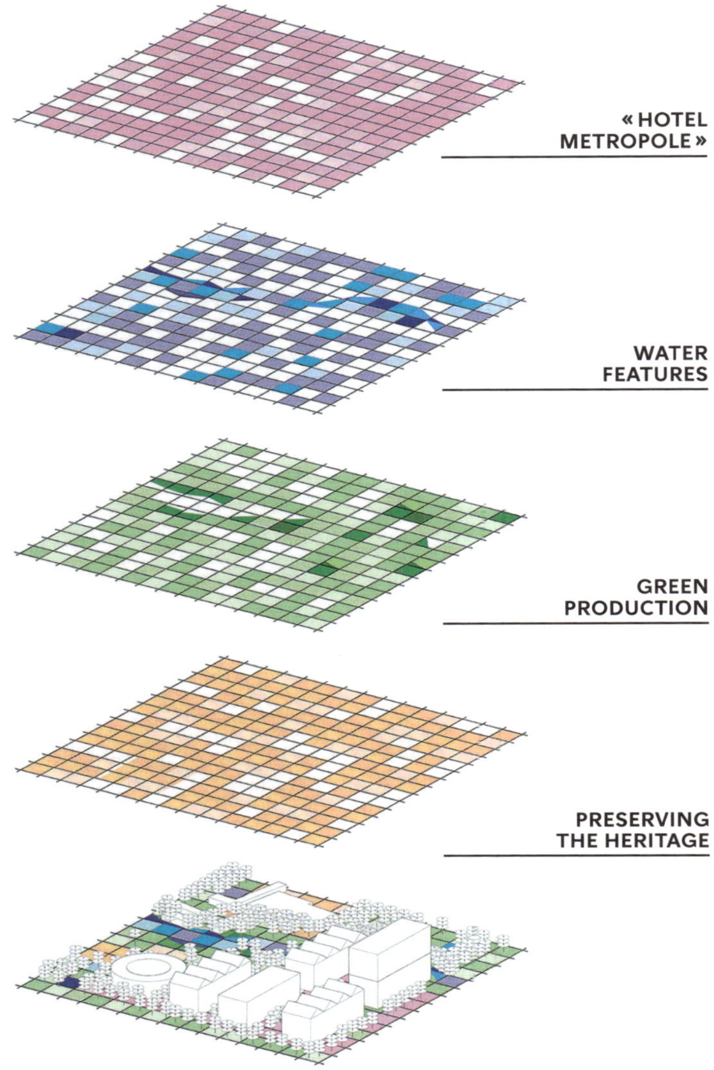
« HOTEL METROPOLE »
WATER FEATURES
GREEN PRODUCTION
PRESERVING THE HERITAGE

2

3

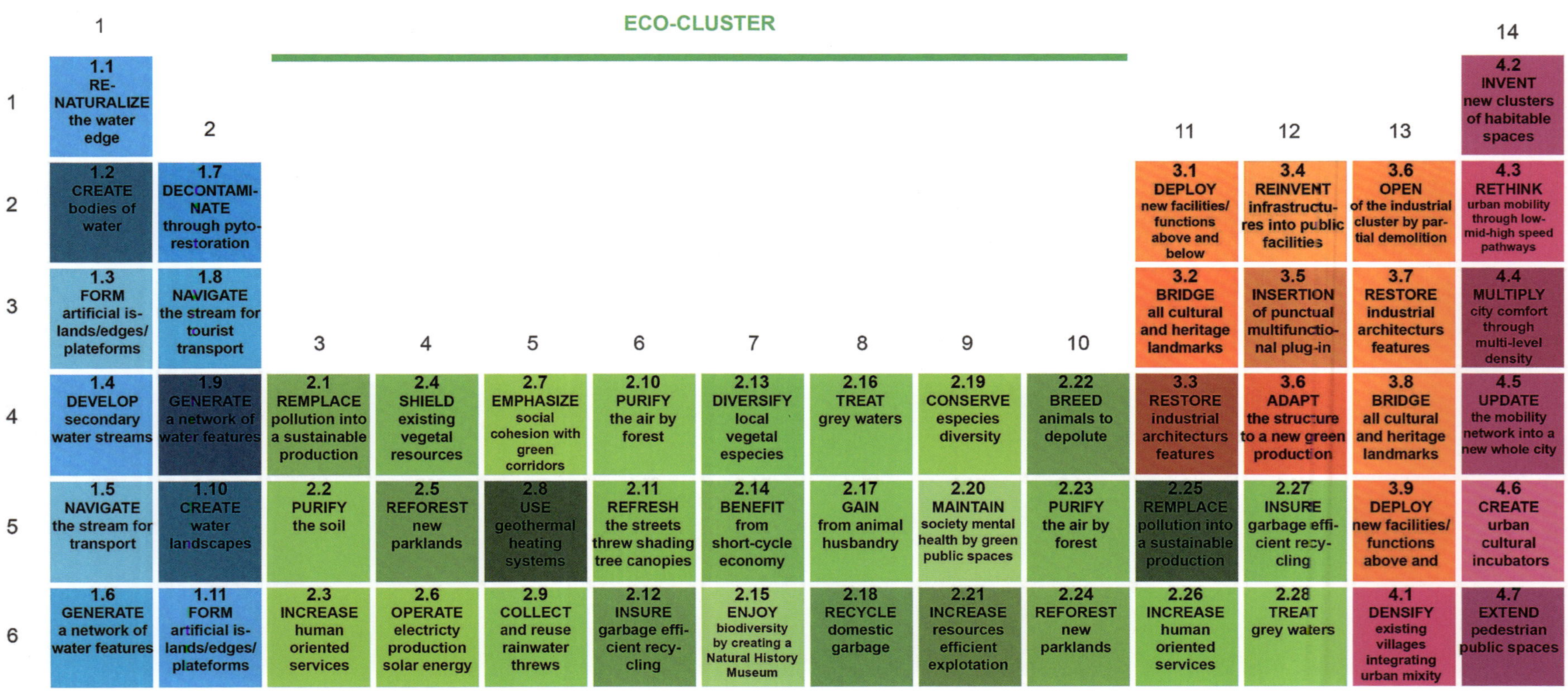
ECO-CLUSTER
1
2
3
4
5
6
7
8
9
10
11
12
13
14
1.1 RE-NATURALIZE the water edge
4.2 INVENT new clusters of habitable spaces
1.2 CREATE bodies of water
1.7 DECONTAMINATE through pyto-restoration
3.1 DEPLOY new facilities/ functions above and below
3.4 REINVENT infrastructures into public facilities
3.6 OPEN of the industrial cluster by partial demolition
4.3 RETHINK urban mobility through low-mid-high speed pathways
1.3 FORM artificial islands/edges/ plateforms
1.8 NAVIGATE the stream for tourist transport
3.2 BRIDGE all cultural and heritage landmarks
3.5 INSERTION of punctual multifunctional plug-in
3.7 RESTORE industrial architecturs features
4.4 MULTIPLY city comfort through multi-level density
1.4 DEVELOP secondary water streams
1.9 GENERATE a network of water features
2.1 REMPLACE pollution into a sustainable production
2.4 SHIELD existing vegetal resources
2.7 EMPHASIZE social cohesion with green corridors
2.10 PURIFY the air by forest
2.13 DIVERSIFY local vegetal especies
2.16 TREAT grey waters
2.19 CONSERVE especies diversity
2.22 BREED animals to depolute
3.3 RESTORE industrial architecturs features
3.6 ADAPT the structure to a new green production
3.8 BRIDGE all cultural and heritage landmarks
4.5 UPDATE the mobility network into a new whole city
1.5 NAVIGATE the stream for transport
1.10 CREATE water landscapes
2.2 PURIFY the soil
2.5 REFOREST new parklands
2.8 USE geothermal heating systems
2.11 REFRESH the streets threw shading tree canopies
2.14 BENEFIT from short-cycle economy
2.17 GAIN from animal husbandry
2.20 MAINTAIN society mental health by green public spaces
2.23 PURIFY the air by forest
2.25 REMPLACE pollution into a sustainable production
2.27 INSURE garbage efficient recycling
3.9 DEPLOY new facilities/ functions above and
4.6 CREATE urban cultural incubators
1.6 GENERATE a network of water features
1.11 FORM artificial islands/edges/ plateforms
2.3 INCREASE human oriented services
2.6 OPERATE electricty production solar energy
2.9 COLLECT and reuse rainwater threws
2.12 INSURE garbage efficient recycling
2.15 ENJOY biodiversity by creating a Natural History Museum
2.18 RECYCLE domestic garbage
2.21 INCREASE resources efficient explotation
2.24 REFOREST new parklands
2.26 INCREASE human oriented services
2.28 TREAT grey waters
4.1 DENSIFY existing villages integrating urban mixity
4.7 EXTEND pedestrian public spaces

1 Database: range of urban tools
2 Axonometric view of the periodic table of urban tools, organized by program on the site.
3 Mendeleev's table reinterpreted.
4 Map of the various programs on the site.
5 Plan showing the distribution of urban tools on the map, indicating their integration with the existing fabric.

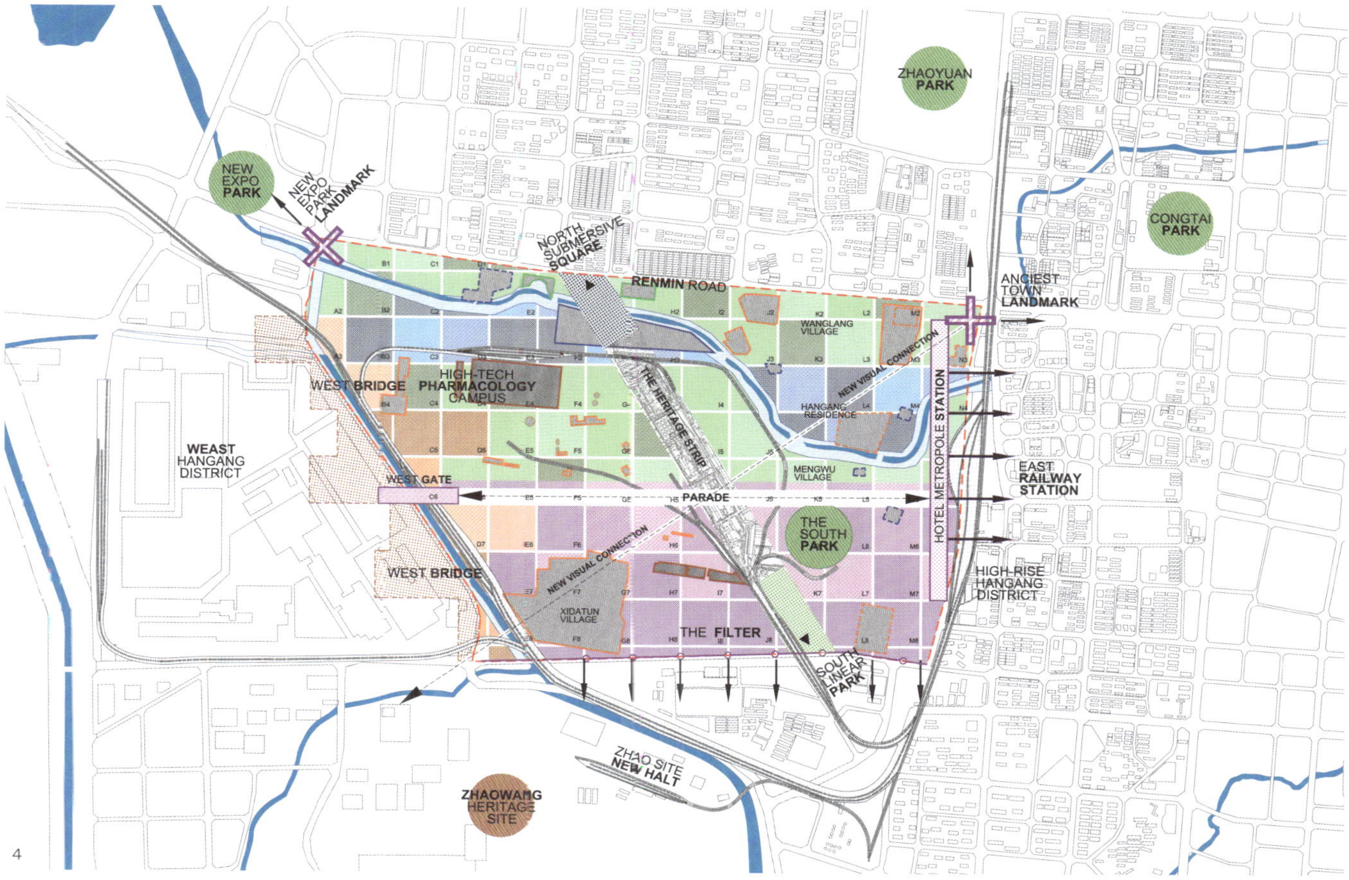

4

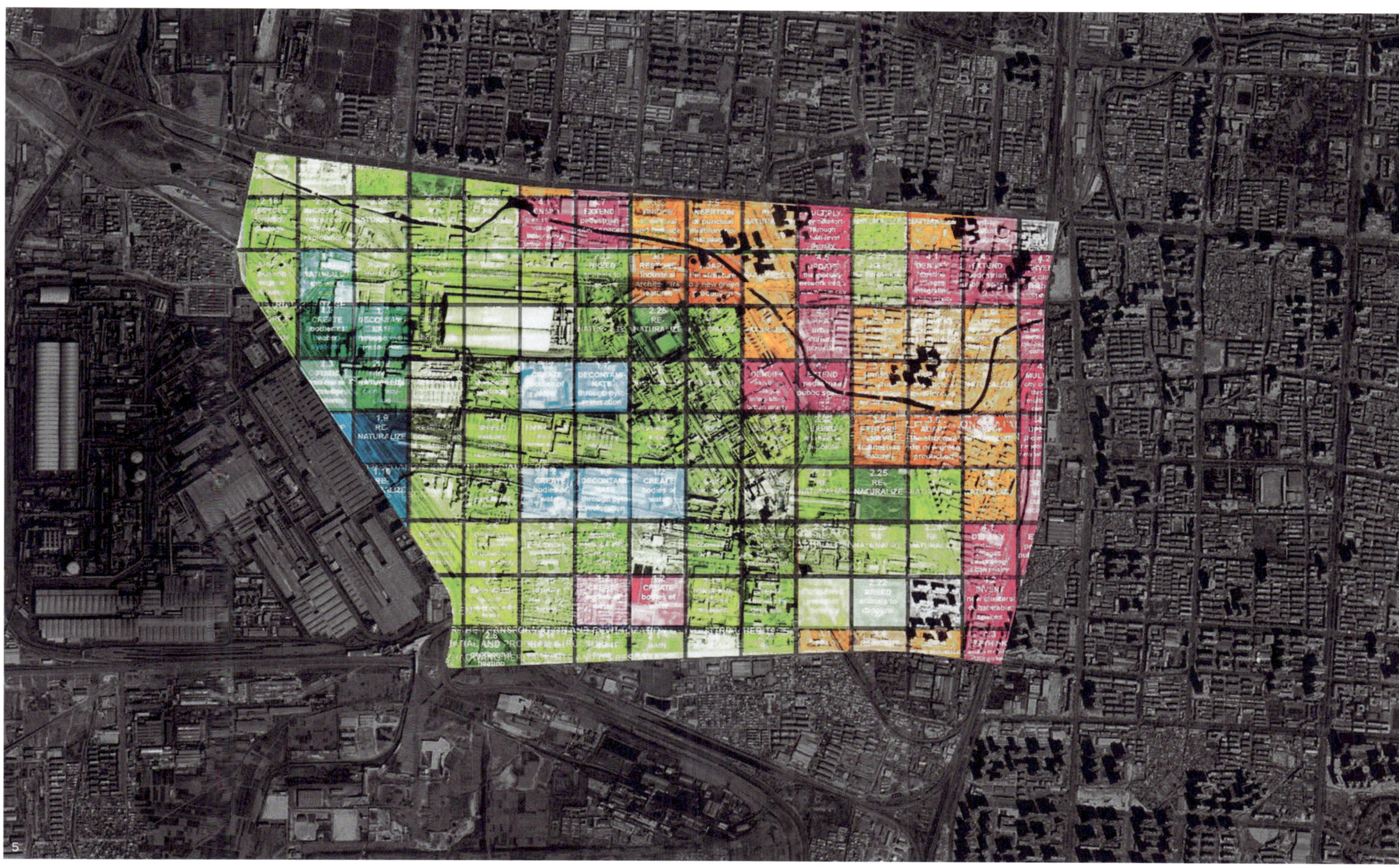
5

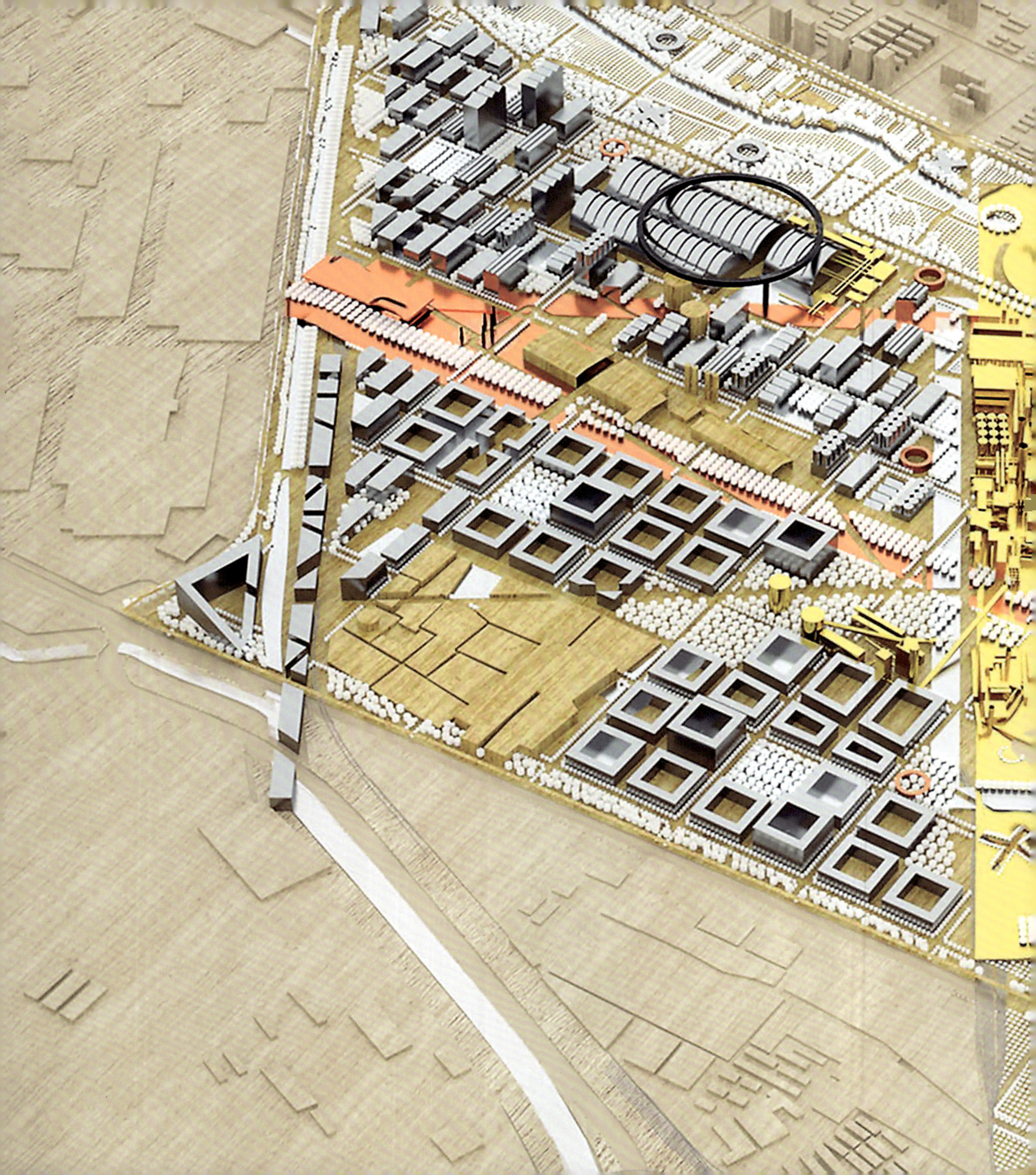

1

2

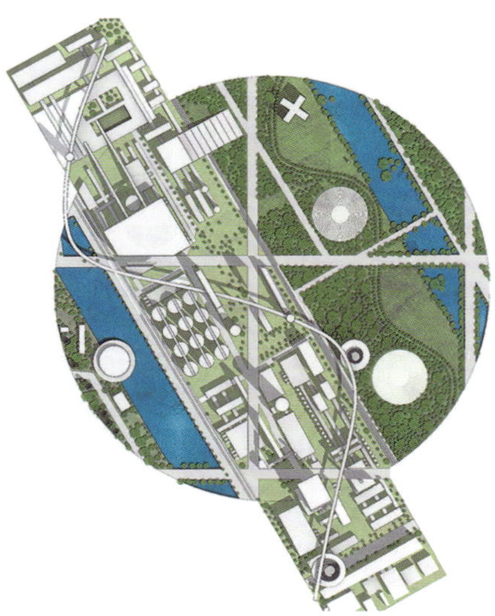

3

1 The backbone of the project is the preservation and cultural enhancement of the industrial heritage of "Heritage Island," former factories rehabilitated as cultural, meeting, and leisure venues.
2 Life on "Heritage Island."
3 Architectural and urban conservation and creation on "Heritage Island."

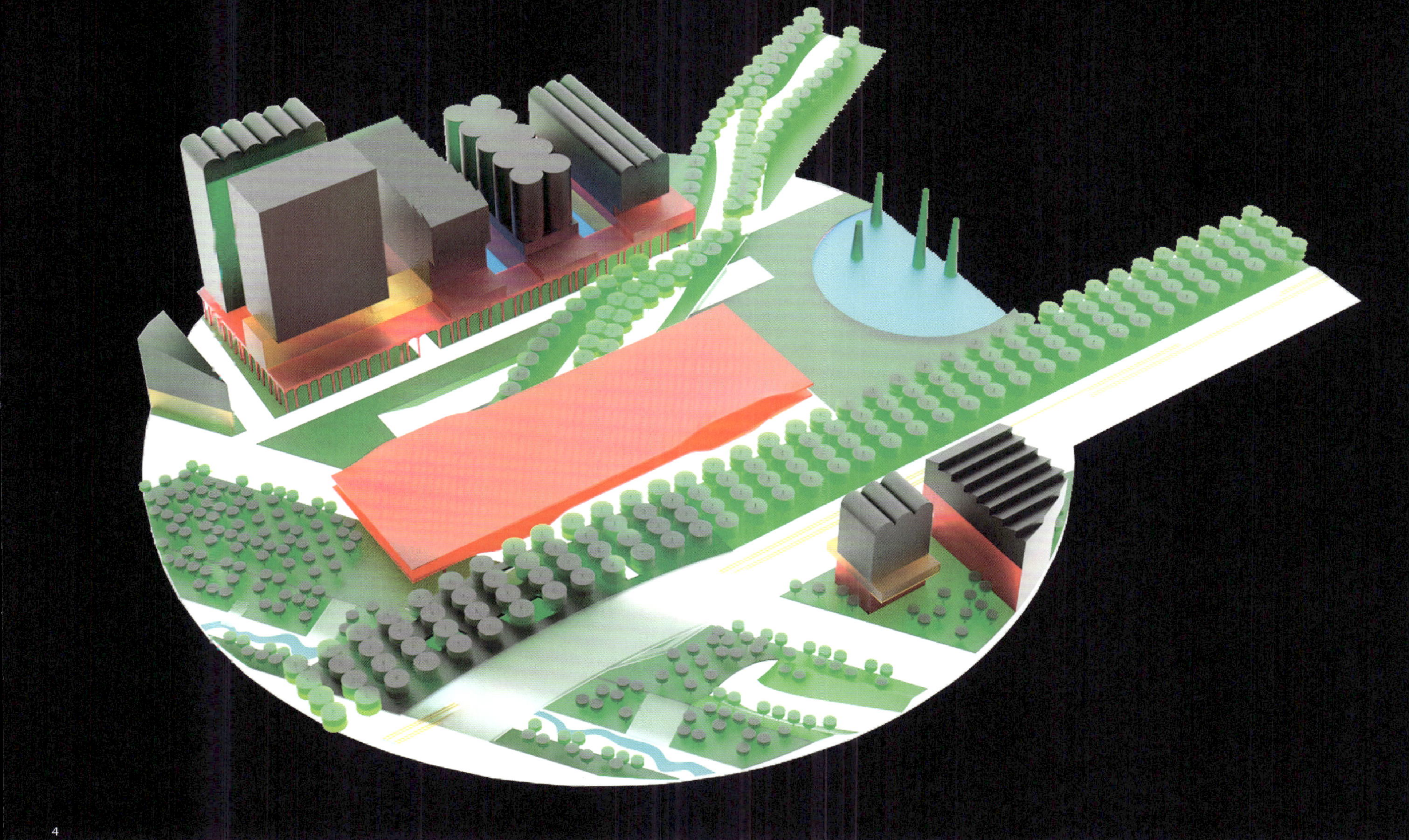

4

5

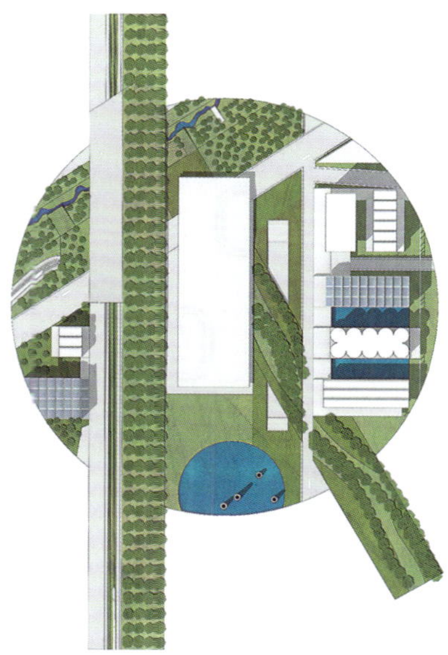

6

4 Between industry and landscape, the emergence of new possibilities.
5 New perspectives and urban promenades.
6 Nature enters the industrial site.

1

2

3

1 Weaving the blue thread of water with the green thread of plantings.
2 The site gradually regenerates along the waterside.
3 The landscape draws the map.

4

5

6

4 A more complex density, with greater diversity.
5 New structural arteries crisscross the neighborhoods.
6 Nature remains present, spreading not on the ground but at altitude.

"ÎLE DE LA CITÉ 2040" MISSION

PARIS, FRANCE

2016

"A territory that forgets its map starts to forget its own geography."

The "Île de la Cité 2040" project was an initiative of French President François Hollande, a study of the future of this institutional territory through the year 2040. The Île de la Cité is an urban paradox: in the center of Paris but outside the world. There is no map, no coherent interpretation of this territory that is the very foundation of Paris. Absent this shared narrative, the "Île de la Cité 2040" mission proposed a project based on an essential gesture: redrawing the map of the island. The maps are concrete fictions combining true and false and current, past, or imaginary projects, in order to produce a possible narrative of the future: mapping as a way of revealing the island's invisible strata, opening up and entering the voids, reconnecting spaces, revealing the potential of underground space, proposing new passages, moving freely between institutions, monuments, and public spaces, rediscovering a relationship with the Seine. The project is based on a meticulous process of montage and collage, following a creative logic close to the palimpsest. Each drawing is a fragment of reflection, a way of re-examining reality and provoking new visions for this frozen island. This project is a manifesto that recasts the geography of the heart of the capital to give it a future as the heart of Paris, beating once again.

1 Collage by DPA. The monumentality of the various entities on the Île de la Cité gives the illusion of high density, whereas in reality this is one of the least densely populated areas in Paris.

2 Fiction by DPA. The island-monument is the emblematic visual of the "Île de la Cité 2040" mission, symbolically associating the island with a ship, a metaphor for its singularity and unity.

3 Reclaiming the south banks.

4 Presentation model, 2016.

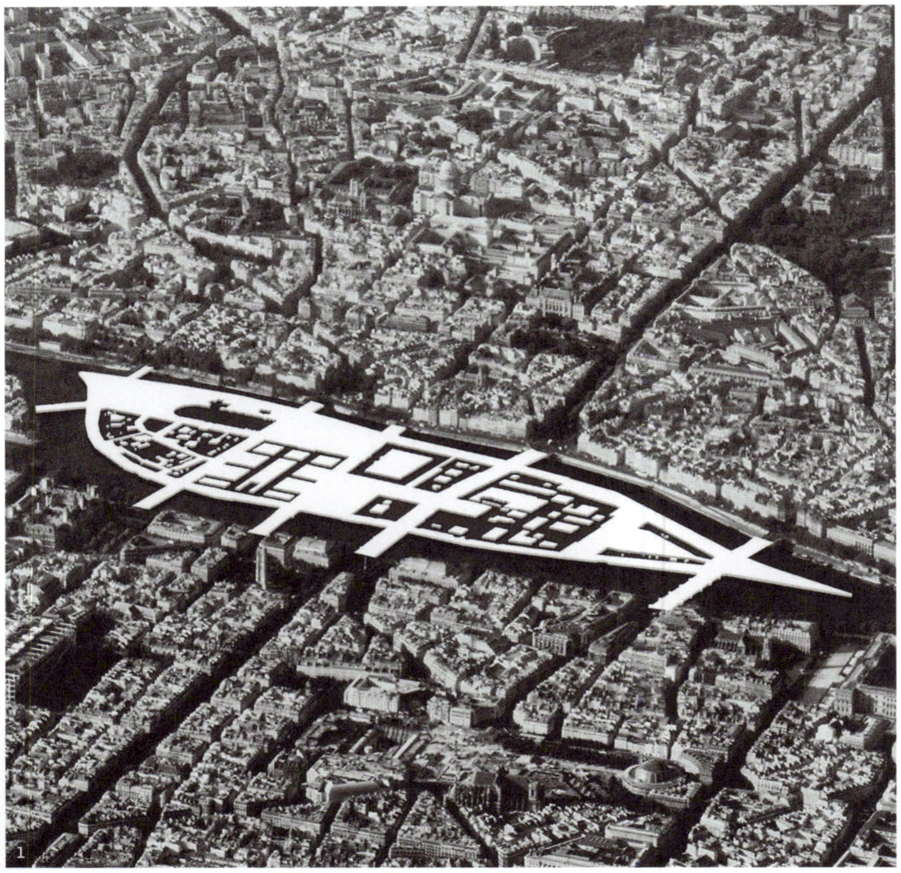

1

2

3

4

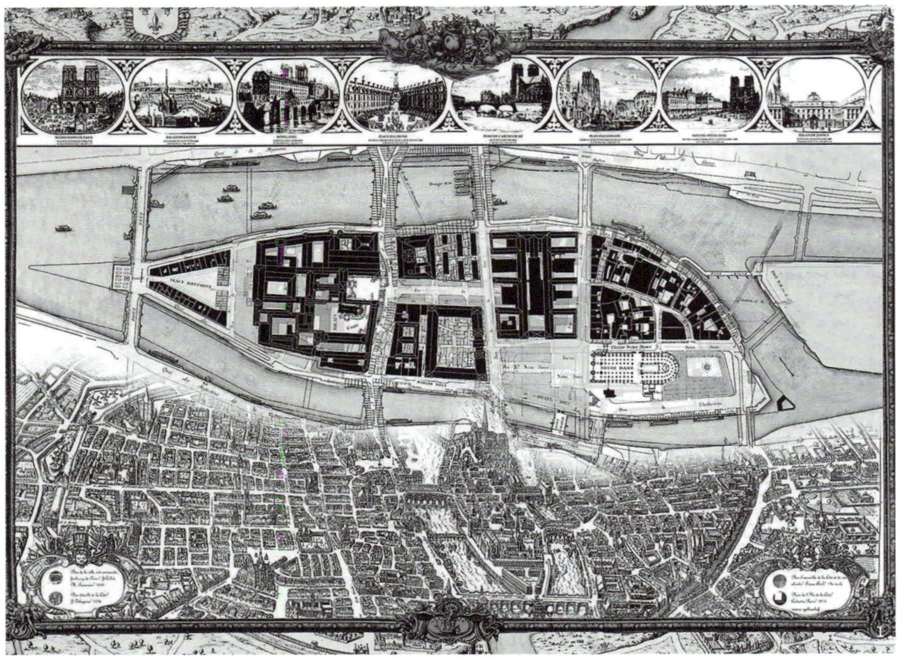

2

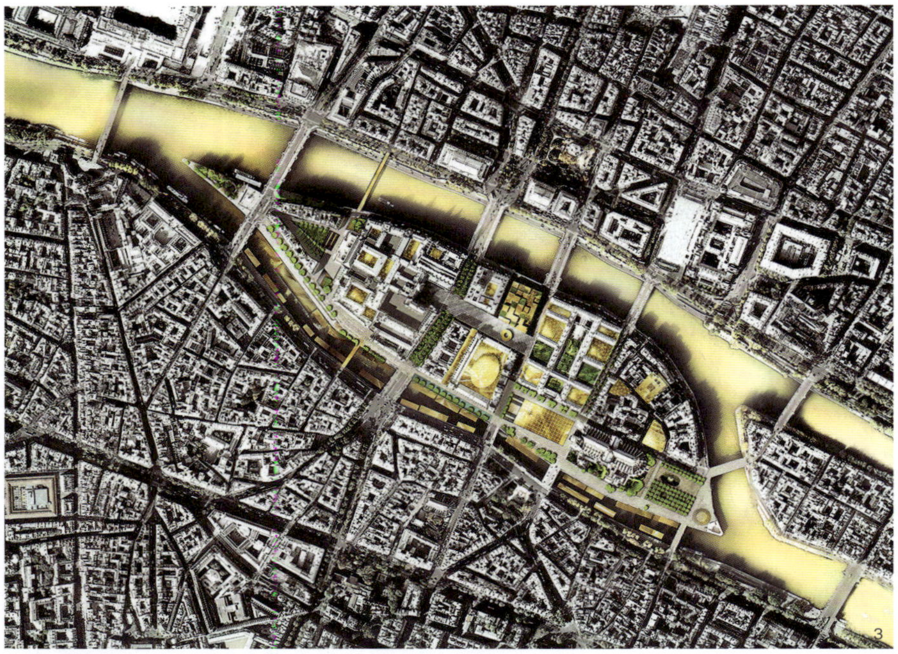

3

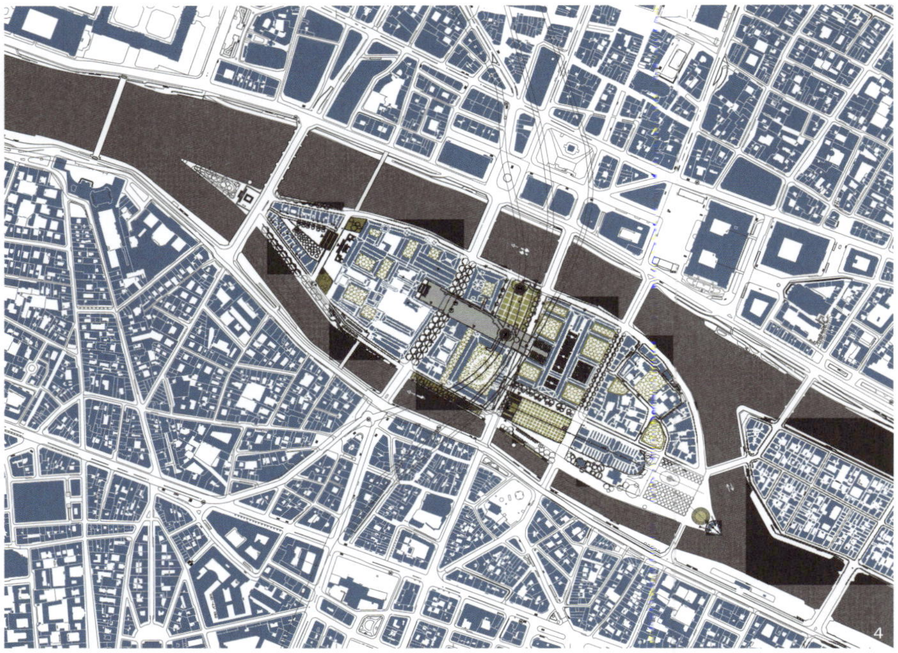

4

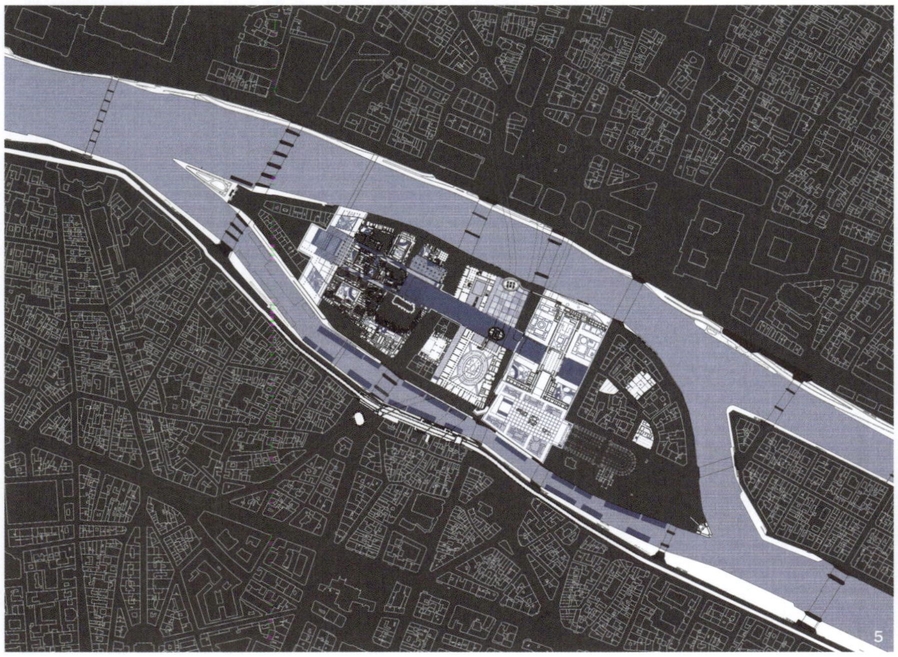

5

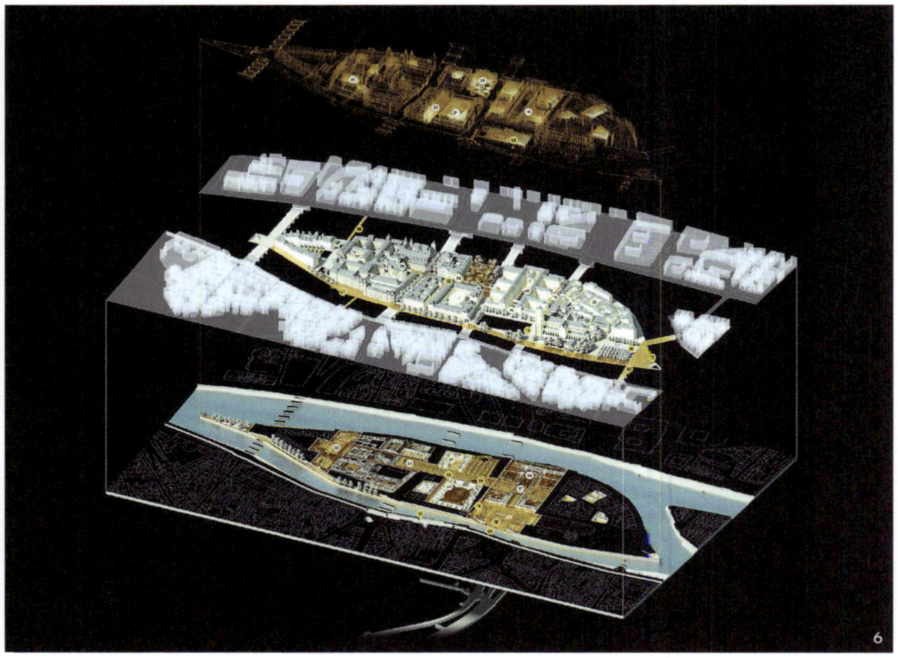

6

“Architecture constructs voids,
time turns them into places,
inhabitants turn them into stories.”

1 The sedimentary layers of the Île de la Cité are represented by the superimposition of three cadastral maps from three eras: the seventeenth century, the eighteenth century, and the present day.
2 Nature on the island.
3 Orthophotograph.
4 Masses: prospective cadastral plan of the island and its surroundings circa 2040.
5 Monument island. Plan of underground levels in 2040: the aim is to reappropriate underground spaces and optimize flows between the different parts of the island.
6 Monument island. Intervention strategies: this map illustrates the project's 35 key proposals across the three layers of the projected island in 2040: the underside, the stone island (existing buildings), and the glass island (contemporary additions).
7 Monument island. Program: a series of commitments concerning the future uses of the island for 2040. Distinction between cultural, public, and activity hubs on one side, and public spaces on the other.

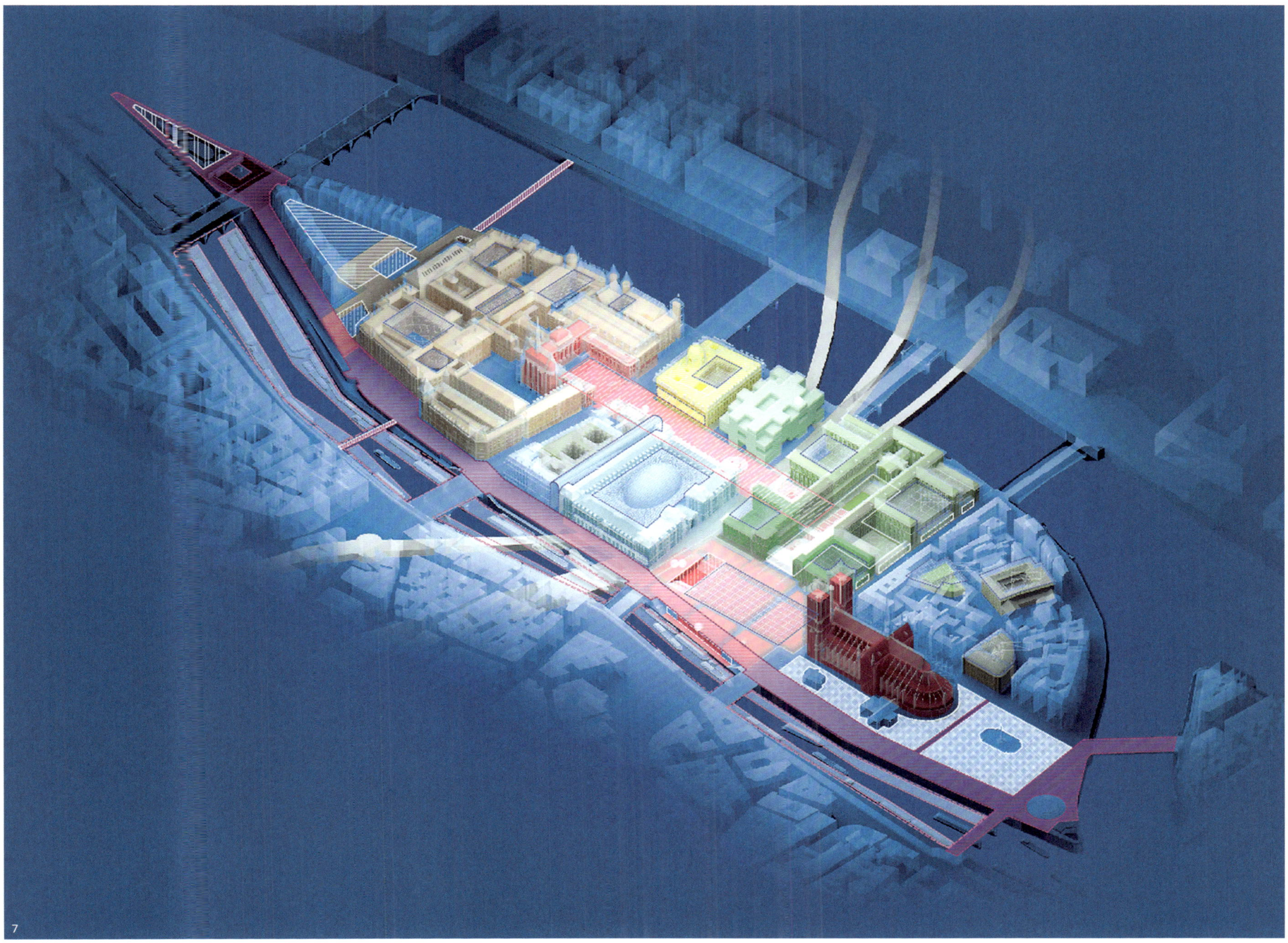
7

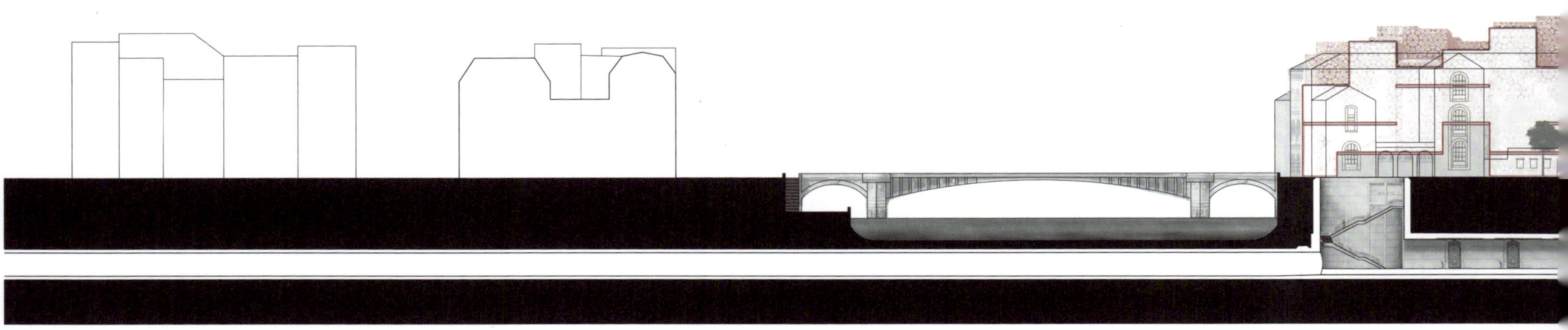

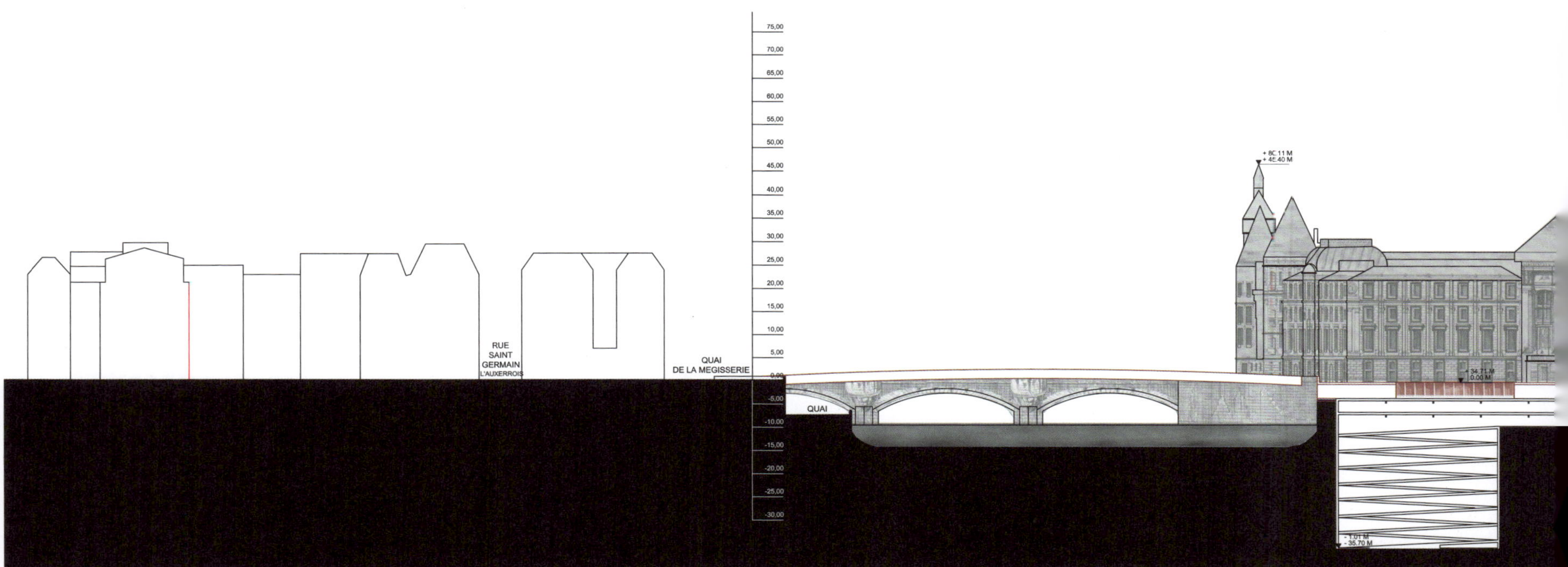
75,00
70,00
65,00
60,00
55,00
50,00
45,00
40,00
35,00
30,00
25,00
20,00
15,00
10,00
5,00
0,00
-5,00
-10,00
-15,00
-20,00
-25,00
-30,00
RUE
SAINT
GERMAIN
L'AUXERROIS
QUAI
DE LA MEGISSERIE
QUAI
+ 34.71 M
0.00 M
- 1.01 M
- 35.70 M

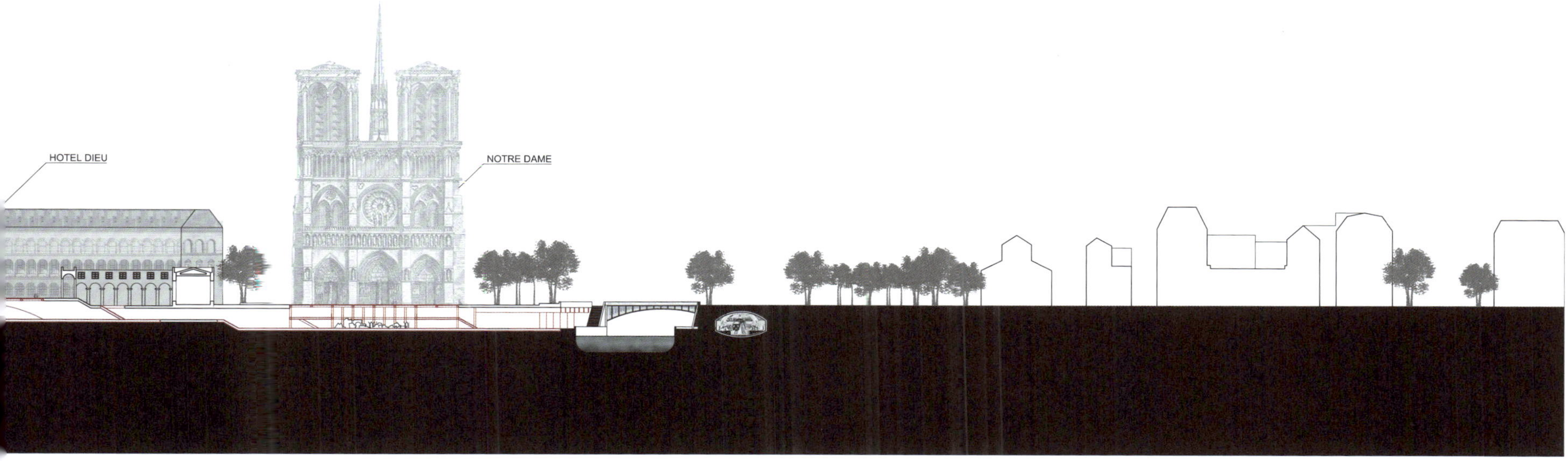
HOTEL DIEU
NOTRE DAME

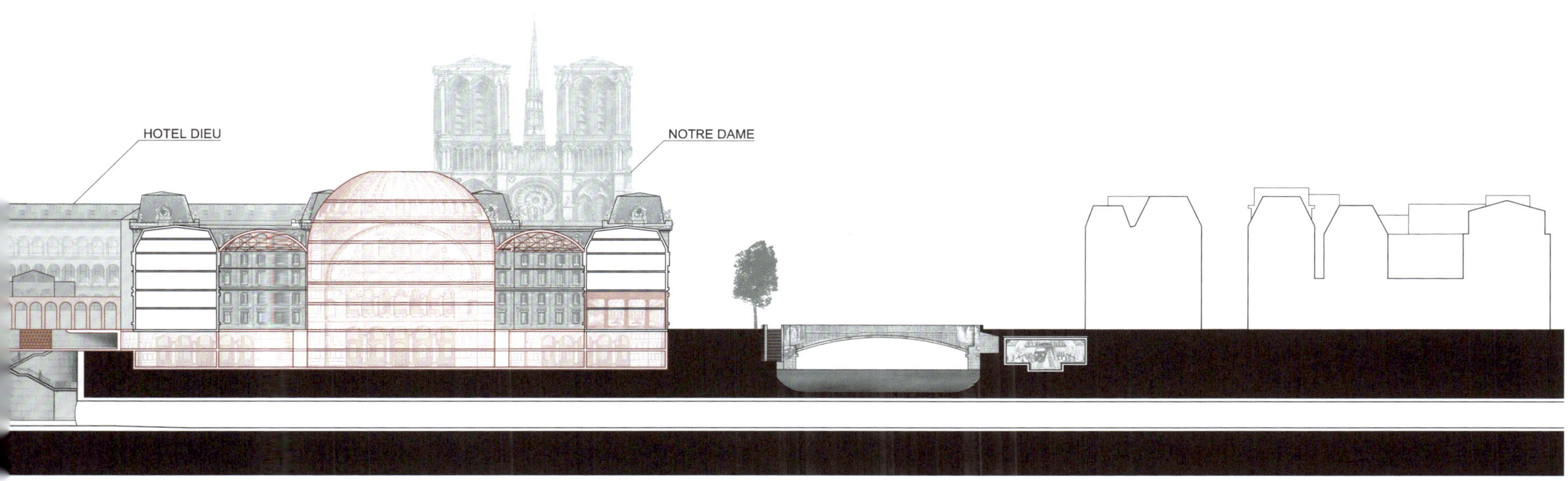
HOTEL DIEU
NOTRE DAME

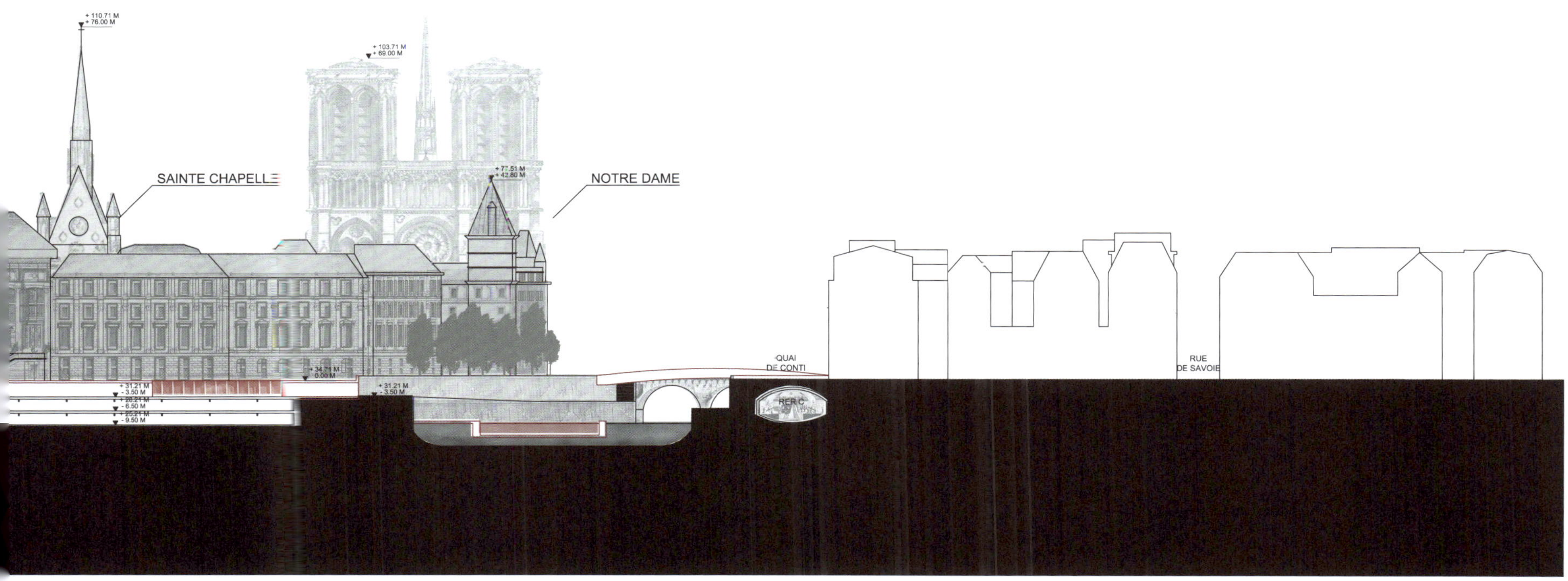
+ 110.71 M
+ 76.00 M
+ 103.71 M
+ 69.00 M
SAINTE CHAPELLE
+ 77.51 M
+ 42.80 M
NOTRE DAME
+ 34.71 M
0.00 M
+ 31.21 M
- 3.50 M
- 6.50 M
+ 25.21 M
- 9.50 M
+ 31.21 M
- 3.50 M
QUAI
DE CONTI
RER C
RUE
DE SAVOIE

1

2

3

4

5

“Architecture is indebted
to urban civility, it translates
the demands of the commons.”

1 Fiction by DPA. Place Dauphine. The creation of a low plaza linking the new entrance to the Palais de Justice to the Place Dauphine reshapes access and flows.
2 Place Dauphine, 2010.
3 Fiction by DPA. Place Dauphine. The layering of contemporary architectural interventions with the emblematic spaces of the Île de la Cité proposes a reflection on heritage as a legacy that accepts the future.
4 Fiction by DPA. The Pont Saint-Louis is a social space between the Île de la Cité and the Île Saint-Louis.
5 Pont Saint-Louis, 2010.

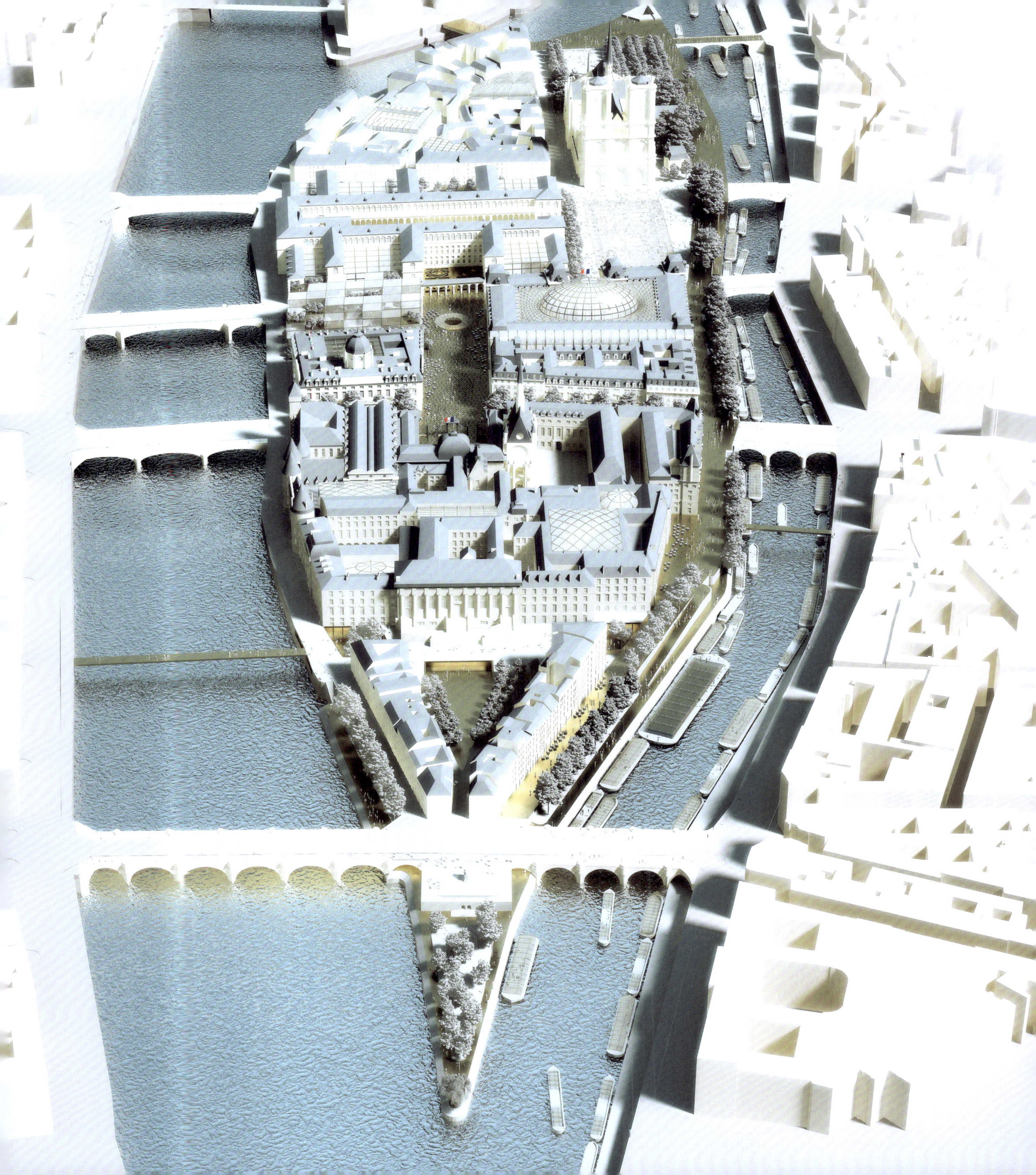

"HOTEL MÉTROPOLE"

PARIS, FRANCE

2013

"Hôtel Métropole" is a project born of the Atelier International du Grand Paris, which set out to rethink the fragmented map of the Greater Paris metropolis around its major facilities—hospitals, prisons, courts, universities, shopping malls, etc. These form a constellation of places that are essential but lack structures to live in. Wherever the metropolis forces people to go, "Hôtel Métropole" invents the right to stay. This is a response to forced mobility, to the displacements of real life, both endured and chosen, which are reshaping the geography of the metropolis. Around these functions, the "Hôtel Métropole" concept imagines a network of places to sleep, remote work, receive guests, take shelter, a room open to the metropolis, designed to reduce forced travel and to inhabit the map of uses in a different way. More than just a building, it is a minimal, flexible system that can be installed on existing buildings awaiting change: a way of infiltrating the urban, of accompanying real lives, without imposing a single urban model. Fictional cartographies offer a reading of metropolitan constellations to draw a map of services rather than a political or administrative map. Because the metropolis is not a continuous city, but a collection of scattered histories and needs. It is a tool for making the city habitable where it is not, a project for urbanity that is mobile, pragmatic, and profoundly human.

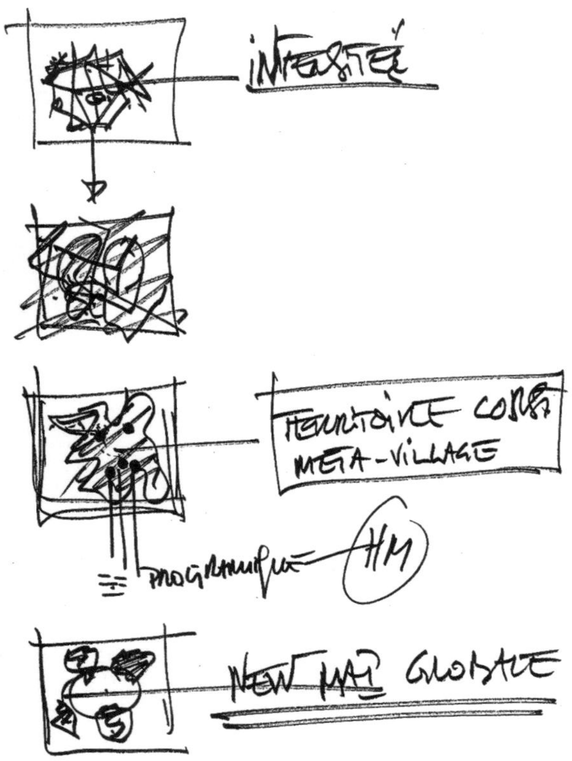

1

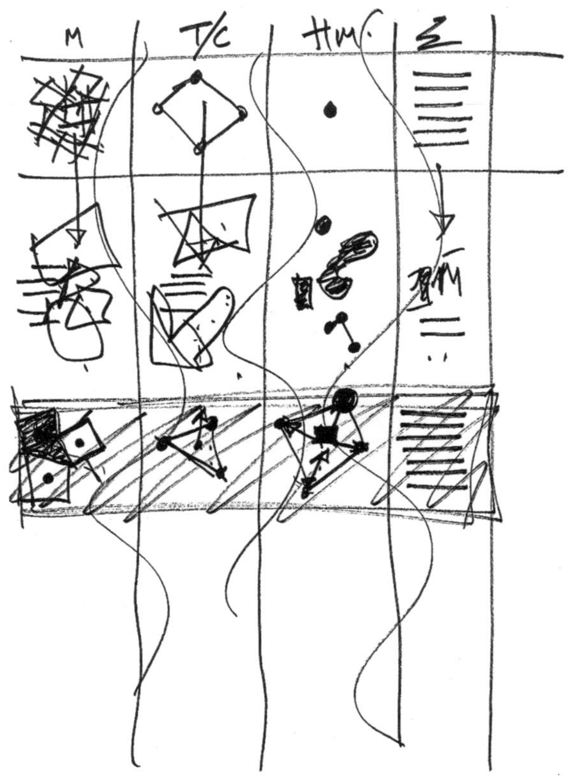

2

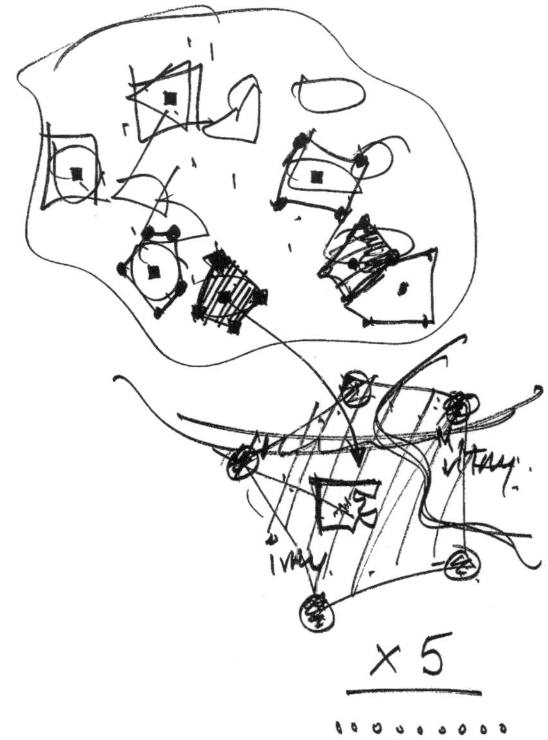

3

1-3 Sketches, 2013.
4 Fiction by DPA. “Hôtel Métropole : superimposed sections of the Pos[illegible] u Louvre and Villejuif-Gustave Rous[illegible]ation.

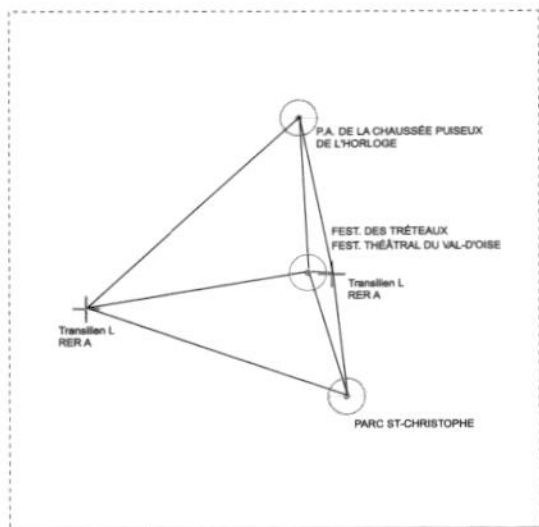
001.B2 CERGY, VAUREAL, OSNY

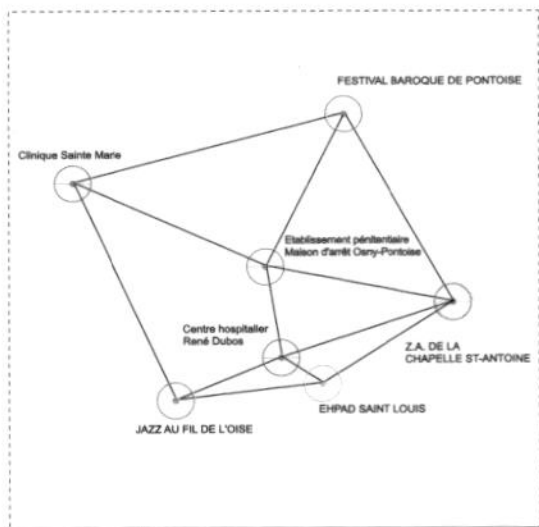
002.B3 OSNY, PONTOISE, ENNERY

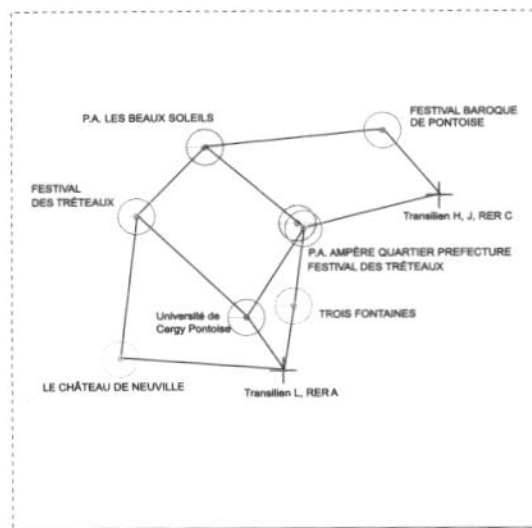
003.B3 PONTOISE, CERGY

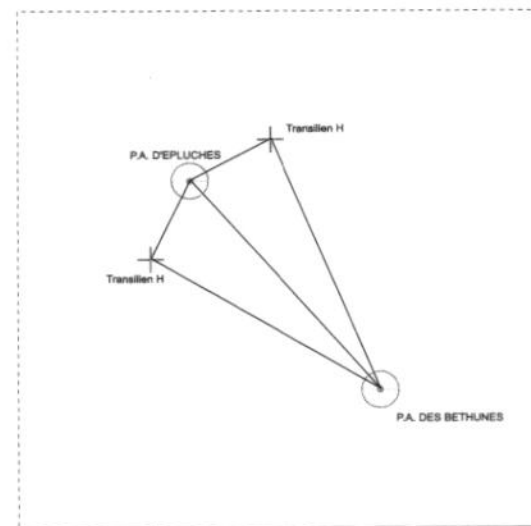
004.B3 SAINT-OUEN-L'AUMONE

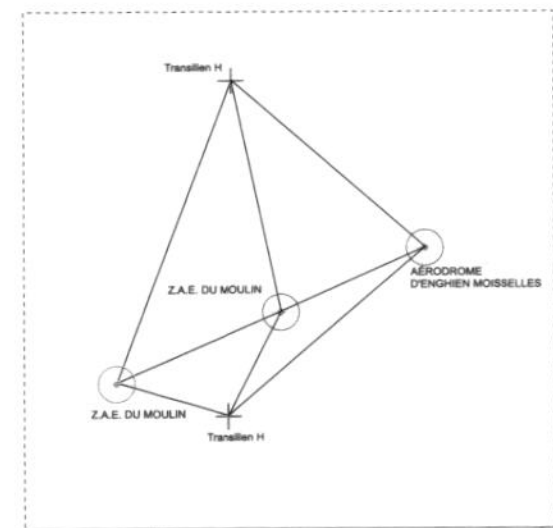
005.B6 MOISSELLES, ATTAINVILLE, BAILLET-EN-FRANCE, EZANVILLE

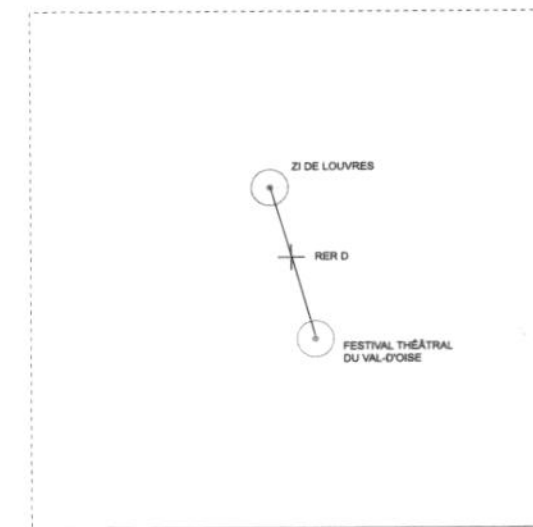
006.B9 LOUVRES

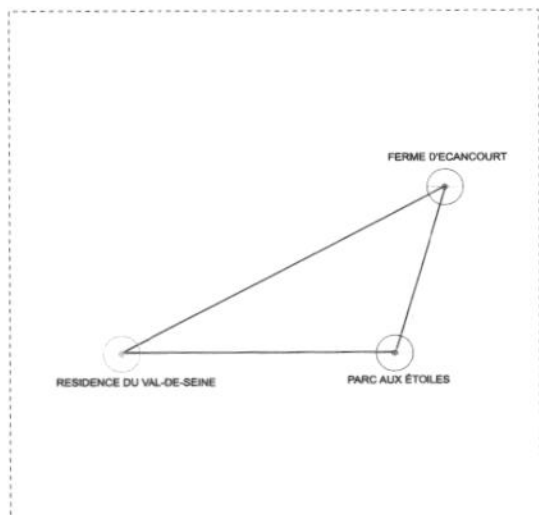
007.C1,C2 JOUY-LE-MOUTIER, TRIEL-SUR-SEINE

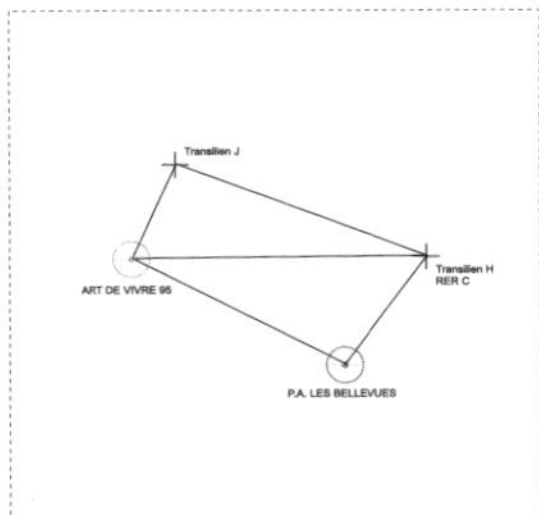
008.C3 SAINT-OUEN-L'AUMONE, ERAGNY

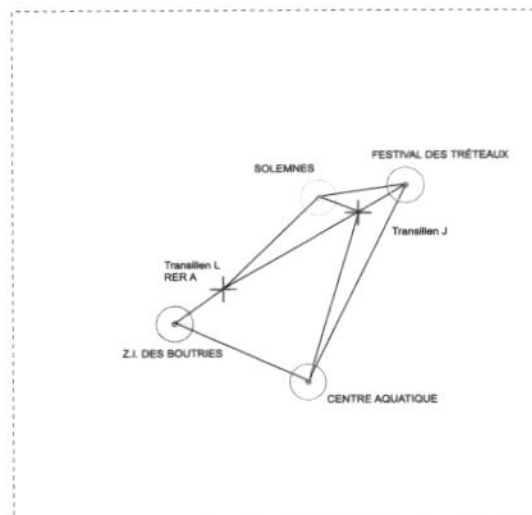
009.C3 CONFLANS-SAINTE-HONORINE, ERAGNY

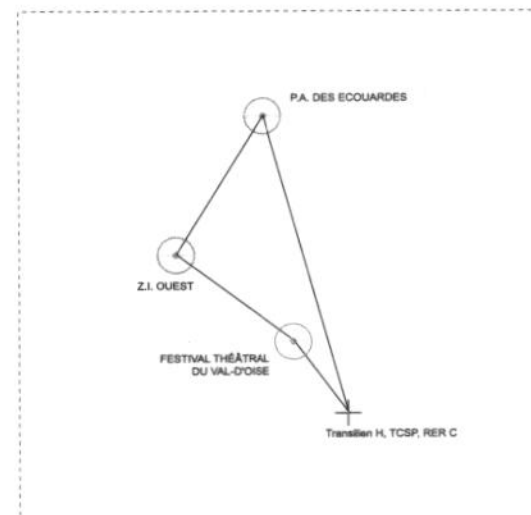
010.C4 BEAUCHAMP

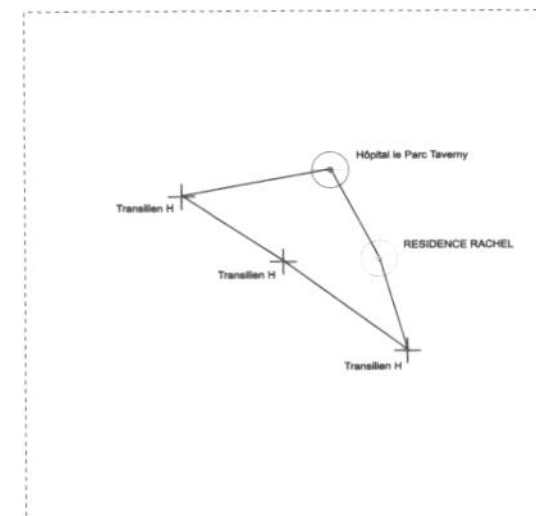
011.C5 TAVERNY

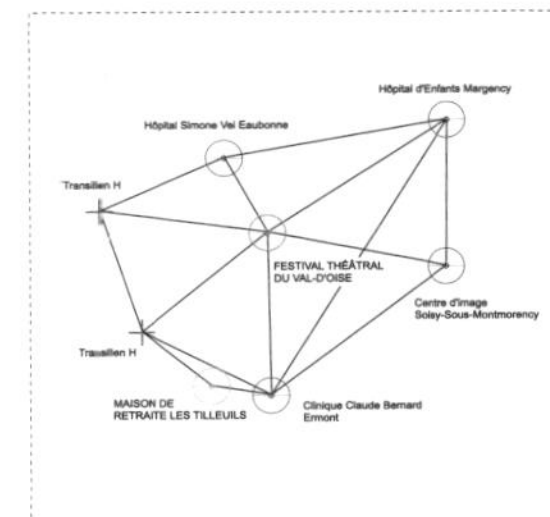
012.C5,C6 MARGENCY, EAUBONNE, ERMONT

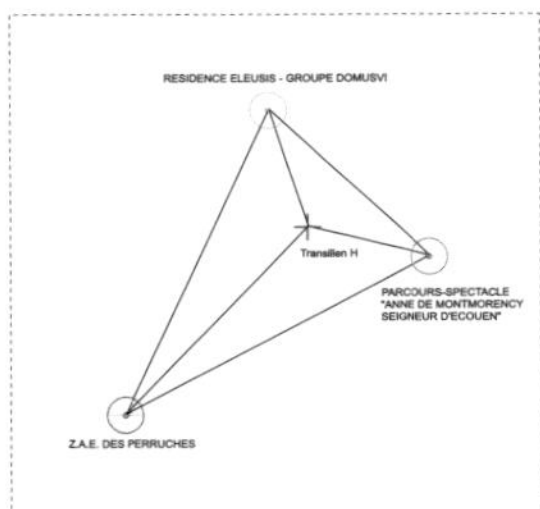
013.C7 SAINT-BRICE-SOUS-FORET, ECOUEN, PISCOP

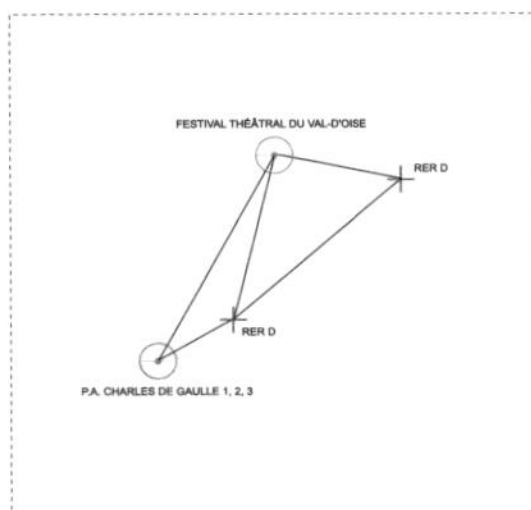
014.C8 GOUSSAINVILLE

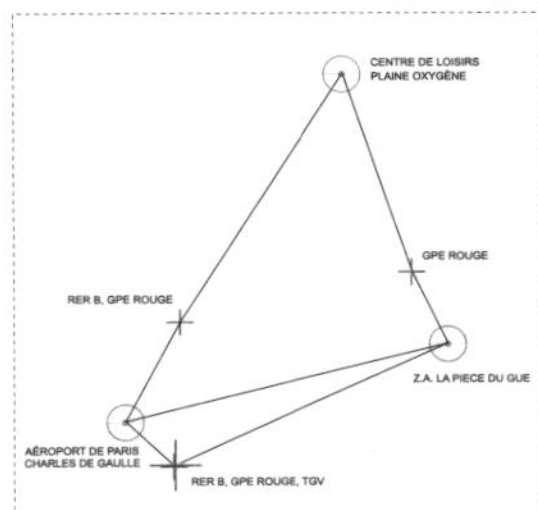
015.C10 LE MESNIL AMELOT

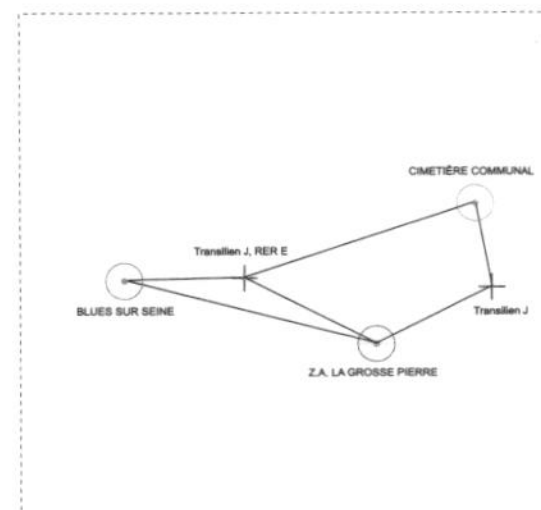
016.D1 VERNEUIL-SUR-SEINE, TRIEL-SUR-SEINE, VERNOUILLET

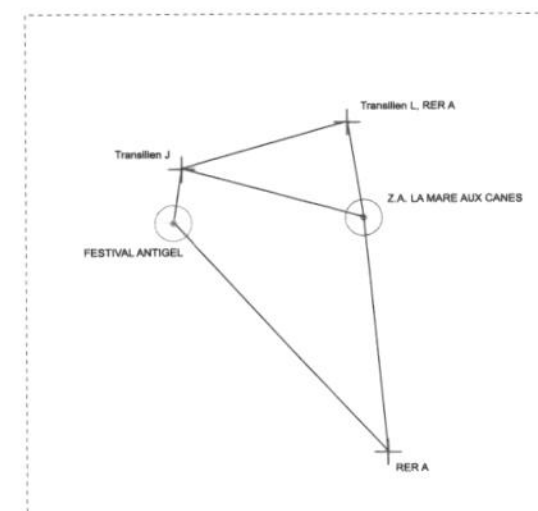
017.D2,D3 ANDRESY

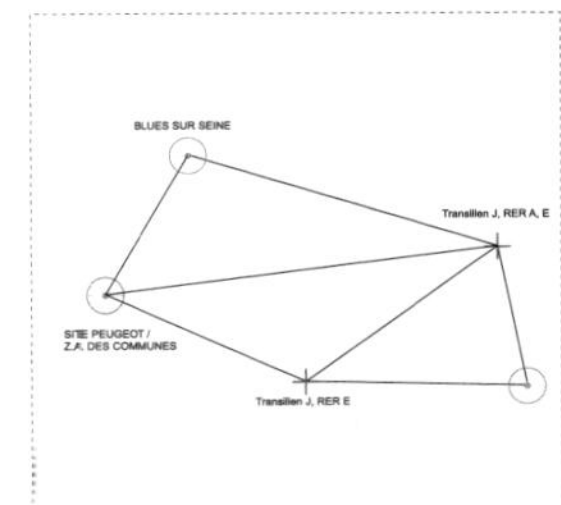
018.D2,D3 ACHERES, POISSY, SAINT-GERMAIN-EN-LAYE

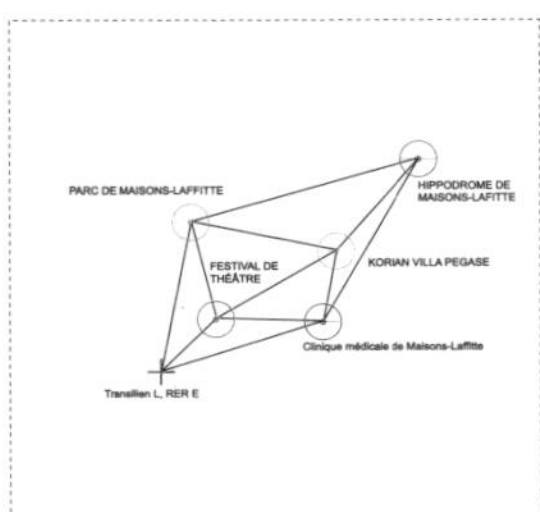
019.D4 MAISONS-LAFFITTE

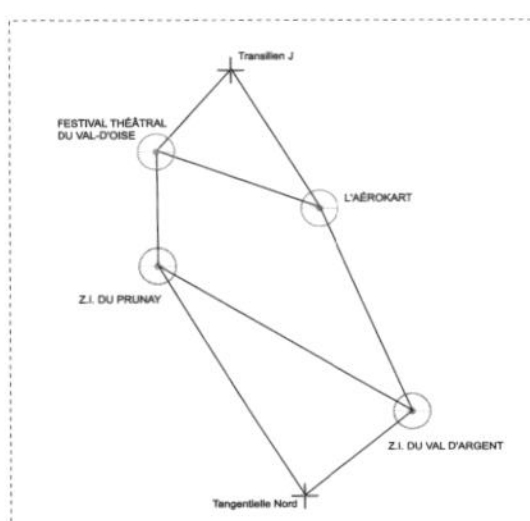
020.D4 LA FRETTE-SUR-SEINE, SARTROUVILLE, ARGENTEUIL

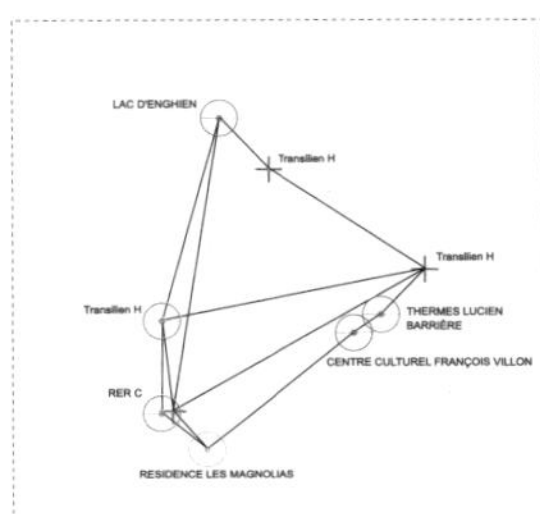
021.D6 SAINT-GRATIEN, ENGHIEN-LES-BAINS

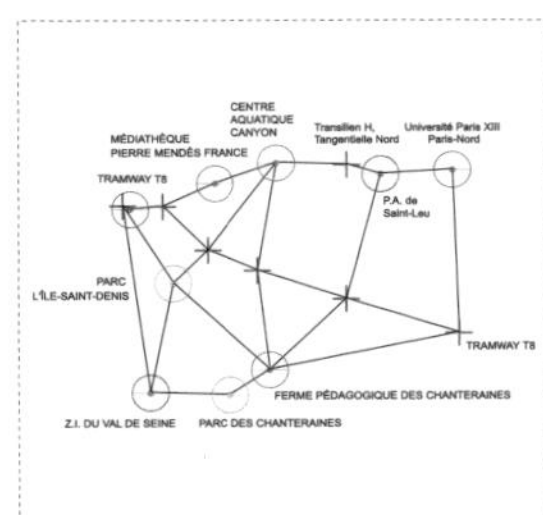
022.D6, E6 VILLETANEUSE, EPINAY, VILLENEUVE-LA-GARENNE

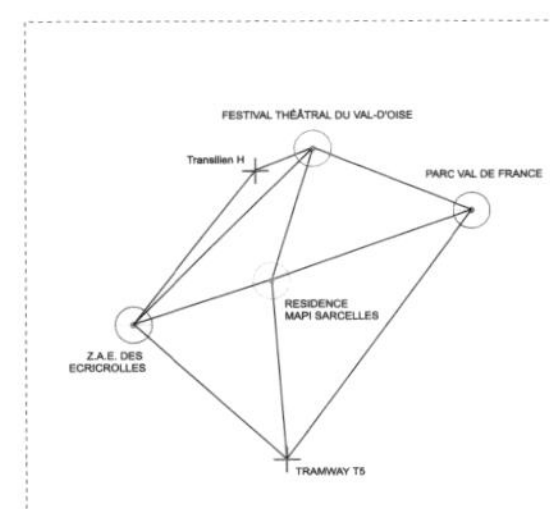
023.C7,D7 GROSLAY, SARCELLES

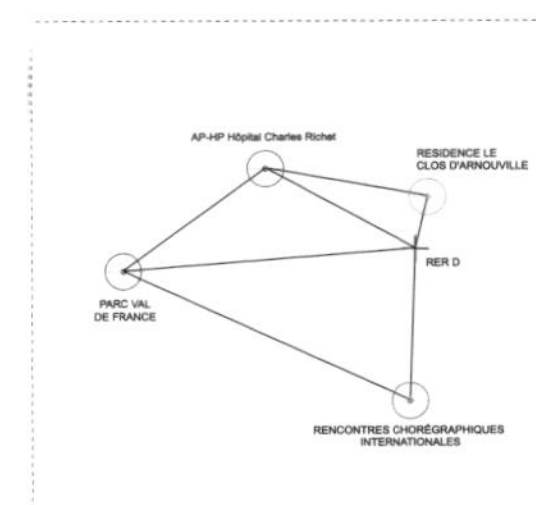
024.C7,D7 SARCELLES, VILLIERS-LE-BEL, ARNOUVILLE-LES-GONESSE

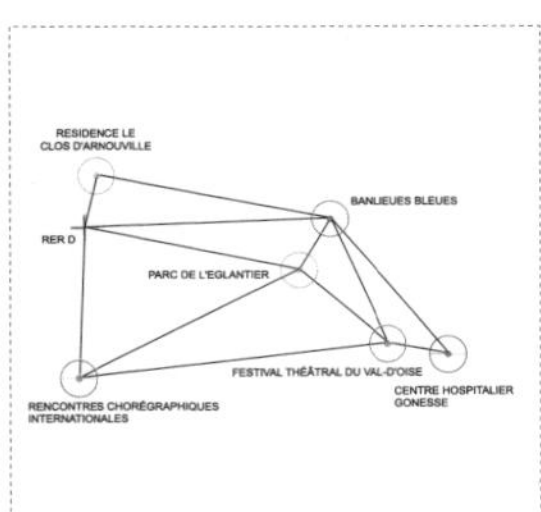
025.C8,D8 ARNOUVILLE-LES-GONESSE, GONESSE

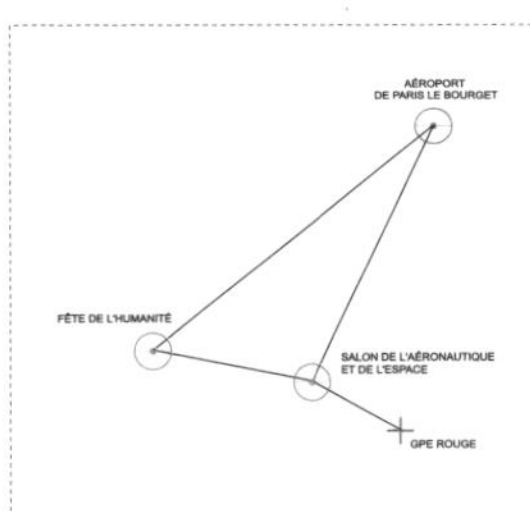
026.D8 DUGNY, BONNEUIL-EN-FRANCE, LE BOURGET

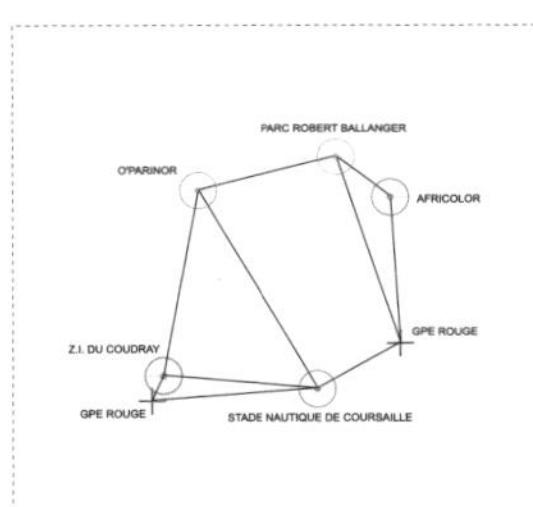
027.D8,D9 LE BLANC-MESNIL, AULNAY-SOUS-BOIS

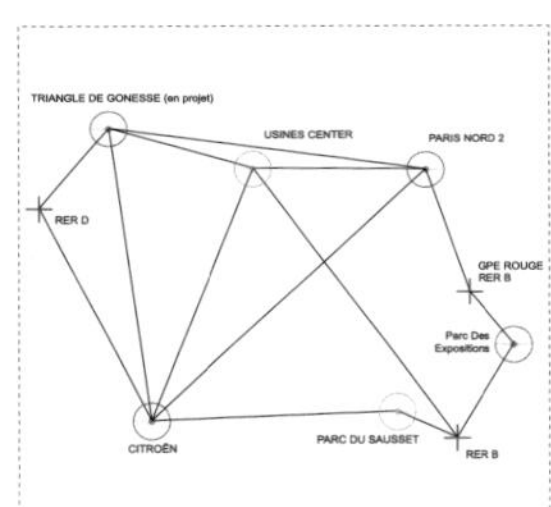
028.D8,D9 GONESSE, VILLEPINTE, AULNAY-SOUS-BOIS

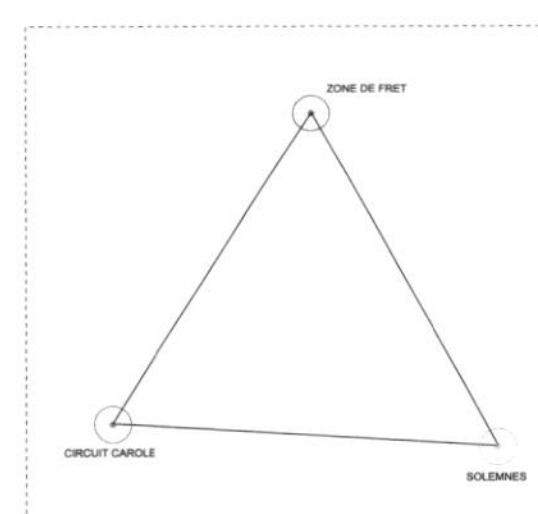
029.D9,D10 TREMBLAY-EN-FRANCE

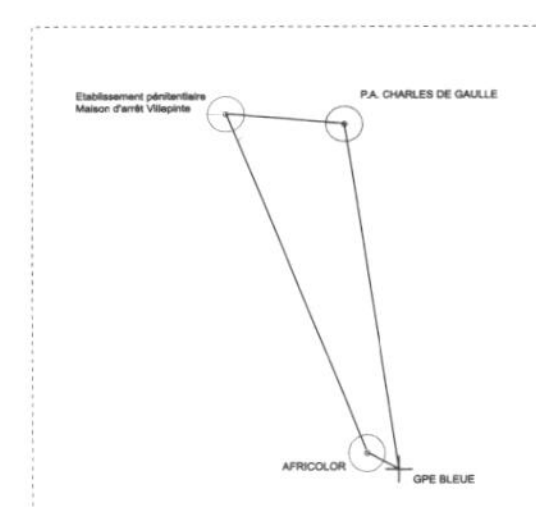
030.D10 TREMBLAY-EN-FRANCE, VILLEPINTE

The "Atlas of 100 Possible Situations" presents a method of reading and representing the territory through 100 possible situations. It highlights 100 territories to be reoccupied, 100 polarities to be strengthened, 100 urban ecosystems to be made more autonomous, more visible, and better able to concentrate urbanization efforts. Faced with the fragmented immensity of the Île-de-France region (1,301 municipalities, 317 cantons, 8 departments, and nearly 150 intercommunal entities), this atlas sketches out a different narrative of Greater Paris, made up of 100 places, 100 constellations to orient oneself, 100 priorities for building a shared vision of the metropolis.

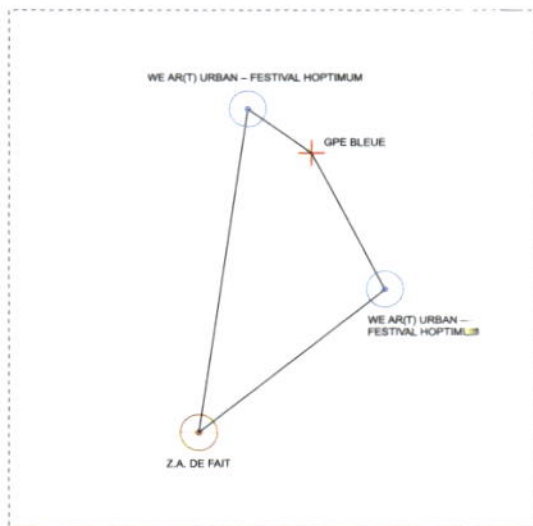

031. D10,E10 VILLEPARISIS, MITRY-MORY

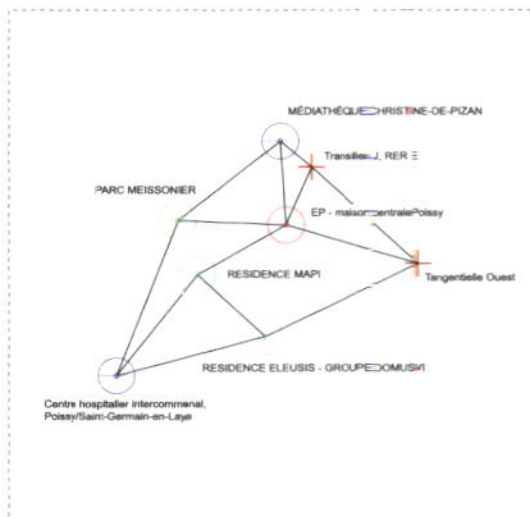

032. E2 POISSY

033. E5 ARGENTEUIL

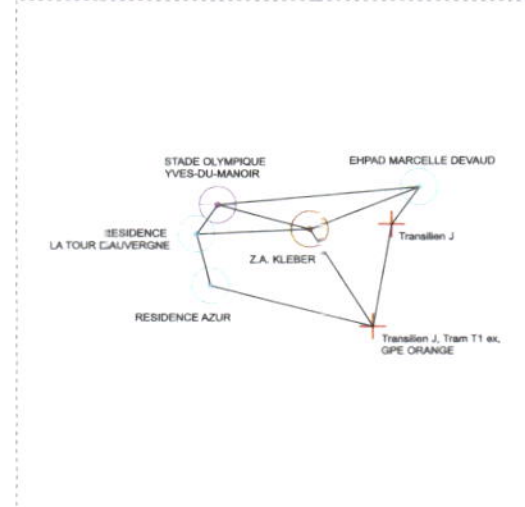

034. E5 COLOMBES

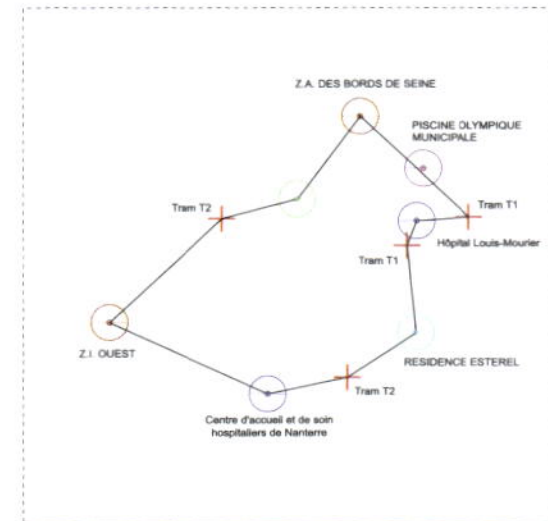

035. E5 BEZONS, COLOMBES, NANTERRE

036. E5 COURBEVOIE

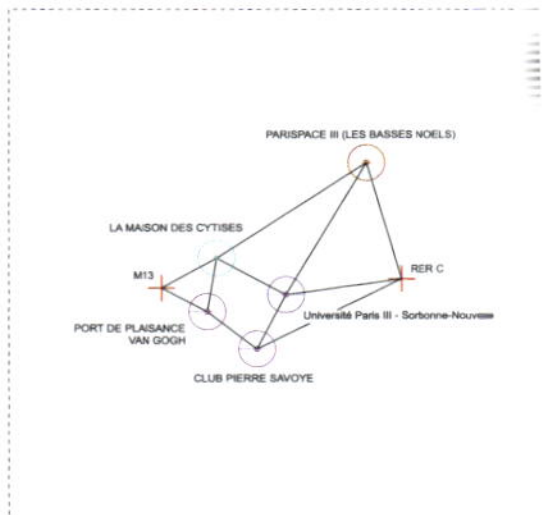

037. E6 GENNEVILLIERS, CLICHY, ASNIERES-SUR-SEINE

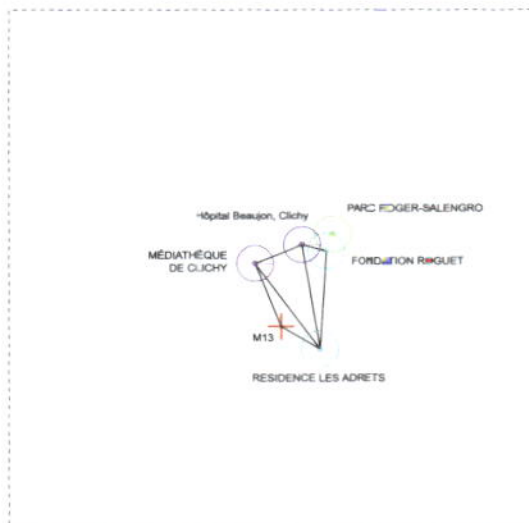

038. E6 CLICHY

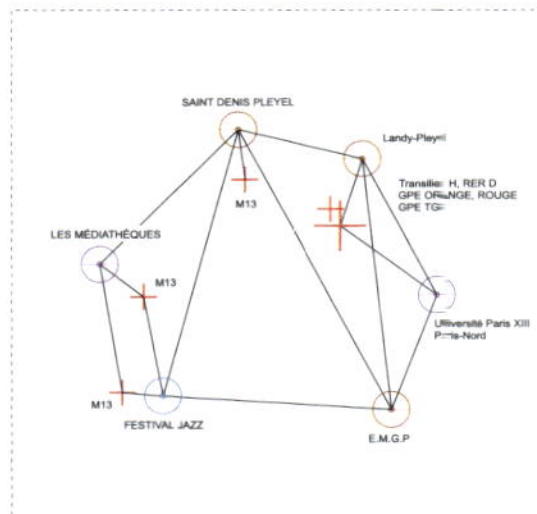

039. E6,E7 SAINT-OUEN, SAINT-DENIS

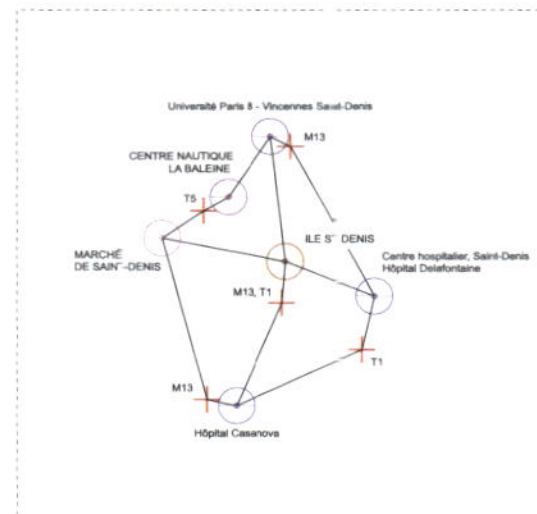

040. E7 SAINT-DENIS

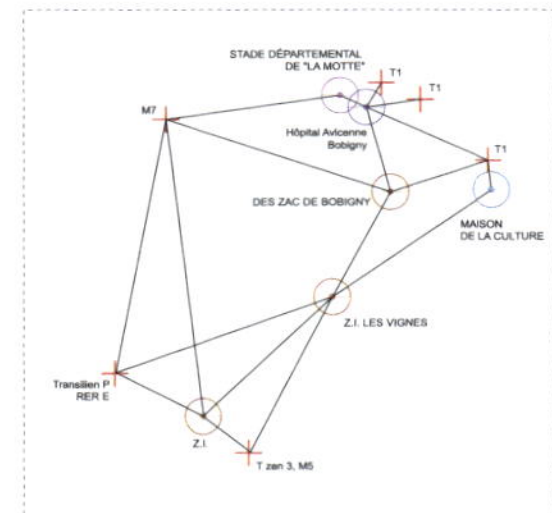

041. E7,E8 AUBERVILLIERS, PANTIN, BOBIGNY

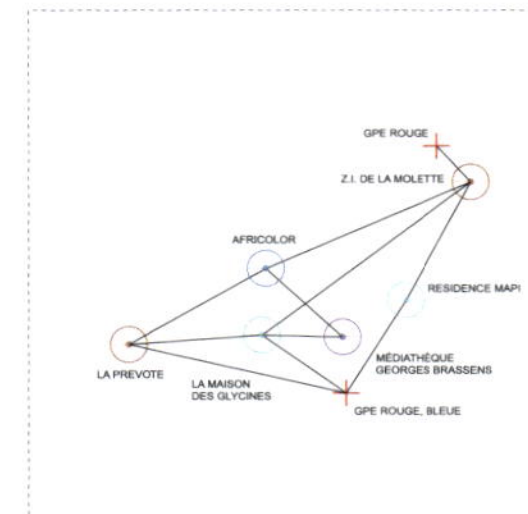

042. E8 DRANCY, LE BOURGET, LA COURNEUVE

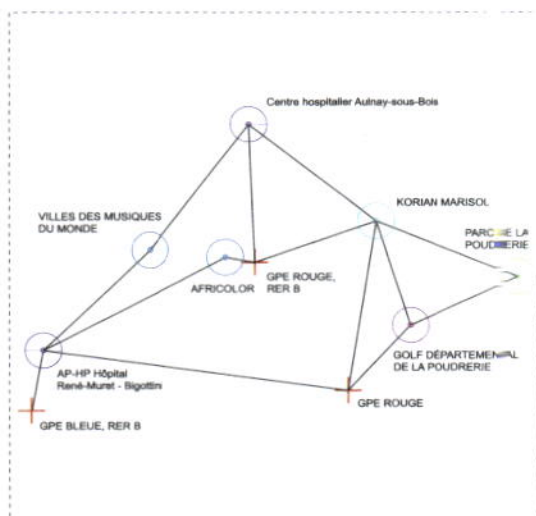

043. E9,E10 SEVRAN

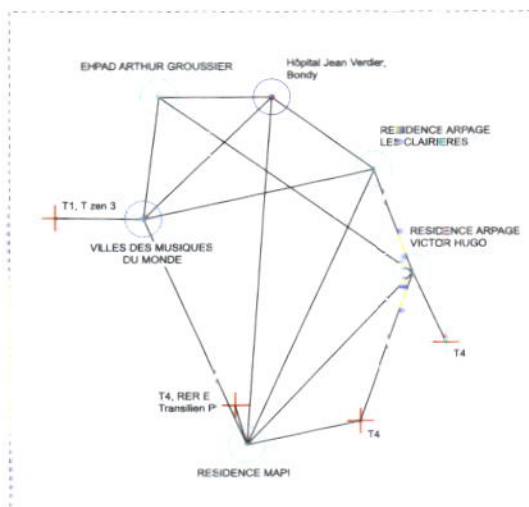

044. E9,F9 BONDY, LES PAVILLONS-SOUS-BOIS

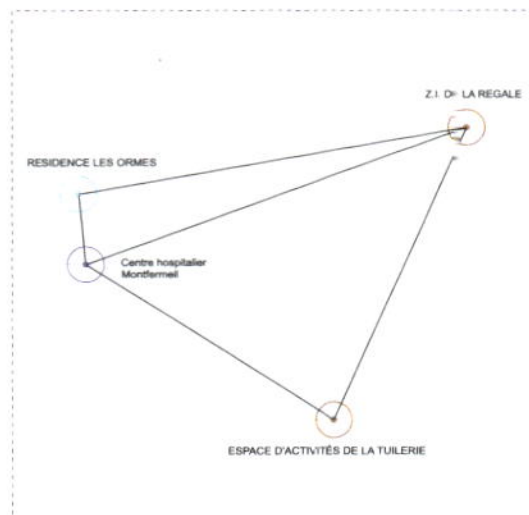

045. E10,F10 CHELLES, MONTFERMEIL, COURTRY

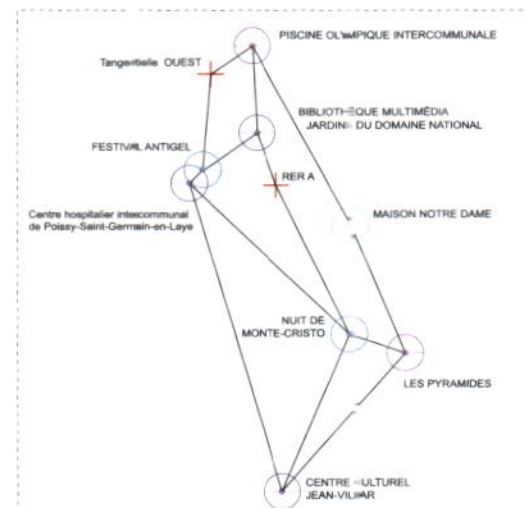

046. F3 SAINT-GERMAIN-EN-LAYE, LE PECQ, MARLY-LE-ROI

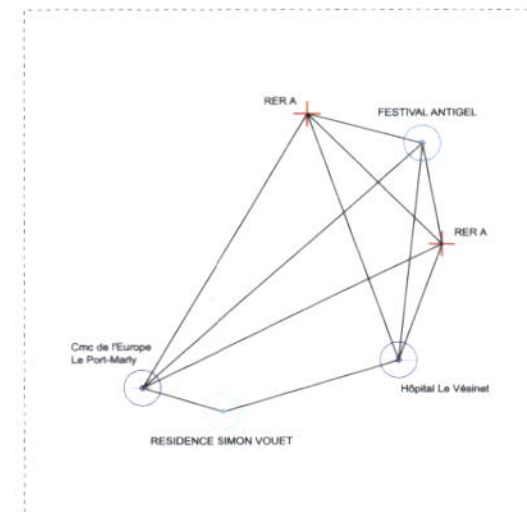

047. F3 LE VESINET, LE PORT-MARLY, CROISSY-SUR-SEINE

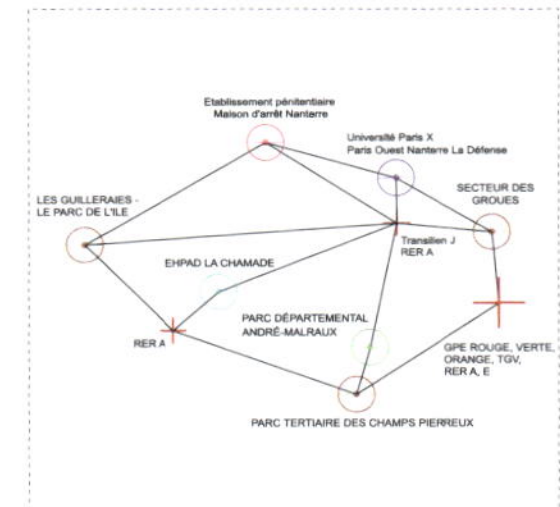

048. F4,F5 NANTERRE

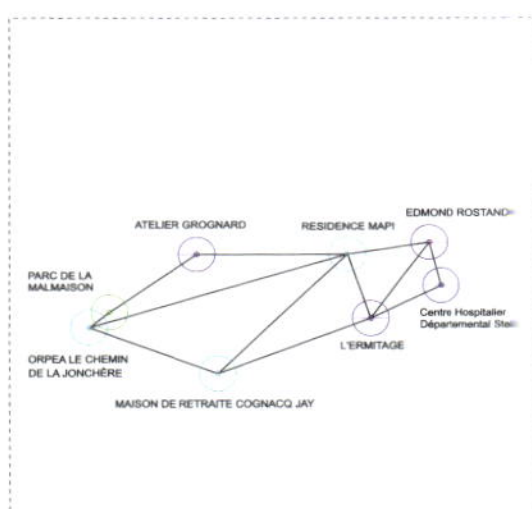

049. F4 RUEIL-MALMAISON

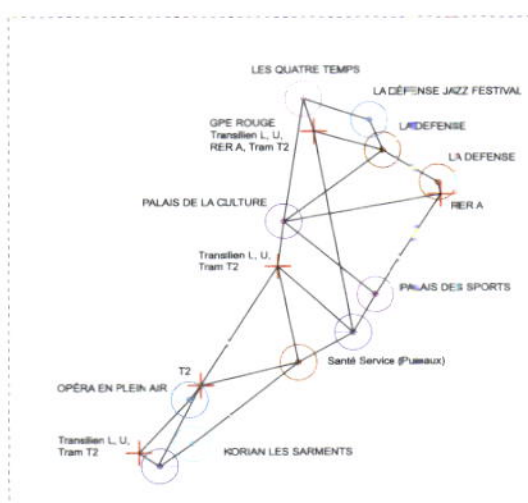

050. F5 PUTEAUX, SURESNES

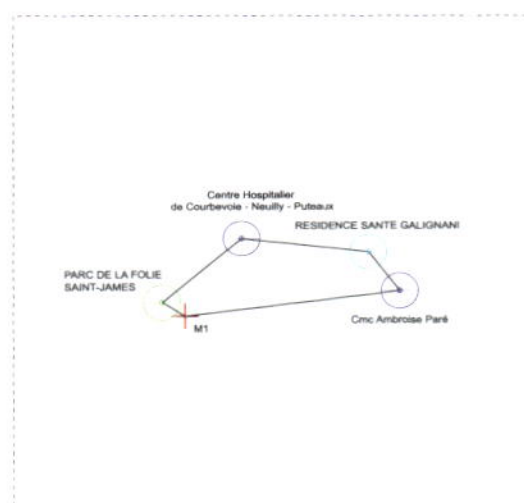

051. F5 NEUILLY-SUR-SEINE

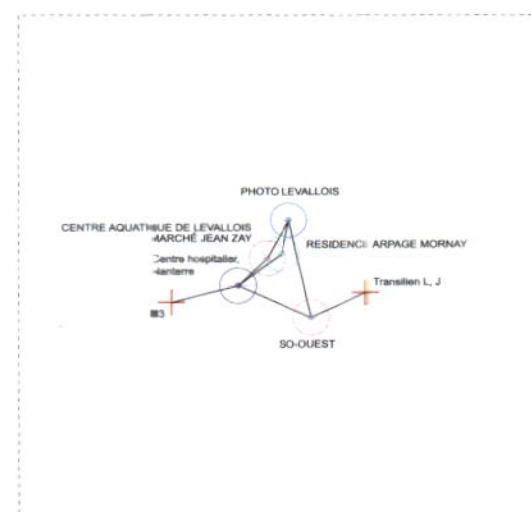

052. F6 LEVALLOIS-PERRET

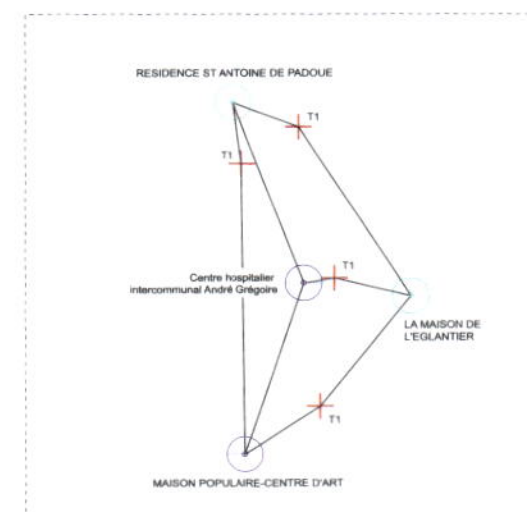

053. F8 MONTREUIL, ROMAINVILLE

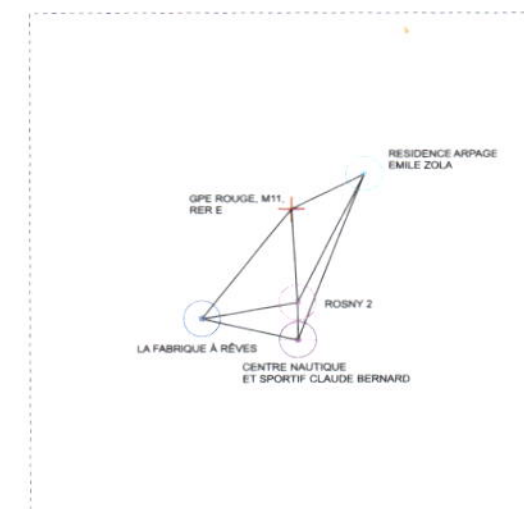

054. F8,F9 ROSNY-SOUS-BOIS

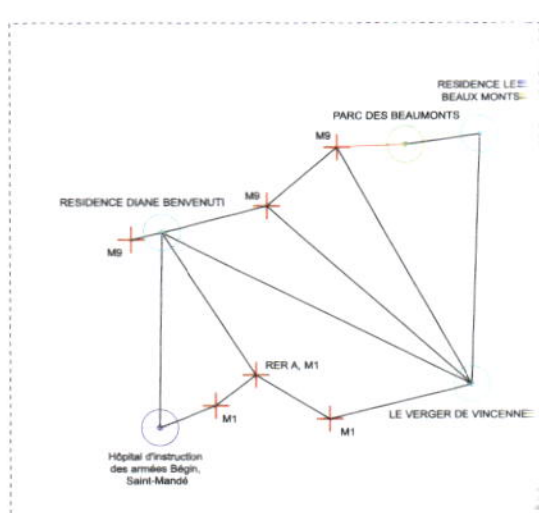

055. F8,G8 MONTREUIL, VINCENNES, FONTENAY-SOUS-BOIS

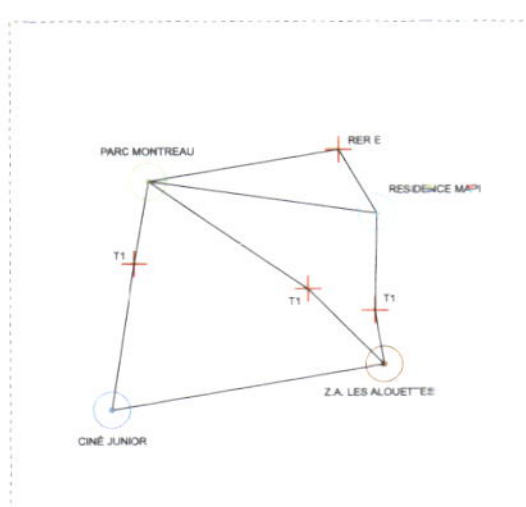

056. F8,F9 MONTREUIL, FONTENAY-SOUS-BOIS

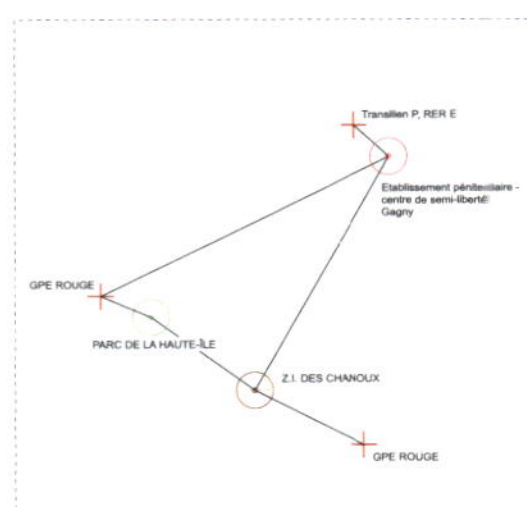

057. F9 NEUILLY-PLAISANCE, NEUILLY-SUR-MARNE

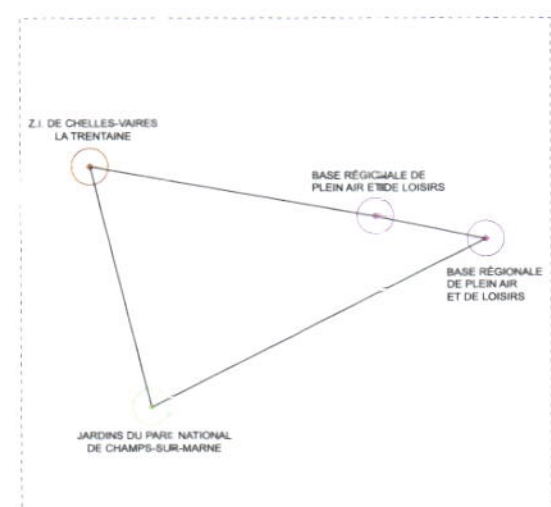

058. F10,F11 CHELLES, CHAMPS-SUR-MARNE, VAIRES-SUR-MARNE

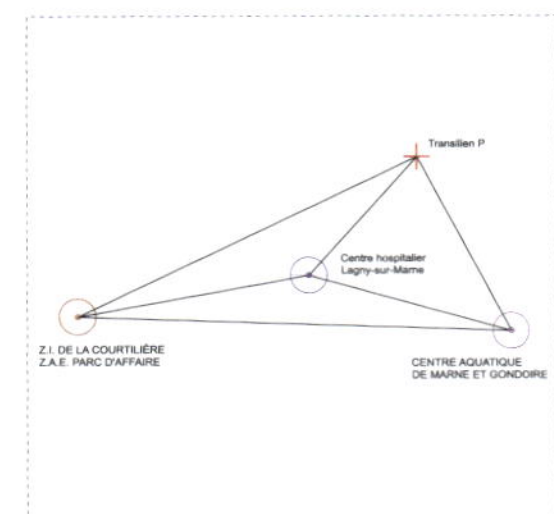

059. F12 LAGNY-SUR-MARNE

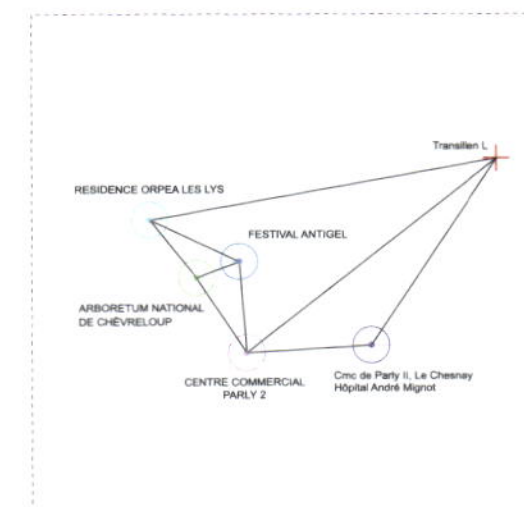

060. G3 ROCQUENCOURT, LE CHESNAY, LA CELLE-SAINT-CLOUD

1

2

3

4

"The map surpasses the plan, just as geography transcends urbanism. Whoever conceives only in terms of the plan is blind to the pulsations of the territory."

1 David Hockney, *The Room Manchester Street*, 1967. Case study 1: Weaving urbanity – Orsay/Gif-sur-Yvette.
2 Edward Hopper, *Morning Sun*, 1952. Case study 2: Metropolitan polarities – Créteil-L'Échat, Créteil.
3 David Hockney, *Christopher Isherwood and Don Bachardy*, 1968. Case study 3: Industrial wasteland – Former Seine paper works, Nanterre.
4 David Hockney, *Model With Unfinished Self-Portrait*, 1977. Case study 4: Rehabilitation – Sagep, Ivry-sur-Seine.

5-8 Schemas of the scenarios developed from the Atlas of 100 Metropolitan Tensions. These chronicles experiment with a system that is both generic and adaptable, rooted in the specificities of the urban typologies encountered. Demonstrating the flexibility of a system capable of building on what is already there—those structures that are present but silent—and weaving new synergies between infrastructures that are geographically close, but disconnected in practice.
9 Map of the "Atlas of 100 Possible Situations." Stressing the metropolitan fabric in order to reveal new urbanities.

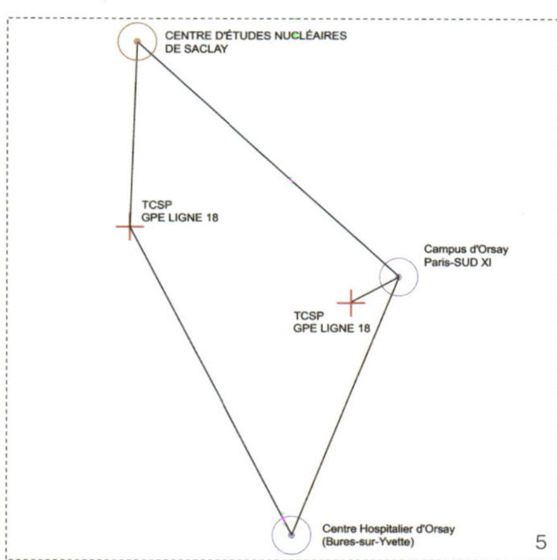

5

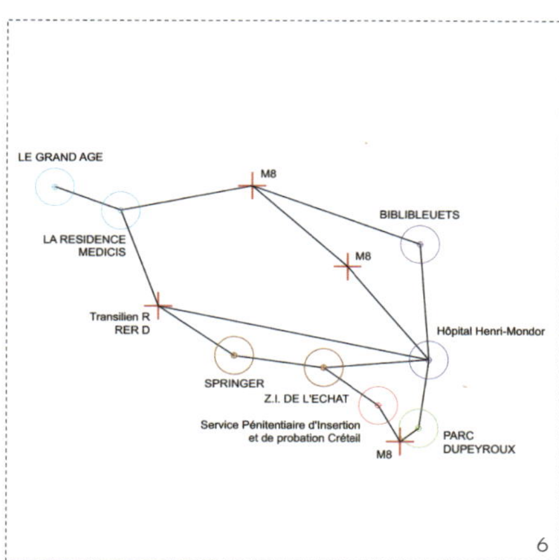

6

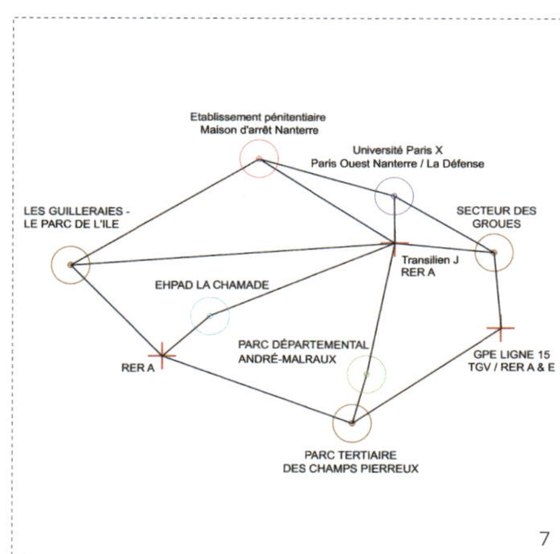

7

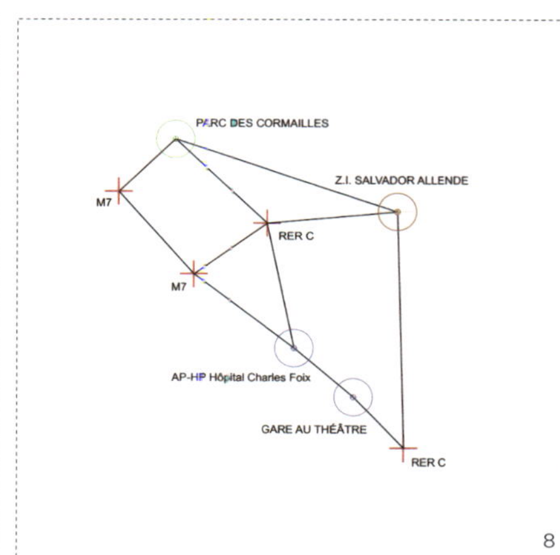

8

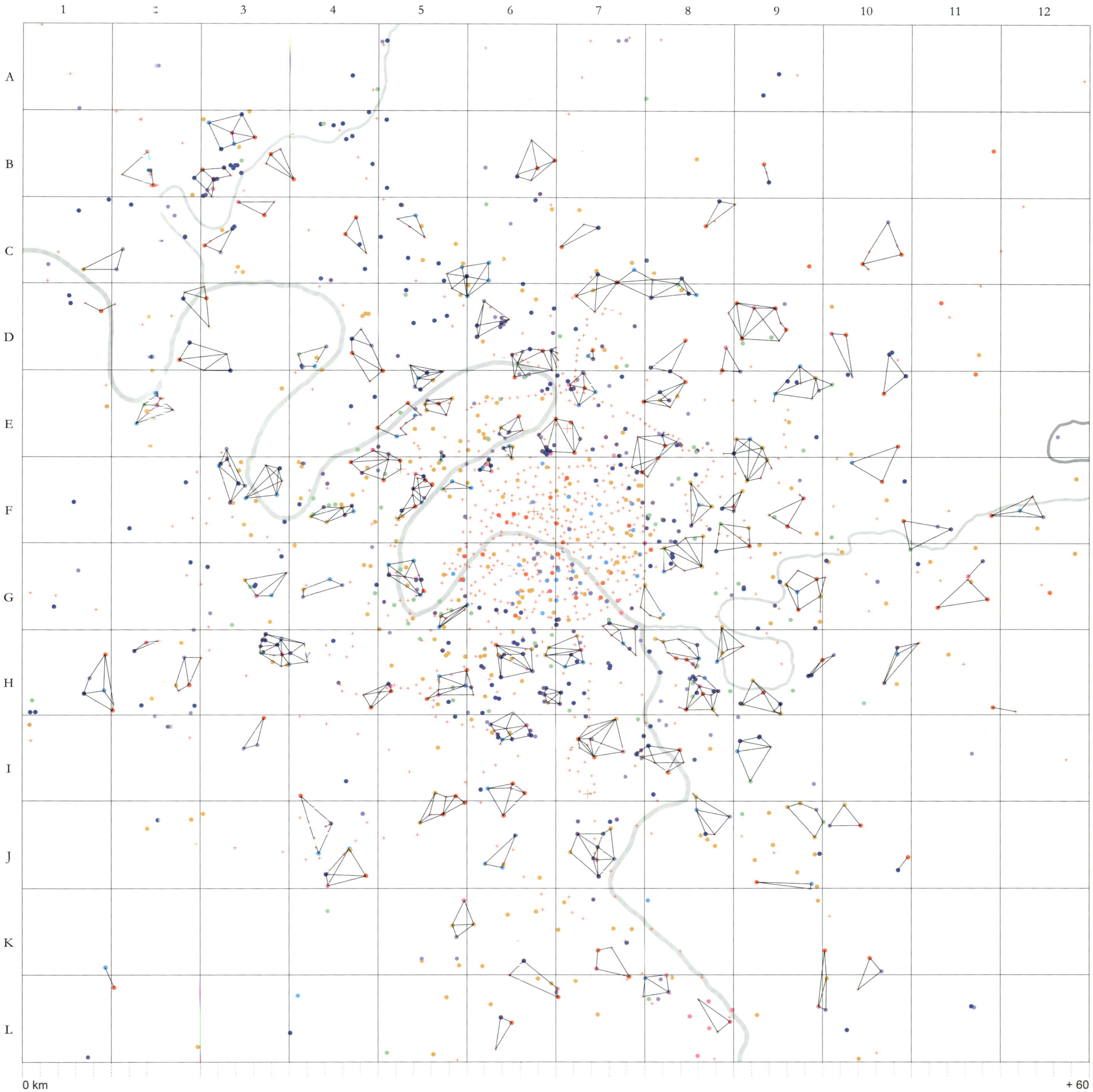

9

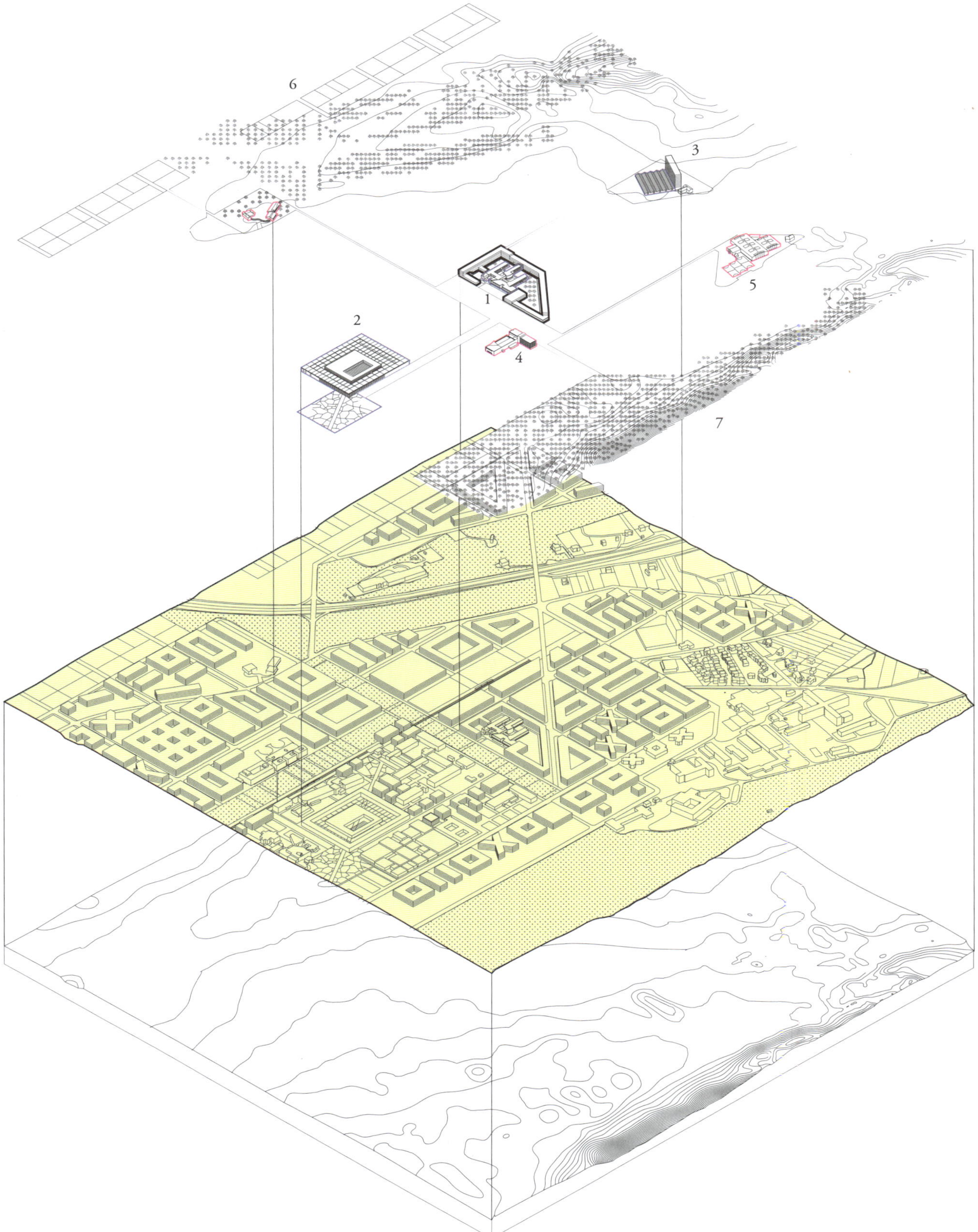

EDUCATION
1. Paris-Sud 11 University
2. École centrale (project)

SERVICES
3. B&B Saclay
4. Forum Engineer
5. Sportsgrounds

TERRITORY
6. South Saclay Plateau
7. La Guyonnerie wood

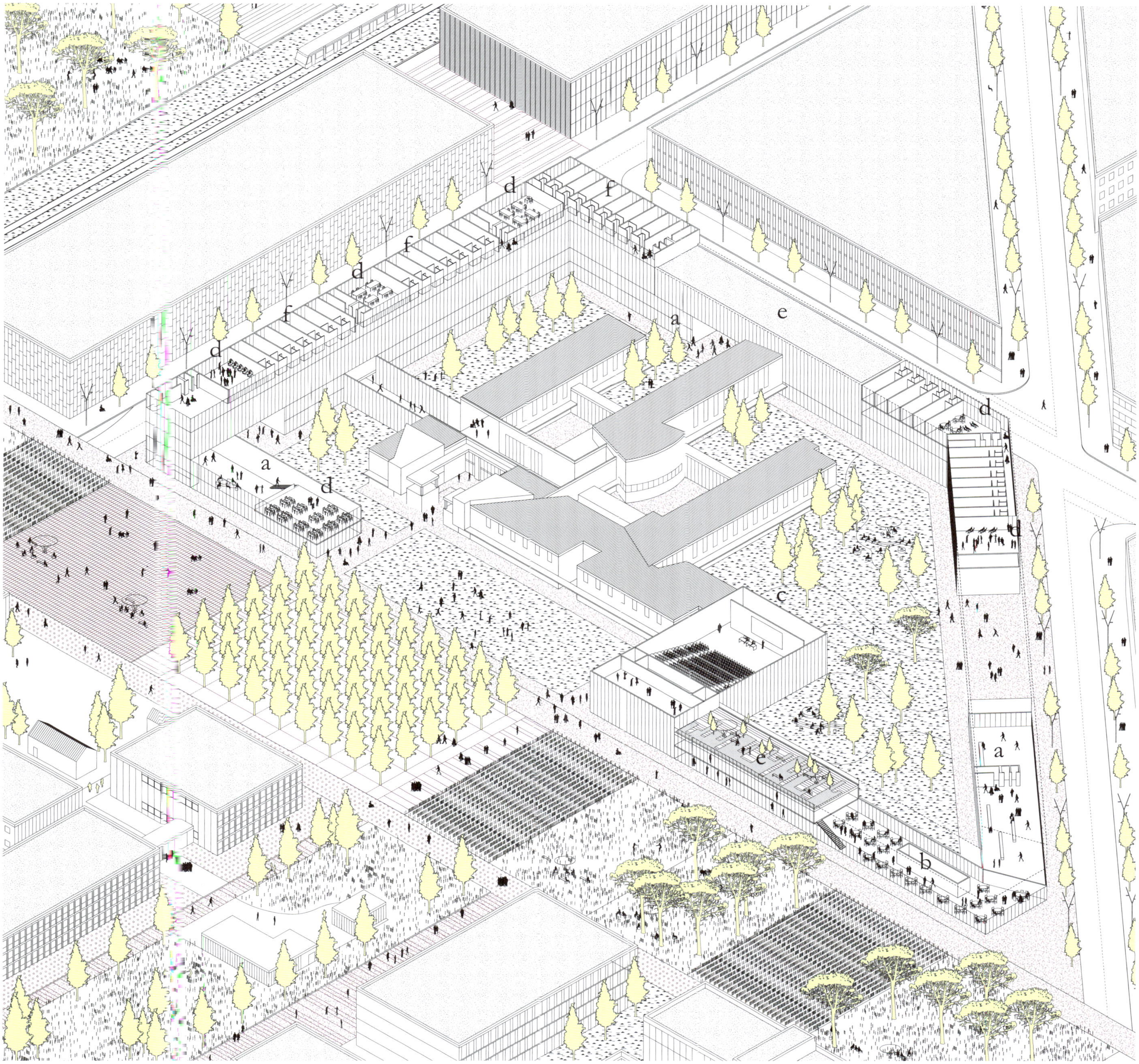

PUBLIC

a. Lobby

b. Restaurant / Café

c. Auditorium / Cinema

SHARED

d. Coworking spaces

e. Terrace

PRIVATE

f. Hotel

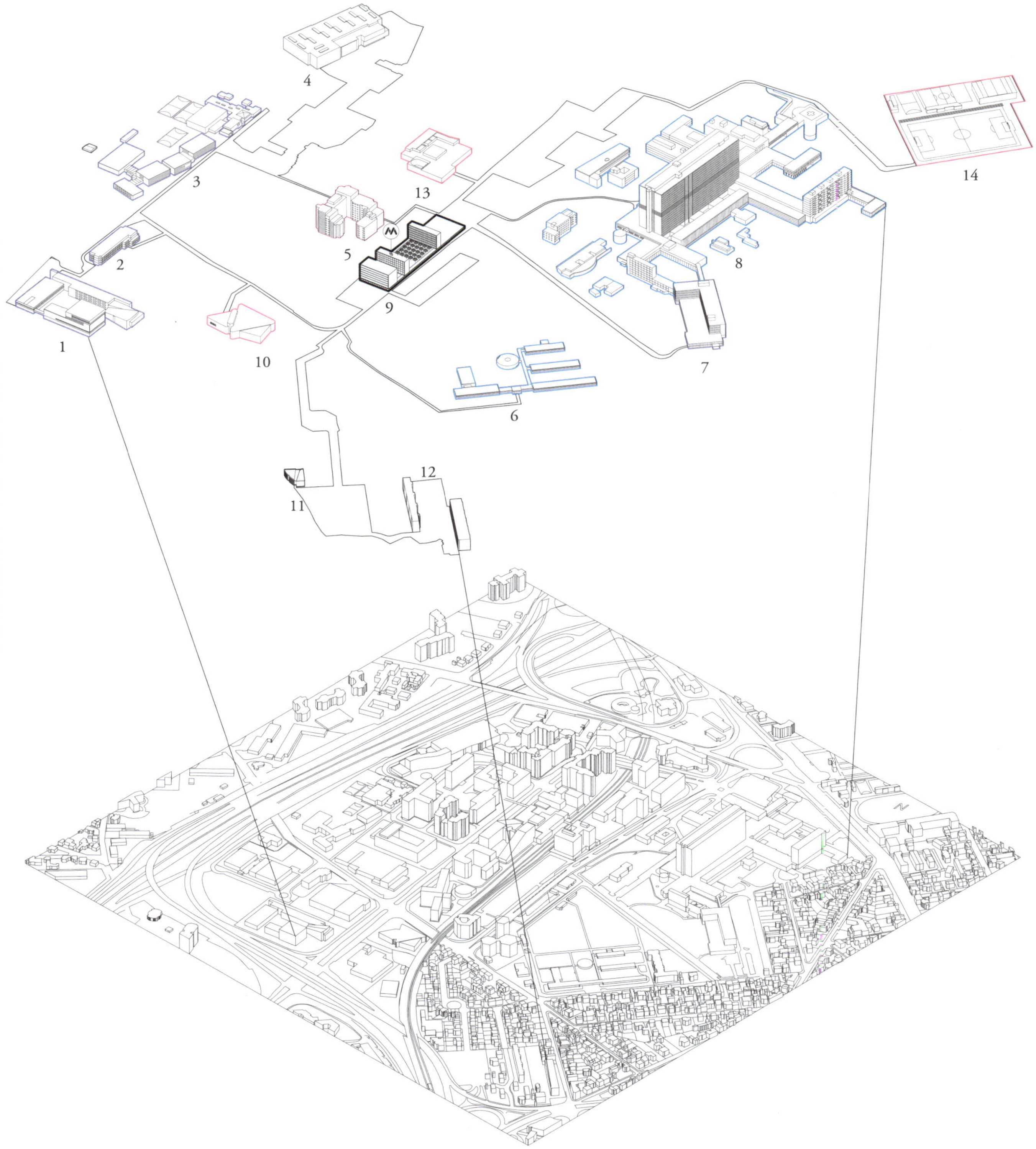

EDUCATION
1. Law faculty
2. Junior and high schools
3. School buildings
4. Sports center

PENITENTIARY
5. Penitentiary service

HEALTH
6. Day hospital – AAE
7. Medical faculty
8. Henri-Mondor teaching hospital

SERVICES
9. Bus terminal
10. Giga Store
11. Christian church
12. Garden / Public space
13. Shopping mall
14. Desmont stadium

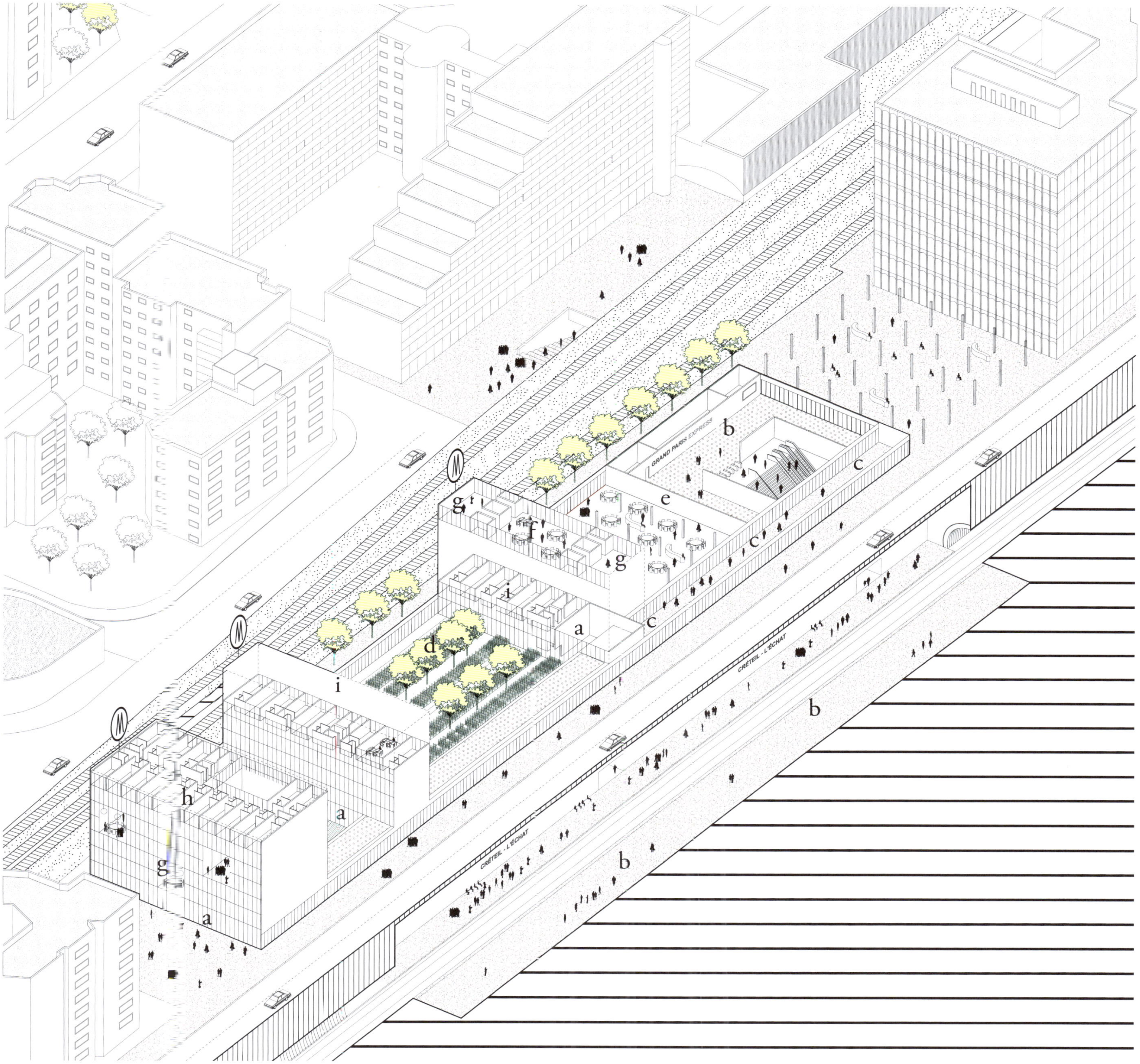

PUBLIC
a. Lobby
b. GPE station (to come)
c. Public gallery

SHARED
Vegetable gardens
Restaurant / Café
Coworking spaces
Collective kitchen

PRIVATE
h. Hotel
i. Student residences

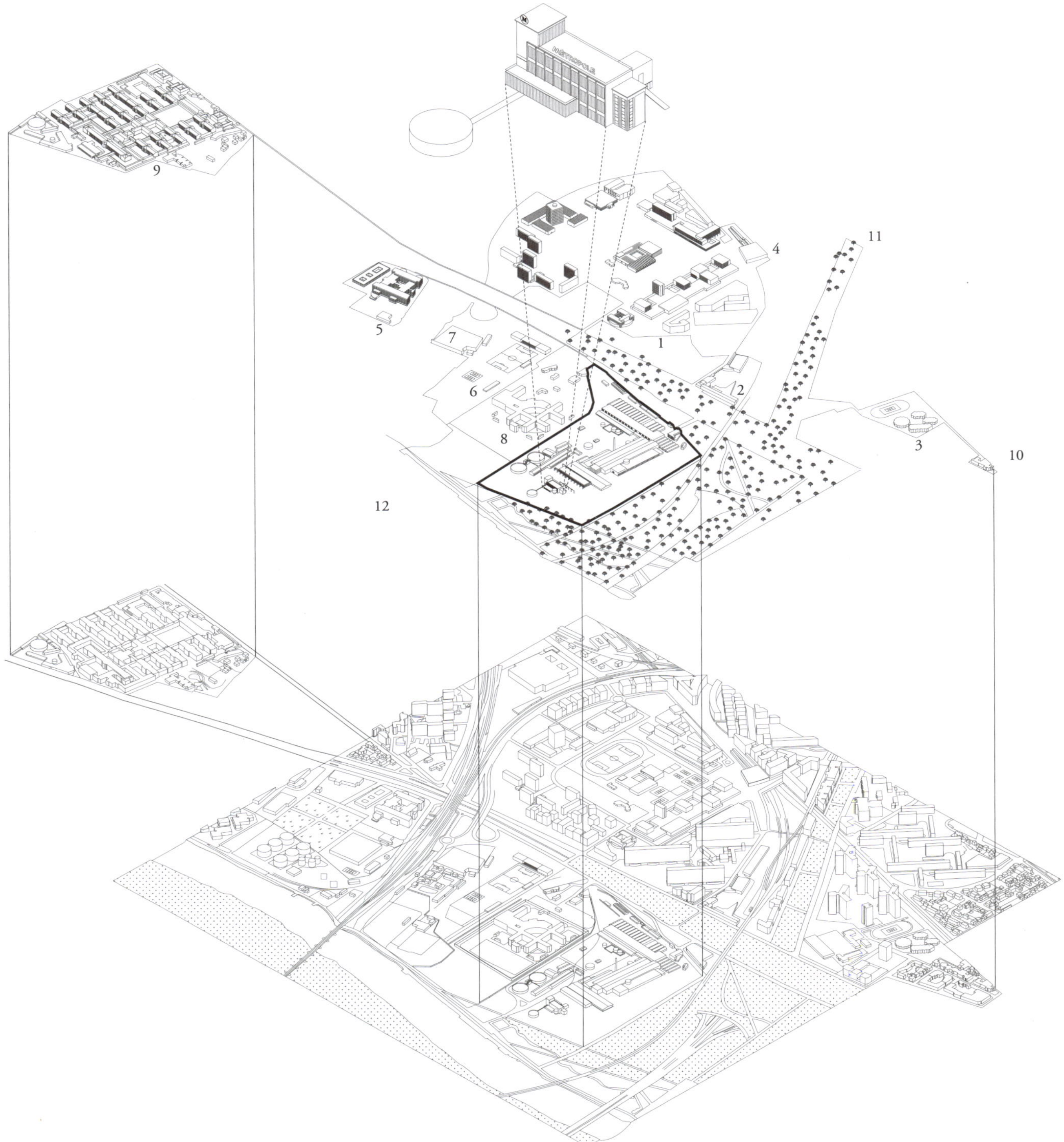

EDUCATION	SERVICES	PENITENTIARY	HEALTH	RETIREMENT HOME	TERRITORY
1. Paris-Nanterre University	4. Multimodal transport hub	8. Penitentiary service	9. Hospital Max-Fourestier	10. La Vie active	11. Nanterre Terraces
2. Junior and high schools	5. Axe Seine shops				12. Seine
3. School buildings	6. Bords de Seine stadium				
	7. Leisure center				

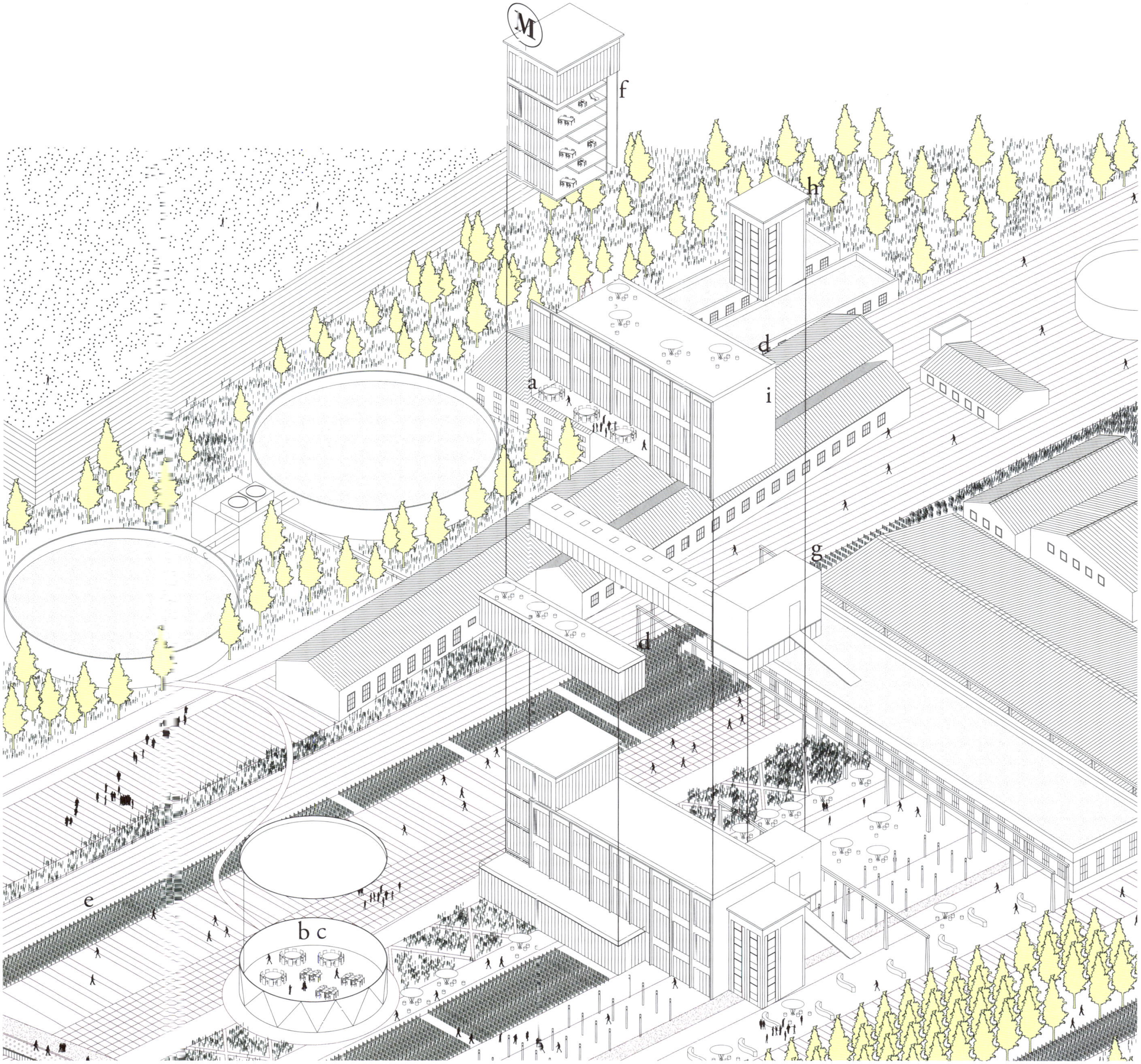

PUBLIC
a. Lobby

SHARED
b. Coworking spaces
c. Collective kitchen
d. Terrace
e. Vegetable gardens

PRIVATE
f. Very small businesses (VSB)
g. Students
h. Short-stay apartments
i. Hotel

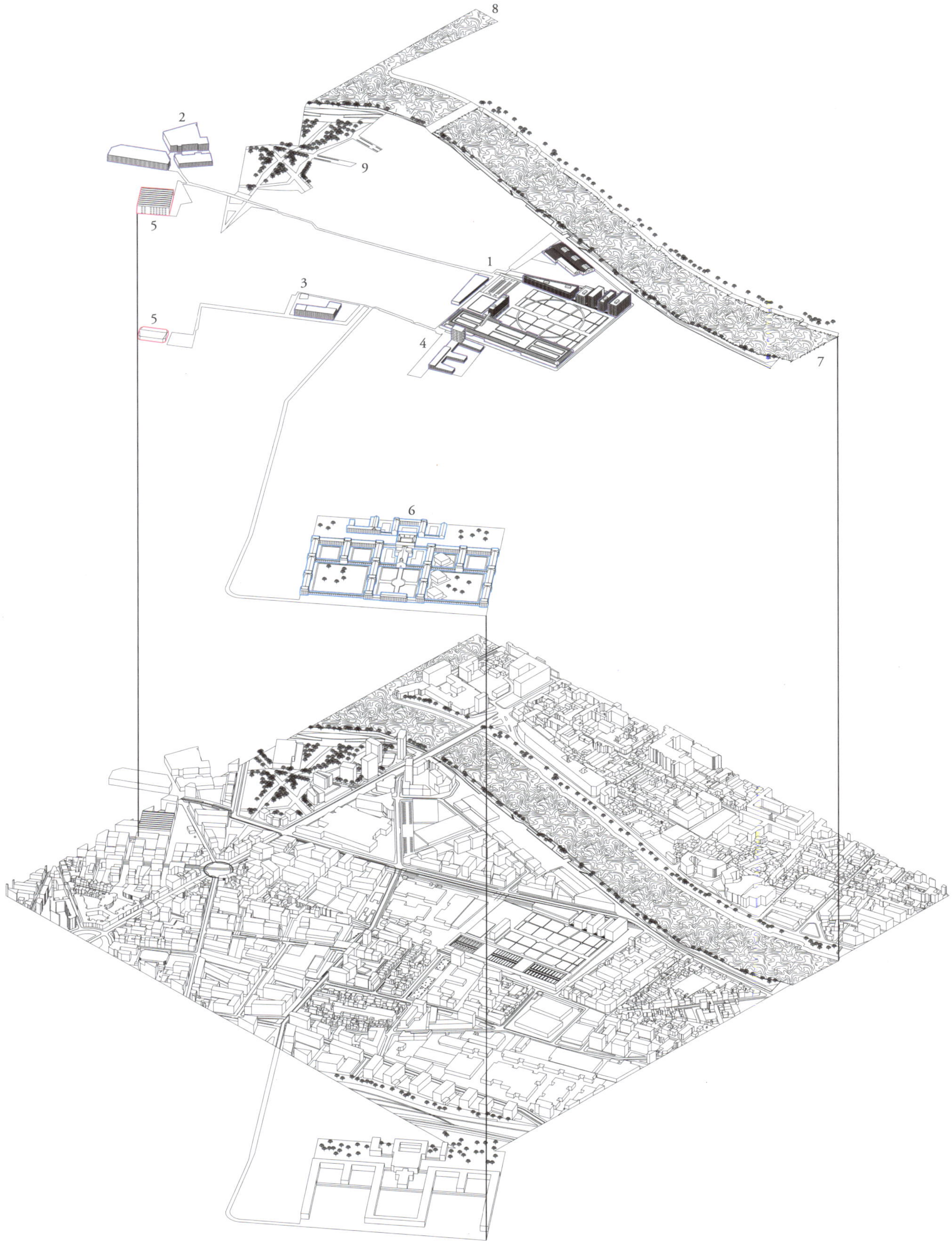

EDUCATION

1. Paris University
2. Paris-VII University
3. School
4. School buildings

SERVICES

5. Sports facilities

HEALTH

6. Charles-Foix Hospital

TERRITORY

7. Seine
8. Marne
9. Parc de la Confluence

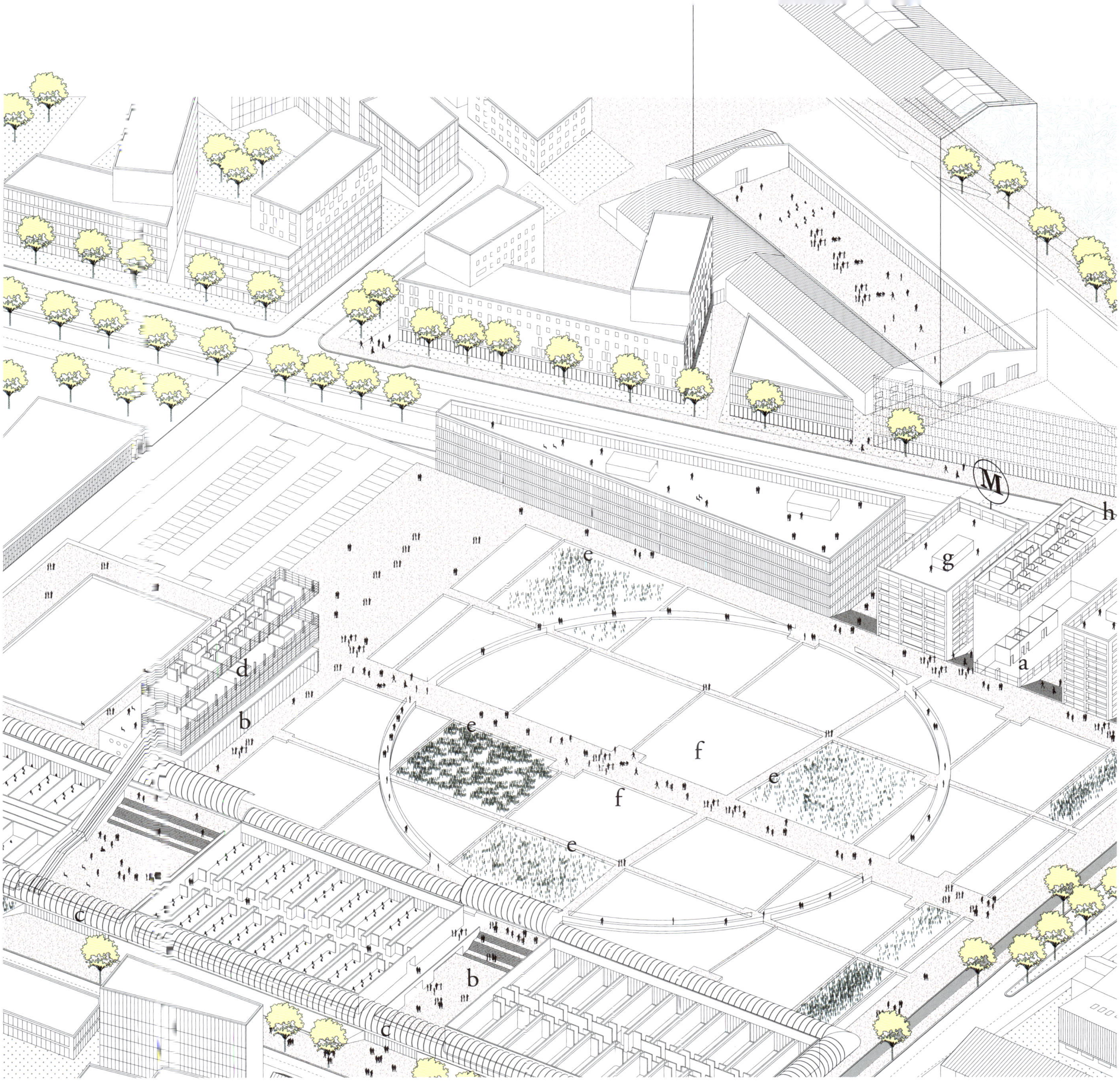

PUBLIC

a. Lobby
b. Restaurant / Café
c. Public gallery

SHARED

Coworking spaces
Urban agriculture
Water garden

PRIVATE

g. Very small businesses (VSB)
h. Students

WRITING

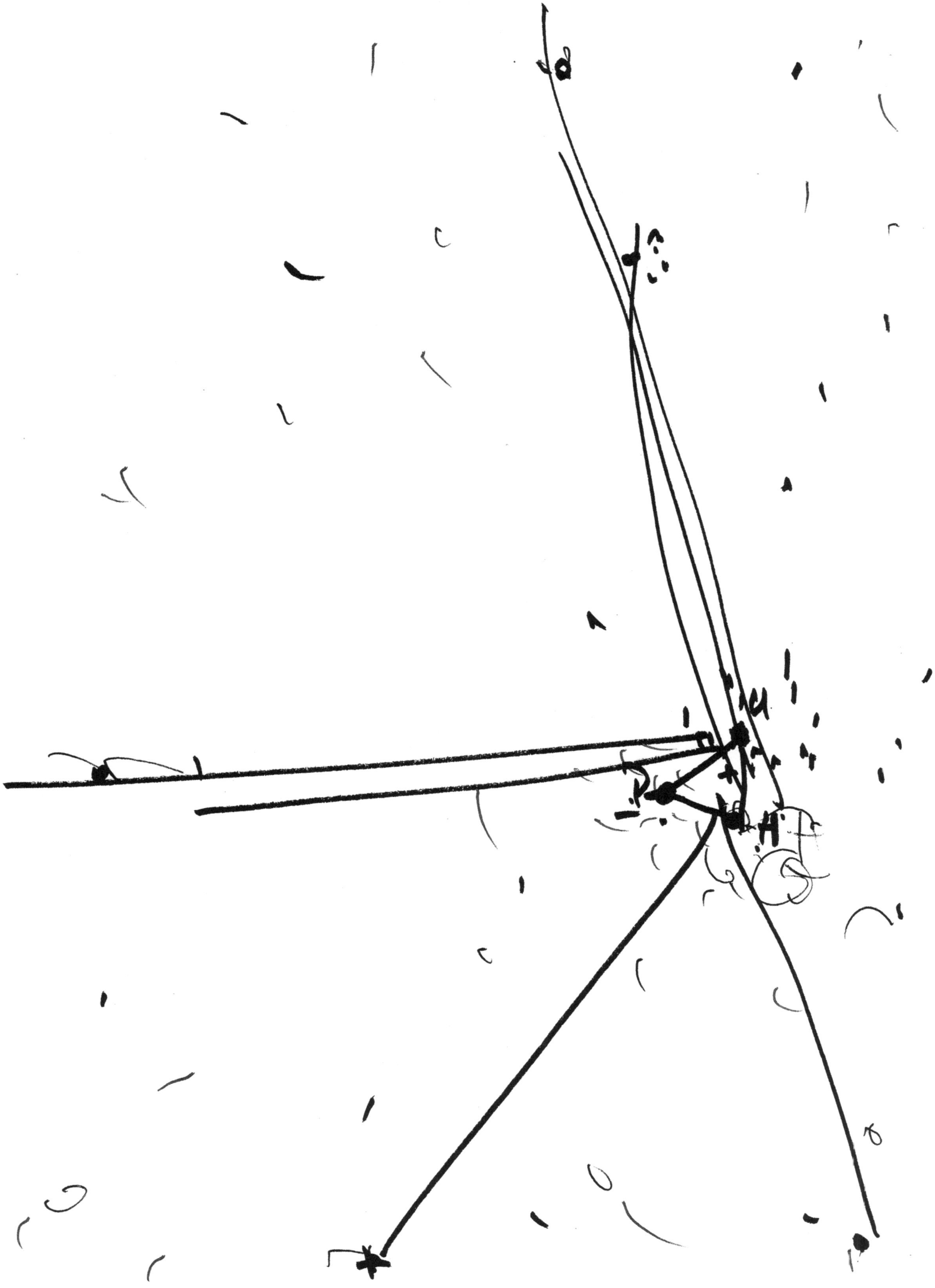

The attitude of writing

Setting the tone with a black felt-tip pen. First gesture, first territory. Defining principles on the fly. The hand investigates. Reprises. Paper absorbs. Lines go to the essential. Writing a building is a manual craft. More than a shape, a silhouette, what we are looking for is its attitude.

Geometry is a defined language. Concise, elementary, it forms a generative grammar ready to take form. A matrix-language that allows the architectural concept to emerge. Just as, in mathematics, we speak of the beauty of an equation, certain plans aim for figurative limpidity, a trigonometry erecting the void. With the void, full powers.

A building must achieve a quality of self-evidence. Good architecture is understood without instructions, in a direct physical and visual relationship. We have to be able to decipher its rules without even thinking about them, and feel at ease spontaneously. Even as the shape of a building is determined in the strong sense of the word, it in turn must never determine the way it is used and inhabited. Architecture becomes rigid as soon as it assigns roles. Whereas, if its language is atmospheric, if it is absent from itself and allows itself to be appropriated, the building begins to speak to each and to all. It is shared. This is architecture that takes the first step.

The application of a clear and total logic, maintained from start to finish, constructs a spatial order in which sensibility and reason resonate. Architectural geometry should be grasped only through direct experience. The diagonal running through Le Corbusier's Carpenter Center at Harvard (1959–61) is a philosophical proposition about continuity and rupture. It is exact. It is complete. There is nothing to add. The concept is tangible. In real generative geometry, human experience is able to unfold its complexity. If the individual is not allowed embodiment and freedom of interpretation, there can be no living architecture.

With architects, attitude is key. They do not dictate it. Nor do they precede it. Architecture is not a question of style, but of strategy, of a situational and territorial approach to the project.

Architecture must be free and appropriable in its very radicality, rather than in its formal grandiloquence. A perceptual vitality of the abstract. Geometric neutrality makes it possible to eschew statements, descriptions, styles, and epochs. It is often confused with minimalism. The term *écriture blanche* would be more appropriate.

Subtractive densification and abstinence can countervail the authority of architecture, its self-centered formal solipsism. It is suspended. Reduced writing purifies it, unclutters it.

Architecture must have the power to be out of time. It must think with its times and against them. The untimely, in the Nietzschean sense, is a mode of authority whereby architecture establishes its living autonomy in the world in which it exists. Not an autarky, but an intractability in the ultra-present. A resistance to the times. To write is to step back.

Sign and phenomenon

Working on the phenomenology of envelopes. Combining their sensory interface with a critical stance. Architecture always benefits from challenging the intangible, from contesting definitive definitions.

Making a black crystal emerge from the land, a tectonic equalizer with frequency processing. Transforming towers draped in glass skin into optical instruments that reconstruct the landscape and create a new one run through with vibrations. A crystal blade erected in the sky like a scything purity.

With the addition of light a precise geometry becomes an exact geometry. A gesture brought to completion, finished and alive. Light transfigures the authority of architecture.

Creating façades with simple skins or with double structures involves architecture in the effects of deepening. Skin is the deepest part of a human being. By virtue of architectural design, some skins take the light as a photogenic phenomenon, traversed by the cycles of day. Kineticism introduces a fourth dimension into architectural conception: time. The building no longer imposes its logic, but gradates its aspects, transitioning them in time with the movements of the light.

In architectural writing, function is an element of consistency, but not a determinant. Certain kinds of writing are there to thwart attributive readings and presumptions of function. A building is first and foremost a complex of potentialities, an operator.

Writing is an exercise in constraint and freedom. The link between the two is a constructive one. Constraint is not an obstacle to overcome. It is the very medium in which thought germinates. It is in the tight space of parameters that the architectural concept is chiseled. If we correctly assimilate the complete frame, then we are perfectly able to accommodate our space for action, as in a sonnet, a programmatic and generative model conducive to the emergence of meaning. The quatrains embrace the situation, the tercets come the *relève* [shift] and the *pointe* [punchline]. A dialectic is tension sustained from beginning to end.

Abstraction, a partial landscape

Radicality is a modality of intensity. The architectural operations of paring and subtracting sophisticate writing to a peak of concision. If abstraction is a critical gesture, it is because its writing posits a differential language. Abrupt confrontation becomes creative. When a building adds an entity to the landscape, it inserts a sign into the geography. Both are measured and magnified, pushed to their limits in an indivisible logic. Where does the project begin and end? The limit is undecidable.

Abstraction is an extraction from nature. It transcends it in a kind of synthetic and analogical harmony. Its language is mediatory. Through it, architecture asserts its integral nature. Not a simulacrum. Not factitious transposition or imitation, but mimesis.

For architectural ideas to find their way, a cutting edge is needed. At Paris-Longchamp, sheets are cut like flint blades. Clean surfaces. Long spans, superimposed and staggered. No vertical to impede the horizontality. Transparencies. A grandstand gliding to its cantilever in a single breath. Air and light flow right through it. The architecture is not an obstacle. It is written in landscape format in the great landscape of the Bois de Boulogne. A limpid plan.

Groundscape writing is a subterranean poetics that transcends the question of architecture's embedding, its incrustation in the subcutaneous layers of earth and rock. The Pantheon in Rome is a subterranean world raised, erected from the ground as a prototype of space. A lair that looks up to the oculus. A self-contained landscape, paradoxically, with no discernible limits.

Generative writing

The purpose of architecture is not to create a figurative work of art, but to produce a sensory concept in tune with the commission. The form is the medium, and the idea the operator.

Generative design uses computing power to formulate working hypotheses based on pre-established constraints, just as the three-dimensional grids of the Dunamu and Twin Peaks towers develop a serial logic as a self-generating principle. Here, the cube is a constructive and mental module. Neutral. Space is no longer thought of simply as a material form, but as an intellectual structure.

Architects today can work with the same generative simulation tools as mathematicians, biologists, and physicists, capable of probing the boundaries between nature and artifice. Computational morphogenesis algorithms generate writing close to biomimicry. The honeycomb vegetality of the balconies and terraces metonymizes architecture's ability to synthesize geometric programming and the indeterminacy of organic growth. Work on the evolutivity of a building's interior spaces (structural flexibility, reversibility, modular variability, adaptability to different uses) itself has affinities with behavioral simulation programs.

Biomimicry can be transposed to the field of urban planning, the generation of territories and metropolitan growth. Just as the urban landscape has been transformed into a global datascape because the nature of geography has changed and has brought forth other realities that can be translated into kinetic and forward-looking maps, so computational architecture makes it possible to model complex buildings, in analogy with living models.

Crystal clear

Crystals, in their smooth or fragmented forms, are associated with the ideality of form and the authenticity of matter. They also raise questions about the scale of nature in relation to the human scale. Their structure provides architectural writing with a paradigm of the processual aspect of forms.

The fractal geometry at play in crystallogenesis effects a radical synthesis: form becomes structure, structure becomes performance. It transforms natural complexity into clarity and beauty that we can grasp. Architecture does not copy crystal. It extracts its internal logic. Crystal growth and spatial design share the same mathematical rigor. Harmony is no longer sentiment but structure.

The properties of fractal objects (self-similarity, infinite iteration, self-affinity, measurable complexity, entropy) are of interest to architecture.

The fractal formation of crystal integrates context without losing its internal coherence. These crystal-shaped architectures embody the fractal process at play in the formation of complex natural objects: snowflake or cloud. Volumetry, structure, and skin grow simultaneously in a single system of self-similar and multi-scalar organization.

An operator of conversions

Metal mesh is a form of writing in its own right, an architectural material. Between it and the wall a conflict of spaces and perceptions plays out. A critical relationship between the limit and transparency, materiality and dematerialization, the static and the metamorphic. Architecture is never definitively designed or written.

The wall has an unquestionable authority, a static quality, a form that is always too fixed. Mesh does not, because ambiguity is its core value. It delimits without dividing or excluding. It works on structural and spatial syntax at the root, on visual lexicons, predicates, aspects, and perceptions.

The critique of the limit is the thinking matter of the mesh. There are many names that could reflect the nature of the median places it invents, belonging neither to the outside nor to the inside: threshold, interface, in-between, embrasure. A fold in architecture, like in a sheet of paper, is both its front and back. Zones of simultaneous spatialities. Planes of interior-exterior permutation. An interlayer. A transitional filter. So many allusions to an architecture whose extreme value would be incompleteness. Spacing in space.

Oxymoronic throughout, reactive, and woven with ambivalence, mesh introduces paradoxes into space, optical games, and successive impressions. Saturated with reversible properties, whether steel, aluminum, copper, or bronze, it is a material of variable phenomenality. Photosensitive, it turns sensuous under the stimuli of light, sometimes opacifying, sometimes transparent.

The material comes to architecture when architecture appropriates it for its project. Metal mesh is nothing but a weave of cables, rods, wires, and coils, but when involved in an exact and rigorous architecture, it becomes a tool of indeterminacy, vibratory and sensorial. It resonates with its nature as an industrial artefact transformed into a material for design. There is a blurring in the categorical boundaries between architecture and conceptual art, design and scenography, installation and urban landscape. Shaped by architects and industrial engineers using 3D modelling software and digital previsualization, metal mesh brings back the *tekhnè*, the source of poetry. Steel has its own technological fictions. Each new construction material opens up a creative field that is conducive to emergences, singularities, interdisciplinarities, and subversion: all so many architectural and tectonic investigations into connections and scansions, serial musicalities and rhythms.

Ductile and malleable, metal mesh abounds in transfigurative properties. Its functionality is surpassed in the sculptural realm through kinetic constructions and visual aspirations, iridescence and diffraction. As an element of landscape, it enters the sensory realm of Land Art.

If, by day, the writing of metallic fabric is held taut, in the evening, when interiors are lit up, it becomes immaterialized in the backlight, projecting onto the floor like a magic lantern, a spectacle of images passing through its skin. Light is a gift. Architecture, a slow and heavy art, is enchanted. The unexpected bestows on it brilliance and transport.

Like autonomous units, the mesh panels stretched over frames create an ephemeral space that can be dismantled, transposed, and moved around. The space seems provisional, evolving. Whereas the wall, firmly integrated into the structures, is held entirely within the register of immovability and separation, mesh gives rise to fictions. It posits an unfixed experimental space, a poetics of transitions. Through its permeability, its virtual mobility, it resolves the negativity of the wall, which then dreams of itself as a thin and light element, dematerialized, open and evident in space, capable of linking the intimacy of the built environment with the exteriority of the world. A plane of contact. A supplement to architecture and even a spirit of architecture. A style that carves out space as if each piece of mesh were an extract from its expanse.

The limit is not defined

Architecture is a synthesis of discontinuity and continuity. It is up to the writer to define it in terms of plans, volumes, structures, and forms. The Teaching Lab at the École Polytechnique Fédérale de Lausanne is a computational *cloud* that could continue to expand through self-similarity. Inside, there are no corridors. There are fluid platforms and flexible spaces conducive to flows and collaborations. Function enters another dimension. Architecture exceeds itself, like the sheet of photovoltaic metal unfolded over the convention center and exhibition hall in León, Spain, like an abstract fractal relief extending beyond the building's rectangular footprint.

Architecture must not abide within the limits of its functions. It believes in its unlimited possibilities.

P. 214 Sketch, concept/context, 2000.

TWIN PEAKS – BONGEUNSA-RO 120

SEOUL, SOUTH KOREA
2023–29

1

Twin Peaks is landscape-architecture, a vertical echo of the lines of the mountain backdrop to the city of Seoul. Anchored by a walkable porous base, the building opens up to the public space of the street before soaring towards the sky. Its twin peaks fan out along a diagonal axis that defies the grid of the city. This calculated torsion captures the light and views while minimizing the shadows cast on its built neighbors. The sloping façades carve out a cascade of terraces that benefit each program equally. With its stepped lines reminiscent in their baroque gesturality of the elegance of the Chrysler Building in New York, Twin Peaks is becoming a geographical beacon on Seoul's South Bank.

1 Sketch, 2023.
2 Satellite view.
3 The project is situated on an intermediate scale between the mountains and the river. It is a geographical beacon, a landmark on Seoul's southern shore. Model, scale 1:1,000, 2022.
4 Glass cascades on the façade.

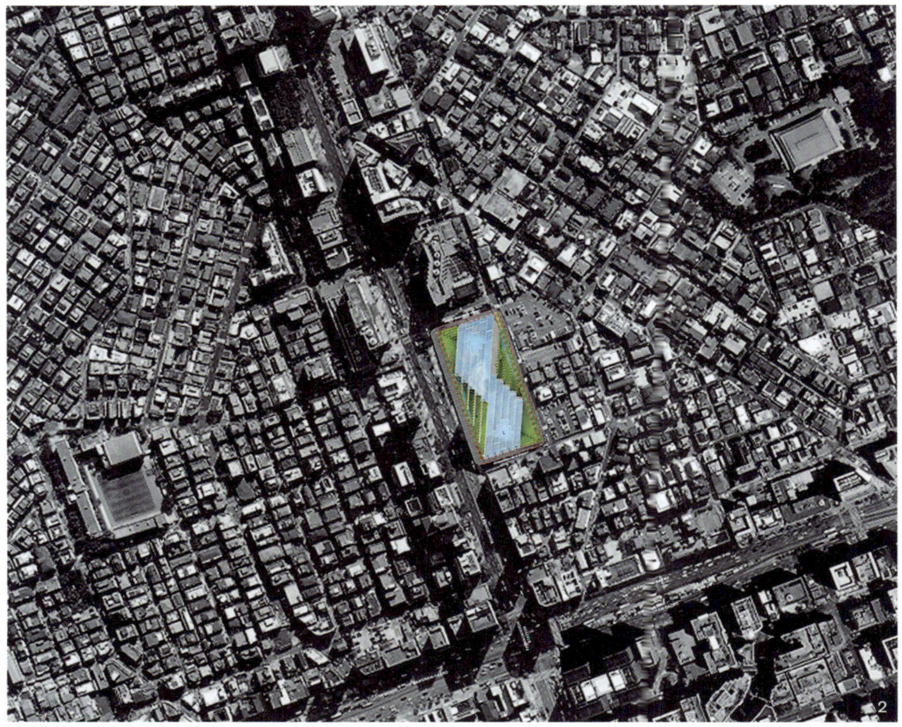

2

3

4

WEST CROWN

HOTEL AMENITIES

HOTEL
11 LEVELS

SKYLOBBY

REFUGE

TECHNICAL

RESIDENCE AMENITIES

RESIDENCE
16 LEVELS

RESIDENCE AMENITIES
2 LEVELS

LOBBY HOTEL / RESIDENCE

COMMERCIAL FACILITIES

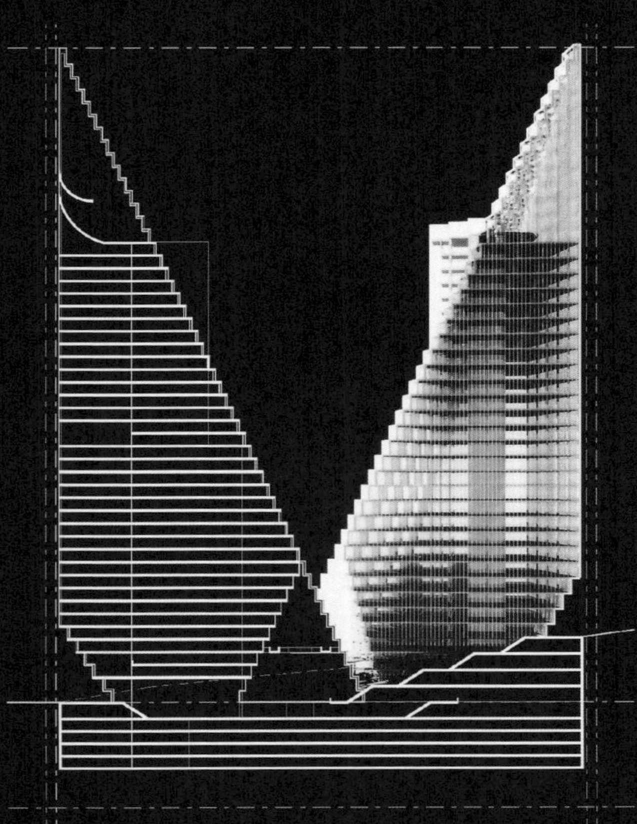

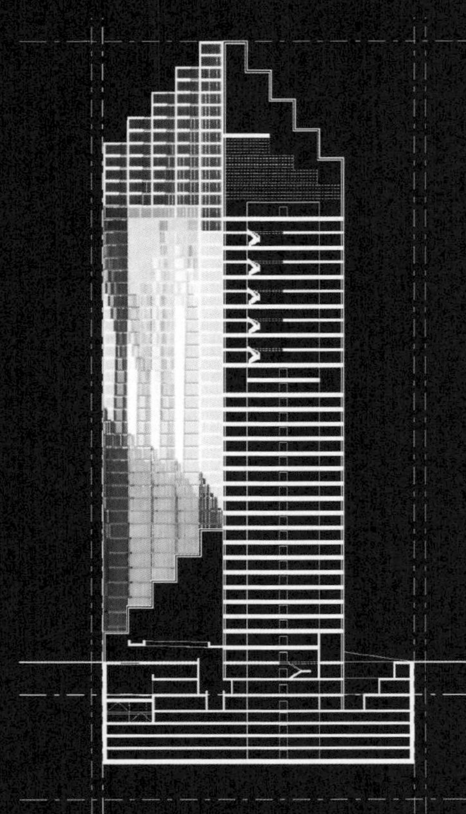

THE BLADE TOWER B2-2

SEOUL, SOUTH KOREA

2011–12

1

With its rhomboid shape and sharp-edged silhouette, the Blade is a landmark in the skyline of Seoul's new Yongsan international business center. The result of the conversion of a former railyard, the tower is part of an urban project comprising an archipelago of vertical buildings linked by a big park. Lean like a sharp blade, it stands out against its surroundings, its crystalline façades intensely reflecting the light. Like an optical prism, the Blade captures, fragments, and reconstructs the landscape in a play of appearances, contrasts, and reflections. Its appearance changes with the angle of view and the movement of the sun, constantly transforming the visual experience and redefining the contours of the city.

1 Site plan, a composition of lozenge-based geometric shapes.
2, 3 A project in the heart of Seoul. The silhouette of a new downtown emerges on the banks of the Han River.
4 The Blade's sharp prisms cut through the light.

1 A glass skin whose shine varies, at dusk.
2, 3 Inner structure and outer luminosity.
4 A crystalline skin with perfect geometry, like a cut stone.

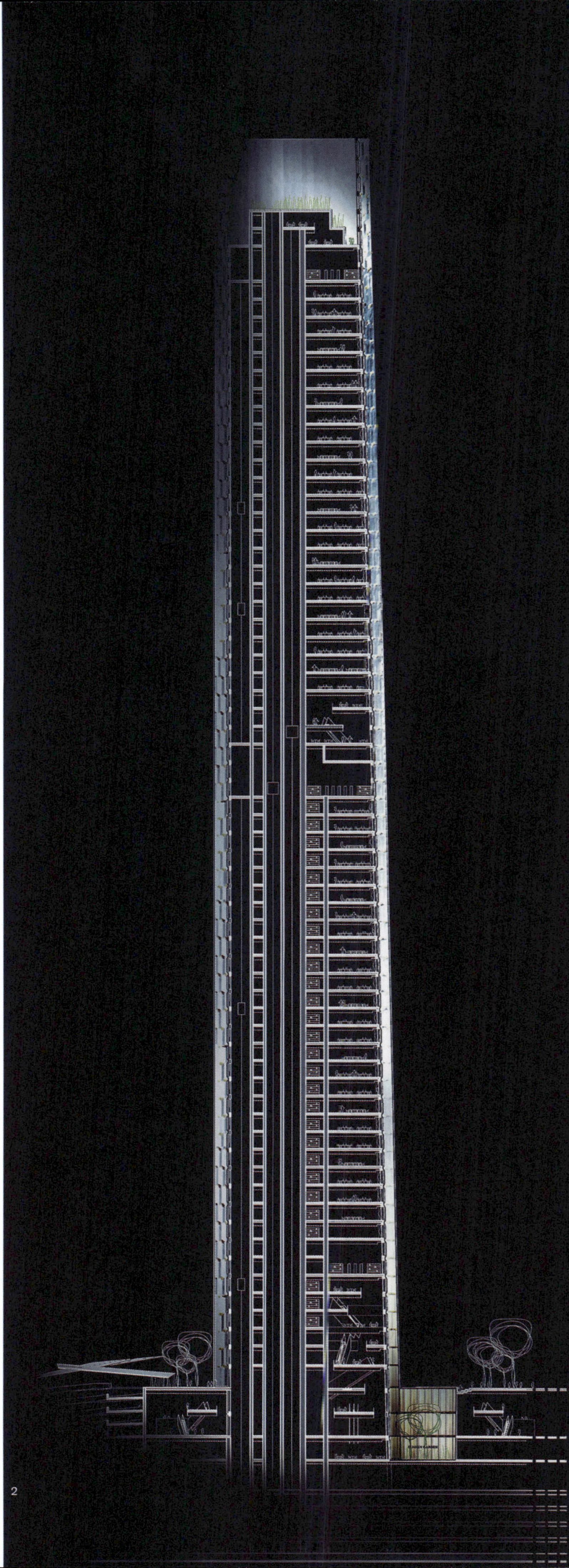

2

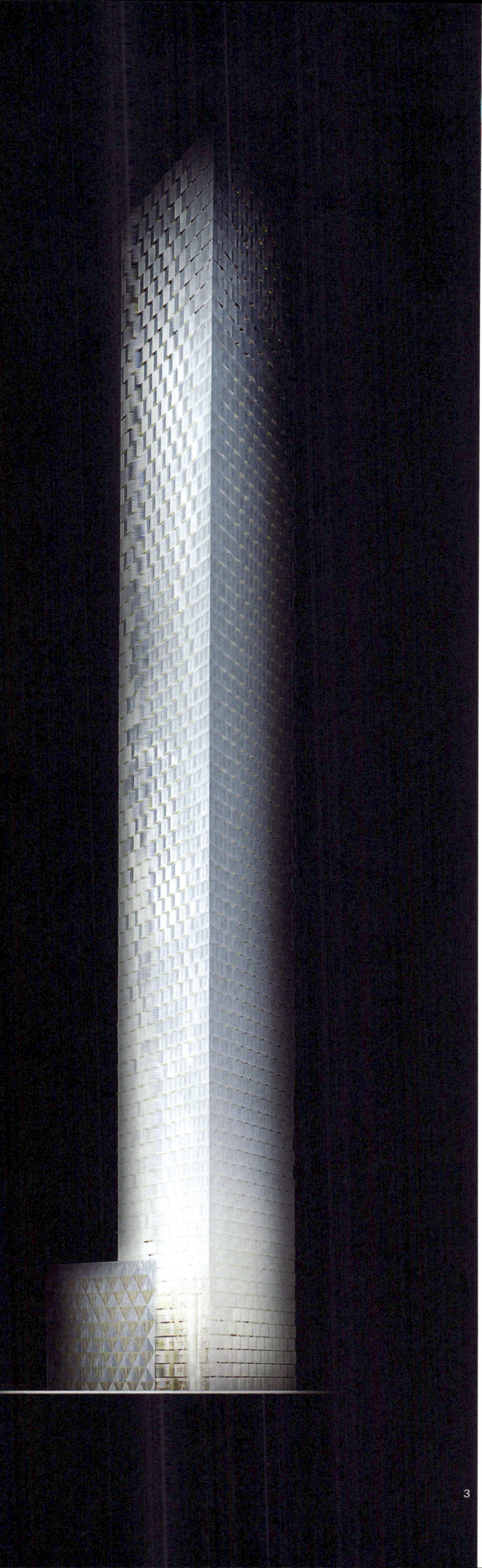

3

4

NATIONAL MUSEUM OF ANDORRA

ANDORRA LA VELLA, ANDORRA
2009

Rooted in the heart of the city of Andorra, this project defies the constraints of urban density by thrusting upwards like a living structure, like a growing tree seeking light. Its fractal architecture unfolds its branches at various angles, freeing up space without extending its footprint. This controlled growth creates a unique space: at the points where the branches cross and form a knot, two large exhibition galleries spread out. At the base, the trunk of the tree houses a five-story vertical library, while, poised at the top, a restaurant overlooks a unique panorama. The volume is both organic and structured, marked by sloping walls that carve out singular spaces, projected towards the city of which it is a symbolic landmark.

1

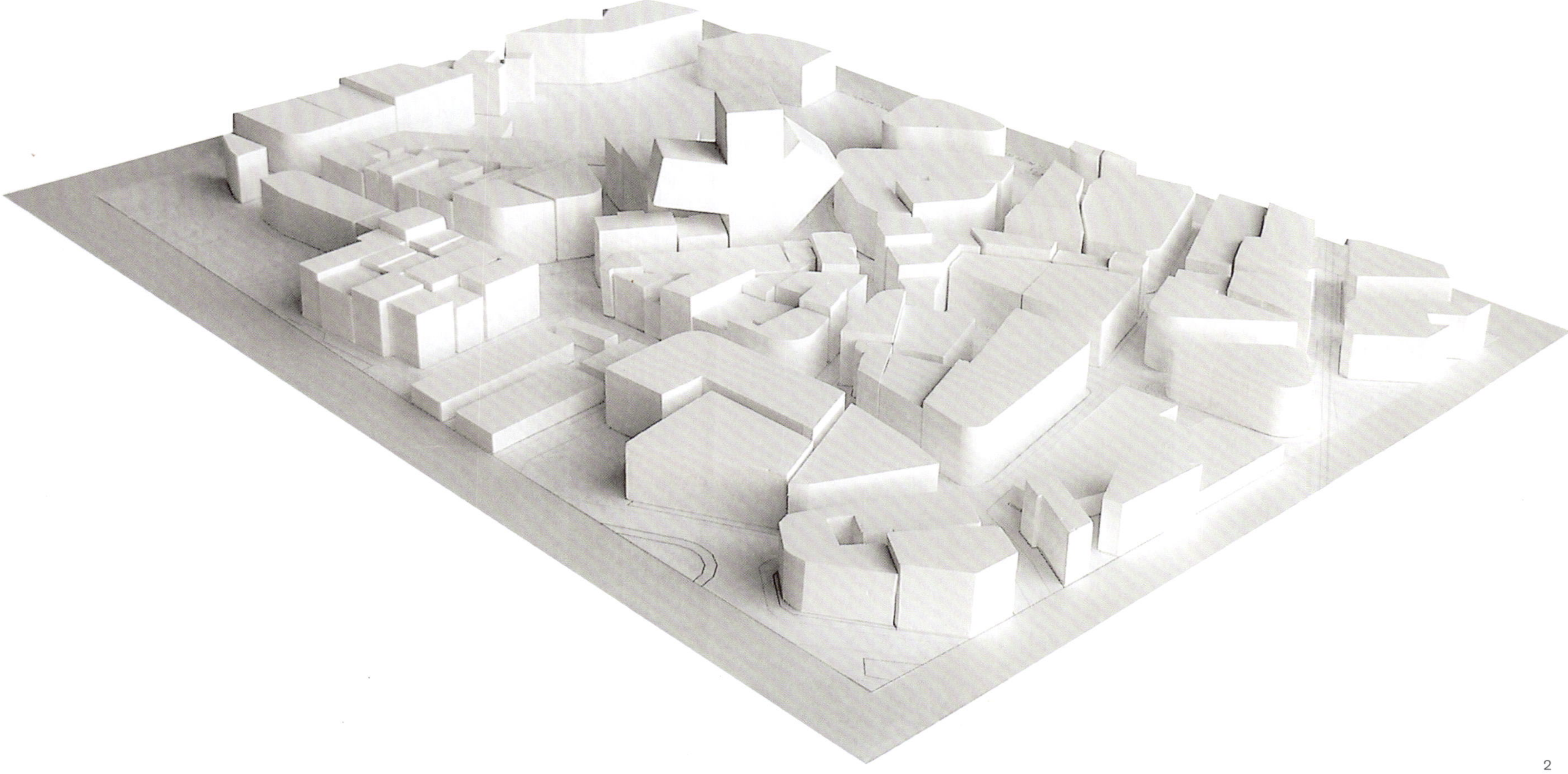

2

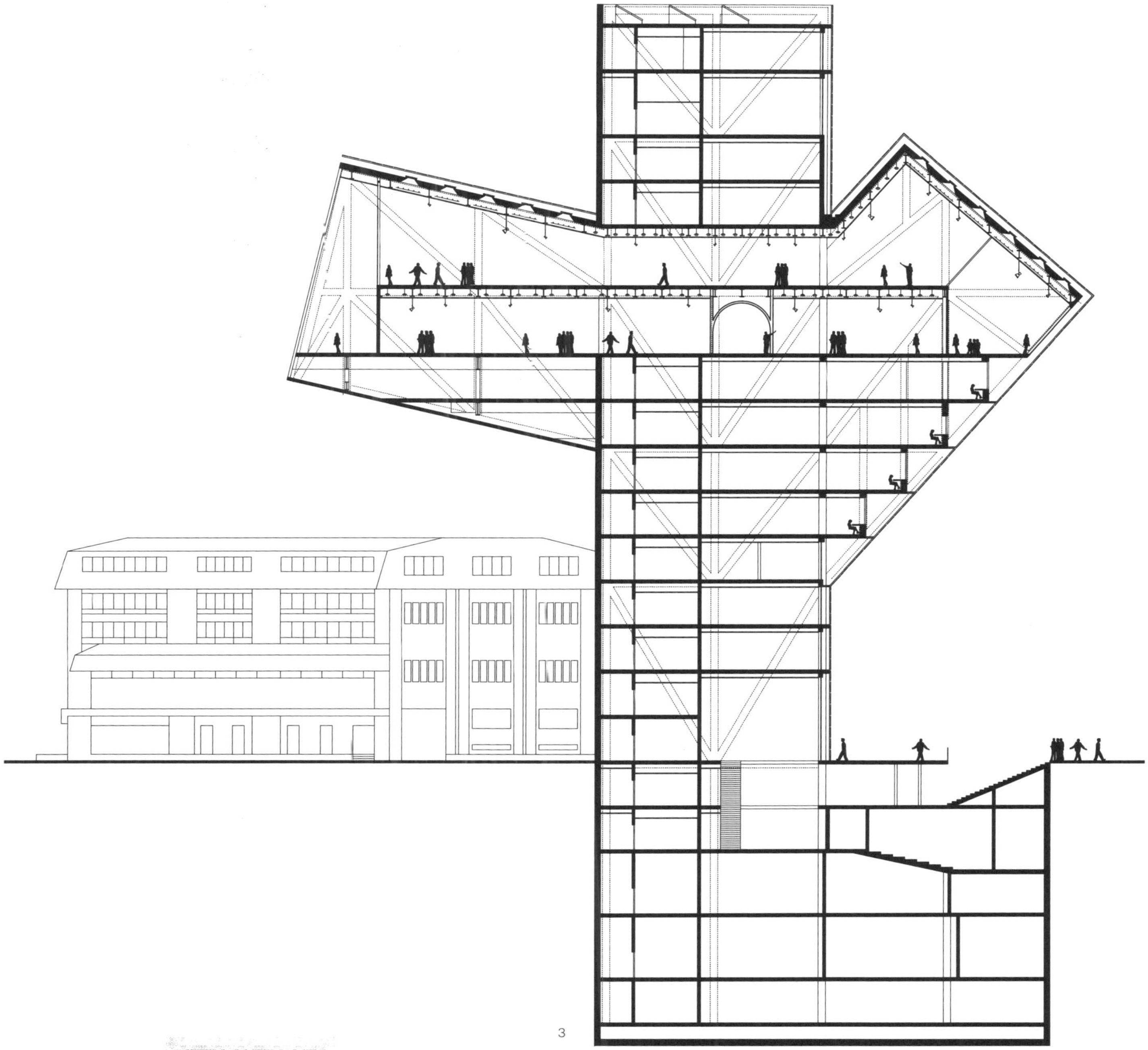

3

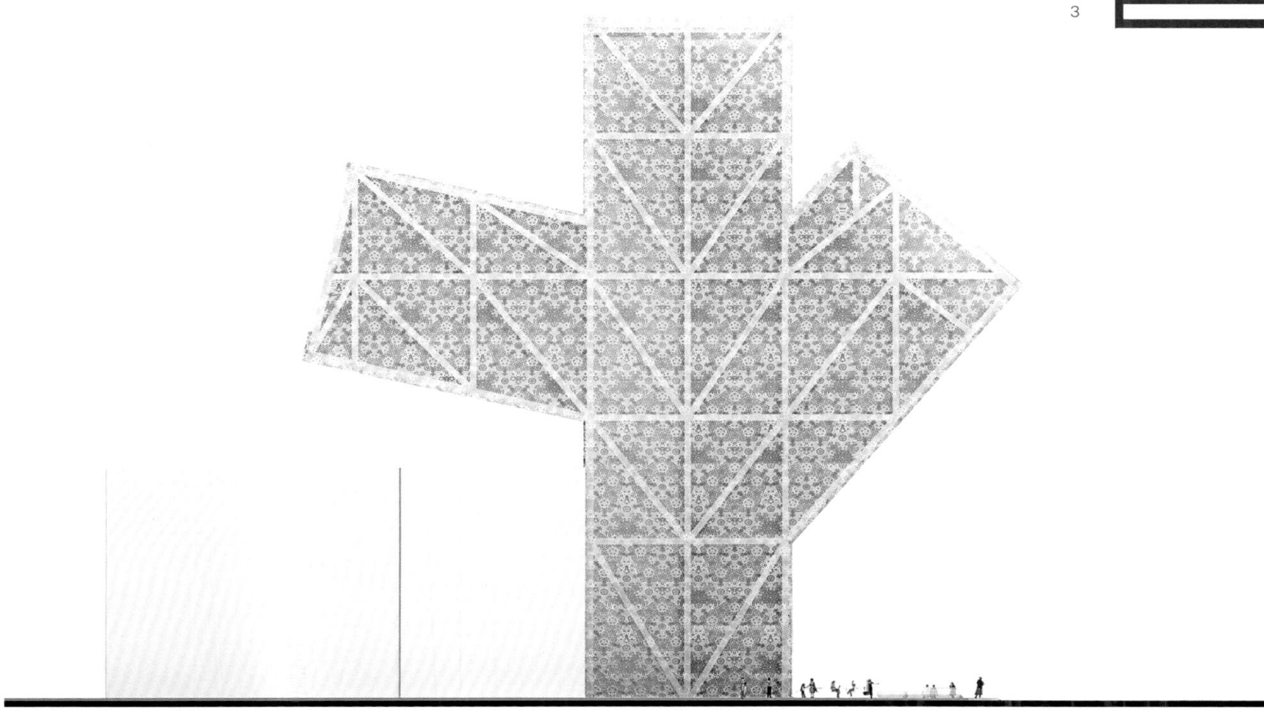

4

1, 2 The museum on a scale with its city and neighborhood.
3 The building rises above the rooftops, freeing views and welcoming light.
4 A biomorphic design, somewhere between a tree and a snowflake.

VINCI HEADQUARTERS

RUEIL–MALMAISON, FRANCE
2009–10

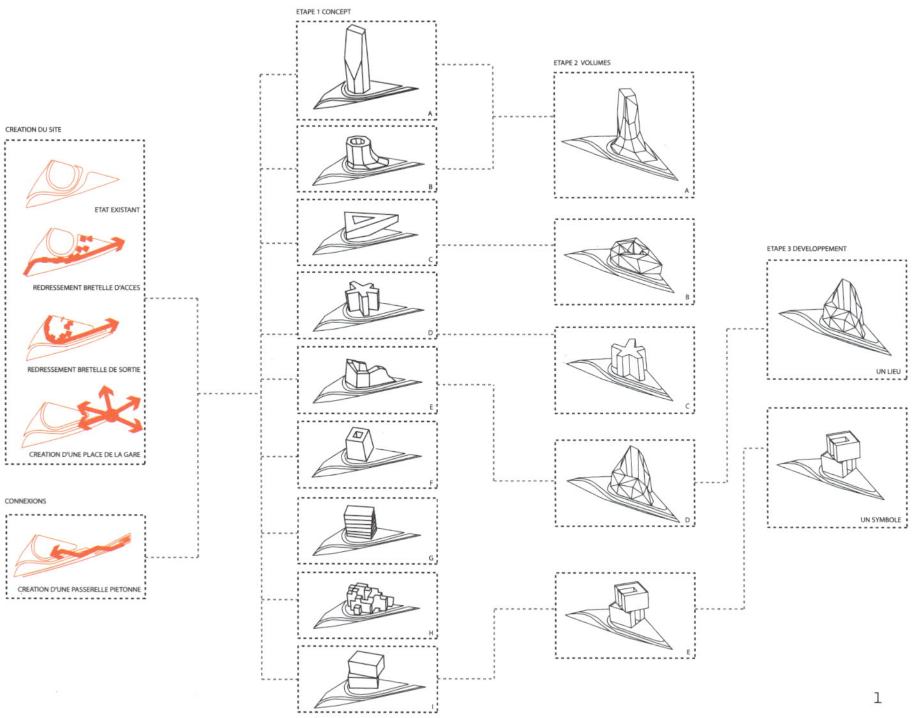

1

2

3

Vinci's headquarters are located at the heart of a motorway interchange on the A86, on disused road. Faced with a marked duality—an opening onto the city on one side, the pressure of a road network on the other—the building adopts a protective posture, like a rock sculpted by its environment. Its curved plan and slender profile sculpt a volume like a massive back, absorbing the dynamics of traffic flows and enveloping a vast interior space, open to the city and protected from the tumult outside. To the rear, the building rests on a thick layer of vegetation, reinforcing this natural envelope that transforms a constrained site into a territory where urban resilience finds its full expression.

1 Typology of possibilities in a place that seems impossible.
2 A "capable" volume protecting a symbolic space at its heart, open to all. Volumetric model, scale 1:500, 2009.
3 The north face of the crystal, a block shaped to offer generous views of the fascinating infrastructure landscape.
4 Cross-section in/out.
5 An opening onto the neighborhood, defining the access and identity of a soothing collective space.

4

5

HOHES DACH – TECHNICAL ADMINISTRATION BUILDING

DÜSSELDORF, GERMANY

2022

With its bold geometry, composed of two sloping and closely linked towers, the Common House marks the skyline of Düsseldorf's IHZ Park. At the heart of this wooden structure, an extruded space creates a monumental hall affording access to the public services located on the lower and upper floors. Walkways, functioning as informal work spaces, cross the volume and connect the two wings of the building. With a public belvedere at the top of the south tower and fully glazed façades, this structure embodies an essential principle of democracy: open and accessible institutions at the service of citizens.

1 The shape of the tower is not the result of a simple triangular extrusion, but of the assembly of two inclined volumes, closely linked, creating a naturally ventilated interior and exterior space, the real beating heart of the project.
2 DPA collage/concept.
3 Nature overtakes the heart of the building.
4 Exploded axonometric view revealing the successive functional layers that ensure the structure's sustainable performance.
5 Silhouette of the Common House and transparency of its central atrium. Model, scale 1:1,000, 2022.

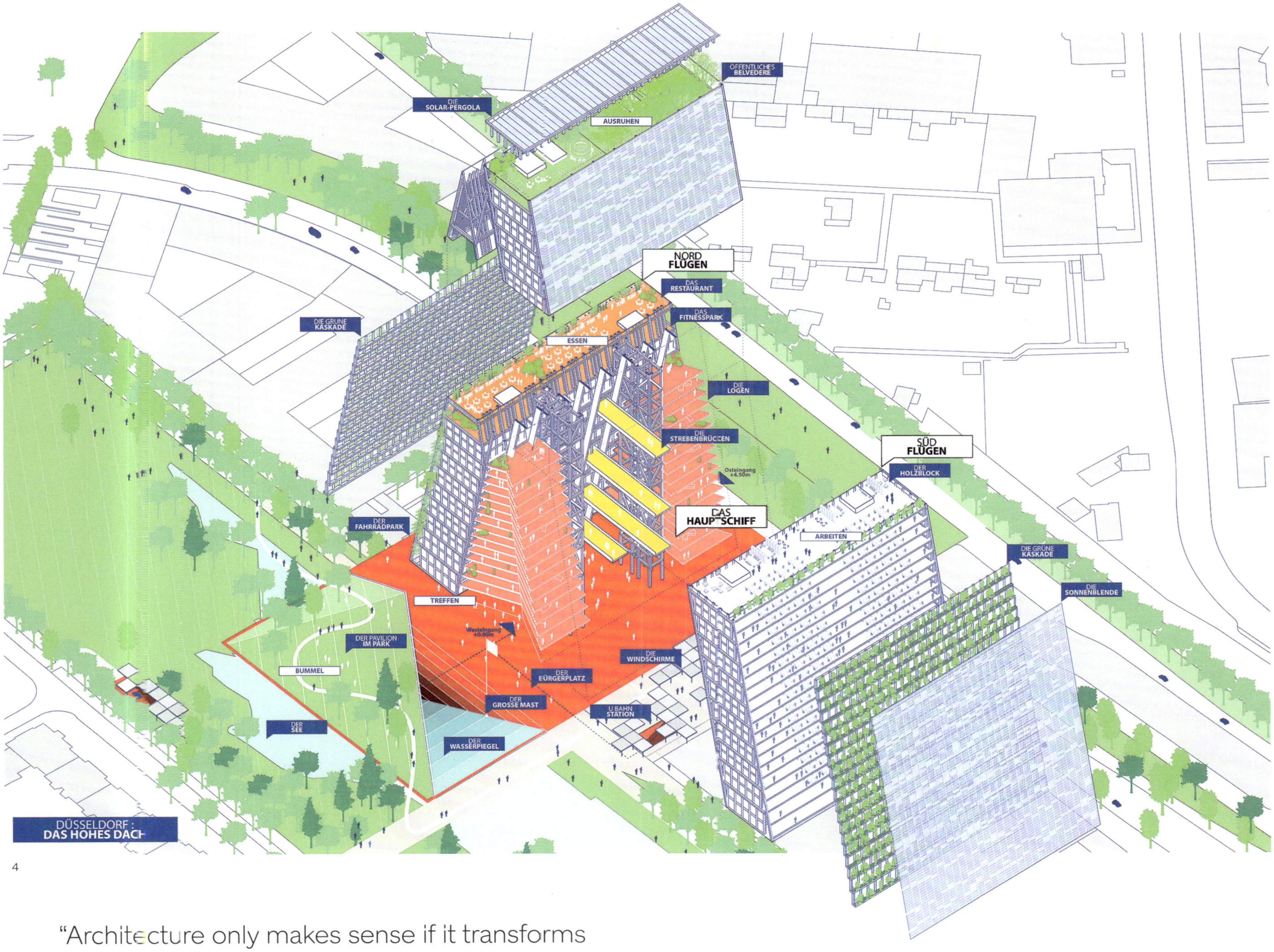

4

"Architecture only makes sense if it transforms one territory into another territory, one nature into another, one place into another."

5

FUKOKU TOWER

OSAKA, JAPAN
2006–10

1

The Fukoku Tower stands like an urban tree deeply rooted in the city, its trunk 133 meters high. Its broad base, anchored in the ground like a network of roots, extends its reach into a series of underground shopping arcades. At the base, the texture of the façade evokes the rough bark of an ancient tree, an effect heightened by a crescendo of inlaid mirrors that reflect and diffract the sky as well as the Osaka landscape. This base gradually gives way to a smooth skin stretching upwards, like a young tree in full growth. At the heart of the building, a spacious atrium immerses visitors in a modern stained-glass window evoking the image of a forest landscape, extending the plant metaphor. The tower has become a landmark at the exit of Osaka's main station.

2

3

1 Sketch, 2007.
2 Glass block made of stacked strata. Study model, scale 1:500, 2008.
3 The main façade features a sculpted base following the geometry of the public space, and a smooth, compact body rising towards the sky.

CITYLIFE RESIDENCES

MILAN, ITALY

2011

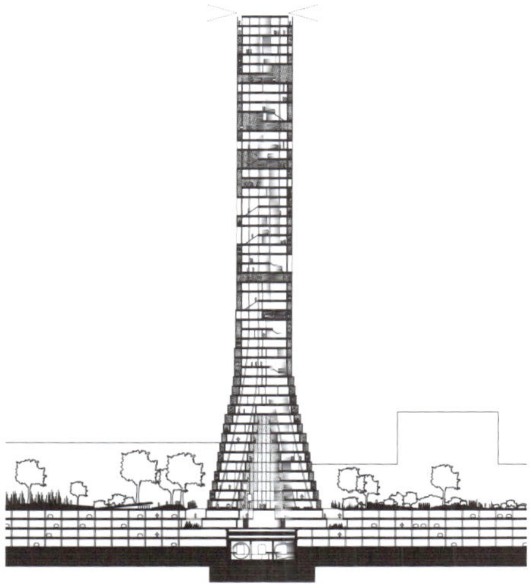

1

With its three emblematic towers, the CityLife district has redefined the heart of Milan, creating a new urban dynamic. The idea is to amplify this initial concept and transform the trio of buildings into a quartet, reinforcing the critical mass of this urban intervention. By layering a mixed program in a single building, the project frees up a maximum amount of space on the ground, making it possible to create large parks. On the façade, a system of planted loggias with alternating depths, widths, and heights naturally regulates the indoor climate. Some of these loggias stretch all the way through the building, providing communal spaces for residents. At its base, the tower splits into two sloping sides, creating a large central nave that links the two parks abutting the tower, along which are a range of services.

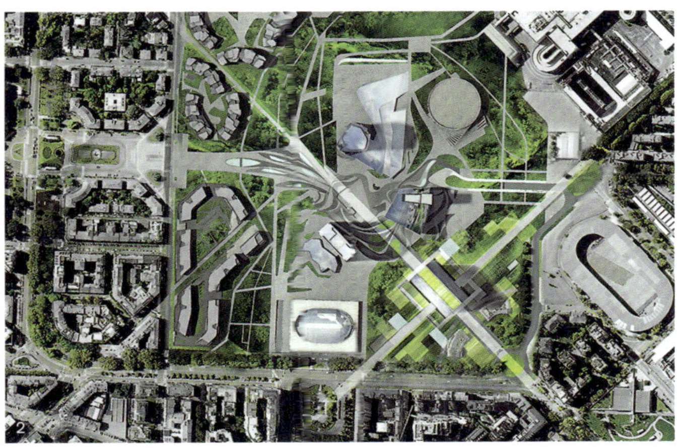

2

3

1 Cross-section of the galleria, a public space crossing the tower base.

2 The site opens up in all directions.

3 Stacking and crystallization of volumes starting from the galleria-public passage. Model, scale 1:500, 2011.

VULCANO

ZURICH, SWITZERLAND
2012–18

"Architecture attains its true power when it ceases to be an object and becomes a phenomenon."

1

2

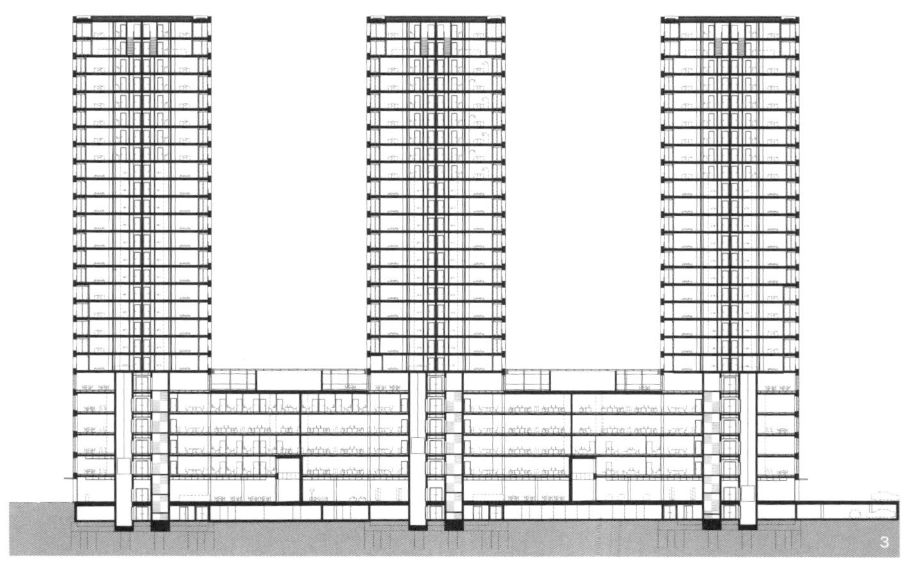

3

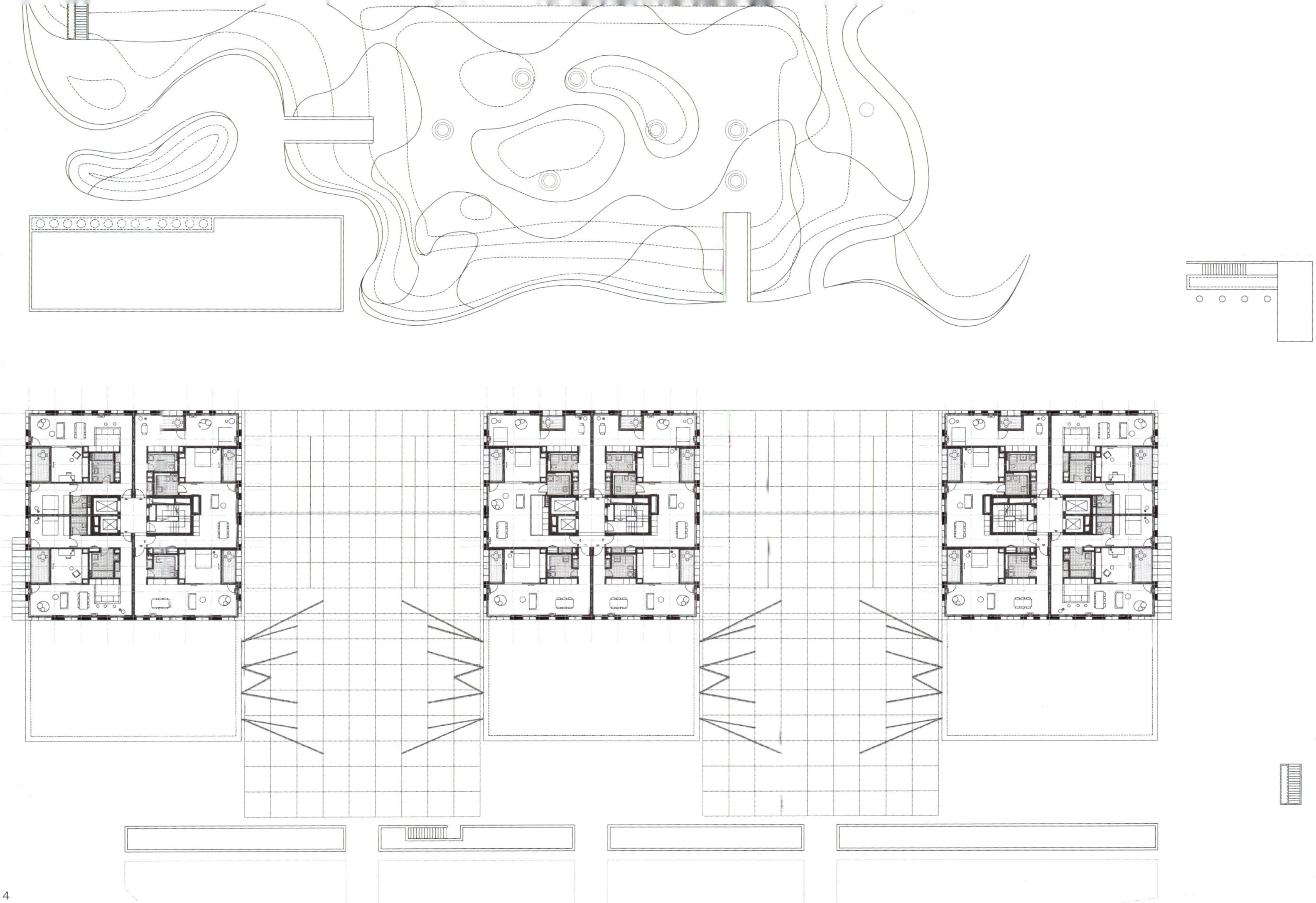

4

Vulcano redefines the urban landscape of the Zurich metropolis by integrating a multi-program volume that combines horizontality and verticality in a dynamic composition closely connected to the city and its new transport infrastructures. The building is constructed around a five-story base with a hotel, retail and office spaces, supporting three identical residential towers. To the rear of the site, their façades rise in continuity with the horizontal volume and open onto a park. On the street side, they are set back, leaving plenty of room for the base, which houses a number of walkways. These porosities invite us to enjoy the protected interior gardens. By its articulation of full and empty spaces, Vulcano engages with the different scales of the site, weaving a dialogue between density and breathing space, between nature, the city, and architecture.

1 Mixed-use development positioned along the railway line to Zurich. Site model, scale 1:500, 2012.
2 Concept for the base and canopy between the foot and body of the towers. Model, scale 1:500, 2013.
3 Cross-section of base and towers.
4 Floor plan of residential units.
5 Vertical city: towers; horizontal city: base.
6 Sculpted façade with loggias.

5

6

DUNAMU HEADQUARTERS
SEOUL, SOUTH KOREA
2023–28

The Pixel Tower is an urban sculpture, a fractured volume in which architectural pixels stack up to create a sophisticated interplay of hollows and reliefs.
At its base, a strategic recess allows for the infiltration of public space: the tower is not an obstacle but a passageway, an urban porosity linking two streets. This base, permeable to the city, is overlooked by the lobby on the first level, suspended above the incessant movement of downtown. Higher up, the structure allows itself to be colonized: terraces and loggias become pockets of vegetation in which a rich natural environment unfolds. The rigorous framework of the tower undergoes a metamorphosis: geometric order gives way to the organic, and architecture becomes landscape.

1

2

3

4

5

6

1 Sketch, 2024.
2 Model of the Gangnam district, scale 1:1,000, 2024.
3 Concept for a pixelated tower alongside the Gangnam Intermodal Transit Center.
4 DPA collage/concept. Structure and landscape.
5 DPA collage/concept. Superimposed programs.
6 Fictional perspective. Animated pixel screens.

1

1 Public passageway crossing the base of the tower.
2 Plan of public space and tower base.
3 Section-elevation of the vertical garden.
4 Axonometric cutaway view of the vertical garden.
5 Top of the tower in the city skyline.
6 Work volume dedicated to open spaces.

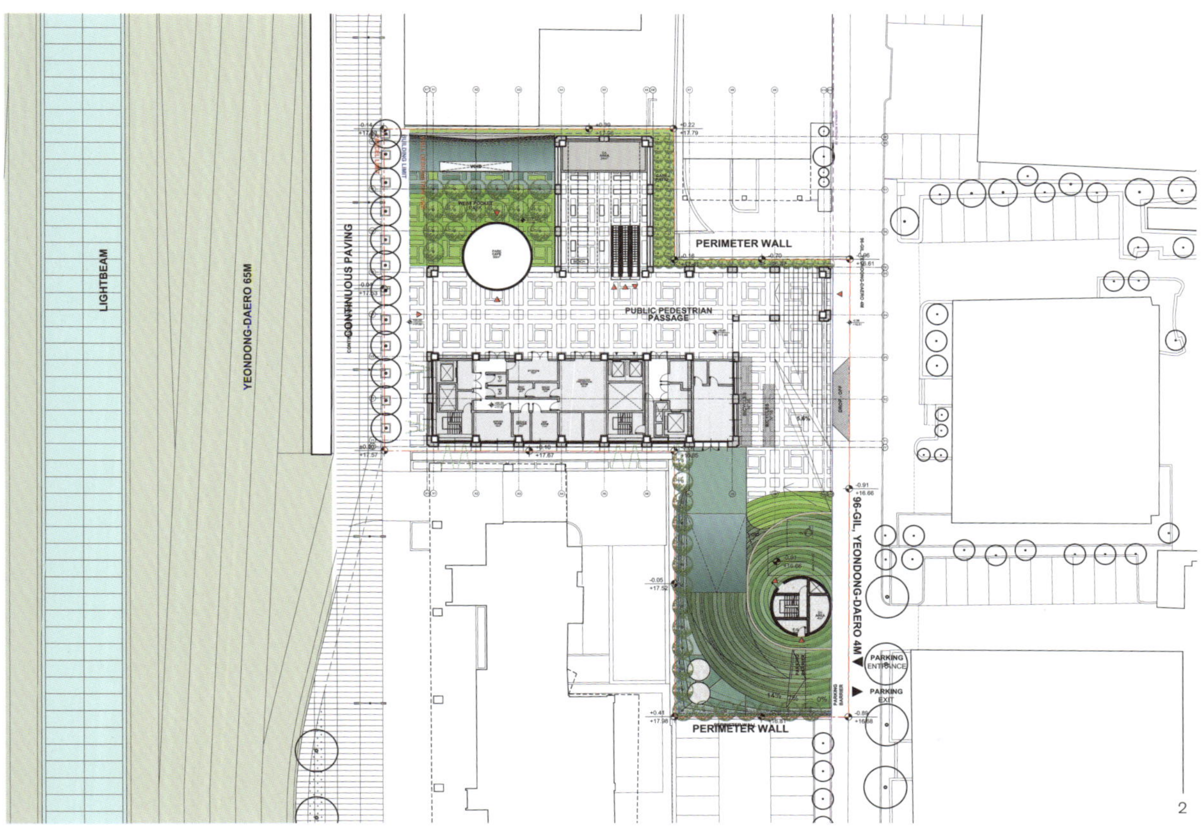

2

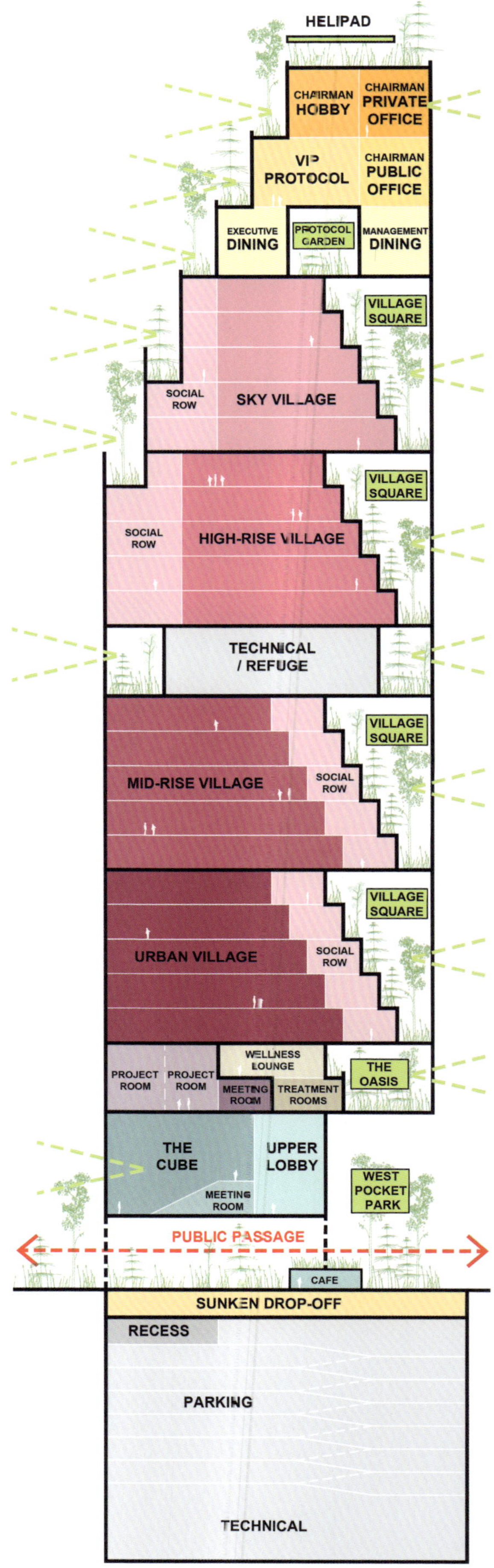

3

4

6

LA LIBERTÉ

GRONINGEN, NETHERLANDS
2007–11

2

3

La Liberté is a new piece of architecture in the urban landscape, a rich addition to a collection of architects' designs scattered across the city of Groningen. This ambitious project superimposes social housing and a hotel over a base of office space. The structure consists of an assembly of stacked cubes, linked by an oblong, aerial platform, marking the transition between the hotel program and the residential area. This composition of balanced volumes gives the building a sculptural dynamic, reinforced by a play of materials: on the different façades appear shades of brick in white, grey, and brown. To catch the northern light and blend the homes into their surroundings, thin volumes of mirror-polished metal are grafted perpendicular to the vertical walls, multiplying reflections and extending the landscape into the very heart of the interior spaces.

1 Plays of volumes articulating the human scale and that of the infrastructure of the adjacent ring road.
2 Plan of a residential level.
3 Mirror-polished steel panels visually extending the interior of the dwelling outwards.

HOCHHAUS GATE 2

VIENNA, AUSTRIA

2014

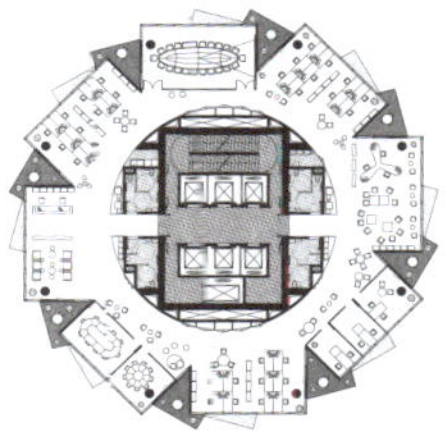

1

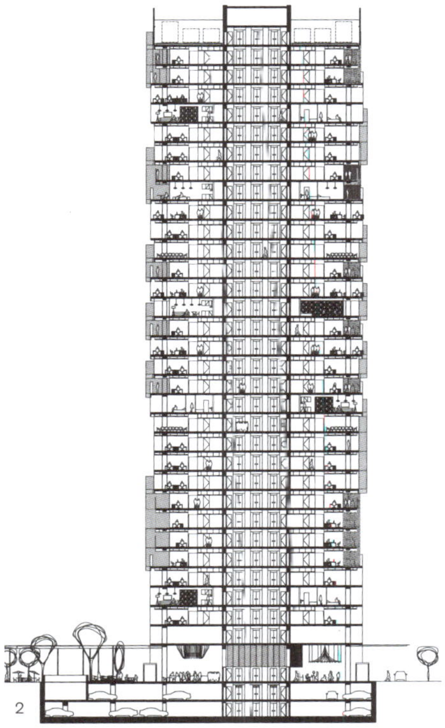

2

Hochaus Gate reinvents the cylindrical tower as an evolving organism. Its circular plan generates a unique flexibility: living modules grafted onto a central core can be combined or separated, creating office and residential spaces that evolve as needs change. The façade is indented by a series of planted terraces, sculpting a vertical landscape in which each balcony forms an inhabited excrescence. The whole complex unfolds in a concretion around the core, giving rise to an expressive play of volumes: visually, Hochaus Gate evokes a mechanism in motion, a stack of rotating gears that breathes kinetic energy into the Viennese skyline and the district marked by the presence of the famous gasometers.

3

1, 2 This hybrid tower consists of a central circular core, retaining the advantages of the cylinder, surrounded by eight rectangular modules offering efficient office floors without loss of space.

3 The mechanics of the volumes allow for the flexible and rational interlocking of a variety of uses.

TIMBER MARINA TOWER

VIENNA, AUSTRIA

2019–28

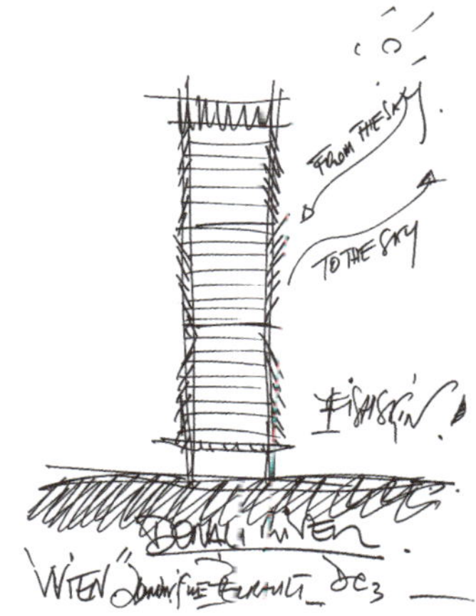

1

This enigmatic tower rises up like a totem emblematic of the new Marina district, on the banks of the Danube. Beyond its height, it stands out for the materials of its façades. Supported by a wooden structure, it is made up of four stacked prisms, whose slightly sloping sides evoke sails of fabric lifted by the wind. Clad in copper-tinted metal brise-soleils, they create a constantly changing play of golden-brown lines. The choice of smoked glass accentuates the vibration of these reflections, so that perception of the building varies with the angle from which it is approached. Like a minimalist art installation, the building subtly and with great economy of means transforms its environment, producing a powerful visual and emotional impact.

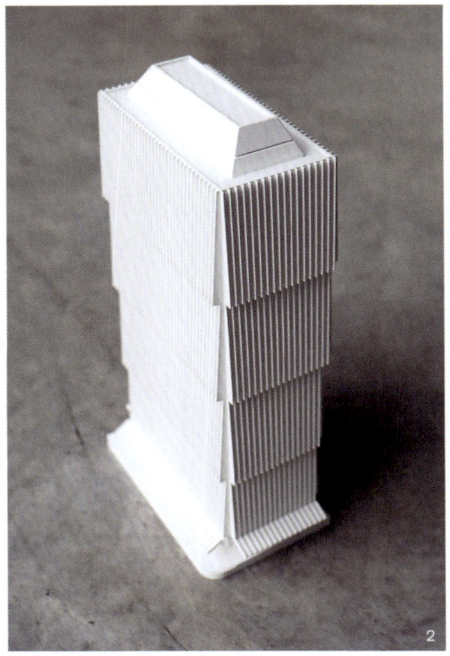

2

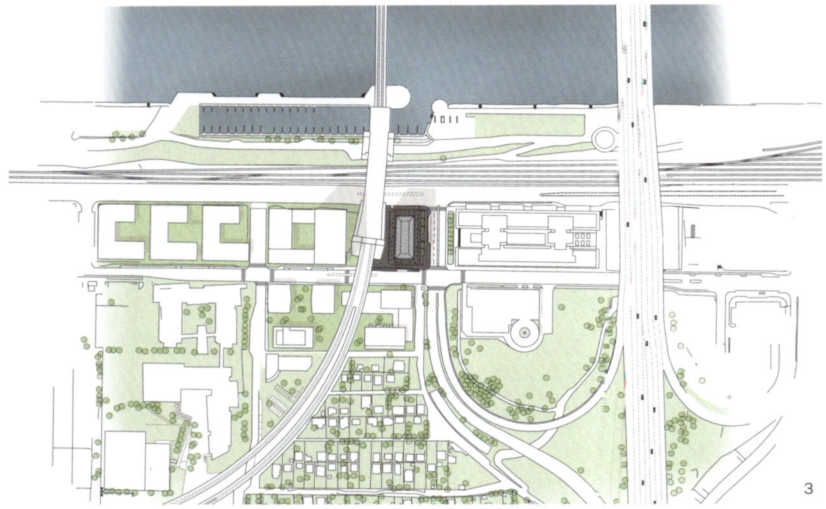

3

4

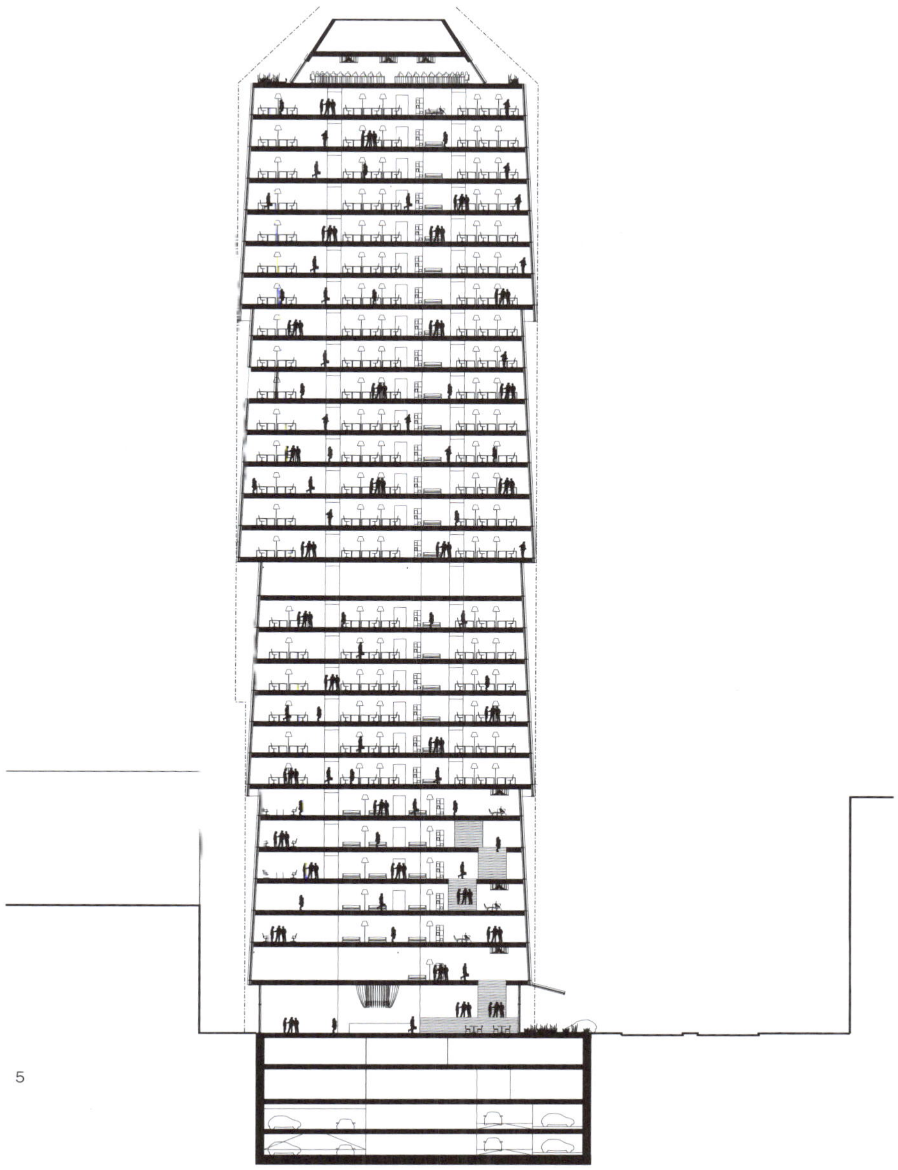

5

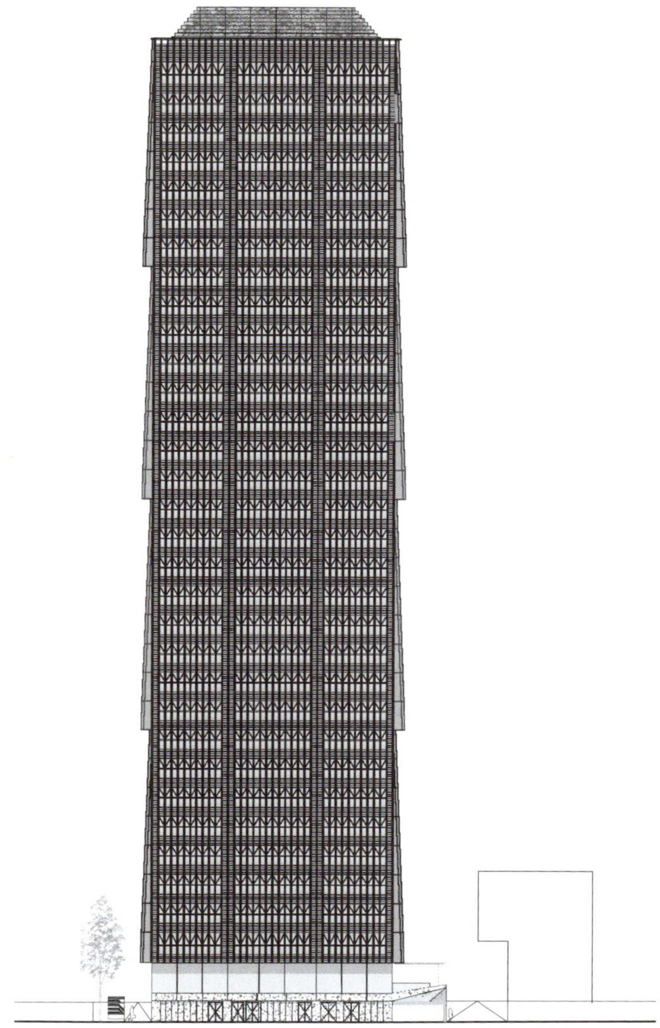

6

1 Sketch, 2020
2 Volumetric model, scale 1:500, 2019.
3 Layout of the tower abutting Donaumarina metro station.
4 The Timber Marina Tower, a 120-meter tower built in timber.
5, 6 Elevation and cross-section over the Danube.
7 Volumetric studies illustrating the evolution of the tower's form.

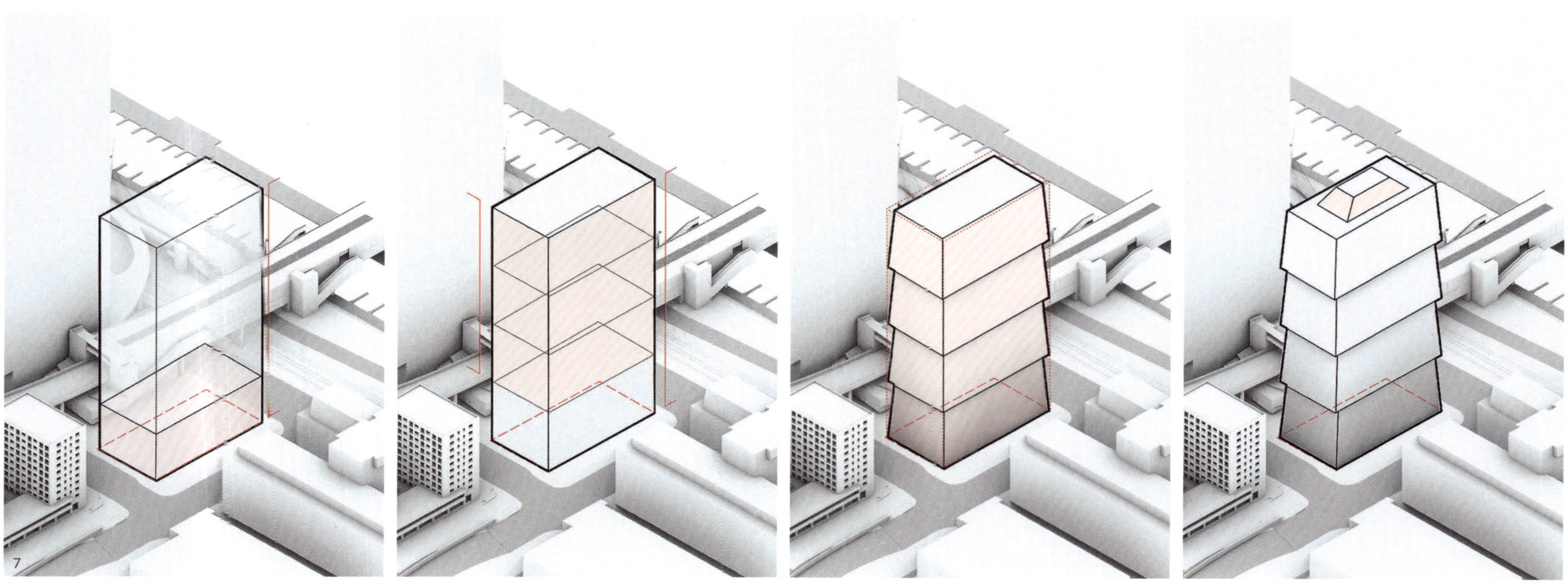

7

1

DYAD – ONE CHEONGDAM-DONG

SEOUL, SOUTH KOREA

2022–25

With its marbled façades, the Cheongdam-dong tower comes across as a timeless monolith, between gravity and lightness, closure and openness. Its structure, composed of a stack of stone blocks, blurs the coordinates, defying both spatial scale and the perception of time. This raw material, carved from the mineral earth, will evolve over the years: its natural patina, far from altering its character, will give it depth and authenticity, like a work of art or a vintage wine that improves with age, with the strength of a vestige and the modernity of an architectural gesture. Inside, wide windows frame the city like an ever-changing painting. On the roof terrace, the architecture recedes into the background: the ground merges with the horizon, fading naturally into the sky.

1

2

3

1 Ivory Rocks echoes the stone surfaces of the surrounding hills.
2 This project is rooted in its context and offers its users an interior luxury: the comfort of seeing without being seen.
3 The sculptural work.

DANCING TOWER – EUROVEA CITY

BRATISLAVA, SLOVAKIA
2024

Standing on the banks of the Danube, this sculptural tower is the first vertical figure in the urban renewal of Bratislava's Eurovea City district. Composed of stacked layers, their plans progressively staggered, it forms a moving, dancing silhouette, evoking the fluidity of the river. Each floor becomes a distinct gesture, a precise spatial variation, while the subtle interplay of recesses and projections creates a kinetic façade that changes constantly with the light and vantage point. Anchored in a base that extends out into the landscape, the tower establishes an active relationship with its surroundings. With its free, organic form, combining context and architectural expression, it rethinks vertical living by offering everyone, at each level, balconies that open onto the city and the Danube.

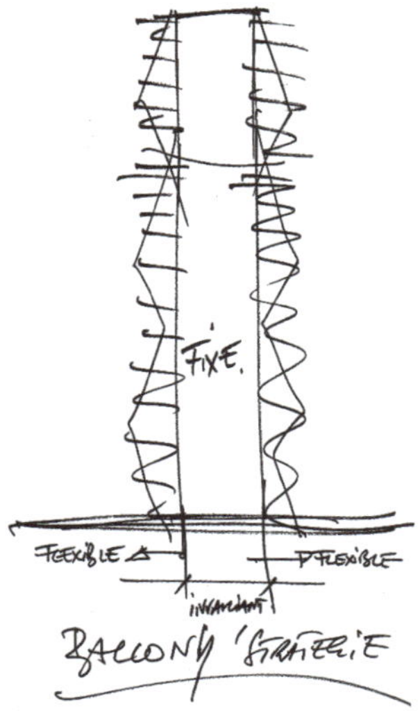

1

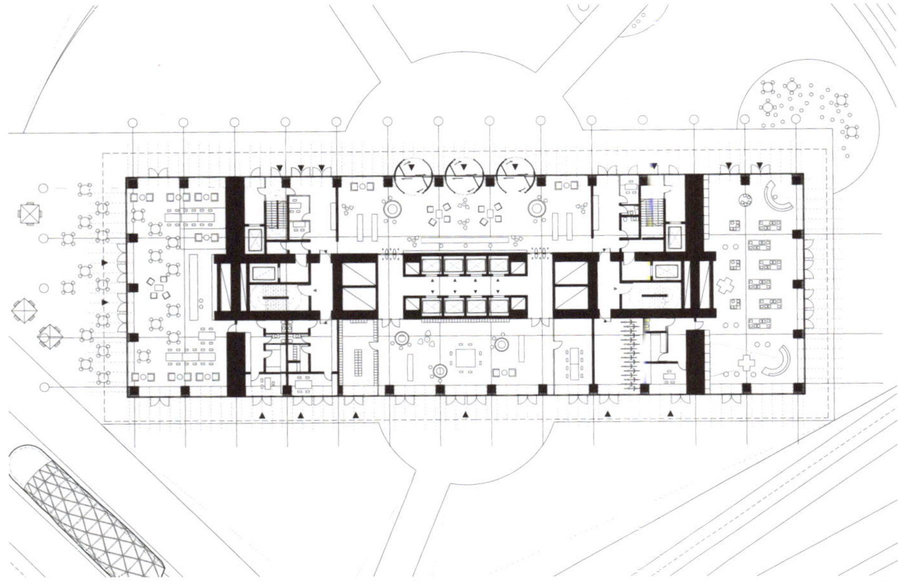

2

3

4

1, 4 Sketches, 2024.
2 Plan of garden level.
3 View of the industrial harbor.
5 Model of the site, scale 1:2,000, 2024.
6 Stereolithography 3D model, scale 1:1,000, 2024.

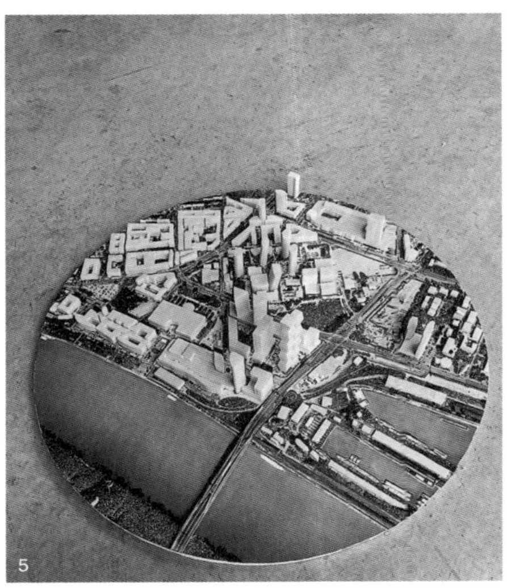

5

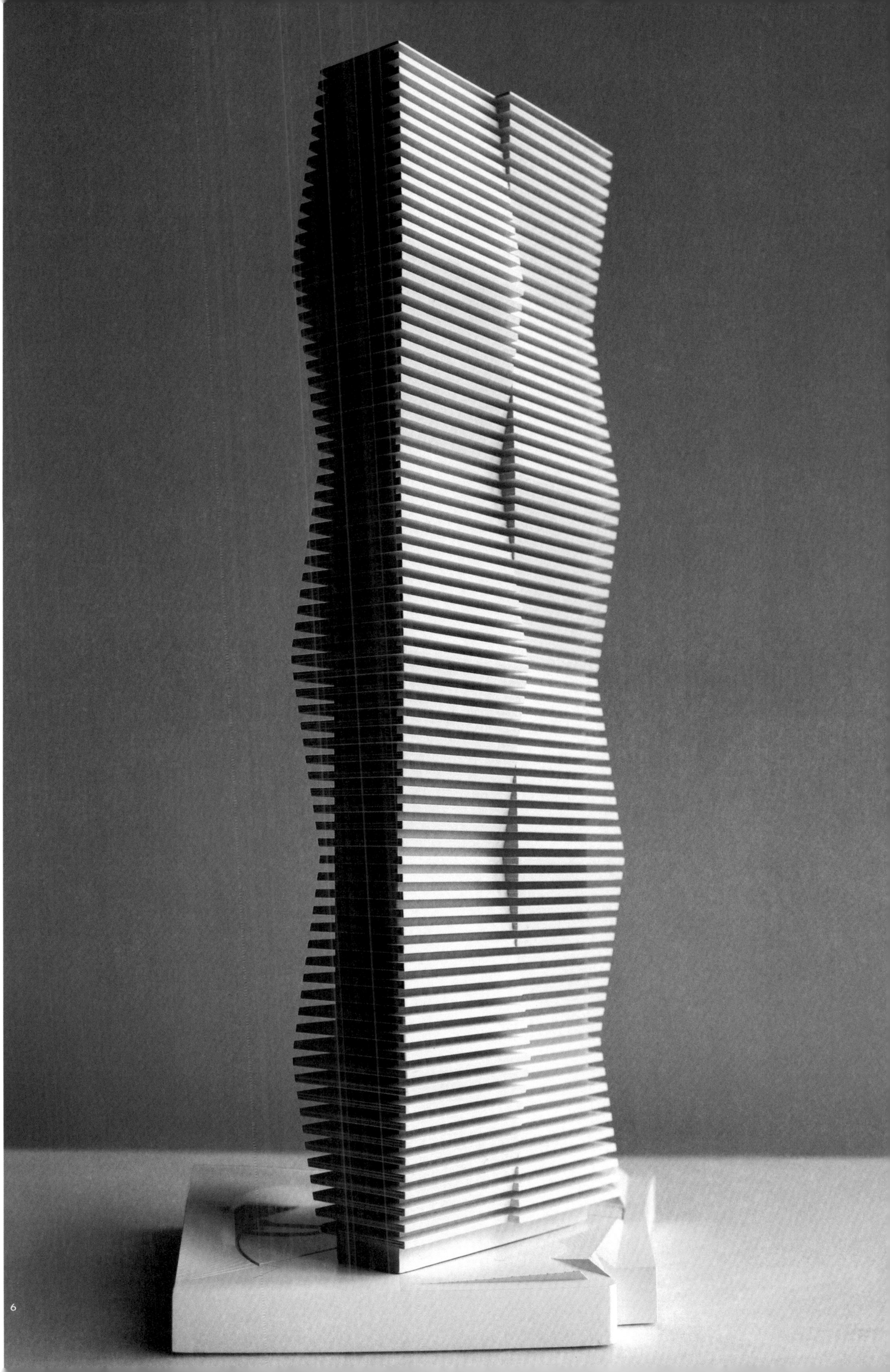

6

DONAU CITY TOWER I

VIENNA, AUSTRIA

2002–14

The first tower to be built in this fast-growing area on the banks of the Danube, DC Tower I was conceived as the first of a pair of towers. The gateway to Danube Island, it turns slightly towards the river and features a pleated façade with a cascade of folds, evoking the movements of a waterfall. Clad in deep black glass, it captures the light of the sky and, at dusk, is transformed into a golden surface, vibrating in the last rays of the sun.

1

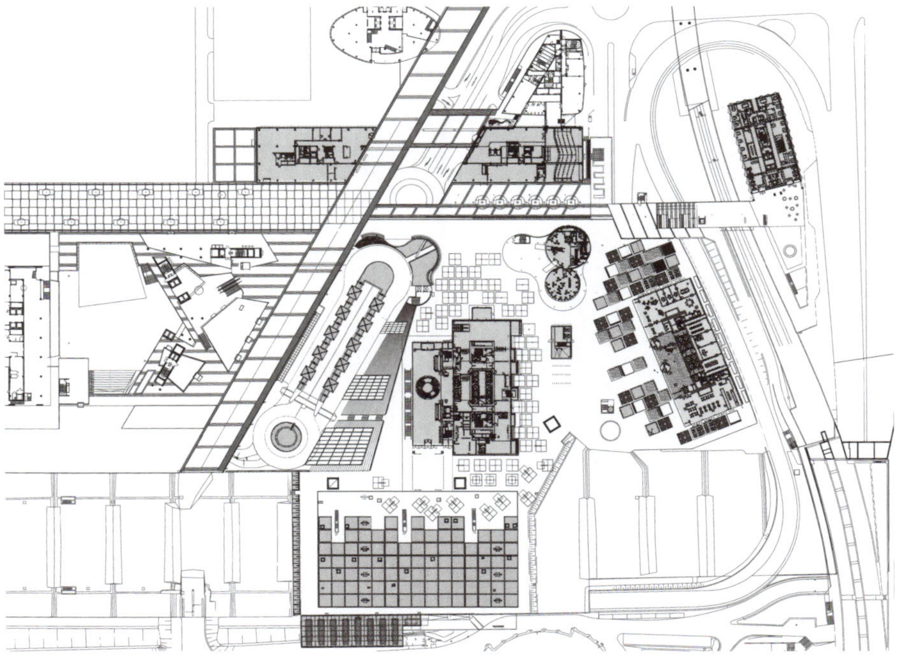

2

1 Sketch, concept of fractured block, 1+1=1, 2005.
2 Plan of the Donau City district.
3 Donau City Tower I, on the banks of the Danube.
4 Reflections on the surface of the water and on the façade of the tower.

3

1

1 The folds of glass contrast with the other rectilinear façades.
2-5 Diversity of programs and uses: restaurants, services, hotel, residences, offices, rooftop.
6 Reflections on the black pleated façade at sunset.
7 Concept of fracture between two blocks. Model, scale 1:500, 2005.

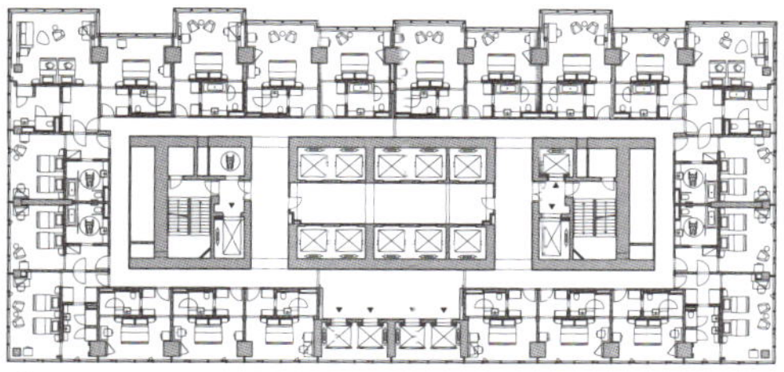

2

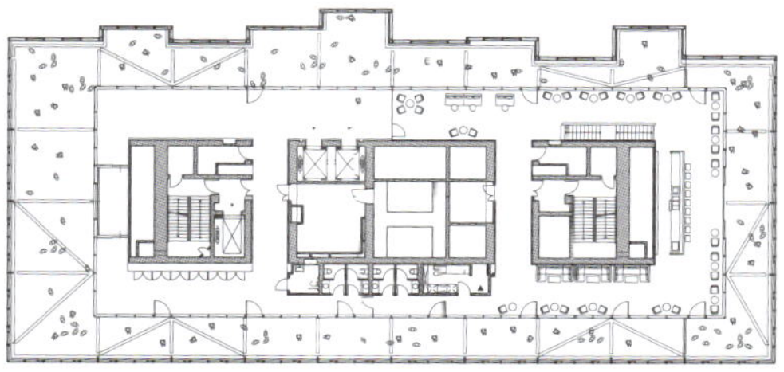

3

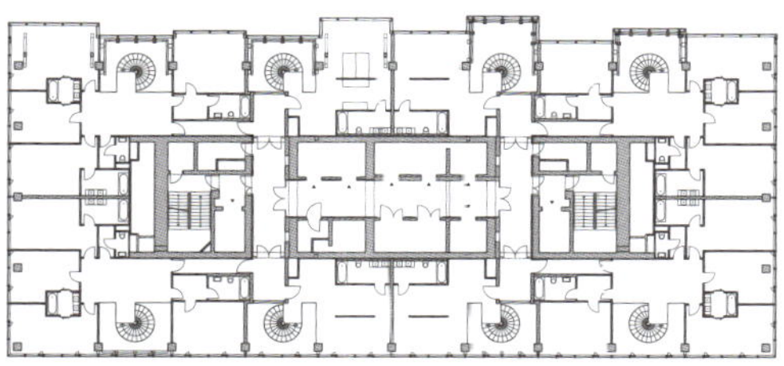

4

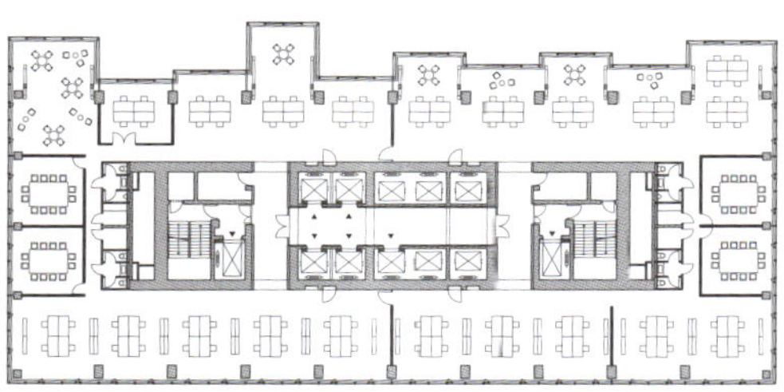

5

7

6

"Geometry carries with it a political writing that is never neutral."

1

3

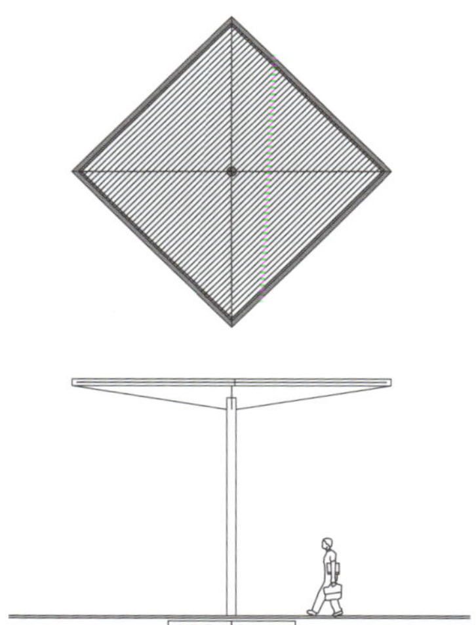

2

4

5

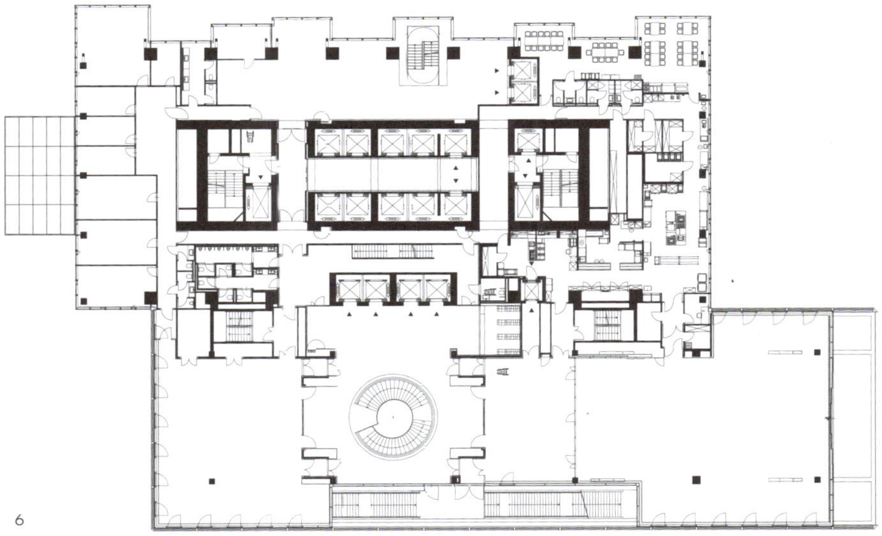

6

7

1-2 Array of canopies/windbreaks at the foot of the tower.
3 Rooftop terrace protected from the wind, offering a view over Vienna.
4 Interior view of the filter façade, with sunlight and reflections on the metal mesh imprinted on the glass.
5 Play of blacks and transparencies in the entrance lobby.
6 Plan of the public square.
7 Play of darkness and light on the floor landings.

DONAU CITY TOWER II

VIENNA, AUSTRIA
2002–27

Alongside DC Tower I, DC Tower II imposes an equally assertive silhouette, but with a different vocabulary. Clad in an envelope of solar panels, it has an extended outer layer of wide balconies that wrap around its entire perimeter, on every level, regardless of whether it is used for residential or office purposes. Free of any spatial hierarchy, it offers unique potential for flexibility.

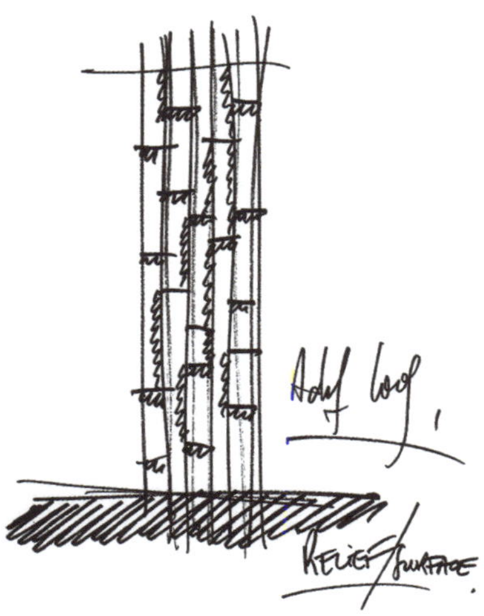

1

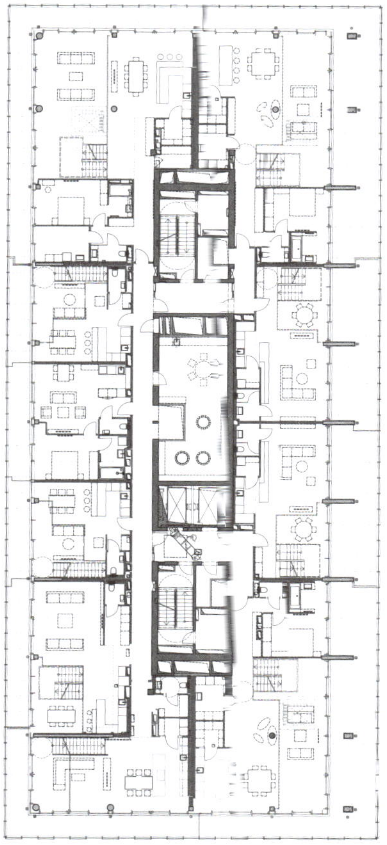

4

5

6

1 Sketch, 2006.
2 Ten years after Tower I, Donau City Tower II rises up opposite.
3 The façade of woven railings and solar panels wraps around the tower's balconies at every level.
4 Plan of a standard residential floor with peripheral balconies.
5 View of the balconies.
6 The rigorous geometry of the façade elements.

TO-LYON

LYON, FRANCE
2012–24

This tower is a major element in the transformation of the Part-Dieu district, enhancing the architectural heritage of the 1970s while regenerating public spaces and transport. With a view to preserving the land, the project is high-density and set in a prominent position on the new central square, opposite the station. Its eight-story, mixed-use plinth meshes with the horizontality of the city and connects directly to the station's main gallery. The vertical part, housing offices and coworking spaces, becomes a metropolitan landmark. Its faceted black façades, inspired by the region's volcanic stones, particularly obsidian, catch the light from all angles, emphasizing the site's geographical identity.

1

1 View from station forecourt.
2 L-shaped tower, with a mixed-use program at the base and office space at the top.
3 The tower's morphology creates a link between the horizontal and vertical city.
4 Lighting study.
5 Development scenario for the new station square. Model, scale 1:500, 2018.

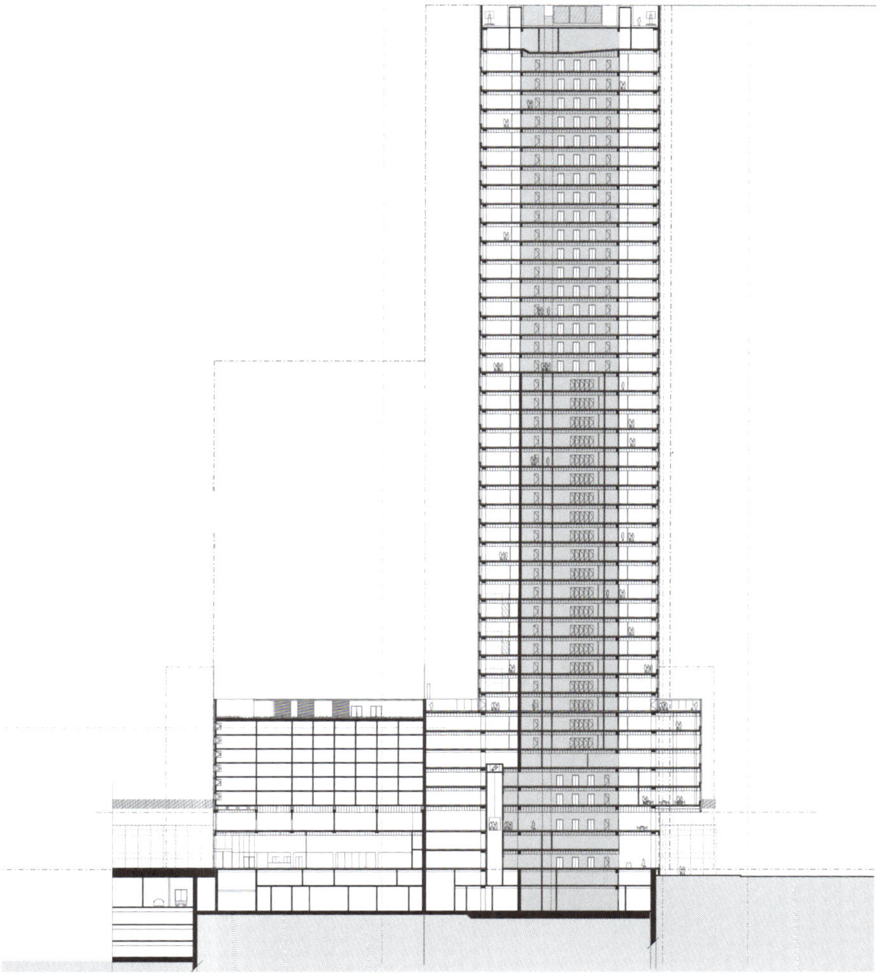
2

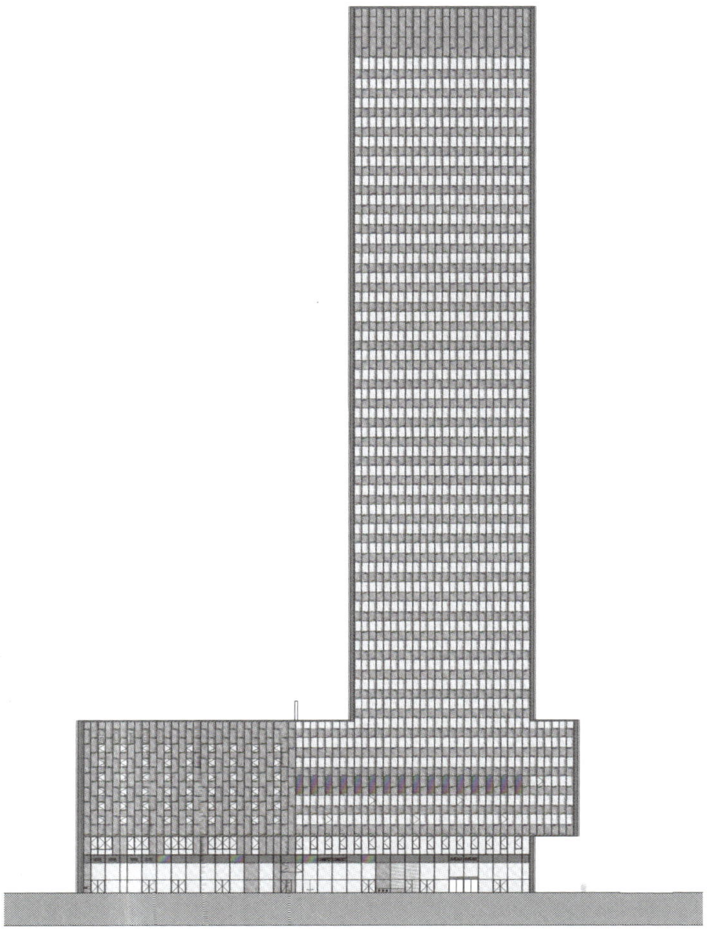
3

4

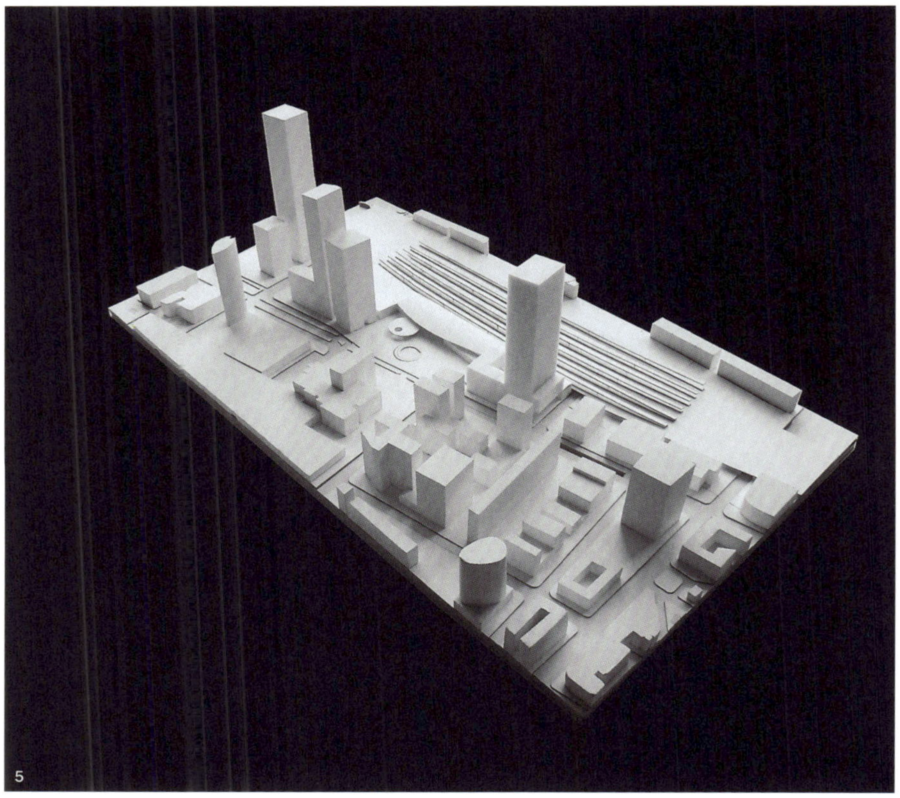
5

1

2

1 The mosaic of façade panes forms a skin sensitive to variations in light.
2 The head-to-tail arrangement of a repeated motif imparts vibrancy to the façade.
3-6 Relief studies of the façade, sculpted like obsidian.

3

4

5

6

PARISLONGCHAMP HIPPODROME

PARIS, FRANCE

2011–18

1

Longchamp is as much a landscaping project as an architectural one, involving rethinking the grandstand, equestrian infrastructure, and green spaces of the racecourse. First, 55,000 square meters of grass were replanted, erasing the asphalt surfaces and reintegrating the racecourse into its green setting. The new grandstand extends the historic structures, incorporating the dynamics of racing into its design. Comprised of open, staggered platforms, it has neither a front nor a rear but unfolds to embrace the landscape at three hundred and sixty degrees: Paris and the Eiffel Tower, the racetrack, the parade ring, the stables and the Bois de Boulogne, designed in the nineteenth century by Adolphe Alphand. The architecture blends into its surroundings: its golden-brown hue, inspired by the colors of autumn, echoes the season of the Prix de l'Arc de Triomphe, a high point in the life of the racecourse.

2

3

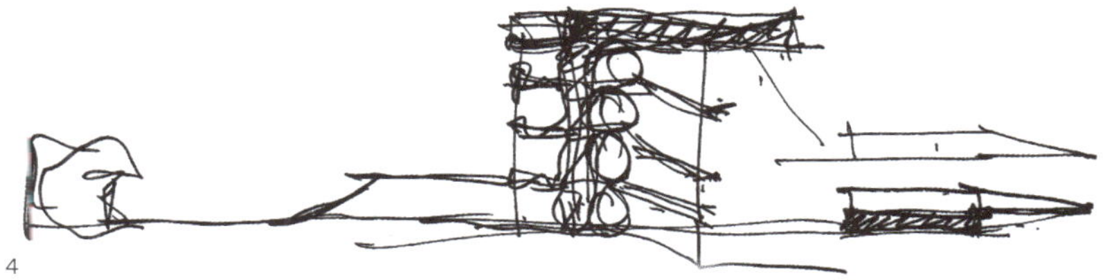

4

5

1 Aerial view of the 60-hectare Longchamp racecourse in the heart of the Bois de Boulogne.
2 Paul Marmuse, historical view of the pavilion grandstand.
3 Guesnu, “Bois de Boulogne,” engraving *in Les Promenades de Paris*, early 19th century (Paris, Musée Carnavalet). General view and detail of the site of the future Longchamp racecourse.
4 Sketch, 2011.
5 The main entrance to the racecourse.
6 Cross-section of the presidential lounge and grand staircase.

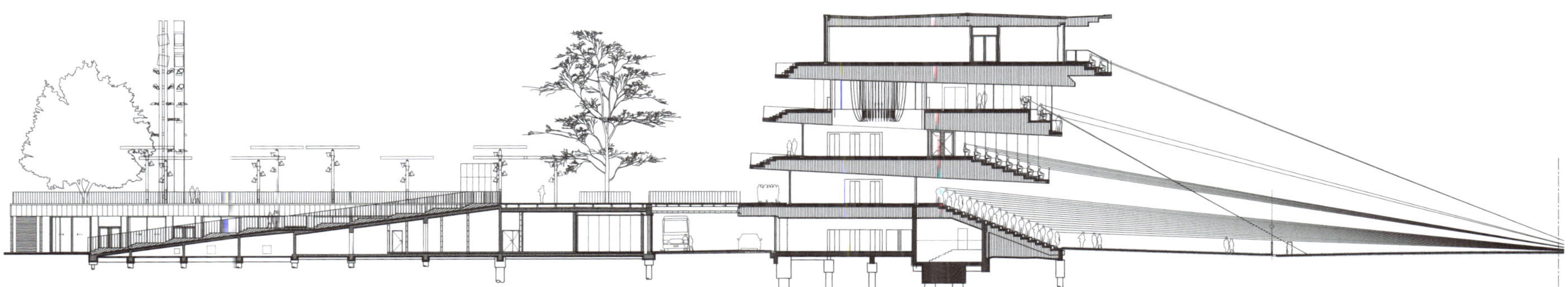

6

1 Cantilever: movement and lightness.
2-4 Light-filtering metal fabric: opaque seen from outside, transparent from the inside.
5 The élan of the grandstand reaching towards the racetrack.
6-9 Kinematics of the architecture: movements of planes, orientations and framing of views.
10 Schematic cross-section showing neither front nor back, but visual transparencies.

5

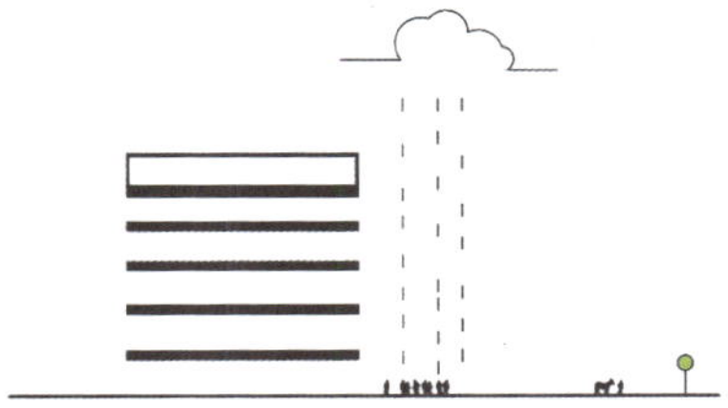

6

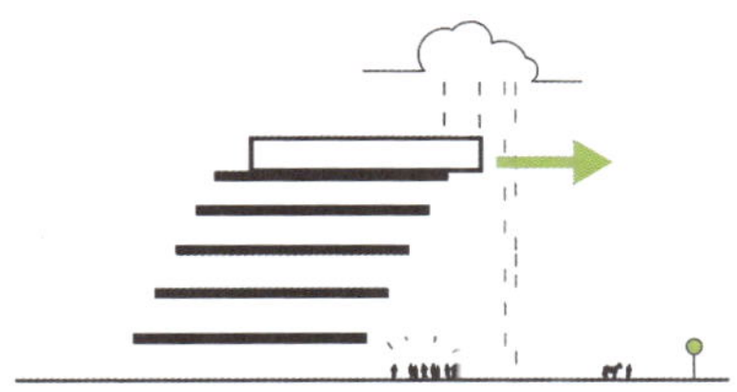

7

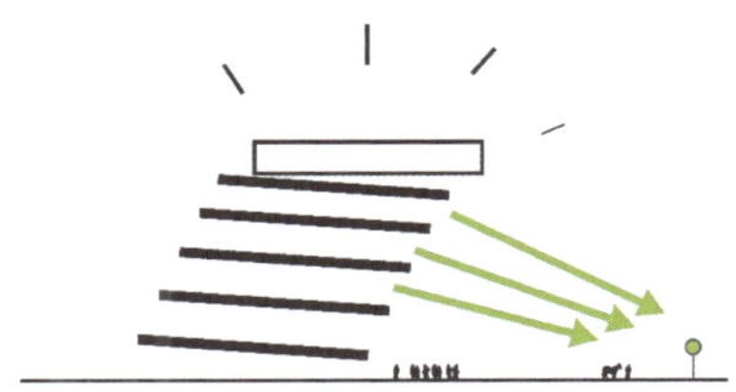

8

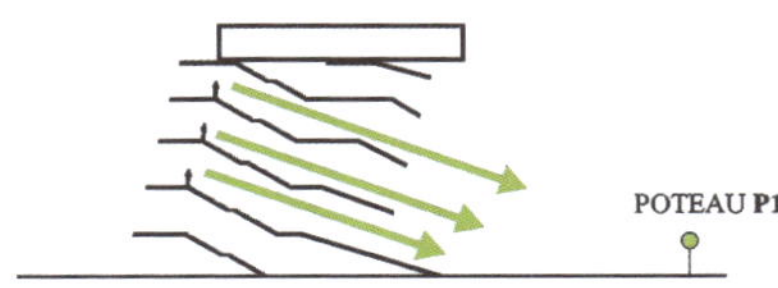

9

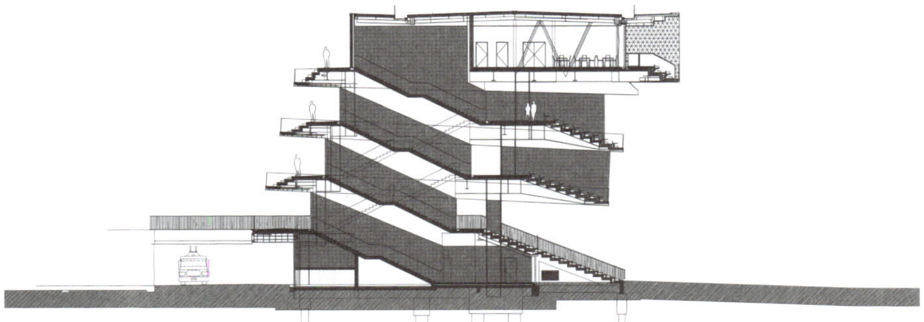

10

"Architectural biomimicry does not copy nature—it extracts its logics in order to create a second nature."

FRANCE GALOP

FRANCE GALOP
19

SEJONG INTERNATIONAL GARDEN CITY EXHIBITION

SEJONG, SOUTH KOREA
2024–26

1

2

3

4

5

6

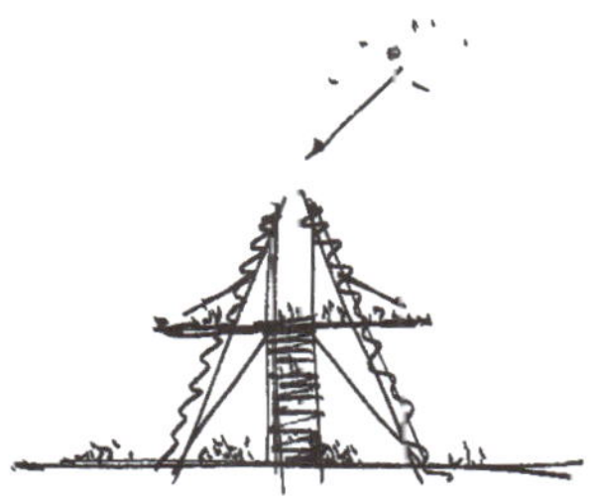

7

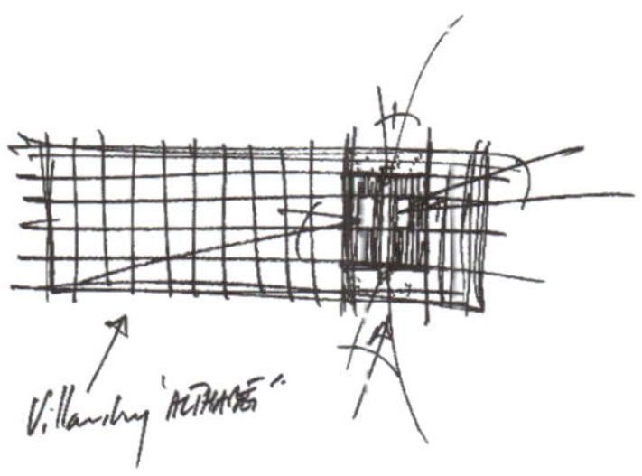

8

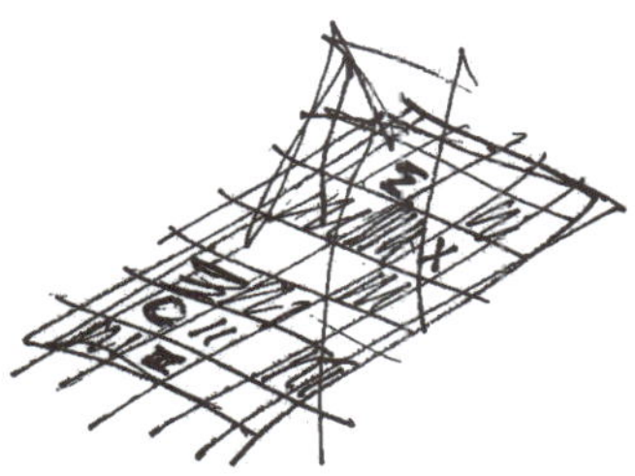

9

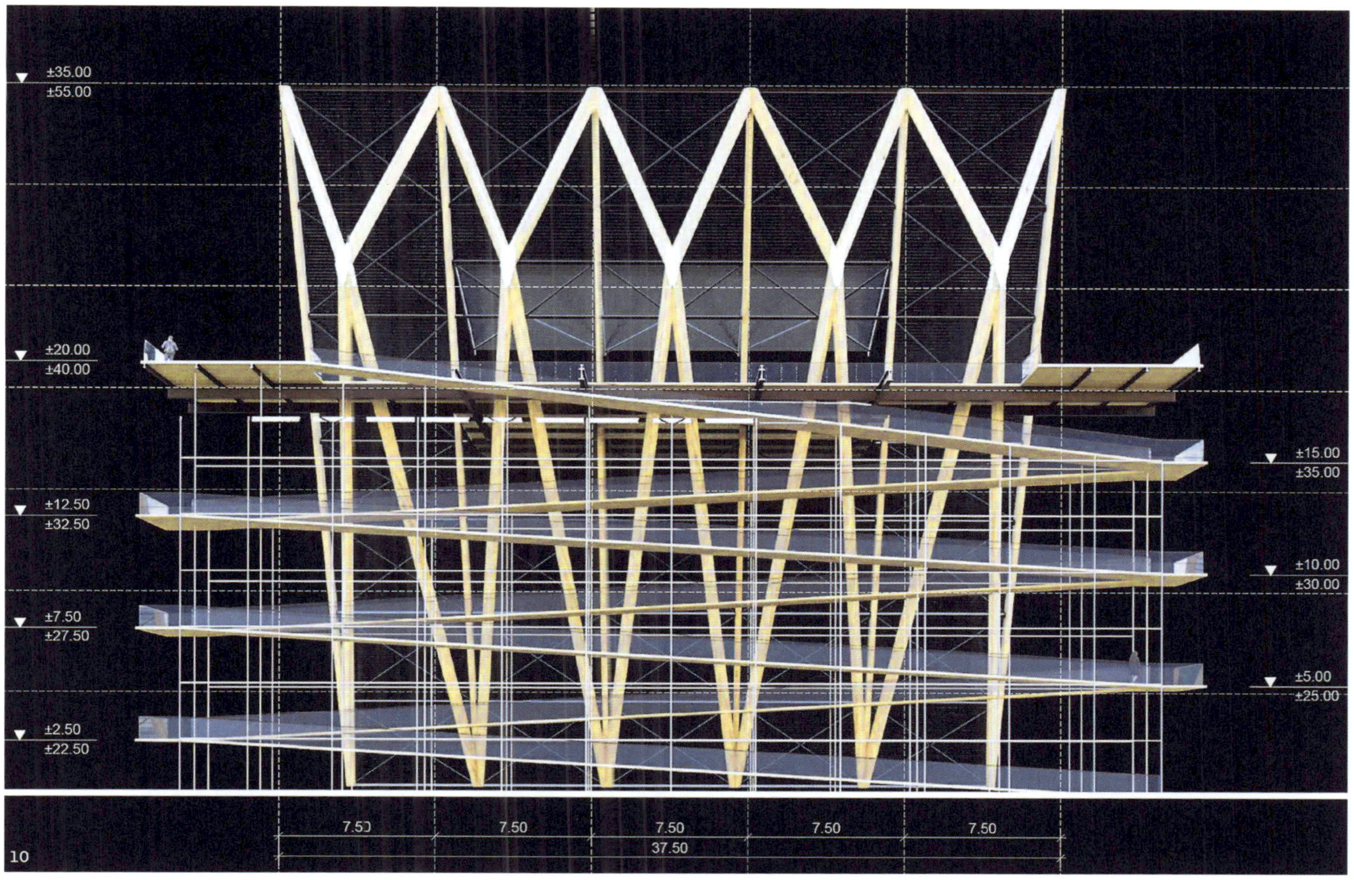

10

11

In the heart of the new town of Sejong, surrounded by mountains, this observatory emerges like a structure woven into the landscape. Overlooking the lake and botanical gardens, it is reminiscent of nineteenth-century factories. Its light structure skims the ground, like a butterfly alighting on a flower. Its sloping wings are clad in a metal veil, a trellis over which luxuriant foliage unfurls, fusing architecture and nature. A spiral ramp guides the visitor, gradually revealing the panorama and leading to a cross-shaped belvedere facing the four cardinal points. At a height of twenty meters, this aerial landmark offers a view of the city, the lake, the mountains, and the gardens, arranged in a majestic composition, where the plant representation of Hangul calligraphy takes on its full dimension in the immensity of the landscape

1 A hut-like silhouette emerges from the heart of the botanical garden.
2 Nature appropriates the façades, clinging to them and climbing up the metal fabric.
3 The belvedere, seen from the garden.
4 View of the city from the belvedere.
5-9 Installation sketch, 2024.
10 All-wood structure.
11 Structure covered with metal mesh.

KINDARENA

ROUEN, FRANCE

2006–12

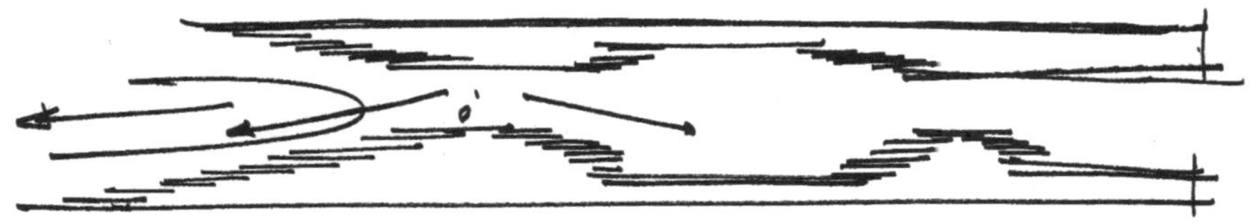

1

The Palais des Sports in Rouen is designed as if it were a theatre, skillfully staged: it comes across as free, defined by ground and sky whose play of light and reflections are constantly generating life. The city's ground is transformed into a new topography of tiered steps leading to a public esplanade that acts as an agora. This space with extended opening hours can be used for cultural events.

Visitors climb these wide stairs to enter the structure and pass the glass enclosure, where they are faced with the depth of the sports arenas below. The cantilevered roof is the counterpart of the plinth: it projects a gigantic canopy in the form of an inverted pyramid, whose mirrored stainless-steel cladding multiplies the movements of the city in spectacular staccato movements.

1 Sketch, 2006.
2 Demountable model showing superimposed ground layers. Scale 1:200, 2008.
3 Extension of the public space to the main entrance at the top of the steps.
4 Location of the project on the edge of the infrastructure zone.

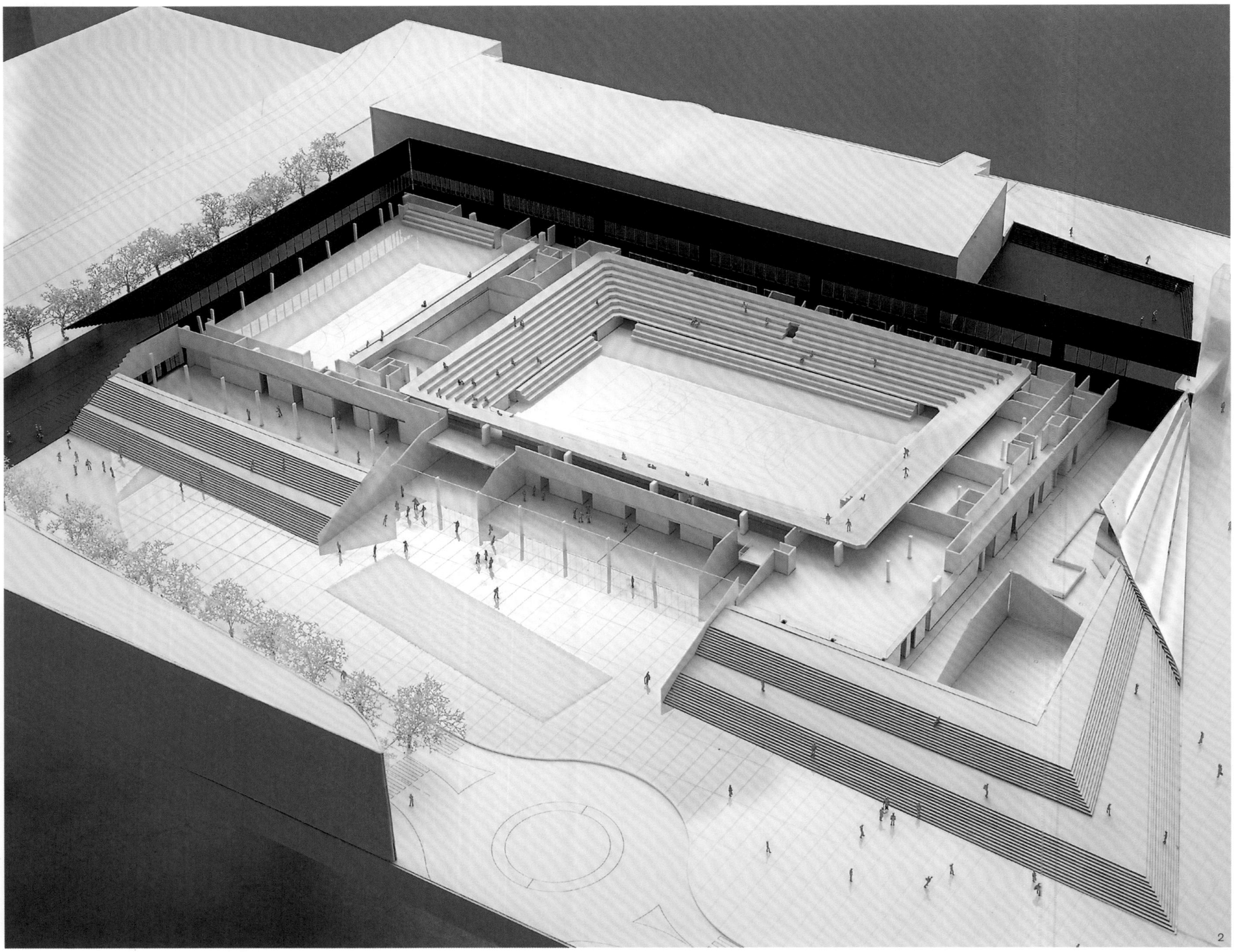

2

3

“Architecture must take root in the common ground where urban substance is found.”

4

BILLETTERIE

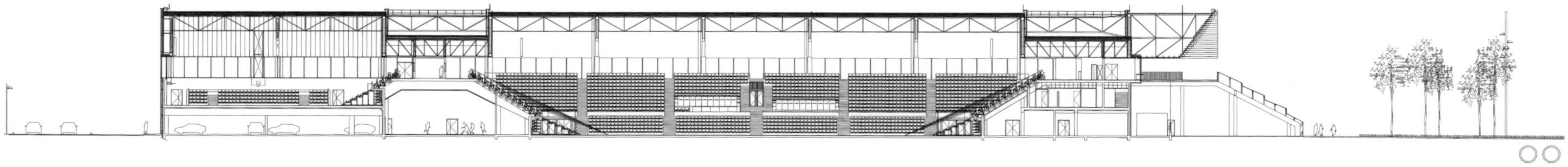

1

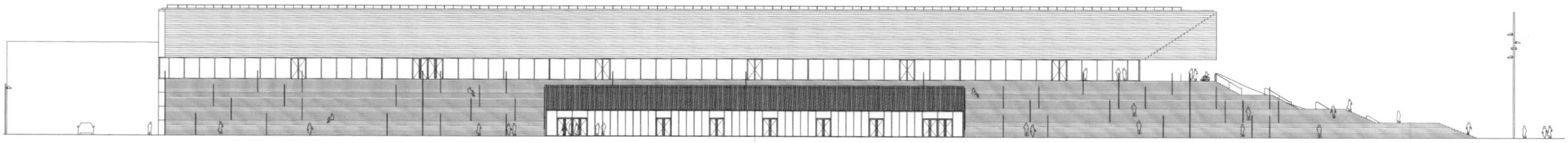

2

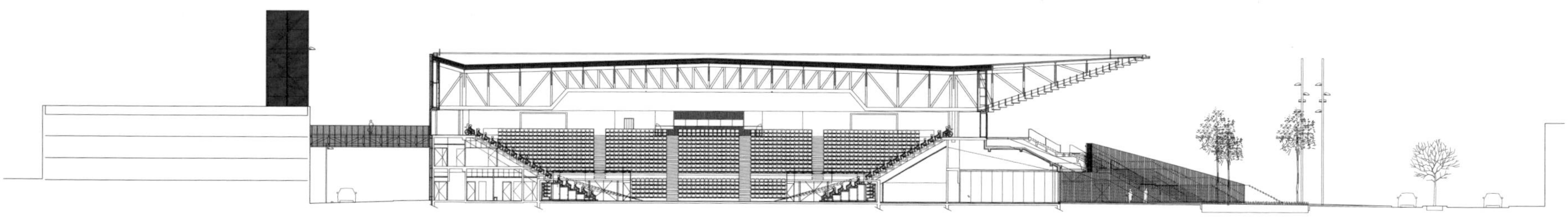

3

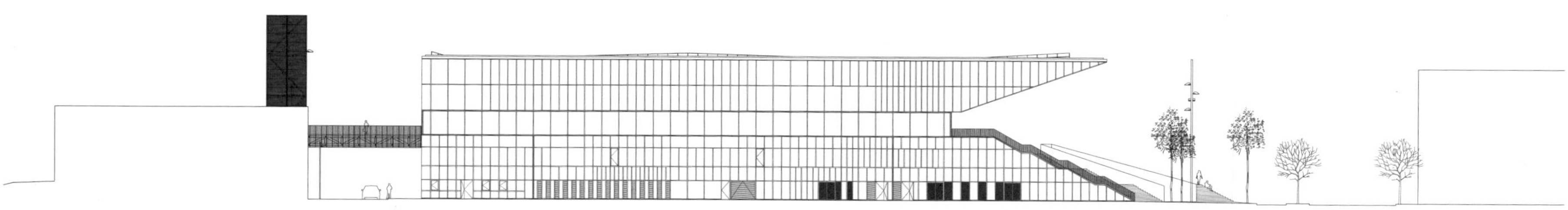

4

1 A topography housing several sports programs under one roof.
2 An immobile volume: a stable base anchored to the ground.
3 Dialogue between heavy and light.
4 The façade design unifies roof and base in a single volume.
5 Main sports hall with bleachers.
6 Balcony-belvedere.
7 Ticket booth.

5

6

7

ARGANZUELA FOOTBRIDGE
MADRID, SPAIN
2008–11

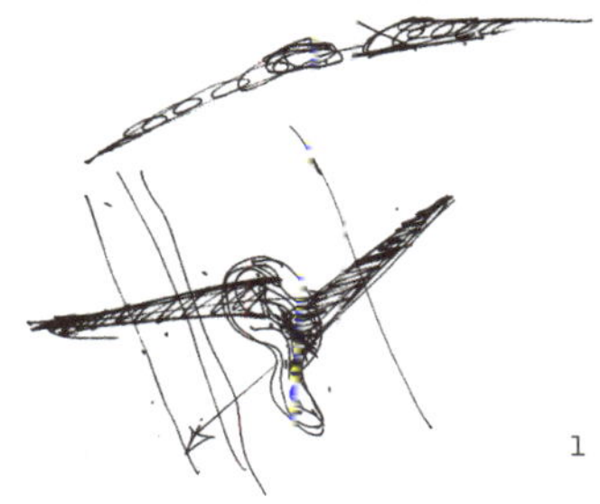
1

2

Moving the roads running alongside the Manzanares river underground freed up a new area, transformed into a green lung in the heart of Madrid: Arganzuela Park, which extends over twenty-three hectares on both banks. In the heart of this natural setting, an extraordinary footbridge crosses the river. Suspended in mid-air, it is made up of two slender cones, slightly offset from each other, opening up a central void that serves as a public square and point of access to the park. Its structure is created by interweaving metal spirals clad in a fluid, openwork veil, like a twisted ribbon. At once protective and ethereal, this metal mesh filters the light, offering shade and glimpses of the urban landscape.

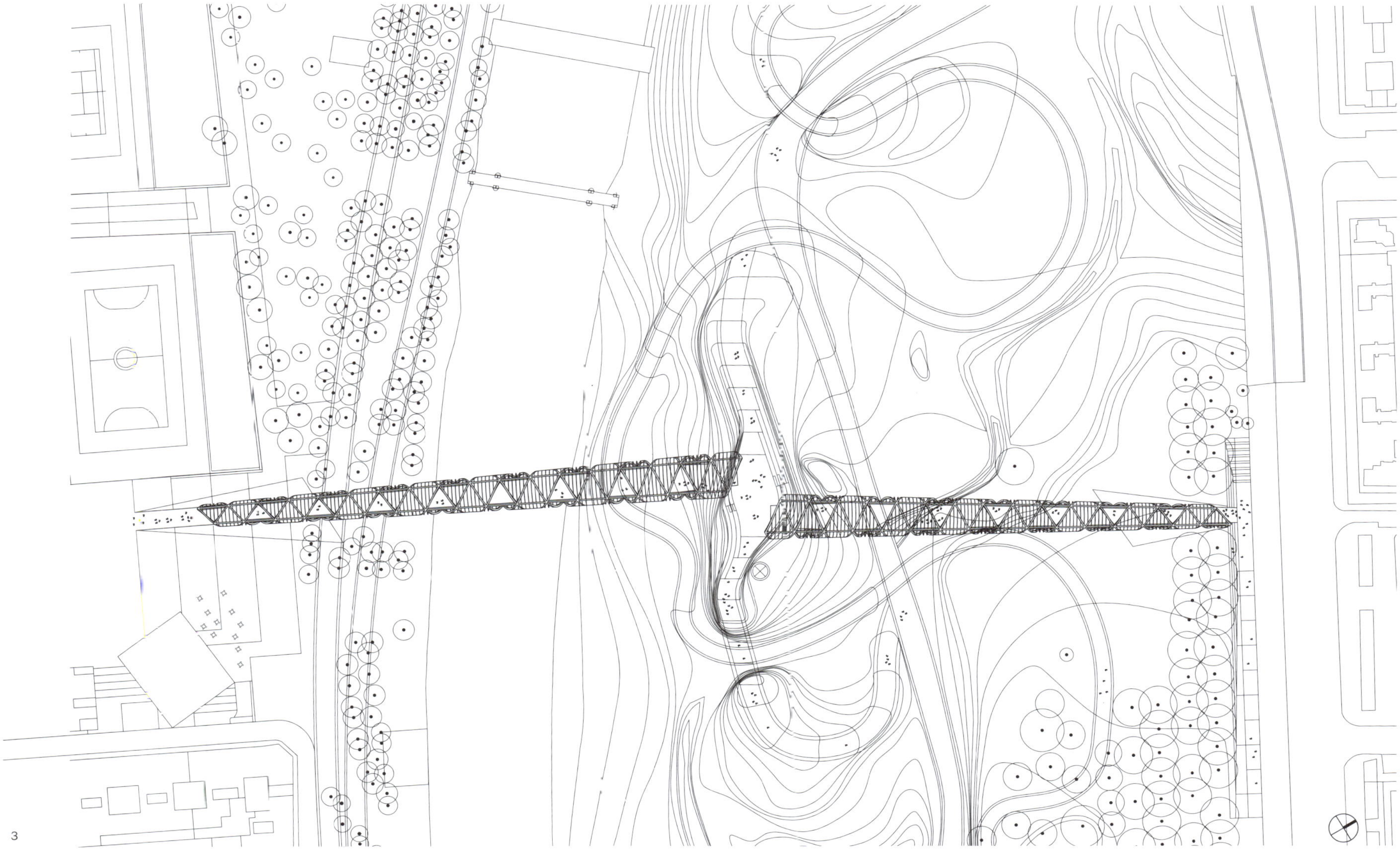

3

1 Sketch, 2005.
2 The footbridge, with its play of light and shadow, spans the Rio Manzanares.
3 Composition: two elongated cores, facing each other but not exactly aligned.
4 Double spiral, on which a metal mesh wraps like a ribbon. Research model, 2006.
5 The gap between the cores opens up access to the surrounding park.

4

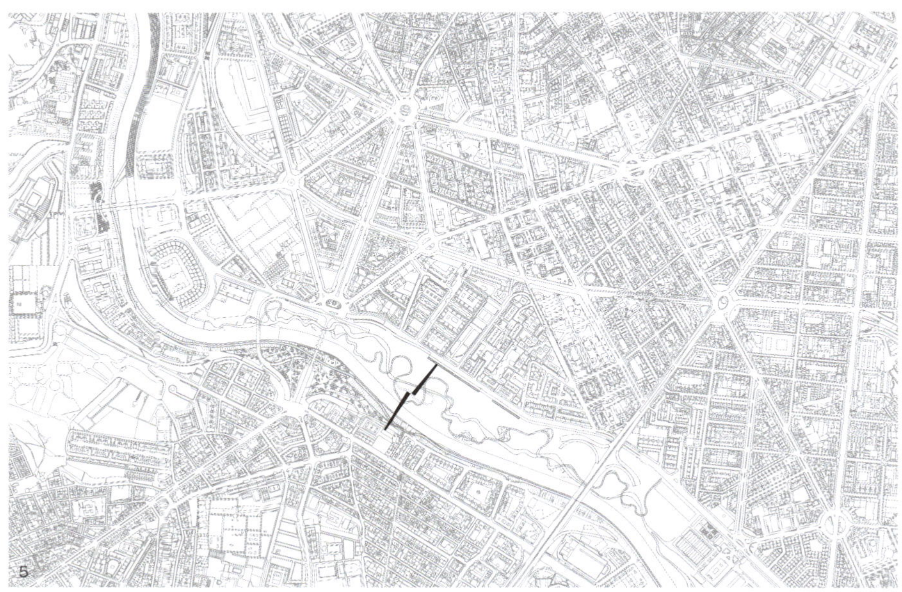

5

NEW MECHANICAL HALL (ME)
ÉCOLE POLYTECHNIQUE FÉDÉRALE DE LAUSANNE

LAUSANNE, SWITZERLAND

2011–16

Lausanne's historic mechanical hall brought together the two autonomous buildings around a central atrium, forming a complex of research laboratories open around the clock. The buildings are united by a uniform shell. This is made up of robotized metal mesh panels that open and close in keeping with the weather. Inclined at five degrees to the façade, on an alternating oblique axis, this automated metal weave interprets the experimental vocation of the hall and represents a milestone in the history of the EPFL campus. The atrium at the heart of the building is a true cognitive space. With its synaptic walkways, it is the beating heart of this brain dedicated to research. It is a meeting place for researchers, students, and anyone else involved in the various laboratories.

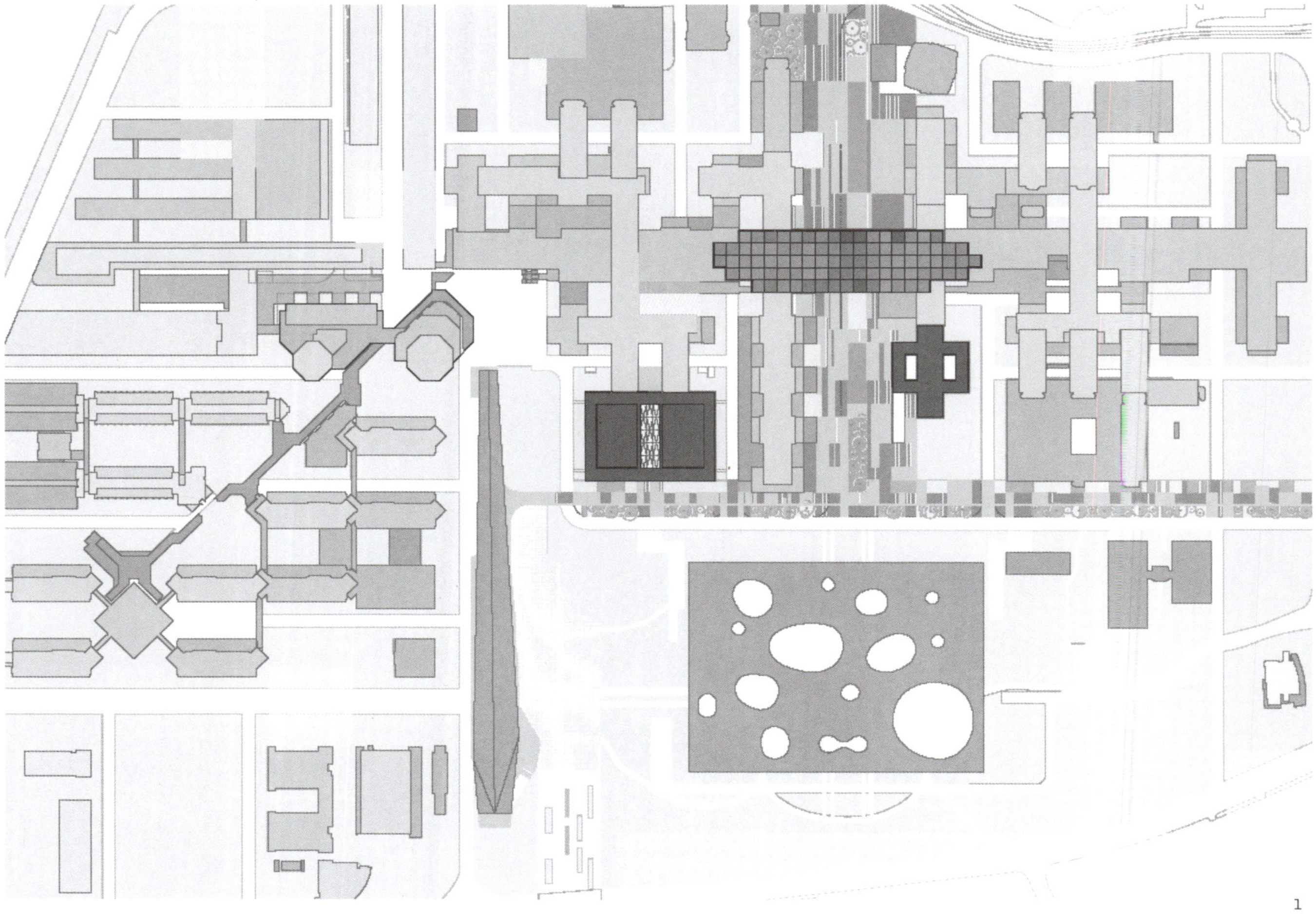

1

3

1 Block plan of the campus.

2 Dedicated to mechanical engineering, the ME building was erected in the early 1970s during the first phase of campus development, by the Zweifel + Strickler + Associés team.

3, 4 To the south, east, and west, the façade is composed of prefabricated factory modules, whose dimensions are determined by the EPFL's historical grid. Each element is made up of metal mesh panels. This system unfolds to form the entrance canopy.

1

1 The main façade.
2 Side façade and interplay of metal mesh panels.
3, 4 The atrium forms the heart of the building, with staircases and passageways crossing the central space.
5 The experimental building for researchers, comprising two wings linked by a large central atrium.

2

3

4

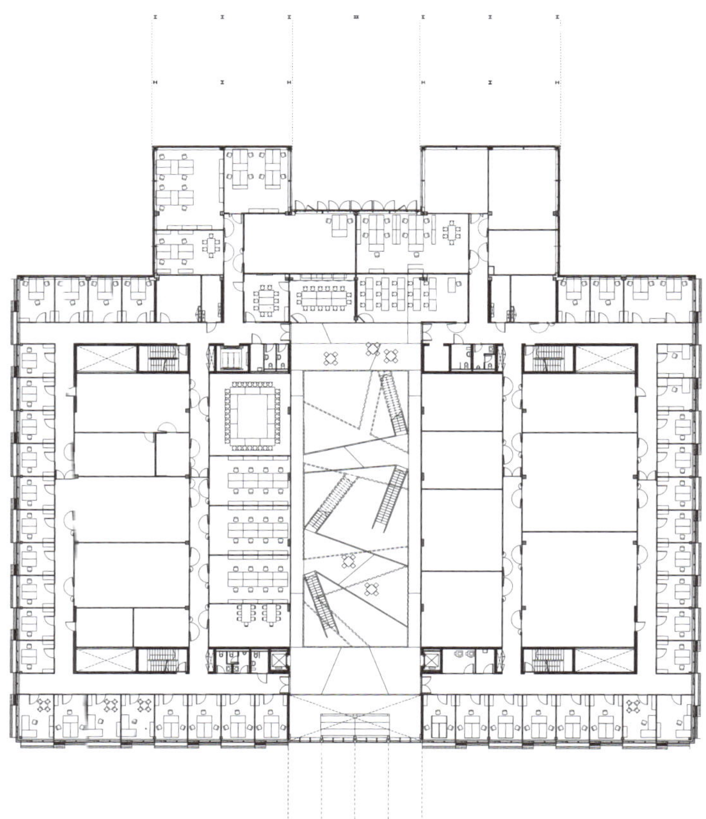

5

TEACHING BRIDGE
ÉCOLE POLYTECHNIQUE FÉDÉRALE DE LAUSANNE

LAUSANNE, SWITZERLAND

2011–19

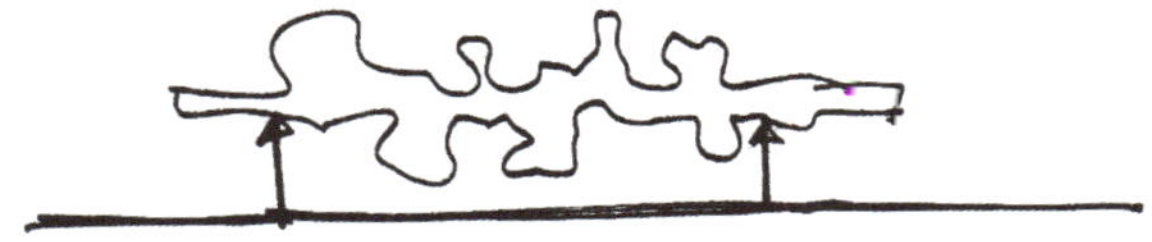

1

Floating like a cloud above the avenue linking the site from south to north, the Teaching Bridge is the tallest building on the campus.
This bridge-building, made up of an accumulation of modules where the subtle interplay between full and empty creates a pixelated effect, houses laboratories and teaching spaces dedicated to research. In order to encourage informal exchanges between researchers, the layout is atypical, far from the traditional layout with a corridor leading to a series of partitioned rooms. Here, the spaces intersect, overlap, and communicate with each other thanks to a succession of tiered terraces. This layout reflects an innovative educational vision of decompartmentalized, perpetually evolving knowledge, which the EPFL places at the heart of its academic project.

3

4

5

6

1 Sketch, 2011.
2, 3 Interior volumes, from level to level.
4 The Teaching Bridge spans Avenue Picard and links the two parts of the campus.
5 Principle of the bridge construction.
6 Geometric research on "chained" pixels. Study model, scale 1:200, 2011.

SHANGHAI LIBRARY

SHANGHAI, CHINA

2016

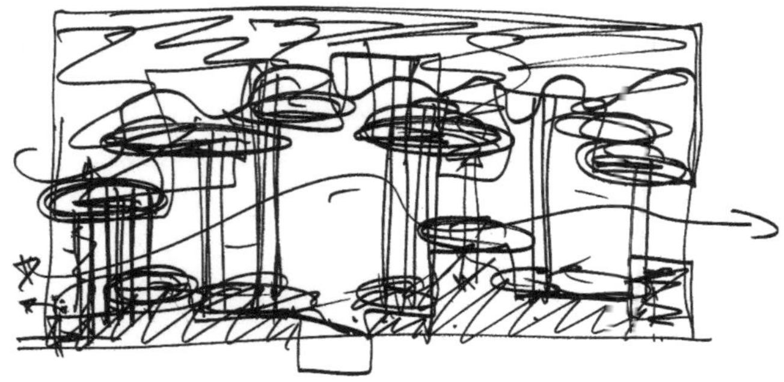

1

Shanghai Library East aspires to become a major cultural center that is inclusive and accessible to as many people as possible. Its architecture reflects this ambition by creating a Reading Square at the heart of the building, a vast open-access room where cultural experiences converge. Against a backdrop of technological change, the library's design allows it to evolve flexibly over time. Within a compact structure, its modular system, based on a grid measuring 10 meters by 10 meters and 5 meters in height, works like a puzzle game, offering an infinite number of configurations. Silent reading, exhibitions, conferences—each space can be transformed, interlocked, and reorganized to meet the needs of readers.

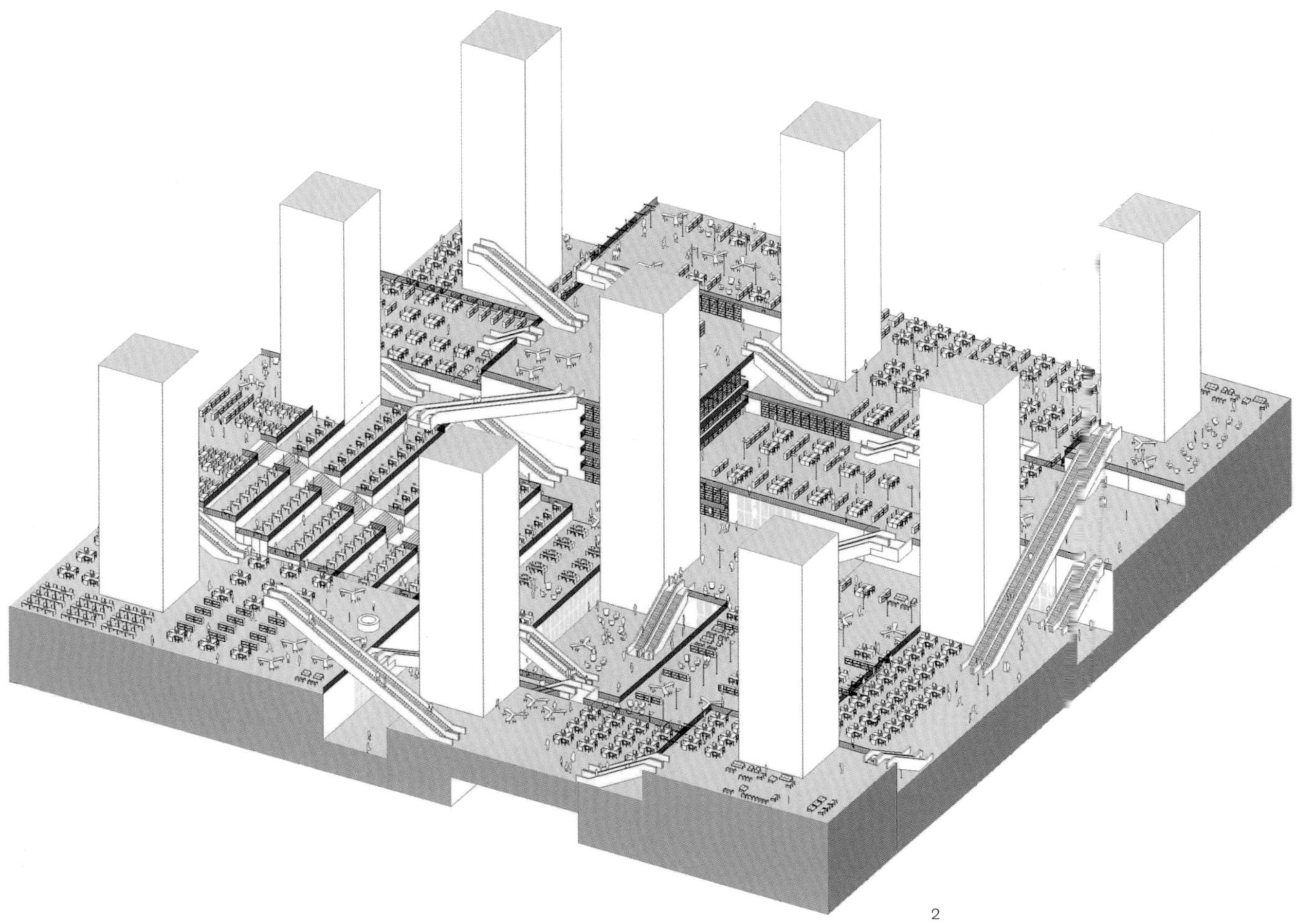

2

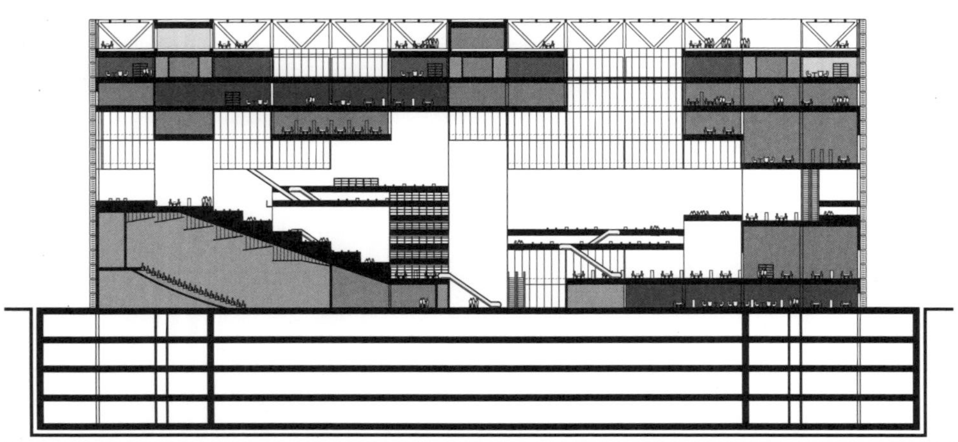

3

1 Sketch, 2016.
2 Exploded views of the reading rooms.
3 Cross-section illustration of the stratification principle.
4 Chinese vernacular architecture is often structured around three symbolic elements: the roof, representing the sky; the base, the earth; and the intermediate space, the world.
5 Completely open and fluid, the library is articulated without partitions, with direct connection to all accesses and functions.

4

5

"It is in this alchemy between mass and immateriality that light is born—architecture becomes enchanted."

GRAND THÉÂTRE

ALBI, FRANCE
2009–14

Elegant and compact, the Grand Théâtre in Albi is designed as a discreet but vibrant presence, set against the city's historic center. To avoid any architectural heaviness, it is wrapped in a golden metallic veil, an airy scarf floating around it, filtering the light and interacting with the city.
This shimmering skin captures the colors of Albi's heritage—bronze, brick, ochre, and pink—blending into its surroundings while asserting its contemporary character. Inside, the warm hues are extended and echoed, offering total sensory immersion. This place of culture and experimentation houses a large auditorium, an experimental studio theatre, an underground multiplex cinema, and a rooftop restaurant overlooking the city.

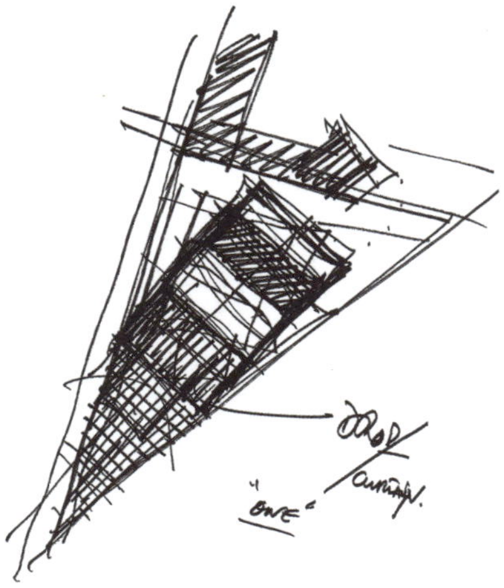

1

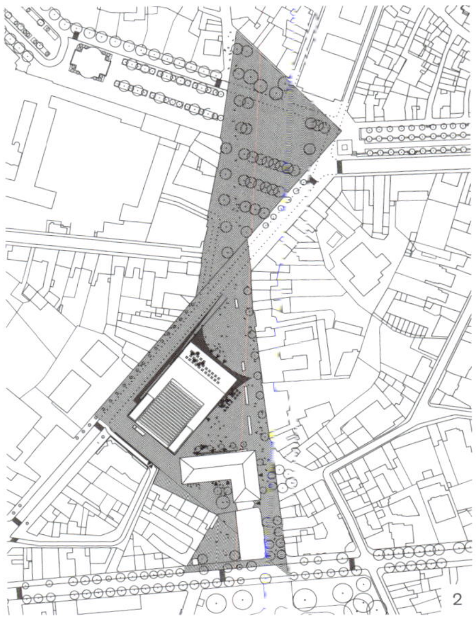

2

4

1 Sketch, 2009.
2 Urban plan.
3 View from the cathedral.
4 View from the theater square.
5 The metal mesh "scarf."

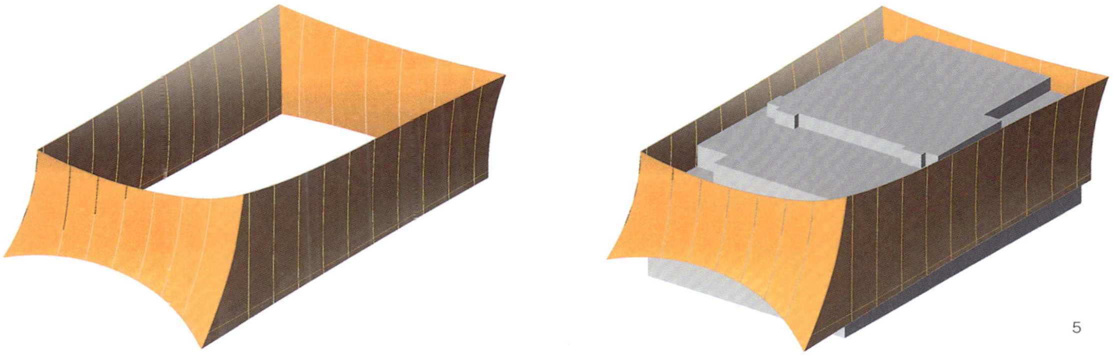

5

1

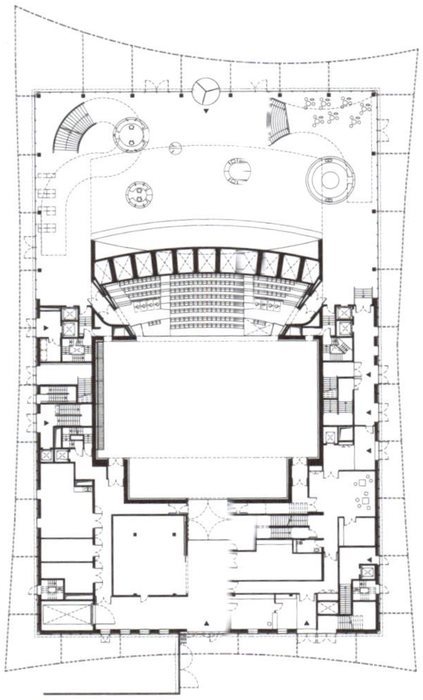

2

3

4

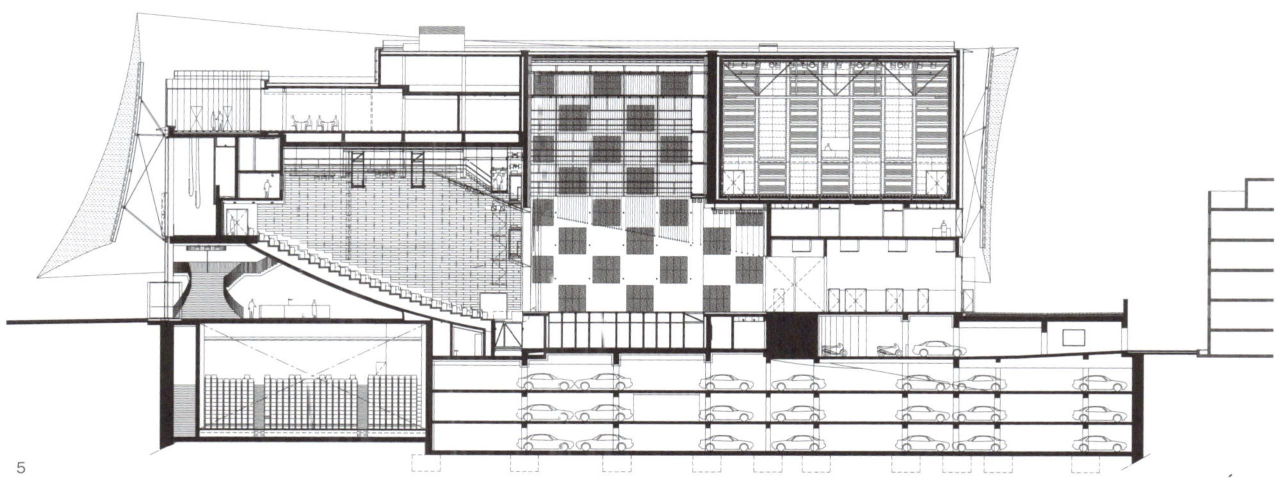

5

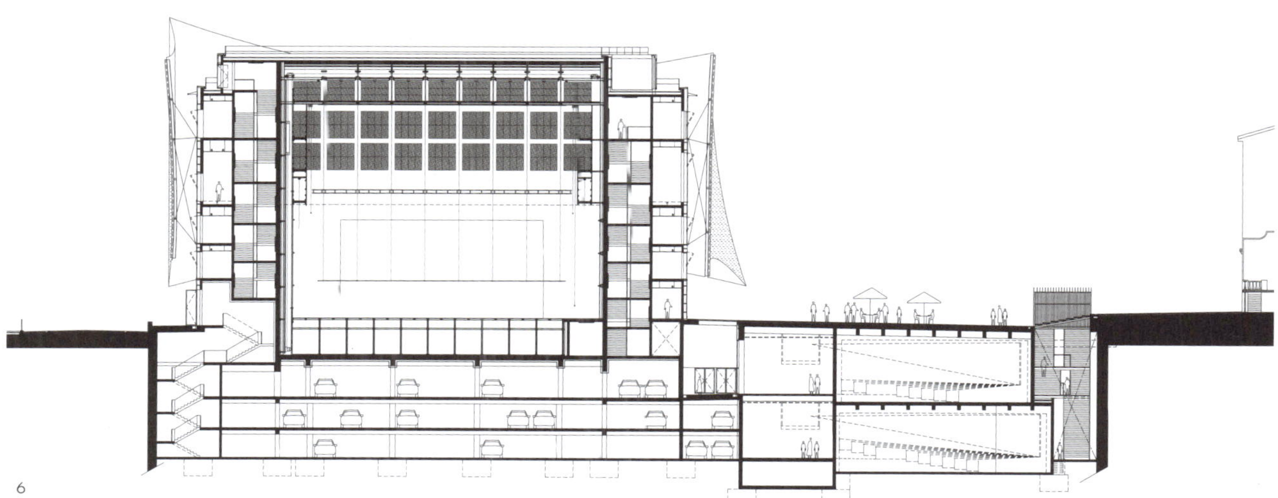

6

1,3 Detail of the façade from the theater forecourt: the metal veil flexibly peels away, marking the entrance to the building.

2 Plan of the first floor.

4 The main auditorium, designed to accommodate 900 spectators.

5,6 Longitudinal and cross-sections reveal the complex superposition of programs: parking, multiplex theater, experimental studio, restaurant, and rooftop.

CONVENTION CENTER AND EXHIBITION HALL

LEÓN, SPAIN

2005–18

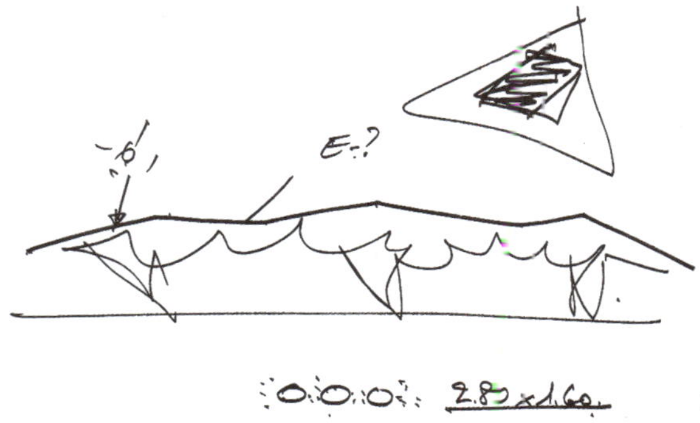

1

With the arrival of the high-speed train, freeing up of foremer railway land, the León Convention Center and Exhibition Hall has become an essential urban catalyst for the transformation of the city. Integrating the renovation of a former sugar factory that houses the palace, the project installs the exhibition hall under a gigantic folded sheet, suspended above the space uncluttered by load-bearing columns. This floating roof, covered in solar panels, ensures the building's energy autonomy, while a black metal lattice, spread out like a canopy of monumental trees, forms its structure. Adding a flamboyant dimension to the façades, the sun blinds draped in the vibrant colors of Spain infuse the whole with a singular identity.

2

3

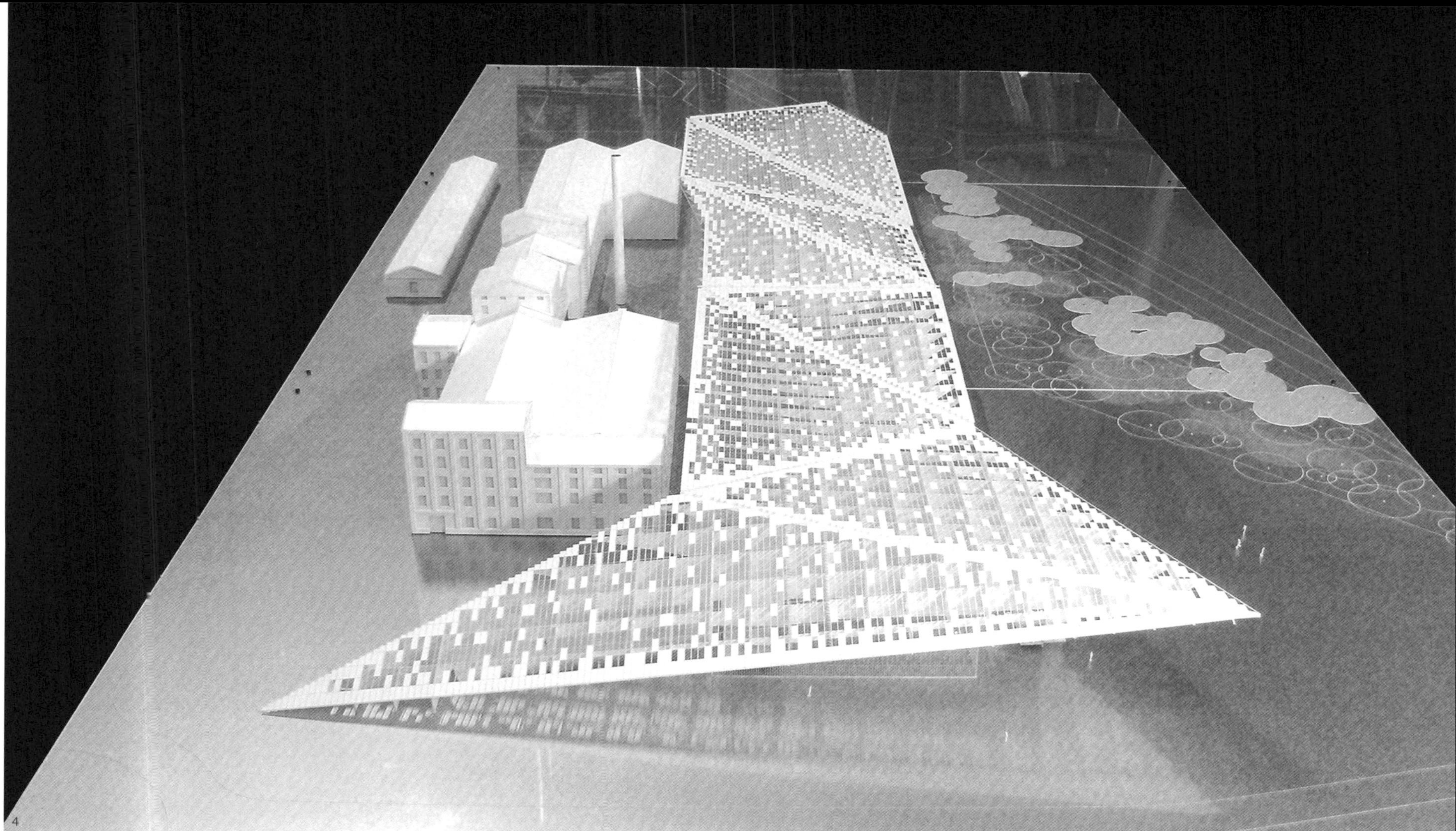

4

1 Sketch, 2005.
2 Historical view of the former sugar refinery, 2001.
3 A new volume of glass and steel envelops the former Santa Elvira sugar refinery bringing together past, present, and future.
4 The building is topped by an extensive photovoltaic metal roof, ensuring its energy autonomy. Model, scale 1:200, 2008.
5 General plan of the first floor.

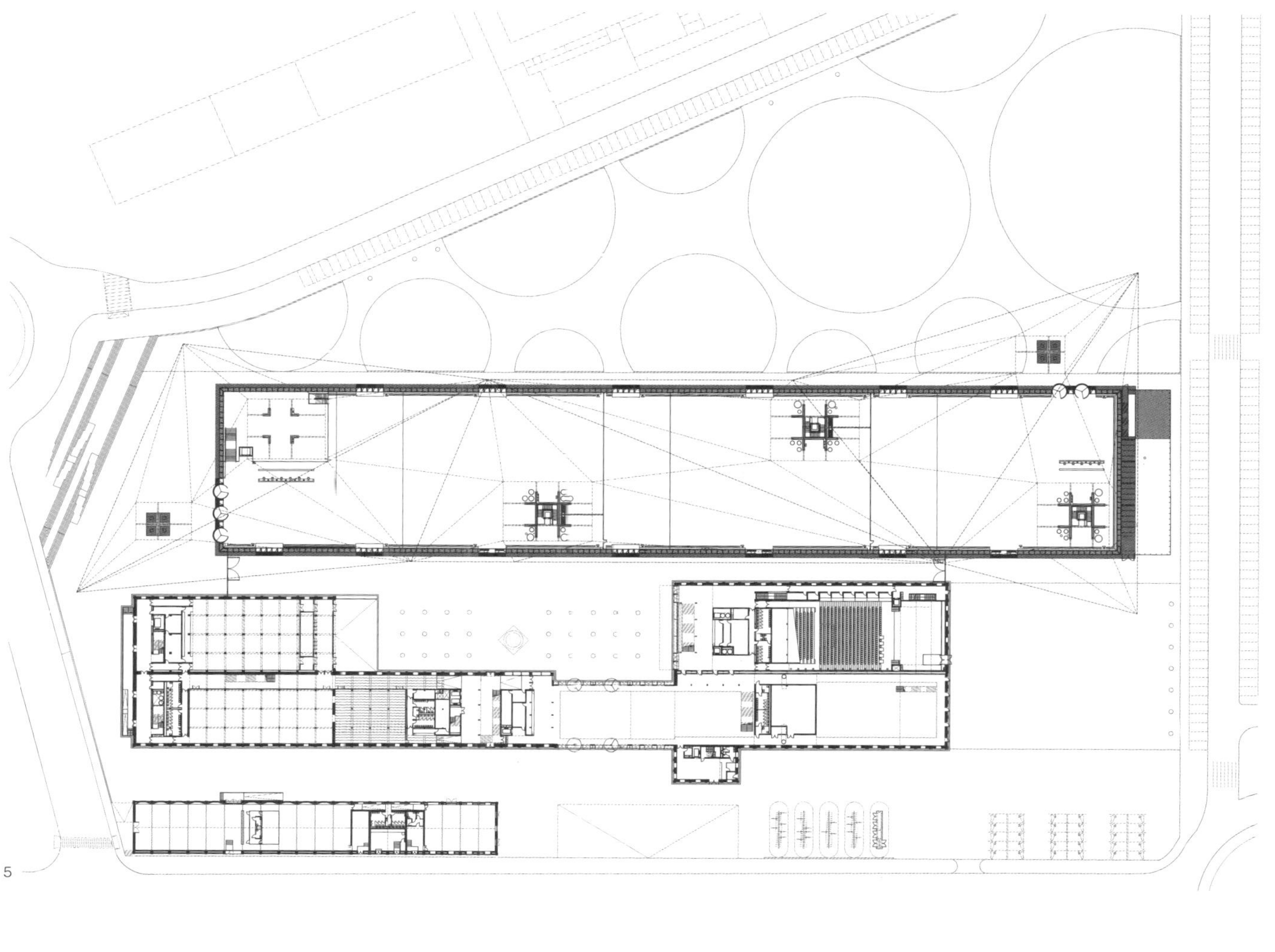

5

1

2

3

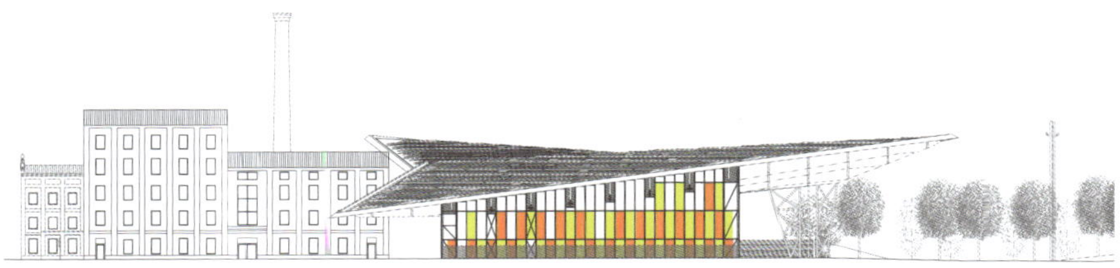

4

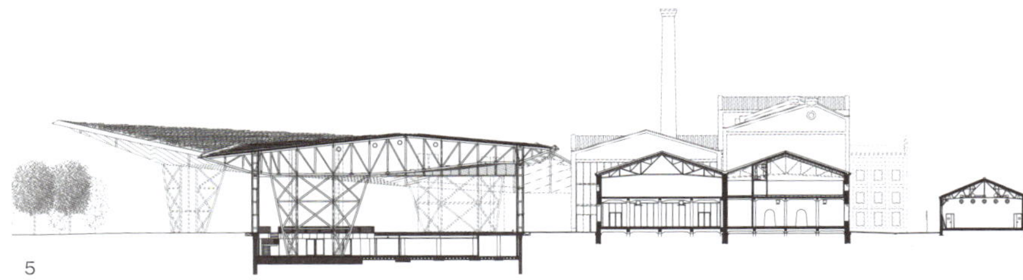

5

1,6 Exhibition hall entrance canopy.
2-5 Elevations and sections of the project.

6

04

REWRITING

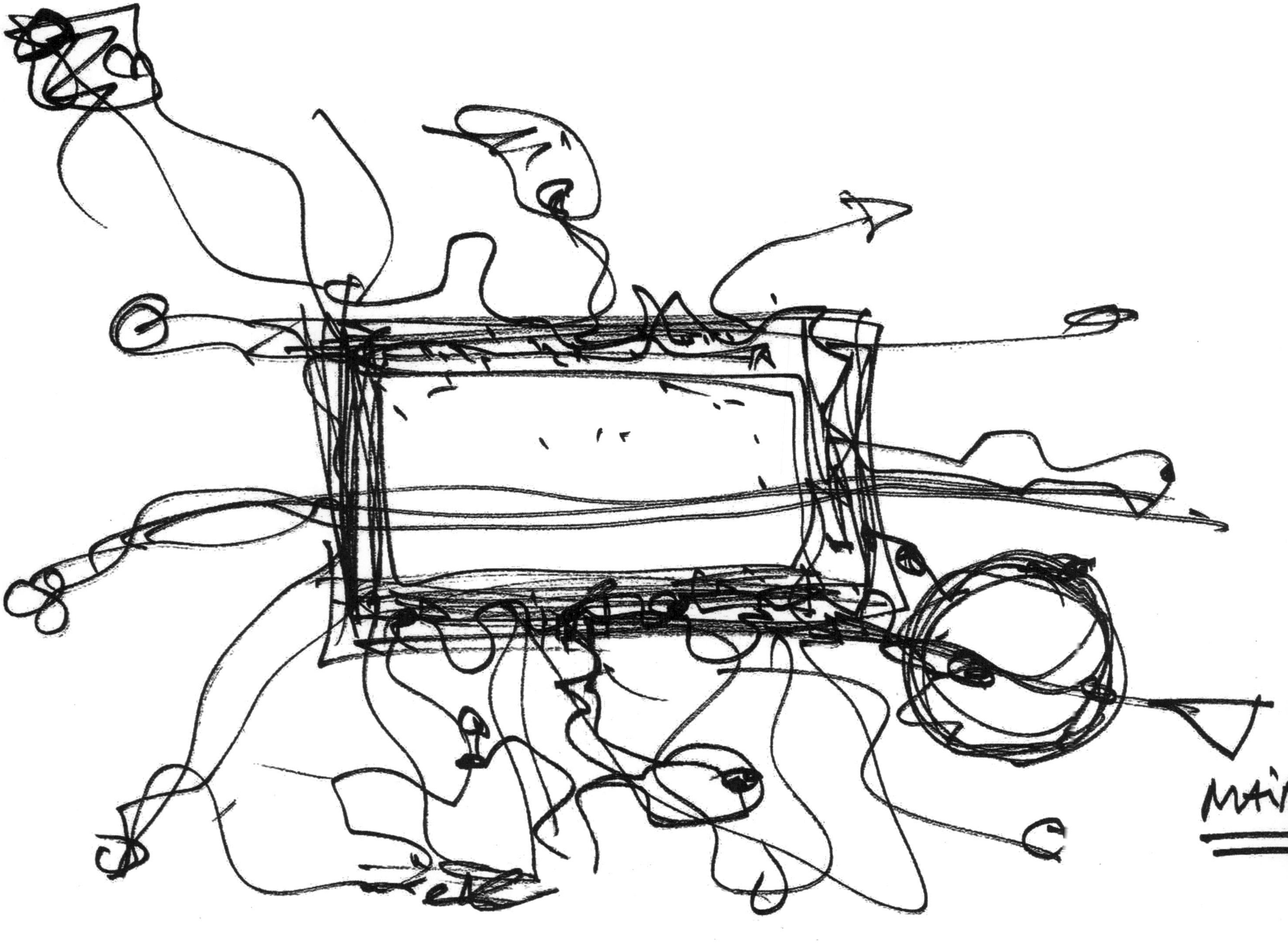

Another multiple

Restructure, restore, transmute, reprogram. There are several ways of approaching rewriting. But there are three basic principles: a building cannot be separated from its site; to reprise a work of architecture is to carry out a comprehensive, critical action on it; and radicalism does not mean a blank slate. What is the goal? Reinscribing the object to create a new singularity. To achieve this requires two things: the dialectical moment and intuition It is through the construction of tensive concepts that something felicitous and exact can be created. Then the *encounter* is authentic.

To rewrite is to raise a question. To reveal a new multiple at the heart of the building.

Reading a building, a site, is already in itself the start of rewriting. Signs are analyzed, connected, and subjected to a critical anatomy. We move, we remove, we add, we work on variances. Architecture never has a stable, univocal, or definitive meaning. It does not exist without interpretation.

Objects can be anemic, illegible, or desolate, but just as in urbanism no place is beyond redemption, so are there no ungrateful buildings. In the architecture of reprises, attitude is the key to everything else. If the architect fails to adopt a narrative, they cannot restructure, but merely conserve, redevelop. Each rewrite is a contemporary redefinition, open to incompletion, to the work in progress.

Who is who?

What is already there has a nourishing value. The important thing is to establish a reciprocal relationship. It's all about weaving threads, about transition, going beyond.

Rewriting is not the same as restoring, let alone substituting by means of reset. It is a matter of bringing something back to life in contemporary times. An update? A modernization? No. That would be the degree-zero of intervention. What we're aiming for is a reset at a higher level.

The reprogramming of the Poste du Louvre is, so to speak, a joint creation. Julien Guadet's building from 1880–88 had availability built into its genome. A mutuality thus occurred, through understanding. A symbiosis of objective sympathy. A four-handed concerto. A dialectic between Guadet and Perrault that led to a form of singularity. Where does one begin and the other end?

The radicalism of this manifesto-building, conceived as a prototype, has a truly conceptual and theoretical dimension.

A method was established: the Poste du Louvre was conceived as a *tool*—Guadet's own word—that could change in accordance with uses and needs. Transience became a constructive principle. This value of autonomous evolution (adaptability, reversibility) is powerfully contemporary. An interior structure that can accept any type of program: that is ultimately the definition of a neutral, a-programmatic building. A typology of subtle spaces. Architecture left to the discretion of the interpreter-occupier. The structures are both complete and unfinished, with no ultimate definition. The Poste du Louvre has an identity that is both fixed and constant, by virtue of its very constructive logic. Because they are rigorous, its structural and spatial principles deliver optimal flexibility and ductility. Rewriting is written into the building's source code. We are dealing here with a functionalism that is free of mono-functionality. The space is complex and receptive. It generates its own multiples. The Guadet building acquires a kind of de-indexed, a-historical classicism, a sort of a-historicism.

Challenging the statement

The Aplix factory near Nantes articulates an orthogonal syntax of square modules that, like a crossword puzzle, can grow in any direction, according to production requirements. As with Guadet, industrial open-endedness is an aesthetic axiom. The activity space disappears behind a façade of multi-folded mirror-polished stainless steel in which the landscape is diffracted.

This rejection of statements and normativity in favor of the sheer phenomenality of architecture transforms it into an instrument for understanding its environment. The writing of Aplix invites us all to forge sensitive links with its kinetic façade. When you walk alongside it, it produces an analytical and syncopated image of its landscape.

A building's identity does not depend on the simple assertion of its model. It must derive a specific form of singularity by seeking an original type of response to the context. In this way, the concept frees itself from abstraction and becomes sensorial. The experience takes place in daylight, through movement, matter, and anamorphosis. It is a poetics.

On the folds of the mirror cladding, the landscape amplifies and intensifies. The architecture becomes absent. The wall dematerializes into a reflective skin.

The rewriting is effected in a blankness of style, an *écriture blanche*, amplifying the reflective object by a few thousand extra scales, like an invisible reptile sloughing off its skin.

The gap

The very possibility of rewriting a heritage suggests that the past is never completely finished. The son begets the father. A heritage does not just involve conservation issues, matters of preservation. First of all, it puts forward, a difference in relation to which we can situate ourselves. If we are to change, we need a reference point that is as assured as possible, from which deviations can be made. The contemporary is measured in this difference. It happens that the reprising of buildings confuses radicality with rupture. By opting for this equivalence and this arbitrary gesture, we deprive rewriting of all its resources.

Textuality of design

The literary fabric of Versailles is at the heart of the rewriting of the Pavillon Dufour. Classical signs and the metamorphic play of the Baroque, in the weft, interweave with abstraction in the warp. There is also an architextuality in the relation to the historical genre: here, the writing reflects its own historicity. The contemporary takes its place in a continuum. The revolution of forms does not exclude a certain durability.

A true *classic* can never be reduced to a self-contained model. It is always open to being reworked *within a form of difference*. Which is how the contemporary is given a say. Perpetually in the process of being born, becoming, and declining, a *classic* speaks to all times, always in a state of incompleteness. So many open virtualities. Changeless under different lights. As long as there is openness, authenticity, and coherence in the encounter, it welcomes rewriting.

The new extension to the Pavillon Dufour—built in 1814–17 following plans drawn up in 1770 by Ange-Jacques Gabriel—works on the underside of the building. A completely new volume has been dug from the ground. A Groundscape[1] in a classical context. Reprogramming is impossible in an unchanged configuration.

Intact on the surface, the Cour des Princes gains depth below. The only thing visible above is a prism of glass panels, which brings the daylight streaming underground. The sides, made of slats of bronze-anodized aluminum, read like a "stack" by Donald Judd. But rather than a contemporary soliloquy, this is a dialogue between the rhythmic weave of the seventeenth-century façades and architectural minimalism: a block of emptiness and light crossing the line of the ground.

The emblematic "Versailles parquet" becomes a composition of iridescent black steel slats in earthy and bluish tones. Like Carl Andre's *5x20 Altstadt Rectangle* (1967), it establishes the space. The infra-thin density of a sculpture deployed horizontally and merged with the materiality of the ground. Conceived for the site, it is made from an industrialized, de-specified, and mass-produced material.

Design transfigures the writing of Versailles in a scenographic flight of light-sculptures. The decorative syntagma and syntactic patterns of Classicism are re-enunciated in a program in which metal is king: mesh (drapes, gadrooned ceilings, carpet-grilles, passementerie-effect banners, ruffs for light tubes), projectors with shutters, poles and slats. In all these different spatial scansions the industrial object reveals its noble lineage.

Geometric hypermediation

At Court Suzanne-Lenglen, the reworking of geometries creates a tension between two architectural styles in order to create a new architectural unity. Metal mesh is a building material in its own right. It is a conduit for shapes, a skilled mediator in reconciling contradictory geometries. Structural and polymorphic, it can be stretched, tightened, stiffened, curved, and counter-curved. On the main façade of Court Suzanne-Lenglen, strips of mesh cling to a concrete arch structure, then rise in oblique lines to the roof cornice. Straight and clean as an equation, it softens orthogonal transitions, resolving structural hardness. Sensuous material, purity of plan. Heterogeneous forms and eras settle and harmonize. From the melting pot of contradictions a singularity is born. The mesh unites like a nuptial tool, in a way which differs from the mode of commentary.

The legacy building acts as a counterweight with its levitating material. Everything is pulled together, unified. It vibrates like the string of a bow.

No rewriting is worthwhile if it does not commit to what is already there. The main conviction, a recurring conviction in the approach to a site when conceiving a project, is to consider the context as an architectural material, a starting point. What we encounter is both an inheritance and a (re)launch pad.

Continuous transformation

Any reprising of an already existing work starts from the premise that architecture is incomplete. The process is always open, in the reprogramming, reinscription, and transtextualization of structural and spatial morphologies, materialities. The architectural object is not fixed, any more than its urban environment. A rewriting operation involves a number of contemporary urbanistic, social, economic, ethical, and environmental issues: the intensification of the city rather than sprawl, mixed-use strategies, the reversibility and mutability of spaces, the problem of obsolescence, energy conservation, and adaptation to global warming.

The rewrite of the Montparnasse Tower (1973) is a manifesto project. The aim is to regenerate a "heritage building" that has little empathy with the city. The new building, designed as an E+C (energy positive + carbon negative) vertical city, demonstrates that it is possible to construct high-rise buildings that are responsible, resilient, reversible, economical, sustainable, and integrated into their environment. The project is also a manifesto in terms of the materials used and the way the structures are reworked. A second tower with a concrete spine is

1 This strategy of building infrastructure is reflected in the new Aérog'Art at Les Invalides and 83 Marceau.

attached to the first, with a protruding structure in wood, dry-fitted and assembled like Meccano. Following a perfect constructive logic that flies in the face of conventional wisdom, the transformation is made by going beyond the perimeter. Once again, reprogramming is impossible in an unchanged configuration.

The new Montparnasse Tower proceeds by palimpsest: the 1973 hypo-script is covered by a "breathable skin" running its full height, made of extra-clear glass scales and an amorphous photovoltaic layer. Ventilation, insulation, autonomous energy production—the new building relaunches the old back into the most imperative contemporaneity. A raw phenomenality of architectural reality.

Resituating, reterritorializing: urban material

Reprogramming a building means exploring a field of possible futures. In order not to hinder them, we have to neutralize assignments, restrictions, and all forms of confinement. The meaning of a building is never given once and for all. Its durability depends on its receptiveness. An architectural project must also confront the contingencies of the site, both its determinations as well as its hazards. In a strategy of reconnection, the goal is to share resources and pool skills. Territorializing a building means stimulating its sociability and urbanity.

Site diagnosis. Value mapping. Assessment of conceptual, contextual, symbolic, social, economic, and political resources. Architecture does indeed extend its field into a number of disciplines. Each with its own methodology of approach. To consider the already-there as a reserve of assets is to think of something other than just a building. It means accepting the site in its complex reality as a human geography, a total environment, a global landscape.

The Citylights complex on the Pont de Sèvres is a new architectural landmark for Boulogne-Billancourt. Built in 1975, this complex of towers had to find its place in a territory that lacked maturity. As part of the Greater Paris metropolitan development strategy, Citylights provides the city with a territorial design and a signpost. The complex marks the entrance to the city like a prow, an epigraph, reflective by day and luminous by night. Rewritten internally by design, it is also reconnected to its new Trapèze district by pedestrian routes, a forecourt, passageways, and gardens. An intensified urbanity. Here, reprising is a process of revelation.

In its relationship with the city, architecture is in itself a metonym for its history and its space. The Court of Justice of the European Union in Luxembourg is a case in point. A monumental palace of steel and glass on a concrete floor, designed in 1973 in the spirit of the Athens Charter. An institutional site with a tight, juxtaposed structure, which has undergone three extensions. As a mirror of the growth of the European Economic Community, and later the EU, the Court has regularly been rebuilt and made more dense, in successive layers. This prior encumbrance is not a hindrance or a handicap: on the contrary, it is a source of interest.

"Work with what you have." Relaunch. Since the 1950s, the development of the Kirchberg Plateau in Luxembourg—originally agricultural land—has always been part of an urban development plan. The aim now is to continue this program through a fourth and a fifth extension: three new towers in the skyline, concise and made for the place. Rewriting this complex also means shifting from the logic of an architectural object to the logic of a neighborhood. Creating the city. Clarifying and reconnecting spaces and streets. Redefining public space. Working on the topography. Unifying. Pacifying the site, which is crossed by a motorway and interchanges—the notion of landscape integration is not an empty word here. Injecting a new urbanity. Creating a European quarter.

For the architect, the already-there is a *material*, always exact. A constructed identity. It determines the possibilities for work. Composite, it is made up of coherences and discontinuities, viscosities and solidifications, fractures.

A building is not just a precipitate of its environment, but a mediator, as in the case of the Hôtel Industriel Berlier, located between an interchange on the Paris ring road, the Quai d'Ivry, and the Austerlitz station railyards. A cross between office space and industrial premises, it is positioned as catalytic architecture. The site is transfigured by glass prism-cum-sheath, its structures emerging as analogues of the urban fabric. The building's reflective curtain wall captures the continuous movement of the landscape. It is here and nowhere else, in its own dedicated geography. A living optical machine. A conceptual manifesto. Intact in its rewriting. A simple glass skin that doubles as an invisible, painless but oh-so-protective inner lining. Another roll of the dice.

P. 306. Sketch "Starting from..." Court of Justice of the European Union, Villejuif, 2010.

PAVILLON DUFOUR

CHÂTEAU DE VERSAILLES, FRANCE
2011–16

1

2

The reorganization of the reception area at the Château de Versailles was carried out from the inside, without compromising functional requirements or betraying the spirit of the place. A new chapter in the complex and ongoing chronology of the château, the intervention marks a clear milestone in the visitor's itinerary. The Pavillon Dufour was extensively redesigned, with the attic converted into an auditorium and an extension built under the Cour des Princes. The integration of a glass prism and a new staircase redefines the geometry of the Cour des Princes and serves to capture light and diffuse it down to the lower levels. The ensemble orchestrates a fluid link between the different architectural styles in the château's east wing while revealing the layers of time that make up Versailles.

3

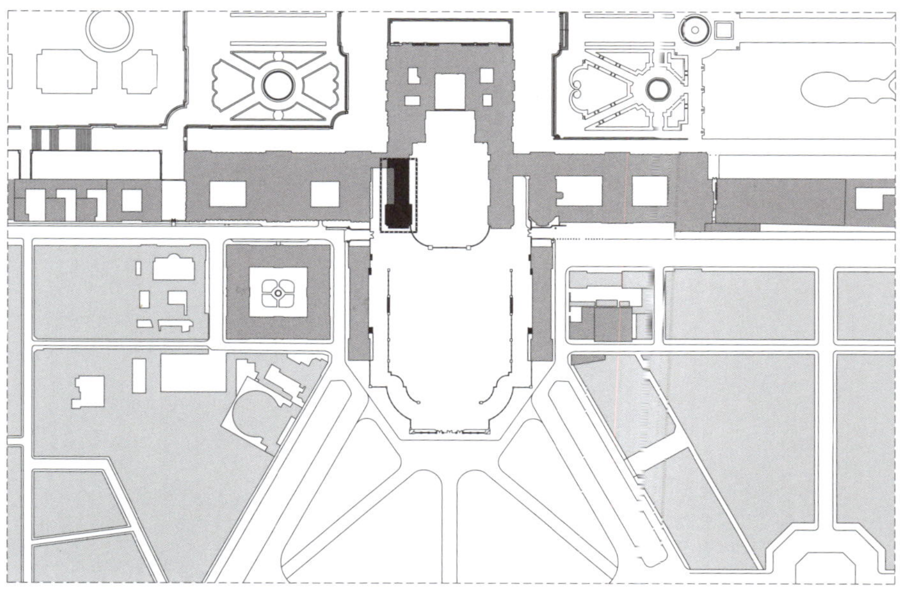

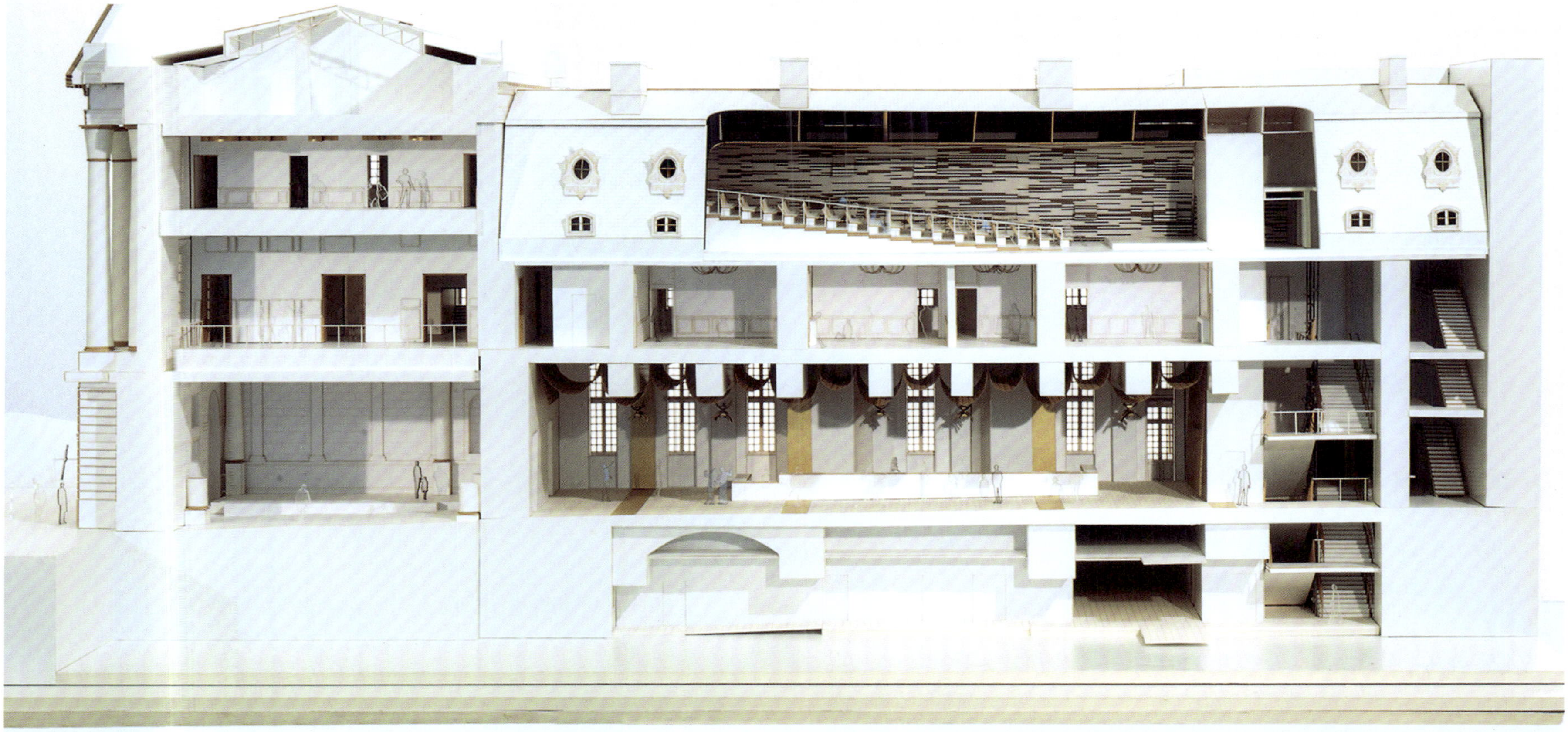

4

5

6

1 Postcard of the Court de Marbre and Pavillon Dufour, published by Ernest Le Deley.
2 The royal courtyard and its two pavilions, Gabriel and Dufour.
3 Site plan.
4 Cutaway view of the Pavillon Dufour, scale 1:50, 2012.
5, 6 Study for embedding of the glass prism, scale 1:50, 2011.

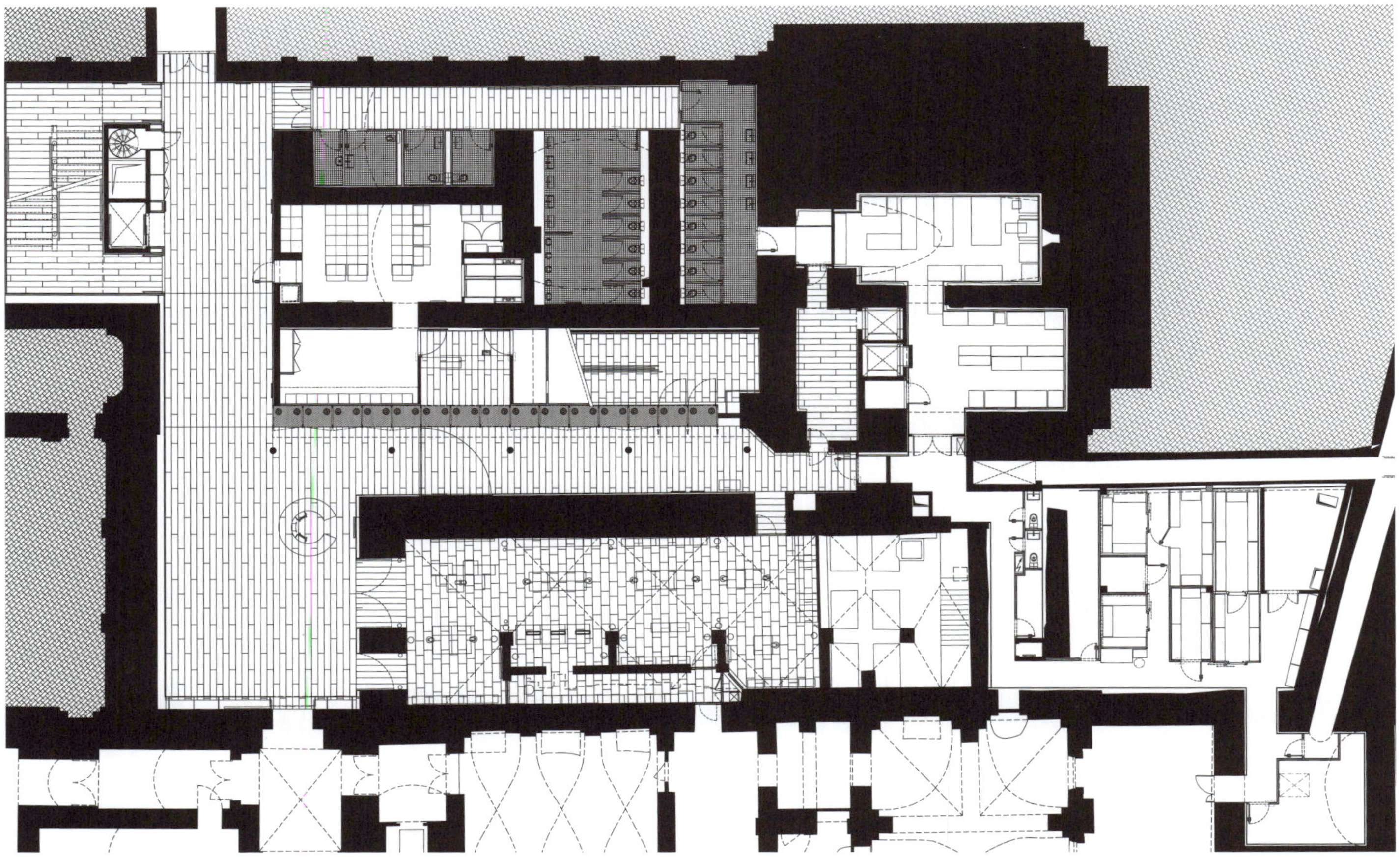
1

"An authentic classic is always indefinitely unfinished."

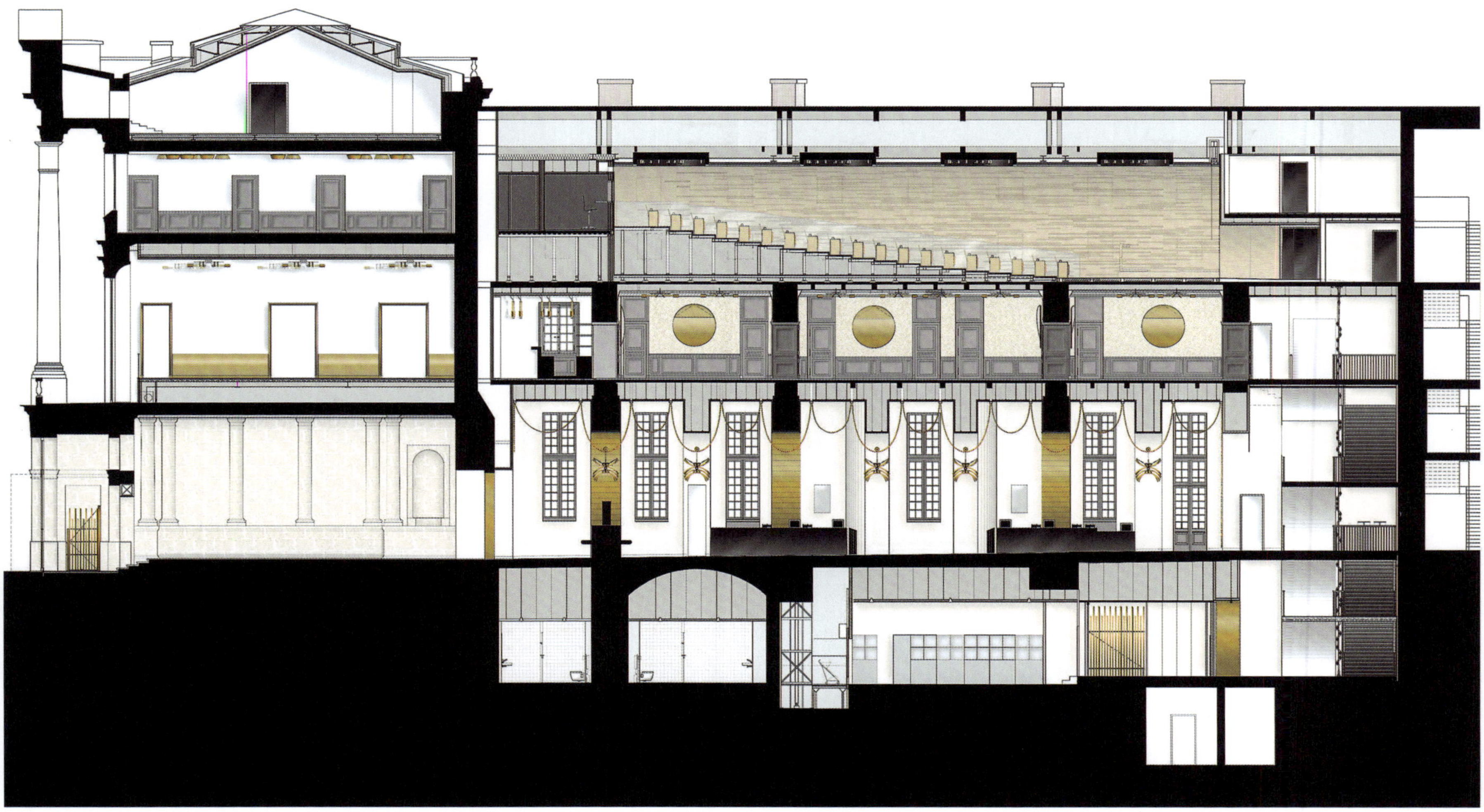
2

4

1, 2 Plan and section of the Pavillon Dufour and the Cour des Princes.
3 Foundations of the Cour des Princes.
4 Foundations of the Pavillon Dufour.

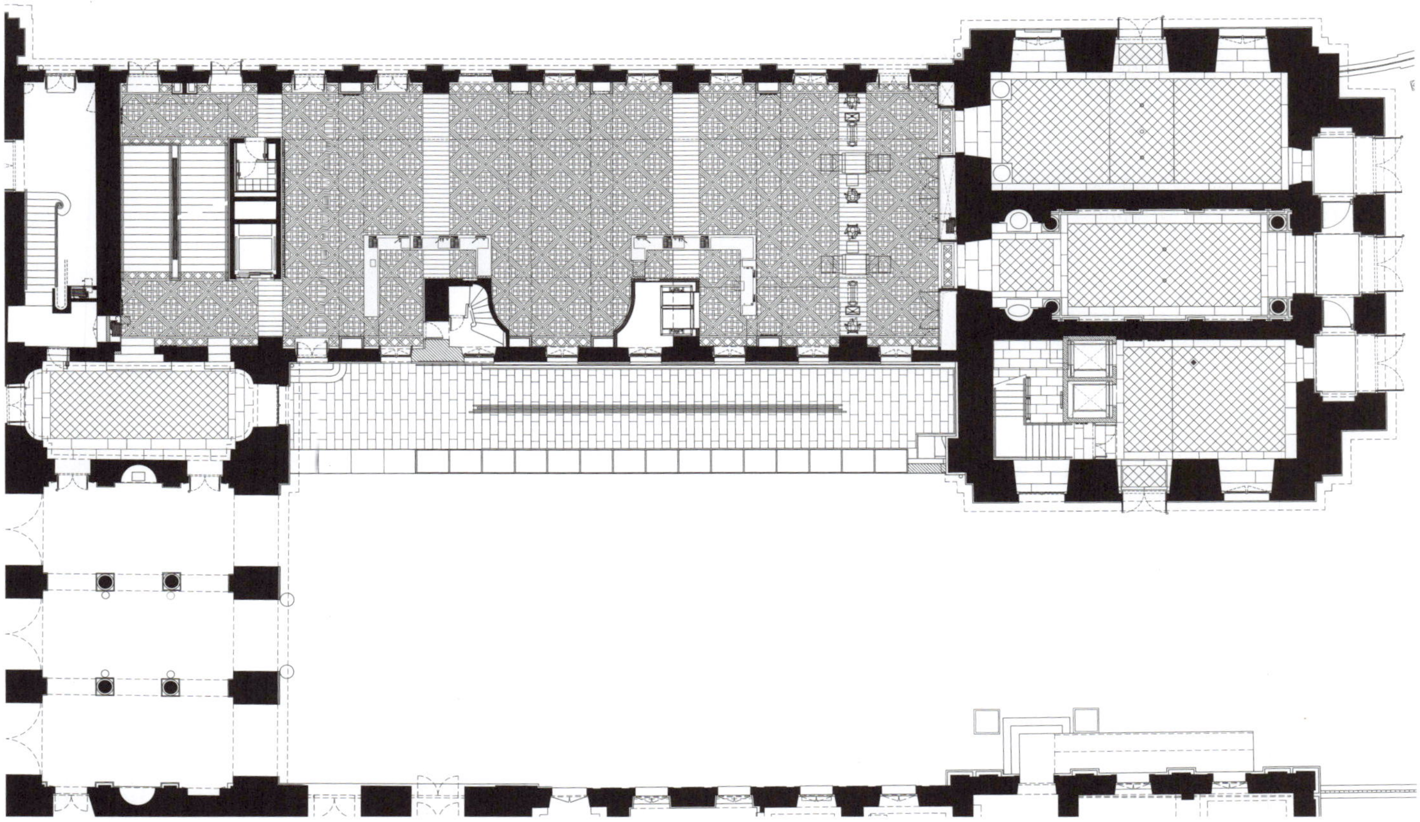

1

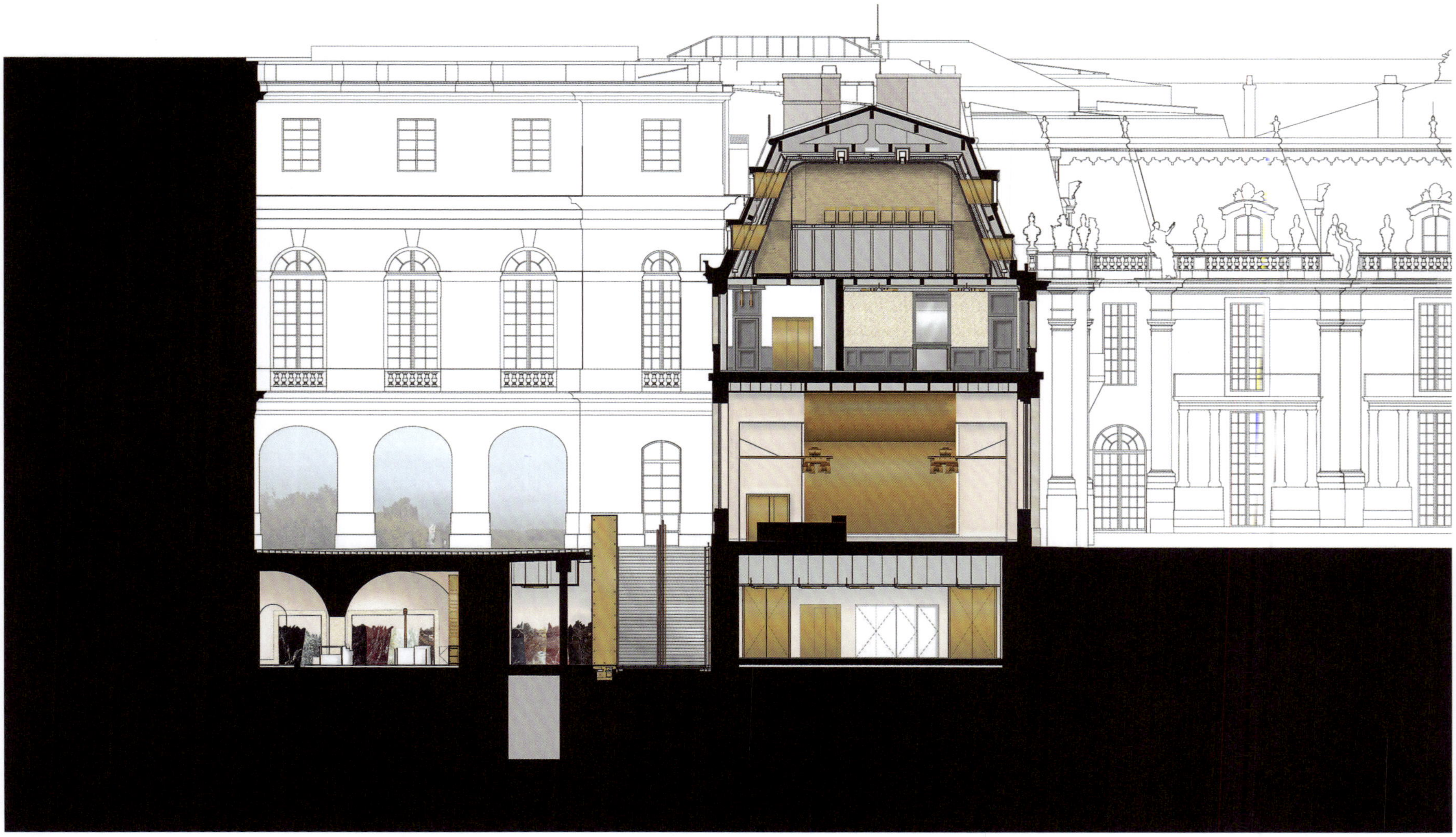

2

3

4

1 Plan of the public reception level.
2 Cross-section from the Cour Royale to the Cour des Princes.
3 Pavillon Dufour, the narthex.
4 Public reception gallery.
5, 6 Public exit via the Perrault staircase along the old wing to the Cour des Princes.

5

6

AÉROGARE DES INVALIDES, FONDATION GIACOMETTI

PARIS, FRANCE

2017–30

The project involves transforming the Esplanade des Invalides, an artificial structure that includes the old *aérogare* (air terminal), the last vestige of the 1900 Universal Exhibition. It begins by restoring the large historic openings that were once essential for ventilating the underground spaces. Reactivated, these openings are transformed into sunken gardens, weaving a link between surface and underground levels, reconnecting the visible city and its subterranean architecture. The *aérogare* building, erected on this slab, will also be redesigned: the pavilions on either end have been faithfully reconstructed, while the central structure has been updated with the addition of floors and a roof, opening the possibility for new uses. Each architectural gesture is based on respect for what is already there, while reviving the historic memory of the site.

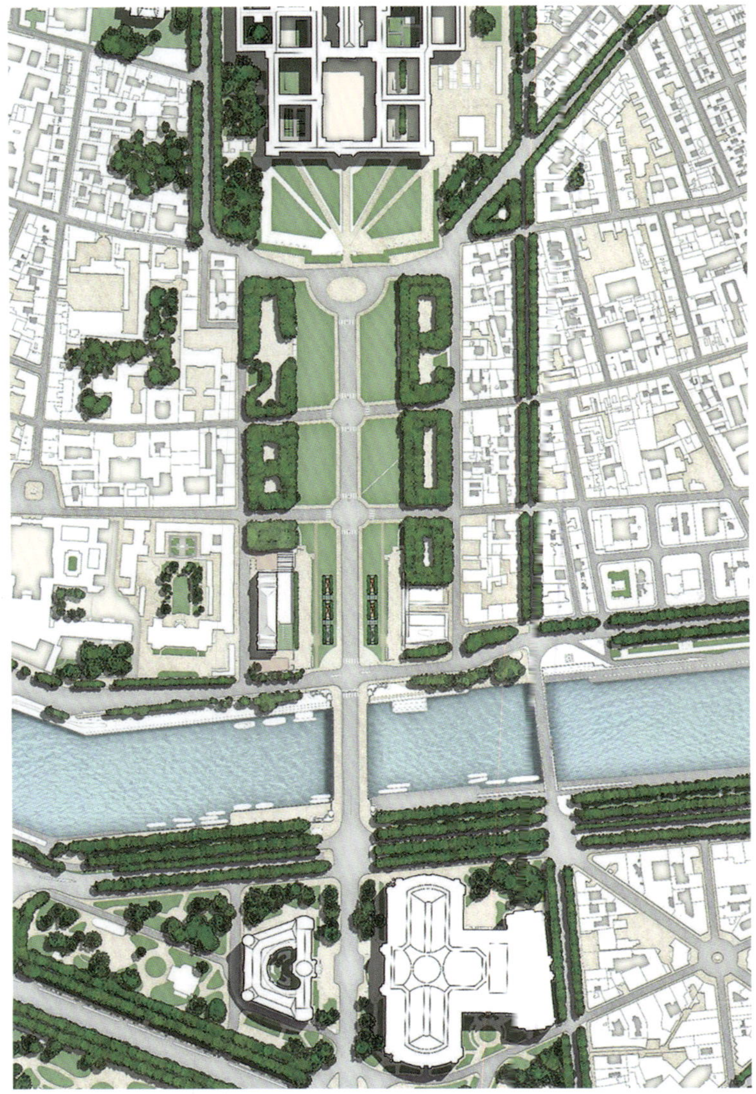

1

2

1 Urban plan.
2 New Invalides station building, within the grand vista of the esplanade.
3 Integrating the project into the monumental architecture of Les Invalides.
4 Juste Lisch (architect), elevation of the historic façade of the Invalides station, 1897.
5 Redevelopment of Place des Invalides and new roof for the historic building

1

2

3

4

1 North pavilion, looking towards the central gallery.
2 North pavilion, looking towards the esplanade.
3 The exhibition hall: plaster decorations and screen-printed glass façade.
4 Interior view of the Invalides terminal before construction by Air France, 1946.
5 Elevation of the north façade.
6 Cross-section of the north façade.
7 Upper gallery, openings with views of the Eiffel Tower.

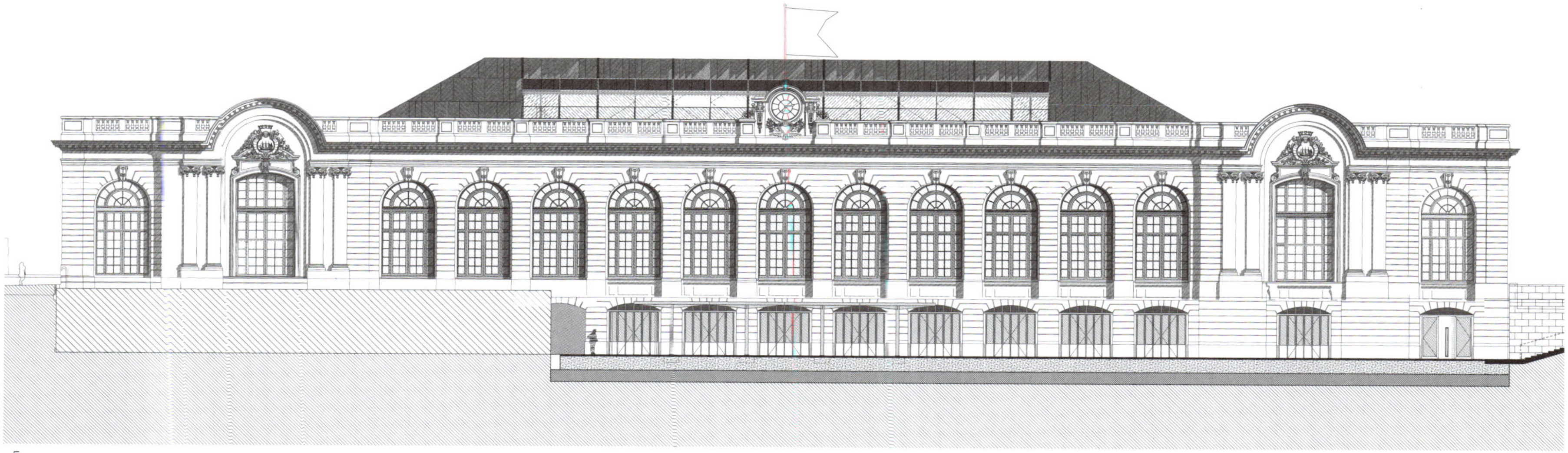

5

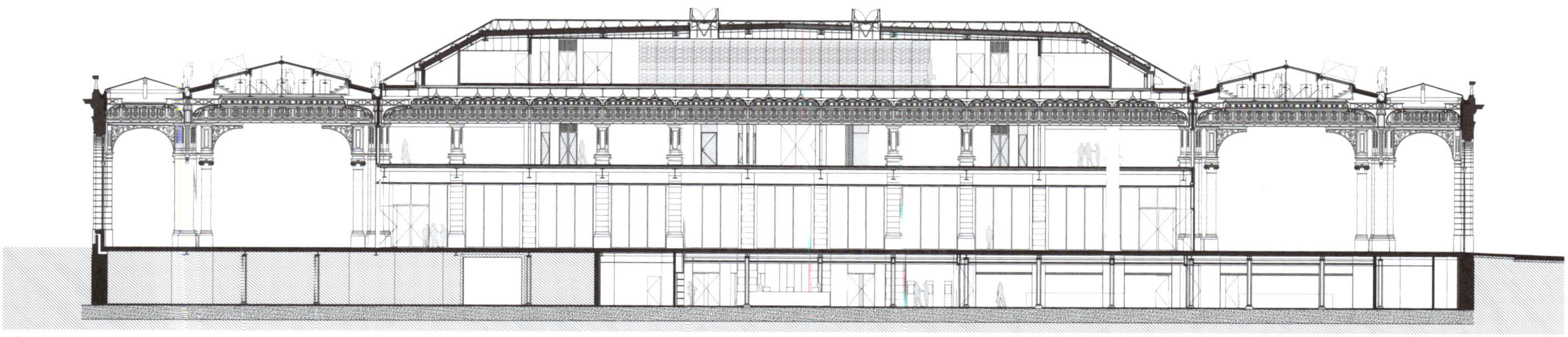

6

7

“The building that embraces its own rewriting agrees to become an open work.”

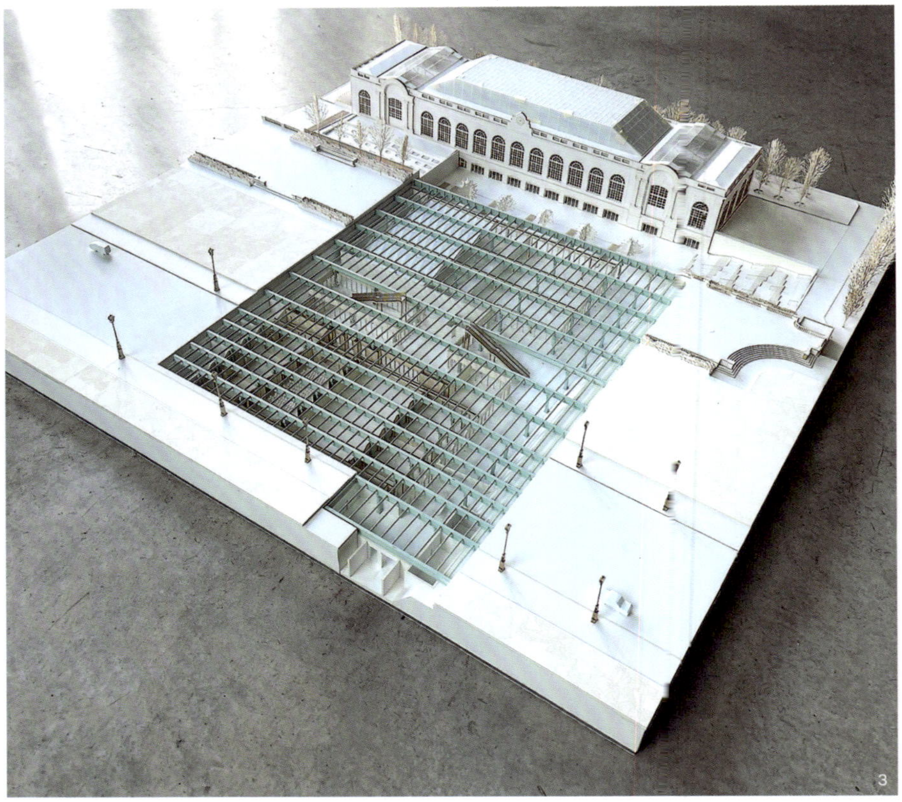

1 Henry de Lestrange, Construction of the railroad tracks at the Gare des Invalides, 1898–1900.
2 Regeneration of the space under the slab.
3 Cutaway of the esplanade revealing its metal structure, scale 1:100, 2024.
4 The main staircase opens onto the surrounding area, linking esplanade and underground spaces.
5 Cross-section of the esplanade infrastructure, from Rue Robert-Esnault-Pelterie to Rue Fabert.

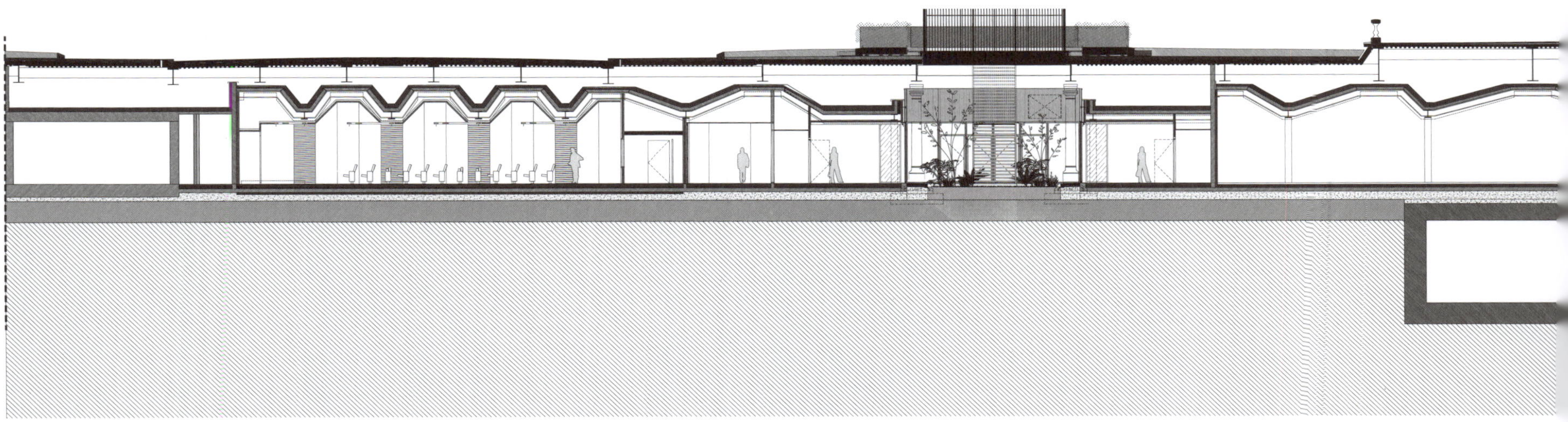

4

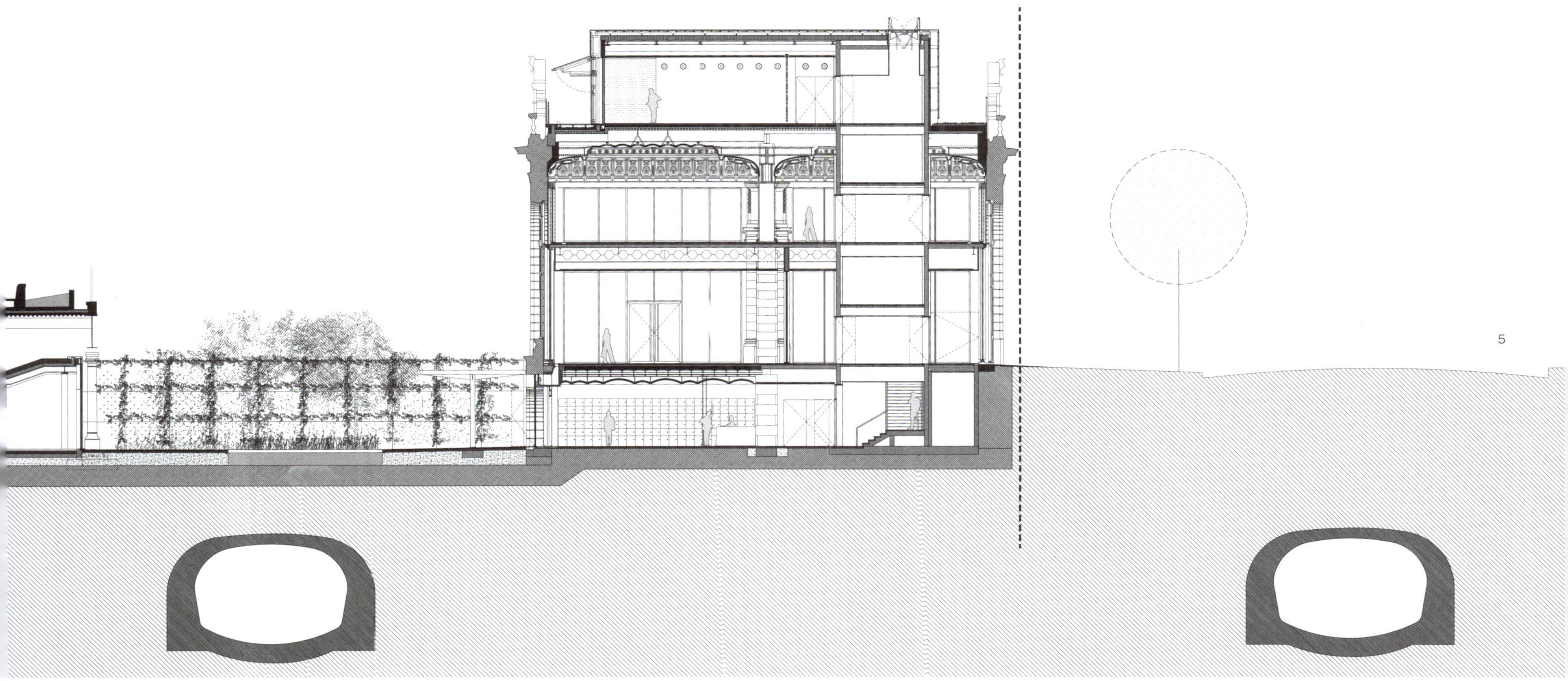

5

1, 2 The original structure of cast-iron posts and lattice girders has been restored and enhanced.
3, 4 Photographs before work, 2017. The project restores the original high ceilings and metal framework.
5 The central courtyard opens on to the sky.
6 Plan of the first floor.
7 Longitudinal section.
8 Cross-section.
9 Façade on Rue Étienne-Marcel.

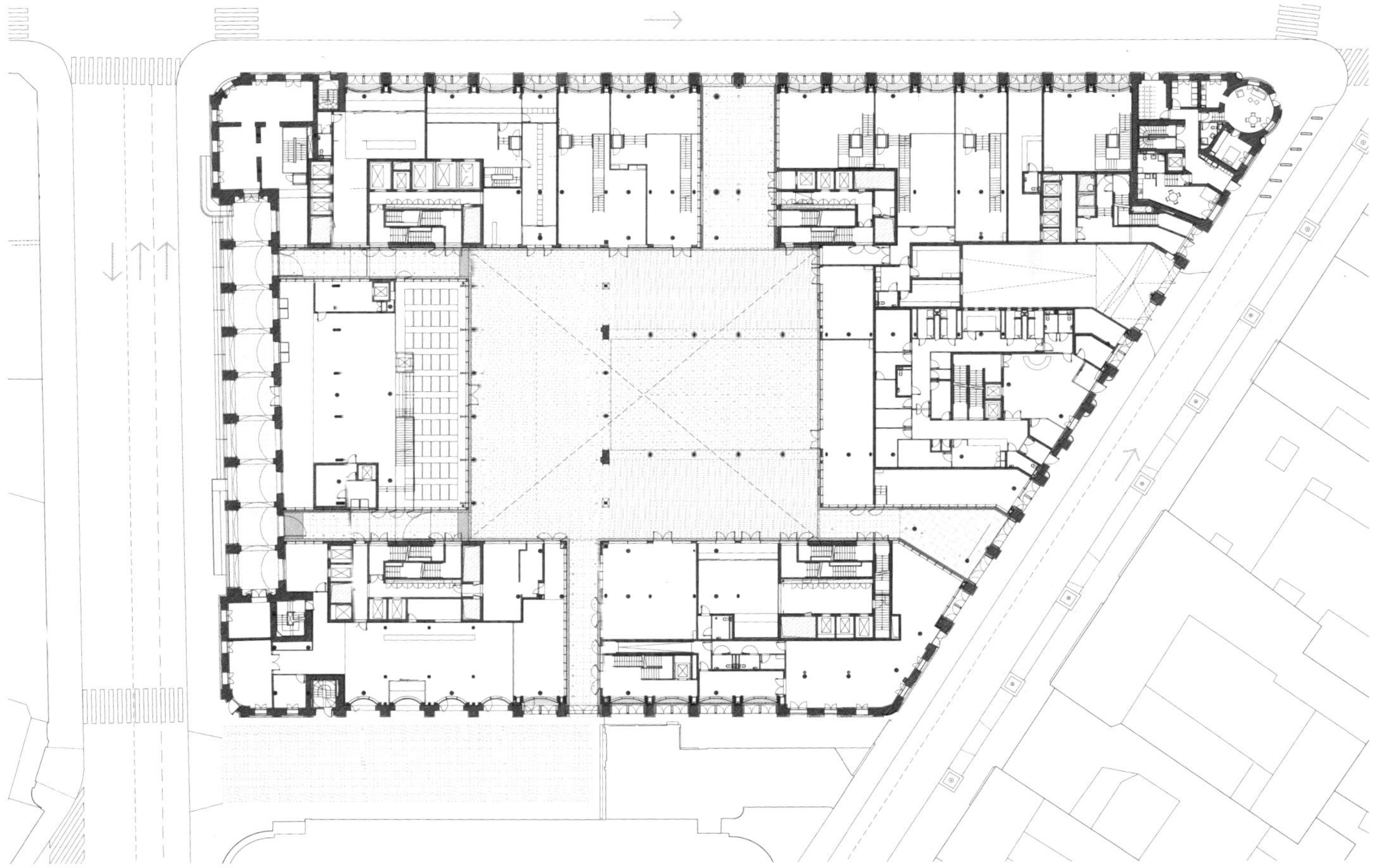

6

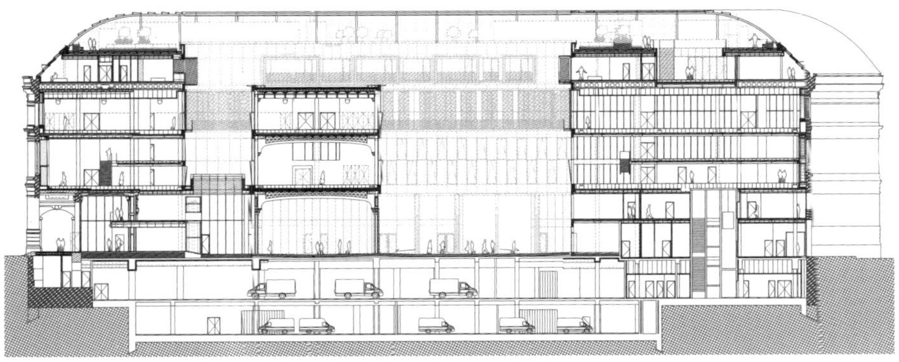

7

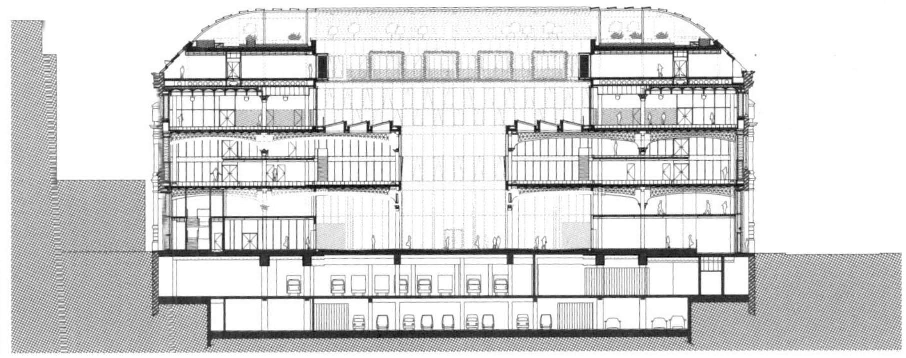

8

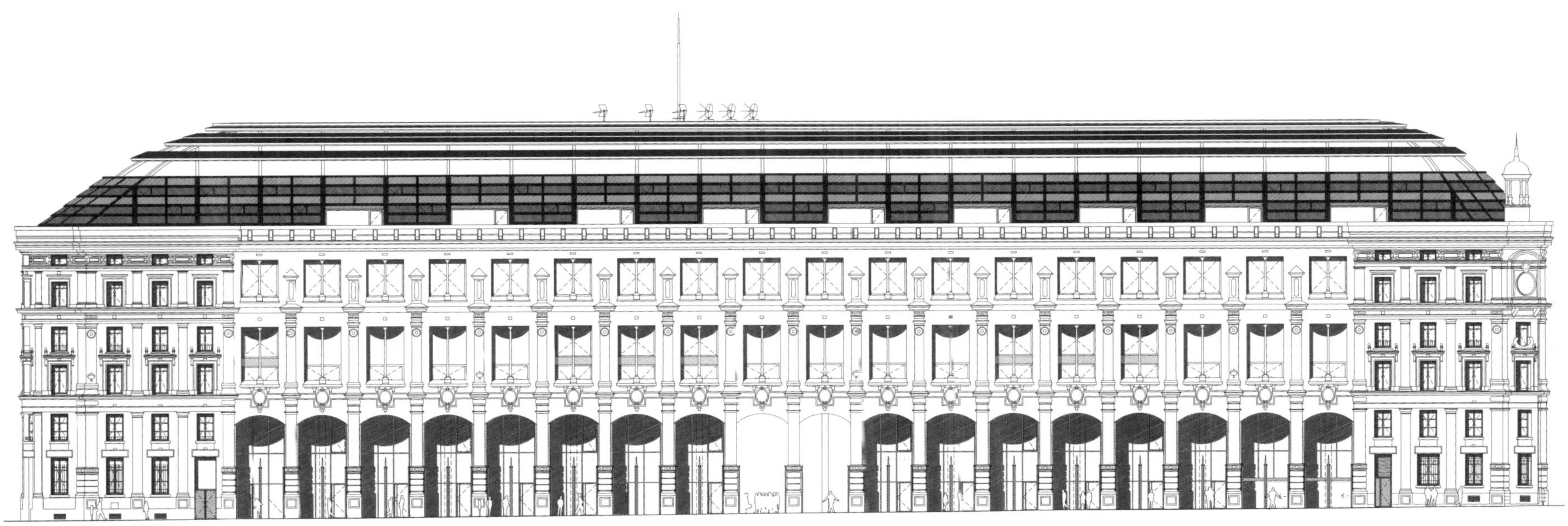

9

1

3

2

1, 2 Lighting and illumination of interior office spaces.
3 Study model of the glazed façade, scale 1:10, 2012.
4 Parisian rooftops and surrounding monuments, including the church of Saint-Eustache.
5 Planted terraces, walkway, and pergola equipped with photovoltaic panels.
6 Reconstruction of the Poste du Louvre roof, destroyed by fire in 1975.

"Transforming heritage into strategy."

COURT OF JUSTICE OF THE EUROPEAN UNION (CJ4 AND CJ8)

LUXEMBOURG, PHASES 1 AND 2

1996–2008 / 2014–19

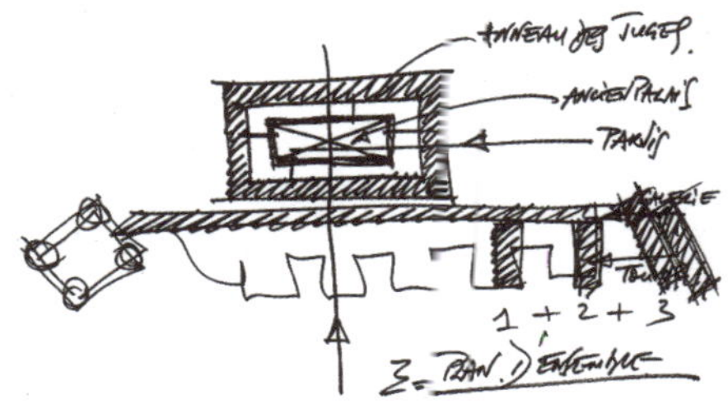

1

Since its creation in 1952, the Court of Justice of the European Union has been constantly reinventing itself, just like the Europe it represents. Housed in various buildings spread out over a single site, it has grown in step with the expansion of the European Community. With the enlargement to twenty-seven member states, the Court embarked on a fourth extension, rapidly followed by a fifth, in line with an injection strategy that emphasizes connecting spaces, rather than simply juxtaposing them. Integrating the markers of its history, the site has been redesigned in relation to the transformation of the original metal palace, built in 1973. Below and linked to it, a 700-meter gallery links all the existing structures, including the three new towers, built gradually to meet the Court's growing needs.

2

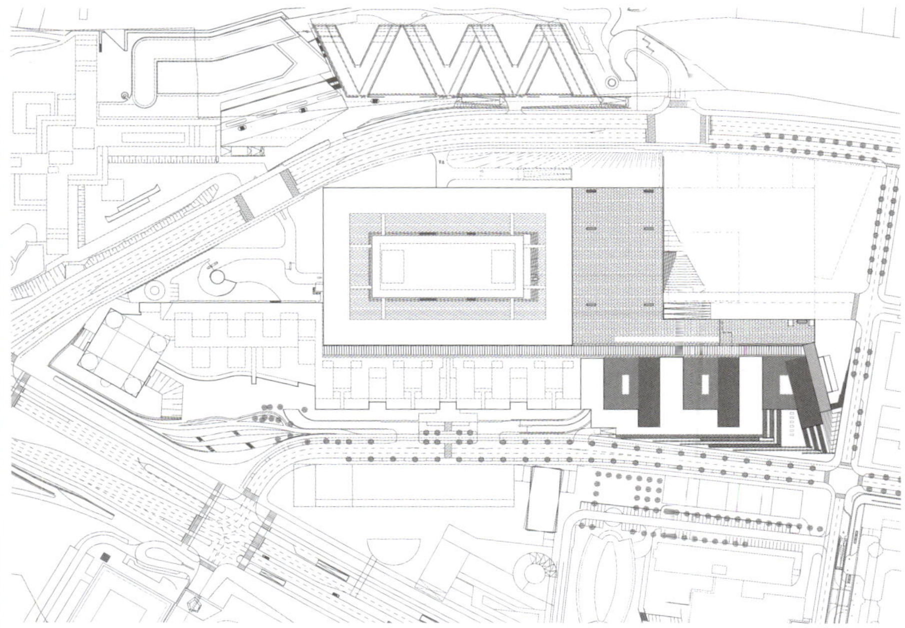

4

1 Sketch, 2018.
2 Kirchberg plateau with palace, 1970.
3 Model of the fourth extension, scale 1:1,000, 2000.
4 Block plan: in black, the various developments carried out between 1996 and 2019, including the refurbishment of the old palace, the extension of the Court through the creation of the ring and the first two office towers (inaugurated in 2008), and the addition of a third tower (inaugurated in 2019).
5 General model of the Court, scale 1:200, 2002.
6, 7 Elevations.
8 Study model, scale 1:1,[illegible]00, 1998.

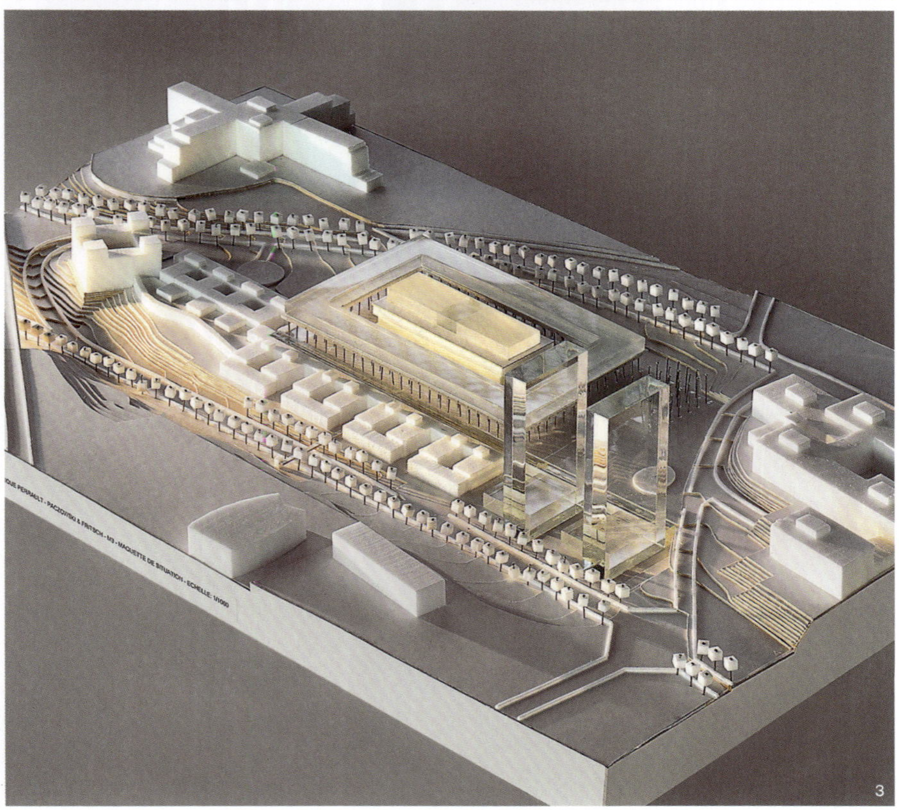

3

"Radicalism is not rupture but conversion. It is the art of bending time between past and present without breaking it."

5

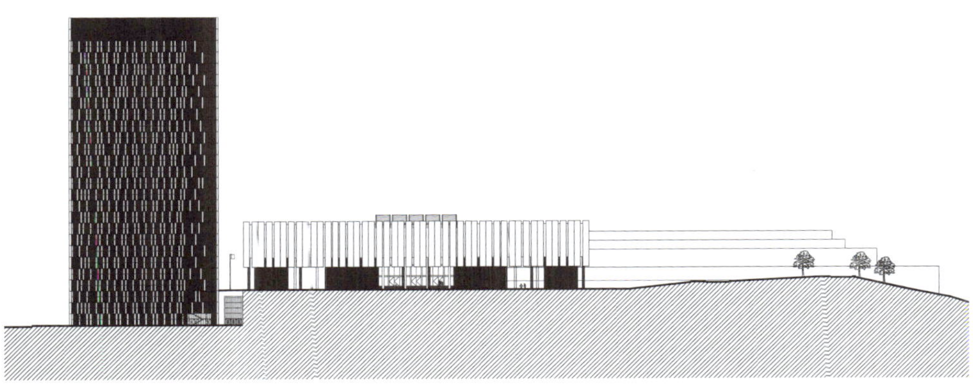
6

8

7

1

2

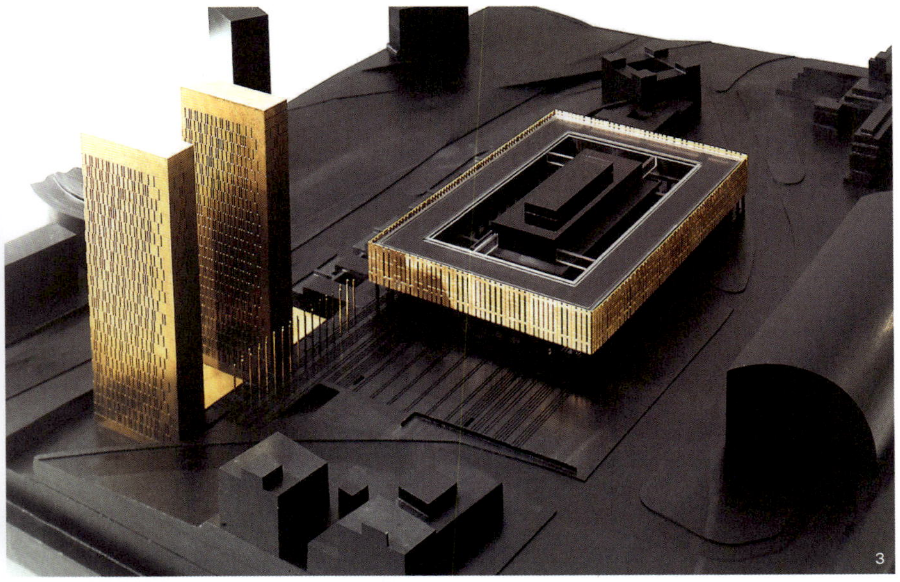

3

1 Surrounding the original building, the new palace features a metal architecture of porticoes and walkways behind a screen of tinted glass. It opens widely onto a vast forecourt to the east.
2 Bridges linking the old palace and the judges' *anneau* (ring).
3 Study model, scale 1:200, 2002.
4 The Court, 2003.
5 Plan of the palace and ring.
6, 7 Glass slats in front of the ring.
8 The façade of the ring consists of a detached and tinted outer layer, acting as a sunshade.

4

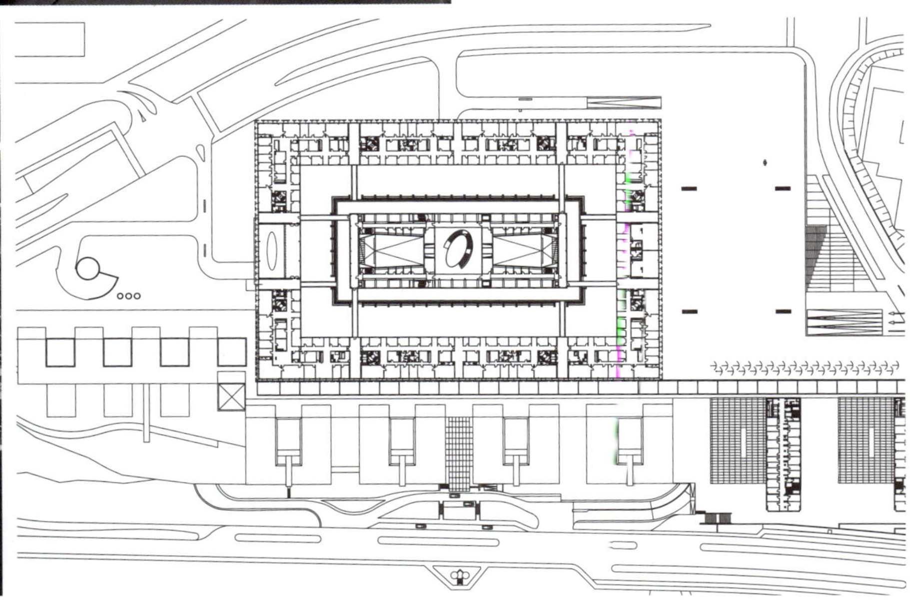

5

6

7

8

1-3 The palace's "salle des pas perdus" (vestibule).
4, 5 The great audience hall with its baldachin in metal mesh.

4

5

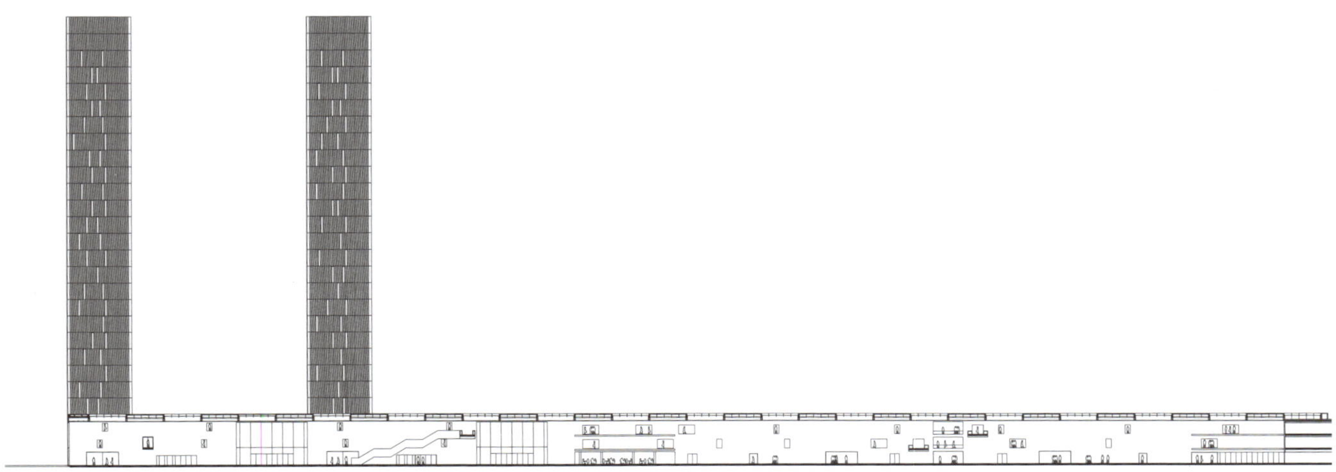

3

1, 2 The backbone of the project, the gallery ensures architectural and functional unity between the old buildings and the contemporary extensions. Study model, scale 1:200, 2004.

3 Cross-section of gallery, palace side.

4 Main staircase linking the gallery to the courtrooms.

5, 6 Large gallery, interior street.

7 Cross-section.

6

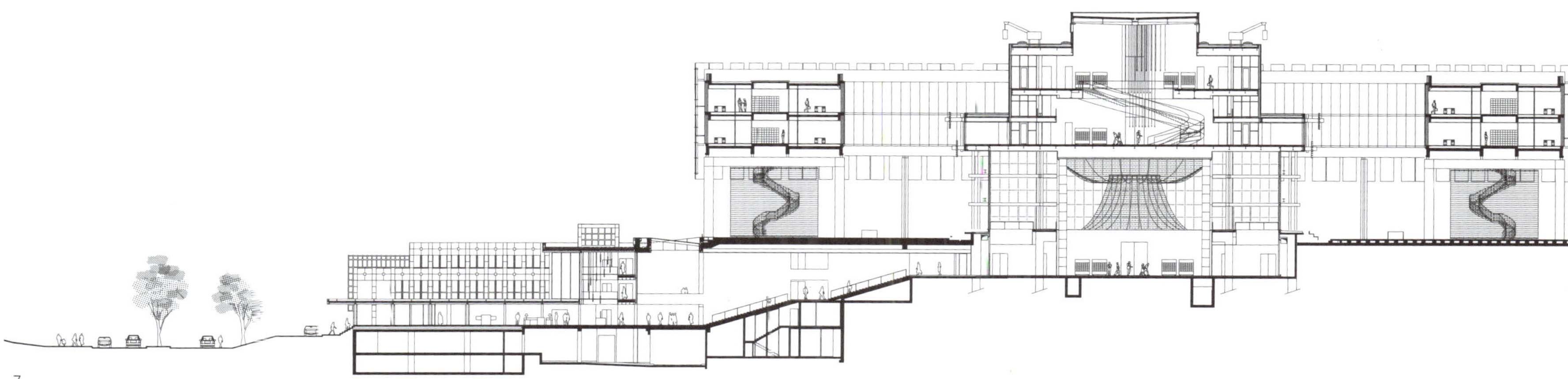

7

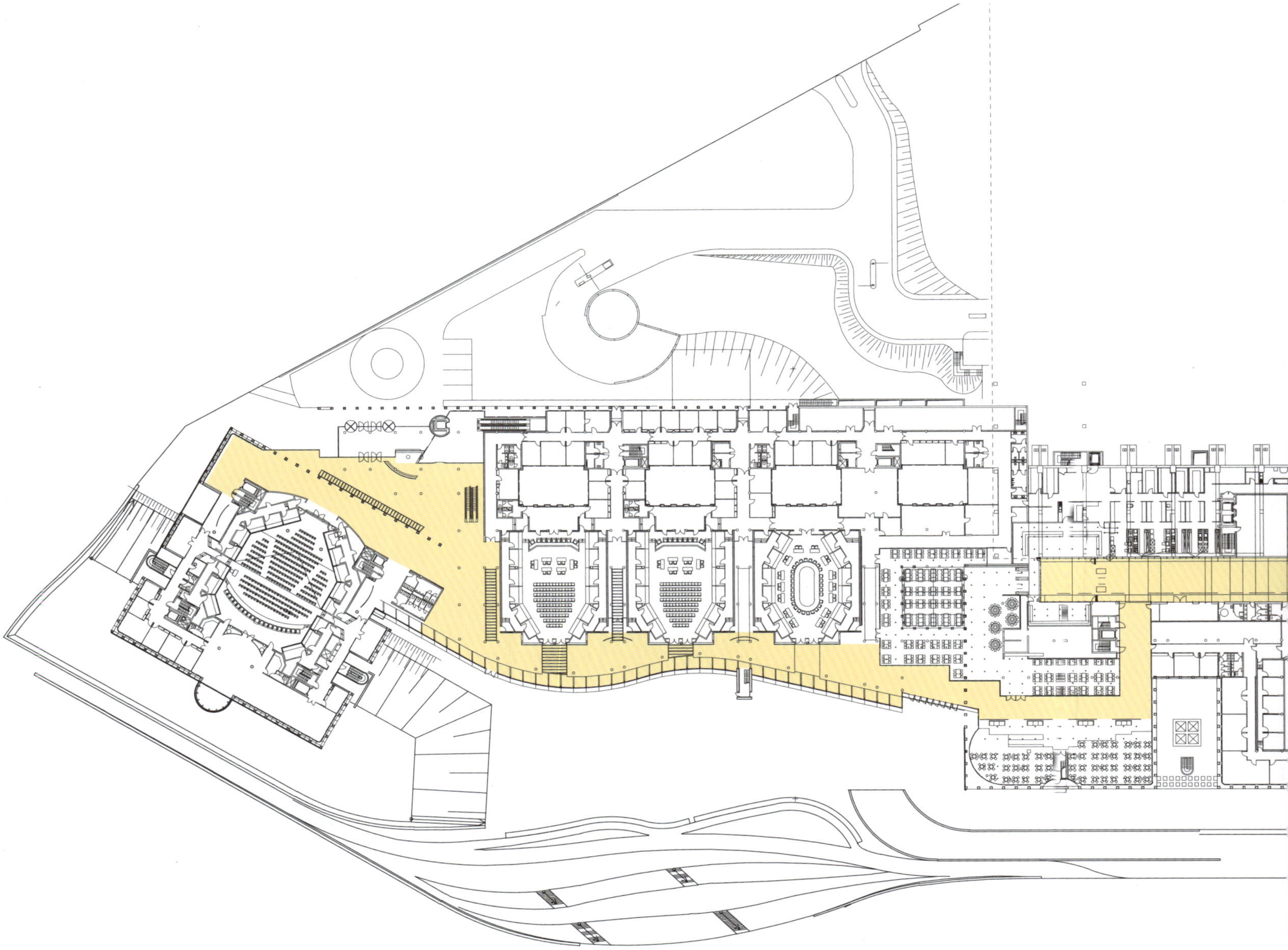

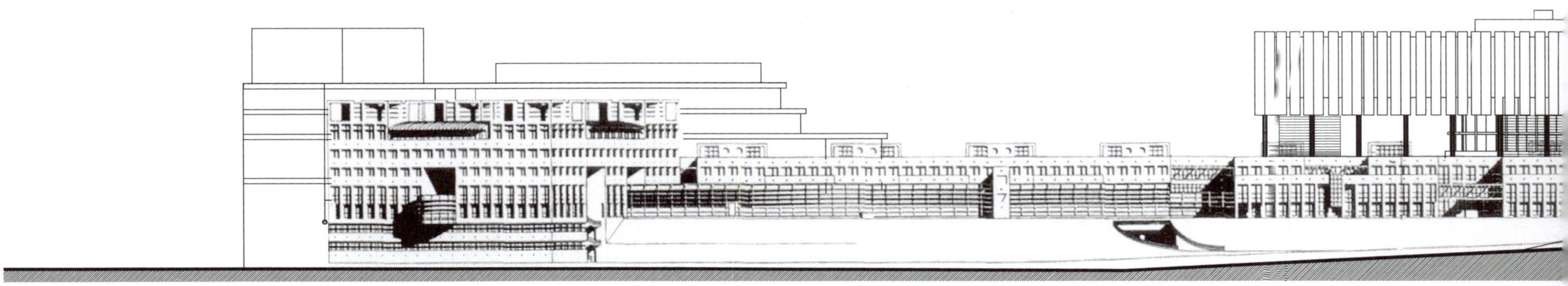

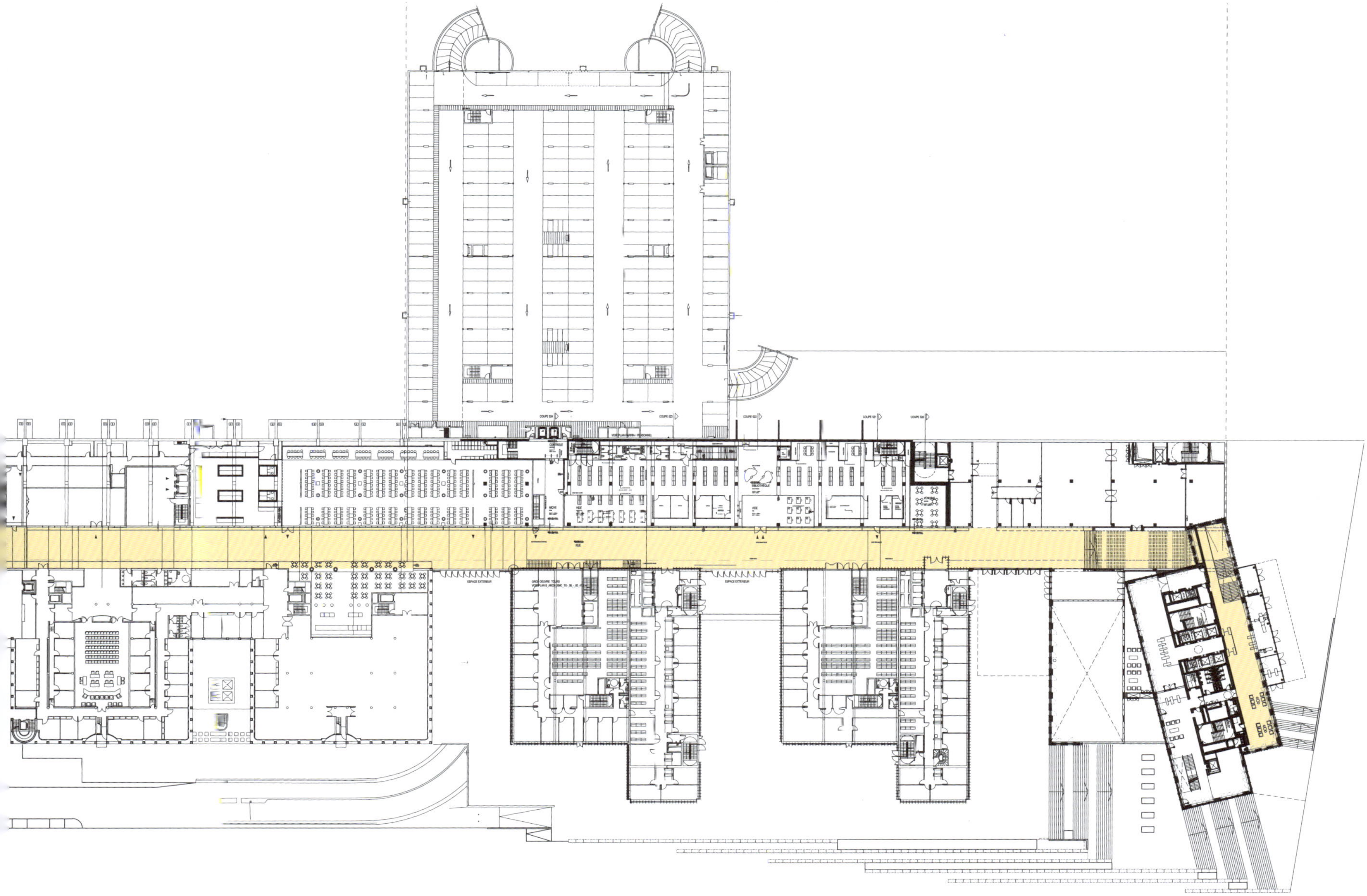

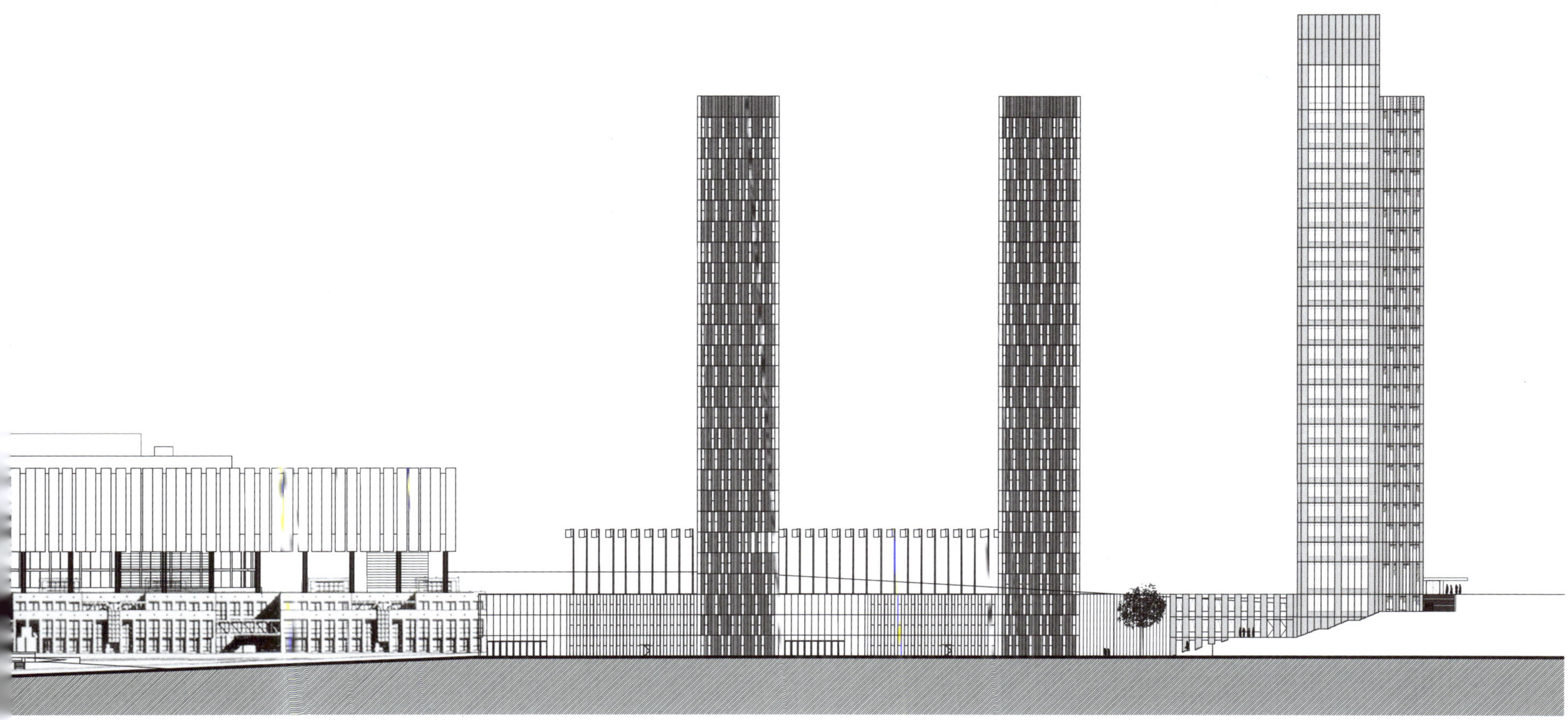

GRANDES ÉCURIES OF THE CHÂTEAU DE CHANTILLY

CHANTILLY, FRANCE

2017

1

The aim of the transformation of the Grandes Écuries at the Château de Chantilly, the emblematic grand stables in this capital of the horse, was to breathe new life into this eighteenth-century masterpiece by making it part of an ambitious Musée du Cheval, telling the story of humanity through man's relation to the horse. The project redefines the heritage of the existing Grandes Écuries and their adjoining courtyards. In a powerful architectural gesture, a monumental staircase rises into the air and its crossing flights form a sculptural X that reconnects the upper part of the stables. This space, formerly reserved for the riders' accommodations, is once again accessible, bringing the vertical dimension back into the visitor's experience. In the courtyard, a new big top houses the equestrian circus, with an overall scenography that restores unity to a previously fragmented system.

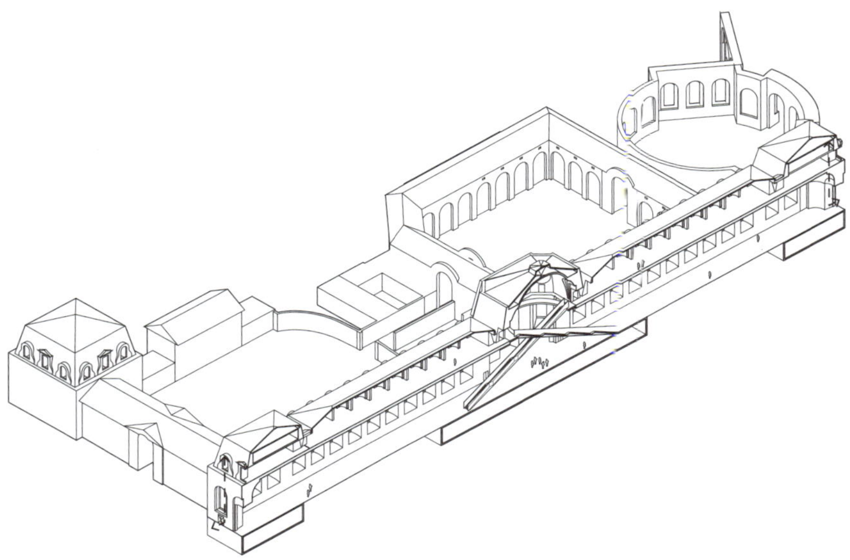

2

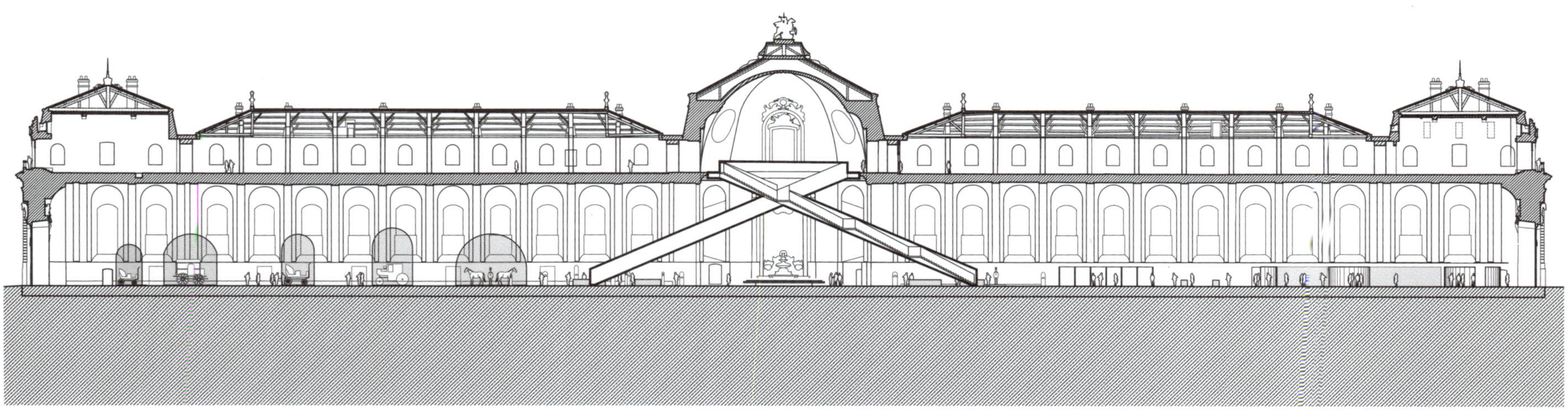

3

1 The Château de Chantilly.
2 The Grandes Écuries (great stables) complex.
3 Longitudinal section of the Grandes Écuries, with the staircase linking the horses to the riders' rooms under the roof.
4 The stables today.
5 The staircase at the heart of the museum's rotunda entrance.
6 Scenography of the museum's great hall.

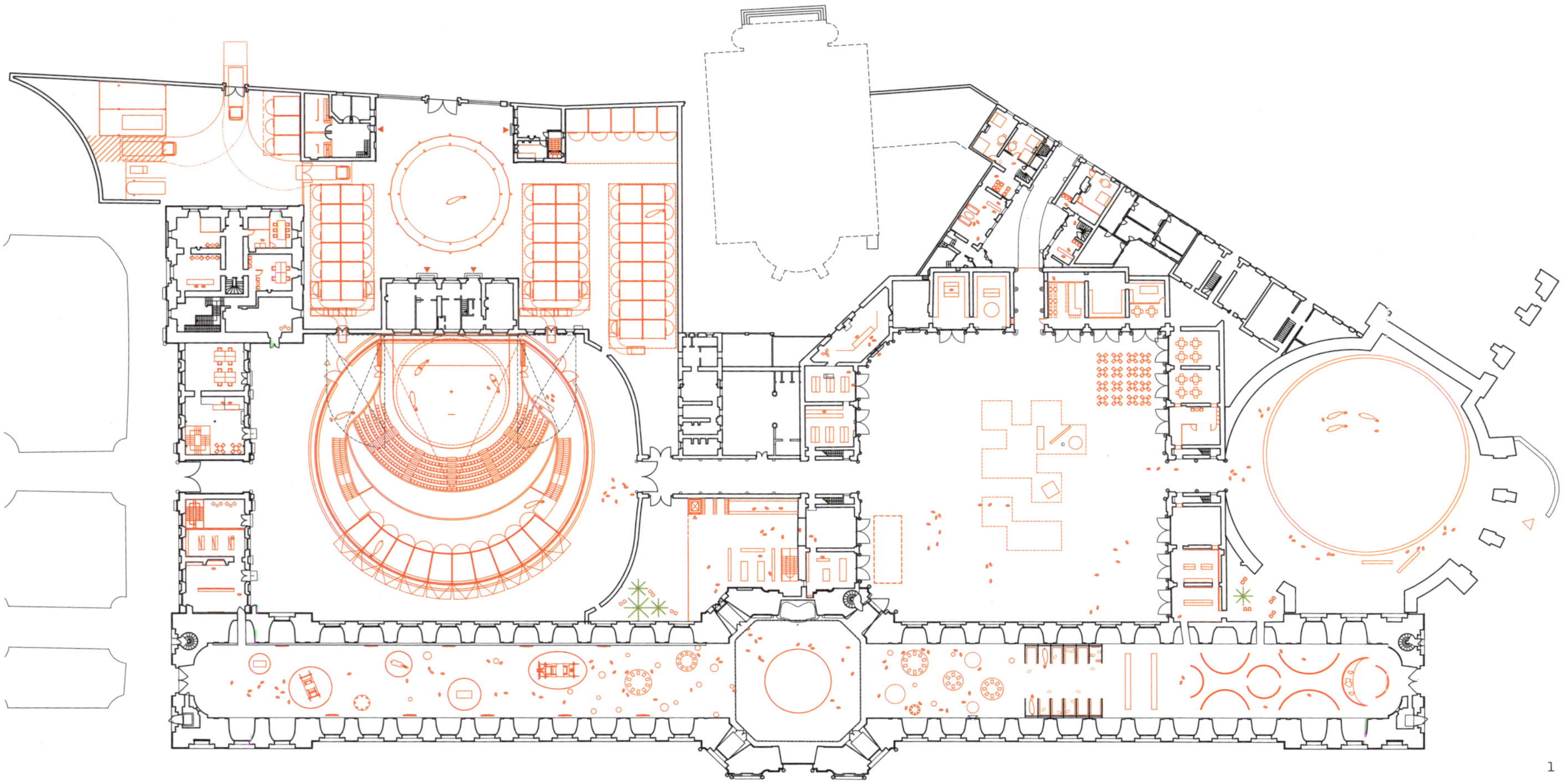

1

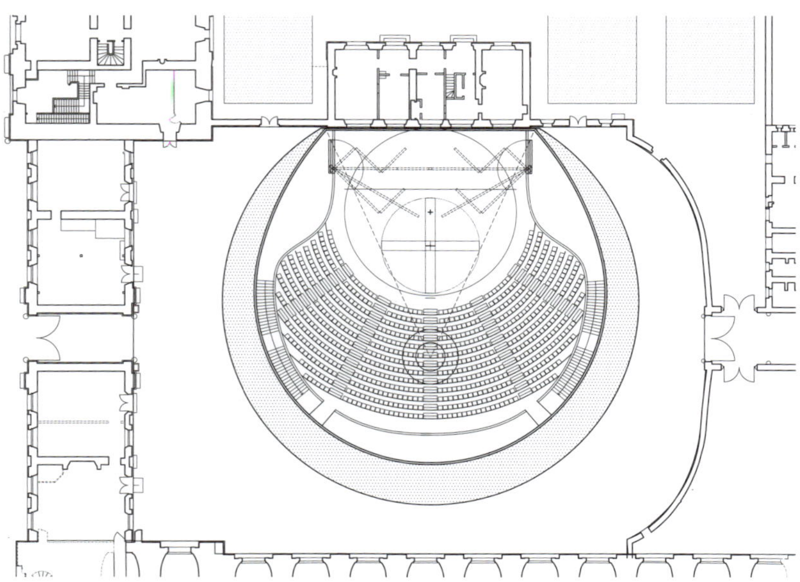

2

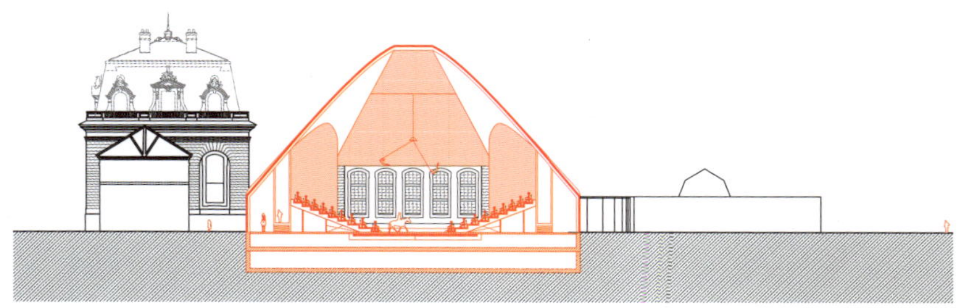

3

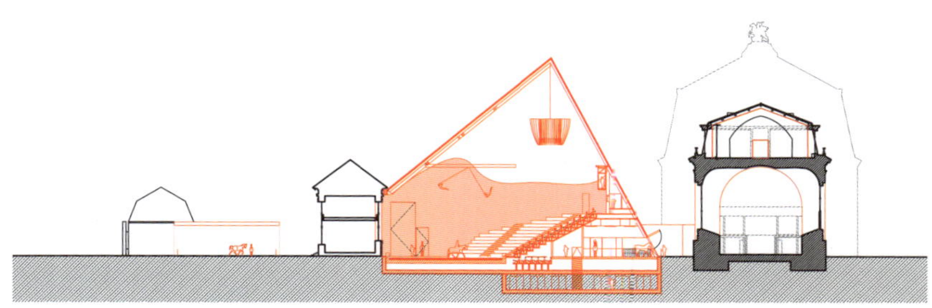

4

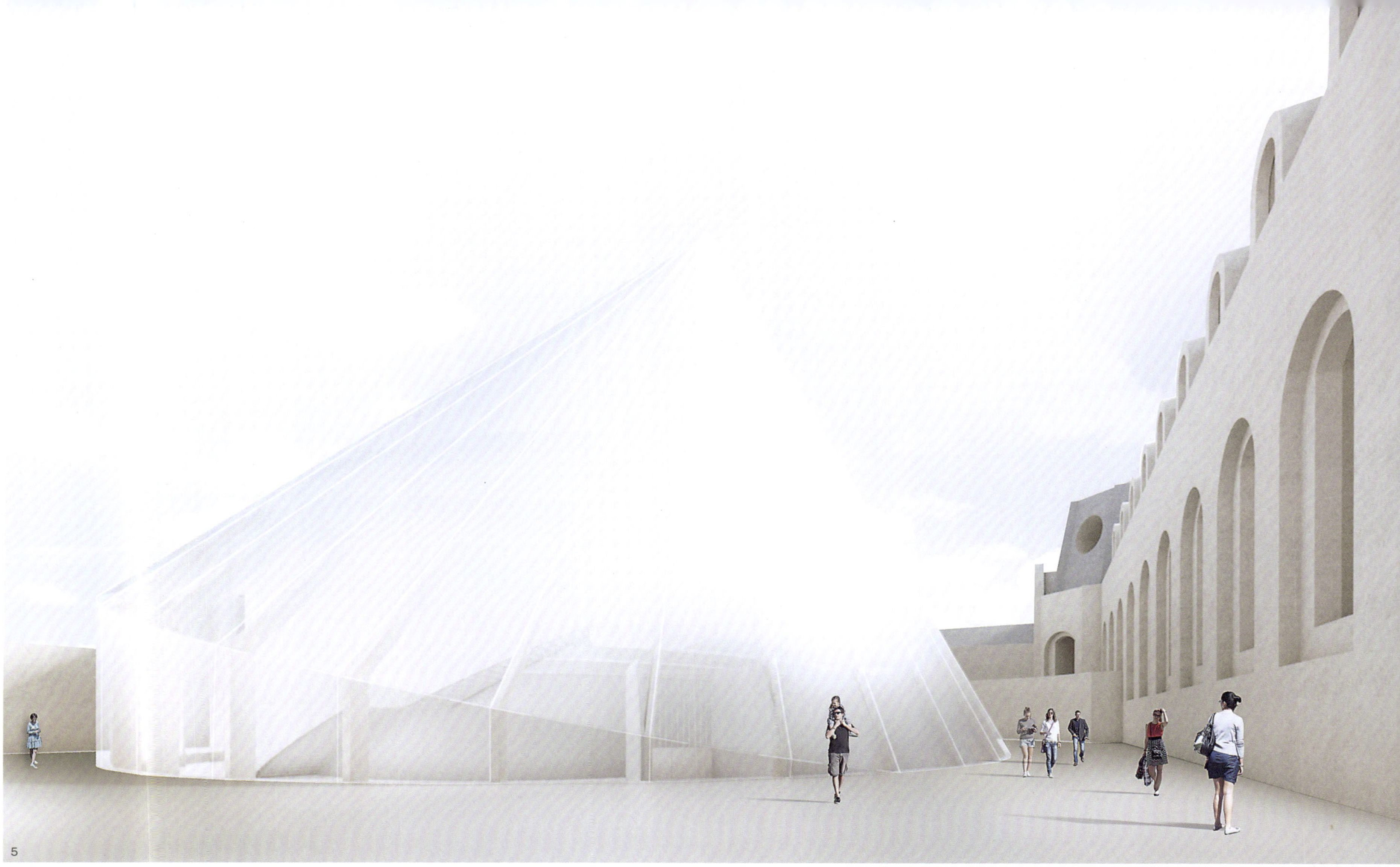

1 Overall layout of the Musée du Cheval, installed both in the buildings and in the three courtyards.
2 Plan of the equestrian theater.
3, 4 Sectional view of the theater and its heritage buildings.
5 The theater marquee, installed in the center of the Cour des Chiens.
6, 7 The theater's construction is backed onto a heritage building, forming a *scaena frons* inspired by Palladio's theater in Vicenza.

LANDSCAPE TOWER

PUTEAUX-LA DÉFENSE, FRANCE
2015–21

Completed in 1983 under the direction of architect Henri La Fonta, the two Pascal Towers, located in the district of La Défense, near Paris, were in need of a thorough transformation.
The reconfiguration of uses and comfort could not be achieved without redefining the built perimeter. The concrete shell has been preserved, but the two towers have been thickened and merged thanks to an extension that combines them into a single coherent building. This shared use of space frees up new areas, breaking with the monotony of repetitive floors. Double-height windows, loggias, and terraces bring in light and air, and accommodate a variety of uses.
The façades, meanwhile, retain the design of the original square grid but are clad in a breathable skin: openable windows on each floor, protected by fixed sheets of glass set twenty centimeters apart, let in natural air while protecting against draughts and rain.

1 General view of the forecourt of La Défense and the Pascal Towers, designed in the early 1980s by Henri La Fonta.
2 The restructuring project combines the two Pascal Towers into a single building.
3-6 Installation of the exterior glass panels to open and ventilate the building naturally.
7, 8 A robe of glass.

1

2

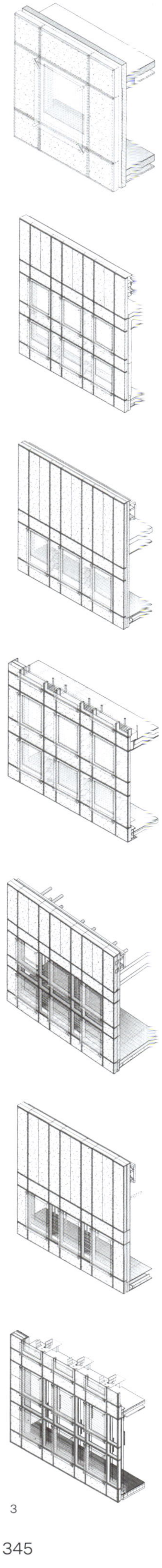
3

4

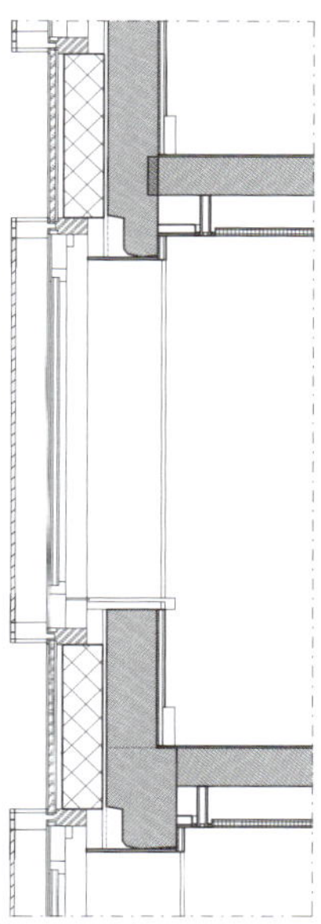
5

6

7

8

CITYLIGHTS

BOULOGNE-BILLANCOURT, FRANCE
2007–16

The Pont-de-Sèvres towers, designed in the 1970s by Daniel Badani and Pierre Roux-Dorlut with efficient hexagonal plans, suffered conspicuously from isolation, both from each other and from their urban environment. The transformation changes this situation: a vast hall of 1,500 square meters now links the towers to a shared base, physically anchoring them in the city.
An additional hexagon, built identically, introduces flexibility to the layout, while the redevelopment of the façades completes the revelation of the building complex: the new crystal-effect metal envelopes transform the towers into powerful light collectors. Thanks to the prismatic shape of the clusters of buildings, light is reflected and diffused, erasing the traditional dichotomy between north and south faces.

2

3

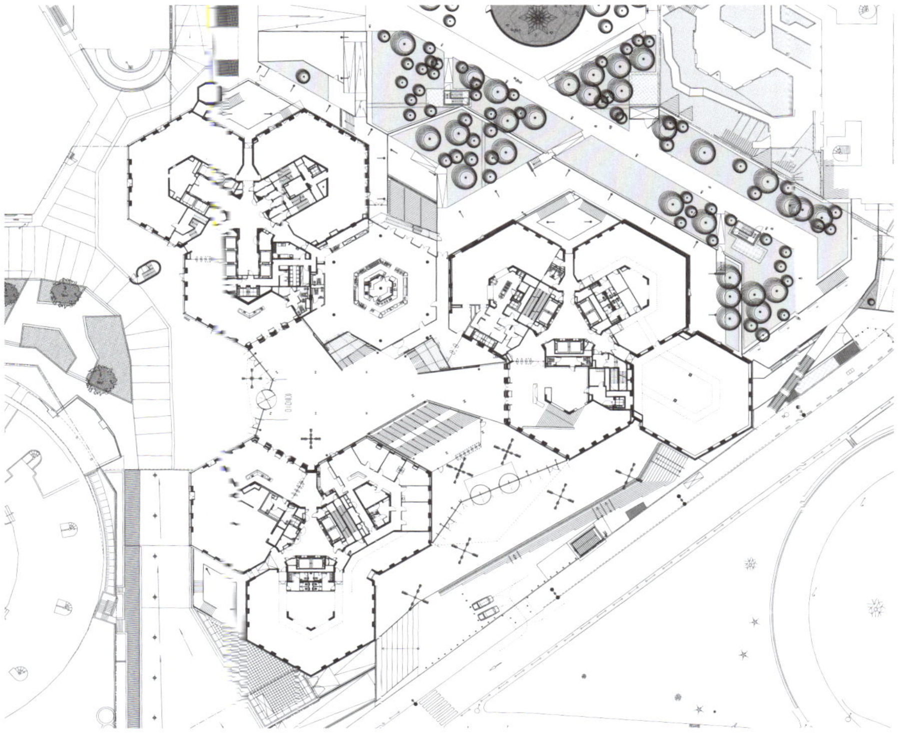

5

4

1 The Pont-de-Sèvres towers, designed in 1975 by Badani and Roux-Dorlut, in an emerging urban territory.
2 Model, scale 1:500, 2015. At the exit of Pont de Sèvres, entering Paris.
3, 4 Inside and outside the towers, metal is multiplied and reflected.
5 Plan of the large lobby linking the lower and upper squares.

1, 2 The prismatic shapes of the façades act as light sensors. Like optical instruments, they allow light to circulate everywhere, ensuring that every office, whatever its orientation, benefits from the reflective effects of the crystal-like façades.
3 Section between the upper and lower plazas.
4 Axonometric view of the breathable façade.
5, 6 Before (2011)/After (2015).

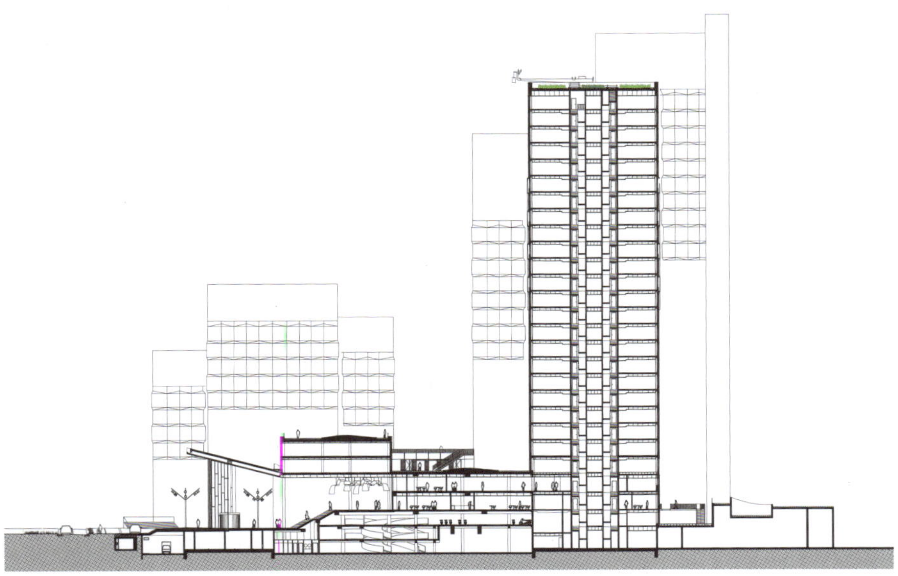

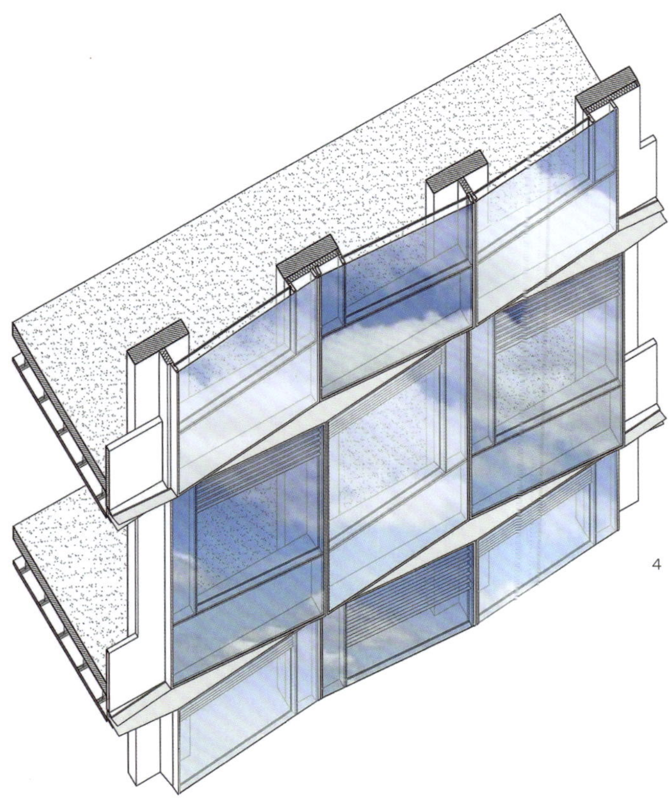

5

6

SUZANNE-LENGLEN COURT COVERAGE

PARIS, FRANCE
2020–24

Confident, pure, and unadorned, the roof structure, the result of precise engineering, consists of a delicate assembly of steel elements that hovers above the original concrete court. A mobile structure ensures that the light, pleated roof can be unfolded elegantly and effortlessly. As soon as it is activated, the show begins: vast canopies in metal fabric, hung from the longitudinal sides of the metal structure, create a link between the existing and the new, between the weight of the concrete and the lightness of the roof, between the flat lines and the curves of the stands. This architecture is designed to be a reflection of the avant-garde and daring character of Suzanne Lenglen, a woman who, almost a century ago, made history with her unique temperament.

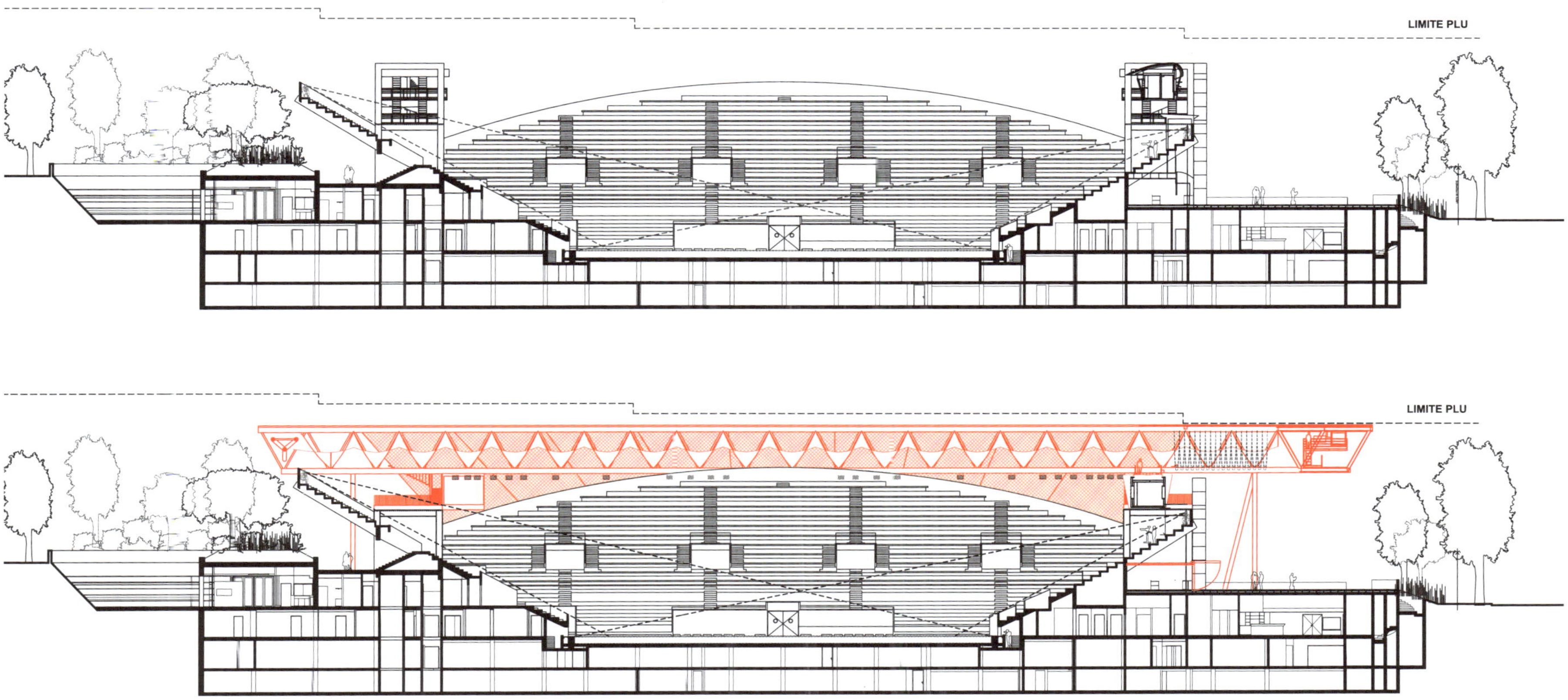

4

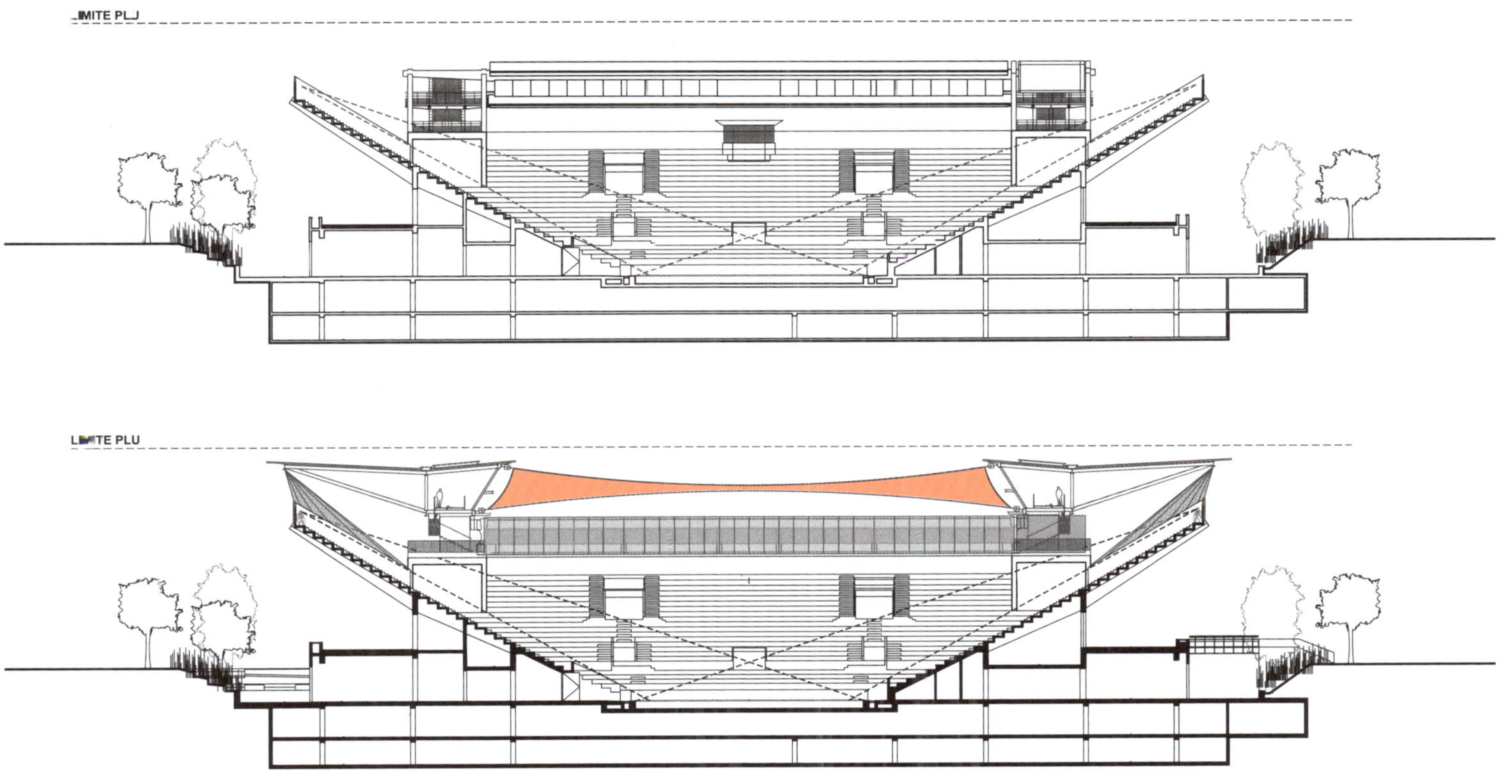

5

1 Initial state, 2018.
2 The Roland-Garros site.
3 Inauguration of Court Suzanne-Lenglen's mobile roof, May 2024.

4 Before and after. The textile roof moves on a metal "table," without touching the concrete structure of the original stadium.
5 Before/after. The membrane floats above the court.

Pages 352-53
1 Inauguration of Court Suzanne-Lenglen mobile roof, May 2024.
2 The diaphanous membrane of the mobile roof.

1

2

1

2

3

4

5

1-4 Stitching detail of the metal fabric
5 The concrete bleachers are connected to the roof line by a metal fabric that follows the shape of the architecture.

"Architectural rewriting is not a graft but a revelation."

EUROPEAN PARLIAMENT – PAUL-HENRI-SPAAK BUILDING

BRUSSELS, BELGIUM
2020

A powerful symbol of the European Union, the European Parliament embodies the postmodern architectural legacy of the 1990s. Its renovation does not seek to erase this memory, but to elevate it by infusing it with new spatial qualities. The transformation takes place within its envelope: the existing levels are maintained, but strategic openings are made, creating visual and spatial connections between the floors.
New walkways on the periphery of the building make it possible to take in views over the city. The roof becomes an active and symbolic space planted with terraced gardens, while the hemicycle—the beating heart of the democratic assembly—is repositioned beneath the dome at the top.
This architectural gesture reinvents the silhouette of the Spaak building while reaffirming its place in the landscape of the European Quarter.

1

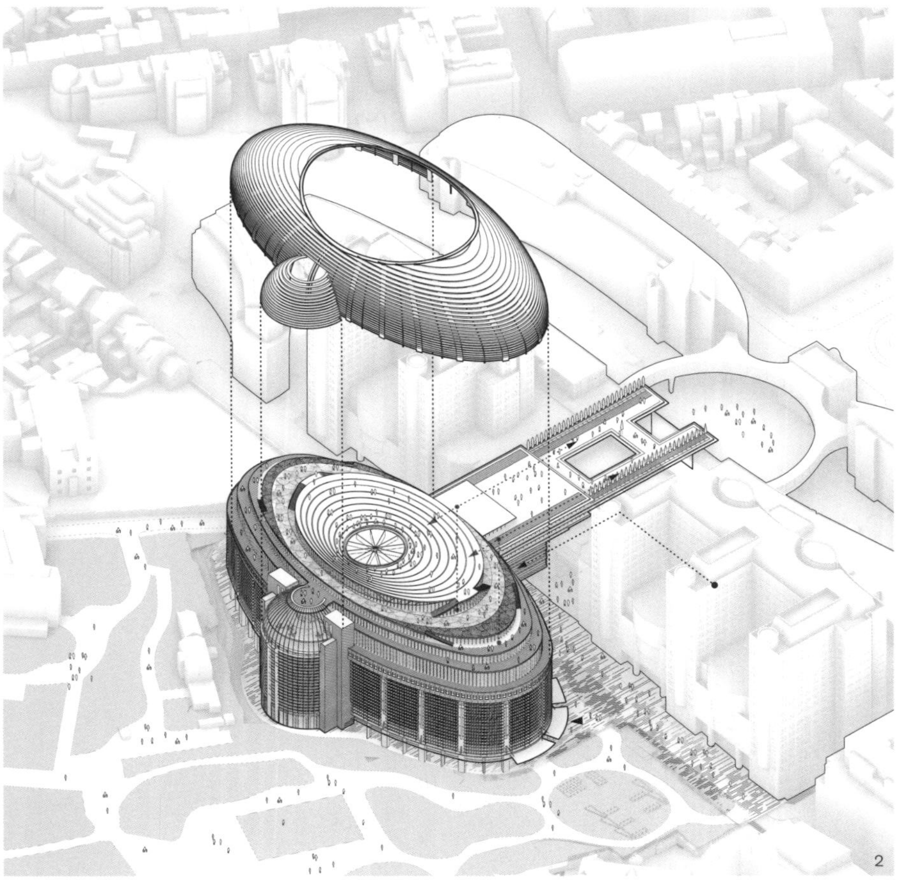
2

3

4

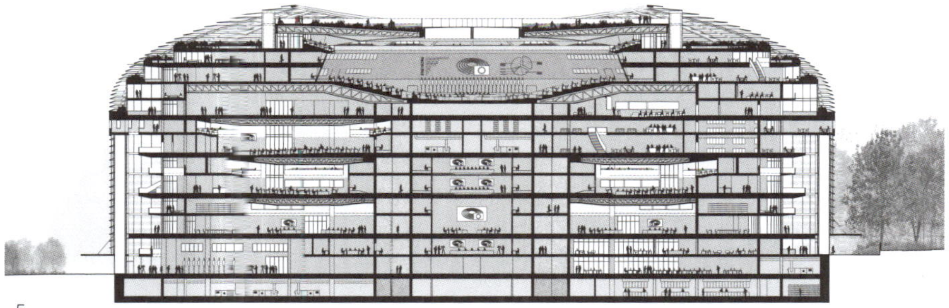

5

6

1 The Paul-Henri-Spaak building at the European Parliament, photograph by Simon Schmit, 2018.
2 A new, more open structure crowns the historic building.
3 Model, scale 1:500, 2021.
4 The compactness and transparency of the proposal allow this initially massive building to settle into the urban landscape of the European Quarter.
5 Longitudinal section, illustrating the redistribution of the program within the building's legacy structure.
6 The hemicycle and oculus.

BANK FOR INTERNATIONAL SETTLEMENTS (BIS)

BASEL, SWITZERLAND

2021

In Basel, the extension to the Bank of International Settlements (BIS) is a continuation of the existing metal building, a subtle design by architect Martin Burckhardt built between 1972 and 1977. The project imagines the current tower as a root from which a twin building emerges, respecting the original architectural style. The two buildings merge in an organic base, sculpted to form a coherent new urban block. This junction gives rise to a structure in which a series of terraced gardens gradually rise up, accompanying the emergence of the twin towers. Beyond the formal intervention, the project carries an ethical message: working with the legacies of the past, to extend and sublimate them.

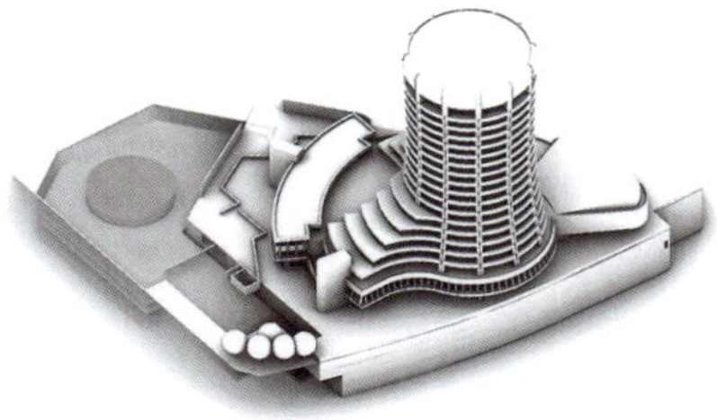

1

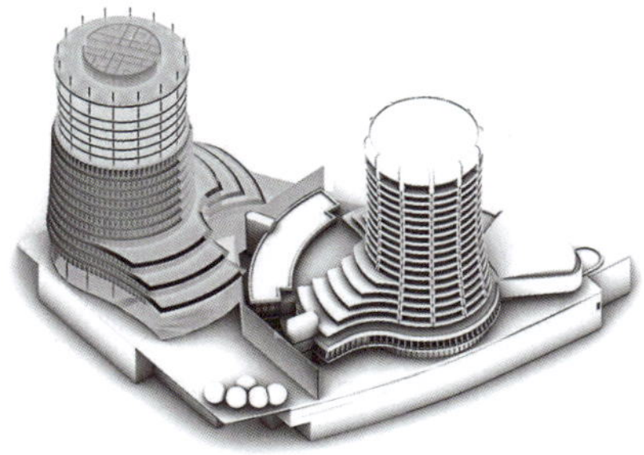

2

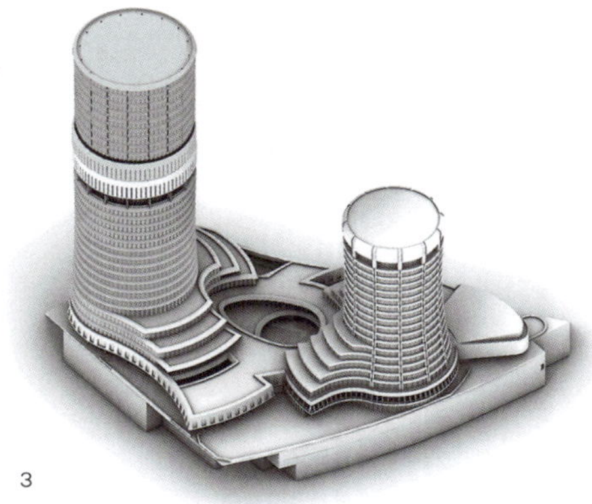

3

4

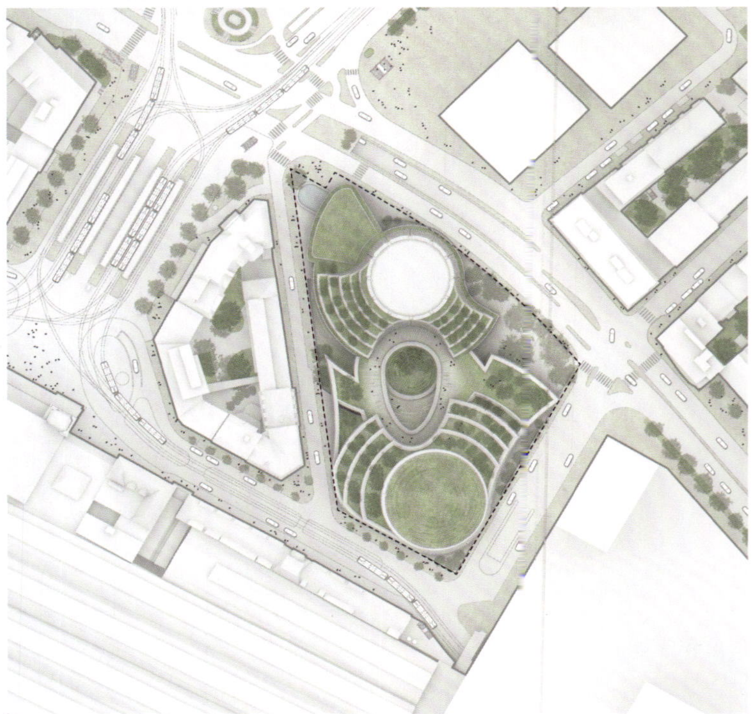

6

5

1-3 The three stages of architectural development.

4 The Bank for International Settlements building, 2021.

5 Elevation of the north façades.

6 The project adds green spaces around the building by means of a series of vegetated terraces and patios.

7 The floor plans are designed to be flexible, sometimes open, sometimes intimate, capable of constantly adapting to changing needs.

8 By reinterpreting and multiplying the original design by Martin Burckhardt in a similar way, a new modernity is created.

9 Detail of the façade envelope of the new towers.

10 The central courtyard and its terraces.

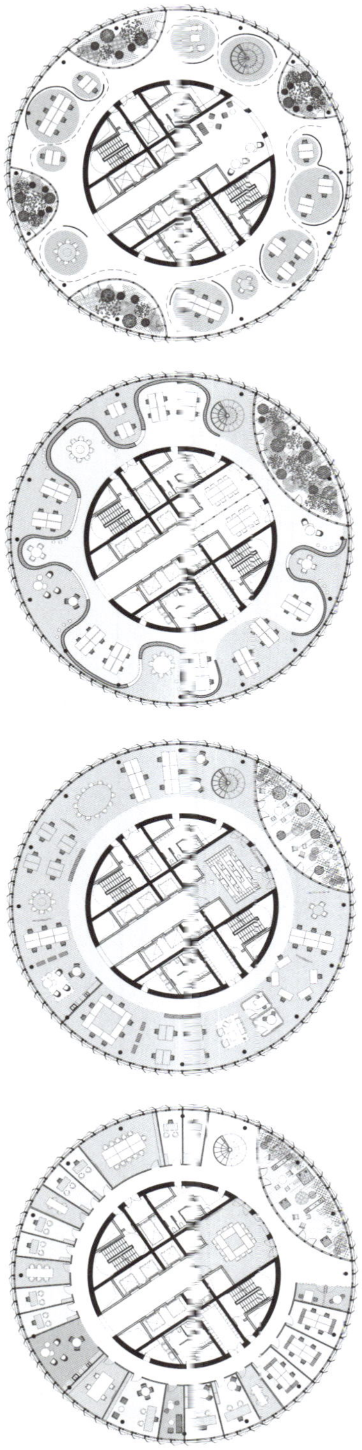

7

8

9

10

1

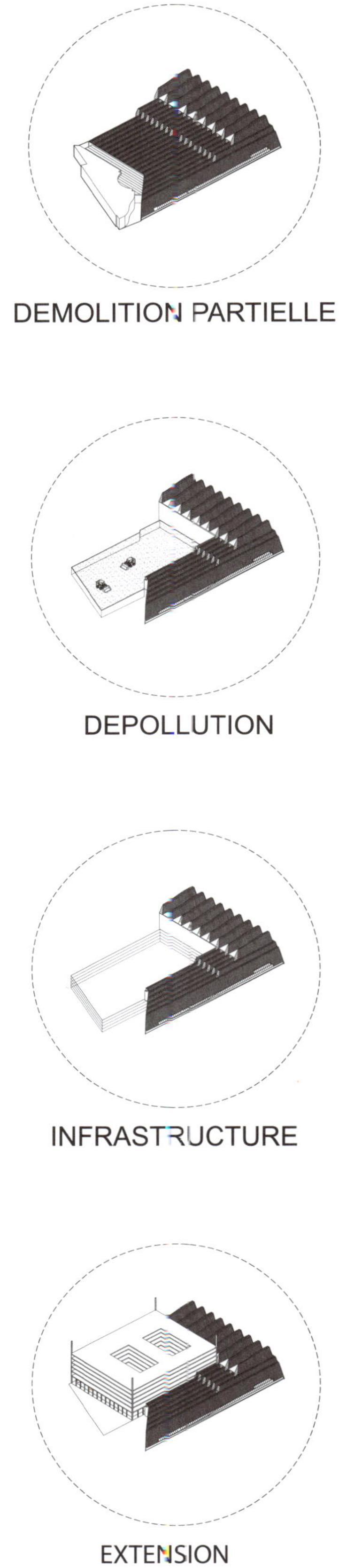

DEMOLITION PARTIELLE
DEPOLLUTION
INFRASTRUCTURE
EXTENSION

3

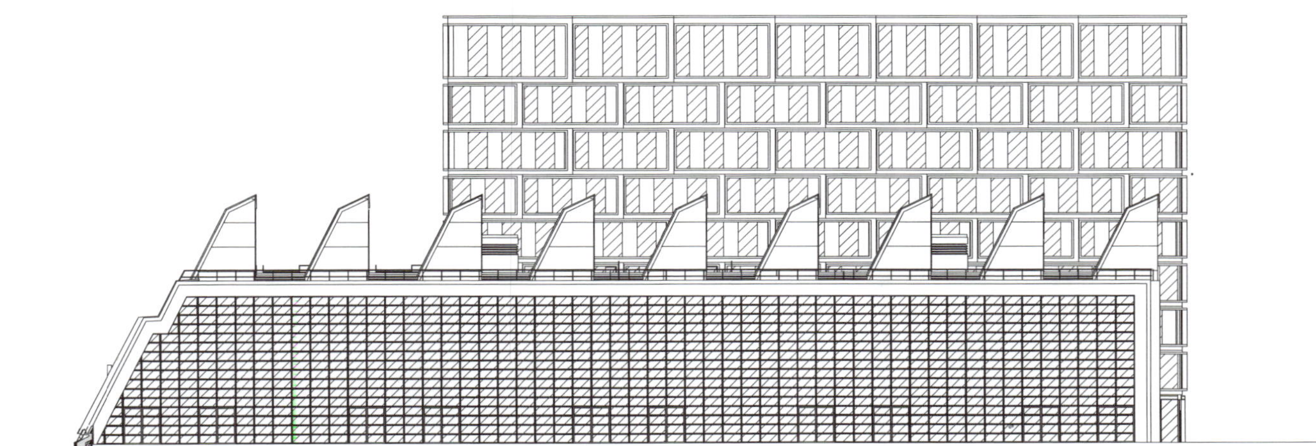

2

1 Highlighting the hangars, evidence of the site's industrial past.
2 Elevation of the east façade
3 Schemas illustrating the intervention process.
4 The hangars introduce natural light into the new spaces.

1

2

3

1 Axonometric view of the junction between the preserved building and the new building.
2 The main central staircase.
3 Geometric meeting of hangars and interior architecture.
4 The plan of the first floor, like a city map.
5, 6 The satin-finish stainless steel façades of the interior patios.

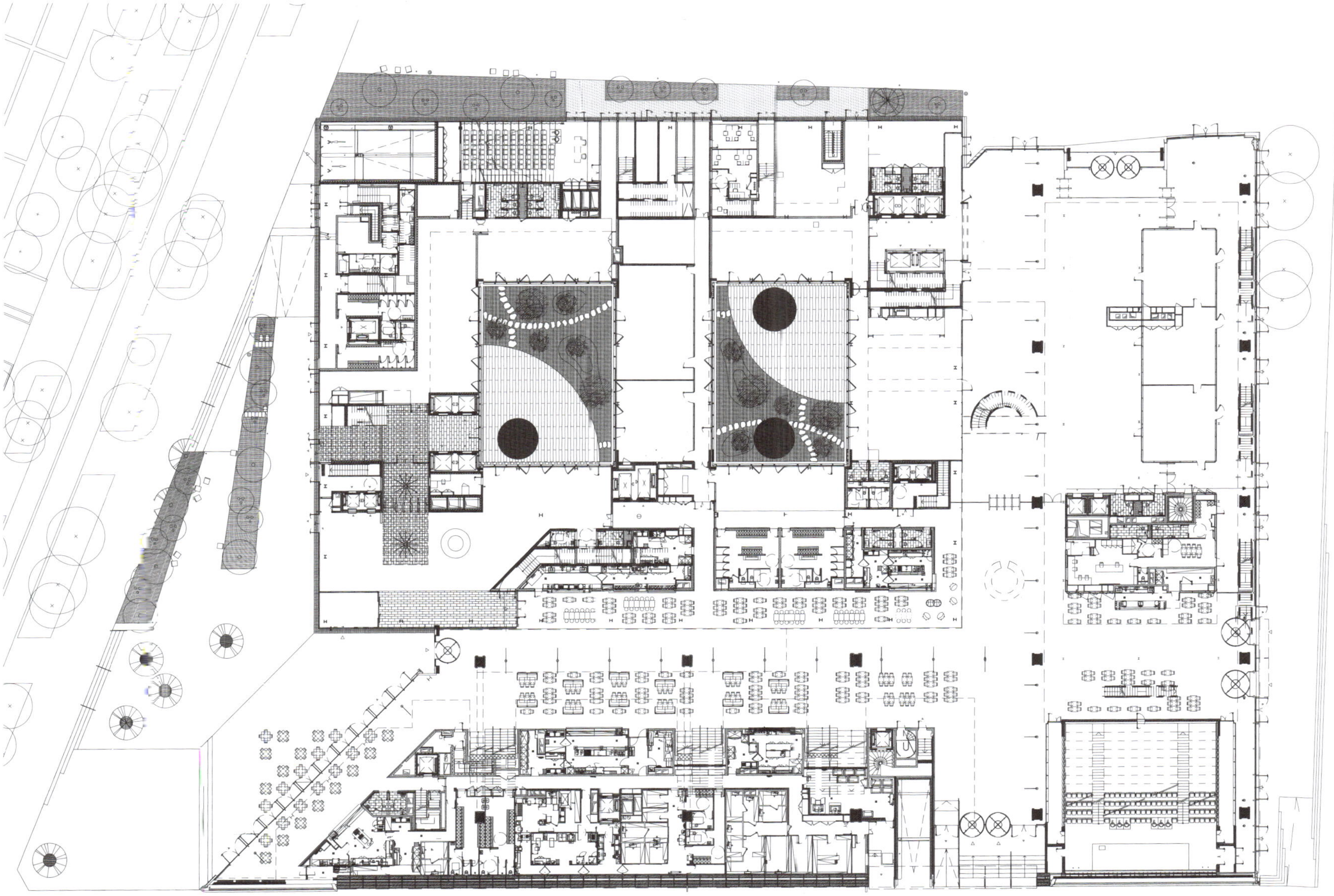

4

5

6

CENTRE POMPIDOU

PARIS, FRANCE

2024

The restructuring of the Centre Pompidou involves a radical move: raising the floor of the interior forum and the car park buried beneath the plaza. This operation opens up the building to natural light, which penetrates the spaces on both sides, fully realizing the founding idea of an active, fluid base permeable to the city. Multiple access points allow visitors to move freely across this vibrant plinth, where the plaza stretches out and becomes a stage open to all forms of art, affirming the principle of art for all. The reinterpreted building seems to float above this living base, magnifying the iconic architecture designed by Renzo Piano and Richard Rogers in 1977, while reaffirming its cultural relevance.

"As it is, even if it's completely different."

2

3

1 Centre Pompidou, 1990
2 View of the new topography of the piazza.
3 Repositioned after being lifted, the building reveals the resources beneath.
4 Redeploying the Centre Pompidou outside its structure to activate a system of squares around its plaza.

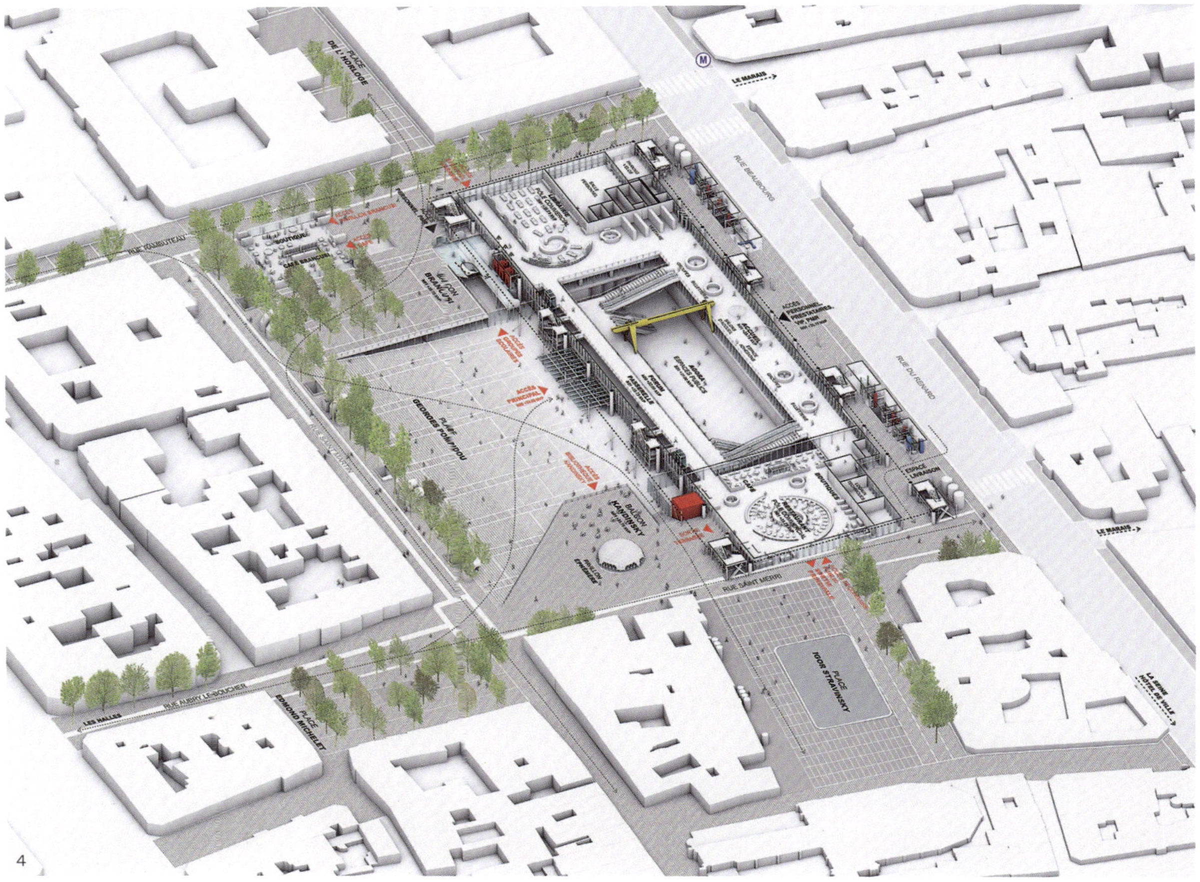

4

APLIX AND APLIX EXTENSION

LE CELLIER-SUR-LOIRE, FRANCE

1997–99 / 2016–20

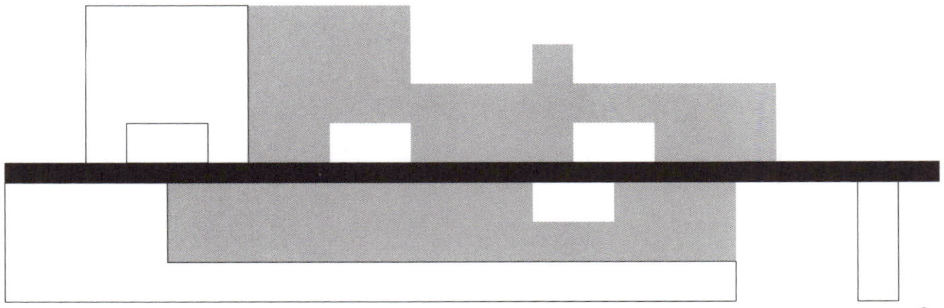

3

The Aplix factory is characterized by a dialectical interplay between appearance and disappearance. Located on a vast, flat plot of land along the RN23 between Nantes and Angers, its façade takes the form of a mirror stretched over a length of 300 meters. Made of polished stainless-steel slats, it literally blends into the green of the lawns and the blue of the sky. The factory seems to come alive, its reflections transforming and multiplying in accordance with the climate, the path of the clouds, and the rotation of the sun.

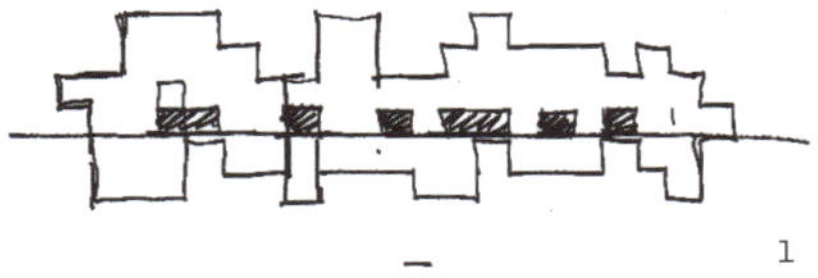

1

1 Sketch, 2016.
2 Concept model, scale 1:500, 1997.
3 The new factory after the extension.
4 The factory façade before the extension, 1999.
5 Block plan, initial state (1999) and extended state (2020). On the ground, a 20 x 20 m grid creates a checkerboard pattern of alternating built and vegetated areas, like a crossword puzzle playing with solids and voids.
6 General plan of the factory, 2020.
7, 8 Elevation and longitudinal section of the factory after extension.

Adding a surface area of 17,000 square meters, the extension to the Aplix factory adopts the same architectural codes as the initial project. This was based around a square grid measuring twenty meters by twenty meters, with some of the hollowed-out cells transformed into patios planted with trees. This modular system opened the way to countless possibilities for extension: a new façade of mirror-polished stainless-steel strips, enveloping the existing structure, plays on the effects of appearance and disappearance, as in the original design. Stretching over 600 meters, it can be seen as a work of Land Art. Inside, a structuring street, lit by the gardens, crosses the entire length of the building. The opacity of the façade keeps the industrial manufacturing secrets and research and development activities of the Aplix factory discreetly hidden, while remaining open to the light at the heart of the building and the plot.

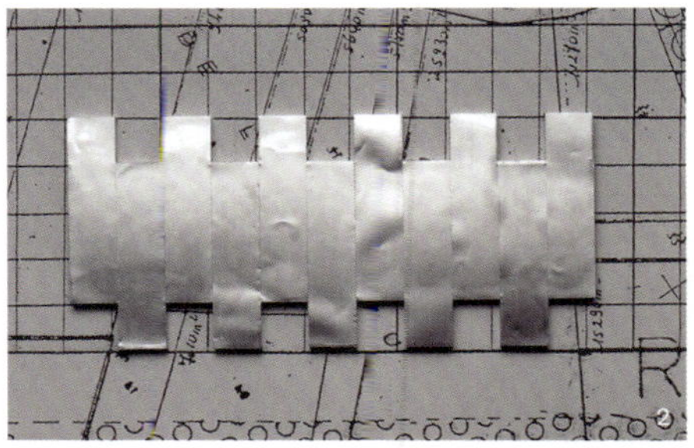

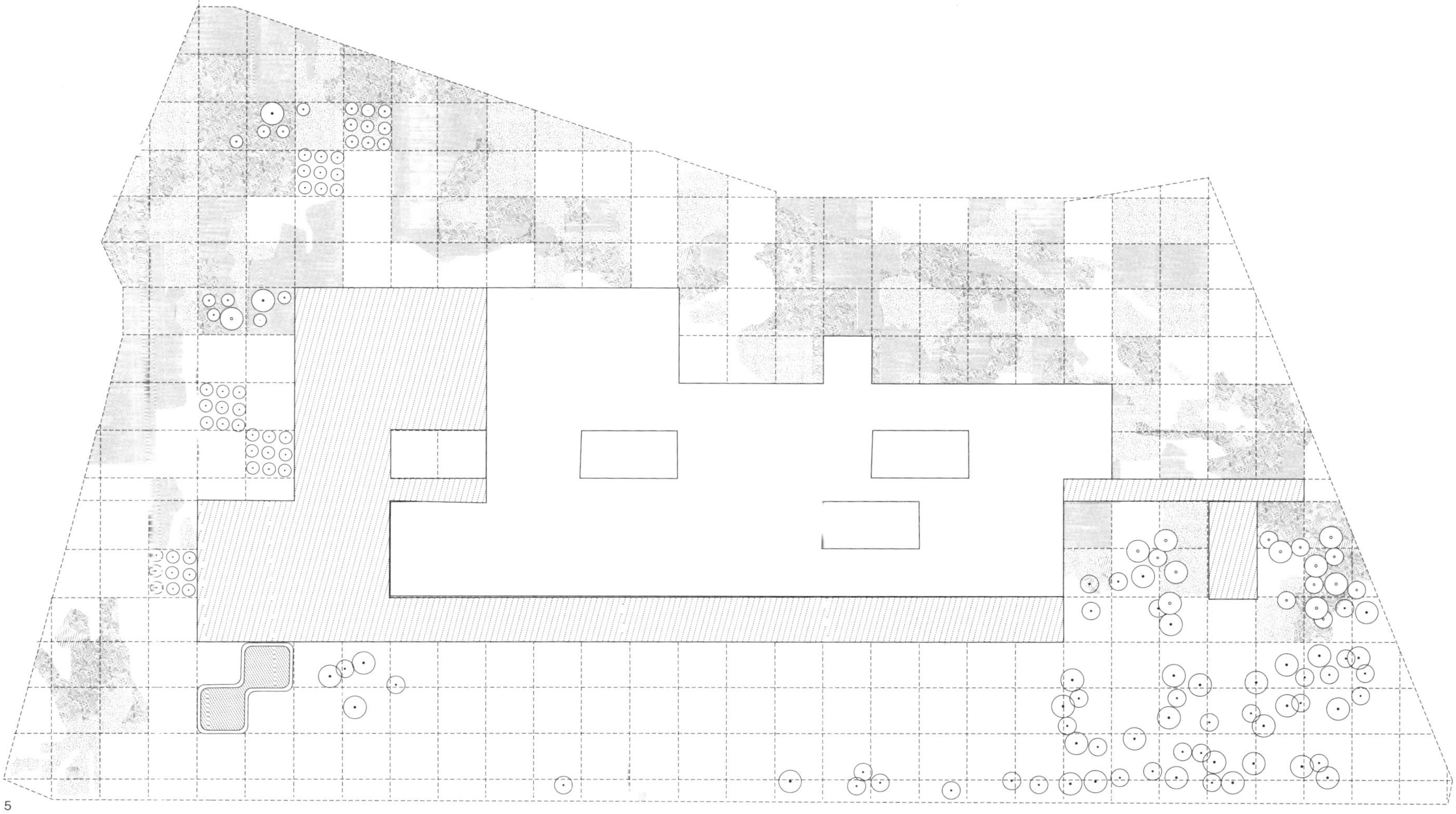

5

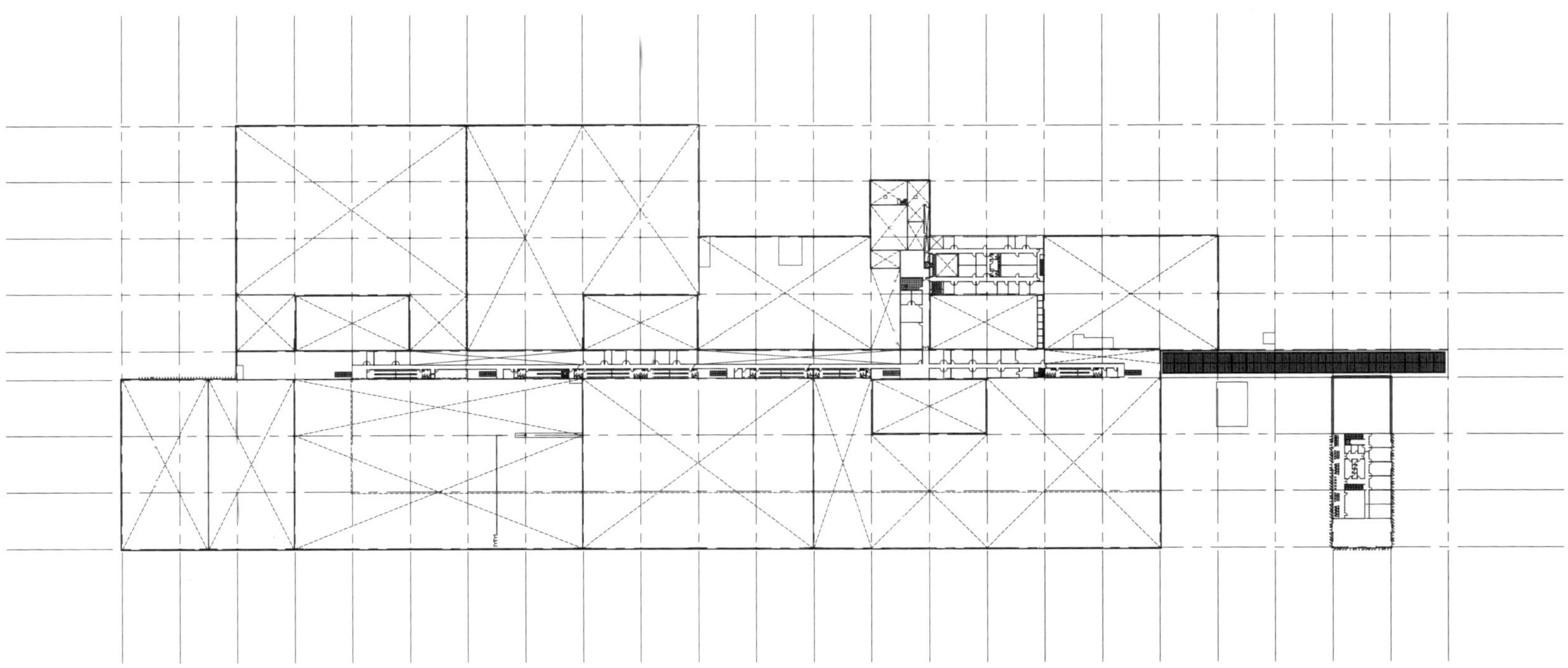

6

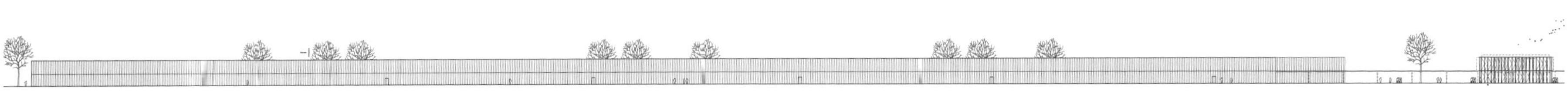

7

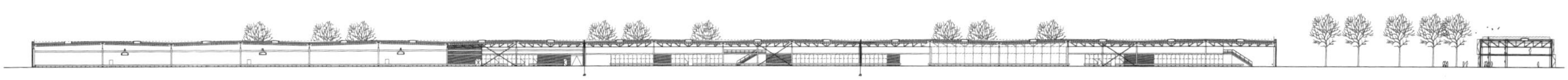

8

HÔTEL INDUSTRIEL BERLIER AND ITS REFURBISHMENT

PARIS, FRANCE

1985–90 / 2014–22

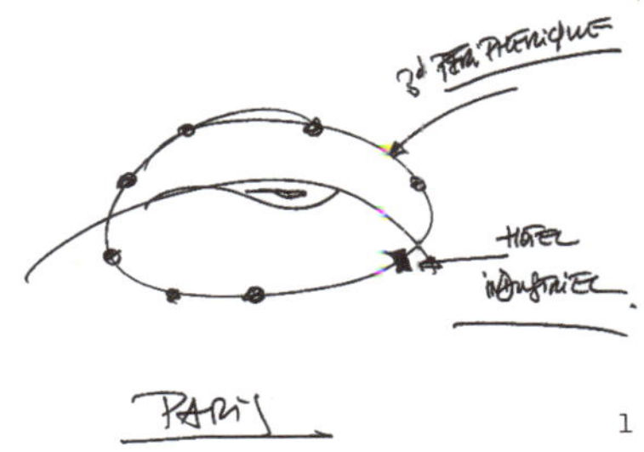

1

Opened in 1990, the Hôtel Industriel Berlier is a major milestone in the history of contemporary architecture. Winner of several awards and internationally acclaimed, it is the forerunner of the Bibliothèque Nationale de France (BnF). It is the first building to feature a curtain wall, with no aedicula or acroteria visible from the street. Each element has been designed and crafted to measure, giving rise to a glass prism of unsettling perfection, inviting the eye to lose itself in the controlled transparency of its lines, where architecture becomes almost immaterial.

2

For the update of the Hôtel Industriel Berlier, innovation is expressed in what cannot be seen: a highly discreet gesture preserves the purity of the original prism while reinventing it from within. The integrity of the envelope, its smooth, immaterial skin, its anchoring in the ground, and its relationship with the environment remain intact. The intervention takes place on the inside: a second skin of glass, modelled on the original façade, slips onto the existing volume. Invisible from the outside, it improves the building's thermal and energy performance. The addition of new vertical walkways improves the building's circulation and adapt it to a mixed program of workshops and offices. This architectural manifesto, a symbol of an era and the transformation of a district, remains visually unchanged.

3

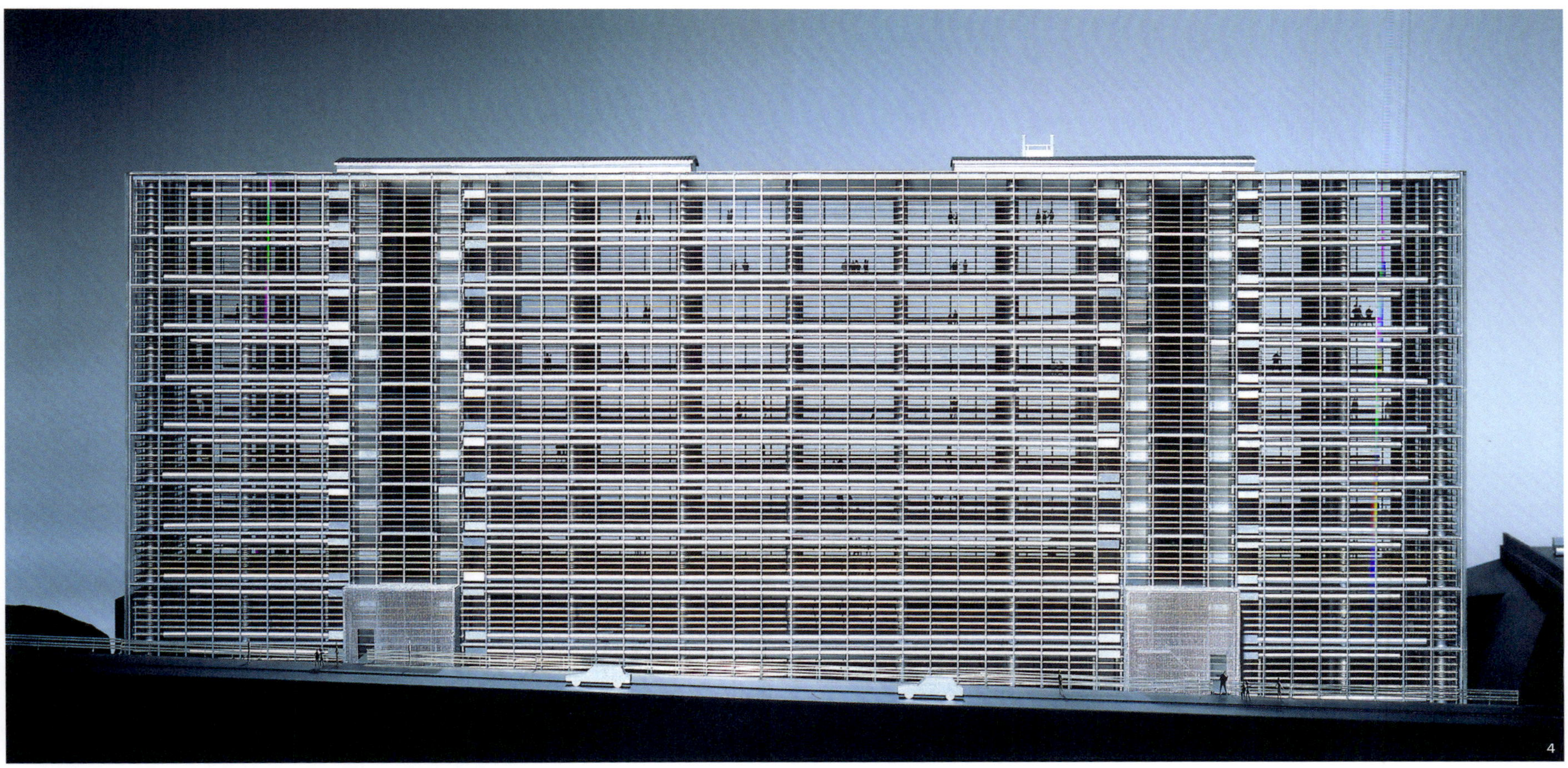

4

6

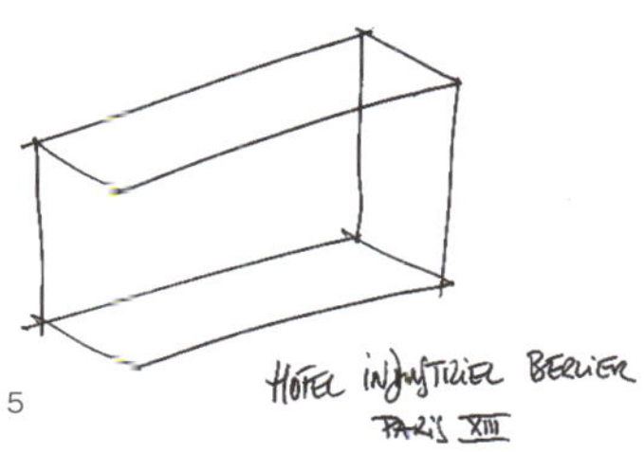

5

1 Sketch, 1986.
2 The Hôtel Berlier, alongside the boulevard périphérique, Paris, 13th arrondissement.
3 Interior view to the west, with the BnF building in the background.
4 The envelope of the Hôtel Industriel displays rich variety of reflections and transparencies. Scale model 1:200, 1989.
5 Sketch, 1986.
6 A block of glass, both solid and immaterial.
7, 8 Elevation and cross-section. Technical equipment is integrated directly into the façade in order to optimize interior floor space.

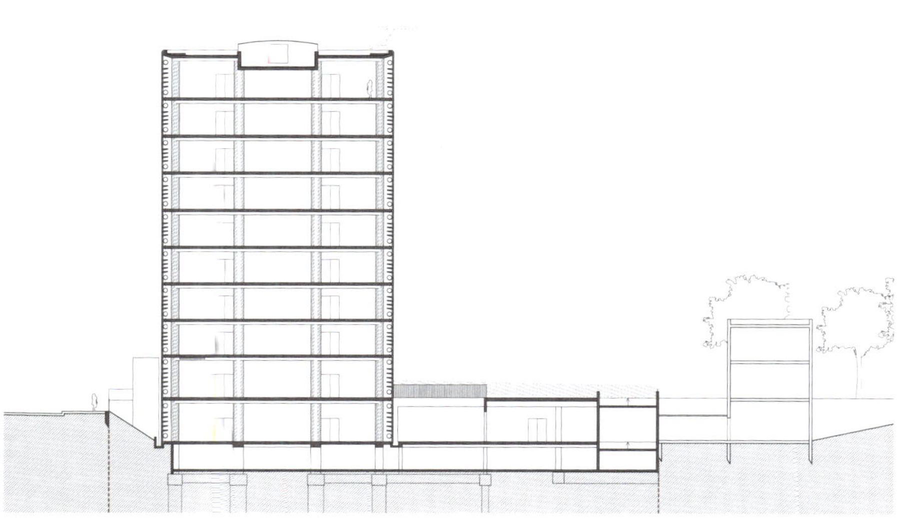

7

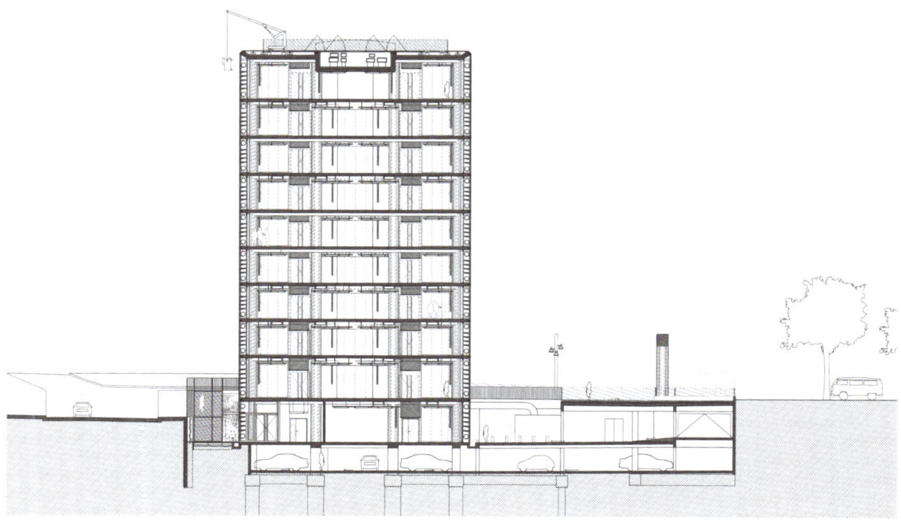

8

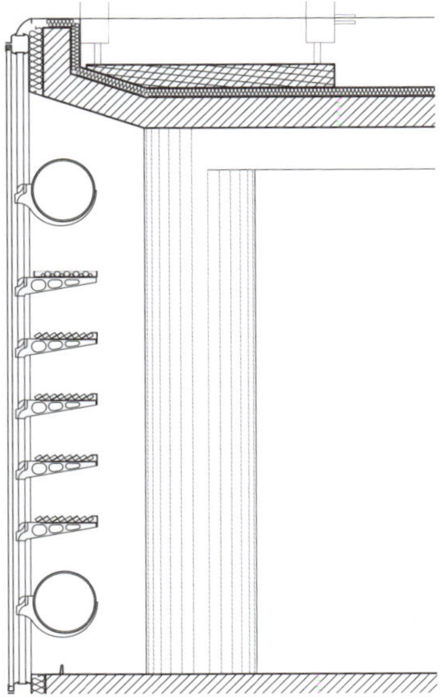

1

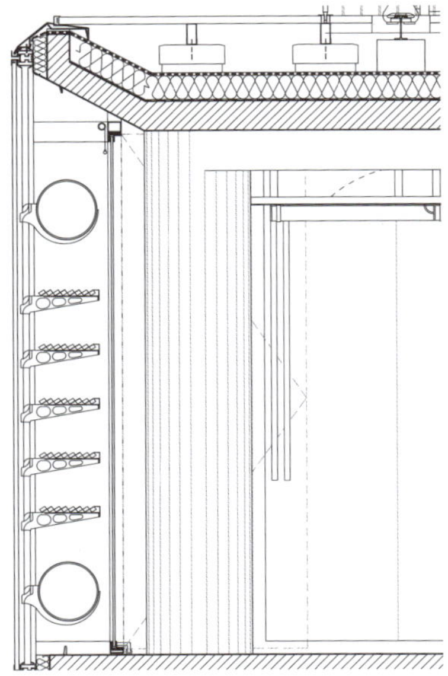

3

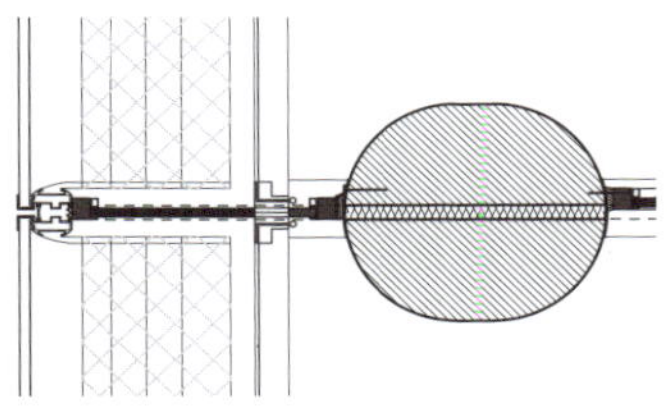

4

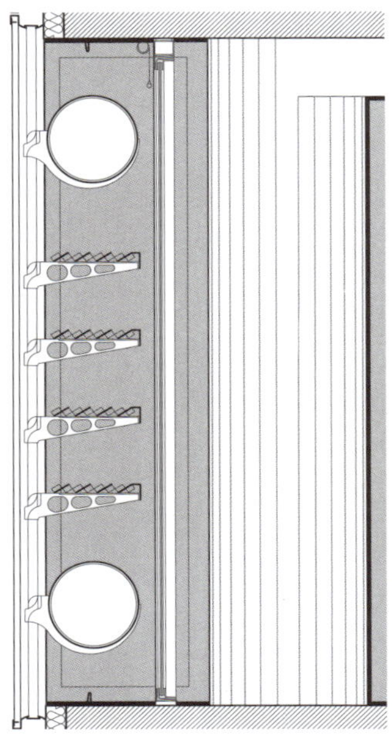

4

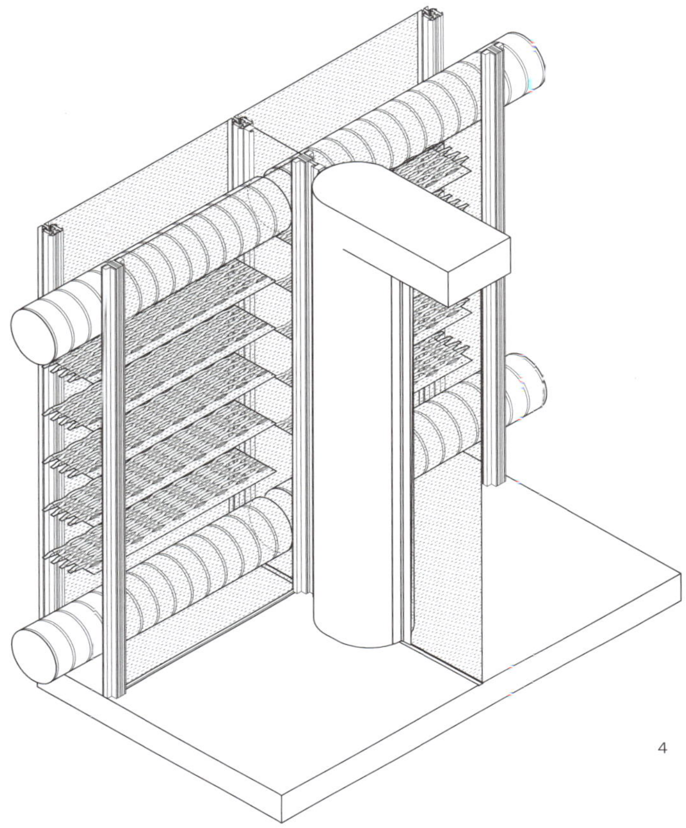

4

2

6

5

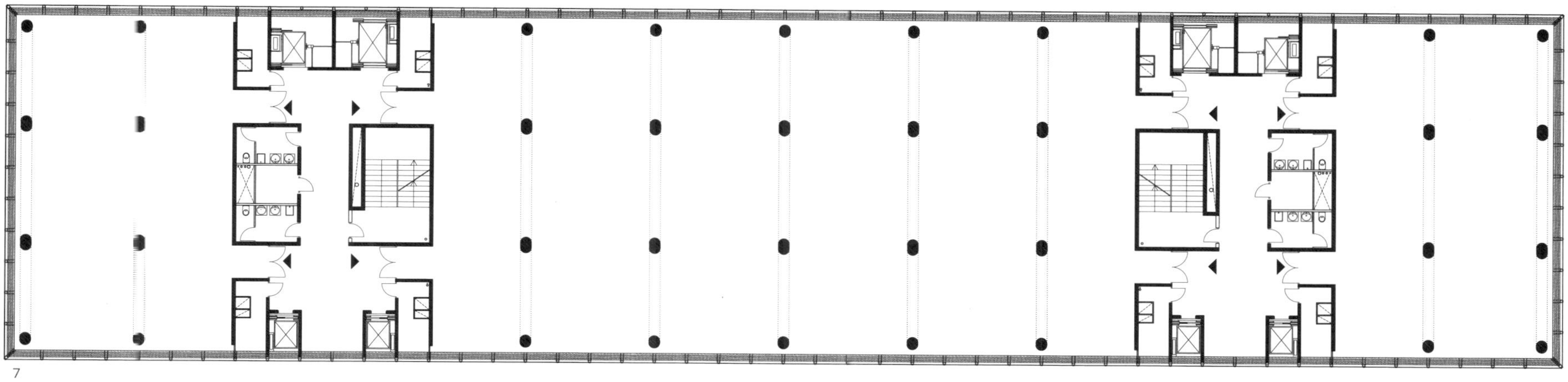

7

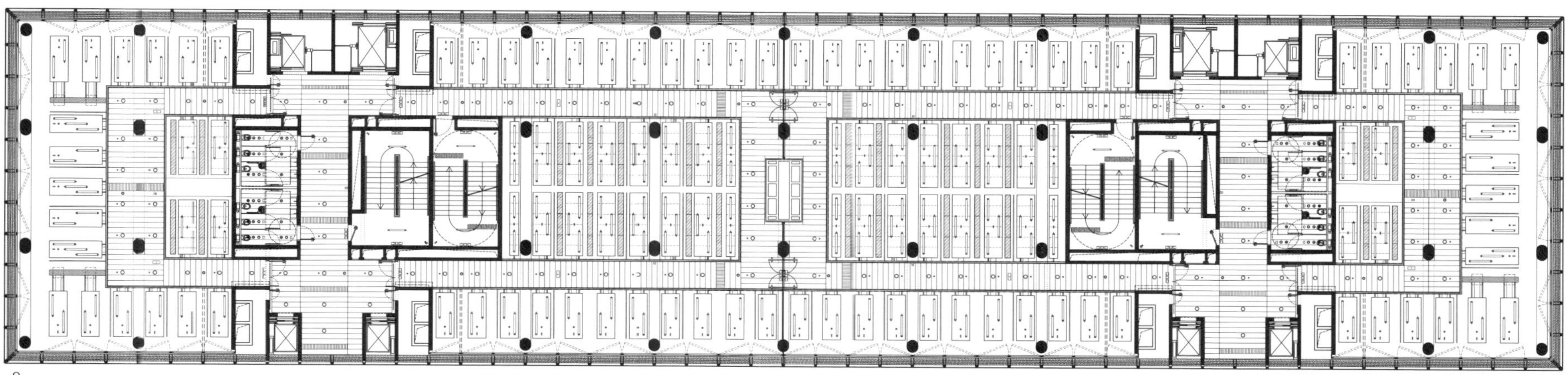

8

1, 2 Initial state, 1990. Expanded metal "shelves" act as sunshades on the façade.
3-5 New state, 2021. A second inner skin is added.
6 View of a typical floor, 2021. Ceiling after rehabilitation, integrating all technical systems.
7 Typical floor open plan, 1990.
8 Typical multi-purpose floor plan, 2021
9 Gable façade, visually unchanged since rehabilitation.
10 Technical area floor plan.

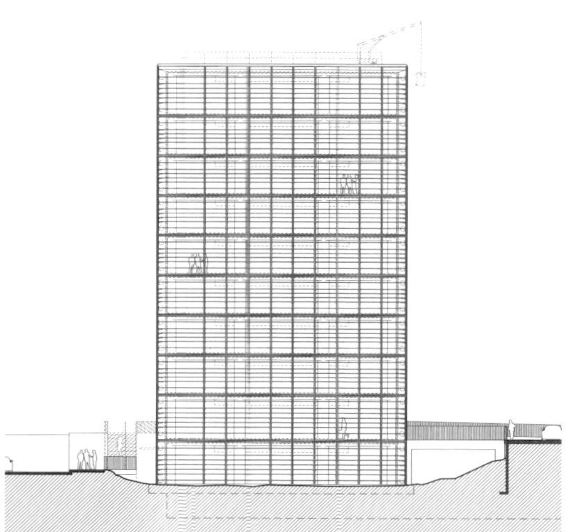

9

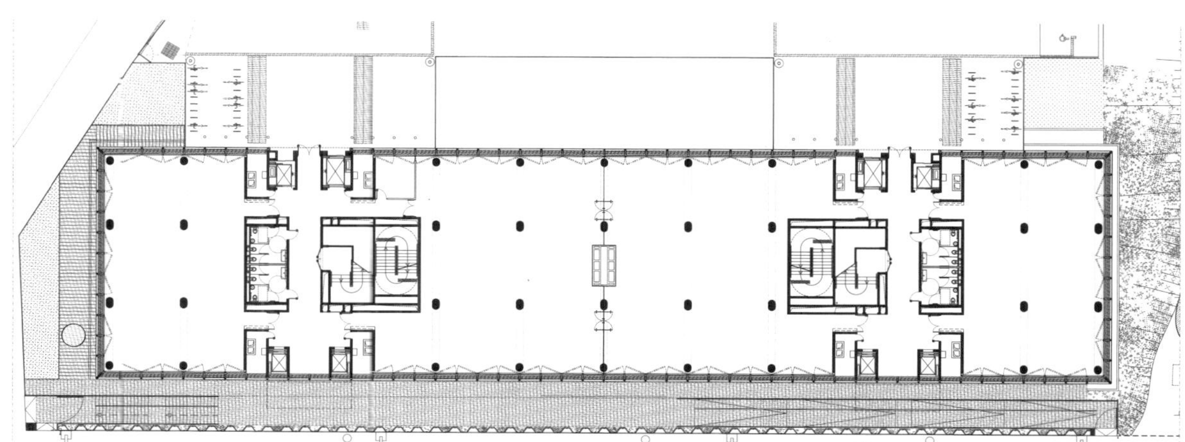

10

1

THE VERTICAL CITY – MONTPARNASSE TOWER

PARIS, FRANCE
2016

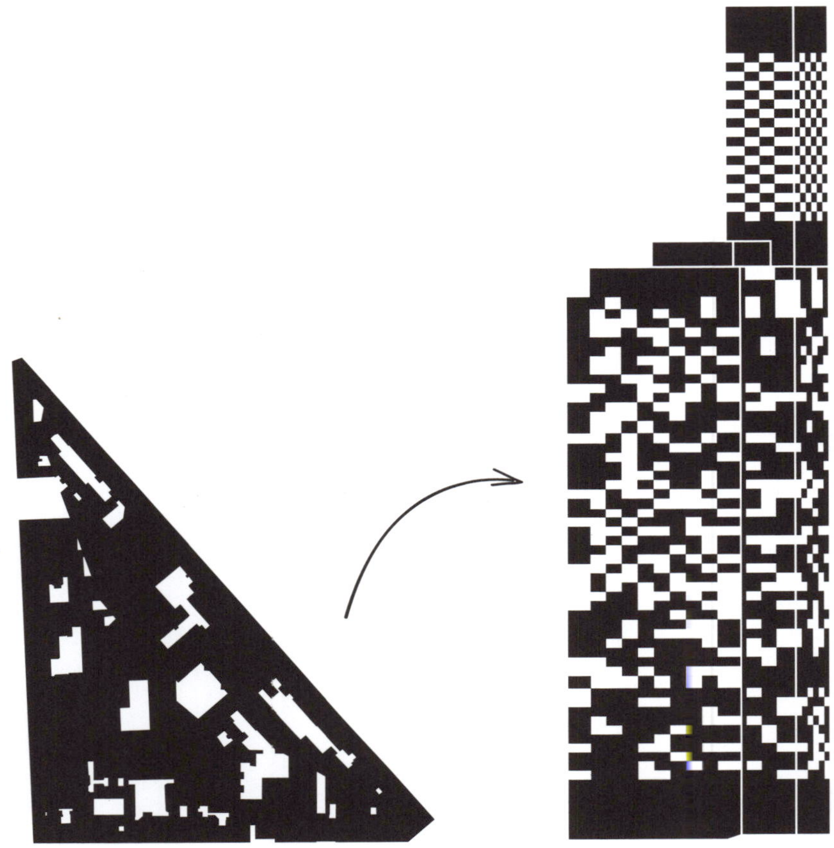

2

The Montparnasse Tower's transformation represents unique opportunity to shape an architectural manifesto: a vertical, positive-energy city that lives day and night, in the heart of Paris. By increasing the surface area and height of the building, while respecting the existing footprint, the project breaks with the repetitive nature of the floors and introduces a diversity of programs. The addition of a slender, 300-meter-high tower, merged with the existing building on one of its sides, increases the total surface area from 100,000 to 135,000 square meters. Inside, structural recesses create double heights, balconies, and loggias, opening up onto the city. The tower, transformed in this way, offers a new symbolic dimension to the city, affirming its status on an international scale.

1 Concept model, 1:200 scale, 1998.
2 Comparison between a Parisian block and the Montparnasse Tower.
3 View from the Pont Alexandre III.
4 The tower in its neighborhood.
5 View from the Jardin du Luxembourg.

3

4

5

CIE
ClubMed
BUS
IVECO
241 FEZ 92

LE ROUGE ET NOIR
CIE
Club Med

“Architecture that thinks of itself solely as a solution is already a problem. True creation invents its own questions.”

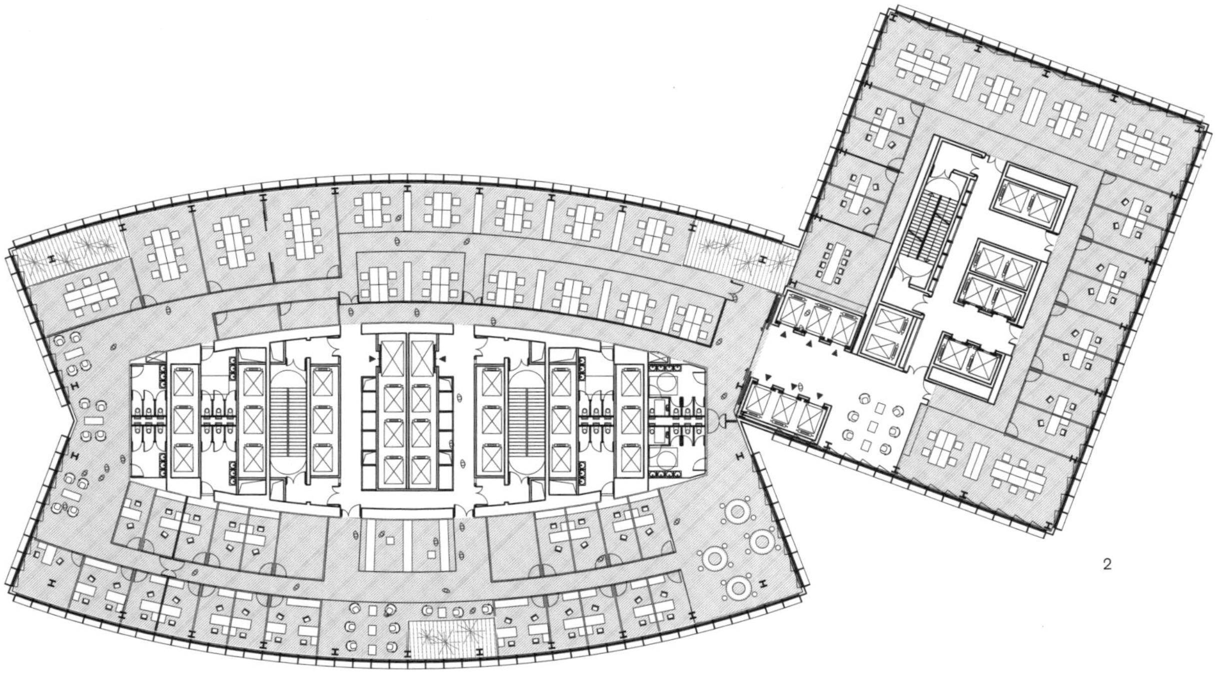

2

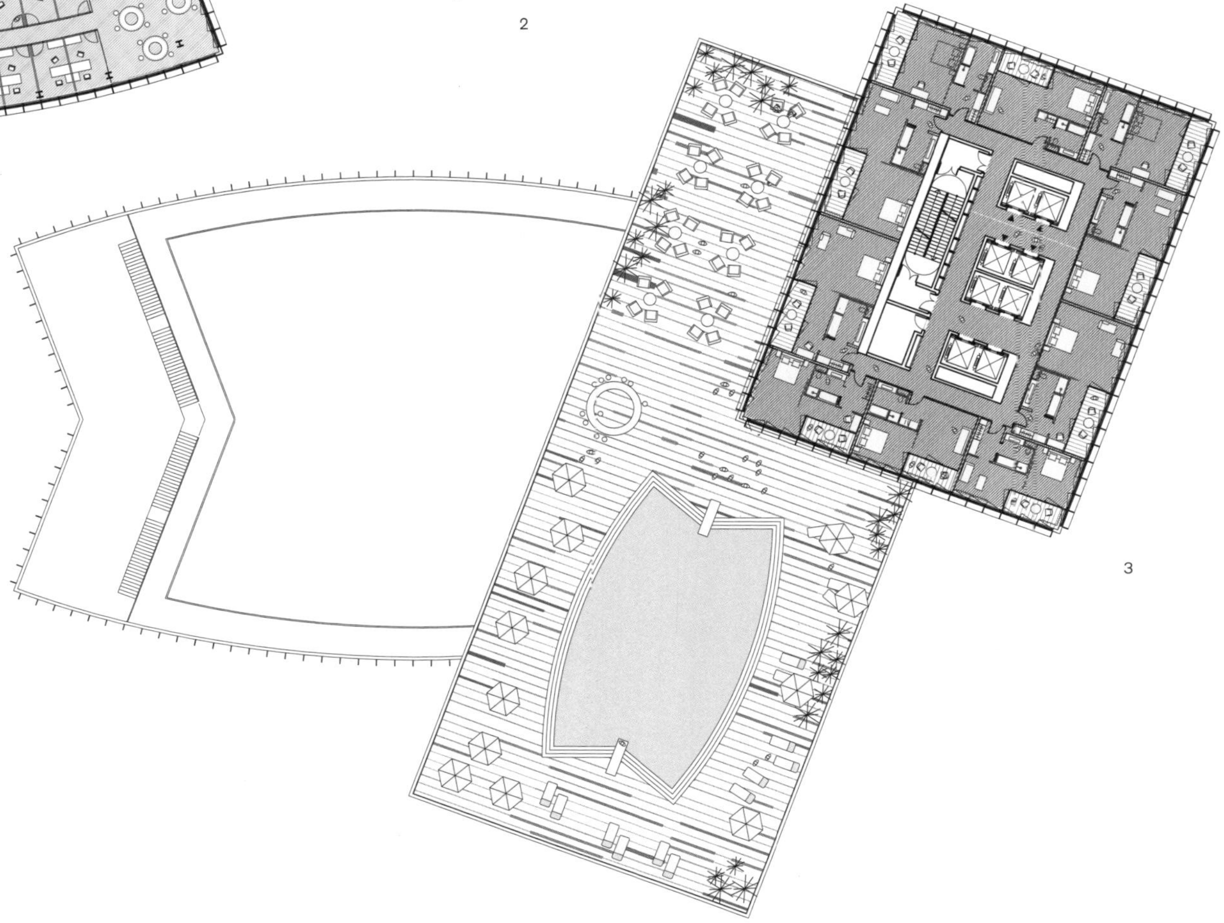

3

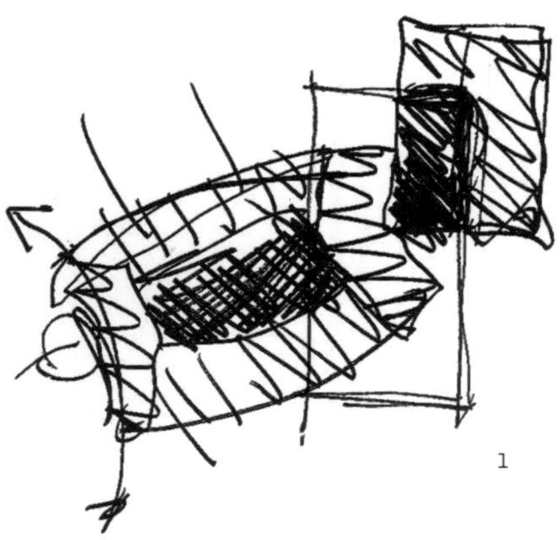

1

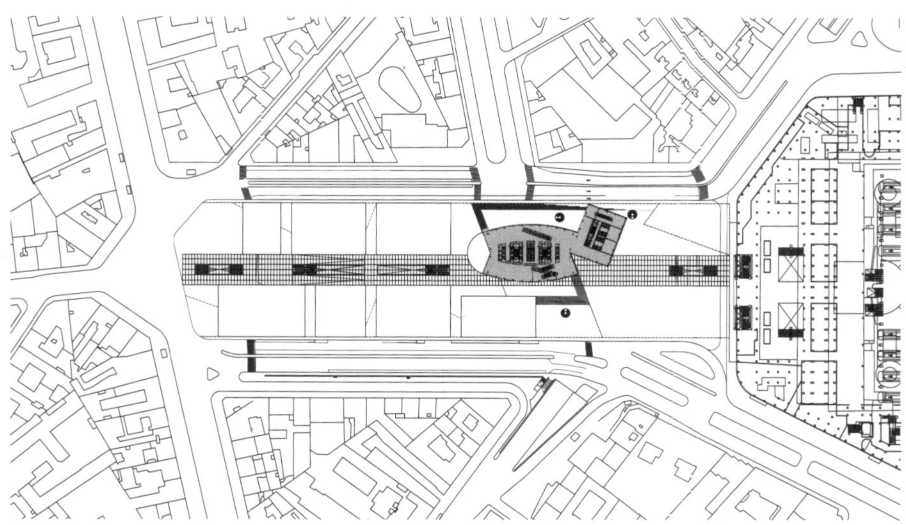

4

1 Sketch, 2016.
2 Principle of an extension while maintain the original footprint.
3 Principle of wooden construction up from the belvedere platform level.
4 Urban strategy, from Rue de Rennes to Gare Montparnasse.
5-8 Presentation model, scale 1:200, 2017.

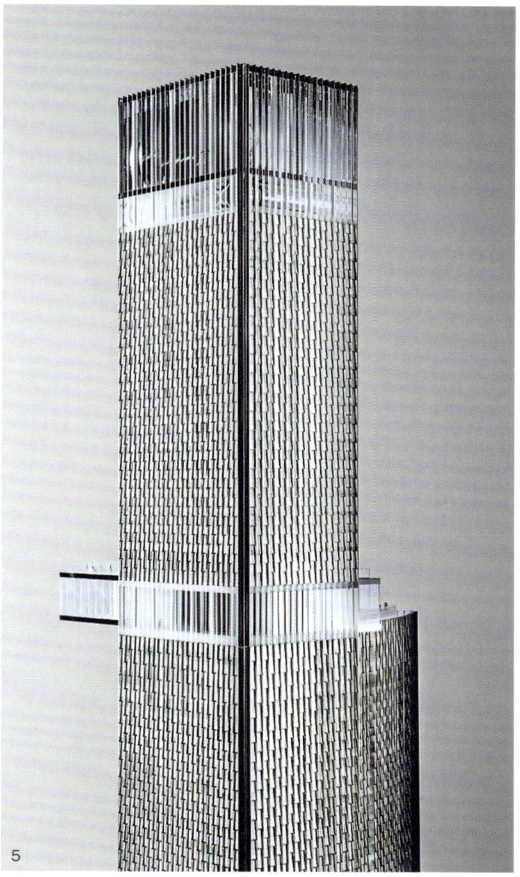

5

6

7

8

1-3 The tower during construction, 1972. The construction of the new station was part of a vast city planning operation aiming to relocate and expand railway facilities, while transforming an insalubrious neighborhood into a complex of offices and shops. Urbain Cassan, Eugène Beaudouin, Louis de Marien, and Jean Saubot built a Parisian skyscraper, inaugurated in 1973.

4 Building more to reduce density in the existing tower and integrate new uses.

5 Sketch, 2016.

6 Connection between Rue de Rennes and Gare Montparnasse.

7 A tower active twenty-four hours a day.

8 Amplifying the building's performance by means of a mixed program.

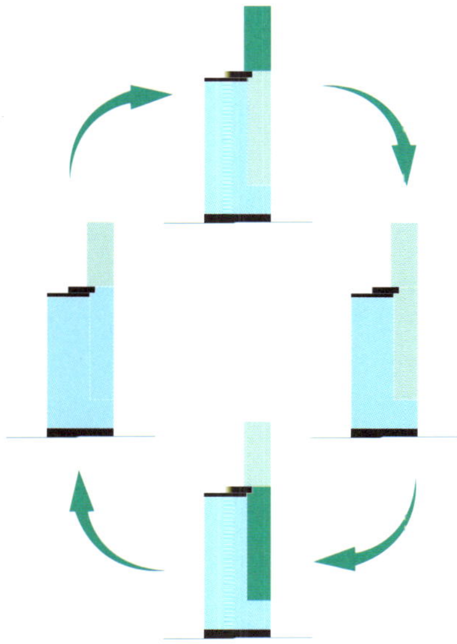

4

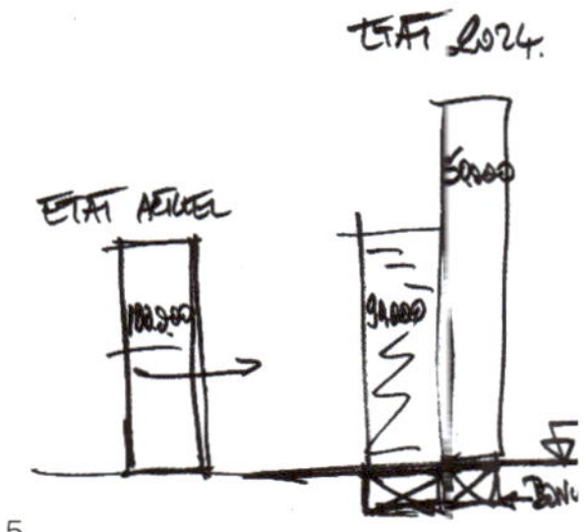

5

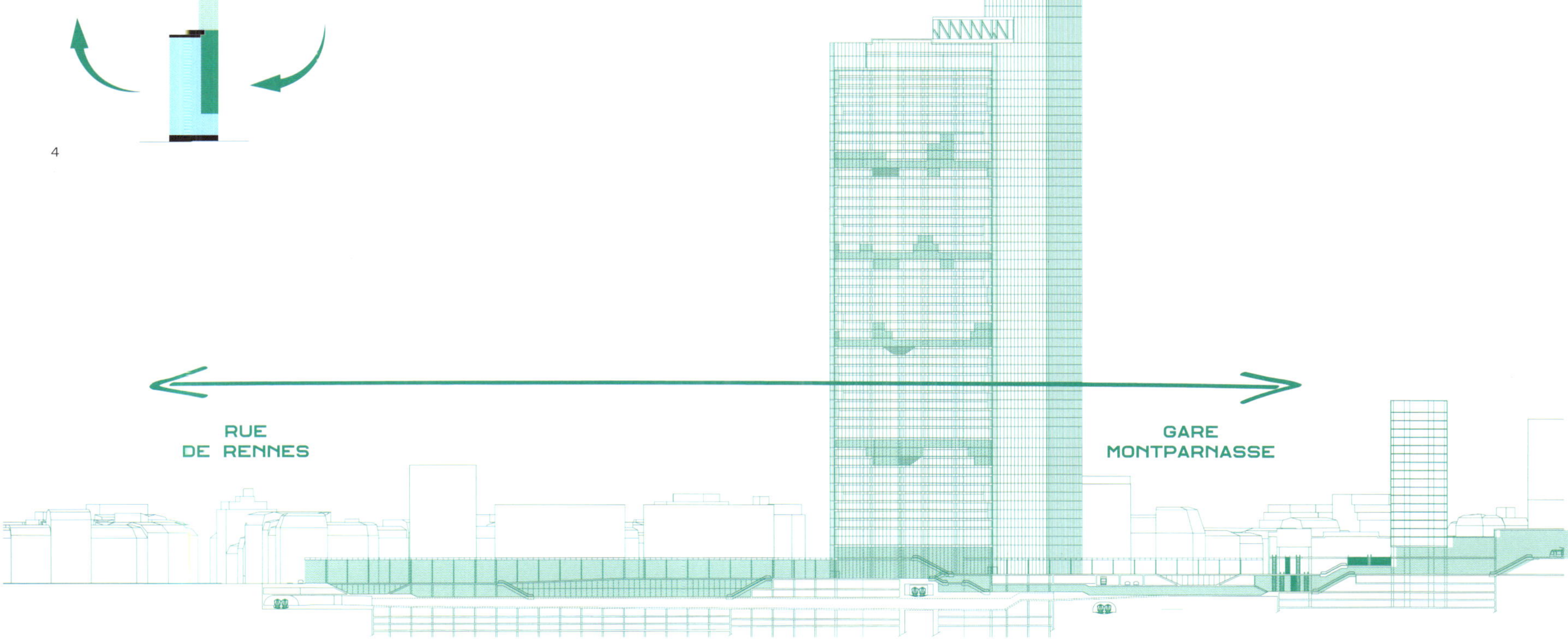
RUE
DE RENNES
GARE
MONTPARNASSE

6

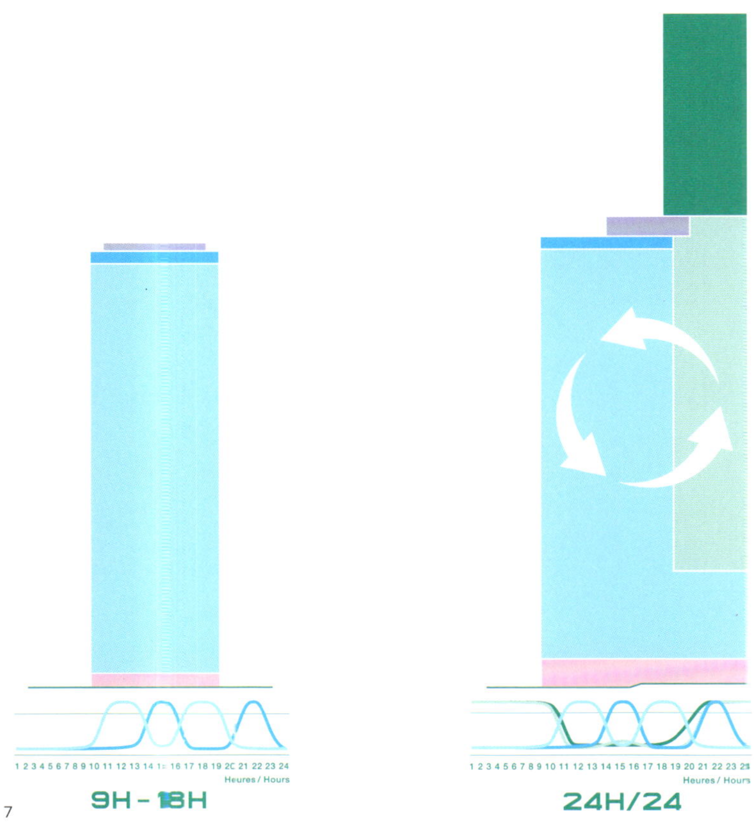
Heures / Hours
9H - 18H
Heures / Hours
24H/24

7

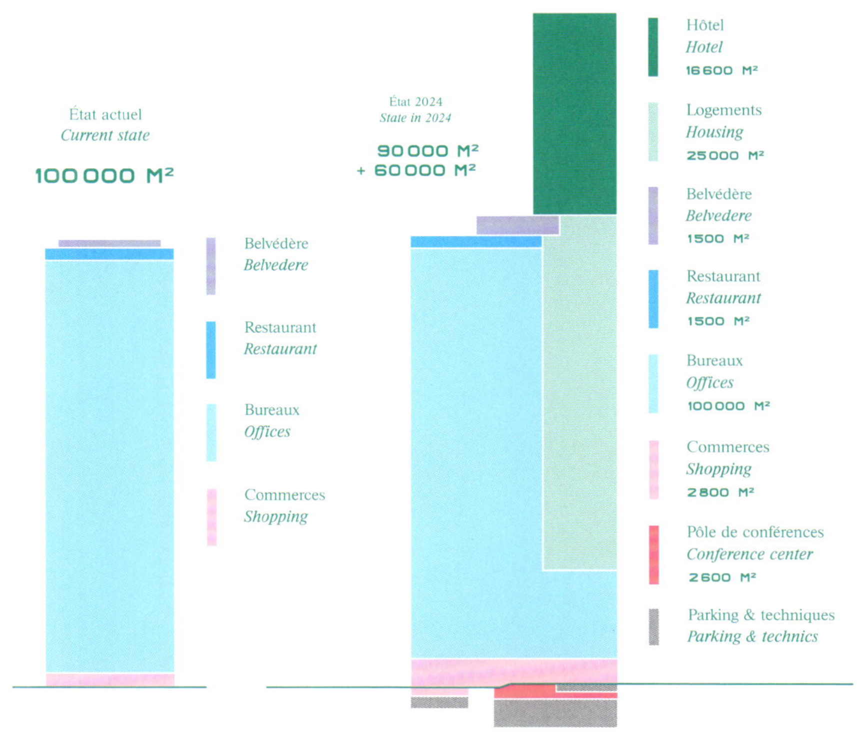
État actuel
Current state
100 000 M²
Belvédère
Belvedere
Restaurant
Restaurant
Bureaux
Offices
Commerces
Shopping
État 2024
State in 2024
90 000 M²
+ 60 000 M²
Hôtel
Hotel
16 600 M²
Logements
Housing
25 000 M²
Belvédère
Belvedere
1500 M²
Restaurant
Restaurant
1500 M²
Bureaux
Offices
100 000 M²
Commerces
Shopping
2800 M²
Pôle de conférences
Conference center
2600 M²
Parking & techniques
Parking & technics

8

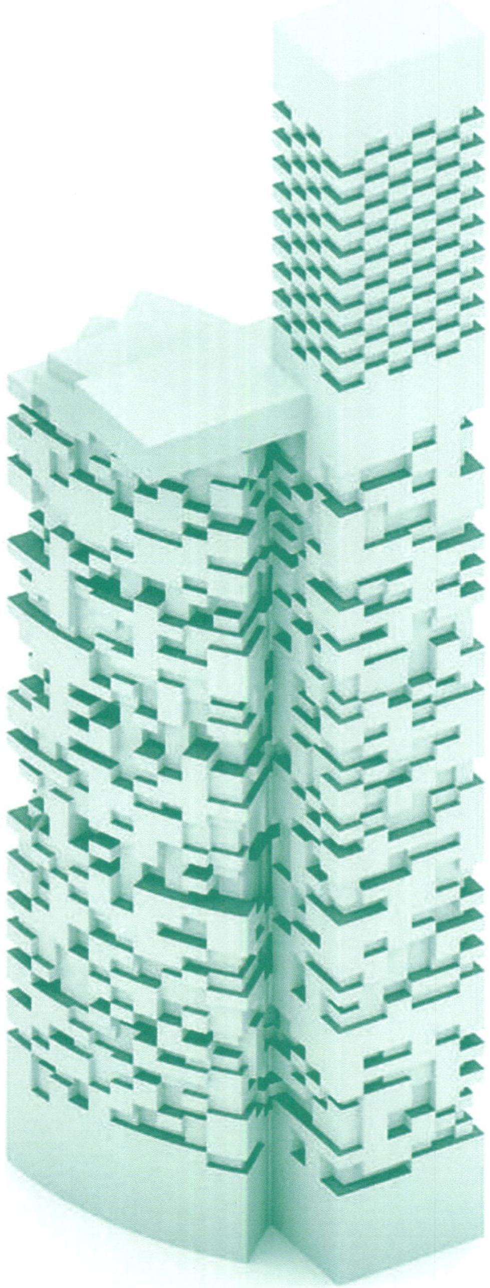

1

Existing structure
Steel/concrete floors
Concrete core
Wood floors
Wood columns
Wood partition walls
Concrete core
Wood floors
Steel columns
Concrete core

2

3

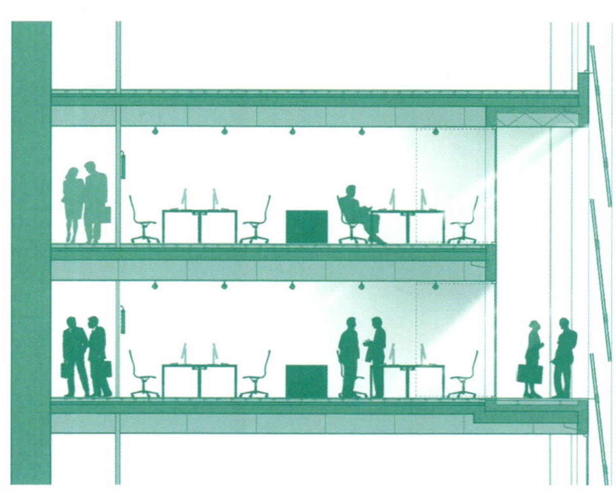

4

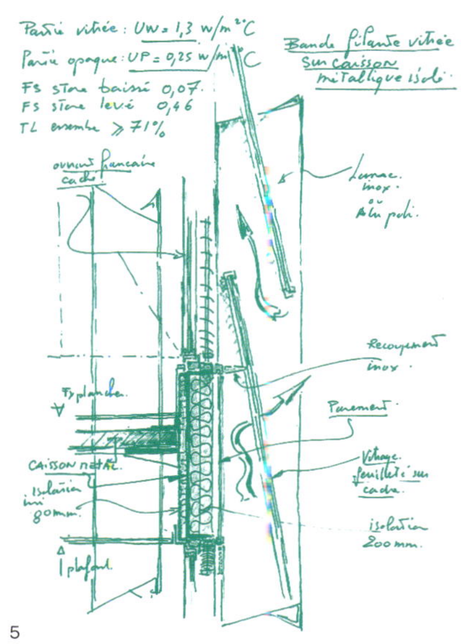
Partie vitrée : UW = 1,3 w/m²°C
Partie opaque : UP = 0,25 w/m²°C
FS store baissé 0,07.
FS store levé 0,46
TL ensemble ≥ 71%
Bande filante vitrée sur caisson métallique isolé.

5

6

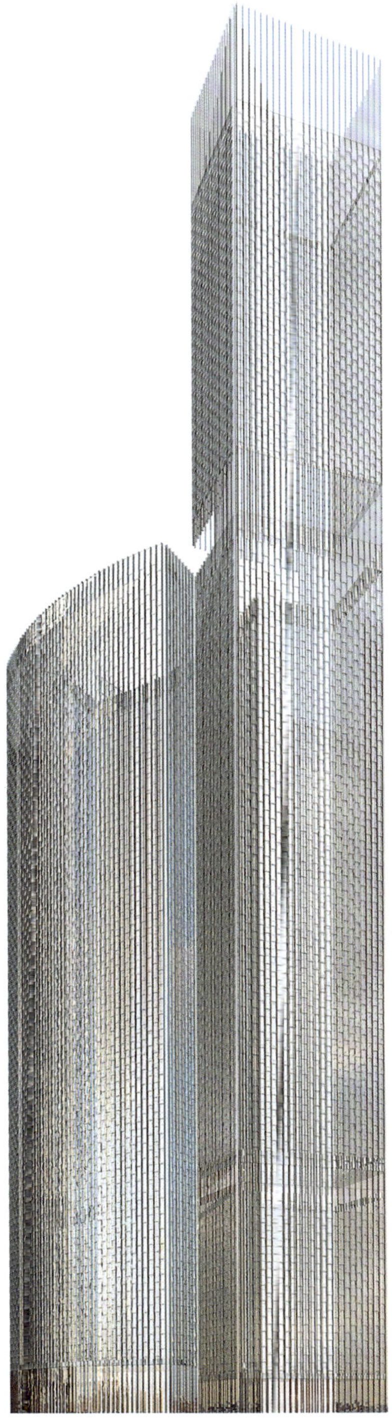

7

8

1,2 The tower is fitted with loggias in order to offer vegetated spaces.
3,4 Cross-section of loggias and winter gardens.
5 Technical study of the double-skin façade designed as a breathable skin. Sketch by Antoine Maufay, Arcora, 2015.
6 De-densify/develop the existing.
7 Cover with a protective sheath.
8 The hollowed-out volume + breathable skin = the living tower.

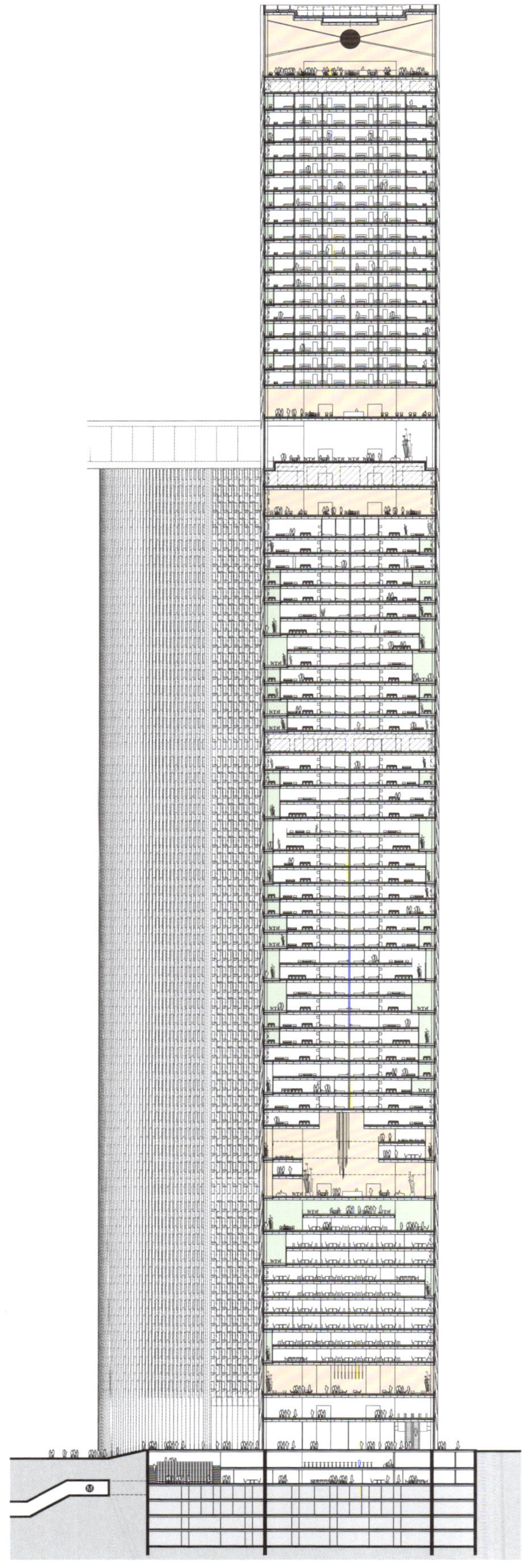

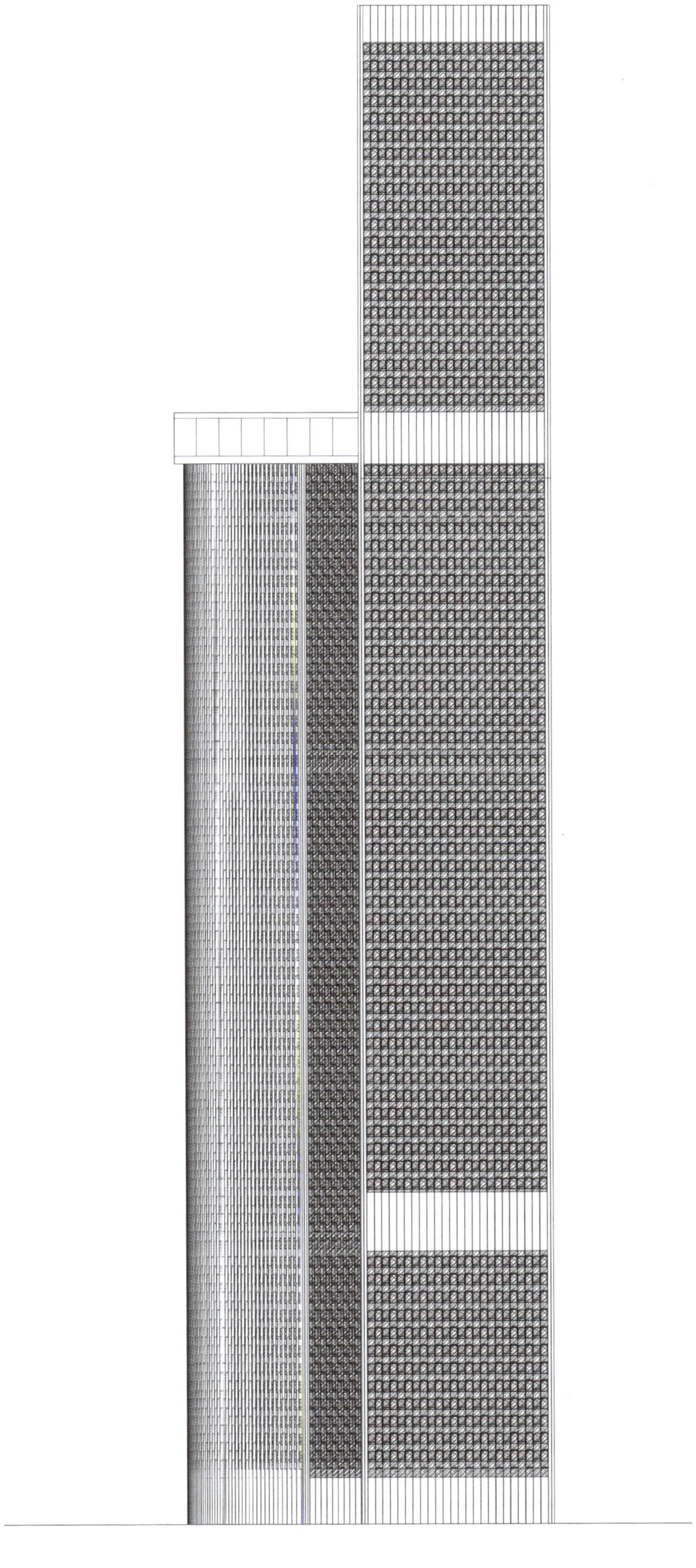

FROM ONE PROJECT TO ANOTHER

1989

Headquarters of JCDecaux, Plaisir, France

ZAC Croix-Blanche, Bussy-Saint-Georges, France

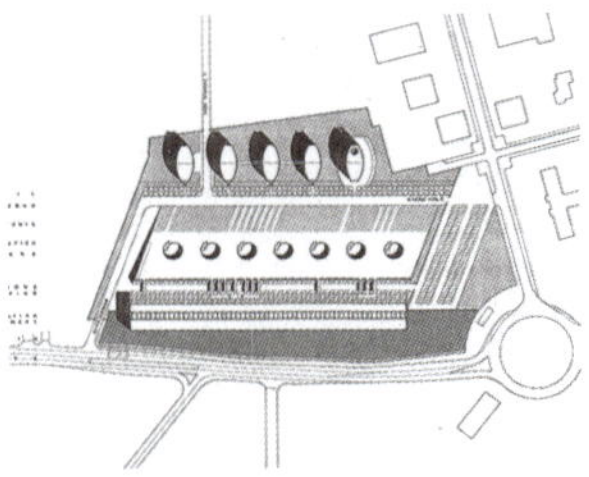
School of technology, Clermont-Ferrand, France

Castelli showroom, Paris, France

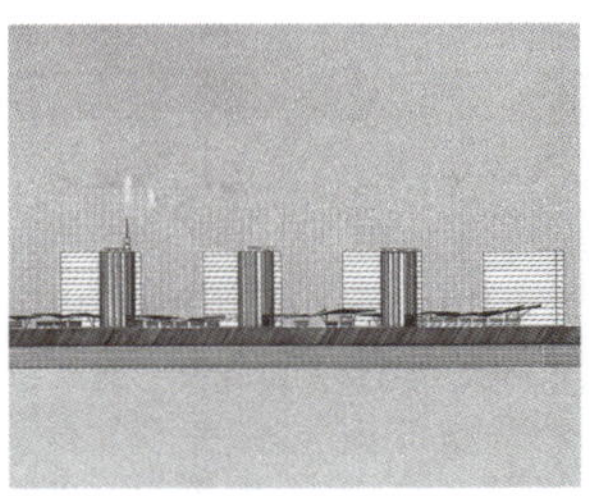
Port of Boulogne-sur-Mer, France

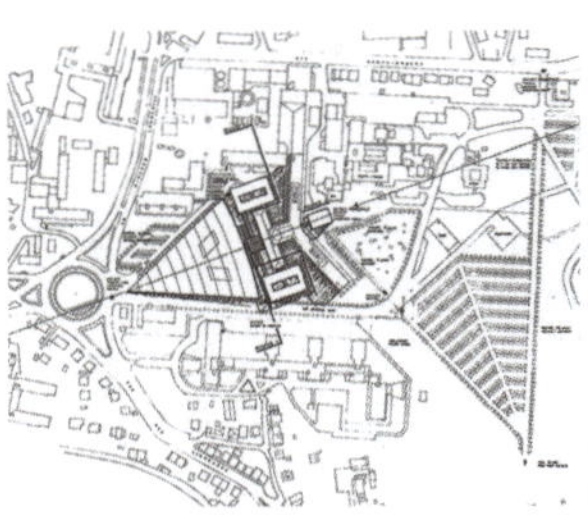
Saint-Jacques hospital, Clermont-Ferrand, France

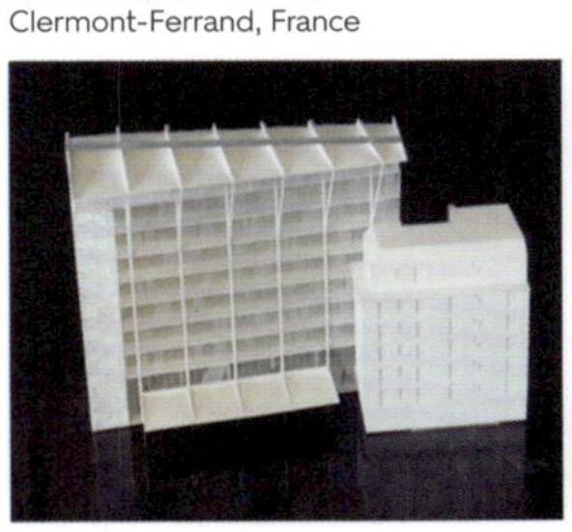
Office building, Porte d'Italie, Paris, France

1990

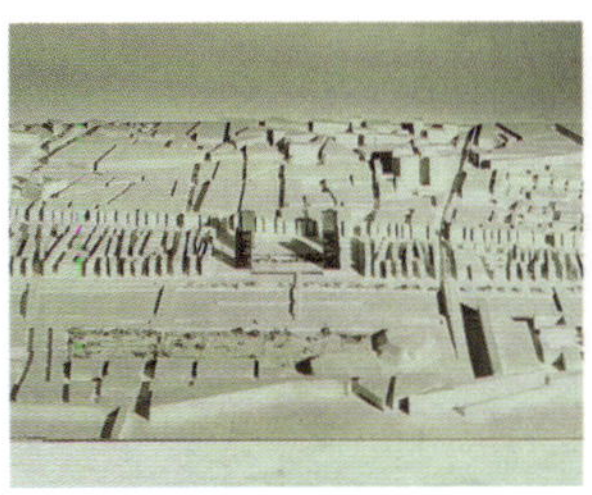
ZAC Tolbiac-Masséna, Paris, France

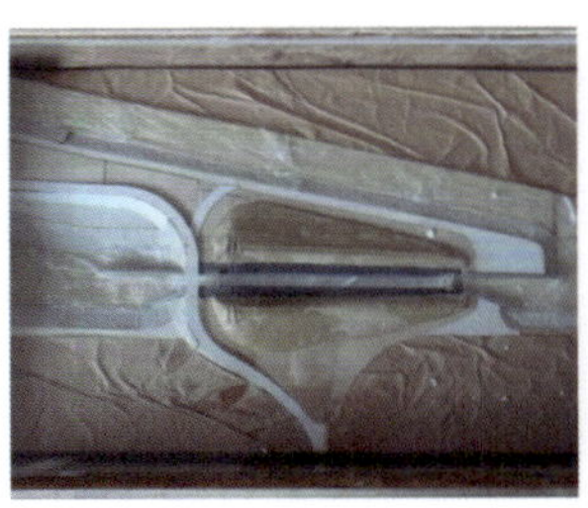
Bief de Niffer, Mulhouse, France

Hôtel Industriel Berlier, Paris, France

1991

Alliance Française, Singapore

Business center, Créteil, France

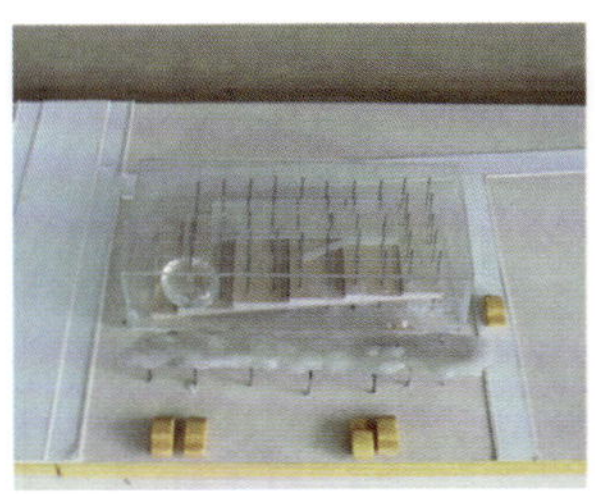
Showcase of the Meuse river in Ile-de-France, Marne-la-Vallée, France

Usinor-Sacilor Conference Center, Saint-Germain-en-Laye, France

Louis-Lumière housing development, Saint-Quentin-en-Yvelines, France

1992

World Center for Peace, Freedom, and Human Rights, Verdun, France

Place d'Youville, Montreal, Canada

École des Mines, Nantes, France

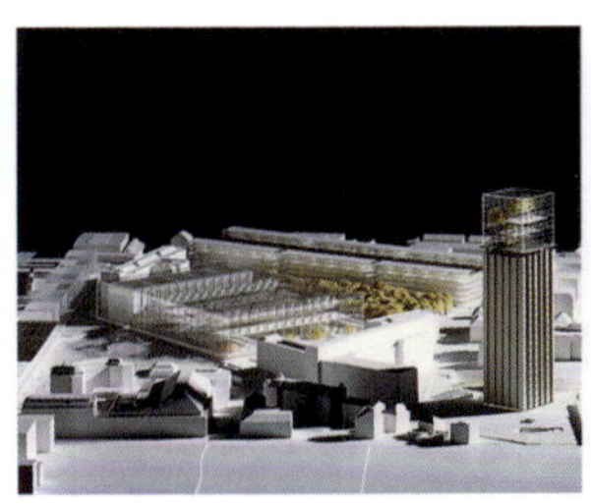
Redevelopment of Sulzer site, Winterthur, Switzerland

Lu Jia Zui financial district of Pudong, Shanghai, China

1993

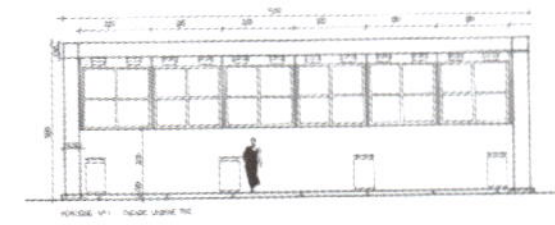
Technal Stand – Bâtimat 93, Paris, France

Wilhelmgalerie, Potsdam, Germany

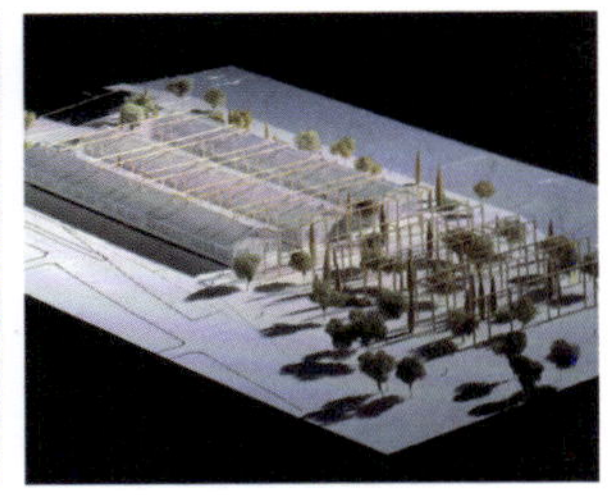
Erol Aksoy Foundation, Istanbul, Turkey

Vincennes Zoo, Paris, France

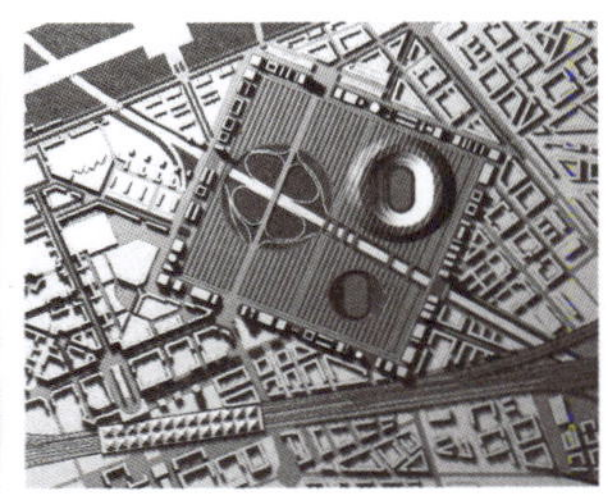
Le Grand Stade, Melun-Sénart, France

SAGEP sewage plant, Ivry-sur-Seine, France

Departmental Archives of Mayenne, Laval, France

1994

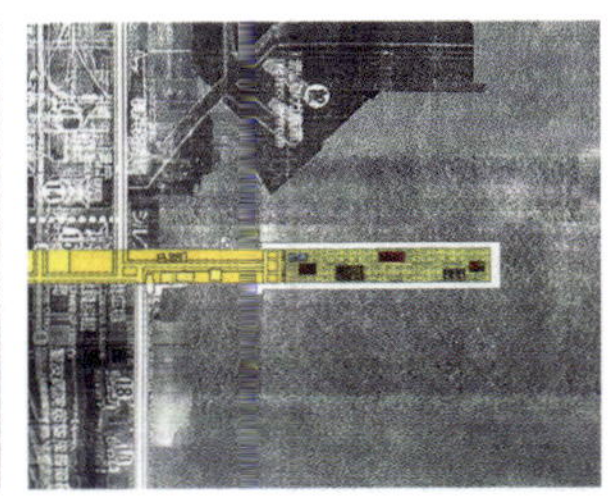
International port terminal, Yokohama, Japan

Hypo-Bank - Theatinerstrasse, Munich, Germany

Salzburg Sparkasse, Salzburg, Austria

1994 | **1995** | **1996**

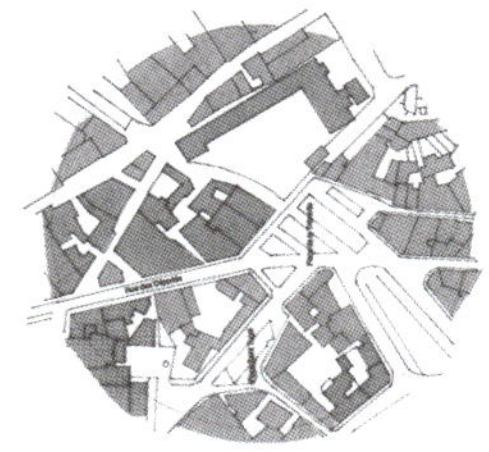
Courthouse, Laval, France

Auditorium, Château-Gontier, France

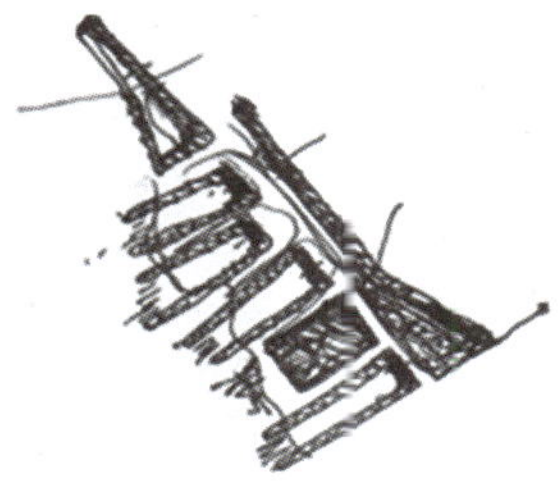
Siemensstadt and Wasserstadt Oberhavel, Berlin, Germany

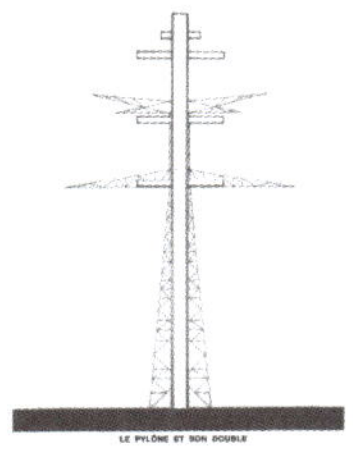
EDF pylon, France

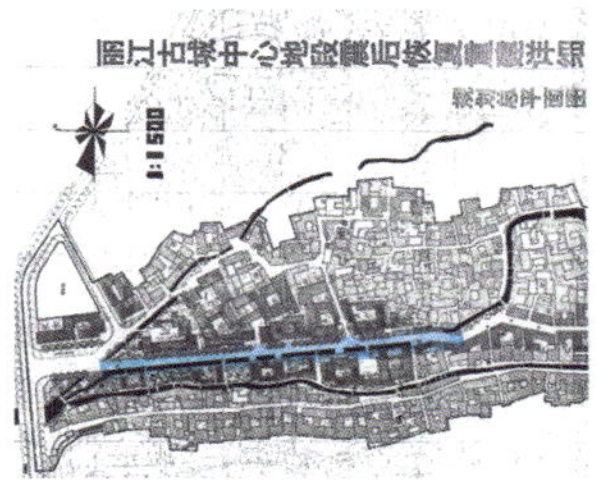
Development studies for the towns of Suzhou and Lijiang, China

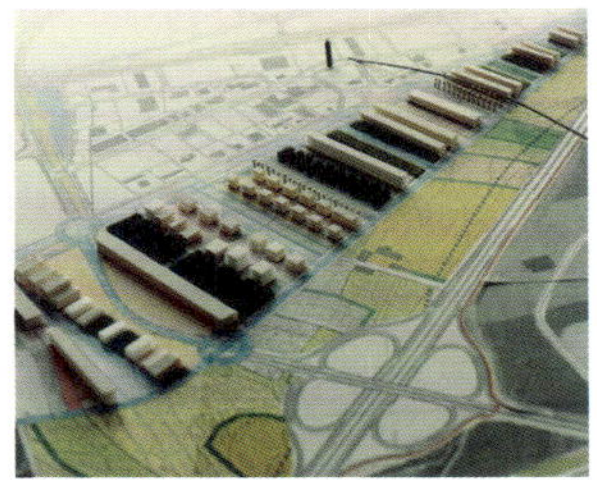
Science park, Sénart, France

Glass House, "Architectural Visions for Europe," Düsseldorf, Germany

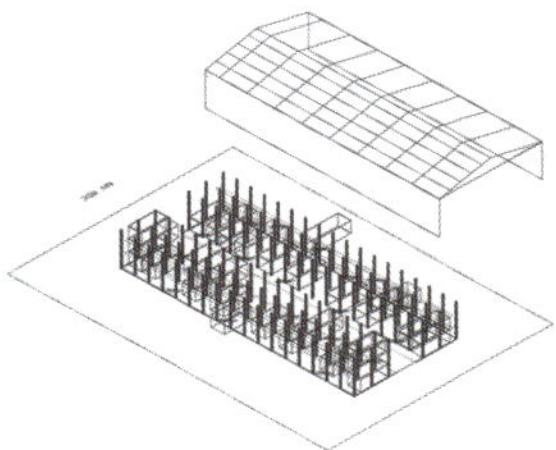
Lognes ZAC, Lognes, France

Center for Books, Bussy-Saint-Georges, France

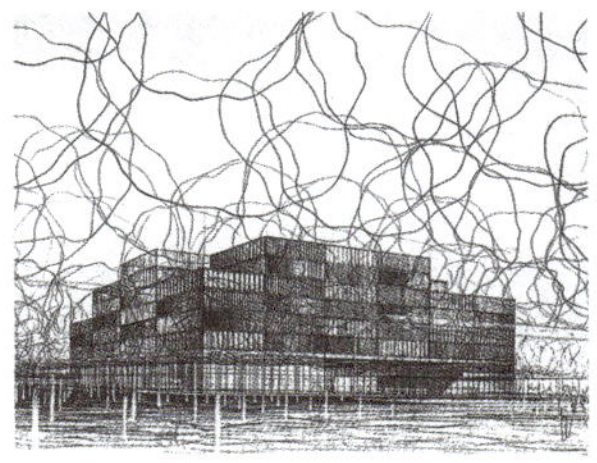
Centre des Archives, Reims, France

Kansai-kan Library, Kyoto, Japan

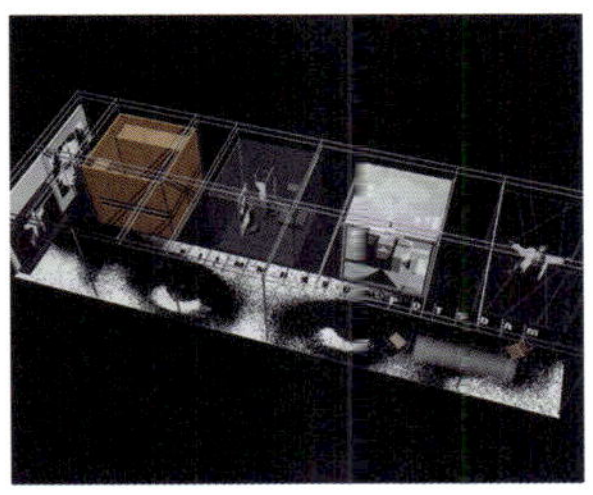
Cinema Museum stands Berlin, Germany

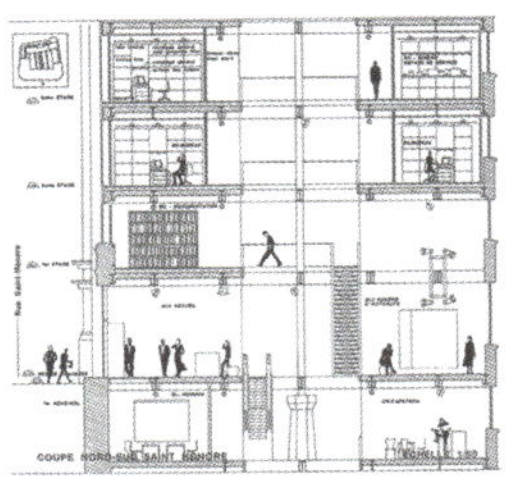
Ministry of Culture, Paris, France

Metro entrance on Leipziger Platz, Berlin, Germany

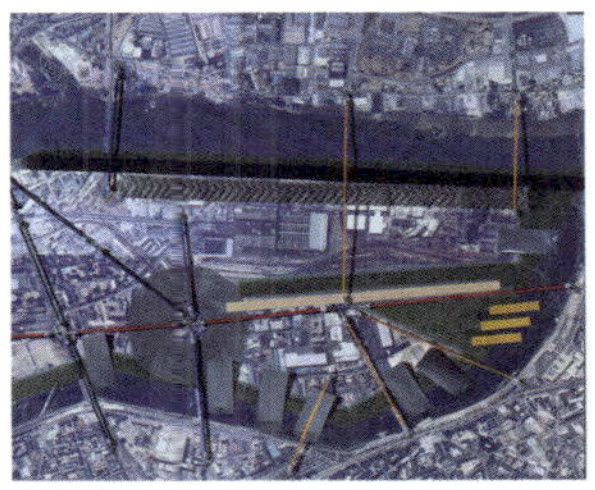
Development of Île Sainte-Anne, Nantes, France

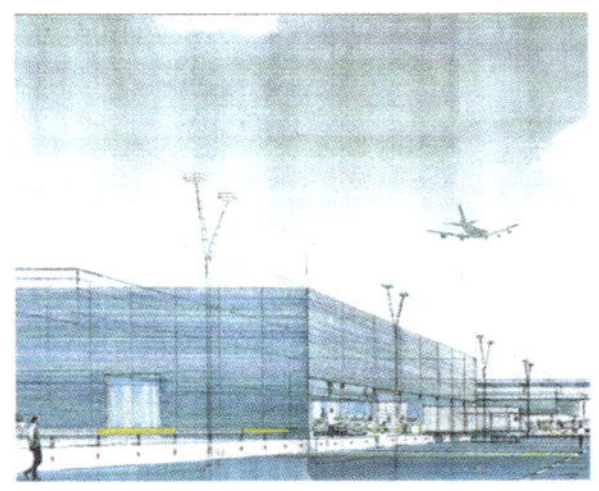
Fedex European Center, Roissy, France

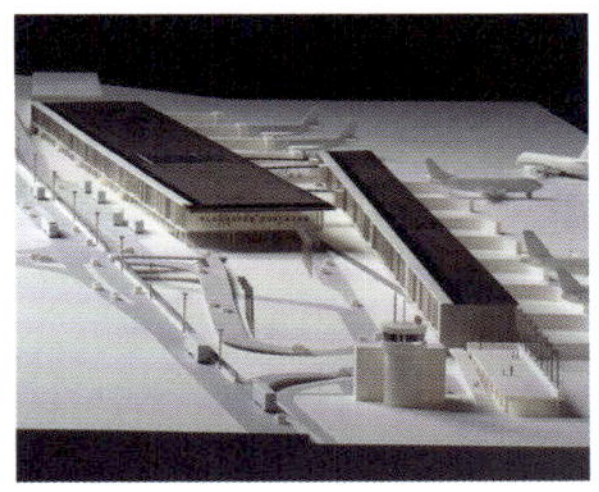
International airport, Dortmund, Germany

Les Balcons du Canal housing, Paris, France

Place des Nations, Geneva, Switzerland

A20 Brive/Montauban expressway, France

Bibliothèque Nationale de France, Paris, France

Place Dr-Franz-Rehrl, Salzburg, Austria

Ministry of Foreign Affairs, Berlin, Germany

Hôtel du Département de la Meuse, Bar-le-Duc, France

Redevelopment of town center, Tremblay-en-France, France

Municipal stadium, Marseille, France

Villa One, Saint-Cast-le-Guildo, France

Kolonihaven installation, Copenhagen, Denmark

Elec'96 central booth, Villepinte, France

1997

1998

1999

La Grande Serre, Paris, France

Messeplatz Tower, Basel, Switzerland

Bordeaux tramway site, Bordeaux, France

Mitra temple, Naples, Italy

Security Policy Center (GCSP), Geneva, Switzerland

Redevelopment of Unimétal site, Caen, France

Corsica cruise terminal, Marseille, France

Maison SCI Les Zèbres, Saint-Mandé, France

Bercy-Tolbiac footbridge, Paris, France

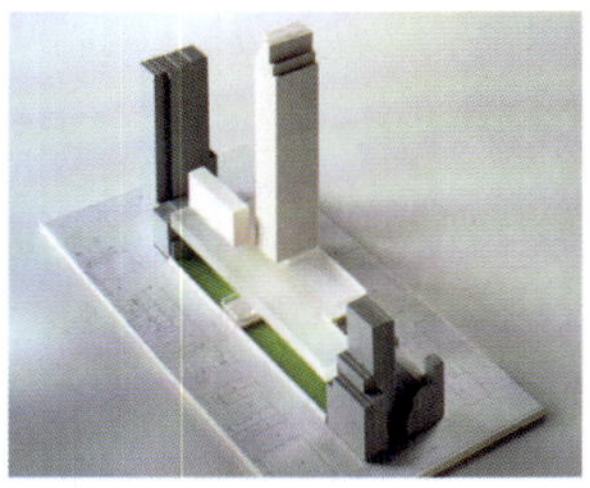
Museum of Modern Art (MoMA), New York, United States

French Embassy, Berlin, Germany

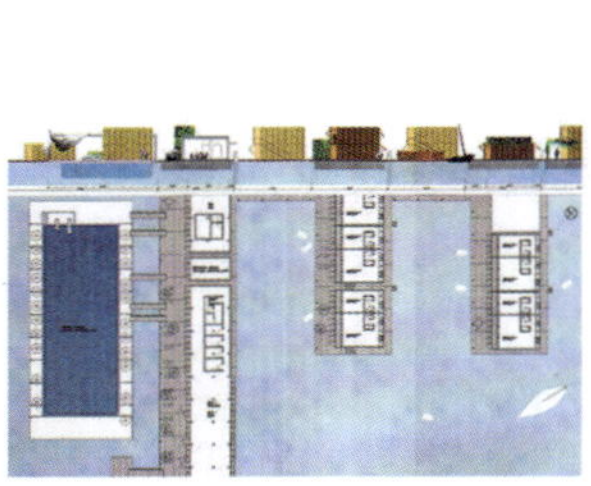
Hotel in Nahuel Huapi national park, Argentina

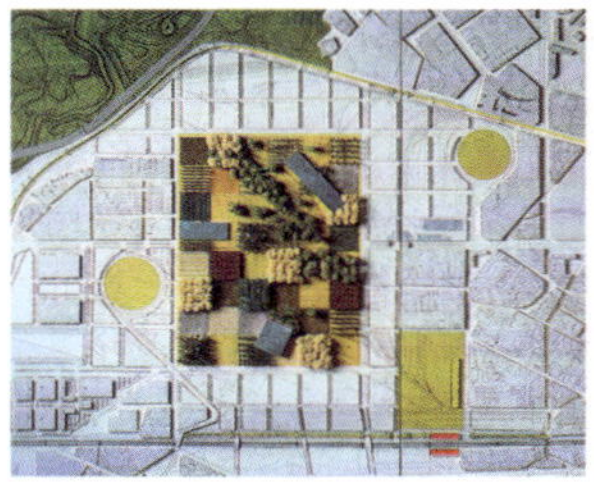
Falck industrial site, Milan, Italy

Montparnasse Tower, Paris, France

Aplix factory, Le Cellier-sur-Loire, France

Development of BLEG land, Berlin, Germany

Le Cargo cultural center, Grenoble, France

Villa La Bouvette, Saint-Cast-le-Guildo, France

Architectural Institute, Venice, Italy

Pfleiderer Bau99 pavilion, Munich, Germany

Courtine peninsula, Avignon, France

Musée Costantini, Buenos Aires, Argentina

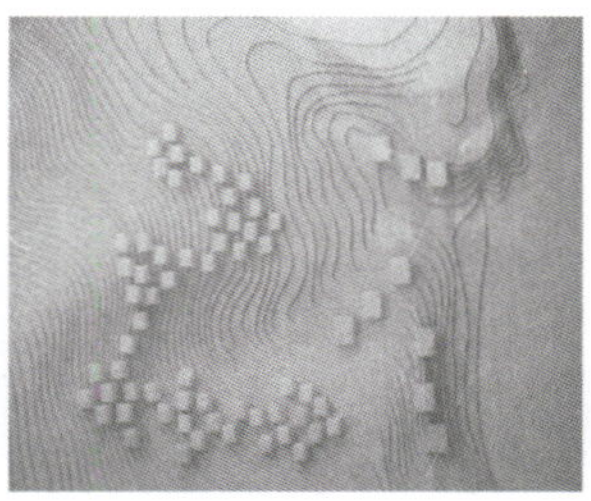
Three hotels: Guadeloupe, Martinique, French Guiana, France

Expressway noise barriers, France

EUR Convention Center, Rome, Italy

Lehrter Bahnof Tower, Berlin, Germany

Light signals, Milan, Italy

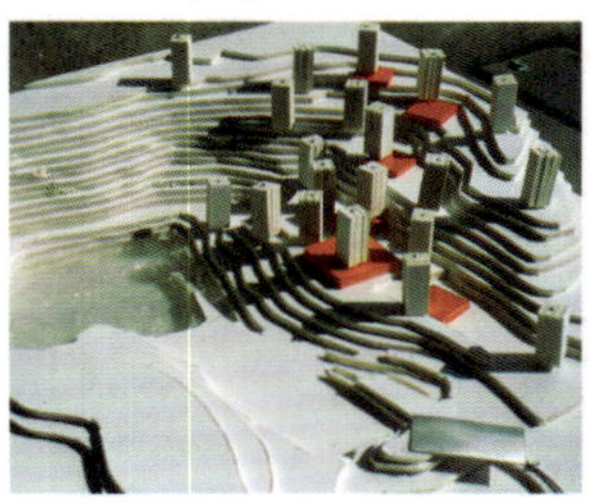
Olympic Village, Kitzbühel, Austria

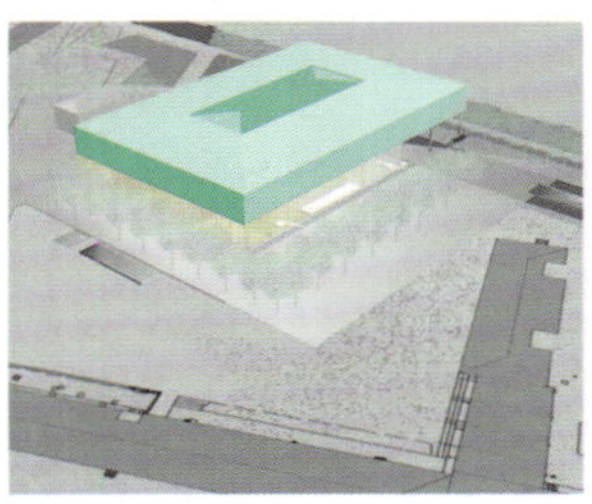
Departmental Archives, Annecy, France

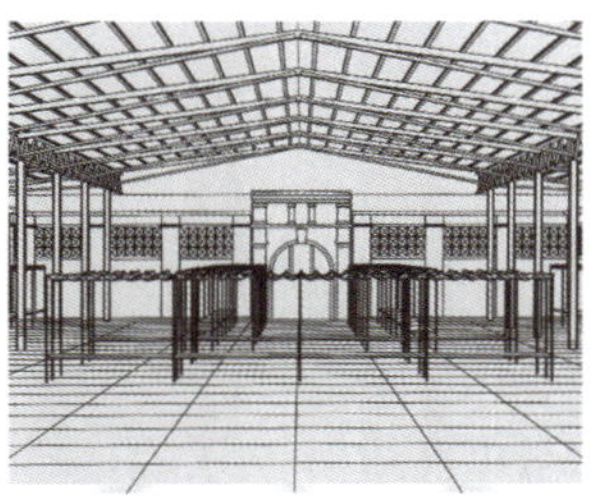
Central market, Nancy, France

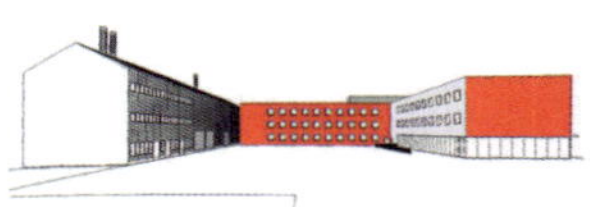
Head office of AMSP, Milan, Italy

Kirchberg plateau cable car, Luxembourg

Development of the two riverbanks, Bordeaux, France

1999

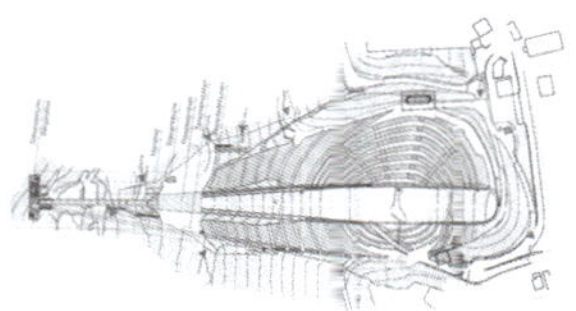
Ski jump, Innsbruck, Austria

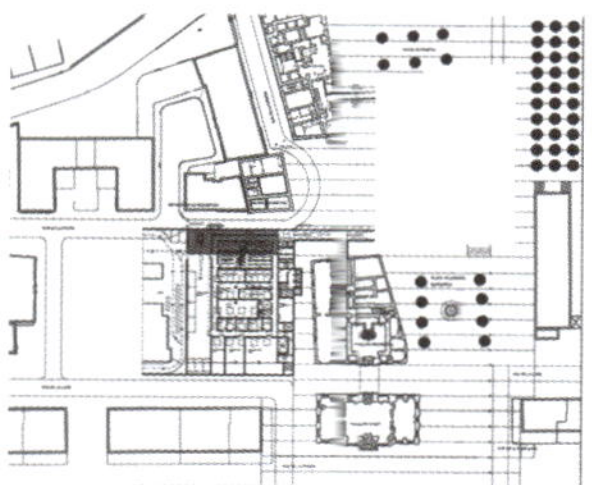
City hall of Marseille, Marseille, France

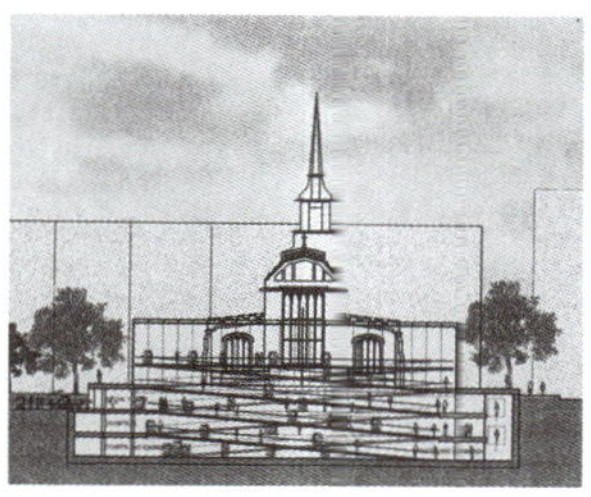
The Tower Environs, London, United Kingdom

Convention center, Graz, Austria

Casa da Musica, Porto, Portugal

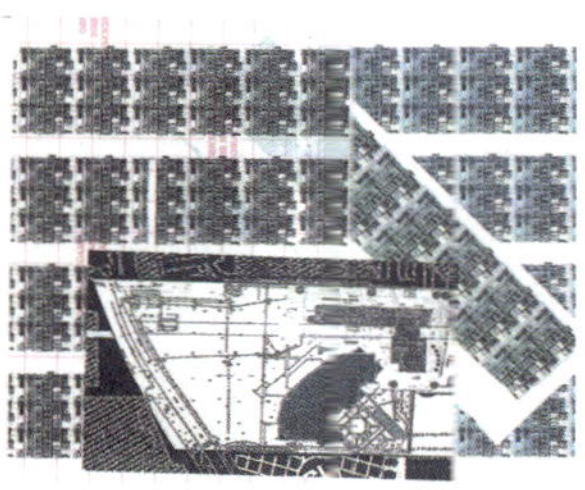
Urban study, Brétigny-sur-Orge, France

Berlin Olympic swimming pool and velodrome, Berlin, Germany

Salerno courthouse, Salerno, Italy

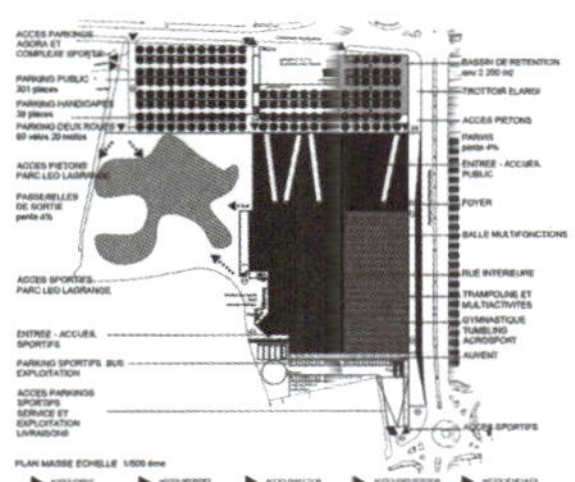
René-Thys sports complex, Reims, France

French Pavilion for Expo 2000, Hanover, Germany

Museo Reina Sofia, Madrid, Spain

Exhibition center, Stuttgart, Germany

Station hall and buffet, Blois, France

Consiag offices, Prato, Italy

Fondation Cognacq-Jay, Paris, France

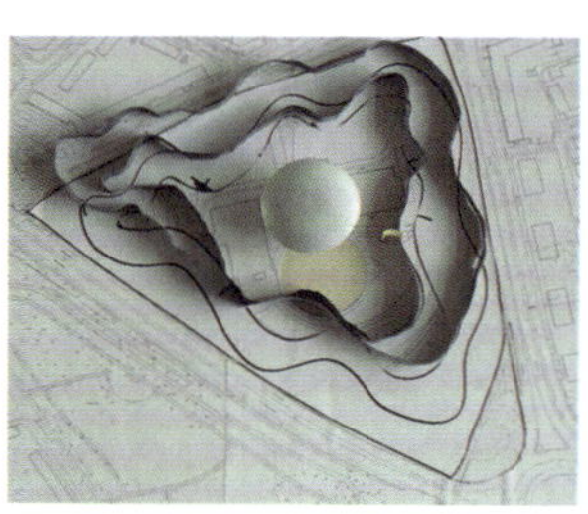
Philips head office, Eindhoven, Netherlands

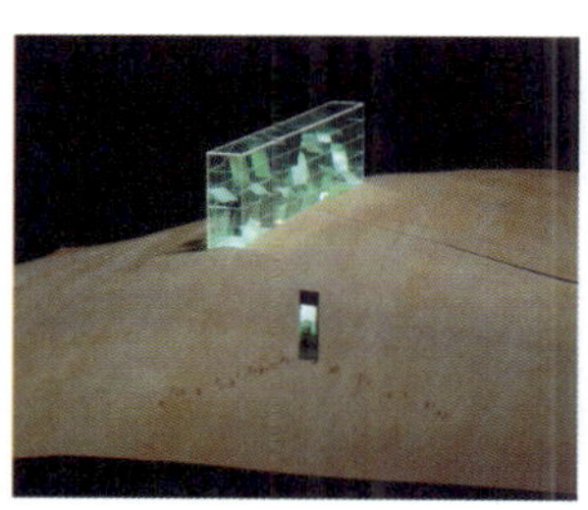
City of Culture of Galicia, Santiago de Compostela, Spain

2000

Stonecutters Bridge, Hong Kong, China

MPreis supermarket WI, Wattens, Austria

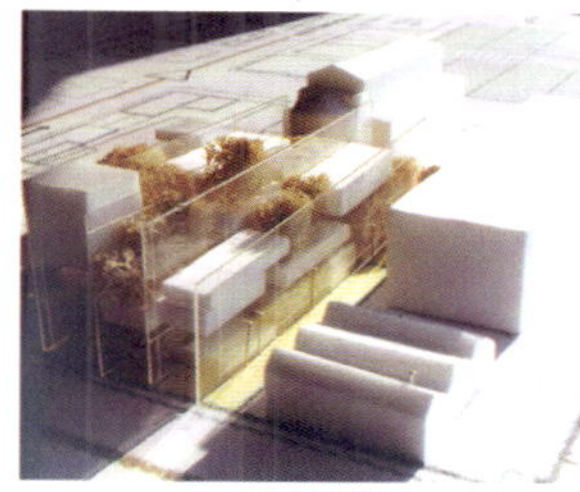
Space Agency, Rome, Italy

Chèvreloup Arboretum, Versailles, France

Head office of Danish radio and television, Copenhagen, Denmark

Old Palace neighborhood, Lugano, Switzerland

Grosser Riederoh district, Frankfurt, Germany

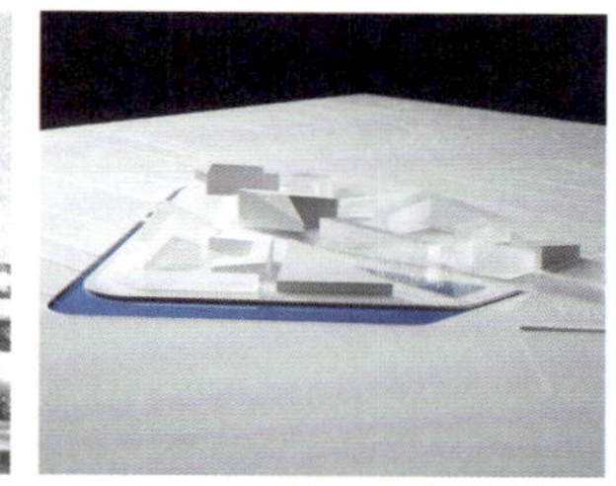
Amsterdam-Schiphol airport, Amsterdam, Netherlands

Galleria Nazionale d'Arte, Rome, Italy

Rue de Bourgogne, Paris, France

Las Teresitas Hotel, Tenerife, Spain

Salmisaari and Ruoholahti districts, Helsinki, Finland

Place du Sarrail, Nantes, France

Landesmuseum, Zurich, Switzerland

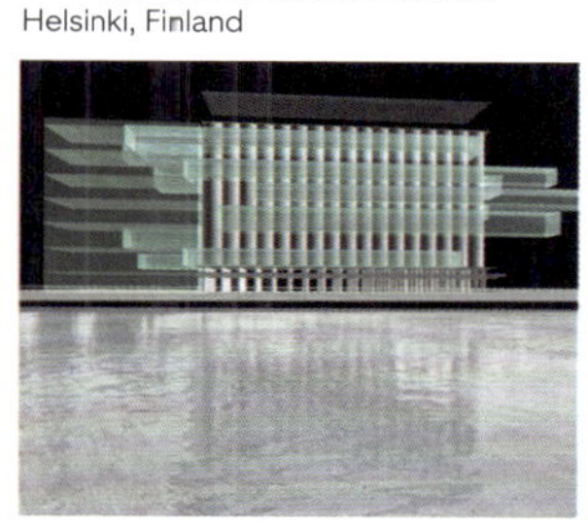
Parodi bridge, Genoa, Italy

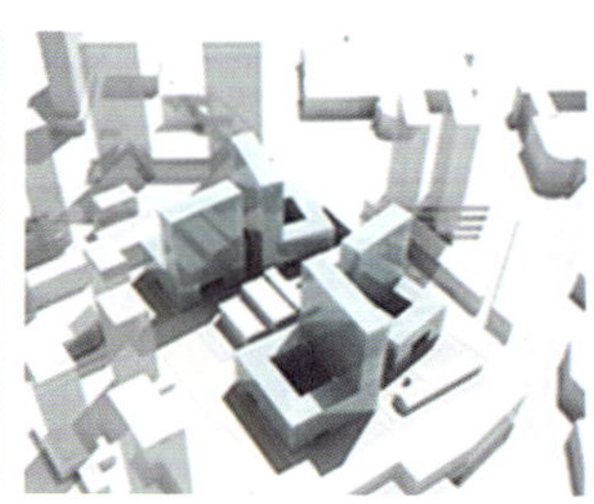
Town center development, Bratislava, Slovakia

Palazzo dell'Arengario, Milan, Italy

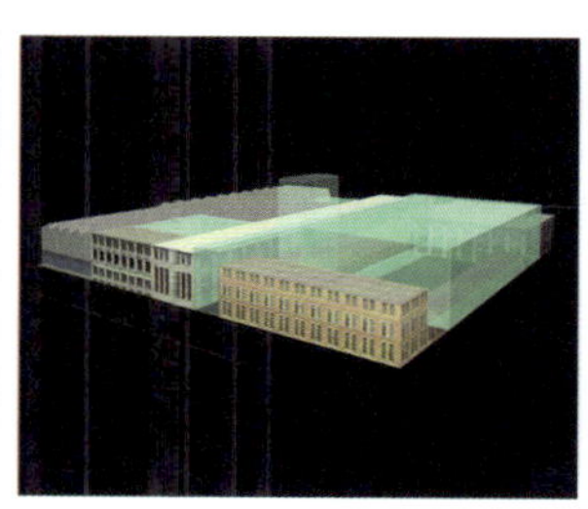
Cultural center, Turin, Italy

Installations for Las Teresitas beach, Tenerife, Spain

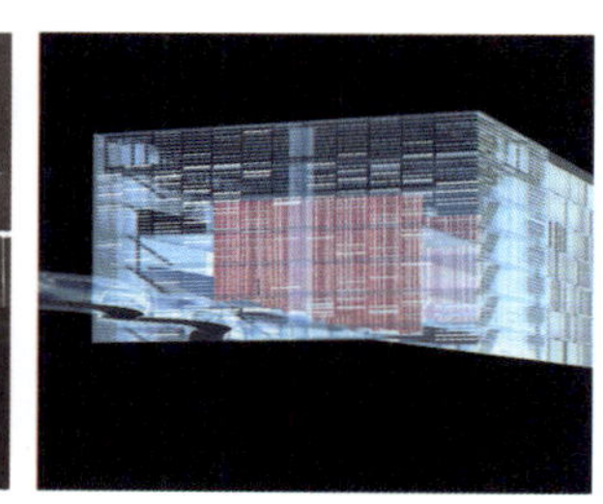
Offices of the World Intellectual Property Organization, Geneva, Switzerland

2001

2002

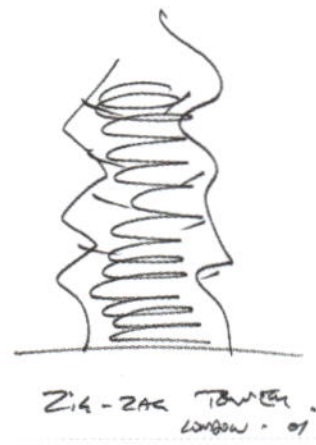

Rolex House, London, United Kingdom

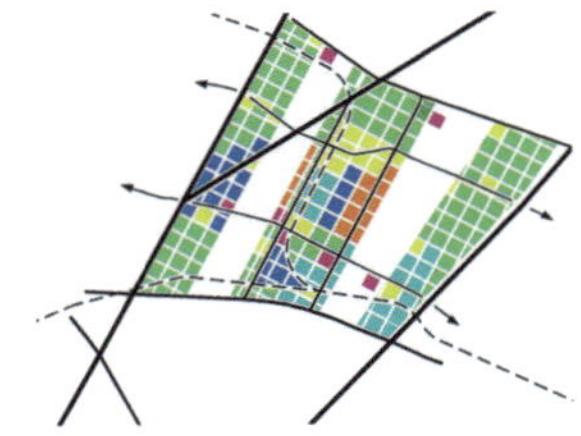

Center of Excellence, Roissy, Gonesse, France

Stade Grimonprez-Jooris, Lille, France

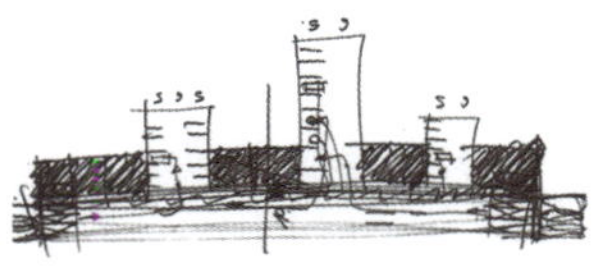

Residences, Aomori, Japan

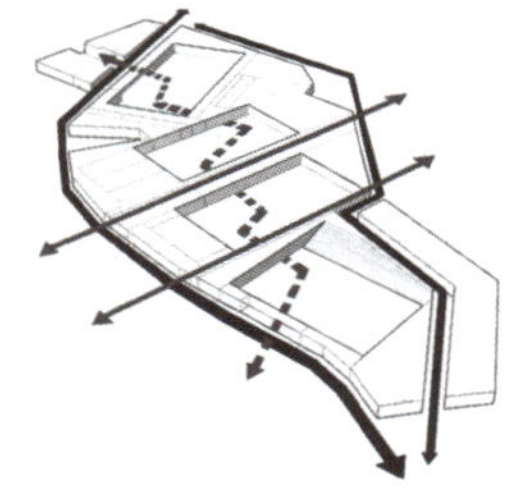

UniPark Nonntal, Salzburg, Austria

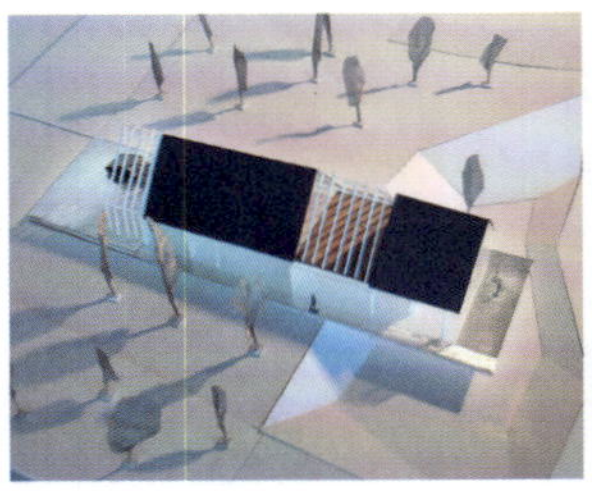

Villa Bonte, Saint-Cast-le-Guildo, France

AMAG-BVK Towers, Zurich, Switzerland

La Praille, business center development, Geneva, Switzerland

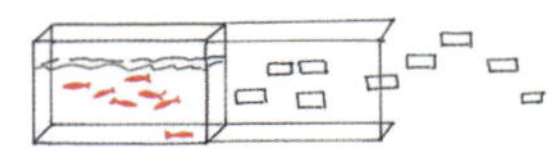

Public reception area, Institut Gustave Roussy, Villejuif, France

Maison Brausch, Luxembourg, Luxembourg

Maison Soto, Issy-les-Moulineaux, France

BMW center, Munich, Germany

Lucie-Aubrac media library, Vénissieux, France

Ordrupgaard Museum, Copenhagen, Denmark

Cable car station, Luxembourg, Luxembourg

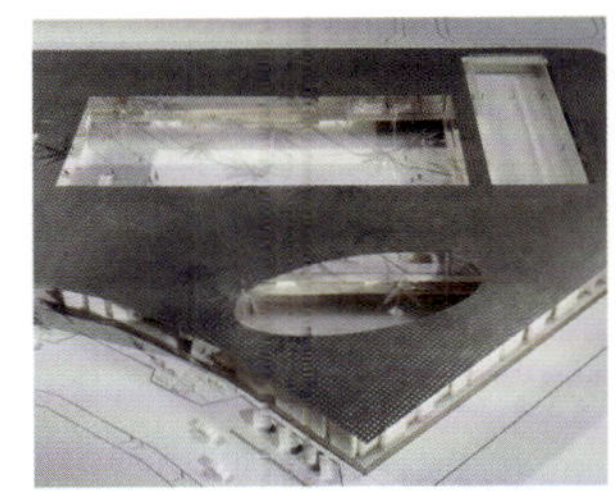

Lycée Français, Cairo, Egypt

Banque Populaire du Sud-Ouest, Bordeaux, France

Mercedes showroom, Salzburg, Austria

Vanity Fair – Tower of Faith, New York, United States

Institute of higher education, Lyon, France

Cuvier block – Université de Jussieu, Paris, France

Donau City district, Vienna, Austria

Mediacity Port, Hamburg, Germany

Wehrhahn metro, Düsseldorf, Germany

Fondation F. Pinault pour l'Art Contemporain, Boulogne-Billancourt, France

Railway zone, Canfranc, Spain

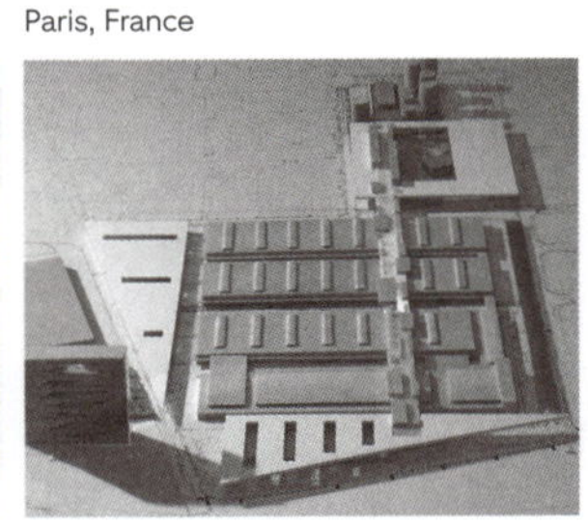

Barcelona Fair, Spain

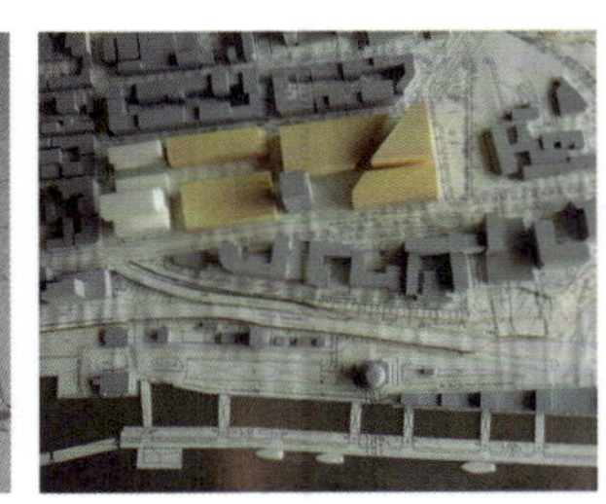

San Pauli Hotel, Hamburg, Germany

International School, Geneva, Switzerland

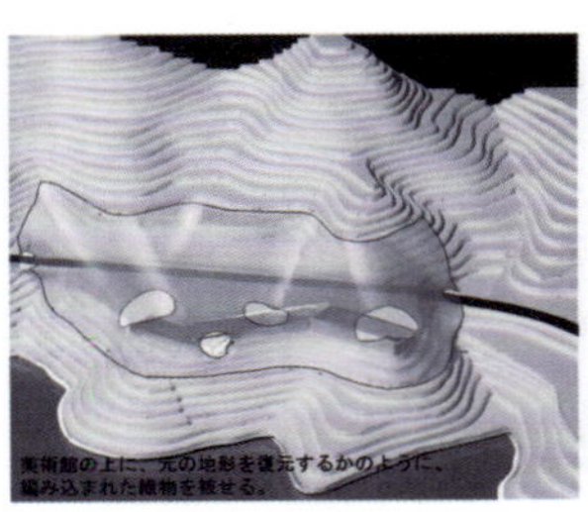

Tomihiro Museum, Midori, Japan

Art Center, Salzburg, Austria

Hesperia hotel and offices, Barcelona, Spain

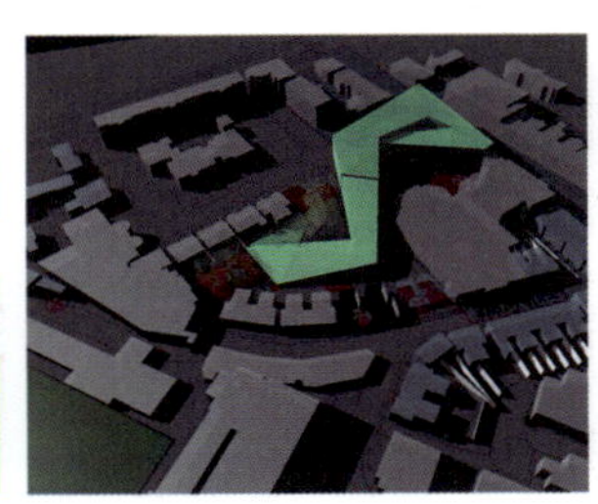

Goldsmiths, University of London, United Kingdom

House of Peace, Geneva, Switzerland

2002

Head offices of Novartis,
Basel, Switzerland

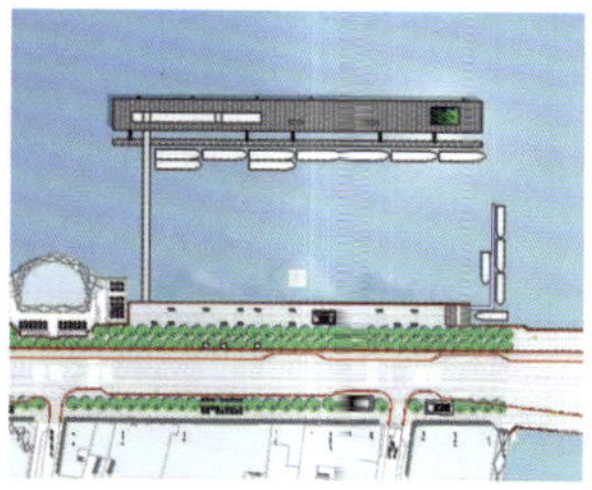
Jungfernstieg promenade,
Hamburg, Germany

Head offices of Chinese Television
(CCTV), Beijing, China

Music Center of North Jutland,
Aalborg, Denmark

Gap 15 offices, Düsseldorf, Germany

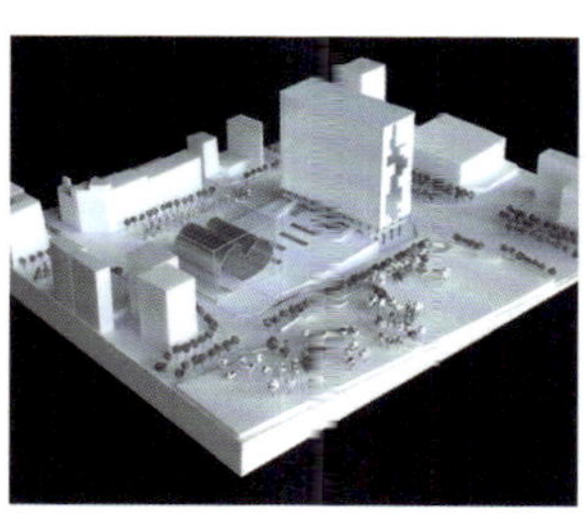
Sabadell Cultural Center,
Barcelona, Spain

Two Velux villas, Malchen, Germany

Casa de Francia, Mexico City, Mexico

Museum of the Palacio Real,
Madrid, Spain

2003

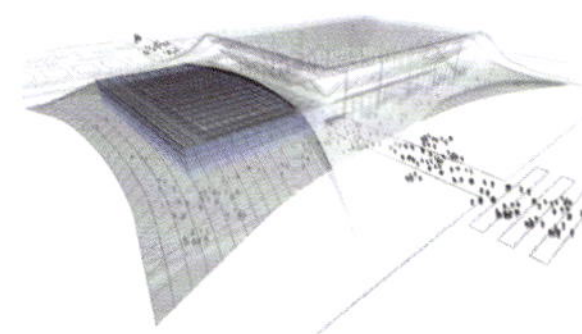
Olympic swimming pool, Beijing, China

Barilla convention center, Parma, Italy

Centre Pompidou-Metz, Metz, France

European Central Bank,
Frankfurt-am-Main, Germany

Ørestad secondary school,
Copenhagen, Denmark

Afragola station, Naples, Italy

City hall, Montpellier, France

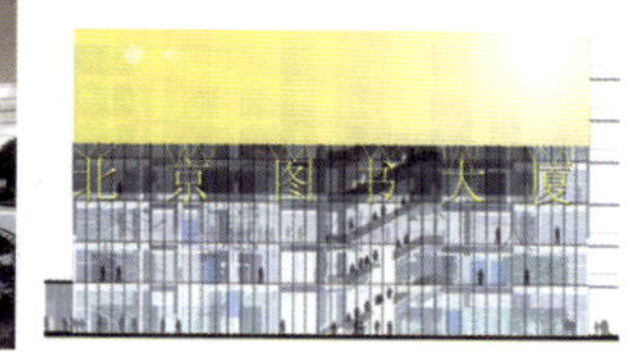
Book Center, Beijing, China

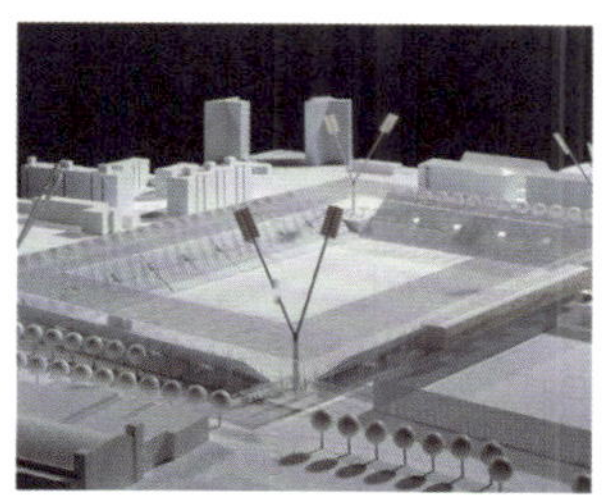
Letzigrund stadium, Zurich, Switzerland

City Gate, Basel, Switzerland

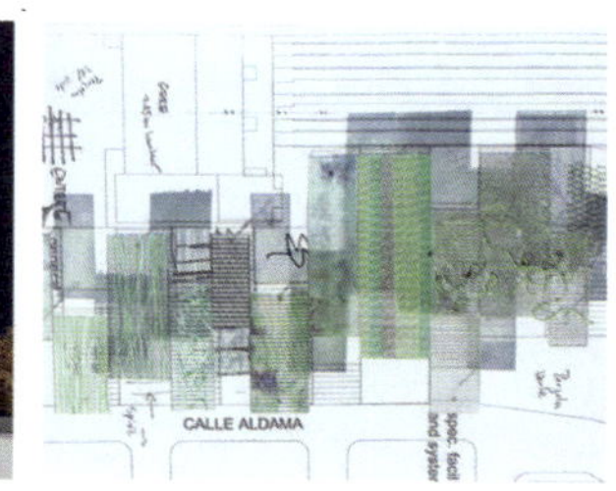
Library, Mexico City, Mexico

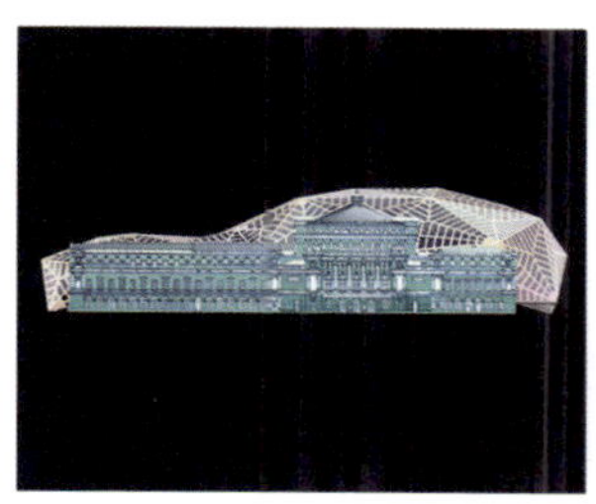
Mariinsky II theater,
Saint Petersburg, Russia

MPreis supermarket, Zirl, Austria

Lexus windows, Aichi, Japan

Industrial engineering and
pharmaceuticals base, Beijing, China

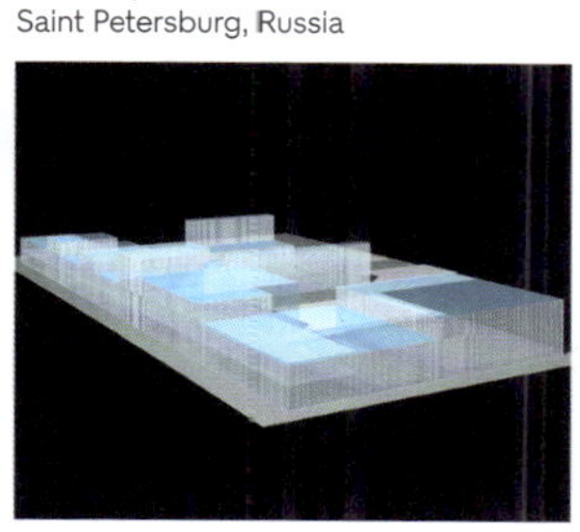
International School, Bonn, Germany

MPreis II supermarket, Wattens, Austria

Anichstrasse building, Innsbruck, Austria

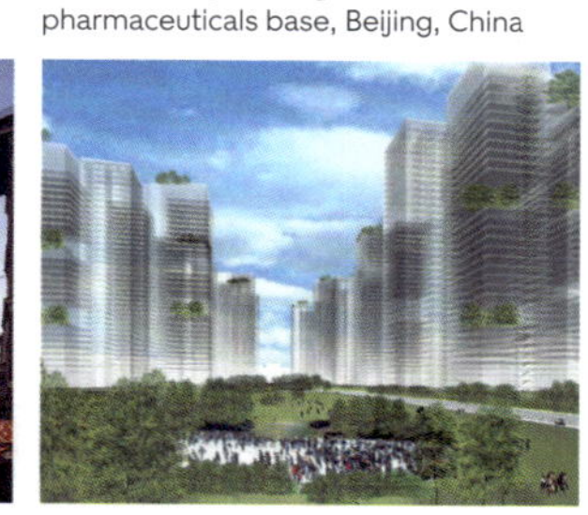
Railway station district, Osaka, Japan

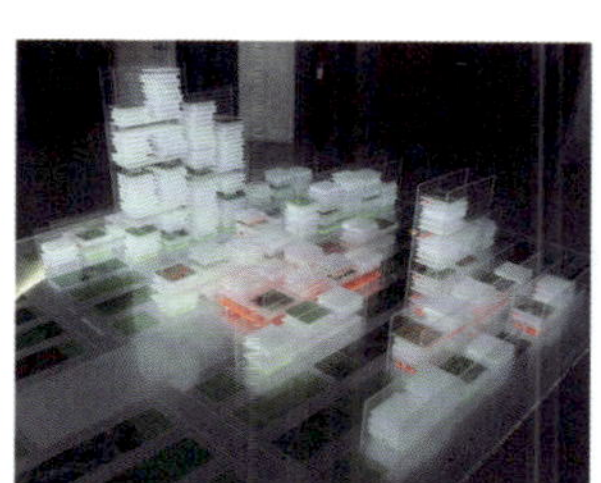
Buildings on Shengming Zhiyuan
Square, Beijing, China

Schindler House, Los Angeles,
United States

Cerisier block, Vénissieux, France

Cité Descartes, Marne-la-Vallée, France

Development of Kirchberg plateau, Luxembourg

Bridge and urban development, Palermo, Italy

Fiera district, Milan, Italy

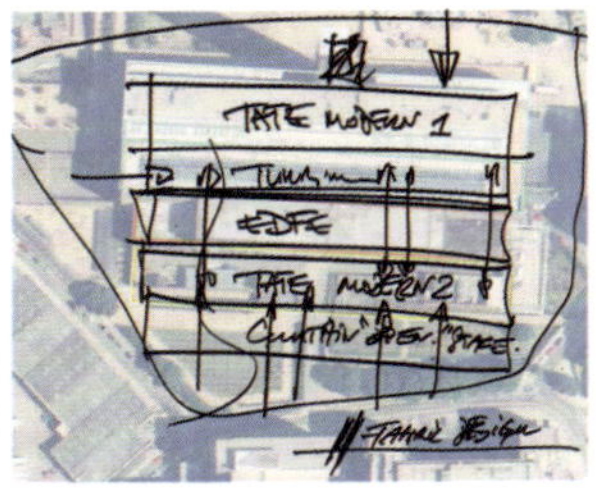
Masterplan for Tate Modern, London, United Kingdom

Olympic Village for Paris 2012, Paris, France

Hungerburg cable car, Innsbruck, Austria

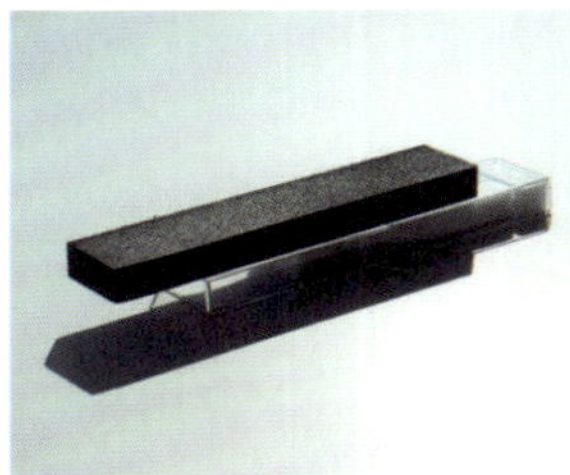
Musée des Beaux-arts, Lausanne, Switzerland

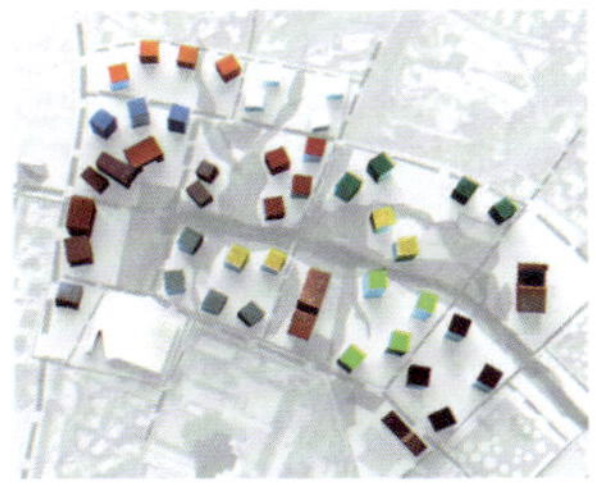
Giustiniano Imperatore district, Rome, Italy

Olympic swimming pool for London 2012, London, United Kingdom

International financial center, Seoul, South Korea

Palais des Festivals de Cannes, Cannes, France

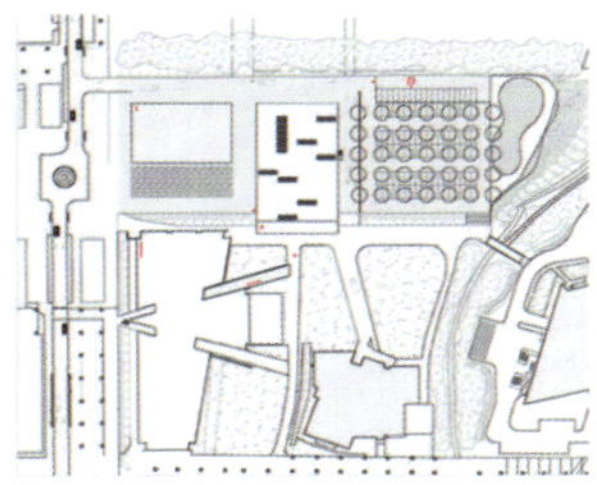
University library, Nantes, France

Porte des Lilas building, Paris, France

Friedrich-Ebert Platz, Düren, Germany

Innsbruck City Hall, Innsbruck, Austria

Museum, Sandnes, Norway

Cologne-Nippes district, Cologne, Germany

EuskoTren central site, Durango, Spain

Lichtblick Café, Innsbruck, Austria

Moscow 2012 stadium, Moscow, Russia

GKD factory, Cambridge MD, United States

Media library, Braunschweig, Germany

Private residence, Moscow, Russia

Housing block, Durango, Spain

Master plan, reception, and library of Cardarelli hospital, Naples, Italy

STIC campus, Sophia Antipolis, France

Sankei building, Osaka, Japan

Globus Provisorium, Zurich, Switzerland

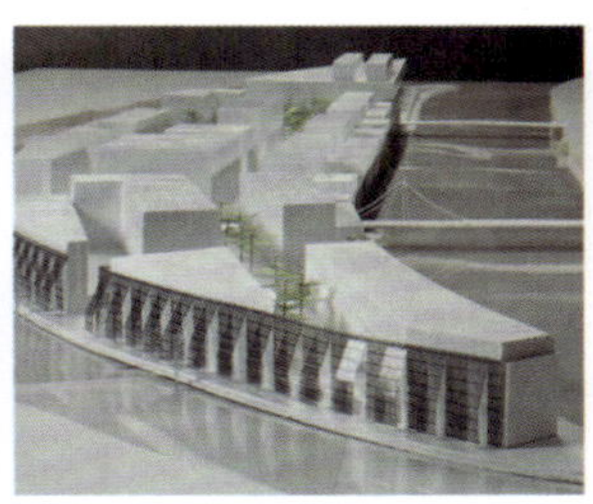
Façade/envelope for Ile Seguin, Boulogne-Billancourt, France

Piazza Gramsci, Milan, Italy

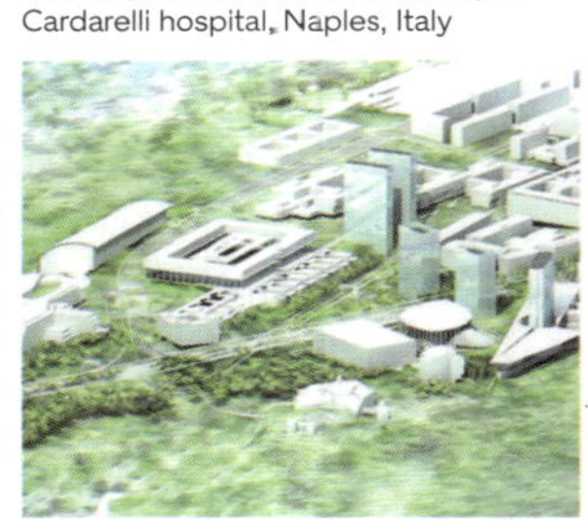
Tramway site on Kirchberg plateau, Luxembourg, Luxembourg

2005

2006

Botanical Garden, Padua, Italy

Airport maintenance installations,
Nice, France

ZAC Thiers, Lyon, France

Nô theater, Tokamachi, Japan

Convention center,
Palma de Majorca, Spain

Lantern Tower, Shanghai, China

Lille Savings Bank Lille, France

Convention center, Zurich, Switzerland

El Canaveral district, Madrid, Spain

Stadthalle, Hamburg, Germany

Historial memorial, Rivesaltes, France

National Digital Library,
Seoul, South Korea

Slovenska Sporitelna (SLSP) bank,
Bratislava, Slovakia

Bois-le-Prêtre Tower, Paris, France

Sully III building, Nantes, France

University library and research center,
Seville, Spain

Office building, Dubai
United Arab Emirates

Watersports Center,
Mantes-la-Jolie, France

León West district, León, Spain

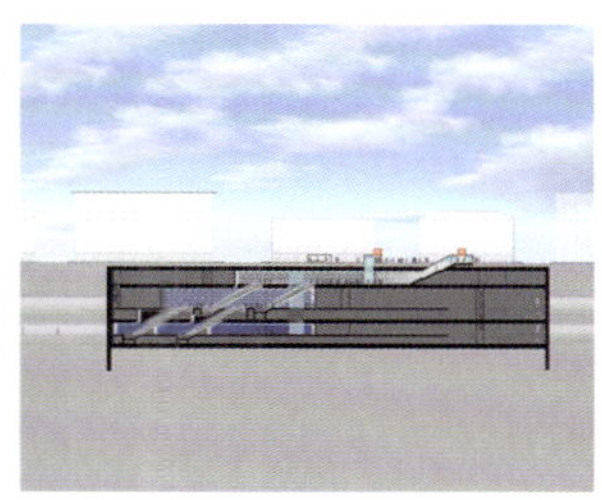
Twelve metro stations, Palermo, Italy

Maxim casino and swimming pool,
Las Vegas, United States

ARos – The Skyspace, Aarhus, Denmark

Manica Lunga library, Venice, Italy

Airbus Delivery Center, Toulouse, France

Terrace for the Kastner & Ohler building,
Graz, Austria

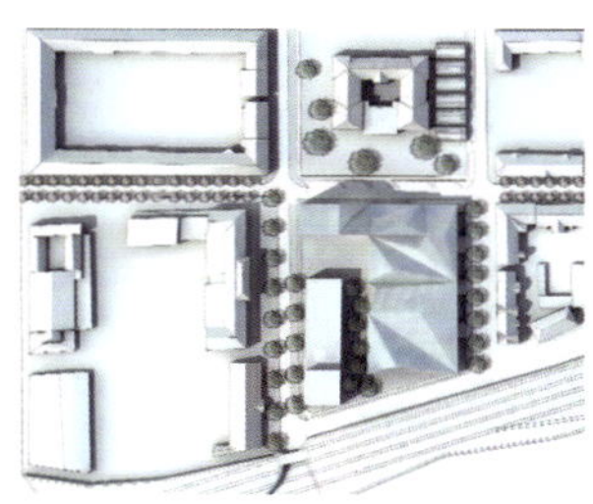
Convention Center, Krems, Austria

Artem program, Nancy, France

Opera house, Seoul, South Korea

Development for the banks of
the Manzanares river, Madrid, Spain

Domplatz, Hamburg, Germany

Centro de Creación Contemporánea
de Andalucía, Cordoba, Spain

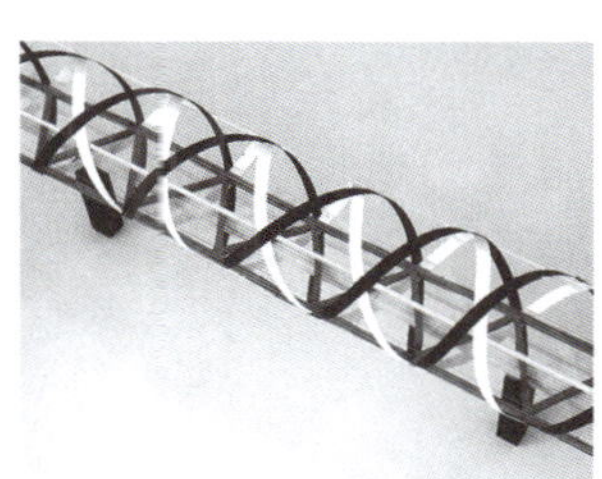
Bridge over the Arno, Florence, Italy

Phare Tower, La Défense, France

Sanpaolo IMI Tower, Turin, Italy

2006

2007

Headquarters of the European Food Security Agency (EFSA), Parma, Italy

Museo Goya, Zaragoza, Spain

Ciudad del Motor, Alcañiz, Spain

Pavilions for Bao'an district, Shenzhen, China

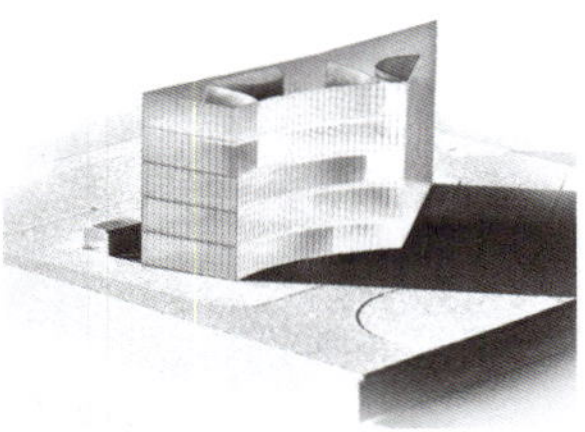

Agelco building, León, Spain

Extension of the Hôtel du Département de la Meuse, Bar-le-Duc, France

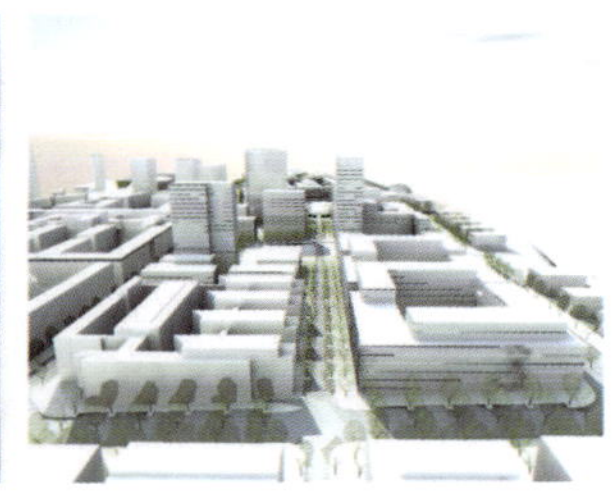

Porte de L'Europe, north sector, Luxembourg, Luxembourg

The Cube, Berlin, Germany

Taivallahti campus, Helsinki, Finland

Ûberseequartier, Hamburg, Germany

French Quarter Towers, Brisbane, Australia

Bernia Hotel, Altea, Spain

Head office of Salewa, Bolzano, Italy

City of the Environment, Soria, Spain

Site of the Neue Sihlpost, Zürich, Switzerland

Chang an Road, Beijing, China

DPA agency, Rue Bouvier, Paris, France

Penz West Hotel, Innsbruck, Austria

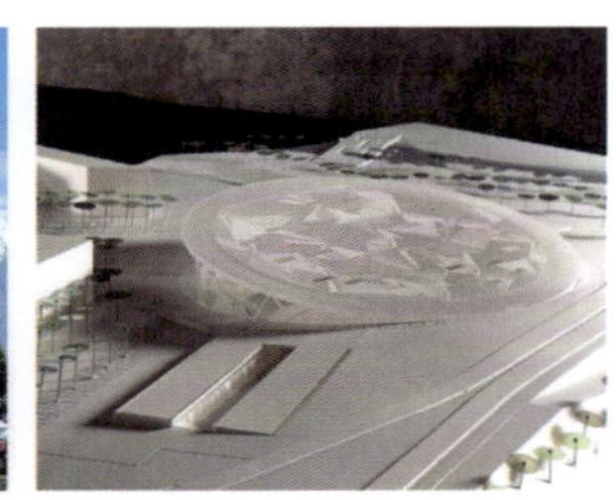

London 2012 Olympic Velopark, London, United Kingdom

Krisztina Palace, Budapest, Hungary

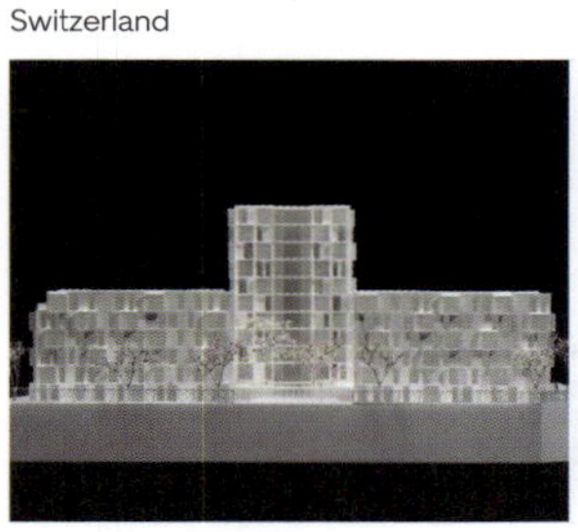

OPAC housing and activity center, Paris, France

Children's courts, Madrid, Spain

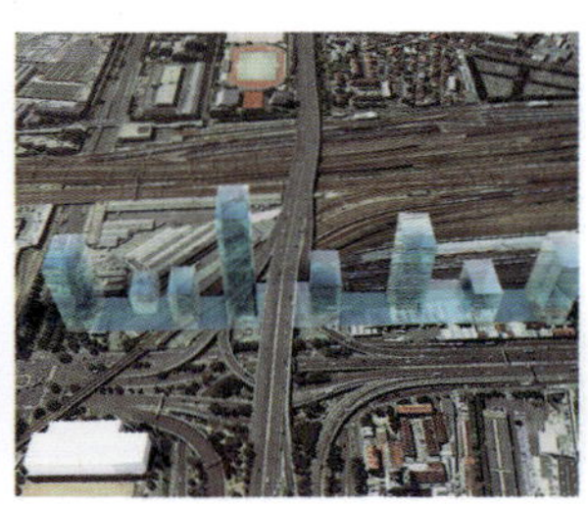

Porte de la Chapelle, Paris, France

Fujimi site, Tokyo, Japan

OCH Handelskai, Vienna, Austria

Landsbanki head office, Reykjavik, Iceland

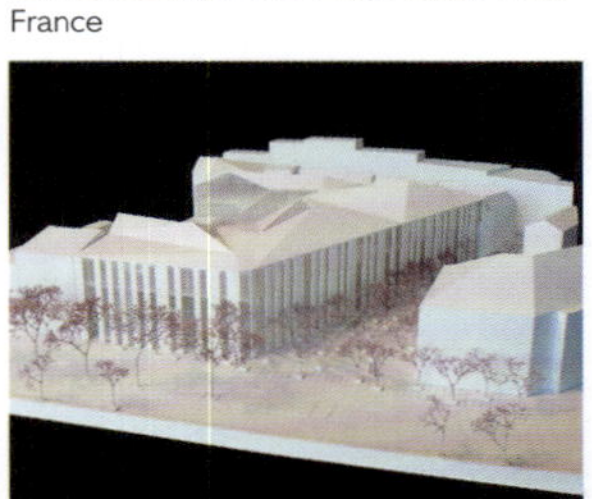

Courthouse, Douai, France

Reception halls of the Bibliothèque Nationale de France, Paris, France

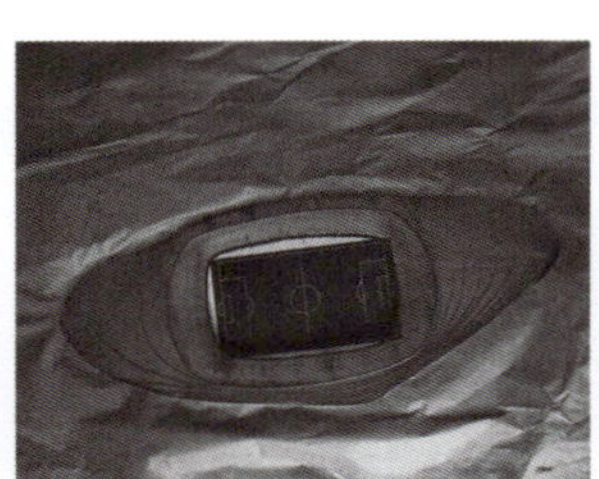

Montigalà sports complex, Badalona, Spain

RWTH campus, Aachen, Germany

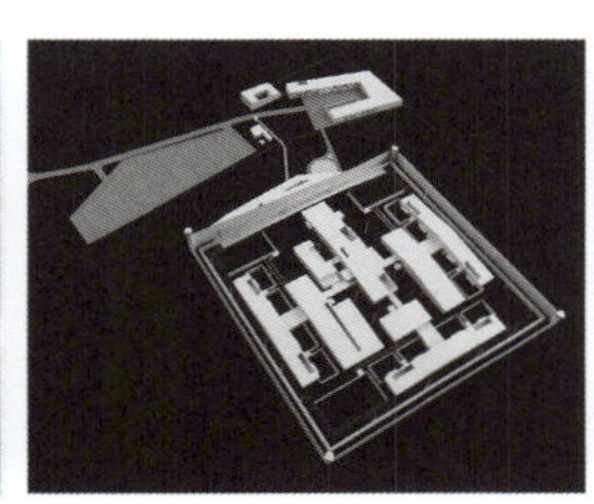

Central prison, Condé-sur-Sarthe, France

Golden Cocoon, Milan, Italy

Olympic aquatic center, Aubervilliers, France

OBB headquarters, Vienna, Austria

Habitat Sky Hotel, Barcelona, Spain

Kobmagergade quarter, Copenhagen, Denmark

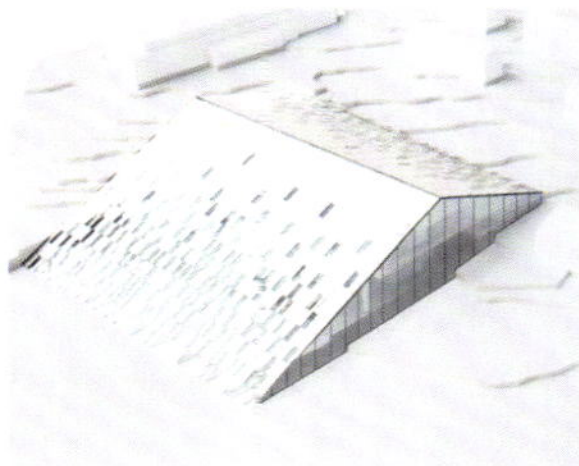
Aquatic center, Qaqortoq, Greenland

Ewha Women's University, Seoul, South Korea

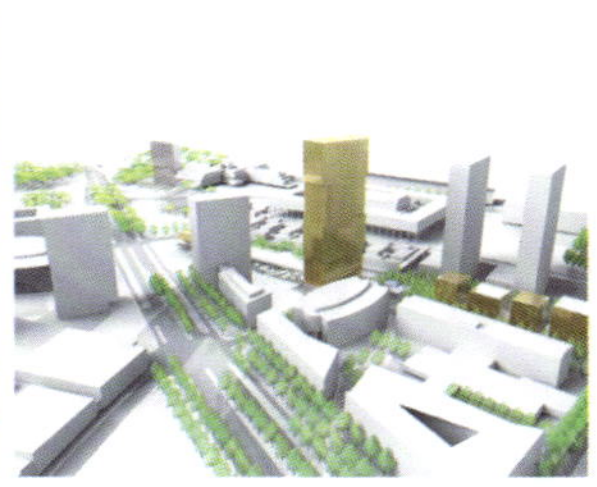
Nierdergunewald and BEI sectors, Luxembourg, Luxembourg

Theater and opera, Cologne, Germany

Cerruti boutique, Paris, France

Icône Tower, Saint-Denis, France

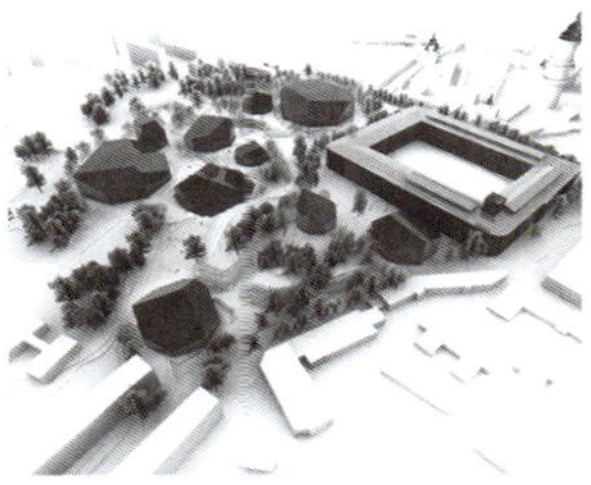
Cultural center and museum, Kyiv, Ukraine

Armonicos theater, Granada, Spain

Priory Park Pavilion, Reigate, United Kingdom

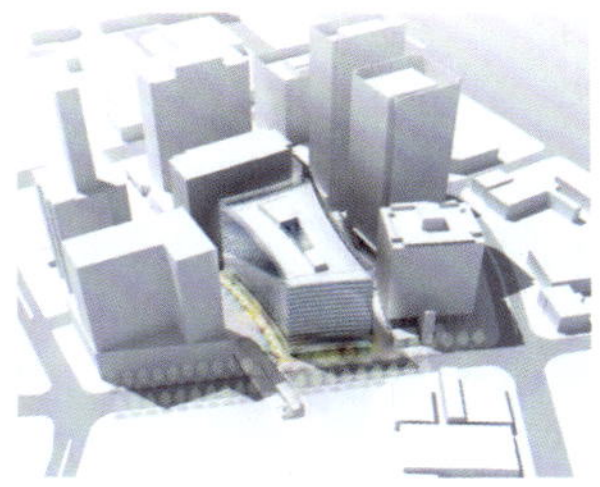
Minato Mirai 21, Yokohama, Japan

New metro, Bologna, Italy

Swiss Re Next, Zurich, Switzerland

Score Tower, La Défense, France

Court of Justice of the European Union (CJ4), Luxembourg, Luxembourg

House of Senators, Seoul, South Korea

Engadine Airport, Saint-Moritz, Switzerland

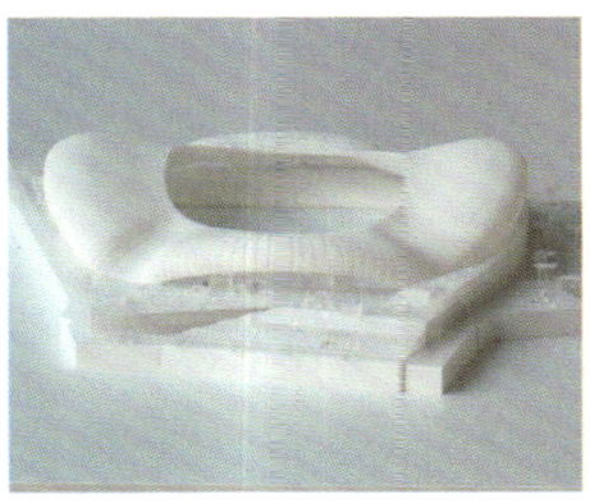
Jean-Bouin stadium, Paris, France

San Pellegrino thermal spa, Bergamo, Italy

Jules-Ladoumègue stadium, Paris, France

Law faculty, Baltimore, United States

Research Tower, Padua, Italy

Piazza della Visitazione, Matera, Italy

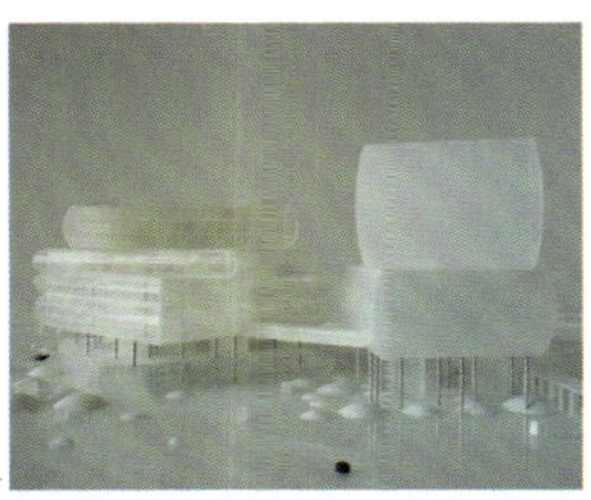
The House of Knowledge, Belval, Luxembourg

Convention center, Lanzarote, Spain

"Dominique Ferrault" exhibition at the Centre Pompidou, Paris, France

Vélodrome, Roubaix, France

Samsung Center, Seoul, South Korea

Erasmus entrance, Luxembourg, Luxembourg

2009

2010

Life science, Basel, Switzerland

Dobrée Museum, Nantes, France

Musée des Beaux-Arts, Nantes, France

Onix building, Lille, France

Multimedia library, Caen, France

The Circle – Airport, Zurich, Switzerland

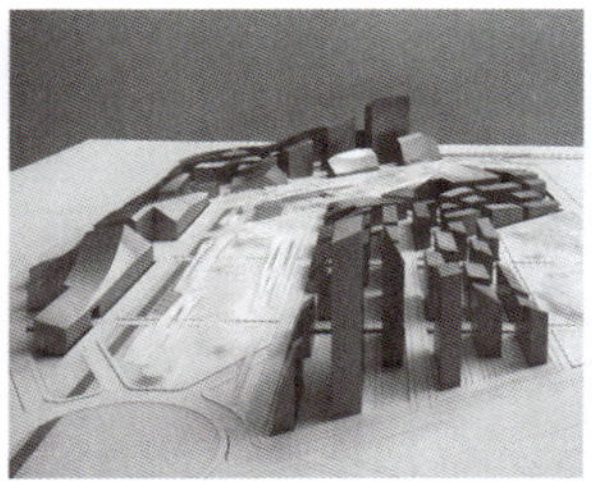
Multifunctional district, Sofia, Bulgaria

Olympic tennis center, Madrid, Spain

University center, Amiens, France

National Museum of Andorra, Andorra la Vella, Andorra

Testimonio II, Monaco, Principality of Monaco

Tesdorpfstrasse, Hamburg, Germany

Diagonal 123 offices, Barcelona, Spain

International Center of Art and Culture (CIAC), Liège, Belgium

Museum of Vega Baja, Toledo, Spain

Porte de Saint-Cloud housing, Paris, France

Octopus – Upgrading the Salerno quarries, Salerno, Italy

New reservoir, Villejuif, France

NH Milano Fiera, Milan, Italy

Ministry of Defense – Balard site, Paris, France

PEMA Nrunecker, Innsbruck, Austria

Sammode offices, Paris, France

Vinci headquarters, Rueil Malmaison, Paris

Dam, Biel, Switzerland

Administrative center, Perpignan conurbation, France

Panum University, Copenhagen, Denmark

Fukoku Tower, Osaka, Japan

Port installations, Granville, France

FFS station precinct, Locarno, Switzerland

Administration for Urbanism and the Environment (BSU), Hamburg, Germany

Aurelium building, Boulogne-Billancourt, France

EDF research center, Palaiseau, France

Metropolis?, Venice Architecture Biennale, Venice, Italy

2011

Institut de France, Paris, France

Arganzuela footbridge, Madrid, Spain

2012

Courthouse, Bobigny, France

Joliot-Curie quarter and École Centrale de Paris (ECP), Chatenay-Malabry, France

Lycée de l'Île de Nantes, Nantes, France

Urban study of the peninsula, Caen, France

La Liberté, Groningen, Netherlands

Andermatt Tourism Resort, Andermatt, Switzerland

Urban study, Neuilly-sur-Seine, France

Monoprix Champs-Elysées façades, Paris, France

Head offices of LMH group, Tourcoing, France

SAV campus, Achères, France

Hôtel Lutetia, Paris, France

The Blade Tower B2-2, Seoul, South Korea

Site of the former drinking water plant of the City of Paris, Ivry-sur-Seine, France

Exhibition hall for street theater, Toulouse, France

Station precinct, Santiago de Compostela, Spain

Courthouse, Caen, France

Euratlantique – Garonne-Eiffel Sector, Bordeaux, France

Eurojust offices, The Hague, Netherlands

Yeulmaru City of Culture and Arts, Yeosu, South Korea

Zurich Assurances, Zurich, Switzerland

Contemporary Art Museum (OCAT), Shenzhen, China

Hôtel de la ZAC Nouveau Saint-Roche, Montpellier, France

Plaza 66, Shanghai, China

160 housing units, Nanterre, France

ESIEE clean rooms, Marne-la-Vallée, France

Essen Fair, Essen, Germany

ENI production center, Milan, Italy

Gateway, Paris, France

Convention center, Berlin, Germany

Lyon Confluences, Lyon, France

Le Vérose, Lille, France

Bridge of Saint-Lazare, Clichy-Batignolles, France

Urban Folly, Gwangju Biennale, Gwangju, South Korea

CityLife residences, Milan, Italy

King Tree, Garden Festival, Chaumont-sur-Loire, France

Teaching Bridge of EPFL, Lausanne, Switzerland

Exhibition and convention center, Annecy, France

City hall, Chartres, France

2012 | **2013** | **2014**

New entrance to the Bibliothèque Nationale de France, Paris, France

Esplanade Tower, Fribourg, Switzerland

Musée des Beaux-Arts, Reims, France

Odysseum station, Montpellier, France

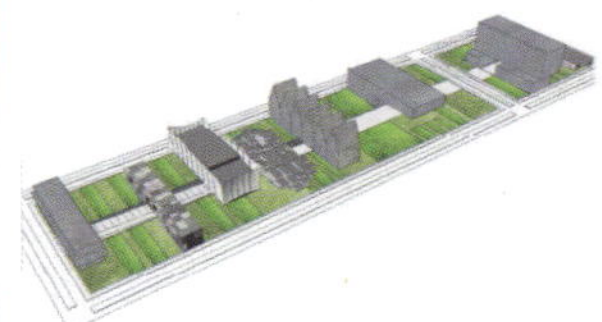
Park Russia, Moscow, Russia

Le Silo – Collection Billarant, Marines, France

Kindarena, Rouen, France

Arena, Zurich, Switzerland

Village 104, Seoul, South Korea

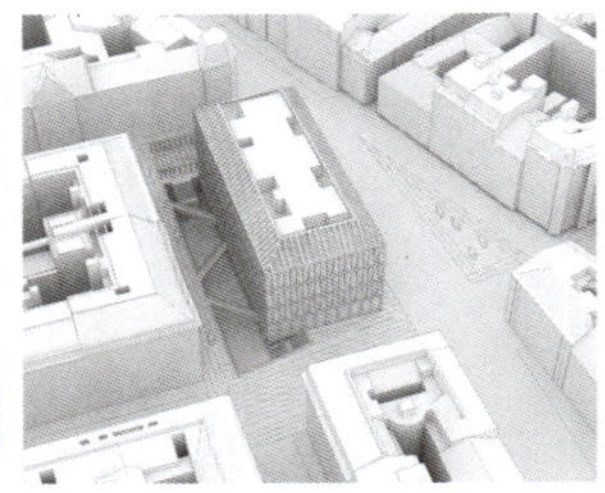
Neubau Rathausstrasse, Vienna, Austria

Confidence Towers, Tokyo, Japan

Hôtel des Lilas, Paris, France

Convention center, Angers, France

96 Iéna, Paris, France

Garage, Zuoz, Switzerland

Vetropack Areal head office, Zurich, Switzerland

Frankfurt Business School, Frankfurt, Germany

Grand Théâtre, Albi, France

Cité Musicale de l'Île Seguin, Boulogne-Billancourt, France

Villas Lotte resort, Jeju, South Korea

Hôtel Industriel enterprises, Geneva, Switzerland

Umekita Masterplan, Osaka, Japan

"Hôtel Métropole," Paris, France

Aman Paris Penthemont, Paris, France

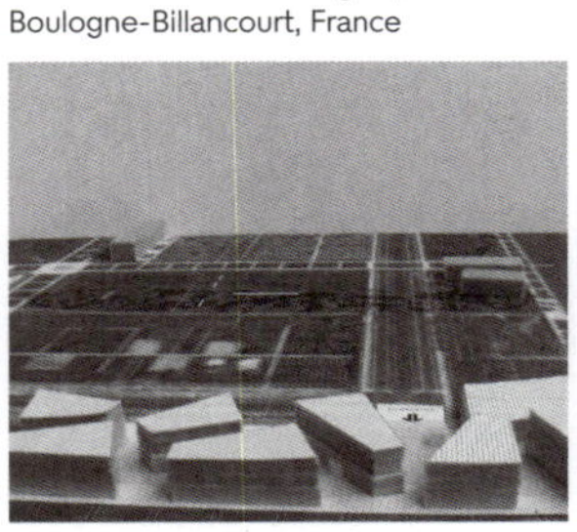
Carré Sénart, Melun, France

Studio Molière, Vienna, Austria

Restaurant Grand Saint-Michel, Chambord, France

Montagne du Parc, Brussels, Belgium

Lighting of the Eiffel Tower, Paris, France

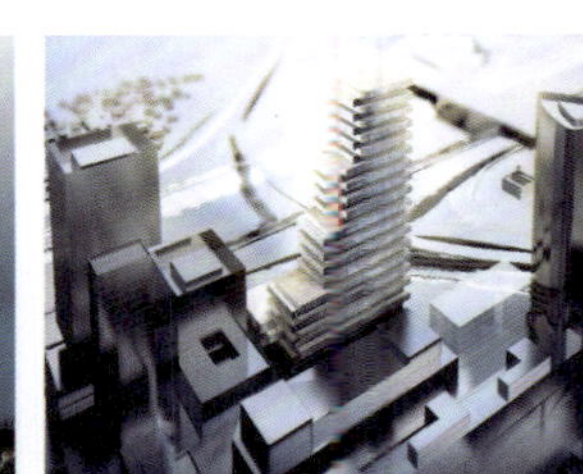
Extension of the Austro Control, Vienna, Austria

Mercedes-Benz campus, Stuttgart, Germany

Sanctuary of Notre-Dame-du-Laus, Saint-Étienne-le-Laus, France

EPFL central administrative building, Lausanne, Switzerland

Cultural Center, Gold Coast, Australia

Antuoshan Museum Park, Shenzhen, China

Hochhaus Gate 2, Vienna, Austria

2014

Housing block,
Chêne-Bourg, Switzerland

2015

Underground project for Avenue Foch,
Paris, France

AgroParisTech, Palaiseau, France

2016

Mechanics center of Polytechnique,
Paris-Saclay, Palaiseau, France

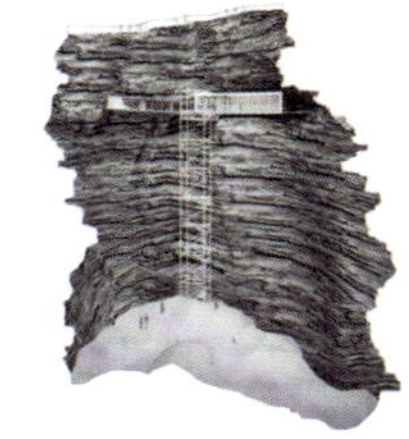

Gouffre de Padirac, Padirac, France

Agglolac, Biel, Switzerland

Museum center, Lausanne, Switzerland

Abbaye du Thoronet,
Le Thoronet, France

Valentino campus, Turin, Italy

Horizon line 17, Paris, France

Staatstheater, Karlsruhe, Germany

Donau City Tower I, Vienna, Austria

Morland administrative block,
Paris, France

ECA headquarters,
Lausanne, Switzerland

Haie-Coq, Aubervilliers, France

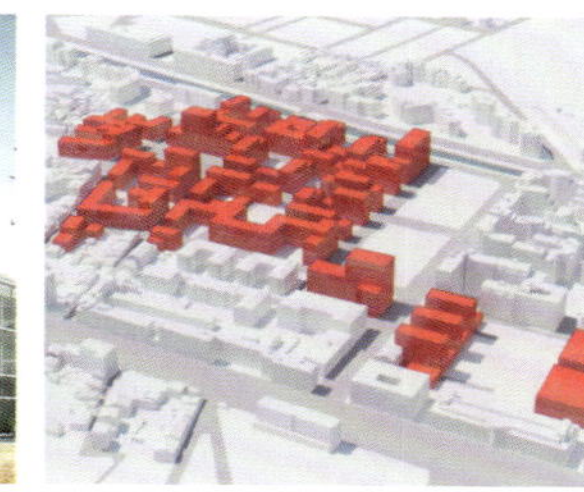

Brouardel sector, Toulouse, France

Paris-Sorbonne Picpus, Paris, France

Grand Arenas, Nice, France

Porsche Design Tower,
Frankfurt, Germany

Clichy-Batignolles, Paris, France

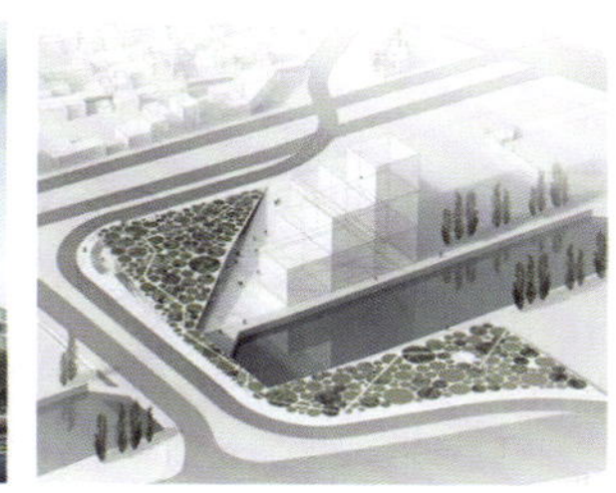

Bondy bridge, Noisy-le-Sec, France

Quai d'Orsay, Paris, France

Seosomun-Bakk historic site,
Seoul, South Korea

Building INL-BPE, Villeurbanne, France

La Pala, Lausanne, Switzerland

Head offices of the Keran Group,
Nantes, France

Shanghai Library, Shanghai, China

New Mechanical Hall of the EPFL,
Lausanne, Switzerland

Haus der Musik, Innsbruck, Austria

Campus of the Euro-Mediterranean
University, Fes, Morocco

Bricks – Old clay tile works,
Allschwill, Switzerland

Citylights, Boulogne-Billancourt, France

Museum of the 20th Century,
Berlin, Germany

Olympic skating rink, Beijing, China

Moosach bus depot, Munich, Germany

Aerial Tower, Santiago de Chile, Chile

Vinci headquarters, Nanterre, France

Copa Cagrana, Vienna, Austria

Carantec, Geneva, Switzerland

Museum of Ethnography,
Budapest, Hungary

2016

2017

Swiss Radio and Television, Zurich, Switzerland

Cité Internationale du Grand Morillon, Geneva, Switzerland

2018

Catalinas Norte II, Buenos Aires, Argentina

The Vertical City – Montparnasse Tower, Paris, France

La Maison du peuple, Clichy, France

Babcock, La Fabrique des Cultures, La Courneuve, France

Alexanderplatz building, Berlin, Germany

The Westin Josun Hotel, Seoul, South Korea

Shinsegae master plan, Seoul, South Korea

Villa Ramier, Toulouse, France

Station canopy, Fribourg, Switzerland

Westin Josun Busan palace hotel, Busan, South Korea

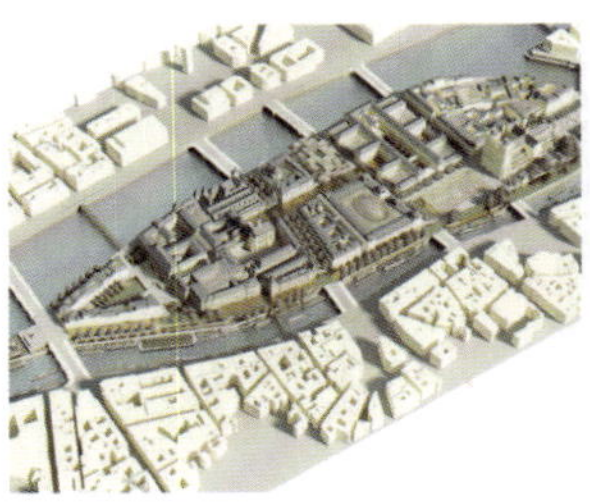
"Ile de la Cité 2040" mission, Paris, France

Grandes Écuries of the château de Chantilly, Chantilly, France

Banque Lombard Odier, Geneva, Switzerland

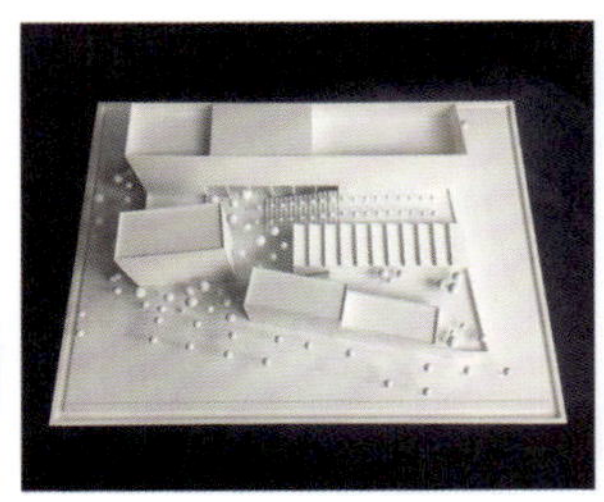
National Apprenticeship Campus, Nice, France

Grand Hôtel Kempinski, Geneva, Switzerland

Vulcano, Zurich, Switzerland

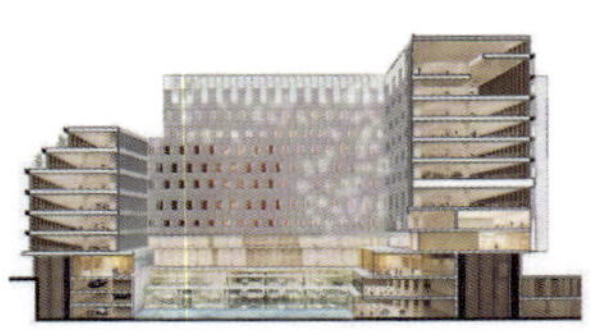
116 Avenue Emile Zola, Paris, France

Hôtel EuropaCity, Gonesse, France

Courthouse, Lille, France

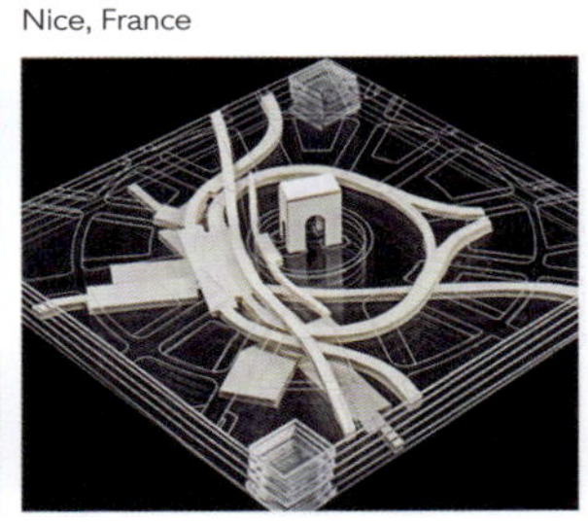
Passage de l'Étoile – Arc de Triomphe, Paris, France

Convention Center and Exhibition Hall, León, Spain

Drape House, Echigo-Trumari Triennale, Niigata, Japan

Grande Armée building, Paris, France

Yvon Lambert bookstore, Paris, France

Picpus building, Hôpital Rothschild, Paris, France

Center for the Protection of the Shore, Wadden See, Wilhelmshaven, Germany

Government headquarters, Sejong, South Korea

ParisLongchamp hippodrome, Paris, France

Pavillon Dufour, Château de Versailles, Versailles, France

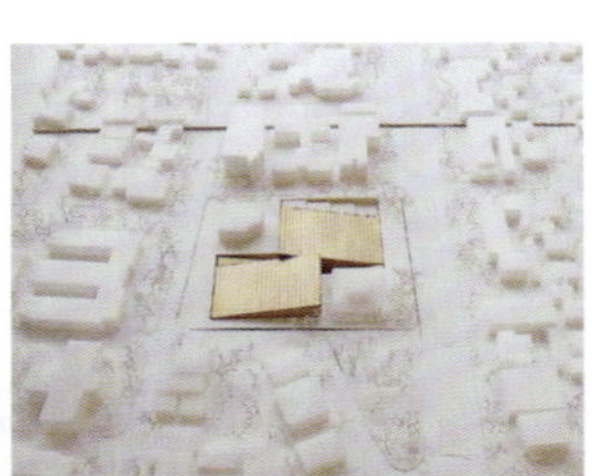
Campus of Gadjah Mada University, Yogyakarta, Indonesia

Yellopark, Nantes, France

Casa Pastors, Girona, Spain

Tempelhof Airport, Berlin, Germany

Connexe project, Aulnay-sous-Bois, France

2018

2019

2020

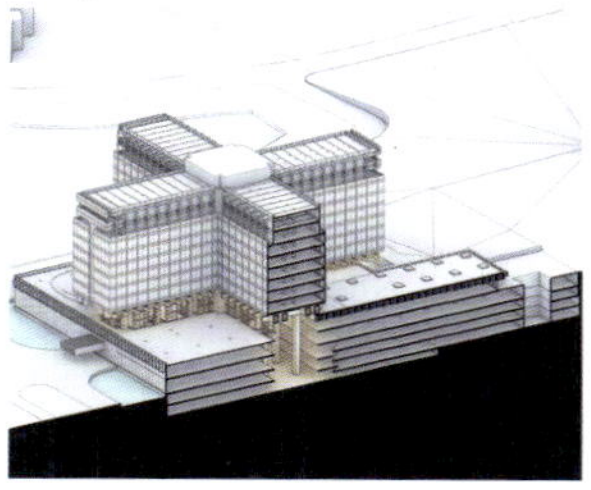
Souverain 25, Brussels, Belgium

Les Acacias quarter,
Geneva, Switzerland

Piazza Garibaldi, Naples, Italy

Shenzhen Institute of Design and
Innovation, Shenzhen, China

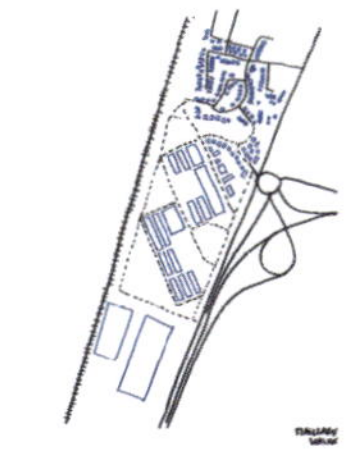
Etamat B sector, Le Mans, France

Milano Gioia district, Milan, Italy

Zurich Stadelhofen station,
Zurich, Switzerland

Samsung Life complex,
Seoul, South Korea

Diamonds, Hanoi, Vietnam

Total Tower, Puteaux, France

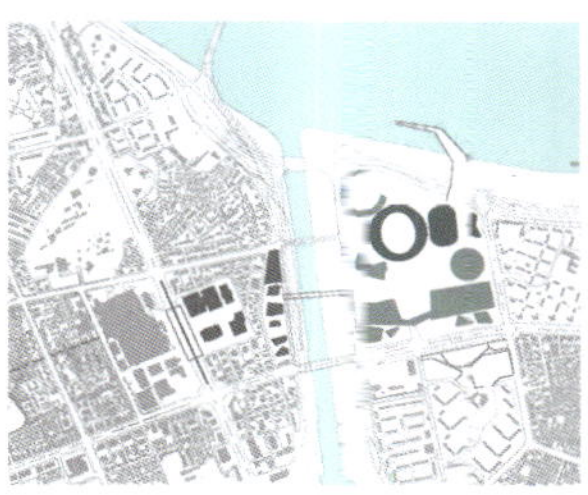
Masterplan Gangnam Jamsil,
Seoul, South Korea

Tiny House Monoprix, Paris, France

Harbor design, Toulon, France

Aplix extension,
Le Cellier-sur-Loire, France

Hangang District master plan,
Handan, China

Hôtel Dieu, Paris, France

Roche Diagnostics, Meylan, France

Court of Justice of the European Union
(CJ8), Luxembourg, Luxembourg

Future parking lot, Paris, France

Council chamber, Hôtel du Département
de la Meuse, Bar-le-Duc, France

Entenwerdern bridge,
Hamburg, Germany

Arsenal, Geneva, Switzerland

CityLife 2 residence, Milan, Italy

Head offices of World Car Center
(WCC), Vigo, Spain

Masterplan 24H du Mans,
Le Mans, France

Natural History Museum,
Shenzhen, China

European Parliament – Paul-Henri Spaak
Building, Brussels, Belgium

Grand Palais Éphémère, Paris, France

Chanel factory, Venette, France

MK2 cinema at BnF, Paris, France

Modernization of Geneva International
Conference Centre, Geneva, Switzerland

City hall, Cheongju, South Korea

Étang Quarter,
Vernier-Geneva, Switzerland

2020 | 2021 | 2022

Park of Villa Tertrais-Chailley, Les Sables d'Olonne, France

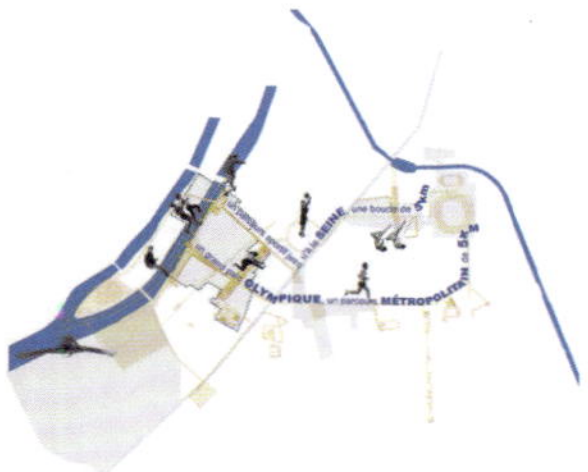

Fitness loop on the territory of La Plaine, Saint-Denis, France

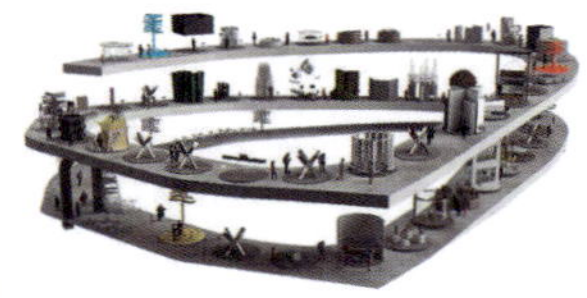

Crossroads, Building the Resilient City, SBAU, Seoul, South Korea

Tilia Tower, Lausanne, Switzerland

Landscape, Puteaux – La Défense, France

Magnifica Fabbrica, Milan, Italy

Women's housing – Association Basiliade, Paris, France

Hanwha life insurance Yongin training institute, Yongin, South Korea

83 Marceau, Paris, France

Bourse parking lot, Paris, France

Hohes Dach – Technical Administration Building, Düsseldorf, Germany

Bank for International Settlements (BIS), Basel, Switzerland

Galerie des Champs-Elysées, Paris, France

Pavilions 1 – Parc des Expositions, Paris, France

Poste du Louvre, Paris, France

Head offices of Medef, Paris, France

Métal 57, Boulogne-Billancourt, Paris, France

Nauentor, Basel, Switzerland

Gold Pavilion – Parc de la Villette, Paris, France

Cupola of La Défense, Puteaux, France

Chamartin station, Madrid, Spain

Cœur des Sources site, Saint-Germain-en-Laye, France

Folies de Neuilly, Neuilly, France

Saint-Eutrope restaurant, Clermont-Ferrand, France

Connected Parasport Health Institute, Les Muraux, France

Auteuil Hippodrome, Paris, France

Archeology Museum, Rostock, Germany

La Cité du Cinéma, Saint-Denis, France

Guide plan of the Hôtel du Département de la Meuse, Bar-le-Duc, France

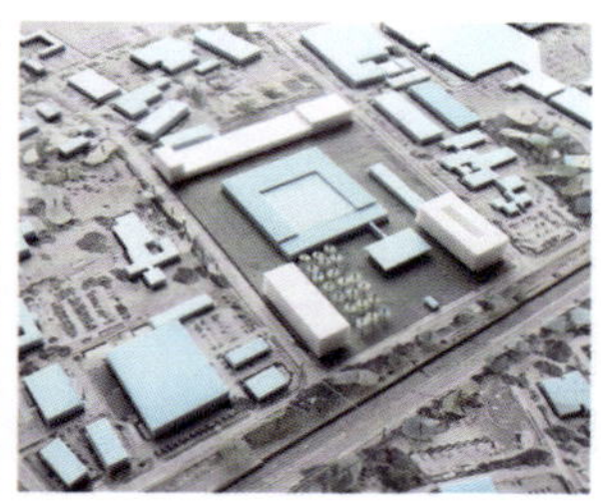

Monnaie de Paris, Pessac, France

Multisports complex, Plan-les-Ouates, Switzerland

Urban study, Minori and Mairoi, Italy

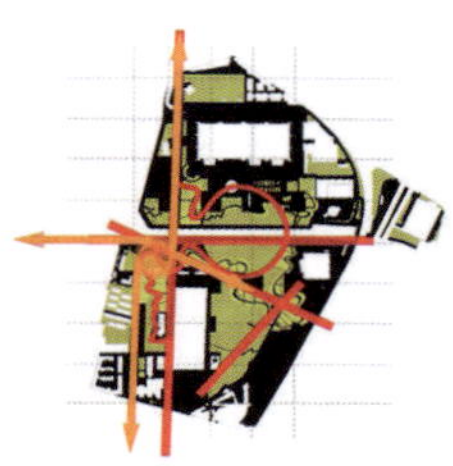

Parc de la Villette, Paris, France

Fitness loop, Berlin, Germany

Refurbishment of the Hôtel Industriel Berlier, Paris, France

Donau Zentrum, Vienna, Austria

Lagardère Paris Racing, Paris, France

2023

District II of Apgujeong
Seoul, South Korea

Campus of the École Polytechnique,
Palaiseau, France

Geneva Library, Geneva, Switzerland

Busan Expo 2030 master plan,
Busan, South Korea

Portal UZH, Zurich, Switzerland

To-Lyon Tower, Lyon, France

Chonbang and Ilshin textiles site,
Gwangju, South Korea

2024

Sejong International Garden City
Exhibition, Sejong, South Korea

Club Mouton, Bordeaux, France

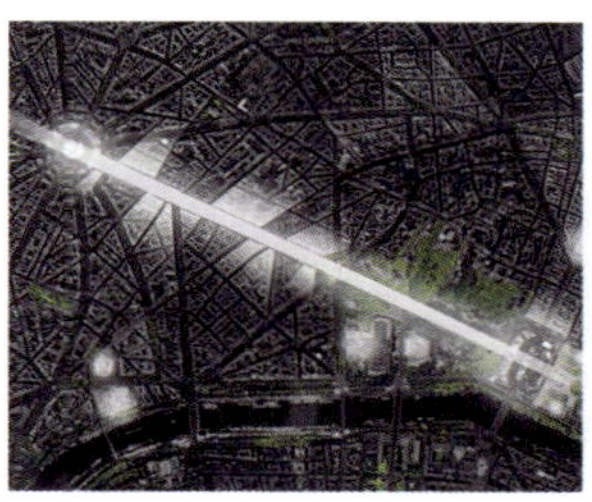

Les Champs de Lumière, Paris, France

Centre Pompidou, Paris, France

Suzanne-Lenglen Court coverage,
Paris, France

Dancing Tower – Eurovea City,
Bratislava, Slovakia

Dyad – One Cheongdam-dong,
Seoul, South Korea

The Athletes' Village – Paris 2024,
Saint-Denis and Saint-Ouen, France

Offices of the Colline Saint-Cloud,
Saint-Cloud, France

Three Trees Tirana, Tirana, Albania

2025

Villejuif-Gustave Roussy station,
Villejuif, France

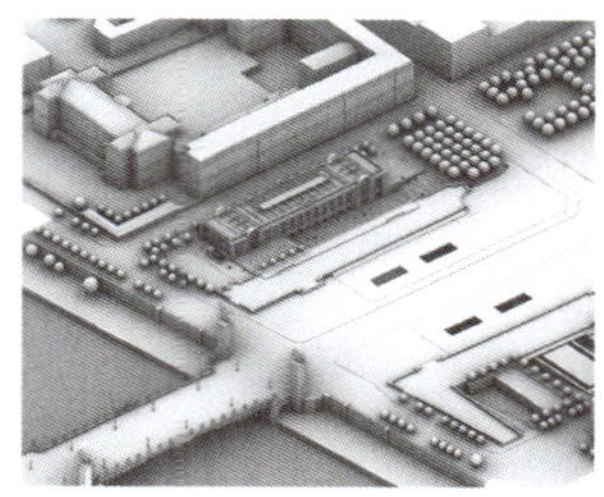

Les Invalides waste plant, Paris, France

Citylights, Boulogne-Billancourt, France

Landscape Tower, Tirana, Albania

Namcheon District, Busan, South Korea

2026–2030

Saint-Martin building, Paris, France

Paris Raspail, Paris, France

Extension of the Olympic Tennis Center,
Madrid, Spain

Aérogare des Invalides,
Fondation Giacometti, Paris, France

Double Deck – Dome-esplanade of
EPFL, Lausanne, Switzerland

Donau City Tower II, Vienna, Austria

Hôtel des Téléphones Gutenberg,
Paris, France

Timber Marina Tower, Vienna, Austria

Twin Peaks – Bongeunsa-ro 120,
Seoul, South Korea

Arc of Light – Nonhyun 114,
Seoul, South Korea

Dunamu headquarters,
Seoul, South Korea

Lightwalk – Gangnam Intermodal
Transit Center, Seoul, South Korea

APPENDICES

BIOGRAPHY
DOMINIQUE PERRAULT

Born in 1953 in Clermont-Ferrand, France, lives and works in Paris.

1973
Begins studies at the École d'Architecture of the École Nationale Supérieure des Beaux-Arts de Paris, attends Martin van Treck's and Antoine Grumbach's studios.

1978
Graduates as an Architecte DPLG (Government Certified Architect), École Nationale Supérieure des Beaux-Arts de Paris (UP4).

1979
Graduate certificate in urban planning, École Nationale des Ponts et Chaussées.

1980
Master of advanced studies in history, École des Hautes Études en Sciences Sociales.

1981
Creation of Dominique Perrault Architecture (DPA) agency in Paris, followed by agencies in Berlin (1992), Luxembourg (2000), Madrid (2006), and Geneva (2013).

1983
Winner of the Albums de la jeune architecture, Ministère de l'Équipement.

1990
Installation of the DPA agency in the Jean-Baptiste-Berlier industrial hotel, Paris (13th arrondissement).

1993
Grand Prix national d'architecture.

1997
Mies van der Rohe Award, for the Bibliothèque Nationale de France.

1998–2001
President of the Institut Français d'Architecture (IFA).

2007
Establishment of DPA at 6, rue Bouvier, Paris (11th arrondissement).

2008
Seoul Metropolitan Architecture Award, first prize for Ewha Women's University, Seoul, South Korea.

2010
Grande Médaille d'or d'architecture, Académie d'architecture.

2012
Member of the Scientific Council of the Atelier International du Grand Paris.
Officer of the Légion d'Honneur.

2015
Winner of the Praemium Imperiale 2015, Architecture section, Japan.
Member of the Academy of Fine Arts, Architecture section.

2016
Commandeur of the Ordre des Arts et des Lettres.

2019
President of the UIA-Unesco International Committee.
Winner of the Observatorio d'Achtall Prize, Architecture section, Spain.

2020
President of the Association pour la Conservation du Domaine de Frapotel.

2024
Member of Seoul City Architect Partners, Seoul, South Korea.

TEACHING AND RESEARCH

1995–96
École d'architecture de Rennes, France.
1997
Tulane School of Architecture, New Orleans, US.
1998
University of Illinois Urbana-Champaign, US.
1999
École Technique Supérieure d'Architecture, Barcelona, Spain.
2000
Institut Victor-Horta, Brussels, Belgium.
2000–03
École Polytechnique Fédérale, Zurich, Switzerland.
2013
Honorary doctorate from the Ion-Mincu Academy of Architecture and Urban Planning, Bucharest, Romania.
2013–18
École Polytechnique Fédérale, Lausanne (SUBLab), Switzerland.
2015
Launch of the research platform DPAx, Paris, France.
2018
Launch of a MOOC on subterranean architecture.
2018–ongoing
Honorary professor, École Polytechnique Fédérale de Lausanne, Lausanne, Switzerland
2022
Launch of the International competition d'Architecture Carpark Futures, Paris-Lille, France.

EXHIBITIONS

2010
Curator of "Métropolis?", French Pavilion at the Venice Architecture Biennale.
2019
Curator of the exhibition "Chambord 1519-2019, l'utopie à l'œuvre," Chambord.
2021
Managing Director of the Seoul Biennale of Architecture and Urban Planning.
2022
Curator of the exhibition "District 2024: Beyond the Athletes' Village," Biennale of Architecture and Landscape, Versailles.
Curator of the Pavillon du Grand Paris Express, traveling exhibition, Paris-Versailles-Dubai.
2023
Curator of the exhibit on "Métro! Le Grand Paris en mouvement" exhibition, Cité de l'Architecture et du patrimoine, Paris.

AWARDS

1983
Winner of the Architecture nouvelle-PAN XII program.
1984
Prix AMO (Architecture et Maître d'Ouvrage), first prize for the Someloir factory, Châteaudun, France.
1990
Prix AMO (Architecture et Maître d'Ouvrage), first prize for the Hôtel Industriel Berlier, Paris, France.
Équerre d'Argent du Moniteur for the Hôtel Industriel Berlier, Paris, France.
1992
Constructa Preis' 92 for the Hôtel Industriel Berlier, Paris, France.
Silver medal for urban planning for the Bibliothèque Nationale de France, Paris, France.
1996
Constructec-Prize, special mention European Prize for Industrial Architecture, for the Sagep water treatment plant.
1999
Deutscher Preis für Architektur, second prize for the Olympic velodrome and swimming pool, Berlin, Germany.
2000
AIT competition, first prize for office furniture, for the reading chairs designed for the Bibliothèque Nationale de France, Paris, France.
2001
World Architecture Award, first prize for the Aplix factory, best industrial building, Le Cellier-sur-Loire, France.
2002
World Architecture Award, first prize for the Vénissieux Multimedia Library, best European public building.
2003
BTV Bauherrenpreis, Austria, for MPreis II supermarket, Wattens, Austria.
BTV Bauherrenpreis, Austria, for City Hall, Innsbruck, Austria.
2005
Best Industrial Building 2005 AIA Maryland USA, for the GKD factory, Cambridge, US.
2006
New Alpine Architecture Award for the MPreis supermarket, Zirl, Austria.
Dedalo-Minosse International Prize, special award for the Town Hall, Innsbruck, Austria.
2008
Reigate Society Award 2008, prize for the Priory Park pavilion, Reigate, UK.
2009
European Steel Design Award 2009 for the European Court of Justice, Luxembourg, Luxembourg.
Concours Construction Acier 2009, award for the European Court of Justice, Luxembourg, Luxembourg.
Green Good Design, Environment/Landscape Architecture Award for Ewha Women's University, Seoul, South Korea.
American Institute of Architects, AIA Design Award for the University of Law Competition, Baltimore, US.
2010
Afex Award, for Ewha Women's University, Seoul, South Korea.
Silver Pyramid, Commercial Property category, Fédération des Promoteurs-Constructeurs (FPC), for the Onix building, Lille, France.
Silver Pyramid, Innovation category, FPC, for the Vérose building, Lille, France.
2011
"Patrimoine du xxe siècle" label for the Archives départementales de la Mayenne, Laval, France.
2014
Grand Prix d'Architecture et d'Urbanisme de Haute-Normandie.
Prix de l'Équipement Public for the Palais des Sports, Rouen, France.
Emporis Skycraper Award, 2nd prize for DC Tower I, Vienna, Austria.
2016
"Patrimoine du xxe siècle" label for the Bibliothèque Nationale de France, Paris, France.
2017
Building of the Year Award from Archdaily for the Pavillon Dufour, Versailles, France.
BCV Foundation Award, for the Groundscape research project.
2019
Euro-China Green & Smart City Award for the development of the parking lot of the future, Paris, France.
2020
Trophées Eiffel, architecture and engineering category, for the Paris-Longchamp racecourse, Paris, France.
2021
Idea-Tops Award, public architecture category, for the ParisLongchamp racecourse, Paris, France.
2022
"Remarkable Contemporary Architecture" label for the Hôtel Départemental de la Meuse, Bar-le-Duc, France.
2024
"Remarkable Contemporary Architecture" label for the École Supérieure d'Ingénieurs en Électrotechnique et Électronique (ESIEE), Marne-la-Vallée, France.

MONOGRAPHIC EXHIBITIONS

1991
"Études pour la Bibliothèque Nationale de France," Galerie Denise René, Paris.
"Concept/Contexte," Galerie Denise René, Paris.
1992
"Dominique Perrault. Morceaux Choisis," Institut français d'architecture, Paris.
1996
"Paris... Berlin. Dominique Perrault," Aedes Architecture Forum, Berlin.
"Des natures, au-delà de l'architecture," Architekturgalerie de Lucerne, Suisse.
1998
"Dominique Perrault. Des natures," Galerie TN Probe, Tokyo.
1999
"Dominique Perrault, Arquitecto Urbanista," galerie du Ministerio de Fomento, Madrid.
2002
"Dominique Perrault. Morceaux Choisis," traveling exhibition, AFAA (Association française d'action artistique du Ministère des Affaires étrangères, France) and DAPA (Direction de l'architecture et du patrimoine du Ministère de la Culture et de la Communication, France),
"Mesh," galerie Anne de Villepoix, Paris.
2006
"Metabuildings," Architekturzentrum, Vienna.
2007
"DPA Dominique Perrault Architecture," Arc en rêve, Bordeaux.
2008
"DPA Dominique Perrault Architecture," Centre Georges-Pompidou, Paris.
2009
"DPA Dominique Perrault Architecture," Fondation ICO, Madrid.
2010
"Urban Landscape," Opera City Art Gallery, Tokyo.
2013
"Dominique Perrault Architecture, Territoires et horizons," EPFL, Lausanne.
2014
"Groundscape. Chroniques et fictions," DPA agency, Paris
2017
"Mission Île de la Cité, le cœur du Coeur," Conciergerie, Paris.
2018
"Dominique Perrault. La Bibliothèque Nationale de France, Portrait d'un Projet 1988–1998," BnF, Paris.
2019
"Esprit des Lois, Génie des Lieux: The Time of a Work. Building a Courthouse for the European Union," Court of Justice of the European Union, Luxembourg.

DOMINIQUE PERRAULT ARCHITECTURE AGENCY

Dominique Perrault is surrounded by a team of some fifty professionals (architects, engineers, designers, model makers, archivists, etc.) from all over the world.
After more than fifteen years on the seventh floor of the Hôtel Industriel Berlier, a building he designed himself in 1990 and which the agency moved into after winning the competition for the design of the Bibliothèque Nationale de France, the agency moved in 2007 to a former twentieth-century factory on rue Bouvier, in eastern Paris. Completely redesigned, the new premises house the architectural studio and a multi-purpose exhibition space of over 500 square meters.

DPA – DOMINIQUE PERRAULT ARCHITECTURE
Partners:
Dominique Perrault, architect, urban planner
Gaëlle Lauriot-Prévost, architect-designer, artistic direction

COLLABORATORS SINCE 1980
Camille Abeille, Andreea Adam, Shubham Agarwal, Chara Agnanti, Akanksha Agrawal, David Agudo, Jueun Ahn, Jean-François Aimé, Stéphani Alary, Magda Aleksiejuk, Daniel Allaire, Anaïs Allard, Michel Alluyn, Claude Alovisetti, Ilena Altmann Berneau, Javier Alvarez Urrutia, Luis Alves Da Silva, Marina Alves Rosa, Quitterie Amiel, Emmanuelle Andreani, Nicolas Andreatta, Chiara Angeli, Viet Anh Nguyen, Esther Anthony, Aymeric Antoine, Jacopo Anzelin, Paolo Apicella, Pedro Araujo, Augustin Ardaillon, Fadi Ariss, Raphaël Arlot, Victor Armas Crespo, Stella Armeli, Shoghah Armoudjian, Idoia Arrazola, Anna Artemeva, Richard Asmar, Leyla Assef, Luc Augustin, Nicolas Ayoub, Nina Azinovic, Concepcion Badia Herrera, Laura Bagdonaite, Martina Baldin, Yvan Balp, Sreoshy Banerjea, Shreya Bansal, Léo Bansaye, Judith Barber, Erik Barbette, Ana Barbier, Thomas Barra, Maud Barthelmé Sitar, Camilla Bartz-Johannessen, Christian Basset, Léa Baudat, Clémentine Baudon, Petra Baumgarten, Francesca Becchi, Manuel Becerra, Serge Bedoukian, Astrid Beem, Jean- Yves Beetschen, Aïcha Belaïche, Geoffroy Belmont, Ekatérina Bélozérova, Augustin Bentz, Philippe Berbett, Nicolas Berdon, Sylwester Beres, Antonio Bergamasco, Pascale Berlin, Tommaso Bernabo Silorata, Ronnie Bertocchi, Jerôme Besse, Jad Beyrouti, Sonal Bhadauria, Jean-Luc Bichet, Marcello Biffi, Quentin Blaising, Isabelle Blancke, Annabelle Blin, Guillaume Bloget, Marie Bodénès, Gerhard Bodenmüller, Iren Böhme, Julien Boitard, Thimothée Boitouzet, Nadina Bold, Élise Bon, Louis-Olivier Bonay, Luca Bonazzi, Raphaël Bonsang, Anne-Laure Borel, Vincent Boreux, Tommaso Borghesi, Giulia Borghi, Thomas Bormann, Thomas Bosi, Yves Bour, Augustin Bourgeois, Amata Bouscein, Laurent Boutin-Neveu, Estefania Branco, Dieter Brandt, Mark Breidy, Luca Brichese, Florian Brillet, Adrien Brunel, Eliott Brunet, Agne Budryte, Geert Buelens, Lucie Bulot, Mattia Buonriposi, Lucile Buquet, Nicolas Bur, Daniela Burkardt, Daniela Busch, Adele Busschaert, Jacques Cadilhac, Mariana Caetano, Antoine Calcagno, Pietro Calusi, Beatriz Calvete, Jean-François Candeille, Carl Cantin, Carla Carboni, Cinzia Casale, Antoine Casanova, Rémi Castello, Francesco Cataldi, Tulio Cathala, Ana Catinca Popovici, Léa Cavelier, Illaria Cazzato, Francesco Cazzola, Maximilien Cecaldi, Rainer Centmayer, Hyemin Cha, Naïs Chamerlin, Édouard Champalle, Aye Chann Mang, Sébastien Chaput, Romain Chassain, Christine Chau, Jean Chaussavoine, Gabriel Chaussée-Jimenez, Jie Chen, Xi Chen, Xingyue Chen, Florian Cherat, Florian Cheraud, Sokman Cheung, Alain Chiffoleau, Giovanna Chimeri, David Chinea, Hristo Chinkov, Eugenio Chironna, Tamara Chitava, Hyunsoo Cho, Ryo Chosokabe, Gabriel Choukroun, Martina Ciet, Hervé Cividido, Anne Claire Saby, Alice Clanet, Anaëlle Clement, Charley Cloris, Louis Clyde Wadell, Rémy Cointet, Sylvain Combaluzier, Fabienne Commessie, Marie-Laure Comon, Yves Conan, Gilbert Corbin, Karen Cornejo Vilchis, Joana Costa, Florine Cottar, Françoise Coulon, Constantin Coursaris, Sandrine Courvoisier, Nathalie Cozic, Patrick Crémel, Maria Cristina Mena Arjona, Nathan Crouzet, Ivana Curic, Bérénice Curt, Bartlomiej Cybula, Griet Daels, Luciano D'Aliéso, Sacha Dalis, Viet Thai Dang, Armando D'Angelo Sante, Malforzata Das, Luis Da Silva, Benjamin Dauby, Sophie Dauchez, Valérie de Calignon, Laurent de Carnière, Jérémy Debois, Marie Debraine, Florian De Clercq, Chiara De Gennaro, Pablo De La Hoz, Fabienne Delandemare, Anne-Sophie Delaveau, Camille Délègue, Nora Delidimou, Anastasia Delinassou, Daniel Del Olmo, Arnaud Delugeard, Bruce Depei, Anne- Mie Depuydt, Chloé de Quillacq, Olivier Desaleux, Benoist Desfonds, Jeanne Despas, Louis Desplanques, François Dessème, Ilaria De Vito, Dieter De Vos, Soetkin Devolder, Divya Dhandapani, Stephani Diaz Gamboa, Rebecca Didier, Claudia Dieling, Alexander Dierendonck, Miriana Di Gioa, Jessica Di Lorenzo, Ludivic Dingreville, Sofia Distefano, Hélène Dittgen, Sandrine Diximus, Renaud Djian, Julie Dobbelaere, Nicolaus Dohrn, Tatiana Dor, Lorenza D'Orazio, Céline Dos Santos, Christine Dos Santos, Marie Doucet, Abderrahmane Douira, Arnaud Drencourt, Laurent Ducourtieux, Marie Ducroc, Bénédicte Duhamel, Ivan Dujic, Niclas Dünnebacke, Antoine Durand, Marie-France Dussaussois, Alex Duzy, Aurélie Eckenschwiller, Peter Edward, Thomas Egret, Miguel Eizmendi Vallés, Elvire Elbourg, Assem El Cheick, Omar El Hassan, Larissa Elschen, Maxime Eon, Alejandro Epstein, Louise Equey, Audrey Errin, Maria Esteban Casanas, Martina Fabris, Raffaella Faccioli, Patrick Fagnoni, Chang Fan, Enrico Fantini, Jérôme Farigoule, Pierre Farkas, Alfio Faro, Valérie Faugeras, Brunello Favilla, Stefan Felber, Ilaria Feltrin, Juan Fernandez Andrino, Anaïs Fernon, Laura Ferreira Sheehan, Évelyne Ferté, Barbara Fetz, Baptiste Fleury, Laurène Flinois, Konstantin Flöhl, Pierre Folens, Sandrine Forget, Andrea Fortunata, Olivier Foucher, Ludivine Foucher, Gabrielle Fournier, Alexandre Franc, Tristan Fricker, Mathias Fritsch, Yaming Fu, Yao Fu, Julien Fuentès, Corinna Fuhr, Shinichi Fukuhara, Mathieu Furlan, Lorenzo Gaetani, Carmelo Gagliano, Romain Galamez, Filippo Galdi, Filippo Galli, Yulia Gandasari, Marcela Garcia, Alvaro Garcia Mendive, Carmen Garcia Pinacho, Laurent Garczynski, Shéhérazade Garmand, Noémi Garrido, Maxime Gaspérini, Alix Gasser, Catriona Gatheral, Caterina Gatti, Valérie Gaydier, Jordan Geiger, Chiara Gelpi, Camille Gerhard, Jérémy Germe, Jeremy Giacomini, Pablo Gil, Sandrine Gill, François Gillet Reto Gmür, Kévin Gillman, Véronique Gillotaux, Paula Gimeno Martinez, Anna Giotakou, Nicolas Girardin, Marine Girault, Bartosz Girek, Sara Girina, Florent Giroguy, Alice Giroux, Theoni Gkesiou, Katerina Gkimizoudi, David Godet, Dimitri Goldenberg, Nilberto Gomes de Souza, Carolina Gomez Muñoz, Anna Gonçalves, Hernan Gonzales Alonso, Alejandro Gonzales Palacios, Cecilia Gonzalez, Maria Gonzalez Oyonart, Marcos Gonzalez Puga, Guillaume Goron, Frank Görge, Leia Gorra, Christina Gortari Chamorro, Katharina Grafi, Gabriel Grandet, Stéphanie Grandjacques, Roger Grass, Camille-Lou Grandrieux, Sébastien Gravier, Constantin Grec, Flavia Greco, Philippe Grégoire, Camille Grégoire, Giulia Grigoli, Nina Grigorieva, Svetla Grigorova, Bernardo Grilli Di Cortona, Gabriel Grandet, Lucie Grimaud, Ulf Grosse, Claire Grossel, Yue Gu, Alban Guého, Nicola Guercilena, Franck Guernieri, Simon Guillemoz, Soner Guner, Chuan Guo, Nicola Gurreiri, Paz Gutierrez Plaza, Frédérick Guy, Serge Guyon, Seyeong Gwan, Andràs Györker, Kristina Hahn, Michael Halter, Philipp Hammesfahr, Florence Hamon, Gwenaël Hamon, Florian Hartmann, Hwang Hee Par, Alix Helard, Luisa Held, Agathe Hemard, Louis Henaux, Evelyn Hendreich, Anna-Ines Hennet, Jorge-Luis Henry, Reiner Herkt, Alicia Hernan Perez, Alfred Heude, Aline Hielscher, Duy Hoang Nguyen, Britta Hohsmann, Sophie-Charlotte Holmlund, Chihiro Homma, Thi Hong Hanh Nguyen, Kotaro Horiuchi, Jan Horst, Pohsien Hou, Weijie Hu, Jean-Jacques Hubert, Christelle-Ségolène Huet, Sarah Hunt, Fatma Hussain, Helmut Hutter, Matteo Ialungo, Caroline Imbert, Tatiana Irintcheeva, Nanako Ishizuka, Louis Isidore, Cyril Issanchou Roman J. Koschut, Philippe Jaby,

Meike Jahn, Jitendra Jain, Arthur Jan, Dominique Jauvin, Charlotte Jean, Julie Jean, Myrlande Jean-Pierre, Kariane Jeaurond, Holm Jellonek, Hyesun Jeong, Gwenaël Jézéquel, Zhi Jian Lin, Alberto Jimenez-Bazo Labrado, Hildegard Jiouo, Thomas Joiret, Caroline Joncourt, Anthony Jorge, Tillmann Jörn Hohenacker, Emma Joynt, Austeja Judzentyte, Christelle Julien, Olivier Jumeau, Ursula Juvan, Dominica Kaczmarczyk, Léonard Kadid, Takayuki Kamei, Sana Kamoun, Hana Kanehisa, Kacper Kania, Anne Kaplan, Tomoko Karakawa, Azadeh Karimi, Abdelkrim Karkach, Genki Kashiwagi, Günter Katherl, Daiki Kato, Mahmut Kemiksiz, Faniel Keppel, Wolfgang Keuthage, David Kevin Longo, Thai Quang Tran, Thi Khanh Anh Tran, Gia Khoa Nguyen, Jouini Khouloud, Tomasz Kieronczyk, Hye-Lee Kim, Hyeseong Kim, Chae-Yeon Kim, Ja Yoon Kim, Jiyeong Kim, Seojung Kim, Tané Kinch, Anette Klatt, Bradley Kligerman, François Koch, Andreas Kofler, Michaël Kohl, Victoria Koppenwallner, Rolf Kopperman, Elena Koropouli, Milana Kosovac, Jack-Louis Kotter, Woyciech Kowalczyk, Katerina Krasteva, Petra Kucerova, Karin Kuhn, Michael Kühnlein, Angelica Kunkler, Martin Kursched, Chanyoung Kwak, Salvatore L'Abbate, Corinne Lafon, Yves Lagache, Christiane Lajeune, Grégory Lalau Keraly, Inés Laloui, Abdallah Lamiri Alaou, Cyril Lancelin, Maryvonne Lanco, Lorena Lannefranque, Catgerine Lanot, Carlos Lapresta, Delphine Larcheres, Thomas Larnicol, David Lasorella, Solène Lavillaureix, Ninon Leal, Filipa Leal de Carvalho, Jean-Jacques Le Berre, Heewon Lee, I-Ting Tina Lee, Yoohnie Lee, Jihye Lee, Jinho Lee, Jinhyuk Lee, Jo Hee Lee, Jun Ho Lee, Junghyun Lee, Mariana Legarve, Pascal Legrand, Alice Legrier, Valérie Lehoucq, Christine Lelong, Jean-Pierre Le Maitre, Philippe Le Moal, Élodie Leneveu, Katarzyna Lesniewska, Simon Lesquelen, Kacem Letaief, Nam Le Toan, Manon Leurant, Aurore Levalois, Ralf Levedag, Mélanie Levet, Michael Levy, Olivier Lidon, Woojin Lim, Klaus Lindenberger, Sara Lipinska, Wenhao Liu, Nacho Lluch, Andy Lockyer, Suzanna Lodde, Aïssa Logerot, Nelly Lopes, Luciola Lopes The Fran, Ramón López Gonzales, Ricardo Lorenzana, Frédéric Louison, Thierry Louvieaux, Gustav Lucas, Jonathan Lucia, Maria Luisa Bongiovann, Irina Lungu, Xiaotian Luo, Lauren Lupa, Alessandro Lunaschi, Nathalie Luyet, Tiago Madeira, Shigeki Maeda, Muriel Maggiol, Baptiste Magnin, Hung-Trung Mai, Nicola Mamel, Gwenaëlle Manach, Natacha Manskowski, Patrice Marchand, Létitia Marcos, Stefania Mariano, Bartlomiej Markowski, Isabelle Marques, Orféo Marques-Mandin, Claire Marrache, Mark-Alexander Marten, Caroline Martin, Elena Martinez Carabello, Maria Isabel Martinez-Cepeda Sevilla, Manuel Martinez Rodriguez, Enrico Martino, Filipe Martins Lourenço, Yves Massardier, Alexandra Da Mata Goncalve, Manuel Mateu Sanchi, Louanne Mayol, Léonor Mayoux, Guillaume Mazars, Giorgia Mazzetti, Piyush Mehra, Stella Melbye, Philip Mellor-Ribet, Isabel Mena, Guilhem Menanteau, Rémi Mendes, Rémi Merchat, Fériel Mestiri, Josiane Mettoudi, Thierry Meunier, Constance Meunier, Frédéric Meurisse, Sofia Micciche, Jérôme Michel, Laura Micheli, Franck Michigan, Julien Milesi, Diana Mingazova, Victor Miton, Martina Dominika Moga, Hugo Moissinac, Jérémy Moles, Stéphane Monfort, Guido Montecchio, Louis Monteils, Alan Moquet, Angelique Morand, Yves Moreau, Guy Morisseau, Alexandre Morizur, Cathy Morot, Joaquín Mosquera, Clara Mosquera Perez, Céline Motte-Moitroux, Jacques Moussafir, Miza Mucciarelli, Caterina Mucignat, Philippe Mueller, Mikel Mujika, Soichi Murai, Thomas Mürrle, Ettore Musso, Caroline Nachtigall-Marten, Filippo Nanni, Heinrich Nau, Frederico Neder, Karine Nedjari, Fabio Negri, Ilga Nelles, Konstanze Neueburg, Matthieu Neufville, Christine Neuhoff, Philipp Neves, Can Nezvat Kutlubey, Richard Nguyen, Thi Hong Hanh Nguyen, Cayetana Nicanor Gonzalez Mulero, Stéphanie Nichols, Kacper Niezabitowki, Mike Nikaes, Georgi Nikolov, Iva Njunjic, Carlos Nogueira De Diego, Marine Norest, Louna Noriega, Misaki Nozawa, Antoine-Frédéric Nunes, Esteban Ochogavia Ascensao, Samuel Odic, Taehun Oh, Taekjun Oh, Jérémy Ohland, Yashuito Ohta, Camille Olsen, Juan Manuel Ortiz Cabeza, Ania Otlik, Marine Oudard, Juan Pablo Paredes Esquivel, Giulia Pace, Ana Maria Padron, Brigitte Paillard, Katia Paola Lopez, Fabio Papandrea, Angeliki Papavasileiou, Arnaud Paquier, Kyoung Park, Cheolgu Park, Hwanghee Park, Kibum Park, Sara Parrinello, Karolina Pawlowska, Léa Pelleteret, Ana Penalba, Ségolène Perennes-Poncet, Morgane Pernot, Vittorio Perotti, Aude Perrault, Christophe Perruche, Camille Petit, Boris Petrovittch Njegos, Monika Pfretzschner, Valérie Phung, Jérôme Picard, Guillaume Picard, Éveline Pichon, Sophie Picoty, Paul Pieffet, Corinne Pierre, Emanuele Piersanti, Léa Pigeon, Pedro Pinto, Geoffroy Piot, Lucas Piquemal, Piero Pivetta, Natalie Plagaro-Cowee, Juliette Planchon, Lars Plugge, Patricia Pluns, Benjamin Porcher, Marcel Portefaix, Guillaume Potel, Iva Potuckova, Leander Praeger, Nicoletta Pramaggiore, Ainoa Prats, Nelly Prazeres Lopes, Rosa Précigout, Delphine Pressevpt, Jules Théodore Prêt, Odile Prigent, Julien Fringuet, Anna Prokudina, René Provost, Marco Punzi, René Puybonnieux, Thai Quang Tra, Andrée Quignon, Sara Quintanilha, Renato Radicella, Vincent Radiguet, Giulia Ragnoli, Carlos Ramirez Pantanella, Astrid Rappel, Neil Rawson, James Read, Martine Recchia, Ute Reh, Patricia Reinhart, Birgit Relsinger, Cédrid Renaud, Hendrix Renonce, Matheus Renno Sartori, François Renson, Panagiota Reppa, François Revel, Julie Revers, Martina Rhür, Nuno Ribeiro, Andreia Ribeiro Dias, Ramona Ribolini, Caterina Ribolla, Léa Richard-Nagle, Christina Ried, Martine Rigaud, Manuel Rigaut, Paolo Righi, Marc-Emmanuel Rihouey, Mariana Riobom Santos, Dominique Rirard, Harold Rivomanana, Teahoon Ro, José Roberto Ramirez Ochoa, Irene Roca Moracia, Dominique Roche-Tessier, Alex Rodriguez, Hella Rolfes, Victor Romero, Bernard Ropa, Marcos Roque, Gilles Roquelaure, Dani Rossello Diez, Alberto Rossetti, Frédérique Roussel, Ludovic Rubbrecht, Manfred Rudolph, Gaëlle Rueff, Sira Ruiz, Lisa Rukavina, Christian Runge, Charlotte Russell, Daniele Russo, Alina Safiullina, Sameh Saad, Alsu Sadrieva, Leilia Sadykova, Éric Saillard, Anne-Virginie Sala, Ramsès Salazar, Mariana Salido Aguilera, Enrico Salvo, Abraham Sancha, Margarita Sanchez, Jakob Sand, Léa Sandberg, Angel San Juan Alvarez, Jérôme Santel, Antoine Santiard, Constanza Santovetti, Roberto Sanz Asensio, Céline Saraiva, Philippe Sarfati, Ileana Savescu, Lavinia Scafi, Stephanie Schleh, Carola Schleiff, Eloisa Schmid, Cornelia Schmitt, Katrin Schmitt, Achim Schneider, Jeffrey Schofield, Kurt Schuessler, Pierre-Yves Schulz, Karin Schumann, Jean-Christophe Schving, Nicolas Schwager, John Sedhom, Matteo Segato, Jung-Soo Seo, Éric Servas, Laurent Sevali Garcia, Iris Sheikh Esmail, Fatih Shakirov, Gentaro Shimada, Derk Sichtermann, Oliver Siekierka, Jan Sienkiewicz, Claudia Siffredi, Kerim Silajdzic, Xavier Simon, Claire Sion, Louis-Grégoire Six, Cris Skenderi, Jan Skuratowski, Elena Slahdji, Christine Sohn, Alexandra Sobczyk, Margaux Solmon, Jooyeon Song, Yooyeong Song, Gaspard Souquiere, Young Soo Kim, Ho Soon Choi, Emmanuel Soyeux, Anne Speicher, Adina Staicu, Petra Steirmayr, Ksenia Stepanova, Élisabeth Stiefel, Daniela Stifter, Bruna Stipanicic, Elke Stoerl, Sandra Stolz, Daniel Sucka, David Tajchman, Tadashi Tamey, Tadashi Tamura, Weikai Tan, Elva Tang, Nicolas Tanquerel, Mohammed-Rabi Tarakji, Jan Taschschingkong, Rémi Taulemesse, Marcello Tavone, Dan Teodorici, Quan Thai, Jérôme Thibault, Simon Thirot, Jacqueline Thition, Sophie Thomas, Olivier Thomas, Veronika Tietmeyer, Yvonne Tietz, Olivier Tinel, Catherine Todaro, Cecilia Tognoni, Ozan Toksoz-Blauel, Patricia Tolentino, Catherine Toporkoff, Michele Torlaschi, Marta Torrecillas Gomez, Sylvain Totaro, Jacques Touchefeu, Iris Toulouse, André Toulouze, Sophie Trelcat, Jeanne Tronquoy, Yumi Tsurumi, Martin Tubiana, Konstantina Tzemou, Anna Ugolini, Marie Urien, Ernesto Urquizar Quesada, Elisabet Uson Maimo, Ryoko Usui, Isaac Vaarzon Morel, Henri Valancogne, Silvia Valencia, Miriam Valiente Ollero De las Nives, Nicolas Valladon, Jerden Van Der Groot, Louis Van-Oost, Radek Vanac, Marie-Pierre Vandeputte, Catherine Vanderslyen, Tiphaine Varigas, Roland Vastra, Pierre Vaubourg, François Vaugoyeau, Stéphanie Vazao Branco, Clara Veci, Richard Veïth, Shriya Verma, Élisa Vernazza, Aurélie Vernon, Nello Verrocchi, Peter Verstraete, Carole Vilet, Roberto Vinante, Francesco Vinci, Ingrid Vindis, Vincent Vinet, Harshil Visrodia, Mariana Volpe, Nora Vorderwinkler, Blin Vose, Inge Waes, Rita Wagner, Brian Wait, Dai Wakabayashi, Guishi Wang, Yan Wang, Birgitt Wassner, Karim Wat, Julien Webb, Tamara Wehner, Gebhard Weißenhorn, Sebastian Welzel, Carlos Wendt Alvarez, Patricia Westerburg, Antoine Weygand, Ewelina Wiciak, Christian Wimmer, Aleksandra Wolffgram, Nichola Woolfenden, Kamil Wrobel, Hao Wu, Chuchu Wu, Yushao Wu, Hanna Wulfing, Marc Wunderlich, Teng Xing, Keita Yamamoto, Takeshi Yamamura, Xinyu Yan, Sizhou Yang, Shenglin Yang, Yino Yang, Yong Yeob Kim, Fook-Wei Yeoh, William Yon, Hajime Yoshida, Airat Zaidullin, Vittoria Zammitti, Lucia Zamponi, Xiaotan Zang, Florentin Zellweger, Hongmei Zhang, Rui Zhang, Xiyuan Zhang, Émilie Zinck, Illaria Zippilli, Gregor Zorzi, Magali Zuercher, Clélia Zurlo, Roberta Zvirblyte.

We apologise for any errors or omissions that may appear in the list of collaborators, despite the care put into drawing it up.

PROJECTS AND ACHIEVEMENTS

SITUATING

MUSEUM CENTER
LAUSANNE
2015

Status: International competition
Location: Place de la Gare 16, Lausanne, Switzerland
Client: État de Vaud, Lausanne
Lead architect: Dominique Perrault Architecte
Interior design: Gaëlle Lauriot-Prévost
Engineer: Basler & Hofmann

Site area: 16,900 m²
Built area: 11,700 m²

Program
The Lausanne Museum Center brings together Photo Élysée (formerly the Musée cantonal pour la photographie) and the Musée de design et d'arts appliqués contemporains (Mudac). Its underground volume accompanies the Musée cantonal des beaux-arts (MCBA), newly built nearby to form a museum complex on a shared site.

USINOR-SACILOR CONFERENCE CENTER
SAINT-GERMAIN-EN-LAYE
1988–91

Status: International competition, winning project
Location: Château de Saint-Léger, Saint-Germain-en-Laye, France
Client: Usinor-Sacilor, Denain
Lead architect: Dominique Perrault Architecte
Consultants: Setec-Foulquier, Arnaud de Bussière

Project area: 4,000 m²

Program
The conference center, dug beneath and around the existing renovated château, accommodates a 200-seat auditorium and exhibition spaces under the glass roof, as well as twelve meeting rooms in the superstructure.

MUSEUM OF ETHNOGRAPHY
BUDAPEST
2016

Status: International competition
Location: Városliget, 1386 Budapest, Hungary
Client: Városliget Zrt., Budapest
Lead architect: Dominique Perrault Architecte

Project area: 26,194 m²

Program
In a 4,558 m² glass prism, the Museum of Ethnography houses reception and information areas that interact directly with the public space. Beneath this prism, a vast foyer, visually open onto the storerooms, links, via large auditoriums, the third and deepest level, which includes the exhibition halls (21,600 m²).

PASSAGE DE L'ÉTOILE – ARC DE TRIOMPHE
PARIS
2017

Status: Competition "Reinventing Paris II-Paris below ground"
Location: Tunnel de l'Étoile, Arc de triomphe, 75008 Paris, France
Client: Ville de Paris et Centre des monuments nationaux, Paris
Consortium leader: Emerige, Paris
Lead architect: Dominique Perrault Architecte
Interior design, signage: Gaëlle Lauriot-Prévost
Landscape design: Vogt
Consultants: Barbanel, Somete, Tribu Énergie, MDS, Jean-Paul Lamoureux, Althing

Built area: 5,300 m²
Length of the tunnel: 380 m

Program
The project proposes to create a new access to the Arc de Triomphe by building a tunnel connected to the Avenue des Champs-Élysées and Avenue de la Grande-Armée. Existing infrastructures will be reinvested to develop new underground circulation areas (3,165 m²), with the reorganization of bicycle lanes and crosswalks, as well as the integration of commercial (1,430 m²) and event spaces (409 m²) and planted areas.

YEULMARU CITY OF CULTURE AND ARTS
YEOSU
2009–12

Status: Commission
Location: Montagne Mangma & Île Jangdo, Yeosu, South Korea
Client: GS Caltex, Seoul
Lead architect: Dominique Perrault Architecte
Local architect: Changjo Architects
Interior design: Gaëlle Lauriot-Prévost

Site area: 70 ha
Project area: 16,000 m²
(+ 10,000 m² parking space)

Program
Set into the hillside landscape, the cultural center includes a large 1,000-seat theater, a small 300-seat theater, 680 square meters of exhibition space, workshops, an energy center, and cafeterias.

EWHA WOMEN'S UNIVERSITY
SEOUL
2004–08

Status: International competition, winning project
Location: 11-1 Daehyundong, Seodaemun-gu, Séoul 120-750, South Korea
Client: Ewha Campus Center Project T/F, Seoul
Lead architect: Dominique Perrault Architecte
Local architect: Baum Architects
Interior design: Gaëlle Lauriot-Prévost
Consultants: VP & Green engineering, HL-PP Consult, Rache-Willms, Jean-Paul Lamoureux
Local consultants: Jeon and Lee Partners, Himec, CG E&C, CnK Associates

Built area: 70,000 m²
Landscaping: 31,000 m²

Program
Founded in 1886, Ewha Women's University is now home to some 25,000 elite female students, and its campus spans 59 hectares. Incorporating a vast public esplanade connected to the city, the Campus Valley project houses a 70,000-square-meter mixed program, both academic (classrooms, amphitheaters, library, computer rooms, study rooms, and public reception and meeting areas) and administrative functions (offices and service premises), as well as numerous related services for site users (restaurants, stores, 750-seat theater, two 162-seat movie theaters, etc.).

LONDON 2012 OLYMPIC VELOPARK
LONDON
2007

Status: International competition
Location: Lower Lea Valley, London, United Kingdom
Client: Olympic Delivery Authority, London
Lead architect: Dominique Perrault Architecte
Interior design: Gaëlle Lauriot-Prévost
Landscape design: Land Use Consultants Ltd.
Consultants: Ove Arup & Partners Ltd., GUS Architekten Ingenieure

METROPOLIS? – VENICE ARCHITECTURE BIENNALE
VENICE
2010

Status: International exhibition
Location: French Pavilion of the 12e Biennale internationale d'architecture, Venice, Italy
Client: Ministère de la Culture et Ministère des Affaires Étrangères et Européennes, Paris
Curator, architect, and scenographer: Dominique Perrault Architecte
Interior design and scenography: Gaëlle Lauriot-Prévost
Curator and editor-in-chief of the magazine ***L'Architecture d'aujourd'hui*****:** Cyrille Poy
Director: Richard Copans, producer and founder of Films d'ici

Program
Transformation of the Pavillon français into a multiplex, with a permanent program of films exploring the question of the metropolis through the study of the cities of Bordeaux, Lyon, Marseille, Nantes, and Saint-Nazaire, as well as the "Grand Paris" project.

CROSSROADS, BUILDING THE RESILIENT CITY – SEOUL BIENNALE OF ARCHITECTURE AND URBAN PLANNING
SEOUL
2019–21

Status: International exhibition
Location: Dongdaemun Design Plaza (DDP), Seoul, South Korea
Client: Seoul Metropolitan Governement, Seoul
General curator and scenographer: Dominique Perrault Architecte

Program
Organization of the 3rd Seoul Biennale, "Crossroads, Building the Resilient City," featuring a series of exhibitions and events structured around five thematic entry points: "Above/Below" (urban planning), "Heritage/Modern" (architecture), "Craft/Digital" (design), "Natural/Artificial" (landscape) and "Safe/Risk" (the city). These themes aimed to explore the world's cities and metropolises. Following a call for ideas, 160 international installations and projects from all five continents were presented. Dominique Perrault, General Director of the Biennial, was also curator of the Biennial's main exhibitions, "Cities" and "Thematic."

HANGANG DISTRICT MASTER PLAN
HANDAN
2020

Status: International consultation, winning project
Location: Usine Hansteel East, Handan, China
Client: Hebei Provincial Housing and Urban & Rural Development Bureau, Hebei Provincial Natural Resources Development Bureau, Handan Municipal People's Government, Handan Natural Resources and Planning Bureau
Lead architect: Dominique Perrault Architecte

Site area: 8.7 km²

Program
The Hansteel East Ironworks urban planning and industrial heritage enhancement project is based on four main principles designed to ensure the coherence of a functional, resilient city deeply rooted in its time: preservation and cultural enhancement of industrial heritage, landscape improvement and creation of new green spaces, optimization and enhancement of water resources through the development of the banks of the Qin River, and the development of mixed, connected and flexible programs.

"ÎLE DE LA CITÉ 2040" MISSION
PARIS
2016

Status: Mission entrusted by President François Hollande
Location: Île de la Cité, Paris, France
Client: Mairie de Paris, entrusted by President François Hollande, Paris
Lead architect: Dominique Perrault, architect and urban planner, and Philippe Bélaval, Président of the Centre des monuments nationaux.

Program
The project explores the future of the Île de la Cité through thirty-five proposals, presented in the form of cartographic fictions, enabling us to envisage the future of this territory by 2040. The aim is to restore the island's role as the beating heart of the capital and the Ile-de-France metropolis.

"HÔTEL MÉTROPOLE"
PARIS
2013

Status: Scientific advisory board, international workshop for research and experimentation
Client: Atelier international du Grand Paris (AIGP), Groupement d'intérêt public (GIP), Paris
Architect and urban planner: Dominique Perrault Architecte
Philosopher: Frédéric Migayrou
Urban planner: Jean-Louis Subileau
Mathematicien: Henri Berestycki
Director and producer: Richard Copans

Program
"Hôtel Métropole" is a research project launched by the Atelier International du Grand Paris (AIGP) to rethink the fragmented map of the Greater Paris metropolis using cartographic fictions. The project's aim is to make use of existing land in anticipation of its eventual mutation, gently infiltrating an urbanity without imposing a unique model of the city.

WRITING

TWIN PEAKS – BONGEUNSA-RO 120
SEOUL
2023–29

Status: International consultation, winning project
Location: Gangnam-gu, Seoul, South Korea
Client: Hyundai E1C/WAD, Seoul
Lead architect: Dominique Perrault Architecte
Local architect: ANU Architects
Interior design: Gaëlle Lauriot-Prévost
Coordination conception: JAD

Site area: 10,300 m²
Built area: 140,000 m²
Elevation: 200 m

Program
"Landscaped-building" consisting of two volumes linked by an active base and hosting a mixed-use program, with a 5-star hotel, offices, shops, a spa, a service residence, and a restaurant.

THE BLADE TOWER B2-2
SEOUL
2011–12

Status: Commission (unrealized)
Location: Tower B2-2 Yongsan International Business Center, Sky Island, Seoul, South Korea
Client: Yongsan Development, Dreamhub Project Financial Investment, Seoul
Lead architect: Dominique Perrault Architecte
Local Architect: SAMOO Architects & Engineers
Interior design: Gaëlle Lauriot-Prévost
Consultants: Bollinger+Grohmann, HI Technik, Jean-Paul Lamoureux

Site area: 2,600 m²
Project area: 131,700 m²

Program
The tower, built in the future Yongsan international business center in Seoul, includes offices, a business forum with reception and conference rooms, a meeting and service center, a fitness lobbym and a panoramic terrace with restaurants, shops, and gardens.

NATIONAL MUSEUM OF ANDORRA
ANDORRA LA VELLA
2009

Status: International competition, winning project (unrealized)
Location: Avenue Meritxell, Andorra la Vella, Andorra Principality
Client: Government of Andorra, Andorra la Vella
Lead architect: Dominique Perrault Architecte
Interior design: Gaëlle Lauriot-Prévost
Engineering: Typsa

Project area: 11,500 m²

Program
Located on the city's main thoroughfare, this new national museum is the region's leading cultural facility, with two exhibition galleries (one for permanent exhibitions, the other for temporary ones) and a specialized library, spread over five floors, as well as a panoramic restaurant.

VINCI HEADQUARTERS
RUEIL-MALMAISON
2009–10

Status: Consultation, winning project (unrealized)
Location: Avenue de Colmar, Rueil-Malmaison, France
Client: Vinci, Paris
Lead architect: Dominique Perrault Architecte

Project area: 60,000 m²
Site area: 8,500 m²
Elevation: 100 m

Program
Public forecourt, private square, conference center, Vinci village (stores, services, businesses), inter-company restaurants, offices, club floor, sky lobby, fitness center, childcare center, terraces, gardens, and parking lots.

HOHES DACH – TECHNICAL ADMINISTRATION BUILDING
DÜSSELDORF
2022

Status: International competition
Location: Moskauer Strass 23, 40227 Düsseldorf, Germany
Client: IPM (Immobilien Projekt Management Düsseldorf GmbH), Düsseldorf
Lead architect: Dominique Perrault Architecte
Associate architect: PSP Weltner Louvieaux Architekten
Consultants: HL-Technik Engineering, Buro Happold Ltd.

Site area: 8,100 m²
Project area: 55,900 m²

Program
Construction of a new technical administration building in Düsseldorf, near the IHZ park and main railway station, to replace the former Auf'm Hennekamp technical town hall. Designed as a bridge building, the new tower will house municipal services and integrate large public spaces.

FUKOKU TOWER
OSAKA
2006–10

Status: International competition, winning project
Location: 2-4, Komatsubara, Kita-ku, Osaka, Japon
Client: Fukoku Mutual Life Insurance Company, Osaka
Lead architect: Dominique Perrault Architecte
Local architect: Shimizu Corporation Ltd.
Interior design: Gaëlle Lauriot-Prévost
Consultant: Mitsubishi Estate Group

Site area: 3,900 m²
Built area: 53,280 m² (excluding parking space)
Elevation: 133 m, 3 stories

Program
At the exit of Osaka's main railway station, a 32-story tower, 28 above ground and 4 underground (excluding parking lots), stands out in the urban landscape. It includes 40,000 m² of office space, a 5,000 m² retail area, 4,000 m² of university laboratories, a lobby, and parking lots.

CITYLIFE RESIDENCES
MILAN
2011

Status: International competition
Location: Largo Domodossola, Milan, Italy
Client: Citylife SRL, Milan
Lead architect: Dominique Perrault Architecte
Consultants: Redesco, Arcora

Project area: 60,000 m²

Program
Hotel, commercial activities, housing, sports facilities, and offices.

VULCANO
ZURICH
2012–18

Status: International competition, winning project
Location: Vulkanstrasse 110, BASF-Areal, Zurich-Alstetten, Suisse
Client: Steiner AG + Crédit Suisse, Zurich
Lead architect: Dominique Perrault Architecte
Partner: Itten+Brechbühl SA

Site area: 12,100 m²
Project area: 50,000 m²
Elevation: 80 m

Program
The three-tower complex is divided into several programs. The plinth, extending from the ground to the fifth floor, houses a 16,000 m² hotel and 1,000 m² of retail and office space. Above the plinth, three identical towers rise from the sixth to the 25th floor to house 300 apartments spread over 25,000 m². Vulcano also includes a large 5,000 m² garden, public passageways, and car and bicycle parking.

DUNAMU HEADQUARTERS
SEOUL
2023–28

Status: Commission
Location: 168-1, 2, 20 Samsaeong-dong, Gangnam-gu, Seoul, South Korea
Client: Capstone Asset Management Co. Ltd, Seoul
Lead architect: Dominique Perrault Architecte
Local architect: Samoo Architects & Engineers
Interior design: Gaëlle Lauriot-Prévost
Consultants: Arup

Project area: 32,000 m²
Elevation: 180 m

Program
The building is designed as a vertical village, with three blocks each housing a specific part of the program. Lobbies to offices, retail and public spaces, as well as a new Dunamu Foundation are located in the lower block, or urban block. The middle block, or city block, houses the main Dunamu offices. The upper block, or sky block, houses conference rooms, dining areas, and a roof top.

LA LIBERTÉ
GRONINGEN
2007–11

Status: Commission
Location: Laan van de Vrijheid, Groningen, Netherlands
Client: Christelijke Woningstichting Patrimonium, Groningen
Lead architect: Dominique Perrault Architecte
Associate architect: Oving Architekten
Interior design: Gaëlle Lauriot-Prévost
Consultants: Dijkhuis, Zonderman B.V., Feenestra, Geveke Bouw B.V.

Site area: 20,000 m²
Tower A: 13,000 m², 80 m, 22 floors
Tower B: 5,000 m², 40 m, 10 floors

Program
La Liberté comprises two buildings, each set on a glass base. They are linked by a footbridge on the third floor and house a mixed-use program comprising residential units (some of which are social housing), a hotel, and offices on the lower level. On the first floor the project includes an ecological garden and a green public space.

HOCHHAUS GATE 2
VIENNA
2014

Status: Competition
Location: Guglgasse 2-4, Vienne, Austria
Client: Austria Immobilien GmbH, Vienne
Lead architect: Dominique Perrault Architecte

Site area: 2,400 m²
Project area: 32,000 m²
Elevation: 120 m, 36 floors

Program
Office, residential, and retail building.

TIMBER MARINA TOWER
VIENNA
2019–28

Status: International competition, winning project
Location: Donaumarina, Vienna, Austria
Client: UBM Development, Vienna
Lead architect: Dominique Perrault Architecte
Partner: Hoffmann & Janz Architects
Interior design: Gaëlle Lauriot-Prévost
Consultants: Bollinger+Grohmann, EUrban, Ingenieurbüro Lakata

Site area: 1,500 m²
Built area: 44,350 m²
Elevation: 110 m, 32 floors

Program
Located in Vienna's Handelskai district, in the waterfront development zone, the Timber Marina Tower will be one of the tallest wooden skyscrapers in the world. Served directly by the Donaumarina U2 metro station, the tower is a ten-minute drive from the city center and airport, and houses a program of offices, shops, restaurants, and parking lots.

ARC OF LIGHT – NONHYUN 114
SEOUL
2024–29

Status: Commission
Location: Gangnam-gu, Seoul, South Korea
Client: Podo Private Residences Seoul Interiors by Fendi Casa, Seoul
Lead architect: Dominique Perrault Architecte
Local architect: Furum Architecture Engineering Construction & Interior Design et Maxtect Architects
Interior design: Gaëlle Lauriot-Prévost, Ewai Interiors

Site area: 3,200 m²
Project area: 3[illegible],350 m²

Program
Luxury residential units with restaurant, coffeeshop, spa, and wellness center.

DYAD – ONE CHEONGDAM-DONG
SEOUL
2022–25

Status: Commission (unrealized)
Location: 1 Cheongdam-dong, Gangnam-gu, Seoul, South Korea
Client: Aster Development
Lead architect: Dominique Perrault Architecte
Associate architect: ANU architects
Interior design: Gaëlle Lauriot-Prévost

Site area: 800 m²
Project area: 5,[illegible] m²
Elevation: 90 m

Program
Luxury residential units with spa, pool, concierge service, studio offices, restaurant, and showroom.

DANCING TOWER – EUROVEA CITY
BRATISLAVA, SLOVAKIA
2024

Status: International competition
Location: Pribinova, Bratislava, Slovakia
Client: JTRE, Bratislava
Lead architect: Dominique Perrault Architecte
Consultant: Bollinger+Grohmann

Site area: 11,400 m²
Project area: 77,200 m²

Program
Erected on the banks of the Danube, this sculptural tower, designed for mixed use, consists mainly of housing, including high-end units, as well as commercial space at the base of the building, leisure areas, and a landscaped park.

DONAU CITY TOWER I
VIENNA
2002–14

Status: International urban planning competition, winning project
Location: Donau-City, Vienna, Austria
Client: WED Wiener Entwicklungsgesellschaft für den Donauraum AG, Vienna
Lead architect: Dominique Perrault Architecte
Partner: Hoffmann & Janz Architects
Interior design: Gaëlle Lauriot-Prévost
Consultants: Bollinger+Grohmann, Gmeiner Haferl Zivilingenieure ZT GmbH, Werner Sobek Ingenieure, ZFG – Projekt, Dr Pfeiler GmbH, Eipeldauer & Partner Ges.m.b.H, AXIS, Ingenieursleistungen ZT GmbH, Wacker Ingenieure

Built area: 229,000 m²
Elevation: 250 m (220 m + 30 m antenna)

Program
A 60-story tower comprising 40,000 m² of office space over 33 floors, a 4-star hotel (254 rooms), 16 duplex apartments (2,400 m²), a sky bar, restaurants on the 57th floor, and an underground parking lot.

DONAU CITY TOWER II
VIENNA
2002–27

Status: International urban planning competition, winning project
Location: Donau-City, Vienna, Austria
Client: Groupe S+B, Vienne
Investor: Commerz Real, Wiesbaden
Lead architect and urban planner: Dominique Perrault Architecte
Partner: Hoffmann & Janz Architects
Interior design: Gaëlle Lauriot-Prévost
Consultants: Gmeiner Haferl & Partner ZT GmbH, ZFG Projekt GmbH, Kunz GmbH, Dr. Pfeiler ZT GmbH

Built area: 59,000 m²
Elevation: 175 m, 53 stories

Program
Mixed-use tower with 36,000 m² of office and coworking space, 470 apartments totaling 23,000 m², and 1,200 m² of retail and restaurant space.

TO-LYON
LYON
2012–24

Status: Commission
Location: Boulevard Vivier-Merle, Lyon Part-Dieu, France
Client: Vinci Immobilier d'entreprise, Lyon
Lead architect: Dominique Perrault Architecte
Infrastructure architect: Sud Architectes
Interior design: Gaëlle Lauriot-Prévost
Consultants: Egis Bâtiments, Barbanel, Setec TPI, Arcora, AE75, Etamine, GLI, Bérim, Bureau Veritas, Cronos Conseil, Socotec

Project area: 80,000 m²
Elevation: 170 m, 43 stories on an 8-story base

Program
Mixed-use real estate program at the heart of the Part-Dieu multimodal hub, featuring 66,000 m² of office and coworking space, a 168-room 4-star Pullman hotel, and a 3,500 m² active base dedicated to shops, lobbies, and services.

PARISLONGCHAMP HIPPODROME
PARIS
2011–18

Status: International competition, winning project
Location: Route des Tribunes, 75116 Paris, France
Client: France Galop, Boulogne-Billancourt
Lead architect: Dominique Perrault Architecte
Interior design: Gaëlle Lauriot-Prévost
Landscape design: Ter
Consultants: Tractebel, Grontmij, RPO, Renaud Pierard, Jean-Paul Lamoureux, Denis Thélot

Site area: 63 ha
Lawn surface: 55,000 m², including 35,000 restored m²

Program
The ParisLongchamp Hippodrome covers an area of 92,000 m²: 22,000 m² are built-up and 70,000 m² are landscaped, with the buildings and gardens forming a single whole. The new Jockey-Club grandstand, with a seating capacity of 10,000 in tiers and including restaurants, terraces, reception lounges, bars, brasseries, and areas dedicated to the press and staff, opens on both sides and offers a 360-degree view of the tracks on one side and the presentation ring on the other. The Pavillon d'Honneur, the renovation and extension of the stables, the presentation ring, the Pavillon des Balances, the Pavillon de Suresnes, and the riding arena—programs related to the grandstand—are linked by the Planches, a 5,500 m² promenade 4.5 meters above ground level, the backbone of the new racecourse. The project also includes the refurbishment of the administrative pavilion and the "totalisateur."

SEJONG INTERNATIONAL GARDEN CITY EXHIBITION
SEJONG
2024–26

Status: Competition (unrealized)
Location: Garden City, Sejong, South Korea
Client: Ville de Sejong, Sejong
Lead architect: Dominique Perrault Architecte
Partner: Baum Architects

Project area: 1,500 m²

Program
Observation lookout made of a 20 m-high structure with a ramp leading to a suspended platform stretching crosswise to the four points of the compass, offering unparalleled views of the botanical exhibition.

KINDARENA
ROUEN
2006–12

Status: International competition, winning project
Location: 40, rue de Lillebonne, Rouen, France
Client: Métropole Rouen Normandie (CREA), Rouen
Lead architect: Dominique Perrault Architecte
Interior design, signage: Gaëlle Lauriot-Prévost
Consultants: Khephren Ingénierie, Alto Ingénierie, RPO, Jean-Paul Lamoureux

Built area: 17,000 m²

Program
The Palais des Sports is envisaged as an urban-planning project. Its interior topography, made up of tiered steps, is reflected in the organization of its surroundings, which open onto the city and provide access to a public esplanade. At the heart of the building are a 4,400 m² modular hall (capacity 6,000 spectators), a 1,700 m² secondary gymnasium (capacity 1,010 spectators), a weights room, warm-up areas and changing rooms, offices, press rooms, and a private area.

ARGANZUELA FOOTBRIDGE
MADRID
2008–11

Status: Commission following an international competition for the development of the banks of the Manzanares river
Location: Parque de la Arganzuela, Madrid, Spain
Client: City of Madrid, Madrid
Lead architect: Dominique Perrault Architecte
Lighting: Gaëlle Lauriot-Prévost
Consultants: MC2/Julio Martínez Calzón, TYPSA, Jean-Paul Lamoureux

Site area: 10 ha
Built area: 1, 684 m²
Dimensions: 158 m (South section), 132 m (North section) in length, width variable, between 6.4 and 12.9 m
Weight: 1,348 tons

Program
The footbridge across Arganzuela Park connects the two banks of the Manzanares, providing a comfortable passage for pedestrians and cyclists. It includes leisure activities and food services and provides a fluid connection with the green spaces it overlooks.

NEW MECHANICAL HALL (ME), ÉCOLE POLYTECHNIQUE FÉDÉRALE DE LAUSANNE (EPFL)
LAUSANNE
2011–16

Status: International competition, winning project
Location: Campus of the EPFL, Route cantonale 1015, Lausanne, Switzerland
Client: Swiss Confederation represented by the Conseil des Écoles Polytechniques
Delegate: École Polytechnique Fédérale de Lausanne (EPFL), Lausanne
Lead architect: Dominique Perrault Architecte
Project conceived/constructed with the Groupe Steiner
Local architect: Architram
Interior design, signage: Gaëlle Lauriot-Prévost
Consultants: Préface Sarl, Betica SA, Daniel Willi SA, d'Silence SA, Duchein SA, Jean-Paul Lamoureux

Built area: 20,800 m²

Program
The Mechanical Hall houses a number of research laboratories: heat and mass transfer, industrial energy, fluid mechanics, mechanical engineering, intelligent systems, robotic systems, as well as a neuroprosthesis center, common areas for students (50-seat auditorium, seminar rooms, dining halls, etc.), and administrative offices.

TEACHING BRIDGE, ÉCOLE POLYTECHNIQUE FÉDÉRALE DE LAUSANNE (EPFL)
LAUSANNE
2011–19

Status: International competition, winning project (unrealized)
Location: EPFL Campus, Route cantonale 1015, Lausanne, Switzerland
Client: Swiss Confederation represented by the Conseil des Écoles Polytechniques
Delegate: École Polytechnique Fédérale de Lausanne (EPFL), Lausanne
Lead architect: Dominique Perrault Architecte
Project conceived/constructed with the Steiner Group
Consultants: Felix construction, Daniel Willi SA, Tecnoservice, Duchein SA

Surface area: 16,000 m²

Program
Multi-level footbridge built over Avenue Picard, housing teaching spaces, part of EPFL's central services, laboratories for the Faculty of Engineering Sciences and Techniques, and a neuroprosthesis center.

SHANGHAI LIBRARY
SHANGHAI
2016

Status: International competition
Location: Century Avenue, Pudong District, Shanghai, China
Client: Pudong New Area Planning and Development Authority, Pudong New District Propaganda Department, Shanghai Architectural Society, *Time Architecture* magazine, Shanghai
Lead architect: Dominique Perrault Architecte
Interior design: Gaëlle Lauriot-Prévost
Consultants: Arup, Jean-Paul Lamoureux

Project area: 110,000 m²

Program
The new Shanghai Library combines its function as a public library with amphitheaters, exhibition rooms, a specialized research center, innovation spaces, and storage areas. At the heart of the project, a large reading plaza establishes a direct visual link with the outside environment.

GRAND THÉÂTRE
ALBI
2009–14

Status: International competition, winning project
Location: Place de l'Amitié-Entre-Les-Peuples, Albi, France
Client: Ville d'Albi, Albi
Lead architect: Dominique Perrault Architecte
Local architect: Christian Astruc Architectes
Interior design: Gaëlle Lauriot-Prévost
Consultants: VP & Green engineering, ETCO, RPO, Changement à vue, Jean-Paul Lamoureux

Site area: 34,000 m²
Built are: 18,000 m²

Program
The Grand Théâtre-Scène nationale d'Albi-Tarn comprises a 900-seat main auditorium, a 250-seat experimental auditorium, a lower entrance foyer and an upper foyer, as well as administrative and logistical areas and an independent panoramic restaurant. The Grand Théâtre also includes an 8-screen cinema complex with a 7,800 m2 infrastructure. The urban design of the Place du Théâtre, Place de l'Athanor, and Place de Lapérouse accompanies the building in its environment, incorporating a work by artist Jeppe Hein.

CONVENTION CENTER AND EXHIBITION HALL
LEÓN
2005–18

Status: International competition, winning project
Location: Avenida del doctor Fleming, León, Spain
Client: City of León, León
Lead architect: Dominique Perrault Architecte
Interior design, signage: Gaëlle Lauriot-Prévost

Site area: 25,000 m²
Built area: 12,700 m²
Urban planning: 30 000 m²

Program
The 12,700 m² exhibition hall can be divided into three 3,000 m² modular sections. The project includes the renovation of part of a former sugar refinery into a small convention center, with a 1,400 m² temporary exhibition space and cafeteria. These buildings form part of the overall urban restructuring of the site, which was created when land formerly occupied by railway tracks was cleared.

PAVILLON DUFOUR
CHÂTEAU DE VERSAILLES
2011–16

Status: International competition, winning project
Location: Château de Versailles, Versailles, France
Client: Opérateur du Patrimoine et des Projets Immobiliers de la Culture (OPPIC) – Établissement public du Château de Versailles, Versailles
Lead architect: Dominique Perrault Architecte
Chief Architect for Historic Monuments: Frédéric Didier
Interior design: Gaëlle Lauriot-Prévost
Consultants: Khephren Ingénierie, Inex SAS Ingénierie, RPO, Thomas Vallette ECBA, Jean-Paul Lamoureux

Project area: 2,900 m²

Program
Restructuring of the Pavillon Dufour to accommodate on the garden level, the entrance and reception area for individual visitors and the information area; on the second floor, Alain Ducasse's Ore restaurant; in the attic, a 150-seat auditorium with interpreters' booths and seminar rooms. The first floor houses the store of the Réunion des Musées Nationaux (RMN), in the château's former cisterns, part of the restaurant's kitchens built in new spaces dug beneath the courtyard, and a grand marble staircase linking the pavilion to the Cour des Princes.

AÉROGARE DES INVALIDES, FONDATION GIACOMETTI
PARIS
2017–30

Status: "Réinventer Paris II – Les dessous de Paris" competition, winning project
Location: Site de l'esplanade des Invalides, quai d'Orsay, 75007 Paris, France
Client: EN Invalides
Lead architect: Dominique Perrault Architecte
Chief Architect for Historic Monuments: Pierre-Antoine Gatier
Interior design: Gaëlle Lauriot-Prévost
Landscape design: Louis Benech
Consultants: Somete, Arcora, Inex, Planibat, MDC Consulting, ODC, Axio, Artelia, Althing, Elan, LM3C, Qualiconsult, Eva, Jean-Paul Lamoureux

Site area: 8,440 m²
Project area: 7,820 m²
Surface of the Aérogare : 4 530 m²
Surface under the Invalides: 3,300 m²

Program
Transformation of the former Invalides air terminal into an innovative building respectful of its history, to house the Fondation Alberto-et-Annette-Giacometti museum. The refurbishment of the terminal is accompanied by the creation of two catering areas under the Invalides esplanade, including the restaurant Chez Françoise, as well as workshops, offices, and a sensory room, operated by the Fondation Giacometti.

POSTE DU LOUVRE
PARIS
2012–21

Status: International competition, winning project
Location: 52, rue du Louvre, 75001 Paris, France
Client: SCI Tertiaire Mixte, Poste Immo, Paris
Lead architect: Dominique Perrault Architecte
Chief Architect for Historic Monuments: Jean-François Lagneau
Interior design: Gaëlle Lauriot-Prévost
Landscape design: Après La Pluie
Consultants: Calq Architectures, Edeis, RPO, Jean-Paul Lamoureux

Site area: 8,240 m²
Built area: 50,069 m²

Program
The restructuring of this historic building, designed and built by architect Julien Guadet (1834–1908) during the Third Republic, will modernize the activities of the historic post office, which remains on the block, and will accommodate offices, social housing, shops, and a five-star rooftop hotel with views of the Eiffel Tower.

COURT OF JUSTICE OF THE EUROPEAN UNION (CJ4), PHASE 1
LUXEMBOURG
1996–2008

Status: International consultation, winning team
Location: Plateau du Kirchberg, Luxembourg, Grand-Duché de Luxembourg
Client: Court of Justice of the European Communities, Administration of Public Buildings, Luxembourg
Lead architect: Dominique Perrault Architecte
Associate architect: Paczowski & Fritsch, m3 architectes
Interior design: Gaëlle Lauriot-Prévost
Consultants: Jacoby & Associés SA, Schroeder & Associés SA, TR-Engineering SA, Felgen & Associés SA, Bevilacqua & Associés SA, Ralf Rache, Jean Schmit Engineering SARL, RMC-consulting, Cabinet Casso et Cie, AIB Vinçotte, Secolux, Jean-Paul Lamoureux

Built area: 100,000 m²

Program
The Court of Justice of the European Union is the only European institution to have built and rebuilt itself since the construction of the palace on the Kirchberg plateau in 1973 by architects Jean-Paul Conzemius, François Jamagne, and Michel Vander Elst.
This is the Court's fourth extension:
– old palace: complete renovation and elevation of 20,168 m², comprising 5 courtrooms, including a large protocol room (41 members and 300 seats), interpreters' booths, deliberation rooms, and the Salle des Pas Perdus;
– the ring: 16,851 m² for the offices of the forty member cabinets;
– the towers: 34,208 m² for the two 24-storey office towers (107 m high) dedicated to translation services, with 1,000 staff providing translations in 23 languages;
– buildings at the foot of the towers: 5,079 m² for administrative offices, ancillary services, and archives;
– the gallery: extension of the existing gallery designed by architects Paul Fritsch and Bohdan Paczowski, a 24,132 m² space that includes company restaurants, a library (84 reading places, 7.5 km of shelving), classrooms, lounges, and public facilities (kiosks, banks, etc.).

COURT OF JUSTICE OF THE EUROPEAN UNION (CJ8), PHASE 2
LUXEMBOURG
2014–19

Status: Direct commission under authorship rights
Location: Plateau du Kirchberg, Luxembourg, Grand-Duché de Luxembourg
Client: Ministry of Sustainable Development, Administration of Public Buildings, Court of Justice of the European Communities, Luxembourg
Lead architect: Dominique Perrault Architecte
Partners: SRA Architectes, Paris/ Jean Petit Architectes, Luxembourg (MOE)
Interior design: Gaëlle Lauriot-Prévost
Consultants: Ney & Partners, Felgen et Associés Engineering SA, Sorane SA, Betavi Ingénieurs Conseils SA, Terrell, Secolux SA, D3 Coordination SA, Pricewaterhouse Coopers, Jean-Paul Lamoureux

Built area: 50,000 m²

Program
The third tower and gallery of this fifth extension follow from the fourth extension, delivered in 2008. The third tower differs from the first two: its layout is slightly offset from the original orthogonal plan, and two slender volumes are juxtaposed. It houses the translators' offices and the institution's services.

GRANDES ÉCURIES OF THE CHATEAU DE CHANTILLY
CHANTILLY
2017

Status: Preliminary study for the Musée du Cheval (unrealized)
Location: Domaine de Chantilly, Chantilly
Client: Domaine de Chantilly, commissioned by prince Aga Khan IV, Chantilly
Lead architect: Dominique Perrault Architecte

Project area: 11,840 m²

Program
The Program includes stables (3,240 m²), the restoration of the Manège (1,250 m²) and the Chenils (2,480 m²), the creation of a tented theater (2,060 m²) and the Musée du Cheval (3,500 m²). It will also incorporate a central square with shops and seminar facilities (1,890 m²), administrative offices (1,200 m²) and rental offices (2,010 m²).

LANDSCAPE TOWER
PUTEAUX-LA DÉFENSE
2015–21

Status: Competition, winning project
Location: 6, place des Degrés, Puteaux-La Défense, France
Client: Altarea Cogedim Entreprises, Paris
Lead architect: Dominique Perrault Architecte
Interior design: Gaëlle Lauriot-Prévost
Consultants: Builders & Partners, Syntesia, Aedis, Gesys, 2F2I, GV Ingénierie, Arcora, Avel Acoustique, Convergence, Apex, Green Affair, Artelia, Socotec

Project area: 72,500 m²
(including a 6,600 m² extension to the original footprint)
Elevation: 100 m, 30 floors

Program
Initially comprised of two office towers designed by Henri La Fonta, the Pascal Towers have now been reunited and transformed into a single complex known as Landscape. This restructuring project involves merging the two volumes into a single building, raising the building by two floors, building the gap between the two original towers, redesigning the lobby, and creating two patios, a conference center with a 200-seat auditorium, and dining areas. This transformation includes a significant improvement in energy performance, with the complete removal of the façades in favor of high-performance envelopes incorporating loggias.

CITYLIGHTS
BOULOGNE-BILLANCOURT
2007–16

Status: International competition, winning project
Location: 204, rond-point du Pont-de-Sèvres, Boulogne-Billancourt, France
Client: SAS des Tours du Pont-de-Sèvres-BNP Paribas Real Estate, Boulogne-Billancourt
Lead architect: Dominique Perrault Architecte
Interior design, architecture, and lighting ("1 immeuble, 1 œuvre" charter) : Gaëlle Lauriot-Prévost
Decoration of service area: Didier Gomez
Consultants: Egis Bâtiments, Eppag, AVLS, AADT, Socotec, Jean-Paul Lamoureux

Built area: 85,400 m² (75,000 m² for the renovation, 10,400 m² for the extension).

Program
Renovation and extension of the Pont-de-Sèvres office towers built in the 1970s by architects Daniel Badani (1914–2006) and Pierre Roux-Dorlut (1919–1995). Creation of a large 1,500 m² lobby, a second entrance to the Forum district, a large restaurant terrace, and a half-hectare garden. The urban evolution of the district and new uses are now examining the hall, which will be redeveloped in autumn 2025, for investors Pimco Prime Real Estate and Gecina.

SUZANNE-LENGLEN COURT COVERAGE
PARIS
2020–24

Status: conception/construction competition, winning project
Location: Roland-Garros, 2, avenue Gordon-Bennett, 75016 Paris, France
Client: Fédération française de tennis (FFT) + Société de livraison des ouvrages olympiques (Solideo), Paris
Contractor: Renaudat Centre Constructions
Subcontractor: Ramery, Taiyo
Lead architect: Dominique Perrault Architecte
Consultants/partners: T/E/S/S, Louise Choulet, Calcul-Meca, Jean-Paul Lamoureux, Element's Ingénieries, Mozaïc, Axio, Aur Blanc

Surface of the permanent roof: 5,200 m²
Surface of the mobile roof: 4,800 m²

Program
Creation of a mobile cover for the Suzanne-Lenglen court to enable tennis matches to be held in rainy weather. Court Suzanne-Lenglen also hosted the boxing and tennis events during the Paris 2024 Olympic and Paralympic Games.

EUROPEAN PARLIAMENT – PAUL-HENRI-SPAAK BUILDING
BRUSSELS
2020

Status: International competition
Location: European quarter, Brussels, Belgium
Client: European Parliament, Brussels
Lead architect: Dominique Perrault Architecte
Associate architect: DDS+
Interior design: Gaëlle Lauriot-Prévost
Consultants: Ney & Partners, HL-PP Consult International Ingenieurgesellschaft mbH, Sorane SA, Arcora, Jean-Paul Lamoureux, Urban Eco

Site area: 17,900 m²
Surface area: 90,900 m²

Program
The project aims to renovate and extend the Paul-Henri-Spaak building, headquarters of the European Parliament designed in 1993 by Michel Boucquillon. Respecting its postmodern identity, the intervention retains the emblematic structural elements for aesthetic and ecological reasons. The envelope has been completely rethought and the structure reconfigured to offer new spatial dynamics. On the roof, a vast dome and terraced gardens complete the building, affirming its institutional and open dimension.

BANK FOR INTERNATIONAL SETTLEMENTS (BIS)
BASEL
2021

Status: International competition
Location: Centralbahnplatz 2, 4051 Basel, Switzerland
Client: Bank of International Settlements (BIS), Basel
Lead architect: Dominique Perrault Architecte
Consultants: Urban Eco, Sorane, HL-Technik, Basler & Hofmann, Gruner

Surface area of the existing tower: 23,000 m²
Elevation of the existing tower: 69.5 m
Surface of the phase 1 and 2 extensions: 45,000 m²
Total elevation of the tower, phases 1 and 2: 195 m
Surface area: 68,000 m²

Program
The extension and modernization of the BIS tower, designed by Martin Burckhardt in the 1970s, takes the form of a twin building connected to the historic building by a shared plinth. The first phase of the extension will bring employees together on a single site, providing 680 additional workstations. A second, subsequent phase will increase this capacity by raising the height of the new tower. Working comfort is enhanced by natural lighting and ventilation, panoramic views and modular meeting and conference rooms equipped with the latest technology.

MÉTAL 57
BOULOGNE-BILLANCOURT
2015–22

Status: Commission
Location: 67, quai Georges-Gorse, 92100 Boulogne-Billancourt, France
Client: BNP Paribas Immobilier, Boulogne-Billancourt
Lead architect: Dominique Perrault Architecte
Interior design and lighting: Gaëlle Lauriot-Prévost
Consultants: Khephren Ingénierie, Barbanel, Arcora, Delporte Aumond Laigneau, Arcadis Esg, Jean-Paul Lamoureux

Site area: 15,127 m²
Built area: 37,900 m²

Program
Designed by architect Claude Vasconi (1940–2009) and delivered in 1984, Métal 57 housed the workshops of the Renault factory. The transformation of the hall and its sheds, framing a new eight-story prism, creates a complex adapted to today's tertiary uses, with offices, catering services, auditoriums, reception areas, and shared landscaped spaces. The complex, previously inward-looking, is now open to the city, thanks in particular to a walk-through interior street accessible to the public.

CENTRE POMPIDOU
PARIS
2024

Status: International competition
Location: Place Georges-Pompidou, 75004 Paris, France
Client: Centre National d'Art et de Culture Georges-Pompidou, Paris
Client's representative: Opérateur du Patrimoine et des Projets Immobiliers de la Culture (Oppic), Paris
Lead architect: Dominique Perrault Architecte
Interior design: Gaëlle Lauriot-Prévost
Scenic design: Cookies
Landscape design: Bureau Bas Smets
Consultants: Buro Happold, Igrec Ingénierie, dUCKS scénc, Atelier Franck Boutté, Cycle Up, Jean-Paul Lamoureux, The Street Society, Axio

Surface area: 72,000 m²

Program
The project involves the complete restructuring of the base of the Centre Georges-Pompidou, a building designed in 1977 by Renzo Piano and Richard Rogers. It aims to reorganize the public and cultural spaces—reception, performances, exhibitions, shops, restaurants, and book store—while renovating the Brancusi pavilion and the Bibliothèque publique d'information (BPI) and relocating the Kandinsky library. The project also includes the creation of a new-generation center, a panoramic terrace, the restructuring of basement workspaces, the redevelopment of logistical areas, and the replacement of Restaurant Georges by an event space.

APLIX
LE CELLIER-SUR-LOIRE
1997–99

Status: International consultation, winning team
Location: Zone d'activités
Les Relandières, Le Cellier-sur-Loire, France
Client: Aplix SA, Paris
Lead architect: Dominique Perrault Architecte
Interior design: Gaëlle Lauriot-Prévost
Consultants: Boplan Ingénierie

Built area: 30,000 m^2

Program
Construction of a woven hook-and-loop fastener factory comprising production and heat-setting workshops, storage areas, laboratories, administrative and social premises, a cafeteria, a restaurant, a shipping and delivery dock (11 stations), and a technical module for the production of electrical energy, heat, and compressed air. The site's landscaping is an integral part of its architecture.

APLIX EXTENSION
LE CELLIER-SUR-LOIRE
2016–20

Status: Direct commission under authorship rights
Location: Zone d'activités
Les Relandières, Le Cellier-sur-Loire, France
Client: Aplix SA, Paris
Lead architect: Dominique Perrault Architecte

Built area: 18,800 m^2

Program
The extension to the Aplix factory, originally designed by Dominique Perrault in 1999, increases the total surface area from 30,000 to 48,800 m^2. The new complex houses industrial areas, a research and development center, as well as a number of facilities dedicated to employees' well-being: a dining room, a sports hall, a rest room, a training area, and an amphitheater.

HÔTEL INDUSTRIEL BERLIER
PARIS
1985–90

Status: National competition, winning project
Location: 26-34, rue Bruneseau, 75013 Paris, France
Maître d'ouvrage: Société anonyme de gestion immobilière (Sagi), Paris
Maître d'œuvre: Dominique Perrault Architecte
Consultants: Technip, Planitec

Site area: 4,700 m^2
Project area: 21,000 m^2

Program
The Hôtel Industriel Berlier, halfway between office and industrial premises, comprises 15,000 m^2 spread over ten levels. It accommodates some forty companies in open-plan structures, and also includes company restaurants and parking facilities.

REFURBISHMENT OF THE HÔTEL INDUSTRIEL BERLIER
PARIS
2014–22
Status: Consultation, winning project
Location: 26-34, rue Bruneseau, 75013 Paris, France
Client: Régie immobilière de la Ville de Paris (RIVP), Paris
Lead architect: Dominique Perrault Architecte
Interior design: Gaëlle Lauriot-Prévost
Consultants: Axio, Edeis, Arcora, Jean-Paul Lamoureux, Atelier Franck Boutté, Frédéric Baudrin

Surface area: 15,912 m^2

Program
The refurbishment of the Hôtel Industriel Berlier, designed by Dominique Perrault and delivered in 1990, transforms this building into a complex of offices and workshops for 1,000 occupants, while updating comfort and energy performance to 2020 standards. Levels RDJ to R+1 house the LEM/LER municipal laboratories, specialized in testing urban materials and equipment. The sixth floor is dedicated to the Rocal pharmaceutical laboratories. Levels R+2 to R+8 (excluding R+6) are home to companies, start-ups, and incubators, in partnership with the City of Paris and local players.

THE VERTICAL CITY – MONTPARNASSE TOWER
PARIS
2016

Status: International competition
Location: 33, avenue du Maine, 75015 Paris, France
Client: Ensemble Immobilier Tour Maine-Montparnasse
Lead architect: Dominique Perrault Architecte
Consultants: Ingerop, Arcora, Transsolar, Jean-Paul Lamoureux, DAL, Omega

Site area: 3,023 m^2
Project area: 150,000 m^2

Program
The project to transform the Tour Montparnasse, designed in 1973 by architects Jean Saubot, Eugène Beaudouin, Urbain Cassan, and Louis de Hoÿm de Marien, calls for the creation of an E+ positive-energy vertical city, hosting a diversity of uses (offices, shops, housing, etc.), as well as tourist areas including a hotel, restaurant, and belvedere.

BIBLIOGRAPHY

DOMINIQUE PERRAULT BOOKS AND MONOGRAPHS

Belmont, Joseph. *Dominique Perrault.* Gros Plan, no. 11. Paris: Institut français d'architecture/Pandora, 1991. 64 pp.

Bernardo, Jordi. *MPreis by Dominique Perrault.* Barcelona: Actar, 2006. 64 pp.

Boeckl, Matthias, Heinz Gappmayr, Edelbert Köb, and Silvia Eiblmayr. *Rathaus Innsbruck.* Barcelona: Actar, 2004. 128 pp.

Bruschi, Andrea. *Dominique Perrault. Architettura assente.* Rome: Edizioni Kappa, 2002. 256 pp.

Bure, Gilles de. *Mesh. Les tissages métalliques de Dominique Perrault et Gaëlle Lauriot-Prévost avec GKD.* Paris: W Éditions, 2002. 91 pp.

—. *Dominique Perrault.* Paris: Terrail, 2004. 304 pp.

—. *Dominique Perrault. 20 purojie = 20 projets.* Tokyo: Kenchiku Journal Editions, 2010.

Bure, Gilles de, ed. *Dominique Perrault. Inspiration and Process in Architecture.* Milan: Moleskine Editions, 2013. 144 pp.

Capitanucci, Maria Vittoria. *Dominique Perrault. Recent Works.* Milan: Skira, 2006. 223 pp.

Champenois, Michèle. *Gaëlle Lauriot-Prévost/Dominique Perrault Architectures.* Paris: Éditions Norma, 2016. 320 pp.

Chancel, Philippe, and Frédéric Prot. *Ouvertement = Openly.* Paris: Dilecta, 2021. 144 pp.

Coleno, Nadine. *Perrault raconte la Bibliothèque nationale de France.* Paris: Éditions du Regard, 2002. 29 pp.

Cook, Peter, Martin Kieren, and Jacques Lucan. *Dominique Perrault.* Exhibition catalogue. Bordeaux: Arc en rêve / Artemis, 1994. 112 pp.

Feireiss, Kristin, and Hans-Jürgen Commerell. *Dominique Perrault. New Mariinsky Theater.* Berlin: Aedes, 2003. 36 pp.

Ferré, Albert, and Gaëlle Lauriot-Prévost, eds. *La Médiathèque de Vénissieux. Dominique Perrault.* Barcelona: Actar, 2002. 79 pp.

Hohler, Anna, ed. *Dominique Perrault Architecture. Territoires et horizons.* Exhibition catalogue. Lausanne: Presses polytechniques et universitaires romandes (PPUR), 2013. 112 pp.

Jacques, Michel, and Gaëlle Lauriot-Prévost, eds. *Bibliothèque nationale de France 1989–1995. Dominique Perrault, architecte.* Bordeaux: Arc en rêve; Basel: Birkhäuser, 1995. 208 pp. + XXIV pp.

Krüger, Thomas Michael. *Velodrom Landsberger Allee, Berlin.* Berlin: Stadtwandel, 2000. 32 pp.

—. *Schwimm- und Sprunghalle Landsberger Allee, Berlin.* Berlin: Stadtwandel, 2005. 32 pp.

Lauriot-Prévost, Gaëlle, and Dominique Perrault. *Maille métallique. L'histoire d'un tissage = Metal Mesh. The Story of a Weave.* 2 vols. Paris: Gallimard, 2025. 304 pp.

Mancini, Daniele. *Dominique Perrault. La seconda natura dell'architettura.* Milan: Postmedia Books, 2007. 80 pp.

Migayrou, Frédéric, Dir. *With: Dominique Perrault Architecte.* Basel: Birkhäuser Verlag, 1999. 392 pp.

Migayrou, Frédéric, ed. *Dominique Perrault Architecture.* Exhibition catalogue. Orléans: Hyx, 2008. 208 pp. + 1 DVD.

Migayrou, Frédéric. *Dominique Perrault. The Bibliothèque Nationale de France. Portrait of a Project 1988–1998.* Orléans: HYX, 2018. 454 pp.

Perrault, Dominique. *La Bibliothèque de France.* Exhibition catalogue. Paris: Institut français d'architecture; Rome: Éditions Carte Segrete, 1989. 47 pp.

—. *Des natures. Au-delà de l'architecture.* Exhibition catalogue. Basel: Birkhäuser, 1996. 88 pp.

—. *Dominique Perrault. Des natures.* Exhibition catalogue. Tokyo: TN Probe, 1998. 56 pp.

—. *Nature-architecture. Olympic Swimming Pool and Velodrome.* Barcelona: Actar, 2001.153 pp.

—. *Morceaux choisis.* Exhibition catalogue. Paris: Sens & Tonka, 2002. 141 pp.

—. *Groundscapes. Other Topographies.* Orléans: HYX, 2016. 208 pp.

Perrault, Dominique, ed. *Carpark Futures. Opportunities in the Underground.* Paris: DPA-Indigo Group, 2019. 112 pp.

Perrault, Dominique, Georges Fessy, and Hubert Tonka. *ESIEE. École supérieure d'ingénieurs en électrotechnique et électronique, Marne-la-Vallée/Cité Descartes.* Seyssel: Champ Vallon, 1988. 67 pp.

Perrault, Dominique, and Gaëlle Lauriot-Prévost. *Meubles et tapisseries = Furniture and Fabrics = Möbel und Wandbehänge.* Basel: Birkhäuser, 1997. 103 pp.

Perrault, Dominique, and André Morin. *GKD-USA.* Paris: Dominique Perrault Architecture, 2006. 47 pp.

Perrault, Dominique, Hubert Tonka, Michel Denancé, and Georges Fessy. *L'Hôpital du livre. Centre technique de la Bibliothèque nationale de France.* Parole à... Paris: Sens & Tonka, 1998. 45 pp.

Rambert, Francis, ed. *Métro ! Le Grand Paris en mouvement.* Exhibition catalogue. Paris: Réunion des musées nationaux, Cité de l'architecture, 2023. 288 pp.

Redecke, Sebastian, ed. *Dominique Perrault, architecte.* Exhibition catalogue. Paris: Sens & Tonka, 1996. 74 pp.

Ruby, Alexandre, Hans Ulrich Obrist, and José María Ezquiaga. *La caja mágica = The Magic Box.* Madrid: Q! estudio, 2011. 208 pp.

Ruby, Ilka, and Andreas Ruby. *Dominique Perrault. Meta-Buildings.* Cologne: Walther König, 2006. 96 pp.

Rutault, Claude, Dominique Perrault, and Bernard Blistène. *Claude Rutault chez Dominique Perrault.* Dijon: Le Consortium, 2000. 31 pp.

Schaer, Roland, and Dominique Perrault. *Chambord, 1519–2019: Utopia at Work.* Exhibition catalogue. Paris: Faton, 2019. 420 pp.

Stalder, Laurent. *Dominique Perrault. Progetti e architetture.* Milan: Electa, 2000. 179 pp.

Whyte, Andy, ed. *Dominique Perrault. Selected and Current Works.* Master Architects Series, vol. IV. Mulgrave: Images Publishing, 2001. 236 pp.

Zabalbeascoa, Anatxu, ed. *Dominique Perrault. Small Scale = Pequeña escala.* Barcelona: Gustavo Gili, 1998. 64 pp.

Zamboni, Andrea. *Dominique Perrault.* Arles: Actes Sud, 2010. 120 pp.

"Dominique Perrault." *L'Arca plus*, no. 20 (March 1999).

"Dominique Perrault, 1990–2001." *El croquis*, no. 104 (2001).

"Dominique Perrault/Tissus." *a+u*, no. 391 (April 2003).

"Dominique Perrault." *World Architecture*, no. 3 (2004).

"Dominique Perrault." *Contemporary Architecture*, no. 64 (January 2006).

"Dominique Perrault. Arquitectura 1997–2007." *TC Cuadernos*, no. 77–78 (2007).

"Dominique Perrault. 1990–2009." Monografías/Monographs. *Arquitectura Viva*, no. 134 (2008). 512 pp.

"Dominique Perrault/DPA Today." *a+u*, no. 468 (2009). 132 pp.

"Dominique Perrault." *World Architecture Masters (WAM)* (2009)

"Dominique Perrault. Arquitectura 2008–2018." *TC Cuadernos*, no. 136–137 (2018).

"Écoles invitées." *Frapotel*, no. 1 (2024).

"Fictions." *Frapotel*, no. 2 (2025).

ARTICLES AND ESSAYS ON THE WORK OF DOMINIQUE PERRAULT

Adriá, Miquel. "Dominique Perrault: el arte de lo neutro." *Letras libres*, no. 23 (November 2000): 102–103.

Albert, Marie-Douce. "L'utopie selon… l'architecte Dominique Perrault." *Le Monde*, November 2012: 12–14.

Amiguet, Lluís. "La contra: Dominique Perrault." *La vanguardia*, October 24, 2004: 12–13.

Bankhamer, Alfred. "Der Maulwurf." *Bau & Immobilien Report*, January-February 1999: 24–31.

Bojardi, Gilda. "Dominique Perrault." *Interni*, no. 530 (April 2003): 276–283.

Boyer, Charles-Arthur. "Le projet, acte fondateur." *L'Architecture d'aujourd'hui*, no. 282 (September 1992).

Brausch, Marianne. "Le contexte selon Dominique Perrault." *d'Land*, no. 23 (June 6, 2003): 23.

Brausch, Marianne, and Marc Emery. "Dominique Perrault." In *Fragen zur Architektur. 15 Architekten im Gespräch*, edited by Marianne Brausch and Marc Emery, 175–183. Basel: Birkhäuser, 1995.

Buica, Viorica. "Dominique Perrault: Meta-arhitectura." *Igloo*, May 2007: 114–130.

Bure, Gilles de. "Dominique Perrault, l'homme qui scintille." *Technikart*, no. 31 (April 1999): 32–37.

—. "L'espace, par Dominique Perrault." *Psychologies Magazine*, special issue (November-December 2007): 36–37.

Cambert, Mary. "Dominique Perrault." In *Les Plus Grands Architectes du monde*, edited by Mary Cambert, 38–67. Barcelona: Atrium, 2005.

Capitanucci, Maria Vittoria. "Dominique Perrault profile." *Materia*, no. 50 (August 2006): 76–97.

Coen, Lorette. "Dominique Perrault revisite les villes suisses." *Le Temps*, July 16, 2012: 19.

Colafranceschi, Daniela. "Dominique Perrault." In *Sull'involucro in architettura. Herzog, Nouvel, Perrault, Piano, Prix, Suzuki, Venturi, Wines*, 34–49. Rome: Edizioni Librerie Dedalo, 1996.

Collyer, G. Stanley. "Interview: Dominique Perrault." *Competitions*, Summer 1994: 52–57.

Couceiro, C. Joana, and Pedro Baía. "O desaparecimento da arquitectura, entrevista a Dominique Perrault." *Nu*, no. 4 (October 2002): 16–22.

Czaja, Wojciech. "Baumeister des grossen massstabs." *Falstaff Living*, May 2024: 182–185.

Desmoulins, Christine. "Parla Dominique Perrault: 'Nella Biblioteca ho messo tutti gli elementi della mia architettura'." *Il giornale dell'architettura*, no. 93 (April 2011): 12.

Haberlik, Christina, and Gerwin Zohlen. "Dominique Perrault." In *Die Baumeister des Neuen Berlin*, edited by Christina Haberlik and Gerwin Zohlen, 144–149. Berlin: Nicolai, 1997.

Hakelová, Lucia. "Dominique Perrault: Verejná zakazka má byť príležitosťou na tvorbu verejného priestoru." *asb.sk*, February 20, 2008.

Hosch, Alexander. "Der Bic-Bauer." *Architectural Digest* 60, no. 5 (May 2003): 36–40.

Ji, Eunkyung. "Dominique Perrault." *Clayarch*, no. 25 (July-August 2006): 36–41.

Killory, Christine, and René Davids. "GKD-USA, Inc. Headquarters Building." In *Details in Contemporary Architecture*, 128–137. New York: AsBuilt, 2007.

Koch, Katrin. "Architektur und Landschaft in ökologischer und poetischer Beziehung." *DBZ*, no. 17 (December 1993): 31–38.

Koivisto, Maritta. "Arkkitehti Dominique Perrault." *Betoni*, no. 1 (January 1999): 24–27.

Lamarre, François. "Dominique Perrault, l'architecture vue d'en haut." *Les Échos*, December 7, 2009: 12.

Laubadère, Bruno de. "AD exclusif." *Architectural Digest*, no. 25 (September 2002): 78–80.

Leboucq, Brice. "Entretien avec Dominique Perrault." *Études*, no. 401 (July-August 2004): 77–88.

Lesnikowski, Wojciech. "Dominique Perrault." In *The New French Architecture*, 170–179. New York: Rizzoli International Publications, 1990.

Lichvárová, Mária. "Dominique Perrault." *Projekt*, no. 2 (July 2007): 60–67.

McCulloch, Patricia. "Architect of controversy." *Paris Boulevard*, no. 17 (December 1992–January 1993).

Messerschmidt, Eric. "Dominique Perrault." In *Arne Jacobsen. Absolutely Modern*, edited by Michael J. Horn, 86–89. Humlebæk: Louisiana Museum of Modern Art, 2002.

Meyhöfer, Dirk. "Dominique Perrault." In *Architectural Visions for Europe*, edited by Dirk Meyhöfer, 102–119. Wiesbaden: Vieweg, 1994.

Michel, Florence. "Les villes de demain." *Enjeux du monde*, no. 22 (November 1994): 39–42.

Molina, Vis. "Personaje Dominique Perrault." *Fuera de serie*, November 2004: 6–8.

Moncan, Patrice de, and Philippe Chiambaretta. "La ville utopique vue par des architectes d'aujourd'hui : Dominique Perrault." In *Villes rêvées*, 166–175. Paris: Les Éditions du Mécène, 1998.

Nottrot, Ina. "Ich arbeite, was ich lebe." *Die Zeit*, December 8, 1995.

Paczowski, Bohdan. "Na nowy wiek Bohdan Paczowski rozmawia z Dominikiem Perrault." *Architektura Murator*, no. 4 (April 2003): 21–31.

—. "Bohdan Paczowski s'entretient avec Dominique Perrault, fragments." In *Doką zmierza architektura?*, 47–60. Warsaw: Wydawnictwo Murator, 2005.

Paoletti, Ingrid. "Le tele metalliche importate dal settore manifatturiero: il caso Dominique Perrault." In *Una finestra sul trasferimento. Tecnologie innovative per l'architettura*, 111–118. Milan: Libreria Clup, 2003.

Quinton, Maryse. "Dominique Perrault, l'homme pressé." *Ideat*, no. 81 (December 2010–January 2011): 303–305.

Redondo, Paloma. "Dominique Perrault: el arquitecto 'mágico'." *Fuera de Serie*, no. 169 (December 5, 2007): 20–22.

Régnier, Philippe. "L'actualité vue par Dominique Perrault, architecte." *Le Journal des arts*, no. 269 (November 16–29, 2007): 6.

Rochebouët, Béatrice. "Les manifestes de Dominique Perrault." *Le Figaro*, January 30–31, 2010.

Roulet, Yelmarc. "'Apprenons à construire la ville souterraine'." *Le Temps*, August 23, 2013: 7.

Roselieb, Arnd, and Daniel Tournier. "The Master Builder." In *Encounters. Visionaries and Architects*, 66–83. Düsseldorf: Egon Zehnder International, 2001.

Roth, Bernard. "Entretien avec… Dominique Perrault." *Réflexions immobilières*, no. 39 (December 2004): 65–73.

Schuh, Karin. "Nur Architekt sein reicht nicht." *Die Presse*, March 18, 2012: 14.

Sfar, Éric. "Architecture et construction de l'œuvre. Entretien avec Dominique Perrault." *Archistorm*, May-June 2008: 36–41.

Slavid, Ruth. "The Architect of absence." *Architects' Journal*, September 28, 1995: 20–21.

Stimmann, Hans. "Dominique Perrault." In *Babylon, Berlin, etc. Das Vokabular der europäischen Stadt*, 210–217. Basel: Birkhäuser, 1995.

Tabak, Ebru. "Perrault'nun sezgisel akli." *Art+Decor*, no. 129 (December 2003): 132–135.

Thiba, Marion. "L'architecture de Dominique Perrault." *Le Temps stratégique*, no. 83 (September-October 1998): 8–30.

Veda, Minoru. "Dominique Perrault, l'architecte de l'invisible." *AT*, May 1993: 5–17.

Vignal, Marion. "Dominique Perrault : archi couture." *L'Express*, June 28–July 4, 2004: 18–19.

Walker, Enrique. "Dominique Perrault." In *Summa + Reportajes. Arquitectos y obras*, 108–111. Buenos Aires: Donn, 2005.

Wierre, Florence. "La production d'archives d'une agence : un entretien avec Dominique Perrault." *Colonnes*, no. 23 (November 2006): 37–44.

"À conversa con… Dominique Perrault." *Mais Arquitectura*, no. 17 (October 2007): 52–59.

"An Interview with Dominique Perrault." *Detail*, no. 5 (September-October 2007): 476, 479.

"Architecture : Dominique Perrault." *Le Moniteur*, November 12, 1993: 84–85.

"Bibliothèque nationale de France." *Connaissance des arts*, special issue, no. 99 (1996).

"Cover interview: Dominique Perrault." *Axis*, no. 88 (November-December 2000): 2–6.

"Der Grossmeister." *Das Ideale Heim*, September 2006: 2–4.

"Die Dimension des Einfachen." *Leonardo*, no. 4670 (May 1993): 38–41.

"Dominique Perrault." *World Architecture Review*, August 1999: 76–97.

"Dominique Perrault." In *World Architects in their Twenties*. Tokyo: University of Tokyo / Toto, 1999.

"Dominique Perrault." *IAOC*, August 2004, 134–136.

"Dominique Perrault." *Interni & Decor*, no. 10 (October 2005): 226–233.

"Dominique Perrault." In *Only With Nature*, 219–224. Barcelona: Collegi d'Arquitectes de Catalunya / Fundación Caja de Arquitectos, 2006.

"Dominique Perrault." *Plus*, no. 8 (2002): 23–47.

"Dominique Perrault." *Archicrée HS Collector 2016* (2016): 70–75.

"Dominique Perrault." *Arquine*, no. 82 (Winter 2017): 97–100.

"Dominique Perrault." *Noblesse China-Korea*, no. 2 (February 2025): 46–49.

"Dominique Perrault: Bes Yeni Proje." *Arredamento Mimarlik*, September 2006: 38–53.

"Dossier Dominique Perrault." *AV Proyectos*, no. 81 (2017): 5–27.

"Elementary Dispositions: Dominique Perrault." In *Anymore*, 272–282. New York: Anyone, 2000.

"France: Dominique Perrault." In *Award Winning Architecture 96*, edited by Frantisek Sedlacek, 106–111. Munich: Prestel, 1996.

"Housing Offices and Commercial Building." In *Cooperative Housing*, 222–229. Seoul: Archiworld, 2007.

"Office Building at Boulogne-Billancourt." In *Ultimate Paris Design*, 108–113. Kempen: teNeues, 2007.

"Où sont les monuments d'aujourd'hui? Table ronde animée par François Chaslin, avec Jean Nouvel, Dominique Perrault, Christian de Portzamparc." In *L'Abus monumental? Actes des Entretiens du patrimoine*, edited by Régis Debray, 389–408. Paris: Fayard-Éditions du Patrimoine, 1999.

PROJECTS

SITUATING

Usinor-Sacilor Conference Center
Saint-Germain-en-Laye, France, 1988–91

Vital-Durand, Brigitte. "Le château au lac de verre." *Libération*, May 17, 1991.

Yeulmaru City of Culture and Arts
Yeosu, South Korea, 2009–12

Perrault, Dominique. *GS Caltex Yeosu Art Park*. Paris: Dominique Perrault Architecture, 2009.

Ewha Women's University
Seoul, South Korea, 2004–08

Accorsi, Florence, and François Lamarre. "Université féminine Ewha Séoul/Corée-du-Sud." In *Exo-architectures. Paris autour du monde en 80 projets*, 257. Paris: Éditions du Pavillon de l'Arsenal, 2007.

Bahamón, Alejandro, and Patricia Pérez. "Campus de la Universidad Femenina Ewha." In *Arquitectura mineral*, 74–81. Analogías. Barcelona: Parramón Ediciones, 2007.

Choi, Won Sok. "Ewha Campus Center Invited – International Design Competition." *Architecture & Culture*, no. 274 (March 2004): 150–157.

Descombes, Mireille. "Construire en Corée du Sud : une aventure riche et troublante." *L'Hebdo*, no. 52/01 (December 28, 2006): 34–37.

Dubois, Marc. "Kracht van de leegte." *de Architect*, no. 37 (September 2006): 15.

Ehret, Gabriel. "À Séoul, Perrault, souterrain et aérien, l'emporte !" *ArchiCréé*, no. 313 (February-March 2004): 8.

Fontana, Jacopo della. "La Strip ipogea." *L'Arca International*, no. 195 (September 2004): 58–63.

"Centro del campus de la universidad de EWHA." *Pasajes Arquitectura y Crítica*, no. 60 (October 2004): 12–13.

"Dominique Perrault : Ewha Campus Center." *a+u*, no. 413 (February 2005): 58–63.

"Interview: Dominique Perrault." *Space* (January 2006): 151–160.

"Centre du campus, université Ewha, Séoul, Corée." *L'Architecture d'aujourd'hui*, no. 364 (May-June 2006): 78–81.

"Dominique Perrault : Ewha Womans University Campus Center, Seoul." *Mais Arquitectura* (March 2007): 38–51.

Double Deck – Dome-Esplanade of the École Polytechnique Fédérale de Lausanne
Lausanne, Switzerland, 2023–27

Scoffier, Richard. "Exercices de haute couture. Concours pour la restructuration de la coupole et de l'esplanade du campus de l'École polytechnique de Lausanne." *d'architectures*, no. 314 (February-March 2024): 42–45.

Octopus – Upgrading the Salerno quarries
Salerno, Italy, 2009

Dragone, Roberta. "Salerno transforma cava dismessa in polo turistico." *archiportale.com*, May 8, 2009.

Sanctuary of Notre-Dame-du-Laus
Saint-Étienne-le-Laus, France, 2012

Pousse, Jean-François. "Notre-Dame-du-Laus." *Arts sacrés*, no. 25 (September-October 2013): 68–75.

Lightwalk – Gangnam Intermodal Transit Center
Seoul, South Korea, 2017–30

Allix, Grégoire. "L'urbanisme souterrain fait son trou." *Le Monde*, November 25, 2017: 4–5.

Park, Yuna. "Without light, Lightwalk will not be architecture: Dominique Perrault." *koreaherald.com*, November 6, 2023.

Perrault, Dominique. *Lightwalk Seoul Gangnam Intermodal Transit Center*. Paris: Dominique Perrault Architecture, 2017.

Perrault, Dominique. "Lightwalk. Gangnam, Seoul, South Korea." *L'Arca International*, no. 140 (January-February 2018): 63–71.

Proux, Fabienne. "Corée du Sud. Le Lightwalk de Dominique Perrault illumine le cœur de Séoul." *urbanutopia*, February 9, 2018.

Zylberman, Joris. "Séoul allie data et multimodal pour de meilleurs services." *lesechos.fr*, May 22, 2018.

Piazza Garibaldi
Naples, Italy, 2004–15 / 2017–19

Cuozzo, Paolo. "Verde e senz'auto: è la piazza Garibaldi del futuro." *Corriere del Mezzogiorno*, April 14, 2005: 5.

De Simone, Dario. "Ecco la nuova piazza Garibaldi." *Il giornale di Napoli*, April 14, 2005.

Guardigli, Decio. "La qualità dello spazio." *L'Arca International*, no. 207 (October 2005): 48–53.

Roano, Luigi. "Garibaldi : due piazze in una nella matita di Perrault." *Il mattino*, April 16, 2004.

"Dominique Perrault: Plaza Garibaldi, Nápoles." *AV Proyectos*, no. 15 (May-June 2006): 26–29.

"Piazza Garibaldi Station." *Plus* (April 2007): 142–145.

Villejuif Gustave-Roussy station
Villejuif, France, 2013–25

Albert, Marie-Douce. "Le Grand Paris Express s'offre un puits de lumière." Le Moniteur, no. 6338 (January 24, 2025): 60–63.

Annicchiarico, Silvana. "Ceci n'est pas un métro. Storia e futuro della fitta rete di strade che fa vivere il sottosuolo di Parigi." repubblica.it, November 8, 2023.

Ayers, Andrew. "Interchange brings the drama to Paris's new suburban orbital metro." ribaj.com, March 27, 2025.

Baumann, Olivier. "Grand Paris Express. 2 tunneliers se croisent au fond d'un puits géant." Construction moderne, no. 163 (2021): 42–45.

Bernau, Nikolaus. "Ein sehr tiefer Tiefbahnhof. Metrostation in Paris von Dominique Perrault." baunetz.de, January 20, 2025.

Gent, Sara, and Minerva García de Castro. "Difuminar los límites de la ciudad. Estación Gustave Roussy por Dominique Perrault Architecture." metalocus.es, February 2, 2025.

Guo, Beini, Jiaxi Wang, and Eugenio Lux. "Parigi si muove sottoterra: Villejuif e la stazione di Perrault." ilgiornaledellarchitettura.com, February 17, 2025.

Monier-Vinard, Bruno. "Le ciel en rosace de la gare de Villejuif." lepoint.fr, January 26, 2025.

Perrault, Dominique. "El groundscape y el territorio." arquine.com, July 8, 2024.

Regnier, Isabelle. "À l'exposition 'Métro ! Le Grand Paris en mouvement', une épopée souterraine du réseau francilien." Le Monde, December 21, 2023.

Rocheboüet, Béatrice de. "'Grand Paris' : ces nouvelles gares qui vont révolutionner l'Île-de-France." Le Figaro, June 17, 2019.

—. "Du métropolitain au Grand Paris, la Cité de l'architecture nous embarque pour un long voyage." Le Figaro, November 24, 2023.

Serafin, Amy. "The Grand Paris Express, Europe's largest urban design project, is en route to success." wallpaper.com, June 23, 2024.

Zabalbeascoa, Anatxu. "La monumentalización del metro." elpaís.com, February 18, 2025.

MAPPING

The Athletes' Village – Paris 2024 Olympic and Paralympic Games
Saint-Denis and Saint-Ouen, France, 2017–26

Bermejo, Rafael F. "Dominique Perrault: conoce al arquitecto (y genio) que ha pensado la Villa Olímpica de París." *Arquitectura y Diseño*, June 27, 2024.

Crook, Lizzie. "Paris 2024 aftermath 'most dangerous time' for Olympic Village says Dominique Perrault." *Dezeen*, July 30, 2024.

Czaja, Wocjciech. "Dominique Perrault: Baumeister von Olympia." *Falstaff Living*, August 6, 2024.

Giovannini, Joseph. "The view from here." *Air Mail*, July 20, 2024.

Kuper, Simon. "Paris, the Olympics and the reinvention of a city." *Financial Times*, July 12, 2024.

Leray, Christophe. "Pour les Jeux Olympiques, Paris est un village." *Chronique d'architecture*, September 19, 2017.

Meister, Martina. "'Der Begriff Banlieue wird bald nicht mehr existieren, glauben Sie mir'." *welt.de*, July 26, 2024.

Perrault, Dominique. *A village and its double, urban planning manual Olympic and Paralympic Games Paris 2024*. Barcelona: Actar, 2024.

—. "Village olympique Paris 2024." *L'Arca Internazional*, no. 139 (November-December 2017): 24–29.

Regnier, Isabelle. "Un quartier durable accueillera le village olympique." *Le Monde*, March 11, 2019.

Sandberg, Britta. "'Der Pariser Snobismus ist nicht mehr zeitgemäß'." *spiegel.de*, October 11, 2023.

Wainwright, Oliver. "Plastic-bottle seats and wooden pools: can Paris deliver the leanest, greenest Olympics yet?" *theguardian.com*, July 15, 2024.

"Design and architecture projects to look out for at the 2024 Paris Olympic Games." *stirworld.com*, May 13, 2022.

Shenzhen Institute of Design and Innovation
Shenzhen, China, 2021–23

Figuet, Léo. "Perrault lauréat du concours pour le nouvel Institut du Design à Shenzhen." *darchitectures.com*, March 31, 2023.

Mora, María Fernanda. "Shenzhen Institute of Design and Innovation. 'Horizon' by Dominique Perrault + Zhubo Design Co." *metalocus.es*, April 5, 2021.

Multifunctional District
Sofia, Bulgaria, 2009–10

Calabrese, Rossella. "Sofia: Perrault firma la Cittadella del Governo." *archiportale.com*, May 25, 2009.

Perrault, Dominique. "Sofia City Center." *Space*, no. 499 (June 2009): 38–41.

—. "Sofia Business Centre." *L'Arca International*, no. 254 (January 2010): 56–63.

"Tsarigradsko Shosse. Perrault gewinnt Wettbewerb in Sofia." *baunetz.de*, May 4, 2009.

"Bauvisionen bis 2020 Facelifting für Europas Städte stockt." *kleinezeitung.at*, August 6, 2009.

Metropolis? – Venice Architecture Biennale
Venice, Italy, 2010

Fèvre, Anne-Marie. "'Metropolis' aère la ville." *Libération*, August 26, 2010, 21.

Lenne, Frédéric. "Bien habiter la ville." *AMC*, no. 199 (September 2010).

Magrou, Rafaël. "Venise 2010, une Biennale mature." *L'Architecture d'aujourd'hui*, no. 380 (November-December 2010): 192–193.

Perrault, Dominique. *Metropolis ? Bordeaux, Lyon, Marseille, Nantes-Saint-Nazaire, Paris. Cinq métropoles en regard du Grand Paris*. Exhibition catalogue. Paris: Dominique Carré / Institut Français, 2011. 295 pp.

Perrault, Dominique, Michal Bogár, Lubomir Kralik, Ludovít Urban, et al. *Bratislava Metropolis*. Bratislava: Spolok architektov Slovenska, 2014. 268 pp.

Soulez, Juliette. "La métropole par le vide, Dominique Perrault à Venise." *Archistorm*, no. 44 (September-October 2010): 20–21.

Trétiack, Philippe. "Dominique Perrault à l'assaut du vide." *Beaux-Arts Magazine*, no. 317 (November 2010).

"Dominique Perrault. Pour une nouvelle architecture." *Le Nouvel Observateur*, no. 2392 (September 9, 2010): 14.

Crossroads, Building the Resilient City – Seoul Biennale of Architecture and Urban Planning
Seoul, South Korea, 2019–21

Crossroads, Building the Resilient City. Data Books. Exhibition catalogue. 7 vols. Seoul: Metropolitan Government, 2021.

Crossroads, Building the Resilient City. Guide Book. Exhibition catalogue. Seoul: Metropolitan Government, 2021. 608 pp.

Seoul Biennale of Architecture and Urbanism 2021, Picture Book. Seoul: Metropolitan Government, 2021. 231 pp.

Kwon, Mee-yoo. "French architect directs Seoul Biennale of Architecture and Urbanism." *koreatimes.co.kr*, September 13, 2021.

Perrault, Dominique. "Les tribulations d'un directeur de biennale." *lepoint.fr*, September 19, 2021.

Stevens, Philippe. "Interview: Dominique Perrault on plans for 2021 Seoul Biennale of architecture and urbanism." *designboom.com*, June 10, 2020.

"Île de la Cité 2040" mission
Paris, France, 2016

Bélaval, Philippe, and Dominique Perrault, ed. *Paris Île de la Cité. Mission 2040*. Paris: Norma, 2017. 288 pp.

Carrey, Pierre. "Notre drame de Paris. Hollande joue les architectes sur l'île de la Cité : un beau projet… mais trop tard." *liberation.fr*, February 14, 2017.

Geipel, Kaye. "In der Herzkammer von Paris." *bauwelt.de*, September 2017.

Guerrin, Michel. "L'île de la Cité laissée en plans" *Le Monde*, February 5, 2016: 18.

Hanimann, Joseph. "Architektur. Hypothese und Hoffnung." *sueddeutsche.de*, February 16, 2017.

Larrochelle, Jean-Jacques, and Florence Evin. "François Hollande veut redessiner l'île de la Cité, à Paris." *Le Monde*, February 13, 2017.

Rochebcuët, Béatrice de, and Claire Bommelaer. "Le grand pari pour redonner vie à l'île de la Cité." *Le Figaro*, February 14, 2017: 27.

Sornin, Garance. "L'île de la Cité à Paris, revue par Dominique Perrault." *amc-archi.com*, January 10, 2017.

"Hôtel Métropole"
Paris, France, 2013

Perrault, Dominique. "Le dispositif Hôtel Métropole." In *Habiter le Grand Paris*, 154–165. Paris: Archibooks, 2013.

WRITING

Twin Peaks – Bongeunsa-ro 120
Seoul, South Korea, 2023–2029

Lee, Soo-jung, and Hee-chul Moon. "New skyscraper to replace Seungri's disgraced Sun club." *koreajoongangdaily.joins.com*, December 29, 2023.

Fukoku Tower
Osaka, Japan, 2006–10

Simenc, P. "L'arbre de verre." *Architectural Digest*, no. 95 (September-October 2010): 78.

"Siège de la compagnie d'assurance Fukoku – Tokyo. Dominique Perrault." *AMC*, special issue (September 2011): 118–119.

"Tour Fukoku." *Detail Japan*, no. 207 (January 2016): 70–71.

Vulcano
Zurich, Switzerland, 2012–18

"Drei neue Wahrzeichen in Zürichs Westen." *Neue Zürcher Zeitung*, January 29, 2015.

"Vulcano: Urbanes Wohnen im neuen Trendquartier Zürich-Alstetten." *Neue Zürcher Zeitung*, special issue (January 13, 2019).

"Vulcano-Türme im gläsernen Kleid." *Fassade/Façade* (March 2013): 33–38.

"Vulcano: Drei neue Wahrzeichen für Zürich." *kmu-magazin.ch*, February 28, 2019.

La Liberté
Groningen, Netherlands, 2007–11

Perfetti, Silvia. "Social Dimension." *Code15*, no. 15 (September 2011): 83.

"Dominique Perrault. 120 logements à Groningue." *AMC*, no. 217 (September 2012): 86–87.

Arc of Light – Nonhyun 114
Seoul, South Korea, 2024–29

Bahng, Youngdouk. "'No one can go in.' Fendi's super-luxurious house, built in Gangnam." *mk.co.kr*, May 1, 2024.

Kim, Byunggyu. "Golden Tree Development Signs Strategic Partnership with Fendi Casa." *Herald Corp*, February 1, 2024.

Son, Ji-su. "The first Fendi house in Asia." *noblesse.com*, May 24, 2025.

Donau City Tower I
Vienna, Austria, 2002–14

Albert, Marie-Douce. "Du haut de la DC Tower 1, DPA domine l'Autriche." *lemoniteur.fr*, February 27, 2014.

—. "Dominique Perrault. Tour DC I, Vienne, Autriche." *AMC*, no. 234 (June 2014): 38–45.

Berger, Michael. "Donau City: Der höchste Turm Kommt erst." *Kurier*, June 13, 2002.

Bucci, Federico. "Dominique Perrault, la nuova torre di Donau City: un'architettura per l'altro centro di Vienna." *Casabella*, no. 838 (June 2014): 46–53.
Griffiths, Alyn. "Dominique Perrault's DC Tower 1 now Austria's tallest building." *dezeen.com*, February 28, 2014.
La Fata, Laura. "La première tour de la Donau City à Vienne est signée Dominique Perrault." *connaissancedesarts.com*, March 3, 2014.
Lalueta, Inés. "The DC Tower 1 by Dominique Perrault, is Austria's tallest building." *metalocus.es*, March 2, 2014.
Perrault, Dominique. "Orizzontale e verticale: Donau City Sky Towers." *L'Arca International*, no. 215 (June 2006): 32–37.
—. "DC Tower 1." *L'Arca International*, no. 118 (May-June 2014): 22–32.
—. "DC Tower I + II." *Architecture and Urbanism (a+u)*, no. 525 (June 2014): 146–147.
—. "Torres DC en Viena." *Arquitectura Viva*, no. 164 (June 2014): 86–91.
—. *Not twins, but one tower split in two.* Photographs by Markus Krottendorfer. Berlin: Distanz Verlag, 2017. 156 pp.
Quinton, Maryse. "Un Français au sommet de l'Autriche." *Ideat*, special issue (April 2014): 28.
Rosenberger, Werner. "Entwürfe sind zu wenig." *Kurier*, July 7, 2006: 21.
Stuhlpfarrer, Martin. "Mega-Türme für Donaucity." *Die Presse*, February 18, 2006.
Taillandier, Ingrid. "L'Europe des tours." *AMC*, special issue (December 2003): 86–90.
"Dominique Perrault talks about Danube City, Vienna." *Axis* (June 2004): 38–39.
"Dominique Perrault: Vienna DC Sky Tower." *GA Document*, no. 91 (June 2006): 120–125.
"Donau-City." In *Architektur Aktuell*, no. 2452023 (March 2005): 59.
"Hochhaus in Wien." *Detail*, no. 6/2015 (June 2015): 577–581.
"Türme im Dialog: Auf der Platte entsteht ab 2007 das höchste Haus Wien." *derstandard.at*, February 20, 2007.

Donau City Tower II
Vienna, Austria, 2002–27
Kanfer, Roland. "Der schlichte Charme der Bohemien." *architecktur-online.com*, May 13, 2024.
Putschögl, Martin. "Der DC Tower 2 wächst, ein Roboter hilft beim Bau mit." *derstandard.at*, February 18, 2025.
Savage, Adam. "Inside Austria's (Terrifying) New Skyscraper Build." *the b1m.com*, April 2, 2025.
Schaur-Wünsch, Teresa. "Vom Tor zum Sonnenturm: Zweiter DC-Tower wird riesige Fotovoltaik-Anlage." *Die Presse*, April 19, 2024.
"DC Tower 2 bekommt Photovoltaik-Fassade." *derstandard.at*, October 25, 2023.

To-Lyon
Lyon, France, 2012–24
Allix, Grégoire. "À Lyon, un monolithe noir pour marquer le renouveau de la Part-Dieu." *lemonde.fr*, September 10, 2019.
Charbonnier, Vincent. "Avec To-Lyon, Vinci Immobilier participe à la requalification de la gare de la Part-Dieu." *lesechos.fr*, September 11, 2019.
Collomb, Gérard. "Tour To-Lyon : Vinci frappe un grand coup." *Le Progrès*, September 10, 2019.
Ehret, Gabriel. "La Part-Dieu s'ouvre sur la ville et se densifie." *AMC*, no. 242 (May 2015): 12–15.
Perrault, Dominique. "To-Lyon." *L'Arca International*, no. 139 (November-December 2017): 92–93.
—. "To-Lyon." *L'Arca International*, no. 152 (January-February 2020): 82–83.
Thibert, Julien. "Dominique Perrault : 'ToLyon, une tour qui s'enracine dans les usages de la ville.'" *mesinfos.fr*, September 9, 2019.
"À la Part-Dieu, la tour To-Lyon a atteint sa hauteur définitive." *leprogrès.fr*, January 18, 2023.
"Pose de la première pierre d'une nouvelle tour à Lyon." *barinfo.com*, September 9, 2019.

ParisLongchamp Hippodrome
Paris, France, 2011–18
Boccara, Laurence. "Le nouvel hippodrome de Longchamp, un chantier à 125 millions d'euros." *Le Monde*, March 19, 2016.
Boudet, Antoine. "France Galop a le feu vert du gouvernement pour relancer l'hippodrome de Longchamp." *lesechos.fr*, August 25, 2018.
Capitaine, Christian. "Béton. Galop d'essai réussi pour la préfabrication." *Le Moniteur*, no. 5941 (September 22, 2017): 78–79.
Duckworth, Amanda. "The Prix de l'Arc de Triomphe Returns to ParisLongchamp." *The New York Times*, October 5, 2018.
Duffé, Julien. "Premier coup de pioche pour le futur Longchamp." *Le Parisien*, no. 22102 (September 30, 2015): 4.
Girard, Laurence. "France Galop fait le pari d'un nouveau Longchamp." *Le Monde*, September 30, 2015.
Hamon, Christine. "L'hippodrome de Longchamp rendu aux Parisiens." *leparisien.fr*, March 22, 2018.
Hitomi, Saito. "Dominique Perrault. New Longchamp Racecourse." *GA Document*, no. 120 (January 2012): 120–125.
Hugron, Jean-Philippe. *L'Hippodrome de ParisLongchamp, Dominique Perrault Architecture*. Paris: Archibooks, 2019. 126 pp.
—. "Longchamp-Bois de Boulogne, Paris, par Dominique Perrault Architecture." *Archistorm*, no. 93 (November 2018).
Luquain, Amélie. "Le nouveau Longchamp, une course hippique." *ArchiCréé*, October 2, 2015.
Miguet, Laurent. "L'hippodrome de Longchamp recompose une lisière du bois de Boulogne." *lemoniteur.fr*, November 18, 2016.
Minutillo, Josephine. "Longchamp Racecourse by Dominique Perrault." *architecturalrecord.com*, August 1, 2018.
Palierse, Christophe. "À Longchamp, France Galop lance la modernisation." *Les Échos*, September 30, 2015, 22.
Périnel, Quentin. "L'hippodrome de Longchamp, dernier acte avant démolition." *immobilier.lefigaro.fr*, September 29, 2015.
Perrault, Dominique. "Paris Longchamp." *L'Arca International*, no. 144 (September-October 2018): 47–57.
Ponsford, Matthew. "Paris' Longchamp racecourse gets ready for 'the best race in the world.'" *CNN*, October 4, 2019.
Robert, Martine. "Voici le nouveau Longchamp." *lesechos.fr*, August 18, 2014.
"France Galop mise sur Dominique Perrault pour rénover Longchamp." *lemoniteur.fr*, October 26, 2011.
"Grandstand in Motion." *SB Magazine*, November 1, 2018: 28–31.
"Sponsored feature: GKD metal fabric gives racecourse a golden glow." *The Architects' Journal*, November 27, 2018.

Kindarena
Rouen, France, 2006–12
Dana, Karine. *Le Palais des sports de Rouen. Dominique Perrault Architecte.* Paris: Archibooks, 2013. 80 pp.
Delacourt, Thierry, and Alain Geslin. "Un Palais des sports à Rouen oui, mais en 2010." *Paris Normandie*, September 14, 2006, 23.
Goasguen, Richard. "Rouen : un palais des sports pour 2010." *Le Moniteur*, no. 5367 (October 5, 2006): 42.
Monier-Vinard, Bruno. "Rouen : le nouveau palais des sports." *Le Point*, November 1, 2007, 24.
Perrault, Dominique. "Kindarena." *L'Arca International*, no. 115 (November-December 2013): 60–67.
Scoffier, Richard. "Le Kindarena à Rouen." *d'architectures*, no. 212 (October 2012): 66–71.
Sfar, Éric. "Stairway to Rouen." *Archistorm*, no. 23 (January-February 2007): 28–29.

Arganzuela footbridge
Madrid, Spain, 2008–11
Ferren, Andrew. "The Madrid Waterfront: Who Knew?" *New York Times*, July 8, 2011: 6.
Medialdea, Sara. "El puente mágico del Manzanares." *abc.es*, March 25, 2011.
Morales, R. "El icono de Madrid Río." *larazon.es*, March 25, 2011.
Serna, Carmen. "Pasarela de diseño en el río." *M2–El Mundo*, June 14, 2008: 4.
Zabalbeascoa, Anatxu. "Por Madrid pasa un río: en el Mananares con Perrault." *El País*, February 28, 2011: 52.
"Le pont Arganzuela, joyau du rio." *Journal des arts*, no. 350, June 24, 2011: 13.
"Les passerelles en acier : la passerelle Arganzuela, Madrid, Espagne, DPA Architecte. Un double cocon en spirale d'acier." *Matières*, no. 19 July 2023: 40.
"Un tirabuzón de 250 metros para cruzar el Manzanares." *El País*, June 14, 2008: 4.

New Mechanical Hall (ME), École Polytechnique Fédérale de Lausanne (EPFL)
Lausanne, Switzerland, 2011–16
Berg, Nate. "Mechanical Humanism. Perrault's School of Engineering." *Architect Magazine* 105, no. 8 (August 2016): 89–101.
Chessa, Milena. "Dominique Perrault campe son architecture à l'EPFL." *lemoniteur.fr*, February 5, 2011.
Hitomi, Saito. "Rehabilitation/Extension of the Mechanical Hall and Library, EPFL." *GA Document*, no. 120 (January 2012): 126–129.
Perrault, Dominique. "Edificio de mecanica de la EPFL (Lausana)." *Arquitectura Viva*, no. 186 (July–August 2016): 74–75.
—. "ME Building." *L'Arca International*, no. 132 (September–October 2016): 34–41.

Grand Théâtre
Albi, France, 2009–14
Berger, Éric. "La future salle de spectacles dévoilée." *La Dépêche du Midi*, December 15, 2009: 20.
—. "Le multiplexe ouvrira dans trois ans." *La Dépêche du Midi*, May 5, 2010.
Carles, G. "Le futur espace culturel séduit et interroge." *Le Tarn libre*, no. 51 (December 18, 2009): 7.
Constans, Jean-Marie. "Albi – Dominique Perrault pour Les Cordeliers." *Le Moniteur*, no. 5539 (January 22, 2010): 42.
Hirou, Amandine. "Les Cordeliers. Nouveau pôle culturel." *L'Express*, no. 3101 (December 2010): 8–10.
Laval, Gilbert. "Albi, le Grand Théâtre prend son quartier." *Libération*, February 27, 2014, 26.

Perrault, Dominique. "Grand Théâtre, Les Cordeliers." *L'Arca International*, no. 120 (September–October 2014): 26–35.

—. "Maille Enveloppante." *AMC*, no. 236 (October 2014): 94–95.

—. "Velo dorado. Grand Theater in Albi (France)." *Arquitectura Viva*, no. 174 (May 2015): 26–31.

—. "Albi Grand Theater." *C3 Korea*, no. 371 (July 2015): 108–119.

Pousse, Jean-François. "Grand Théâtre des Cordeliers à Albi." *Archiscopie*, no. 1 (January 2015): 18–23.

Ritter, Alison. "Transparency is a question of the light. The new Grand Théâtre in Albi/F by day and night." *Professional Lighting Design*, no. 97 (March-April 2015): 34–41.

"Les Cordeliers, un nouveau cœur de vie." *AlbiMag*, no. 129 (December 2009): 19–26.

Convention Center and Exhibition Hall
León, Spain, 2005–18

Fernández-Galiano, Luis. "León al sol." *Arquitectura Viva*, no. 104 (September–October 2005): 106–107.

"Concurso Palacio de Congresos y Recinto Ferial, León." *AV Proyectos*, no. 11 (September–October 2005): 51–55.

"Concurso de Ideas para el Palacio de Congresos y Recinto Ferial de León." *Arqscoal*, no. 3 (March 2006): 32–37.

"Dominique Perrault proyectará el Palacio de Congresos de León." *Vía construcción*, no. 49 (October 2007): 16.

"Palacio de congresos y recinto ferial." *Pasajes arquitectura y Crítica*, no. 72 (December 2005): 12.

REWRITING

Pavillon Dufour
Château de Versailles, France, 2011–16

Albert, Marie-Douce. "Dominique Perrault aménagera le Pavillon Dufour." *Le Moniteur*, no. 5611 (June 10, 2011): 95.

—. "Dominique Perrault apporte sa touche de soleil à Versailles." *lemoniteur.fr*, January 31, 2014.

—. "Sous les ors de Dufour, le public est roi." *Le Moniteur*, no. 5899 (December 9, 2016): 70–73.

Bialestowski, Alice. "Perrault prépare un accueil royal au château de Versailles." *AMC*, no. 241 (April 2015): 19.

Bommelaer, Claire. "Le pavillon Dufour du Château de Versailles, l'entrée en jeu." *Le Figaro*, March 18, 2016: 32.

Champenois, Michèle. "La pirámide invisible." *Arquitectura Viva*, no. 190 (December 2016): 28–36.

Didier, Frédéric, Dominique Perrault, and Claude Rutault. *Le Pavillon Dufour*. Versailles: Château de Versailles / Direction de l'information et de la communication, 2017. 35 pp.

Edelmann, Frédéric. "Le pavillon Dufour à Versailles, aux marches du palais." *Le Monde*, December 14, 2016.

Giovannini, Joseph. "How do you add to Versailles? Bravely." *International New York Times*, August 6–7, 2016: 19.

Leray, Christophe. "À Versailles, les bons comptes de Perrault." *chroniques-architecture.com*, February 7, 2017.

Mauron, Laurent. "Le château peaufine son nouvel accueil." *Le Parisien*, March 4, 2015.

Tourneboeuf, Patrick. "Château de Versailles : les travaux de la République." *d'architectures*, no. 224 (March 2014): 56–59.

Trétiack, Philippe. "Dominique Perrault redore Versailles." *Beaux-Arts Magazine*, no. 388 (October 2016): 28.

—. "Le pavillon Dufour à Versailles. Le beau conte de Perrault." *Elle Déco*, no. 250 (December 2016): 62–67.

Aérogare des Invalides, Fondation Giacometti
Paris, France, 2017–30

Dagen, Philippe. "Pour Alberto Giacometti, un grand musée de 6 000 mètres carrés au centre de Paris." *Le Monde*, November 14, 2022.

Duponchelle, Valérie. "En 2026, le Musée Giacometti va s'ancrer aux Invalides." *Le Figaro*, November 14, 2022.

Henry, Christine. "Aérogare des Invalides à Paris : après Coca et Air France, quel avenir pour le site 'laissé à l'abandon' ?" *Le Parisien*, September 1, 2024.

Pic, Rafael. "En 2026, un musée Giacometti devant les Invalides." *Le Quotidien de l'art*, no. 2492 (November 15, 2022): 8–10.

Pierre, Lola. "La Fondation Giacometti va ouvrir un musée et une école d'art au cœur de Paris." *vogue.fr*, November 14, 2022.

"Giacometti krijgt eigen museum in Parijs." *De Standaard*, November 15, 2022.

Poste du Louvre
Paris, France, 2012–21

Albert, Marie-Douce. "La poste du Louvre, recto-verso." *Le Moniteur*, no. 6161 (October 15, 2021): 62–65.

Boccara, Laurence. "À Paris, la poste du Louvre se métamorphose." *Le Monde*, April 10, 2016: 7.

Bréson, Martine. "Paris : la mythique Poste du Louvre va devenir un site avec hôtel de luxe, boutiques et logements sociaux." *francebleu.fr*, July 8, 2020.

Delafon, Louis. "Dominique Perraault : 'La Poste du Louvre ressemblera aux bâtiments de Soho'." *paris-match*, July 9, 2020.

Dicharry, Elsa. "Le chantier de la poste du Louvre dans la dernière ligne droite." *Les Échos*, July 8, 2020.

Gutperle, Thomas. "Dernière ligne droite pour le chantier de La Poste du Louvre." *decideurs-magazine.com*, July 8, 2020.

Henry, Christine. "C'est parti pour le gigantesque chantier de la Poste du Louvre." *Le Parisien*, May 19, 2015.

Rochebouët, Béatrice de. "Coup d'envoi de la rénovation de la poste du Louvre." *lefigaro.fr*, September 7, 2012.

—. "La Poste du Louvre révolutionne Paris." *Le Figaro*, July 8, 2020.

Sabbah, Catherine. *Paris. La Poste du Louvre. Révolution urbaine*. Paris: Flammarion, 2022. 79 pp.

Vovos, Joffrey. "La Poste confie son fleuron à l'architecte de la BNF." *Le Parisien*, February 15, 2013: 15.

"La nouvelle vie de la poste du Louvre." *AMC*, no. 218 (October 2012): 32.

"La Poste du Louvre." *Connaissance des arts*, special issue, no. 940 (May 2021). 68 pp.

"La Poste du Louvre, chef-d'œuvre de l'architecture industrielle, va faire peau neuve." *bfmtv.com*, July 8, 2020.

"Le plus grand bureau de poste de France prépare sa métamorphose." *Géo*, no. 497 (July 2020).

Court of Justice of the European Union (CJ4 and CJ8)
Luxembourg, Phases 1 and 2, 1996–2008 / 2014–19

La Cour de justice des Communautés européennes dans son nouveau palais. Luxembourg: Didier Devillez, 2009. 93 pp.

Le Palais de la Cour de justice de l'Union européenne, dix ans. Exhibition catalogue. Luxembourg: CJUE Publishing, 2018. 68 pp.

Braush, Marianne. "La Logique de la justice." *Land*, no. 43 (October 2001): 23.

Brausch, Marianne, et al. *The Major Extension of the Court of Justice of the European Communities: the process of a project*. Luxembourg: Funds for the Urbanisation and Development of the Kirchberg Plateau, 2002. 127 pp.

Bure, Gilles de. "Dominique Perrault: Court of Justice of the European Communities." *a+u*, no. 433 (October 2006): 108–113.

Champenois, Michèle. "À Luxembourg, la justice érigée en Palais." *Le Monde 2*, February 14, 2009: 42–47.

Chessa, Milena. "Dominique Perrault voit triple au Grand-Duché." *Le Moniteur*, no. 6059 (November 29, 2019): 68–72.

—. "À Luxembourg, fin d'une construction européenne." *Le Moniteur*, no. 6067 (January 17, 2020): 60–63.

Cour, Jean-Pierre. "La Justice européenne architecturée." *Tageblatt*, May 8, 2003: 4.

Degioanni, Jacques-Franck. "La justice affirme sa prééminence." *Le Moniteur*, no. 5427 (November 30, 2007): 56.

Fèvre, Anne-Marie. "À Luxembourg, inauguration de la Cour de justice européenne." *Libération*, December 20–21, 2008: 35.

García, Ángeles. "La grandeza de Perrault." *El País*, April 5, 2009: 31.

Glancey, Jonathan. "Let there be light." *theguardian.com*, December 2: 2008.

Hennebert, Jean-Michel. "Cour de Justice de l'UE. Une troisième tour pour 'cimenter' l'Union européenne." *paperjam.lu*, June 27, 2016.

Kaiser, Gérard. "Gerecht Justice." *Staal Acier*, no. 15 (June 2007): 22–27.

Kass, Carlos. "Dominique Perrault zu Besuch in seinem EU-Justizpalast auf Kirchberg." *Tageblatt*, no. 284 (December 2009): 23.

Marteling, Luc. "Groß, teuer, atemberaubend." *Luxemburger Wort*, September 23, 2006: 3.

—. "Wo Luxemburgs höchste Türme entstehen." *Luxemburger Wort*, September 25, 2006: 4.

Miguet, Laurent. "Le Quartier européen accueille des habitants." *Le Moniteur*, no. 5316 (October 14, 2005): 76–79.

—. "Structure préservée dans un palais de justice transfiguré." *Le Moniteur*, no. 5460 (October 17, 2008): 68–69.

Rachet, Jean-Michel, ed. *Construire un palais de justice pour l'Union européenne*. Luxembourg: Fonds d'urbanisation et d'aménagement du Plateau de Kirchberg, 2019. 180 pp.

Regnier, Isabelle. "Tours de force pour la justice européenne." *Le Monde*, September 10, 2019: 19.

Simenc, Christian. "Droite comme la justice." *L'Œil*, no. 729 (December 2019): 14.

Trelcat, Sophie. "Dominique Perrault, Tribunal de Justice des Communautés européennes, Luxembourg." *AMC*, no. 186 (March 2009): 64–73.

"Gerichtshof der Europäischen Gemeinschaft wird rund 400 Millionen Euro kosten." *Tageblatt*, August 29, 2007.

Landscape Tower

Puteaux-La Défense, France, 2015–21

Bocquet, Catherine. "Nouveau look et nouveaux locataires pour les anciennes tours Pascal à La Défense." *lesechos.fr*, December 20, 2022.

"La Défense: les tours Pascal oublient les années 1980." *leparisien.fr*, March 17, 2017.

Citylights

Boulogne-Billancourt, France, 2007–16

Albert, Marie-Douce. "Dominique Perrault revisite les tours du Pont-de-Sèvres." *Le Moniteur*, no. 5647 (February 17, 2012): 66.

Bernatas, Jérôme. "Les tours du Pont-de-Sèvres vont changer de look." *Le Parisien*, September 30, 2011: 3.

Delhumeau, Gwenaël, and Aurélien Lemonier, eds. *Badani/Roux-Dorlut Architectes*. Orléans: HYX, 2016. 175 pp.

Gréco, Bertrand. "Des tours transformées en un kaléidoscope géant." *Le Journal du dimanche*, April 15, 2012: 16.

Laroue-Pont, Thierry, Philippe Zivkovic, Patrice de Moncan, et al. *Citylights*. Paris: Les Éditions du Mécène, 2015. 125 pp.

Perrault, Dominique. "Citylights. Boulogne-Billancourt." *L'Arca International*, no. 131 (July 2016): 58–65.

Pousse, Jean-François. "Citylights, métamorphose des tours du Pont de Sèvres à Boulogne-Billancourt." *Archiscopie*, no. 5 (January 2016): 36–45.

Sabbah, Catherine. "Tours du Pont-de-Sèvres. Les nouvelles lumières de la ville." *Archistorm*, no. 56 (September–October 2012): 48–54.

—. "À Boulogne, Citylights sort de l'ombre." *lesechos.fr*, November 21, 2013.

Véran, Cyrille. "Dominique Perrault. Tours de bureaux, Boulogne-Billancourt." *AMC*, no. 248 (February 2016): 24–31.

"Réhabilitation lourde en vue pour les tours du pont de Sèvres." *lemoniteur.fr*, January 13, 2012.

"Citylights by Dominique Perrault." *domusweb.it*, January 13, 2012.

Suzanne-Lenglen Court coverage

Paris, France, 2020–24

Luquain, Amélie. "Structure: Suzanne-Lenglen déploie son toit." *Le Moniteur*, no. 6235 (March 3, 2023).

Pousse, Jean-François. "L'esthétique de la technique." *Archiscopie*, no. 37 (July 2024): 36–41.

Regnier, Isabelle. "À Roland-Garros, sur le court Suzanne-Lenglen, un nouveau toit plissé comme la jupe de Jean Patou." *Le Monde*, May 27, 2024.

Schneider, Romain. "Roland-Garros: le futur toit du court Suzanne-Lenglen dévoilé." *Le Figaro*, October 2, 2020.

"Dominique Perrault Designs Retractable Roof On Suzanne Lenglen Tennis Court In Paris." *worldarchitecture.org*, October 2, 2020.

"Paris 2024: un nouveau toit à Roland-Garros, conçu par Dominique Perrault." *amc-archi.com*, October 9, 2020.

"Roland-Garros: le nouveau toit du court Suzanne-Lenglen dévoilé pour la première fois." *leparisien.fr*, November 23, 2023.

Métal 57

Boulogne-Billancourt, France, 2015–22

Albert, Laurence. "Boulogne-Billancourt: la deuxième vie du 57 Métal." *lesechos.fr*, April 13, 2016.

Bocque, Catherine. "Carton plein pour Métal 57, l'immeuble de Dominique Perrault à Boulogne-Billancourt." *Les Échos*, no. 25349 (December 8, 2022).

Falzon, Paul. "Métal 57, l'alliage fin du neuf et de l'ancien." *Le Moniteur*, no. 6169 (December 10, 2021): 58–59.

Monier-Vinard, Bruno. "Immobilier de bureau. De l'art de la métamorphose." *Le Point*, no. 2625 (December 1, 2022): 8–11.

Rambert, Francis. *57 Métal – Métal 57. The story of a mutation*. Orléans: HYX, 2018. 256 pp.

—. "Greffe dans le paysage des sheds." *Archiscopie*, no. 30 (July 2022): 96–97.

"À Boulogne-Billancourt, un nouvel espoir pour l'emblématique immeuble 57 Métal." *leparisien.fr*, February 11, 2016.

"Métal 57 à Boulogne-Billancourt. De 57 Métal à Métal 57." *Matières*, no. 9 (February 2021): 52–53.

Aplix and Aplix Extension

Le Cellier-sur-Loire, France, 1997–99 / 2016–20

Cannatà, Michele, and Fátima Fernandes. "Instalações da Fábrica Aplix." In *A tecnologia na arquitectura contemporânea: Dominique Perrault, Baumschlager & Eberle, Mansilla + Tuñón*, 50–63. Lisbon: Estar Editora, 2000.

Dellux, Manuel. "Un bâtiment industriel conçu comme un process." *Le Moniteur*, no. 4981 (May 21, 1999): 34–35.

Fuchigami, Masayuki. "Aplix, l'usine qui discute avec la nature." *Nikkei Architecture*, no. 699 (March 19, 2001): 22–27.

Guimard, Emmanuel. "Dominique Perrault habille d'Inox la nouvelle usine d'Aplix." *lesechos.fr*, September 30, 1999.

—. "L'usine Aplix de Dominique Perrault." *lesechos.fr*, August 18, 2014.

Le Neve, Florence. "Le spécialiste du scratch Aplix agrandit son usine 'miroir'." *lesechos.fr*, October 23, 2021.

Menard, Jean-Pierre. "L'Usine Aplix: brillante et discrète." *Le Moniteur*, no. 4999 (August 17, 2001): 6–7.

Mostaedi, Arian. "Aplix Factory." In *Factories & Office Buildings*, 132–141. Barcelona: Links International, 2003.

Perrault, Dominique, and André Morin. *Aplix*. Baden: Lars Müller Publishers, 1999. 108 pp.

Rambert, Francis. "Quand l'industrie ne pollue pas le paysage." *Le Figaro*, August 7, 2000: 8.

Vögtlin, Rudolf. "Deux œuvres à racines urbaines." *Fassade/Façade*, March 2001: 71–75.

"Détails peaux." *AMC*, no. 99 (June–July 1999): 90–93.

"Dominique Perrault: The Aplix Factory, Le Cellier, France 1997–1999." *a+u*, no. 362 (November 2000): 14–27.

"Fábrica Aplix." In García Cañizares, Ana Cristina, *High-Tech para High-Tech. La arquitectura de la empresas del futuro*, 70–77. Barcelona: Loft Publications, 2001.

"Jeux de miroir." *Techniques & architecture*, no. 444 (August 1999): 26–29.

"Nantes, Diálogo con el paisaje." In *Re-création. 21 architectures en France à l'aube du XXIe siècle*, 84–89. Paris: AFAA/Ministère de la Culture et de la Communication, 1998.

"Perrault fait les mots croisés." *ArchiCréé*, no. 56 (1999): 94–97.

"The Aplix Factory." *ATD*, no. 122 (November 2004): 78–81.

"Une façade miroir en acier poli." *Le Moniteur*, no. 4968 (March 5, 1999): 69.

"Usine de tissu auto-agrippant." *AMC*, no. 103 (December 1999): 190–193.

"Usine. Le Cellier-sur-Loire." In Éric Lapierre, ed., *Architecture du réel*, 236–249. Paris: Éditions du Moniteur, 2004.

"Variazioni di scala: nuove costruzioni." *Casabella*, no. 683 (November 2000): 50–55.

Hôtel Industriel Berlier and its refurbishment

Paris, France, 1985–90/2014–22

Albert, Laurence. "Paris se dote de deux nouveaux hôtels industriels." *lesechos.fr*, March 10, 2023.

Blistène, Bernard, and Xavier Douroux, eds. *Claude Rutault chez Dominique Perrault*. Dijon: Centre d'art contemporain; Paris: Les Presses du réel, 2000. 32 pp.

Duffaure-Gallais, Isabelle. "Un hôtel industriel transparent." *Le Moniteur*, no. 4494 (January 12, 1990): 50–53.

Fillion, Odile. "Les Prix du 'Moniteur'." *Le Moniteur*, no. 4547 (January 18, 1991): 77–81.

Lamarre, François. "Hôtels industriels: la chaîne s'agrandit." *Architectes*, no. 194 (January–February 1989): 16–18.

—. "Lieux d'exception: ... à l'espace minimal de l'hôtel industriel." *Le Magazine de la construction*, no. 31 (January–February 1991).

Lonchamp, Juliette. "Le ventre de l'architecte." *Archi News*, February–March 1991.

Lucan, Jacques. "Phénomène Perrault." *AMC*, no. 17 (December 1990): 40–45.

Lueder, Christoph. "Gläserner Kubus Großartig in seiner Flexibilität." *DBZ*, no. 260 (April 1992): 489–494.

Perrault, Dominique, and Georges Fessy. *Hôtel industriel, Paris treizième*. Architecture & Cie/État & Lieux. Paris: Demi-Cercle, 1993. 48 pp.

Perrault, Dominique, and Marcus Robinson. *L'Hôtel industriel Berlier de Dominique Perrault*. La Figure & le lieu. Paris: Pandora, 1991. 56 pp.

Rougé, Marianne. "Les hôtels industriels." *AMC*, no. 8 (February 1990): 22–27.

Zabalbeascoa, Anatxu. "Dominique Perrault, París, 1990." In *El taller del arquitecto*, 130–133. Barcelona: Gustavo Gili, 1996.

Zoffoli, Paolo. "Edificio industriale a Parigi." *L'industria delle costruzioni*, no. 243 (January 1992): 46–51.

"Gewerbe- und Bürogebäude Berlier, Paris, 1990." *Werk, Bauen und Wohnen*, no. 4/1991 (April 1991): 38–41.

"Gewerbe- und Bürogebäude in Paris." *Baumeister*, no. 1/1992 (January 1992): 12–14.

"Hotel Industrial Berlier." In *Arquitectura francesa. 11 proyectos. Nouvel, Perrault, Hauvette, Architecture-Studio*, 72–81. Seville: Junta de Andalucía, 1993.

"Hôtel Industriel: Dominique Perrault." *de Architect*, no. 1991–10 (October 1991): 90–91.

"Plan et arrière-plan." *Techniques et architecture*, no. 391 (September 1990): 67–74.

The Vertical City – Montparnasse Tower Paris, France, 2016

Perrault, Dominique. *E+ Vertical City*. Paris: Dominique Perrault Architecture, 2017. 55 pp.

Scoffier, Richard. “Nous n’avons jamais été modernes. Concours pour la réhabilitation de la tour Montparnasse.” *d’architectures*, no. 58 (November 2017): 43–47.

Trétiack, Philippe. “À quoi ressemblera la tour Montparnasse en 2024?” *Beaux-Arts Magazine*, no. 402 (December 2017): 24.

FILMOGRAPHY

Boisseau, Lionel. *La BnF, à livre ouvert*. InJam Production, 2025. 52 min.

Copans, Richard. *L’Arbre, le Livre et l’Architecte*. Les Films d’ici / Perrault Projets, 1994. 12 min.

—. *Le Livre, ses tours et ses chiffres. La Très Grande Bibliothèque de France*. Les Films d’ici, 1996. 13 min.

—. *Dominique Perrault*. Les mots de l’architecte. Les Films d’ici, 1998. 53 min.

—. *Caen, le grand plateau*. Les Films d’ici-District du Grand Caen / Perrault Projets, 1998. 14 min.

—. *Hôtel industriel Jean-Baptiste Berlier*. Les Films d’ici / Perrault Projets, 1998. 15 min.

—. *Bibliothèque nationale de France*. Les Films d’ici / Perrault Projets, 1998. 15 min.

—. *Berlin, Vélodrome olympique*. Les Films d’ici / Perrault Projets, 1998. 21 min.

—. *Une maille à l’endroit – Une maille à l’envers*. Les Films d’ici / Perrault Projets, 2002. 3 min.

—. *Competition, Peking Chinese television Center*. Les Films d’ici, 2002. 18 min.

—. *Supermarché MPREIS*. Les Films d’ici, 2004. 7 min.

—. *La Médiathèque de Vénissieux*. Les Films d’ici, 2006. 6 min.

—. *Aplix*. Les Films d’ici, 2006. 6 min.

—. *La Médiathèque Lucie-Aubrac*. Les Films d’ici, 2007. 13 min.

—. *Les Onze Mots de l’architecte*. Les Films d’ici, 2008. 58 min.

—. *Metropolis. Biennale d’architecture de Venise*. Les Films d’ici, 2010. 46 min.

—. *Ewha the Seoul Hidden University*. Arte France, Les Films d’ici, 2010. 26 min.

—. *Le Plein et le Vide. Leçon de géographie*. Dominique Perrault Architecture / Les Films d’ici, 2011. 26 min.

Coudert, Gilles. *The Le Corbusier Spirit*. Mona Lisa Production, 2018. 52 min.

Cubero, Ángel Borrego. *The Competition. Documentary film about an architecture competition*. Office for Strategic Spaces (OSS), 2013. 3 min.

Planchot, Alexandre, and Antoine Prévost. *Dominique Perrault, l’Hôtel du département de la Meuse à Bar-le-Duc, label Architecture contemporaine remarquable*. Drac Grand Est / Lorenzo Diez-Futur antérieur production-Gabriel Scialom, 2023. 81 min.

Puybaret, Vincent. *Olympe-sur-Seine*. BelOrage Productions, 2025. 80 min.

Permanence et discontinuité. Conversation avec Dominique Perrault. Cité de l’architecture et du patrimoine, 2014. 16 min.

PHOTOGRAPHIC CREDITS

All images: © Dominique Perrault Architect, ADAGP, Paris, 2025, except:

- © Francis Alÿs. Digital image, The Museum of Modern Art, New York/Scala, Florence: p. 108 (9)
- © Daici Ano: p. 238 (3), 404 (Fukoku Tower)
- © Tadao Ando. Photography: Ken Conley: p. 114 (9)
- © Archives Départementales de la Seine-Saint-Denis: p. 124 (1)
- © Art © Holt/Smithson Foundation/ADAGP, Paris, 2025: p. 114 (10)
- © Atchain: p. 58 (7), 59 (9, 10), 60 (1), 61 (5), 252 (1, 2, 3) 253 (1), 411 (Dyad, Twin Peaks, Arc of Light, Centre Pompidou)
- © Atchain/Gaëlle Lauriot-Prévost: p. 61 (6)
- © Kader Attia, ADAGP, Paris, 2025, with kind permission from Galleria Continua, San Gimignano/Beijing/Les Moulins: p. 112 (4)
- © Francesca Avanzinelli: p. 159 (4, 5, 6), 160 (1, 3), 161 (6, 9), 404 (*Metropolis?*)
- © Bank for International Settlements (BIS): p. 360 (4)
- © Anne Claude Barbier: p. 94 (1), 101
- © Anne Claude Barbier/Gaëlle Lauriot-Prévost: p. 102, 103 (2, 4), 104-105
- © Gerry Barry Artworks: p. 109 (10)
- © Baum Architects: p. 410 (Yongin)
- © Jean Ber: p. 403 (Centre Pompidou), 404 (Sammode)
- © Luc Besson/EuropaCorp: p. 116 (9)
- © Bibliothèque Historique de la Ville de Paris: p. 321 (1)
- © BnF Gallica: p. 188 (1)
- © Rudi Bohmer: p. 400 (Düren)
- © Vincent Boutin: p. 294 (3)
- © Centre Pompidou/Fondazione Renzo Piano: p. 368 (1)
- © Château de Chantilly: p. 340 (1), 341 (4)
- © 1976 Christo and Jeanne-Claude Foundation, ADAGP, Paris, 2025./Photographic credit: Centre Pompidou, MNAM-CCI/Philippe Migeat/Dist. GrandPalaisRMN: p. 108 (3)
- © 1976 Christo and Jeanne-Claude Foundation. © ADAGP, Paris, 2025: p. 108 (4)
- © Marie Clérin/André Morin: p. 370 (4), 409 (Aplix)
- © Collection Musée Air France: p. 318 (4)
- © Collection Pavillon de l'Arsenal-Préfecture de Police: p. 384 (1, 2, 3)
- © Axel Dahl/Gaëlle Lauriot-Prévost: p. 283 (5)
- © Darshanhr.007 (via Wikimedia Commons), CC BY-SA 4.0: p. 110 (5)
- © Patrice Debois, model maker: p. 126-127
- © Michel Denancé: 272 (1), 274-275, 322 (5), 327 (5, 6), 374 (2, 4), 376 (2, 5, 6), 392 (Châteaudun, Angers), 393 (Canal+), 394 (Zac Tolbiac, Usinor-Sacilor, Sulzer site, Sagep, Hypo Bank, Lu Jia Zui, Mayenne), 395 (Glass House, Île Sainte-Anne, Les Balcons du Canal), 396 (Unimétal), 410 (83 Marceau, La Poste), 411 (Villejuif)
- © Michel Denancé/Gaëlle Lauriot-Prévost: p. 103 (3), 322 (3), 324 (1, 2), 326 (1, 2)
- © Michel Denancé/Dominique Perrault Architect, ADAGP, Paris, 2025: p. 112 (1, 2), 116 (1)
- © Digital image, The Museum of Modern Art, New York/Scala, Florence © Adagp, Paris, 2025: p. 20
- © Do Ho Su: p. 71 (7)
- © Domaine de Frapotel © Philippe Chancel, Courtesy Éditions Dilecta: p. 8
- © D.R.: p. 82 (3), 110 (8), 111 (6), 114 (7)
- © Drac Centre: p. 409 (Bar-le-Duc)
- © DREIF: p. 124 (2)
- © EdC © ADAGP, Paris 2025: p. 14 (2)
- © EdC © DB-ADAGP, Paris 2025/CNAP: p. 18
- © Éditeur Aéro-Photo/Roger-Viollet/Carto.net/Industry-&-Science/Alastair Philip Wiper: p. 184 (2)
- © Ólafur Elíasson. Courtesy of Studio Olafur Eliasson. Photography: Annabel Elston: p. 109 (9)
- © Larry Ellis: p. 113 (9)
- © Epaillard+Machado: p. 98-99
- © Leandro Erlich, with kind permission from 21st Century Museum of Contemporary Art, Kanazawa. Photography: Ajari (*via* Wikimedia Commons), CCBY2.0: p. 109 (7)
- © ESRI: p. 161 (7)
- © Estate of Gordon Matta-Clark/Artists Rights Society (ARS), New York/Scala, Florence: p. 116 (4, 5)
- © Everyday Practice: p. 162 (3)
- © EyeEm/Freepik: p. 110 (9)
- © Ewha Womans University: p. 48 (1)
- © Ewha Womans University/Namhun Sung: p. 403
- © Fancy Digital Technology: p. 174-175, 176 (1, 2), 177 (4, 5) 178 (1, 2), 179 (4, 5), 181, 182-183
- © Georges Fessy: p. 58 (3, 4), 114 (3), 185, 295 (4), 296 (1, 3), 329 (8), 330-331, 332 (1, 2), 333 (6, 7) 336 (4, 5), 337 (3), 370 (2), 372-373, 374 (3), 375 (6), 378 (1), 393 (Clermont-Ferrand), 394 (Zoo de Vincennes, Istanbul, Hôtel Berlier, Logements Louis-Lumière), 395 (Bussy-Saint-Georges, Kansai-kan, BnF, Villa One), 396 (Grande Serre, Temple de Mithra, GSCP, MoMA, Montparnasse Tower, Aplix, Tour Lehrter Bahnof), 397 (Chèvreloup, Casa da Musica, Vélodrome and swimming pool-Berlin, Landesmuseum-Zurich, City of Culture of Galicia), 398 (Vénissieux, Fondation Pinault), 399 (Centre Pompidou Metz), 400 (Seoul), 402 (Montigalá), 403 (Erasmus entrance), 404 (Madrid), 405 (Arganzuela), 406 (Kindarena, Albi), 409 (CJ8)
- © Georges Fessy/Gaëlle Lauriot-Prévost: p. 283 (6, 7), 297 (4), 333 (8), 334 (1, 2, 3), 335 (4, 5)
- © Georges Fessy/Dominique Perrault Architect, ADAGP, Paris, 2025: p. 109 (1), 111 (1), 113 (1, 2, 3)
- © Vincent Fillon: p. 269 (5), 271-272, 286 (3), 287, 288 (1), 310 (2), 315 (6), 324 (3, 4), 347 (5), 348 (1, 2), 349 (6), 364 (1), 366 (2, 3), 367 (5, 6) , 383 (5 à 8), 406 (entrée BnF entrance, EFPI administrative building), 407 (Halle Mécanique, Citylights), 408 (Picpus building, ParisLongchamp, Pavillon Dufour)
- © Vincent Fillon/Gaëlle Lauriot-Prévost: p. 289 (3, 4), 315 (5), 365 (4), 410 (Métal 57)
- © FOA/Farshid Moussavi/AZPML/Marcus Trimble/Flickr: p. 95 (4)
- © Fondazione Lucio Fontana, Milano/by SIAE/ADAGP, Paris, 2025: p. 114 (5, 6)
- © Kirchberg Fund and Court of Justice of the European Union (CJEU): p. 332 (4)
- © Geneanet: p. 67 (4)
- © Henri Germond: p. 286 (2)
- © Eredi Luigi Ghirri: p. 109 (6)
- © Didier Ghislain: p. 128 (4), 395 (Fedex, Salzburg), 396 (Bercy-Tolbiac footbridge, French Embasse in Berlin), 397 (Cognacq-Jay), 398 (Lille stadium, Copenhagen), 402 (BnF entrance hall)
- © GLP: p. 408 (Drape House), 409 (Tiny House), 410 (Basiliade, Saint-Eutrope)
- © Google Earth: p. 54 (5), 56 (2), 58 (2, 5, 6), 62 (2), 64 (2, 3), 38 (2), 144 (3), 154 (3), 168 (1), 184 (1), 188 (3), 218 (2), 228 (2), 268 (3), 279 (4), 328 (2), 346 (4), 350 (2), 379 (3)
- © Google Street View: p. 68 (1), 191 (bottom photo), 194 (2), 195 (5) 316 (2), 317 (3, 5)
- © Miguel de Guzman: p. 234, 404 (Diagonal 123)
- © Michael Halbert: p. 107
- © Matthias Haker: p. 109 (8)
- © 2025 Harald Haraldsson: p. 111 (4)
- © Michael Heizer. Courtesy of the artist and Gagosian. Photo: Michael Heizer: p. 14 (3)
- © Michael Heizer/Triple Aught Foundation, with kind permission from The Museum of Contemporary Art, Los Angeles: p. 108 (6), 115 (9)
- © Michael Heizer/Triple Aught Foundation/The Los Angeles County Museum of Art. Photography: Doug Pray: p. 115 (9)
- © David Hockney, p. 202 (1, 3, 4), 204 (two photos on left), 208 (two photos on left), 210 (two photos on left)
- © Hoffmann Janz/OLN: p. 262 (2, 3), 263 (5, 6), 411 (Donau City Tower II)
- © Edward Hopper, Columbus Museum of Art, p. 202 (2), 206 (two photos on left)
- © Ionomo GmbH/Bloom Images: p. 248 (4), 411 (Timber Marina)
- © Arthur Jan: p. 350 (3), 352, 353, 355 (5 à 10), 356 (1 à 4), 357
- © Arthur Jan/Gaëlle Lauriot-Prévost: p. 100 (1, 2)
- © Thomas Jantscher: p. 399 (MPreiss Zirl)
- © Alain Jaramillo: p. 400 (GKD factory)
- © Magdalena Jetelová: p. 112 (8)
- © Junnglim/Luxigon: p. 71 (9

- © Junnglim/Yayus: p. 86-87
- © Louis Kahn/Mitchell Giurgola Architects/Google Street View/ Iwan Baan: p. 104 (1)
- © Dmitri Kessel: p. 111 (7)
- © Kamel Khalfi: p. 264, 344 (1), 345 (7, 8), 410 (Landscape Puteaux), 411 (To Lyon Tower)
- © Uwe Kils (via Wikimedia Common): p. 116 (6)
- © Jandee Kim, 516 Studio: p. 166, 167 (bottom photos)
- © Nikola Krtolica-Copropriétaires Tour Maine-Montparnasse: p. 379 (3, 5), 380, 381
- © Gaëlle Lauriot-Prévost: p. 60 (3, 4), 100 (7), 167 (top photo) 260 (2), 311 (4), 312 (2), 314 (2), 322 (2), 366 (1), 405 (Urban Folly, Arbre Roi)
- © Le Corbusier) © EdC © F.L.C/ADAGP, Paris 2025: p. 14 (1)
- © Le Corbusier – Fondation Le Corbusier, ADAGP-, Paris 2025: p. 117 (10)
- © Le Corbusier – Fondation Le Corbusier, ADAGP-, Paris, 2025/Dominique Perrault Architect, ADAGP: p. 117 (11)
- © Library of Congress: p. 114 (4)
- © Richard Long/ADAGP, Paris, 2025: p. 115 (10)
- © Richard Long/ADAGP 2025, with kind permission from Lisson Gallery: p. 108 (8)
- © Luxigon: p. 72, 74, 75, 80-81, 82 (1, 2), 83 (7), 131, 145, 219, 220-221, 223, 225 (3), 226-227, 411 (Lightwalk)
- © Tiago Madeira: p. 272 (2), 273 (5), 285 (4), 323 (6), 347 (6), 407 (Yvon Lambert)
- © Tiago Madeira/Gaëlle Lauriot-Prévost: p. 272 (3, 4)
- © Pepe Maisto: p. 92-93, 409 (Piazza Garibaldi)
- © Manfred Sodia photography: p. 110 (3)
- © Frederico de Matteis: p. 50 (4, 7)
- © Elena Matta/damaStudio: p. 116 (8)
- © Antoine Maufray, Arcora: p. 386 (5)
- © Paul Maymont/Paris-Match: p. 113 (8)
- © Microsoft Bing: p. 186-187
- © MiraCosta College staff, from public domain sources (USGS/NASA/NOAA): p. 108 (7)
- © André Morin: p. 47 (5), 49 (5), 50 (5, 6), 52-53, 56 (4, 5, 6), 64 (5, 6), 90 (2), 91 (6), 95 (3), 96 (1), 157 (6, 7), 239 (3), 259 (7), 278 (2), 332 (3), 336 (1), 397 (Graz, Hanover, Frac), 398 (Cairo, Banque Populaire-Bordeaux), 399 (City Gate, Letzigrund, MPreis Wattens, Mexico City), 400 (Cannes, Rathaus Innsbruck, Durango, Île Seguin), 401 (ARos, Seoul Opera, Cordoba, Turin), 402 (Helsinki, - DPA Agency, London 2012, Opac Paris, OCH Handelskai), 403 (Habitat Sky, Granada, Vélodrome Roubaix), 404 (Onyx Lille, The Circle, Sofia, Milano Fiera BSU Hamburg), 406 (Hôtel des Lilas, Vetropack, Mercedes-Benz), 407 (Paris-Saclay)
- © André Morin/Gaëlle Lauriot-Prévost: p. 51 (8, 10, 11), 315 (3)
- © Joaquin Mosquera: p. 298 (3), 300, 301 (5), 310 (1), 407 (León convention center)
- © Joaquin Mosquera/Gaëlle Lauriot-Prévost: p. 302-303
- © Musée de la Poste: p. 322 (4)
- © Musée d'Orsay, documentation, Fonds Juste Lisch, Gare des Invalides, ARO 2000 25: p. 317 (4)
- © Michael Nagl: p. 256 (3), 257, 258, 259 (6), 260 (1, 3), 407 (Donau City Tower I)
- © Michael Nagl/Gaëlle Lauriot-Prévost: p. 260 (4), 261 (5, 7)
- © Ivan Navarro, ADAGP, Paris 2025: p. 111 (8)
- © DR Oscar Newman: p. 113 (7)
- © ORNL Photography: p. 113 (6)
- © Panoramio/All rights reserved by A.M.Z./Microsoft Bing: image bank p. 184 (3)
- © Paris-Match/LVMH: p. 112 (6, 7)
- © European Parliament: p. 358 (1)
- © Dominique Perrault Architecte, ADAGP, Paris, 2025/Raymon Cauchetier for the photograph of Jean-Paul Belmondo and Jean Seberg on the shoot of *À bout de souffle* by Jean-Luc Godard:p. 132
- © Jason Pineau: p. 110 (6)
- © Marta Pirlo/Atelier Misto: p. 405 (ENI Milan)
- © Plaine-Commun:Paris 2024/DPA: p. 125 (3)
- © John Portman: p. 113 (4)
- © Paz Benito del Pozo (personal archives): p. 298 (2)
- © Giancarlo Pradelli: p. 400 (Piazza Gramsci)
- © Philippe Ramette, ADAGP, Paris, 2025, with kind permission from Galerie Xippas: p. 109 (5)
- © Shannon Christine Rankin: p. 115 (5)
- © Realism Noir. © Loris Gréaud, Gréaudstudio, Association pour la Conservation du Domaine de Frapotel, Mondes Nouveaux/ADAGP, Paris, 2025: p. 19
- © Christian Richters: p. 399 (Innsbruck)
- © Élise Robaglia/Potion Médiatique: p. 7 (4), p. 134-135, 327 (4), 411 (Athletes' Village)
- © RSI Studio: p. 150 (4, 5), 151 (6), 152-153, 409 (Shenzen), 410 (Champs-Élysées)
- © Philippe Ruault: p. 395 (Bar-le-Duc), 402 (Bar-le-Duc)
- © Mark Sekuur/Prima Focus: p. 246 (1, 3), 405 (La Liberté)
- © Takuji Shimmura: p. 279 (3), 280-281, 404 (Aurelium), 405 (La Vérose), 407 (Keran)
- © Regina Silveira/Atlas Sztuki Foundation, Łódź: p. 109 (4)
- © Simon Schmitt: p. 403 (CJ4)
- © Donatella Simonetti: p. 241 (6)
- © Steiner/Ralph Bensberg: p. 241 (5) 408 (Vulcano)
- © Mikhael Subotzky/Magnum Photos and Patrick Waterhouse, with kind permission from Goodman Gallery: p. 110 (7)
- © René Sultra © Fondazione Lucio Fontana, Milan/by SIAE/ADAGP, Paris, 2025: p. 14 (4)
- © T/E/S/S: p. 354 (1, 3, 4), 355 (2)
- © The Print Collector. Reproduced with permission from Alamy: p. 111 (5)
- © Patrick Tourneboeuf/Tendance Floue: p. 313 (3)
- © Patrick Tourneboeuf/Tendance Floue/ Gaëlle Lauriot-Prévost: p. 315 (4)
- © Vibhakar86 (via Wikimedia Commons), CCBY-SA 3.0: p. 110 (4)
- © James Turrell: p. 111 (9)
- © Ingel Vaikla: p. 112 (5)
- © Deidi Von Schaewen: p. 393 (ESIEE)
- © Gunther Richard Wett: p. 397 (MPreiss Wattens)
- © Wikimedia Commons: p. 70 (3), 268 (2), 111 (10), 112 (9, 10), 113 (5), 115 (8)
- © Egon Wurm: p. 400 (Café Lichtblick)
- © Tokujin Yoshioka: p. 71 (6)
- © Yoi takes pics (*via* Flickr): p. 115 (4)
- © Carey Young, with kind permission from Paula Cooper Gallery, New York: p. 108 (5)
- © Zabalaga-Leku, ADAGP, Paris 2025: p. 116 (7)

The models reproduced in this book were made by Jean-Louis Courtois, Patrice Debois, Philippe Dubois, Etienne Follenfant, Michel Goudin, Miza Mucciarelli, Atelier Misto, and Nanako Ishizuka.

Every effort has been made to correctly identify and mention the copyright holders of the content reproduced in this book. We would be grateful for notification of any errors or omissions.

ACKNOWLEDGMENTS

I would like to salute all those who, in various ways, have accompanied, supported, and inspired me since the 1980s.

I would like to thank the team at Éditions Gallimard—Antoine Gallimard, Franck Fertille, Manuele Destors, Geneviève de La Bretesche, Anne Lagarrigue, and Faye and Rik Bas Backer—as well as each of the authors—Barry Bergdol, Éric de Chassey, Nina Leger, Fréderic Prot, and Sophie Trelcat—for their contributions to this monograph.

My thanks also go to all those whose advice and conversation have contributed to the realization of this book, in particular Richard Nguyen, who brought to life the Sub Lab research laboratory at the École Polytechnique Fédérale de Lausanne, the "Île de la Cité 2040" mission, and to the 2021 Seoul Biennale of Architecture and Urbanism.

Finally, I would like to express my gratitude to Gaëlle Lauriot-Prévost for our deep friendship, without which this work would not have been possible.

AUTHOR BIOGRAPHIES

Barry Bergdoll

Barry Bergdoll is Professor of Art History at Columbia University. A specialist in the history of modern architecture, from 2007 to 2014 he was Chief Curator of Architecture and Design at the Museum of Modern Art in New York. He has designed and organized several exhibitions in Paris (Musée d'Orsay, Caisse des Monuments Historiques), at the Canadian Center for Architecture, Montreal, and in Mexico City, at the Banamex Foundation.

He is the author of a widely distributed architecture textbook, *European Architecture, 1750–1890* (Oxford University Press, 2000) and of textbooks devoted to Karl Friedrich Schinkel, Mies van der Rohe, Léon Vaudoyer, and Marcel Breuer. He is currently working on an essay on the history of architectural exhibitions, based on the Mellon Lecture given at the National Gallery of Art in Washington.

Éric de Chassey

Éric de Chassey is an art historian who has led several cultural and research institutions. Director of the École Nationale Supérieure des Beaux-Arts since July 2025 and professor of Contemporary Art History at the École Normale Supérieure de Lyon since 2012, he is Honorary Director of the Académie de France à Rome-Villa Médicis, which he directed for six years (2009–15). From 2016 to 2025, he was Director of the Institut National d'Histoire de l'Art (INHA). He has published, in various languages, articles, essays, catalogs, and books on the history of the arts from the nineteenth to the twenty-first century, on the political history of the visual arts, and on the history and theory of art history. He has also curated some fifty exhibitions in France and abroad.

Nina Leger

Nina Leger is a writer and professor of art history at the Beaux-Arts de Marseille. A graduate of the École Normale Supérieure and Paris 8 University, she wrote her thesis on the use of perspective by artists of the American avant-garde. Her fiction writing has been nourished by this research, and her novels, published by Gallimard, take space as their main dimension (*Mise en pièces*, 2017, Prix de la vocation). Her last two published texts are poetic and political investigations into the construction of places and their narratives (*Antipolis*, 2022, Prix Écrire la ville; *Mémoires sauvées de l'eau*, 2024, Prix du roman historique).

DOMINIQUE PERRAULT ARCHITECTURE

Dominique Perrault, architect, urbanist
Gaëlle Lauriot-Prévost, interior architect, designer
with
Marie Bodénès, documentalist, picture researcher
Tulio Cathala, secretary general
Heewon Lee, interior architect
Valérie Lehoucq, documentalist
Louanne Mayol, documentalist
Richard Nguyen, architect, project manager
Nicolas Valladon, project assistant
Tiphaine Varigas, graphic designer, architect

Dominique Perrault, Gaëlle Lauriot-Prévost and les éditions Gallimard warmly acknowledge Marie Bodénès for her commitment in the production of this book.

ÉDITIONS GALLIMARD

Franck Fertille, director of partnerships
Manuele Destors, project manager

Anne Lagarrigue, artistic director
Pascal Guedin, art book coordinator
Faye and Rik Bas Backer, graphic design and layout

Geneviève de La Bretesche, managing editor
Francys Gramet, preparation and correction of French texts
Charles Penwarden, Madeleine Compagnon, and Cerise Fontaine, translation from French to English
Madeleine Compagnon, preparation and correction of English texts
Clorinde Bloc, picture research (pp. 14-27)

Sandrine Lebreton, production manager
Cécile Lebreton and Béatrice Bourgerie, production

Béatrice Foti, press officer, assisted by Laetitia Copin

Les éditions Gallimard would like to thank Dominique Perrault and Gaëlle Lauriot-Prévost for their support in the publication of this book.

The book's paper is made from natural, renewable, recyclable fibers, sourced from sustainably managed forests.

The book is set in Ny. Sans, produced by A2-Type
Paper: Magno Natural 140 g/m^2
Cover: Assuan Canvas
Photoengraving: Printway
Copyright deposit: October 2025
magasin@gallimard.fr
Printed in September 2025 on the presses of Printer Trento for Maestro, Italy.
ISBN: 978-2-07-306775-3 / 631386
Sodis item code: G09106